Alessandro Filippini

The Table

How to Buy Food, how to Cook it and how to Serve it

Alessandro Filippini

The Table
How to Buy Food, how to Cook it and how to Serve it

ISBN/EAN: 9783744643559

Printed in Europe, USA, Canada, Australia, Japan

Cover: Foto ©Lupo / pixelio.de

More available books at **www.hansebooks.com**

How to Buy Food, How to Cook It, and How to Serve It

BY

ALESSANDRO FILIPPINI.

NEW YORK:
CHARLES L. WEBSTER & COMPANY.
1889.

CONTENTS.

	PAGE
FAC-SIMILE LETTERS OF FILIPPINI AND DELMONICO..........	vi-vii
THE PLEASURES OF THE TABLE.........................	1-3
OUR MARKETS...	4-7
VARIETIES OF FISH TO BE FOUND IN THE MARKETS DURING THE DIFFERENT MONTHS...........................	8-14
VEGETABLES...	15-17
WATER-MELONS AND MUSK-MELONS	18
HOW TO SET A TABLE	19, 20
HOW TO SERVE MEALS.................................	20-23
MENUS FOR EVERY DAY IN THE YEAR	25-150
RECIPES	151-392
HOW TO CARVE..	393, 394
CELEBRATED MENUS, MANY OF WHICH WERE PREPARED BY MR. FILIPPINI	395-409
CURIOUS MENUS OF VARIOUS NATIONS	411-418
INDEX...	419-432

THE TABLE.

THE PLEASURES OF THE TABLE.

THE pleasures of the table are enjoyed by all who possess good health. Nothing is more fascinating than to be seated at a well-served, well-cooked breakfast or dinner; and yet, of the immense number that enjoy the good cheer and luxuries of the table, how few, very few, there are who stop to consider the vexatious trouble our host undergoes when arranging the daily bill of fare. "Variety is the spice of life," but nowhere is it more important, aye, actually necessary, than in the getting up of a palatable meal. This pertains not only to the dining-room of a hotel of the least pretensions or to the so-called "grand" restaurant, but particularly to the family table. The writer has known a gentleman who presided over an immense restaurant, and daily provided the supplies therefor. He experienced no difficulty with any single part of his business, yet when he came to arrange the details of his own family's meals, and attempted to practically fulfill them, he was puzzled and annoyed beyond description. And, after all, there is no place in the civilized world where the market for the supply of food is so well provided as in New York, both as to variety and excellence, and even as to luxuries. Educated as thousands of persons have been, in the art of dining, by the famous Delmonico and his able lieutenants, New York, perhaps, contains a larger number of so-called high-livers than any other city.

These "gourmands" (if you please), and their number is legion, have, with the aid of the excellent resources of the American market and the encouragement given to the culinary art of the period, brought the modern American table to virtual perfection. This is saying a great deal, inasmuch as the famed restaurants of London, Paris, and Vienna have ever claimed a reputation and an ascendancy over others that seemed to form a part of history itself.

But as times change, so we change with them. Westward the course of Empire sways, and the great glory of the past has departed from those centres where the culinary art at one time defied all rivals. The sceptre of supremacy has passed into the hands of the great metropolis of the New World. It has been the writer's good fortune to gain experience on this subject from his observations in Europe as well as in this country. He can state, without fear of contradiction, that more first-class, well-fatted, and corn-fed cattle reach the markets of New York, than any other market of the United States. Whenever a first-class article of beef is required by one of the inland hotels, they send to New York for it.

Ask the ordinary traveler, and he will tell you that a first-class steak, an "A 1" chop, or prime roast beef is a *rara avis* in hotels outside of New York. London has excellent mutton and good beef; that is all. Paris gives plenty of variety, but it is all of an inferior quality with the exception of veal, which is good. The same may be said of northern Germany, where, in addition, the larger hotels in Hamburg and Bremen are able to supply good steaks, the cattle in that country being of fine quality.

Yet no American, accustomed to his prime beef at New York, can be pleased at any of these continental hotels, as he loses sight of his favorite roast and steak.

At the extensive cattle yards of Berlin, which are under control of an excellent administration, and perfectly arranged, it was impossible, for instance, on a well-supplied market day to find a single dozen corn-fed young steers that would make good enough beef for first-class custom in New York. The bulk of cattle offered for sale was made up of oxen that had been overworked—they had horns bigger than themselves—and the remainder were old cows and bulls.

Of the bovine family, the branch most celebrated for the good quality of beef is the Durhams or Shorthorns. It is only fifty years ago that the first were imported to this country from England, and so well have they prospered and multiplied that the finest and best specimens of the race are now found in these United States. They are now freely exported, at large prices, to the mother-country, where they are highly prized for breeding purposes. There are farms in Kentucky, Illinois, Indiana, Ohio, and even in Missouri and Kansas, that turn out annually from 300 to 1,000 head of fatted, corn-fed cattle, from two to four years old, and weighing from 1,500 to 2,500 pounds per head.

As to mutton, this country is already beginning to occupy a position second to none. We may probably not as yet surpass England in this respect, but we have learned a great deal on this subject during the past thirty years; hence the American breed of sheep has considerably improved. The quality and flavor of our mutton is improving to that extent that a long time cannot possibly elapse before the prejudice now existing in favor of the English article must give way to the honest acknowledgment that the American mutton, if not superior to, stands at least fully on a par with, the English rival.

Our farmers and agriculturists have learned a great deal on this question. They now know that, as to early lambs, for instance, the ewes should be strong, and kept in good condition, so that they can supply the lambs with plenty of milk. They are now kept in a warm barn where the cold winds do not touch them, and where the sun can shine on them. They commence feeding them by putting a little bran in the lamb's mouth, so that it can taste it, and the lambs commence eating from a box separate from the sheep. They generally feed them with cracked corn or meal, and sometimes oats and corn ground together, with plenty of milk from the ewes. If kept in good order and well fed, they will be ready for market, by the time they are six to eight weeks old. After the month of June, lambs come from New York State—mostly from Dutchess County. They are turned out to graze on the hills, where some cracked corn and meal are put in the fields, so they can eat it at their pleasure. Many of the late sheep and lambs come from Canada. Two of the largest sheep ever sold in New York were raised by Mr. Vail, of Dutchess County, and sold by A. Luyster to Mr. L. Delmonico for the sum of $100. The two weighed, alive, 632 lbs., and dressed, 420 lbs.

One of the leading questions that directly affects the American cuisine is the contest now progressing as to the transportation of animal food to the great Eastern markets. Heretofore live cattle were transported to, and slaughtered at, the places of consumption. This so-called home-slaughtering interest has within the past few years experienced great competition with the slaughterers of cattle in the far West, who have brought their meats to the Eastern market in refrigerator-cars. The great question now is: Which is the better way, and by which method are the public interests served the best, as well as the sanitary condition of this important article of food most improved?

There can be no doubt that, while this controversy lasts, the consumer has already been benefited, and the transportation of live cattle has already been greatly facilitated and improved. The quality of the meat does not depend upon the place where the animal is slaughtered, but it does depend upon the state of the animal's health when it is slaughtered. Let the cattle-cars be improved so that cattle can be transported without being knocked about and bruised, and let them be properly fed and watered while in transit; after making the long journey from the far West, let them be well rested and cooled off before slaughtering.

The Western dressed-beef men will also have to be on their mettle in order to meet the exigencies of the times. Let them keep their wild prairie cattle and their scalawags out of the better markets, handle their beef carefully, keep it subjected to a uniform temperature of about 38° Fahrenheit, discard all artificial preservative means, and all opponents to their interests will be bereft of argument.

OUR MARKETS.

OUR markets contain an abundant supply of poultry and game of an exceptionally fine quality. For superior and palatable chickens we are recommended to those raised about the creameries of New Jersey. The hand-fed geese and ducks of Rhode Island rival in flavor and delicacy the celebrated Caneton-de-Rouen, while the American turkeys are famous the world over. To give any adequate idea of the quantity of game which comes from the vast feeding-grounds of this country, or to enumerate substantially every form in which, during the different seasons, game appears in market, would require too much space.

No game is more highly prized or more eagerly sought after in Europe than our American canvas-back ducks, grouse and wild turkeys. It has become part of our history that during the late war twenty thousand turkeys were shipped by one firm in New York City to supply a Thanksgiving dinner to an army; while at present so plentiful is the supply that but a few days would be required to secure double that number.

Near Rhode Island, on one farm of about fifty acres, twenty thousand geese, and as many ducks, are fattened annually for market. In Vermont and other cold localities during December, when turkeys are full grown and fattest, hundreds of tons of them are dressed, frozen hard in boxes, and preserved in that condition for use in the spring and summer months; when freshly killed, turkeys are tough and unpalatable. Unless well experienced, the purchaser would do better to leave the selection of poultry and game to some reliable dealer, rather than depend upon "signs," which are at times deceiving.

Spring chickens appear in market about May; those hatched in incubators come somewhat earlier. They are very small, weighing about a pound each, and improve in flavor and richness as they increase in size. Tender chickens may be had almost the whole year, but they are not plentiful during the spring months.

Capons are good from December until April.

Young turkeys are first killed in September; they are full grown and fattest in December, and remain good until spring, when they are superseded by frozen turkeys.

Geese and ducks are first brought to market in June, and, if they have been properly fed, are a great delicacy. They may be had through the summer, autumn, and winter months. Geese are called "green" until they are three or four months old.

Guinea-fowls are best in summer and autumn, when young and fat.

Squabs are in market the whole year.

The laws for killing and selling game vary somewhat in the different States, and sometimes in the different counties of the same State. Reference is made principally in regard to the New York City markets. So great are the facilities for forwarding quickly by rail and steamer, that supplies of game are easily obtained from long distances ; and birds killed in southern Texas, or other remote places, may be served perfectly fresh on New York tables a few days later. The flight of birds is greatly controlled by the weather. An early or late season, or a wet or dry one, or even a cold wave, may hasten or retard them, and make game plentiful or scarce, fat or poor ; but an abundant supply of all kinds of game in its best condition is generally to be had in the months it is in season, as follows :

Ruffed grouse, commonly called partridges, are in season from September 1 to February 1.

Pinnated grouse, commonly called prairie-chickens, from September 1 to February 1.

Quails, from November 1 to February 1.

Woodcock are in the market from August 1 to February 1, and are fattest in October.

English snipe appear in the spring, and again in the autumn, when they are in their best condition, and are to be had in smaller quantities during the winter.

Yellow-legged snipe, robin or red-breasted snipe, dowicher and black-breasted or winter snipe, also common snipe, are abundant in the spring, and again from July through October, when they are best.

Upland, grass, or gray plover are in market through the spring and summer months, and are fattest in August and September.

Doe-birds are to be had at about the same time. They are plover of a larger size, and are considered not inferior to any other.

Golden plover, or frost-birds, are plentiful in the spring, and are in fine condition in September and October.

Sora, or Virginia rail, are best in September and October.

Reed-birds, or rice-birds, become very fat in August and September. When found among the reeds of New Jersey they are called reed-birds, and rice-birds when from the wild rice-fields of the South.

Rabbits and hares are in season from November 1 to February 1.

Venison is in market from August 1 to January 1 only, and is good during that time.

Antelope may be generally had through the autumn and winter months.

Wild pigeons appear in the spring and autumn, but no longer in such immense numbers as formerly. It is only possible to obtain them for market when their "nestings" are near a railroad, which facilitates their quick shipment. The young birds (wild squabs), taken from the nest, make a most delicious broil.

Wild ducks, swan, geese, and brant are in season from September 1 to May 1. The choicest of these are : canvas-back, mallard, teal, red-head, widgeon, wood, brant, cygnet or young swan, goose when young and fat.

English pheasants, English hares, and Scotch grouse are to be found in the New York markets in excellent condition during the winter months.

The wild mongrel goose, which appears in our markets about Christmas-time, is, like the canvas-back duck, considered as one of the greatest luxuries, and exclusively American.

The far-famed canvas-back duck is also an exclusively North American species. Closely resembling in appearance and habits the red-head of America and the pochard of Europe, it is still quite distinct from and superior to both these species in the excellence of its flesh. It is found throughout North America, from the Arctic Ocean to Central America, on the interior waters and on both shores. Chesapeake Bay is the most noted ground for canvas-back ducks in the country, but they are especially abundant in Southern California. They breed on the ponds, rivers, and lakes, from Oregon to the more extreme northern portions of the continent. The canvas-back is without doubt the most sought after and widely known of all our ducks, and in localities where it can obtain the root of the *Vallisneria spiralis* (called by some tape-grass, and by others, incorrectly, wild celery), the food to which it owes the peculiarly delicate flavor for which it is so famous. As a highly prized delicacy, it stands without a rival. When, however, it is obliged to content itself with a diet chiefly of animal food, or is not properly handled in the kitchen, it becomes merely a very ordinary table bird. The *Vallisneria* is not found on the Pacific Coast, but in many parts of the interior, and especially in the Chesapeake Bay. The canvas-back being an excellent and strong diver, brings from the bottom the *Vallisneria* by the roots; these it bites off and swallows, while the red-head, black-head, and other ducks feed on the refuse grass, or occasionally a root snatched from the canvas-back. At times the water is covered with grass thus pulled up. By the middle of December the canvas-back becomes so fat as to have been known to burst open in the breast in falling on the water. In New Orleans it is called "canard cheval." The canvas-back is covered somewhat like the red-head, but there is no reason for the confusion which exists in the minds of so many people regarding the two species. A careful comparison of the following descriptions of the two birds will indicate well-marked differences by which they may always be distinguished. The cook of a Buffalo gentleman, when asked if she knew the difference between a red-head and a canvas-back replied, "To be sure! one has the head of a fool!" (meaning the canvas-back).

CANVAS-BACK.	RED-HEAD.
Feathers of the head short and smooth. Male with head and neck of deep chestnut color, the former sometimes quite blackish. Fore parts of body, wings and tail, black,	Feathers of the head rather long, giving it a puffy appearance. Male with head and neck chestnut red. Fore parts of body, wings and tail, black, under parts

under parts white ; back and sides whitish, waved with black, but the white predominates, and the black lines are faint and much broken up. Female everywhere duller in color than the male.

Bill entirely greenish-black, longer than head, nearly as long as middle toe (without claw), narrow, high at base, and nostrils medium.

Iris red.

The weight of a pair of good fat canvas-back ducks with feathers on will average six pounds.

white ; back and sides whitish, waved with black, the dark waved lines unbroken. Female everywhere duller in color than the male.

Bill dull blue, with a black belt across the end, shorter than the head, shorter than the middle toe (without claw), broad, depressed ; nostrils within its basal half. Always to be distinguished from other ducks by shape of the bill.

Iris yellow.

The weight of a pair of good fat red-head ducks with feathers on will average five pounds.

The red-head duck is found in greater or less numbers throughout North America, on the Atlantic and Pacific coasts, breeding in high northern latitudes, and frequenting in winter the southern portions of the continent as far as Mexico. The red-head is not common on the coasts of New England. During the winter months it abounds considerably along the south shore of Long Island, and is extremely abundant from this point south, especially at Chesapeake Bay and Currituck. Its flesh is excellent, and when it is enabled to feed on the well-known *Vallisneria* is almost fully equal in point of flavor to that of the canvas-back. The diet of the red-head is by preference vegetable, but in default of a sufficiency of food of this nature, they will, like other ducks, eat frogs, tadpoles, and various mollusks. In the West they feed largely on corn and wheat, which they glean from the fields, and on wild oats, the seed of the water-lily, and roots and leaves of other aquatic plants.

VARIETIES OF FISH TO BE FOUND IN THE MARKETS DURING THE DIFFERENT MONTHS.

JANUARY.

Live codfish [*Gadus morrhua*]. Haddock [*Melamogramus agle finus*]. Cusk [*Brosmius brosme*]; this belongs to the cod family, and although very little known, is an excellent table fish. Hake [*Phycis chuss*]; this is another of the codfish family, but inferior to any of the other varieties. Halibut [*Hypoglossus vulgaris*]. Small chicken halibut [*Hypoglossus vulgaris*]. Striped bass [*Roccus lineatus*]. Eels [*Arguilla vulgaris*]. Lobsters [*Homarus Americanus*]; very scarce, and in poor condition. Fresh salmon [*Oncorhynchus chouicha*]; these salmon are caught in the Columbia River, Oregon, all the year round, and are shipped in refrigerator-cars, and received daily in the New York markets. Frozen salmon [*Salmo salar*]; caught in the Restigouche River in July, and kept in freezers. Turbot [*Platysomatichthys hippoglossoides*], coming from Newfoundland, are occasionally in market during this month. Frost-fish, sometimes called tomcods [*Microgdus tomcod*]. Frozen fresh mackerel [*Scomber scombrus*]. Frozen Spanish-mackerel [*Scomber omarus*]. Pompano [*Trachynotus carolinus*]; a few occasionally in market, coming from Pensacola, Florida. Red-fish, or channel bass [*Sciæna ocellata*], caught in Florida. Sheep's-head [*Diplodus pobatocephalus*], from Florida. Grouper [*Epinephelus moria*], from Pensacola; a very good fish for boiling, somewhat like the red-snapper, but the meat is of a finer grain. Red-snapper [*Lutjanus Blackfordii*] has become a staple article in our markets during the winter. They weigh from two pounds upward, as much as twenty pounds each. It is good either boiled or baked, but most epicures prefer it baked. In selecting a fish, care should be taken not to buy one that weighs over eight pounds, as anything larger than that is apt to be tough and lacking in flavor. Shad [*Clupea sopidisima*], caught in the St. John's River, in Florida, are to be had nearly every day during this month. Frozen bluefish [*Pomatomus saltatrix*], preserved by being kept in freezers since the previous fall. Herring [*Clupea harengus*], from Nova Scotia. Skate, or ray-fish [*Plerroplatea maclura*]. The demand for this fish increases every year. The American people begin to appreciate its many excellences. Probably the annual dinners of the Ichthyophagous Club, at which this fish is always served, have materially increased the popularity and demand for this fish. Rainbow trout [*Salmo irridea*]. These fish were first marketed during the winter of 1885 and 1886, and they are one of the notable examples of fish-culture, as the following brief history will show. Six years ago Professor Spencer F. Baird, then Commissioner of Fish and Fisheries for the United States, received a lot of eggs of the rainbow trout from California. He presented five hundred of them to the South Side Club, who have one of the most complete fish-cultural establishments in this State. These eggs were hatched and the fish raised in the preserves of the Club, where they increased to such an extent that the Club decided to send their surplus to market, and they have become very popular, and sell readily at one dollar and twenty-five cents per pound. The open season for these trout is from April to September. Salmon-trout, frozen [*Salvelinus namaycush*]. Whitefish, frozen [*Coregonus clupeiformis*]. Pickerel [*Esox reticulatus*], weighing from half a pound to ten pounds each, are very good during the winter months. Wall-eyed pike [*Sticostedium vitreum*]. Catfish [*Ictalurus punctatus*]. Smelts [*Osmerus mordax*] are received from different parts of the East and North during this month. The choicest come from Maine and Massachusetts. Those coming from Canada are always frozen, and are inferior, and sold at a very low price. Green turtle. Diamond-back terrapin. Prawns, from South Carolina. Scallops. Oysters. The following are the best in this month: Blue Points, Shrewsburys, East Rivers, and Mill Ponds. Hard crabs. Crab-meat, fresh picked. Whitebait. Finnan haddie. Smoked salmon. Smoked halibut. Best boneless dried codfish.

FEBRUARY.

Live codfish. Haddock. Halibut. Striped bass. Eels. Live lobsters. Fresh salmon. Frost-fish. Fresh Spanish-mackerel are found occasionally in market, coming from Pensacola, Florida. Pompano. Sheep's-head. Red-fish, or channel bass. Grouper. Red-snapper. White perch [*Roccus Americanus*], from Long Island ; one of the best pan-fish that is found in market. Smelts, green, from Maine, Massachusetts, and Rhode Island, and frozen smelts from Canada. During the latter part of the month very choice smelts are received from Long Island. These fish are large, and are considered the best of all varieties of smelts received. Shad. During the latter part of the month they begin to come from North Carolina. These fish are oftentimes large, weighing six pounds each, and in flavor are equal to those taken in the Connecticut River. Herring. Skate, or ray-fish. Salmon-trout. Whitefish. Yellow perch [*Perca Americana*]. Pickerel. Wall-eyed pike. Catfish. Green turtle. Terrapin. Prawns. Scallops. Oysters. Codfish tongues. Soft shell crabs during this month are in excellent condition, and are considered one of the most seasonable shell fish in market at this time. Hard crabs. Whitebait. Crab-meat, fresh picked. Finnan haddie. Smoked salmon. Boneless dried codfish. Smoked halibut.

MARCH.

Live codfish. Haddock. Halibut. Striped bass. Chicken Halibut. Eels. Live lobsters. Salmon, from the Columbia River. During the latter part of the month a few fish are received from Nova Scotia, weighing about eight pounds each, and are called Kennebec salmon by the tradesmen, although no salmon are caught either in the Penobscot or Kennebec rivers, Maine, until about the 1st of May. Large flounders [*Pseudopleuronectes Americanus*], suitable for making fillet of sole. Spanish-mackerel. Pompano. Sheep's-head. Red-snapper. Grouper. Shad are abundant this month from North Carolina, and about the 25th or 30th of March they make their first appearance in the North or Hudson River. Herring. Skate, or ray-fish. Sturgeon [*Acipencer sturio*]. Salmon-trout. Whitefish. Yellow perch. Pickerel. Cisco [*Coregonus artedi*]. Catfish. Wall-eyed pike. Green turtle. Terrapin. With the month of March closes the terrapin season, as after the 1st of April it seems to be univerally conceded that the weather is too warm, and terrapin are not relished, nor does the palate crave them. Soft shell clams are still excellent this month. Prawns. Scallops. Oysters. Those known as East Rivers, caught on the north shore of Long Island, are considered best in this month. Crab-meat, fresh picked. Smoked haddock. Smoked salmon. Smoked halibut. Smoked mackerel.

APRIL.

Live codfish. Haddock. Halibut. Striped bass. Chicken halibut. Eels. Live lobsters. Tomcods. Salmon, fresh from the Columbia River. Salmon, fresh from Nova Scotia. Flounders. White perch. Fresh mackerel. About the first part of April mackerel make their appearance on our coast, oftentimes in enormous numbers, and are sold in the markets at prices so low as to make them the cheapest food of the season. Spanish-mackerel and pompano are occasionally in the market from Pensacola, Florida. Kingfish [*Menticirrus nebulosus*] ; a few come into market from North Carolina. Sheep's-head, from North Carolina. Smelts ; with the close of this month the fish goes out of season. Red-snapper are to be found in market up to the 15th of April. Sea bass [*Serranus atrarius*] ; a few occasionally come into market from Charleston, S. C. Shad increase in abundance from the North and Hudson rivers. 'Skate, or ray-fish. Bluefish [*Pomatomus saltatrix*] ; a few make their appearance, caught on the Florida coast. Brook-trout [*Salvelinus fontinalis*]. The open season for this fish commences April 1. Salmon-trout. Whitefish. Pickerel. Cisco. Wall-eyed pike. Catfish. Green turtle. Prawns. Crayfish [*Astacus fluviatilus*] are found during this month in the markets ; they are caught in the Potomac River. Scallops ; with the close of this month they are out of season. Oysters are generally better during the month of April than at any other time of the year, but, according to custom, with the close of this month the oyster season ends. Fresh frogs' legs during the latter part of this month are taken, and begin to make their appearance in market at prices of about sixty to seventy-five cents per pound. Codfish tongues. Hard crabs. Crab-meat. Whitebait. Smoked haddock. Smoked salmon. Smoked halibut.

MAY.

Codfish during this month is apt to be poor, as no live fish are brought to the New York markets. It is mostly fish caught off Nantucket and repacked in Boston, and from there shipped to New York. Haddock; the same applies to this fish as to the cod. Halibut is in excellent condition this month, both large fish for steaks, and small chicken halibut for dinner fish. Striped bass. Eels. Lobsters. Blackfish [*Teutogo onitis*]. Salmon from Restigouche make their appearance about the 20th of May. Oregon salmon continue to come during this month, although not in as good order as in previous months. Large flounders for fillet of sole are excellent this month. Fresh mackerel. Spanish-mackerel and pompano from Pensacola, Florida. A few come to market from North Carolina during this month. Butter-fish [*Stromateus triacanthus*] make their appearance in the market this month. Weakfish [*Cyonoscion regale*] plenty and cheap. Kingfish from Long Island make their appearance during this month in the markets, and are an excellent fish, growing better each month till October, when they go out of season. Sheep's-head; a few make their appearance from Long Island. Porgies [*Stenotomus chrysops*], from Long Island. Sea bass during this month are abundant from Narragansett Bay. Shad from Connecticut is probably at its best this month. There is no doubt that shad from this river possesses a flavor superior to all others. Shad from the North River begin to get soft and are not in good condition. Bluefish; there are a few weighing one and a half to two pounds each in market. Squid [*Loligo pealæi*] This is an article of food that Spaniards and Italians think a great deal of, but it is very little used by American people as yet. It has been introduced to the American public by the dinners of the Ichthyophagous Club, which is composed of a few gentlemen connected with the leading newspapers, and some eminent scientific men, whose object is to cultivate a taste and demand for those varieties of fish which are not generally supposed to be good edible food. Brook-trout under the existing law come into market on April 1. Probably the finest flavored trout found on this continent are the wild brook-trout taken in the streams of Long Island. Cultivated brook-trout that are raised in ponds and preserves depend very much upon the character of their food as to what the flavor will be. Trout that are fed entirely upon chopped liver are usually flat and insipid to the taste. But trout that are fed upon small minnows or other fish-food, such as clams, larvae of insects, and small fish of any kind, are always more delicate in flavor. Salmon-trout and whitefish; a few are found in market this month, but during warm weather it is very difficult to obtain them in New York City markets in prime condition. Carp [*Cyprinus carpia*]. These fish are now making their appearance in our markets in considerable quantities, having been introduced into this country through the instrumentality of Professor Spencer F. Baird, late United States Fish and Fisheries Commissioner, some eight years ago.

They have been distributed in nearly every State of the Union, and in the Southern States have grown larger, and are found in better condition, than they are in Germany, where the parent fish came from. The market is principally supplied now with fish caught in the Potomac River, weighing from two to fifteen pounds each, and are selling at present for twenty-five cents a pound ; but in the course of a few years there is no doubt that these fish will be sold for from ten to twelve cents a pound. Green turtle. Frogs' legs. Crayfish during this month come from Wisconsin. They are of very fine flavor, and are the best that are found in this country. Prawns from South Carolina. Crab-meat, fresh picked. Soft crabs grow more abundant during this month, and are in excellent condition. A very choice smoked fish is in season this month, called the roe herring, and by some of the grocers under various names, such as bloaters, Burlington herring, etc.

JUNE.

Codfish may be had, but not in good condition. Haddock may be had, but not in good condition. Halibut. Striped Bass. Eels. Lobsters. Fresh salmon from the Kennebec and Penobscot rivers, Maine, and from the Restigouche and other rivers in Canada, are very abundant this month, and are to be had at the lowest price during the season, selling oftentimes as low as fifteen cents per pound by the whole fish. Large flounders for fillet of sole. Blackfish. Fresh mackerel. Pompano. Spanish-mackerel. Weakfish. Butter-fish. Kingfish. Sheep's-head. Porgies. Sea bass. Sturgeon. Shad from the Connecticut River are still in good condition, but with the close of this month go out of season. Bluefish are larger, sometimes weighing four to six pounds each, and are improving in quality. Carp. Skate, or ray-fish. Black bass [*Micropterus dolomiei*] are in season from the 1st of June until the 1st of January. This is a very choice table fish; probably one of the best of the fresh water fishes. Crayfish. Frogs' legs. Soft crabs. Crab-meat. Whitebait.

JULY.

Cod. Haddock. Halibut. Striped bass. Eels. Lobsters. Kennebec salmon. Pompano. Restigouche salmon. Large flounders for fillet of sole. Blackfish. Fresh mackerel. Spanish-mackerel. Butter-fish; this is a small, sweet pan-fish. Weakfish. Kingfish. Sheep's-head. Porgies. Sea bass. Bluefish. Moonfish [*Choetodipterus faber*]. This fish is somewhat similar in appearance to the sheep's-head, and is a very fine boiling or baking fish. Squid. Skate. Brook-trout. Black bass. Green turtle. Crayfish. Prawns. Frogs' legs. Soft crabs. Whitebait.

AUGUST.

Cod. Haddock. Halibut. Striped bass. Eels. Lobsters. Restigouche salmon. Kennebec salmon. Large flounders for fillet of sole. Fresh mackerel. Spanish-mackerel. Bonito [*Sarda mediterranea*]. This fish is sometimes sold through the country as Spanish-mackerel, but it is a very inferior fish as compared with the Spanish-mackerel. Crevalle [*Caranx hippos*]. This fish is sometimes sold as pompano, but is a very inferior fish, as the pompano is one of the choicest fishes that we have in market. Butter-fish. Tilefish [*Lopholatilus chamaeleonticeps*]. This fish was first discovered in our waters by the United States Fish Commission in 1880. It is very brilliant in color, but the meat is very coarse-flaked, and somewhat resembling the haddock in appearance and flavor. Lafayette [*Liostomus xanthurus*], a small fish weighing about a quarter of a pound each, and a very desirable pan-fish. Sea-robins [*Prionotus palmipes*]. This fish is found very plentifully at this season of the year in the waters of Long Island, and was first introduced as a table fish by the Ichthyophagous Club some five years ago. It is a very fair pan-fish. Sea bass. Kingfish. Sheep's-head. Porgies. Bluefish. Moonfish. Squid. Skate. Brook-trout. Black bass. Catfish. Green turtle. Crayfish. Prawns. Frogs' legs. Soft crabs. White-bait.

SEPTEMBER.

Codfish. Haddock. Halibut. Striped bass. Lobsters. Eels. Salmon from Nova Scotia. During this month the salmon advance very much in price, and with the close of the month fresh salmon caught on the Atlantic coast go out of season. Large flounders for fillet of sole. Blackfish. Fresh mackerel. Spanish-mackerel. During this month the Spanish-mackerel are in their best condition, being fat and of delicate flavor. Cero [*Scomberomorus caballa*]. A large fish, weighing from six to twenty pounds each, resembling the Spanish-mackerel in appearance, but not so fine flavored. Crevalle [*Caranx hippos*]. Pompano. Butter-fish. Tilefish. Weakfish. Lafayette. Porgies. Squid. Smelts make their appearance for the first time in the season during this month. Red-snapper are to be found in market this month, the first of the season. Grouper; a fish somewhat resembling the red-snapper in form, but of a darker red color, and similar in flavor to the red-snapper, and by a great many people thought to be superior to the red-snapper. Sea bass. Skate. Bluefish are in better condition, and in their prime during this month. Salmon-trout. Pickerel. Whitefish. Catfish. Wall-eyed pike. Carp. Green turtle. Crayfish. Prawns. Frogs' legs. Scallops begin to come into market at this time, but are not quite so good as they are a month later. Hard crabs. Whitebait. Soft crabs are in better condition and of better flavor during this month than at any other time of the year. Moonfish. Butter-fish. Bonito. Sea-robins.

OCTOBER.

Codfish; during the latter part of this month codfish are brought alive to the market. Haddock. Halibut. Striped bass. Eels. Lobsters. Blackfish. Columbia River salmon commence to come into market at this time. These salmon are what are known as the steel-head variety [*Salmo gardneri*]. They are not as fine flavored nor as much esteemed as those that are called chinooks, which come earlier in the season. Large flounders for fillet of sole. Fresh mackerel. Cero. Spanish-mackerel. Pompano. Weakfish. Kingfish. Sheep's-head. Grouper. White Perch. Smelts. Red-snapper. Sea bass. Bluefish. Black bass. Salmon-trout. Whitefish. Yellow perch. Pickerel. Cisco. Wall-eyed pike. Green turtle. Carp. Terrapin are caught during every month in the year, but are not considered good for the table until the weather is cold, and with the month of October are first used on the table. Crayfish. Prawns. Frogs' legs. Hard crabs. Soft crabs are to be found in market usually up to the 10th of October. White-bait. Scallops. Redfish, or spotted bass. This is a Southern fish, and is somewhat similar in flavor to the striped bass, but not quite so good.

NOVEMBER.

Live cod. Haddock. Halibut. Striped bass. Eels. Lobsters. Salmon. Cusk. Blackfish. Fresh mackerel. Redfish, or spotted bass. Grouper. White perch. Smelts. Red-snapper. Skate. Black bass. Salmon-trout. Whitefish. Yellow Perch. Pickerel. Cisco. Shad. For the past two or three years, during the month of November, shad have been taken off the coast of Massachusetts in the nets along with the mackerel. These shad are large, weighing five pounds each, and are very fat and of excellent flavor. Bluefish. This month usually closes the bluefish season, but during the months of December, January, and February they are found in market, but always are fish that have been preserved by freezing. Masquallonge [*Esox nobilier*]. This fish weighs from four to twenty pounds each, and is of the pickerel family, and considered the most superior in flavor to all the pickerels. Wall-eyed pike. Catfish. Green turtle. Terrapin. Crayfish. Prawns. Scallops. Frogs' legs. Hard crabs. Whitebait.

DECEMBER.

Live cod. Haddock. Halibut. Striped bass. Eels. Lobsters. Columbia River salmon. Large flounders for fillet of sole. Turbot. These fish are caught in extreme Northern waters. They are somewhat similar in flavor to the chicken halibut, but are black upon both sides. They are of a very peculiar flavor. Tomcods, or frost-fish. A small fish weighing about one-fourth of a pound each; very sweet, and a desirable pan-fish. Cusk. Blackfish. Grouper. Smelts. Mullet [*Mugil albula*]. A Southern fish, sweet and oily, and a good pan-fish. Red-snapper. Skate. Shad are received during this month from St. John's River, Florida. Black bass. Salmon-trout. Whitefish. Yellow perch. Pickerel. Masquallonge. Cisco. Wall-eyed pike. Green turtle. Terrapin. Crayfish. Frogs' legs. Prawns. Scallops. Hard crabs. Soft crabs. This is a different variety of crab than is found in the summer; it is very much smaller, and of a brown color; not equal in flavor to the soft crab found during the summer.

VEGETABLES.

VEGETABLES are grown to such an extent in the South, and also in hot-houses in the North, that we may enjoy, even in the coldest winter weather, nearly every variety.

The growing of vegetables in the South for Northern markets received its impetus through an incident which happened in a then well-known resort in New York. A party of gentlemen, among them a steward on one of the Southern steamers, were seated one day in January conversing, when the steward, who was in the habit of bringing mint with him for this particular resort, ordered a mint-julep; this order, at that time of the year, created a little surprise, especially to one of the party, who was a dealer in vegetables. However, the matter was explained, and the dealer arranged with the steward to bring him some mint, together with whatever vegetables he could get, on each of his Northern trips. The demand for them increased so fast that a great many growers commenced to raise vegetables, so that the business has grown to vast proportions.

The following information may be useful to those who wish to know at what season of the year certain vegetables may be had, and also where they may be had in their prime.

Asparagus. The consumption of asparagus has grown so much during the past few years, partly, perhaps, through the recommendation of physicians, that it might be well here to give an idea as to where and when it is grown. It first makes its appearance in market from the middle of February until the middle of March, according to the condition of the weather.

Occasionally it may be had during the winter from hot-houses, but of inferior quality. The first of out-door growth comes from Charleston, S. C., where there are a number of very large beds, and where it is grown very successfully, both as to quality and quantity. It is shipped from there to Baltimore, Washington, Philadelphia, and New York, arriving at the latter place by express in a little less than forty-eight hours after cutting. Although North Carolina is growing more every year, the next location where it is raised in quantities for market is Norfolk, Va., the quality being of the best. We now reach our own vicinity—Oyster Bay and New Jersey. The former place has long had the reputation of raising the finest asparagus, but as a great many of their beds are getting old, and not receiving the proper attention, they are fast losing their prestige to Jersey, where they are growing more and more every year, and of the very finest quality. Asparagus may be had at its best from the 1st of May, until the 1st of June; after this time it commences to run out until July first, when cutting is stopped. The demand has been so great for the past few years that, although more and more is raised every year, the price advances instead of getting less, and for the large "Colossal" or "Delmonico" asparagus immense prices are paid.

French artichokes may be had all the year round; the quality and size depend on the condition of the weather during their growth. Most of the supply is from France, but occasionally from California and the South.

Jerusalem artichokes appear from the 1st of October until June; they are always good.

String beans can be had from the middle of February until December; they are in their prime during the spring and fall months. Occasionally we receive them in December and January from Havana, but they are not first-class.

Lima beans, which are seldom shipped from the South, can be had from August until frost sets in; they are always good.

Beets all the year round; best in spring and summer.

Cabbage all the year round; always good. The first new cabbage comes from Florida in March. During the winter large quantities of cabbages are imported from Denmark.

Carrots all the year; the small young ones appearing in the spring.

Chives can be had all the year round.

Cucumbers all the year round. In the winter we get them from the hot-houses around Boston; they are of the very finest quality, although rather expensive.

Cauliflower all the year round; we have them in January, February, and March from England and France, and in April and May from the hot-houses on Long Island. They are of fine quality at all seasons except during summer.

Celery may be had in every month but May and June, but is best during the cold weather. It is being extensively raised in Kalamazoo, Mich., for the past three or four years; and as they raise it much earlier than we, and of good quality, it will not be long before we have it all the year round.

Chervil may be had all the year round, but is usually poor during warm weather.

Chicory we have from August until March; best during fall and winter months; occasionally during February and March; a fine quality comes from France.

Corn or winter salad (called by the French *doucette*, and by the Germans *fetticux*) from September until warm weather sets in. It is purely, as its name indicates, a winter salad, as it never grows in the summer.

Cress all the year round; best in the spring.

Dandelion from January 1 to June.

Escarolle salad from August until March.

Egg-plant all the year round; scarce during winter.

Garlic all the year round; in large quantities for the past two or three years during May, June, and July, from New Orleans.

Herbs, such as thyme, sage, sweet basil, borage, dill, lavender, sweet-fennel, sweet-marjoram, rosemary, summer-savory, tansy, etc., may be had green in the summer and fall, and dry during the balance of the year.

Kohl-rabi from May until November.

Knot celery from September until May.

Leeks all the year round.

Lettuce can be had all the year round. In the winter it comes from the hot-houses of Boston, Providence, Long Island, and Jersey, but principally from Providence, as that city for the past few years has made a business of growing lettuce for the New York market. It is best in the fall and spring. It is almost impossible to grow good lettuce in the summer, for, should it head at all, the warm weather would rot it.

Mint can be had nearly all the year round; scarce during December and January.

Mushrooms can be had all the year round; they are raised principally in cellars and hot-houses on Long Island, and the demand for them increases yearly. The people are gradually getting over the fear they once had of the poisonous toad-stools, of which, by the way, there is no danger now, as the mushrooms are carefully picked and sent to market by men who understand the business. They are scarce during the very warm weather.

Oyster-plant can be had from September until June.

Okra appears all the year round; in the winter and spring it comes from Havana.

Parsley all the year round.

Onions may be had all the year round.

Green peppers all the year round. In winter we get them from Havana.

Potatoes all the year round. There need be but little fear of a potato-famine. During the past few years, when our own crop has been light, large quantities were imported from England, Ireland, Scotland, and Germany. The first new potatoes come from Bermuda about April 1.

Sweet potatoes from August until June.

Peas from March until November.

Parsnips from September until June.

Pumpkins from September until February.

Romaine salad can be had in the spring and fall.

Radishes all the year round; they are very scarce in hot weather.

Rhubarb from February until July.

Brussels-sprouts from October until April. We import the very finest from France during March and April, but our growers are improving in raising them from year to year, and we hope before long to rival the French.

Kale-sprouts from November until June.

Shallots all the year round. They are green in spring and summer and can be had dry during winter.

Spinach all the year round; it is covered up in the early winter to keep it from freezing, but occasionally during extreme cold weather the cold reaches it, when it is impossible to cut it, which makes it scarce and high in the markets.

Sorrel can be had all the year round; it is raised mostly by French gardeners.

White and yellow summer-squash from April until October.

Marrow-squash all the year round, except May and part of June; they are used quite generally to make pies instead of pumpkins.

Tomatoes can be had all the year round, except December and part of January. The first new ones come from Key West; they are of excellent quality.

White and ruta-baga turnips can be had all the year round.

Estragon appears from March until December.

WATER-MELONS AND MUSK-MELONS.

WATER-MELONS first make their appearance in market about the first of July, and can be had until the middle of October. Unlike the musk-melon, they are of a rather hardy nature, and after the melon has grown on the vine, the changes in temperature, or rain, have little effect on them. The first in market come from Florida, and as the season advances we get them from further North, until New Jersey is reached. More melons are raised in Georgia than in any other State, and of far better quality. The best variety to be relied on, as to quality, is known as the "Gem."

Musk-melons, although raised in nearly all parts of the country where the climate will admit, are seldom shipped to New York from any distance further than North Carolina, as a musk-melon, in order to be of good flavor, must be ripened, or nearly so, on the vine. When ripe they are so easily cracked or mashed that they would not stand transportation. For the past two or three years, a few, of a rather hard-rind variety, but of excellent flavor, have been shipped from New Orleans, but with only partial success, as the cost of transportation and the loss are so great that it hardly pays. We often hear the remark, "I have not eaten a good melon this season." This can be easily explained.

A melon is of a very sensitive nature, and the delicious flavor is destroyed by rain or cold weather. A melon-patch from which we get finely flavored melons to-day, may be ruined (as to flavor) for a few days, by a heavy rain-storm; for the melon absorbs water like a sponge. When we have hot nights and no rain, we have perfect melons. Invariably, it is during this kind of weather that they are most appreciated. Melons first appear about the middle of July, and last until cold weather.

HOW TO SET A TABLE.

TO set a table seems, perhaps, very easy, but to set it properly and tastily is not such an easy matter. The advice herewith given may prove advantageous to many.

Place the table in the centre of the dining-room, under the chandelier, and see to it that it is perfectly steady; that is to say, that there is no

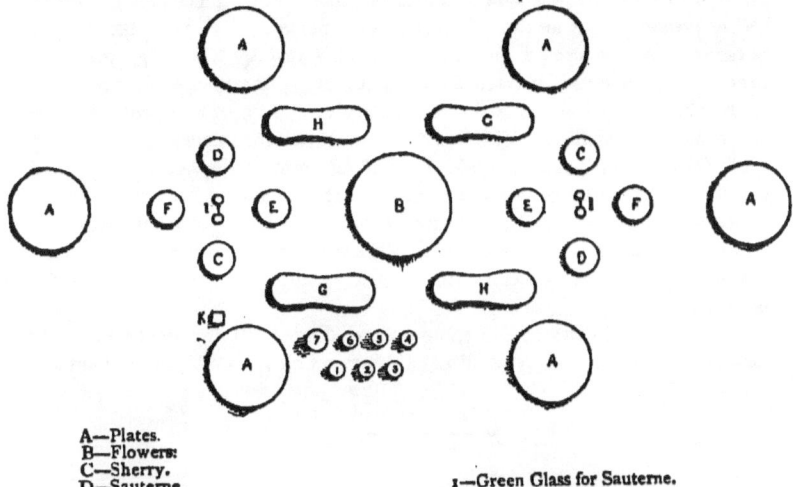

A—Plates.
B—Flowers.
C—Sherry.
D—Sauterne.
E—Fruits.
F—Cakes.
G—Celery.
H—Radishes.
I—Black and Red Pepper.
K—Salt Cellars.

1—Green Glass for Sauterne.
2—Glass for Sherry.
3—Red Glass for Rhine Wine.
4—Glass for Champagne.
5—Glass for Latour.
6—Glass for Chambertin.
7—Glass for Water.

danger of its being shaken while the dinner is in progress. Should it not rest firmly, perhaps an old relic, in the shape of a Bland Dollar, could be made serviceable by placing it under one of the feet. See to it that there is plenty of space between each cover; it is annoying to come in contact with every move of your neighbor.

A table for six persons should be six feet long. Take a woolen cloth and put it over the table, and then place a linen cloth on top of it; this will deaden the noise of plates and glasses.

Flowers should never be absent from the table when you have guests; they can be procured at all seasons. A large basket or bouquet should be placed in the centre of the table; a large bouquet on the right side for each lady, and a small *boutonnière* for each gentleman, also on the right side of the cover.

On each side of the centre-piece place a fruit-stand, nicely arranged with the choicest fruits of the season. Next to this place a *compotier* with assorted cakes. Place celery, olives, or radishes symmetrically in the space that is left between the centre and the covers. Fish-knives, soup-spoons, and oyster-forks must be placed on the right side of the plate, and the fork on the left side. If desired, place fancy pieces on the table, (*pièces montées*); but as the foregoing items pertain only to a dinner for six persons it would crowd out much available space. The diagram on the preceding page will illustrate the arrangement of the glasses on the table.

Napkins can be arranged in various styles and figures; into flowers or any other desired form. The latest and most fashionable way is to arrange them folded plainly, so as to show the monogram of the family. A small salt-cellar should be placed at each cover, to avoid asking the servant for it.

Menus, either printed or written, should be placed at each cover. It is not a breach of etiquette to refuse a course you do not desire; by knowing what is coming, you can with propriety refuse a course, and take the next one.

About ten minutes before commencing dinner, fill the decanters with Sauterne and with sherry, and place the same on the table, as in diagram, marked *C* and *D*.

HOW TO SERVE MEALS.

NEARLY every family of means is in the habit of giving a few dinners to its friends during the year. As a matter of course, the members of the family are, in return, invited to "dine out."

If you invite your friends to a dinner, you should not wish them to go away dissatisfied. After a varied experience of many years, both in this country and in Europe, the author feels that no apologies are necessary if he endeavors to enlighten our epicures and dinner-givers as to how to arrange and serve a fine dinner, from commencement to close, after the manner of the French.

It should not be forgotten that much depends upon the appearance of the table, and the manner of serving the courses. In fact, more success can be attained by studied attention to the room, the table, and the serving of the courses, than in the preparation of costly viands.

On entering a dining-room, the first object which strikes the eye is the table. If the table is void of flowers, and other side decorations, including olives, radishes, and celery, tastefully arranged napkins and wine-glasses, an impression is given of a boarding-house table. On the contrary, when you see a beautifully decorated and artistically arranged table, the heart is immediately gladdened.

A proper regard should be given to the comfort of the guests as regards temperature. Have the room neither too cold nor too warm; the temperature should never exceed sixty degrees. The dining-room should be well aired before dinner commences. Great care should be taken that the dinner be served very hot. Noises with plates and glasses should be avoided.

There is as much system in serving a fine dinner as there is in running a railroad, or in any other business. French dinners are generally served in three main courses, viz., *Relevés, Entrées,* and *Rotis;* all the rest are considered side courses. It depends entirely on the taste of the host as to how many main courses he desires served. The author would suggest two *relevés,* three *entrées,* and one or two *rotis;* this could be made an elaborate dinner.

Naturally, what you shall serve will depend entirely on what there is in market at the season. For instance, you cannot serve brook-trout in January, or canvas-back duck during the months of June, July, August, or September. However, the very best in the market should invariably be selected.

Care should be taken to have the wines at the right temperature. Sherry, Sauterne, Chablis, and Rhine wines should always be served cold. Champagne should be served very cold, almost at the freezing-point. Bordeaux and Burgundy should be kept twelve hours before dinner in a room at a temperature of seventy degrees. Servants should be instructed not to fill the glasses more than three-fourths full; for guests are in danger of soiling their dresses, and, again, it is not considered good form.

The following is a fair menu for a New Year's dinner, with the necessary instructions how to serve it:

Blue Point Oysters, 298. *Haut Sauterne.*

SOUPS.

Consommé Royale, 107. Cream of Asparagus, 70. *Amontillado.*

HORS D'ŒUVRE.

Radishes, 292. Olives.

Timbales à l'Ecossaise, 261.

RELEVES.

Bass à la Régence, 305.

Potatoes à la Windsor, 1008. *Rauenthaler-Berg.*

Fillet of Beef, larded à la Parisienne, 514.

Saddle of Mutton, currant jelly, 666. *Pommery Sec.*

ENTREES.

Sweetbreads, larded à la Colbert, 617.

Terrapin à la Maryland, 397. *Chateau Latour.*

SORBET.

Kirsch Punch, 1305.

RÔTIS.

Canvas-back Ducks, 874.

Celery, Mayonnaise Salad, 1042. *Chambertin.*

ENTREMETS.

Artichoke Bottoms, 897. French Peas, 977.

String Beans, 948.

SWEET ENTREMETS.

Plum Pudding à l'Anglaise, 1163.

ICES.

Vanilla, 1271. Pistache, 1275.

Fruit. Cakes.

Coffee, 1349.

Cordials.

To begin with the oysters or clams: place some finely chopped ice on each soup-plate, with a small fancy napkin on top. Arrange the oysters or clams nicely on top of each plate, with a piece of lemon, and serve. With this course serve also Haut Sauterne. It is understood that the oysters or clams are to be served after all the guests are seated. It should be made a rule never to remove any plates while some of the guests are still eating. When all have finished, remove the oyster-plates and leave dinner-plates in their stead; then serve the soup. The servant is expected to present a plate of each kind to each guest, and ask which is preferred. Serve sherry with the soup. Always serve the plates on the right side, and remove on the left. Serve timbales. First put a spoonful of sauce on each plate, and then the timbale; at the same time you are serving the timbale, remove the cold plates and serve the fish. Put the fish on the plates, then the sauce, with a few potatoes on the same plate. Serve Rauenthaler-Berg. Remove the plates and serve fillet of beef, which should be cut in small, even slices. Put the sauce on the plate, and then the fillet. Place the artichokes on the same plate. Serve Pommery Sec with this and with the other course. Remove the plates and serve saddle of mutton. Cut the loin of the saddle lengthwise, and then crosswise, and serve with a little gravy and a spoonful of string-beans on the same plate. When this course is finished, serve the sweetbreads. Put the sauce first on the plate, as with the fillet, with a spoonful of peas. With this serve Chateau Latour. The next course, terrapin, should be served in a very hot tureen. Before serving, add a little fine sherry; mix well, and give each guest a small portion. Serve more Chateau Latour with this course.

After this comes sorbet. This can be served in glasses or in shells; for instance, take six lemons or six small oranges, cut off the tops, take the soft parts out of them, and in them place the sorbet. Arrange them on cold dessert-plates, decorated with small fancy napkins or fancy paper. While the guests are enjoying the sorbet, remove sherry, Sauterne, and Hock glasses, no matter if empty or full. (Replace knives and forks before serving the sorbet.)

Now come canvas-back ducks. Before serving, place them for a moment before the host, so that all the guests can see them. Cut off only the breasts, and serve with a little of the gravy and a small piece of fried hominy, on very hot plates; then pass around the currant jelly. You can serve a whole breast or a half one; however, during a hearty dinner, a half one is preferable; this is entirely at the disposition of the host. Serve celery salad with mayonnaise dressing on separate dessert-plates, with forks, and then serve Chambertin.

When this course is finished, remove all side dishes, casters, and salt and pepper cruets, and leave nothing on the table but flowers, fruits, and cakes. Clean the table neatly with a brush or napkin, and then place dessert spoons and forks at each cover. Serve plum pudding the same as *omelette au rum*. Pour the rum over the pudding, spread powdered sugar on top, and, with a spoon, keep pouring the burning liquid over it until it ceases to burn. Then cut in slices and serve, putting some of the liquid on each plate.

Vanilla and pistache ice-cream should be served on cold dessert-plates with fancy paper underneath, and with dessert spoons and forks. Serve the cakes with the ice-cream.

When this course is finished, serve to each guest a finger-bowl, with a thin slice of lemon in the water. Small cups for coffee should be passed at the same time. Fruits, nuts, and raisins come next. It is customary with some old American families to introduce at this course a bottle of very old Madeira wine; but this is certainly not necessary.

Now comes the last, the coffee, which must be served fresh and very hot, for the preparation of which the author refers you to page 381. At the same time serve cordials, and the dinner will be completed.

MENUS FOR EVERY DAY IN THE YEAR.

EXPLANATORY NOTE.

While these menus are simple and complete, it is not supposed that they can always be carried out in detail. They will, however, furnish suggestions to house-keepers who are daily perplexed with the question, "What shall we have for breakfast, luncheon, and dinner?" The number placed after each dish refers to the recipe showing how the dish is prepared. The menus are arranged so as to be used for any year. New Year's, 1890, will begin on a Wednesday instead of a Tuesday, as here printed; in that case, use the New Year's menu and then turn to the first Thursday in January and proceed in regular order. Should you come out uneven at the end of the month, through skipping some days at the first, turn back again to the beginning. For instance should Thursday be the 29th of January, instead of the last, as printed, turn back to the first Friday in January, and proceed until the month is completed. Special menus have been prepared for New Year's Day, Washington's Birthday, Fourth of July, Thanksgiving Day, and Christmas.

NEW YEAR'S DAY.

Tuesday, January —.

Breakfast.

Eggs à l'Aurore, 444.
Boiled Haddock, Cream sauce, 352, 181.
Lamb Chops, maison d'or, 683.
Potato Croquettes, 997.
Stewed Prunes à la Général Dufour, 1330.
Wheat Cakes, 1184.

Luncheon.

Stuffed Deviled Crabs, 370.
Chicken Sauté à la Marengo, 771.
Sweet Potatoes Soufflées, 1010.
Macaroni au Gratin, 955.
Maraschino Pudding, 1134.

Dinner.

Blue Point Oysters, 298.   *Haut Sauterne.*
SOUPS.
Cream of Asparagus, 70.
Consommé Royale, 107.   *Amontillado.*
HORS D'ŒUVRE.
Radishes, 292.   *Olives.*
Timbales à l'Ecossaise, 261.
RELEVÉS.
Bass à la Régence, 305.
Potatoes à la Windsor, 1008.   *Rauenthaler-Berg.*
Fillet of Beef, larded à la Parisienne, 514.
Saddle of Mutton, currant jelly, 666.   *Pommery Sec.*
ENTRÉES.
Sweetbreads, larded à la Colbert, 617.
Terrapin à la Maryland, 397.   *Chateau Latour.*
SORBET.
Kirsch Punch, 1305.
ROTIS.
Canvas-back Ducks, 874.
Celery, Mayonnaise Salad, 1042.   *Chambertin.*
ENTREMETS.
Artichoke Bottoms, 897.   French Peas, 977.
String Beans, 948.
SWEET ENTREMETS.
Plum Pudding à l'Anglaise, 1163.
ICES.
Vanilla, 1271.   Pistache, 1275.
Fruit.   Cakes.
Coffee, 1349.
Cordials.

Wednesday, January —.

Breakfast.
Eggs, with brown butter, 414.
Fried Scallops, Tomato sauce, 301-205.
Minced Lamb à l'Anglaise, 688.
Hashed Potatoes, 1002.
Rice and Milk, 1177.

Luncheon.
Lobster à la Bordelaise, 360.
Mutton Chops, Maintenon, 685.
Potatoes Château, 1009.
Herring Salad, 1074.
Galette, 1221.

Dinner.
Oysters, 298.
Mock Turtle, 17.
Celery, 290. Sardines, 283.
Fillets of Sole, Joinville, 322.
Salmi of Duck à la Bourgeoise, 829.
String Beans, with cream, 946.
Venison Steak, Londonderry sauce, 880.
Stuffed Tomatoes, 1023.
Roast Veal, 585.
Escarole Salad, 1055.
Nelson Pudding, 1155.
Coffee, 1349.

Thursday, January —.

Breakfast.
Omelet Raspail, 467.
Fish Balls, 347.
Beefsteak, with Anchovy butter, 524-146.
Potatoes à la Rice, 1007.
Blanc Mange à la Josephine Delmonico, 1270.

Luncheon.
Oyster Patties, 387.
Broiled Kidneys, with Bacon, 713.
Saratoga Potatoes, 1011.
Blanquette of Veal, with Mouilles, 552.
Strawberry Tarts, 1117.

Dinner.
Oysters, 298.
Purée Crécy, 47.
Olives. Radishes, 292.
Salmon à la Régence, 305.
Sweetbreads, with Spinach, 607.
Spaghetti à l'Italienne, 960.
Mignon Filets aux Pommes Parisiennes, 515.
Roast Chicken, 755.
Celery Salad, 1041.
Almond Cake, 1224.
Coffee, 1349.

Friday, January —.

Breakfast.
Eggs à la Bourguignonne, 411.
Whitebait, 301.
Pig's Feet à la Boston, 730.
Succotash, 1022.
Brioche à la Condé, 1203.

Luncheon.
Boiled Skate, cream sauce, 325-181.
Stewed Calf's Liver à l'Alsacienne, 582.
Oyster-Plant Poulette, 1019.
Lobster Salad à la Plummer, 1062.
Vermicelli Pudding, 1142.

Dinner.
Oysters, 298.
Cream of Asparagus, 70.
Celery, 290. Thon, 282.
Smelts à la Toulouse, 354.
Braised Beef à la Flamande, 482.
Artichokes à la Florentine, 903.
Chicken Sauté à la Marengo, 771.
French Peas.
Roast Quail, with Watercress, 834.
Lettuce Salad, 1057.
Pie à la Martha Washington, 1105.
Coffee, 1349.

Saturday, January —.

Breakfast.

Ham Omelet, 462.
Boiled Halibut, butter sauce, 309-157.
Chicken Livers, with Bacon, 769.
Sweet Potatoes Soufflées, 1010.
Corn Fritters, 965.

Luncheon.

Stuffed Oysters à la Mali, 386.
Chicken Pot-pie, 757.
Anchovy Salad, 1037.
Diplomatic Pudding, 1129.

Dinner.

Clams, 300.
Pot-au-feu, 54.
Olives.   Radishes, 292.
Matelote of Eels, 332.
Partridge, braised with Cabbage, 845.
Stewed Tomatoes, 1027.
Calf's Head à la Poulette, 639.
Potatoes à la Bignon, 1001.
Roast Mutton, 585.
Chicory Salad, 1045.
Baked Apple Dumplings, 1122.
Champagne Jelly, 1322.
Coffee, 1349

Sunday, January —.

Breakfast.

Eggs à la Livingstone, 410.
Picked-up Codfish, 346.
Escalops of Veal, Provençale, 573.
Potatoes Julienne, 1013.
Iced Timbale of Rice, 1175.

Luncheon.

Lobster à la Newburg, 359.
Chicken Croquettes à la Périgourdin, 761.
Hashed Potatoes au Gratin, 1004.
Macaroni, with cream, 954.
Chocolate Eclairs, 1243.

Dinner.

Oysters, 298.
Chicken à la Piémontaise, 63.
Radishes, 292.   Celery, 290
Blackfish au Gratin, 319.
Minced Beef à la Catalan, 502,
Cauliflower, butter sauce, 925.
Boiled Leg of Mutton, caper sauce, 651.
Brussels Sprouts, 922.
Romaine Punch, 1304.
Roast Grouse, 852.
Watercress Salad, 1072.
English Pudding, 1137.
Stilton Cheese.
Coffee, 1349.

Monday, January —.

Breakfast.

Omelet, with fine Herbs, 451.
Lobster Cutlets, Victoria, 366,
Sausages au Gastronome, 740.
Carrots and Cream, 927.
Rice à l'Airolo, 1171.

Luncheon.

Broiled Sardines on Toast, 403.
Hamburg Steak, Russian sauce, 526.
Potatoes à la Hanna, 1012.
Chicken Salad, 1044.
Apple Tarts, 1120.

Dinner.

Clams, 300.
Brunoise, 2.
Lyon Sausage, 286.   Olives
Smelts au Gratin, 356.
Stewed Lamb, with Peas, 706.
Potatoes Soufflées, 1010.
Croquettes of Sweetbreads, Périgueux, 619.
String Beans, 946.
Squash à l'Américaine, 820.
Barbe de Capucine Salad, 1038.
Plum Pudding, 1110.
Coffee, 1349.

Tuesday, January —.

Breakfast.

Fried Eggs, 412.
Soles à la Horly, 321.
Mutton Chops, Soyer, 647.
Stewed Potatoes, 995.
Peach Marmalade, 1331.

Luncheon.

Lobster en Chevreuse, 362.
Mignon Filets aux Pommes Parisienne, 515.
Celery a la Bonne Femme, 928.
Apple Pie, 1083.

Dinner.

Oysters, 298.
Chicken, with Leeks, 68.
Radishes, 292.   Thon, 282.
Broiled Sea Bass, maître d'hôtel, 326.
Cucumber Salad, 289.
Hot Patties à l'Anglaise, 266.
Braised Noix of Veal, Morlaisienne, 635.
Stuffed Egg-Plant, 909.
Roast Chicken, 755.
Lettuce, and Egg Salad, 1058.
Charlottes Glacées, 1299.
Coffee, 1349.

Wednesday, January —.

Breakfast.

Eggs à la Tripe, 419.
Porterhouse Steak, with Watercress, 524.
Cold Boiled Ham, 722.
Hashed Potatoes au Gratin, 1004.
Brioche Fluttes, 1204.

Luncheon.

Stuffed Clams, deviled, 376.
Epigrammes of Lamb, with chicory, 690.
Macaroni au Gratin, 955.
French Pudding, 1139.

Dinner.

Oysters, 298.
Consommé Royal, 107.
Celery, 290.   Olives.
Fillets of Bass à la Chambord, 343.
Croquettes of Chicken à la Reine, 758.
Braised Beef à la Mode, 479.
Spinach, maître d'hôtel, 942.
Roast Venison, currant jelly sauce, 878.
Escarole Salad, 1055.
Savarin à l'Anglaise, 1199.
Sherry Wine Jelly, 1318.
Coffee, 1349.

Thursday, January —.

Breakfast.

Scrambled Eggs, with Asparagus tops, 406.
Broiled Sardines on Toast, 403.
Black Sausages, with mashed Potatoes, 719.
Stewed Prunes, 1330.

Luncheon.

Canapé Lorenzo, 391.
Beefsteak Pie à l'Anglaise, 487.
Macédoine Salad, 1063.
Rhubarb Tarts, 1112.

Dinner.

Clams, 300.
Terrapin, 61.
Radishes, 292.   Lyon Sausage, 286.
Sheep's-head au Gratin, 319.
Saddle of Mutton à la Sevigné, 669.
Broiled Fresh Mushrooms on Toast, 916.
Chicken Sauté à la Parmentier, 773.
French Peas.
Roast Partridge sur Canapé, 843.
Celery, Mayonnaise Salad, 1042.
Baba au Rhum, 1217.
Coffee, 1349.

Friday, January —.

Breakfast.
Oyster Omelet, 452.
Pork Andouillettes, 742.
Mutton Chops, maison d'or, 683.
Sorrel, with Croûtons, 974.
French Pancake, 1186.

Luncheon.
Mussels à la Marinière, 378.
Duck à l'Américaine, 823.
String Beans, 947.
Apple Charlotte, 1167.

Dinner.
Oysters, 298.
Bisque of Crabs, 9.
Celery, 290.   Olives.
Broiled Pompano, maître d'hôtel, 329.
Cucumber Salad, 289.
Tenderloin Piqué à la Bernardi, 523.
Stuffed Green Peppers, 975.
Calf's Head en tortue, 641.
Roast Quail, 834.
Watercress Salad, 1072.
Vanilla Ice-Cream, 1271.
Lady-Fingers, 1231
Coffee, 1349.

Saturday, January —.

Breakfast.
Eggs à la Finoise, 424.
Codfish à la Bonne Femme, 345.
Veal Cutlets en Papillottes, 566.
Mashed Potatoes au Gratin, 998.
Milan Cake, 1228.

Luncheon.
Crabs à la St. Jean, 371.
Chicken à la Maryland, 785.
Stewed Tomatoes, 1027.
Anchovy Salad, 1037.
Apricot Tarts, 1108.

Dinner.
Oysters à l'Alexandre Dumas, 299.
Croûte-au-Pot, 11.
Thon, 282.   Radishes, 292.
Fillet of Soles, à la Hollandaise, 317.
Potatoes à la Parisienne, 986.
Shoulder of Lamb Rouennaise, 698.
Spinach, with gravy, 943.
Sweetbreads à la Béarnaise, 610.
Roast Squabs, 816.
Chicory Salad, 1045.
Omelet Célestine, 477.
Lemon Water Ice, 1279.
Coffee, 1349.

Sunday, January —.

Breakfast.
Sausage Omelet, 465.
Fried Smelts, tartare sauce, 301, 207.
Kidneys, stewed with Madeira, 662.
Potatoes, maître d'hôtel, 985.
Preserved Peaches, 1340.

Luncheon.
Stuffed Clams, 376.
Curry of Lamb à l'Indienne, 677.
Spaghetti au Gratin, 961.
Chicken Salad, 1044.
Apple Pie, meringué, 1103.

Dinner.
Oysters, 298.
Consommé Deslignac, 108.
Celery, 290.   Olives.
Bass aux Fines Herbes, 323.
Suprême of Chicken à la Toulouse, 786.
Brussels Sprouts, 922.
Antelope Steak, purée of Chestnuts, 890, 882.
Potatoes à la Bignon, 1001.
Kirsch Punch, 1305.
Roast Beef, 527.
Escarole Salad, 1055.
Diplomatic Pudding, 1129.
Gorgonzolla Cheese.
Coffee, 1349.

Monday, January —.

Breakfast.
Eggs à l'Aurore, 444.
Mackerel aux Fines Herbes, 331.
Minced Beef à la Provençale, 500.
Sweet Potatoes Soufflées, 1010.
Corn Fritters, 965.

Luncheon.
Broiled Florida Shad, maitre d'hôtel, 326.
Cucumber Salad, 289.
Beef Tongue, with risotto, 537.
Macaroni and Cream 954.
Cream Renversée, 1252.

Dinner.
Clams, 300.
Chicken à la Portugaise, 66.
Radishes, 292. Celery, 290.
Lobster au Curry, 358.
Pork Chops, sauce piquante, 745.
Cauliflower, with butter, 925.
Croquettes of Chicken à la Reine, 758.
Stuffed Lettuce, 953.
Roast Turkey, Cranberry sauce, 800, 1329.
Barbe de Capucine Salad, 1038.
Omelet Soufflée, 474.
Kümmel Jelly, 1323.
Coffee, 1349.

Tuesday, January —.

Breakfast.
Oatmeal and Cream.
Sardine Omelet, 468.
Beefsteak, Horseradish sauce, 524-164.
Mashed Potatoes, 998.
German Pancake, with Apples, 1189.

Luncheon.
Broiled Pompano, 329.
Roulade of Beef à l'Ecarlate, 539.
Sorrel, with eggs, 974.
Salad à l'Italienne, 1036.
Peach Pie, 1092.

Dinner.
Oysters, 298.
Cream of Celery, 71.
Thon, 282. Radishes, 292.
Deviled Crabs, 370.
Shoulder of Lamb, jardinière, 696.
Potatoes Duchesse, 1006.
Artichoke Bottoms, Florentine, 903.
Antelope Chops, Currant jelly, 891.
Beans Panachés, 950.
Doe-birds sur canapé, 838.
Celery Salad, 1042.
Cabinet Pudding à la Sadi-Carnot, 1164.
Coffee, 1349.

Wednesday, January —.

Breakfast.
Asparagus Omelet, 458.
Minced Beef à la Catalan, 502.
Turnips, with gravy, 967.
Rice à la Française, 1180.

Luncheon.
Lobster à l'Américaine, 357.
Sweetbread Croquettes à la Périgueux, 619.
Potatoes Julienne, 1013.
Stewed Fresh Mushrooms, with cream, 915.
Sago Pudding, 1140.

Dinner.
Clams, 300.
Purée à la Parmentier, 44.
Radishes, 292. Sardines, 283.
Broiled Blackfish, Shrimp sauce, 325, 178.
Civet of Hare à la Française, 893.
Celery à la Bonne Femme, 928.
Mutton Chops à la Robinson, 682.
Stuffed Tomatoes, 1023.
Roast Red-head Ducks, 876.
Lettuce Salad, 1059.
Charlotte Panachée, 1300.
Coffee, 1349.

Thursday, January —.

Breakfast.
Eggs, with brown butter, 414.
Mutton Hash à la Zingara, 652.
Lima Beans, 952.
Small Brioches, 1202.

Luncheon.
Oysters à la Poulette, 383.
Corned Beef and Cabbage, 490.
Macaroni Napolitaine, 957.
Chicken Salad, 1044.
Cherry Tarts, 1111.

Dinner.
Oysters, 298.
Busecca, 7.
Celery, 290.   Olives.
Salmon à la Génoise, 306.
Boiled Turkey, Oyster sauce, 797.
Spinach à l'Anglaise, 940.
Lamb Steak, purée of Peas, 716.
Potatoes à la Parisienne, 986.
Woodcock sur Canapé, 871.
Tomato Salad, 1070.
Hot Savarin, 1198.
Coffee, 1349.

Friday, January —.

Breakfast.
Eggs à la Bennett, 447.
Fried Smelts, Colbert sauce, 301, 190.
Country Sausages à l'Anglaise, 736.
Beet-roots, with cream, 912.
Stewed Quinces, 1338.

Luncheon.
Stuffed Lobster à la Diable, 367.
Stewed Veal, Solferino, 628.
Fried Egg-plant, 907.
Tongue Salad, 1056.
Caramel Pudding, 1166.

Dinner.
Oysters, 298.
Bouille-à-Baisse, 1.
Olives.   Sardines, 283.
Bass à la Vénitienne, 338.
Beef Tongue à la Chipolata, 532, 232.
Stuffed Green Peppers, 975.
Pigeon Cutlets à la Victoria, 815.
Potatoes à la Windsor, 1008.
Saddle of Antelope, Cranberry sauce, 878, 1329.
Celery Salad, 1041.
Chocolate Ice-Cream, 1272.
Vanilla Eclairs, 1245.
Coffee, 1349.

Saturday, January —.

Breakfast.
Cheese Omelet, 469.
Broiled Spanish-Mackerel, 329.
Breaded Veal Cutlets, tomato sauce, 563.
Broiled Bacon, 754.
Rice au Lait d'Amandes, 1170.

Luncheon.
Oysters en Brochette au Petit Salé, 385.
Broiled Beefsteak, with Watercress, 524.
Brussels Sprouts, 922.
Stewed Lamb à la Parisienne, 708.
Apple Tarts, 1120.

Dinner.
Clams, 300.
Sorrel, with Asparagus tops, 41.
Lyon Sausage, 286.   Celery, 290.
Fried Eels, sauce tartare, 301, 207.
Potatoes, Saratoga, 1011.
Garnished Sour-krout, 924.
Salmi of Duck, with olives, 827.
Celery, with cream, 929.
Roast Leg of Lamb, 648.
Lettuce Salad, 1057.
Pineapple Pudding, 1148.
Coffee, 1349.

Sunday, January —.

Breakfast.

Eggs à la Meyerbeer, 437.
Veal Kidneys, sauce madère, 662.
Stuffed Pig's Feet, 732.
Potatoes à la Rice, 1007.
Fried Hominy, 1035.

Luncheon.

Lobster Croquettes à la Victoria, 365.
Broiled Grouse, bread sauce, 854, 162
Broiled Fresh Mushrooms on Toast, 916.
Boiled Apple Dumplings, 1127.

Dinner.

Oysters, 298.
Chicken à la Hollandaise, 64.
Celery, 290. Radishes, 292.
Red Snapper à la Créole, 339.
Beef Braised à l'Orsini, 481
Stuffed Tomatoes, 1023.
Lamb Croquettes, sauce Robert, 679, 192.
String Beans, 945.
Punch à la Cardinal, 1306.
Canvas-Back Ducks, Currant jelly, 874, 1326.
Chicory Salad, 1045.
Iced Pound Cake, 1193.
Pistache Ice-Cream, 1275.
Imported Brie Cheese.
Coffee, 1349.

Monday, January —.

Breakfast.

Mushroom Omelet, 460.
Cold Bass, Ravigote butter, 352, 147
Hashed Beef à la Zingara, 652.
Broiled Ham, 753.
Milan Cake, 1228.

Luncheon.

Soft Clams à la Newburg, 390.
Chicken Sauté, with Tarragon, 774.
Potatoes à l'Italienne, 990.
Herring Salad, 1074.
Baked Apples, 1124.

Dinner.

Oysters, 298.
Consommé Célestine, 118.
Thon, 282, Celery, 290.
Terrapin à la Maryland, 397.
Compote of Squabs, 822.
Fried Oyster-plant, 1021.
Veal Fricandeau à la Morlaisienne, 579.
Sorrel au Gras, 974.
Roast Saddle of Mutton, 664.
Tomato Salad, 1070.
Pithivier's Cake, 1225.
Peach Marmalade, 1331.
Coffee, 1349.

Tuesday, January —.

Breakfast.

Chicken Liver Omelet, 464.
Broiled Sardines, sauce percillade, 403, 165
Hashed Mutton au Gratin, 653.
Oyster-plant à la Poulette, 1019
Wheat Cakes, 1184.

Luncheon.

Sheep's-head, sauce Hollandaise, 309, 160.
Beefsteak Pie à l'Américaine, 488.
Cauliflower au Gratin, 926.
Lemon Pie, meringué, 1102.

Dinner.

Oysters, 298.
Mulligatawney, 34.
Tomatoes, 288. Olives.
Crawfish à la Bordelaise, 360.
Piloff of Chicken à la Turque, 782.
Succotash, 1022.
Sweetbreads Piqués à la Financière, 603.
Spaghetti à l'Italienne, 960.
Roast Quails, with Watercress, 834.
Escarole Salad, 1055.
Cocoanut Pudding, 1147.
Camembert Cheese.
Coffee, 1349.

MENUS.

Wednesday, January —.

Breakfast.

Eggs à la Valencienne, 421.
Fried Frostfish, sauce Colbert, 301–190.
Mignon Filets à la Bernardi, 512.
Hashed Potatoes au Gratin, 1004.
Stewed Apples, 1332.

Luncheon.

Crabs à l'Anglaise, 373.
Hashed Turkey en Bordure, 805.
Broiled Tomatoes, 1025.
Potato Salad, 1073.
Farina Pudding, 1144.

Dinner.

Clams, 300.
Beef à l'Ecossaise, 6.
Anchovies, 284.   Celery, 290.
Smelts à la Toulouse, 354.
Civet of Hare, poivrade sauce, 886.
Stuffed Cabbage, 919.
Breast of Lamb, jardinière, 702.
Roast Chicken, 755.
Watercress Salad, 1072.
Orange Water-Ice, 1280.
Allumettes, 1205.
Roquefort Cheese.
Coffee, 1349.

Thursday, January —.

Breakfast.

Scrambled Eggs, with Chicory, 409.
Broiled Oysters, 382.
Flat Sausages, with White Wine, 735.
Carrots, with Cream, 927.
Brioche à la Condé, 1203.

Luncheon.

Oysters à la Mali, 386.
Irish Stewed Mutton, 660.
Shrimp Salad, 1067.
French Pancake, with jelly, 1187.

Dinner.

Clams, 300.
Consommé au Vermicelli, 103.
Celery, 290.   Lyon Sausage, 286.
Frogs' Legs à la Geo. Merrill, 1372.
Leg of Mutton à la Condé, 649.
Stuffed Onions, 970.
Suprême of Chicken à la Toulouse, 786.
Fresh Mushrooms on Toast, 914.
Red-head Duck à l'Américaine, 820.
Lettuce and Egg Salad, 1058.
Peach Ice-Cream, 1276.
Almond Biscuits, 1235.
Coffee, 1349.

Friday, January —

Breakfast.

Tomato Omelet, 456.
Black Bass, Oyster sauce, 309, 173.
Chicken Livers en Brochette, 769.
Potatoes à la Lyonnaise, 991.
Waffles and Sugar, 1196.

Luncheon.

Croquettes of Salmon à la Victoria, 365, 208.
Calf's Head à la Vinaigrette, 640.
Okra, stewed with cream, 1031.
Russian Salad, 1065.
Bread Pudding, 1132.

Dinner.

Oysters à l'Alexandre Dumas, 299.
Mulligatawney à la Delmonico, 35.
Olives.   Thon, 282.
Pompano, with fine Herbs, 331.
Broiled Tenderloin, with Mushrooms, 496.
Lima Beans, 952.
Chicken Vol-au-Vent au Salpicon Royal, 810,
Artichokes à la Barigoul, 897.   [255.
Roast Woodcock, 871.
Chicory Salad, 1045.
Iced Timbale of Rice, 1175.
Swiss Cheese.
Coffee, 1349.

Saturday, January —.

Breakfast.
Oatmeal and Cream.
Eggs à la Provençale, 422.
Cod's Tongues, black butter, 349.
Fried Calf's Brains, sauce tartare, 559.
Oyster Plant, with butter, 1018.
Baked Apples, 1124.

Luncheon.
Crabs à la St. Laurent, 372.
Broiled Chicken on Toast, 756.
Brussels Sprouts, 922.
Timbales à la Schultze, 263.
Rum Omelet, 476

Dinner.
Oysters, 298.
Cream of Chicken, 82.
Anchovies, 284.   Radishes, 292.
Sheep's-head, Lobster sauce, 158.
Braised Beef à la Morlaisienne, 478.
Potatoes en Surprise, 1005.
Lamb Chops à la Signora, 681.
French Peas.
Roast Partridge, 843.
Celery Salad, 1042.
Charlotte au Café, 1262.
Coffee, 1349.

Sunday, January —.

Breakfast.
Kidney Omelet, 463.
Broiled Shad, maître d'hôtel, 326.
Hamburg Steak, Madeira sauce, 526–185.
Potatoes Lyonnaise, 991.
Cream Renversée, 1252.

Luncheon.
Truffled Boned Turkey, 813.
Mignon Filets à la Bohémienne, 513.
Potatoes au Gratin, 1004.
Shrimp Salad, 1067.
Chaussons, 1236.

Dinner.
Oysters, 298.
Consommé Colbert, 120.
Olives.   Celery, 290.
Smelts à la Béarnaise, 353.
Grenadin of Veal à la Sevigné, 588.
Celery, with Marrow, 930.
Fried Chicken, Cream sauce, 181.
String Beans. 948.
Punch à la Lallah Rookh, 1308.
Roast Doe-birds à l'Américaine, 840.
Escarole Salad, 1055.
Peach Pudding, 1150.
Gorgonyolla Cheese.
Coffee, 1349.

Monday, January —.

Breakfast.
Boiled Eggs.
Broiled Calf's Liver and Bacon, 584.
Tripe à la mode de Caën, 547.
Potatoes Lyonnaise 991.
Stewed Pears, 1333.

Luncheon.
Fried Oysters, 380.
Veal, stewed with Peas, 631.
Cauliflower Salad, 1040.
Pineapple Pie, 1087.

Dinner.
Clams, 300.
Julienne, 27.
Celery, 290.   Radishes, 292.
Turbot, sauce aurore, 309–182.
Bouchées à la Reine, 270.
Flageolets, 1365.
Epigrammes of Lamb, with Asparagus tops, 690.
Spaghetti à l'Italienne, 960.
Roast Beef, 527.
Tomato, Mayonnaise Salad, 1071.
Champagne Jelly, 1322.
Lady Fingers, 1231.
Coffee, 1349.

Tuesday, January —.

Breakfast.

Scrambled Eggs, with truffles, 407.
Boiled Haddock, Cream sauce, 352-181.
Brochettes of Lamb à la Dumas, 674.
Potatoes Parisienne, 986.
Crême en Mousse au Café, 1253.

Luncheon.

Bluefish à l'Italienne, 337.
Escalops of Veal à la Duxelle, 569.
Stuffed Cucumbers, 937.
Croquettes of Macaroni, 279.
Blackberry Tarts, 1119.

Dinner.

Oysters, 298.
Clear Green Turtle, 18.
Tomatoes, 288. Radishes, 292.
Shad, with fine Herbs, 323.
Broiled Sirloin Steak à la Bordelaise, 491.
Potatoes Bignon, 1001.
Timbale of Foie-gras, Lagardère, 809.
Roast Partridge, 843.
Lettuce, Mayonnaise Salad, 1057-1042.
Apples Meringuées, 1248.
Cheddar Cheese.
Coffee, 1349.

Wednesday, February —.

Breakfast.

Eggs à l'Impératrice, 440.
Mutton Chops, Soyer, with Potatoes, 647.
Broiled Ham, 753.
Milan Cake, 1228.

Luncheon.

Fried Oysters, 380.
Blanquette of Veal, with nouilles, 552.
Fried Sweet Potatoes, 993.
Mince Pie, 1082.

Dinner.

Clams, 300.
Menestra, 36.
Sardines, 283. Celery, 290.
Lobster en Chevreuse, 362.
Tenderloin Piqué à l'Egyptienne, 521.
French Peas.
Broiled Fresh Mushrooms on Toast, 916.
Croquettes of Sweetbreads, with Peas, 620.
Roast Goose, 808.
Watercress Salad, 1072.
Boiled Peach Dumplings, 1125.
Coffee, 1349.

Thursday, February —.

Breakfast.

Omelet Régence, 470.
Boiled Porgies, maître d'hôtel, 329.
Minced Veal à la Discaëmie, 576.
Turnips and Gravy, 967.
Preserved Cherries, 1347.

Luncheon.

Oysters en Brochette au Petit Salé, 385.
Chicken Pot Pie, 757.
Tomatoes à la Marseillaise, 1029.
Beef Salad, 1039.
Stewed Pears, 1333.

Dinner.

Oysters, 298.
Consommé, with Italian paste, 103.
Olives. Tomatoes, 288.
Broiled Spanish-Mackerel, 329.
Cucumber Salad, 289.
Beef Tongue à la Gendarme, 532.
Fried Oyster Plant, 1021.
Salmi of Woodcock à la Chasseur, 873.
Roast Veal, 585.
Lettuce Salad, 1057.
Pistache Ice Cream, 1275.
Bitter Almond Macaroons, 1209.
Coffee, 1349.

Friday, February —.

Breakfast.

Eggs à la Chipolata, 442.
Picked-up Codfish, 346.
Lamb en Brochette, Colbert sauce, 674-190.
Stewed Potatoes, 995.
Rice and Milk, 1177.

Luncheon.

Fillets of Sole à la Vénitienne, 338.
Breaded Veal Cutlets, Tomato sauce, 563.
String Beans, 946.
Crab Salad, 1047.
Plum Pudding, 1163.

Dinner.

Oysters, 298.
Bisque of Lobster, 10.
Sardines, 283.   Olives.
Salmon, en papillotes, 302.
Tenderloin à la Hussarde, 519.
Succotash, 1022.
Coquilles of Chicken, with Mushrooms, 271.
Roast English Snipe sur canapé, 868.
Celery Salad, 1041.
Baba, 1216.
Pont l'Evêque Cheese.
Coffee, 1349.

Saturday, February —.

Breakfast.

Omelet Bonne Femme, 466.
Tripe Sauté à la Lyonnaise, 548.
Beefsteak, with Watercress, 524.
Hashed Potatoes, with Cream, 1003.
Corn Fritters, 965.

Luncheon.

Canapé Lorenzo, 391.
Lamb Chops à la Robinson, 682.
French Peas.
Anchovy Salad, 1037.
Diplomatic Pudding, 1129.

Dinner.

Oysters, 298.
Consommé Tapioca, 104.
Thon, 282.   Celery, 290.
Boiled Sheep's-head, with fine Herbs, 352-323.
Pig's Cheek, Apple sauce, 726-168.
Oyster Plant à la Poulette, 1019.
Piloff of Chicken à la Créole, 783.
Beans à l'Anglaise, 948.
Roast Mutton, 585.
Barbe de Capucine Salad, 1038.
Charlotte Russe, 1261.
Coffee, 1349.

Sunday, February —.

Breakfast.

Eggs à la Turque, 439.
Hashed Lamb, 700.
Sausages, with White Wine, 735.
Potatoes Julienne, 1013.
Peach Marmalade, 1331.

Luncheon.

Broiled Spanish Mackerel, maître d'hôtel, 329.
Cucumber Salad, 289.
Stewed Veal à la Marengo, 624.
Rhubarb Pie, 1085.

Dinner.

Oysters, 298.
Consommé Douglas, 114.
Celery, 290.   Lyons Sausage, 286.
Croquettes of Lobster, sauce Colbert, 365-190.
Sweetbreads à la Duxelle, 608.
Broiled Tomatoes, 1025.
Chicken Sauté à l'Hongroise, 772.
Spinach, with croûtons, 943.
Romaine Punch, 1304.
Roast English Snipe, 868.
Watercress Salad, 1072.
Croustade of Rice, 1176.
Imported Brie Cheese.
Coffee, 1349.

Monday, February —.

Breakfast.
Omelet Mexicaine, 473.
Broiled English Breakfast Bacon, 754.
Calf's Liver Sauté à l'Italienne, 580.
Stewed Tomatoes, 1027.
Preserved Plums, 1343.

Luncheon.
Soft Clams à la Merrill, 389.
Curry of Chicken à l'Indienne, 792.
French Peas.
Salad Suédoise, 1069.
Mille-feuilles, 1223.

Dinner.
Clams, 300.
Consommé Printanier, 109.
Celery, 290.   Caviare, 281.
Broiled Smelts, Béarnaise, 353.
Broiled Lamb Chops, Bordelaise sauce, 647-186.
Spaghetti à l'Italienne, 960.
Antelope Steak, Currant jelly sauce, 884.
Sweet Potatoes, Hollandaise, 999.
Roast Teal Ducks, 859.
Chicory Salad, 1045.
Tapioca Pudding, 1141.
Coffee, 1349.

Tuesday, February —.

Breakfast.
Eggs au Miroir, 425.
Broiled Deviled Mutton, Kidneys, 715.
Hamburg Steak, Russian sauce, 526.
Lima Beans, 952.
German Pancake, 1188.

Luncheon.
Broiled Shad, maître d'hôtel, 326.
Cucumber Salad, 289.
Salmi of Duck, Rouennaise, 825.
Onions, with Cream, 968.
Greengage Pie, 1093.

Dinner.
Oysters, 298.
Chicken à la Richmond, 62.
Celery, 290.   Radishes, 292.
Stuffed Lobster, 367.
Tenderloin, piqué à la Portugaise, 517.
Potatoes Duchesse, 1006.
Squabs en Crapaudine, 819.
Brussels Sprouts sautés au beurre, 922.
Roast Chicken, 755.
Celery, Mayonnaise Salad, 1042.
Sponge Cake, 1195.
English Cheese.
Coffee, 1349.

Wednesday, February —.

Breakfast.
Tomato Omelet, 456.
Broiled Smelts, Béarnaise, 353.
Chicken Livers en Brochette, 769.
Potato Croquettes, 997.
Preserved Apricots, 1340.

Luncheon.
Lobster en Brochette, 361.
Beefsteak Pie à l'Anglaise, 487.
Spinach, with eggs, 943.
Macédoine Salad, 1063.
Huckleberry Tarts, 1113.

Dinner.
Oysters, 298.
Giblet à l'Anglaise, 22.
Sardines, 283.   Celery, 290.
Bass à la Chambord, 343.
Stewed Veal à la Grecque, 626.
Edible Snails à la Bourguignonne, 393.
Artichokes, Barigoul, 897.
Roast Plover, 865.
Lettuce Salad, 1057.
Crème en mousse, 1260.
Sweet Almond Macaroons, 1210.
Coffee, 1349.

Thursday, February —.

Breakfast.

Eggs à l'Impératrice, 440.
Broiled Pig's Feet, maître d'hôtel, 727, 145
Smoked Beef, with Cream, 486.
Potatoes Hollandaise, 999.
Brioche, 1201.

Luncheon.

Oyster Patties, 387.
Sirloin Steak à la Duchesse, 494.
Potatoes Château, 1009.
Lobster Salad à la Plummer, 1062.
Vanilla Eclairs, 1245

Dinner.

Clams, 300.
Consommé Rachel, 123.
Radishes, 292.   Olives.
Crabs, St. Laurent, 372.
Panplette of Veal, purée of Chestnuts, 594.
Fried Oyster-plant, 1021.
Chicken Sauté, with tarragon, 774.
Asparagus à la Tessinoise, 906.
Roast Beef, 527.
Celery, Mayonnaise Salad, 1042.
Parfait au Café, 1295.
Coffee, 1349.

Friday, February —.

Breakfast.

Omelet, with fine Herbs, 451.
Haddock, Cream sauce, 352, 181.
Brochette of Lamb à la Colbert, 674, 190
Saratoga Potatoes, 1011.
Buckwheat Cakes, 1183.

Luncheon.

Fried Smelts, Tomato sauce, 301, 205.
Leg of Mutton, Bretonne, 650.
Spaghetti à l'Italienne, 960.
Russian Salad, 1065.
Blackberry Pie, 1097

Dinner.

Oysters, 298.
Bisque of Clams, 8.
Celery, 290.   Olives.
Lobster à l'Américaine, 357.
Broiled Tenderloin à la Nivernaise, 505.
Stewed Tomatoes, 1027.
Stuffed Pig's Feet, Périgueux, 732.
Goose, stuffed with Chestnuts, 808.
Romaine Salad, 1064.
Custard Pudding, 1154.
Brie Cheese.
Coffee, 1349.

Saturday, February —.

Breakfast.

Eggs à la Reine, 438.
Broiled Fresh Herrings, anchovy butter, 329.
Minced Veal à la Catalan, 575.   [146.
Stewed Carrots, and Cream, 927.
Peach Marmalade, 1331.

Luncheon.

Broiled Lobster, Tomato sauce, 364, 205.
Stewed Lamb, and Potatoes, 708.
Broiled Fresh Mushrooms on Toast, 916.
Apples, with Rice, 1169.

Dinner.

Oysters, 298.
Cream of Cauliflower, 73.
Celery, 290.   Radishes, 292.
Bluefish à l'Icarienne, 336.
Roast Sucking Pig, Apple sauce, 720.
Stuffed Green Peppers, 975.
Turkey's Legs à la Diable, 766.
Beans Panachés, 950.
Roast Spring Lamb, Mint sauce, 1361, 169.
Lettuce Salad, 1058.
Charlotte Russe, 1261.
Coffee, 1349.

MENUS.

Sunday, February —.

Breakfast.
Omelet, with Cheese, 469.
Broiled Mutton Chops, Parisian potatoes, 647.
Tripe Sauté à la Créole, 545. [986.
Wheat Cakes, 1184.

Luncheon.

Canapé Madison, 260.
Broiled Sirloin à la Moëlle, 493.
Spaghetti Napolitaine, 959.
String Bean Salad, 1068.
Frangipani Tarts, 1121.

Dinner.
Oysters à l'Alexandre Dumas, 299.
Consommé Châtelaine, 128.
Radishes, 292.   Tomatoes, 288.
Bass à la Vénitienne, 338.
Chicken Sauté à la Marengo, 771.
Sweet Potatoes Hollandaise, 999.
Sweetbreads, larded à la Soubise, 606.
Carrots, with Cream, 927.
Punch à la Lorenzo Delmonico, 1303.
Roast Beef, 527.
Barbe de Capucine Salad, 1038.
Cabinet Pudding à la Sadi-Carnot, 1164.
Strachino Cheese.
Coffee, 1349.

Monday, February —.

Breakfast.
Eggs à la Bonne Femme, 432.
Cod's Tongues à la Poulette, 351.
Tenderloin of Pork, sauce piquante, 741, 203. Olives.
Fried Oyster-plant, 1021.
Waffles, with Sugar, 1196.

Luncheon.

Hashed Lamb à la Polonaise, 700.
Escalops of Veal, Jardinière, 568.
Succotash, 1022.
Shrimp Salad, 1067.
Pear Pie, 1084.

Dinner.
Clams, 300.
A la Russe, 55.
Bologna Sausage, 286.
Halibut, Lobster sauce, 309-158.
Corned Beef, with Kale sprouts, 490.
Potatoes à la Windsor, 1008.
Sweetbreads à la Béarnaise, 610.
Green Peas à la Bourgeoise, 970.
Roast Chicken, with Watercress, 755.
Doucette Salad, 1052.
Apple Charlotte, 1167.
Coffee, 1349.

Tuesday, February —.

Breakfast.
Omelet Régence, 470.
Broiled Ham, 753.
Lamb Chops à la Robinson, 682.
Lima Beans, 952.
Stewed Plums, 1337.

Luncheon.

Broiled Deviled Lobster, butter sauce, 364, 159.
Stewed Tripe à la Lyonnaise, 548.
Fried Egg-plant, 907.
Apple Fritters, 1191.

Dinner.
Oysters, 298.
Crabs, with Gumbo, 24.
Radishes, 292.   Olives.
Smelts, Toulouse, 354.
Tendron of Veal à la Chipolata, 636.
Chicken Sauté à la Parmentier, 773.
Tomatoes à la Bock, 1026.
Roast Squabs, 816.
Beet-root and Doucette Salad, 1053.
Almond Cake, 1224.
Neufchatel Cheese.
Coffee, 1349.

Wednesday, February —.

Breakfast.

Eggs à la Hyde, 448.
Broiled Boned Smelts, tartare sauce, 354, 207
Escalops of Veal au Jus, 568.
Hashed Potatoes, 1002.
Milan Cake, 1228.

Luncheon.

Welsh Rarebit, 294.
Bass, with fine Herbs, 323.
Broiled Porterhouse Steak, 524.
Macaroni Croquettes, 279.
Pumpkin Pie, 1099.

Dinner.

Oysters, 298.
Brunoise, with Sorrel, 4.
Celery, 290.   Olives.
Salmon Cutlets, Victoria, 366.
Antelope Steak, Currant jelly, 890.
Oyster Plant à la Poulette, 1019.
Mignon Filets, with Marrow, 510.
Cauliflower, sauce Hollandaise, 925.
Upland Plovers, sur canapé, 865.
Escarole Salad, 1055.
Coffee Ice Cream, 1273.
Fancy Almond Cakes, 1239.
Coffee, 1349.

Thursday, February —.

Breakfast.

Omelet, with Chicken Livers, 464.
Broiled Sardines on Toast, 403.
Broiled Calf's Liver and Bacon, 584.
Watercress Salad, 1072.
Brioche Fluttes, 1204.

Luncheon.

Soft Clams à la Newburg, 390.
Lamb Stewed à la Créole, 711.
Herring Salad, 1074.
Cherry Tarts, 1111.

Dinner.

Clams, 300.
Cream of Barley, 77.
Radishes, 292.   Cucumbers, 289.
Shad, with Sorrel, 327.
Chicken Sauté à la Bohemienne, 778.
Stuffed Tomatoes, 1023.
Coquilles of Sweetbreads à la Dreux, 621.
New Peas, with cream, 980.
Roast Turkey, oo.
Lettuce Salad, 1059.
Baked Apple Dumplings, 1122.
Coffee, 1349.

Friday, February —.

Breakfast.

Hominy and Cream, 1034.
Scrambled Eggs, with Truffles, 407.
Picked-up Codfish, 346.
Sausages, with White Wine, 735.
Potatoes, maître d'hôtel, 985.
Corn Fritters, 965.

Luncheon.

Skate, with black butter, 325, 159.
Corned Beef Hash en Bordure, 531.
Stuffed Egg-plant, 909.
Stewed Peaches, 1334.

Dinner.

Oysters, 298.
Consommé à l'Africaine, 116.
Radishes, 292.   Caviare, 281.
Bluefish à l'Italienne, 337.
Tenderloin Piqué à la Provençale, 518.
Cauliflower au Gratin, 926.
Veal Cutlets à la Maréchale, 562.
String Beans, 948.
Doe-birds à l'Américaine, 840.
Chicory Salad, 1046.
Apples Meringuées, 1248.
Coffee, 1349.

MENUS.

Saturday, February —.

Breakfast.
Omelet Raspail, 467.
Hashed Mutton au Gratin, 653.
Pig's Feet à la Boston, 730.
Succotash, 1022.
French Pancake, 1186.

Luncheon.
Cromesquis aux Truffes, 268.
Calf's Head à la Financière, 637.
Stewed Sweet Potatoes, 995.
Rum Omelet, 476.

Dinner.
Clams, 300.
Purée of Chestnuts, 91.
Celery, 290.   Olives.
Sole à la Normande, 318.
Antelope Chops, port wine sauce, 891.
Potatoes Château, 1009.
Chicken Sauté à la Bordelaise, 776.
Asparagus, drawn butter, 904-157.
Roast Mutton, 585.
Celery Salad, 1042
Savarin à l'Anglaise, 1199.
Coffee, 1349.

Sunday, February —.

Breakfast.
Oatmeal, with Cream.
Eggs à la Meyerbeer, 437.
Broiled Deviled Kidneys, 715.
Potatoes à la Rice, 1007.
Malaga Grapes.

Luncheon.
Broiled Pompano, maître d'hôtel, 329.
Cucumber Salad, 289.
Mutton Chops, Soyer, 647.
Spaghetti au Gratin, 961.
Sago Pudding, 1140.

Dinner.
Oysters, 298.
Cream à l'Allemande, 84.
Radishes, 292.   Celery, 290.
Lobster à la Newburg, 359.
Broiled Tenderloin à la Trianon, 507.
Potatoes à la Hanna, 1012.
Lamb Chops, maison d'or, 683.
Spinach, with Croûtons, 943.
Punch à la Française, 1311.
Roast English Snipe, 868.
Barbe de Capucine Salad, 1038.
Macédoine Glacée à la Cavour, 1298.
Stilton Cheese.
Coffee, 1349.

Monday, February —.

Breakfast.
Omelet, with Smoked Beef, 461.
Fried Oysters, 380.
Lamb Steak à l'Américaine, 718.
Lima Beans, 952.
Brioche, 1201.

Luncheon.
Timbales à l'Ecossaise, 361.
Tendron of Veal, Morlaisienne, 635.
Sweet Potatoes Soufflées, 1010.
Lobster Salad, 1061.
Apple Pie, 1083.

Dinner.
Clams, 300.
Consommé d'Orléans, 110.
Olives.   Cucumbers, 289.
Shad, vert pré, 328.
Cromesquis of Chicken à la Richelieu, 764.
Calf's Liver, braised, Bourgeoise, 583.
Potato Croquettes, 997.
Roast Beef, 527.
Lettuce Salad, 1057.
Maraschino Pudding, 1134.
Coffee, 1349.

Tuesday, February —.

Breakfast.
Lobster Omelet, 454.
Hashed Turkey à la Crême, 804.
Lamb's Tongues, sauce piquante, 203.
Stewed Potatoes, 994.
Stewed Quinces, 1338.

Luncheon.
Oysters à la Baltimore, 388.
Brisotin of Veal à l'Ecarlate, 555.
Macaroni au Gratin, 955.
Baked Apples, 1124.

Dinner.
Oysters, 298.
Cream of Celery à l'Espagnole, 86.
Celery, 290.   Radishes, 292.
Oyster Crabs à la Poulette, 374.
Civet of Hare à la Française, 893.
Brussels Sprouts, 922.
Squabs en Compote, 822.
String Beans à l'Anglaise, 948.
Roast Capon, 755.
Dandelion Salad, 1048.
Baba, with Rum, 1217.
Domestic Brie Cheese.
Coffee, 1349.

Wednesday, February —.

Breakfast.
Eggs à la Tripe, 419.
Calf's Brains, brown butter, 557.
Lamb Chops à la Signora, 681.
Hashed Potatoes au Gratin, 1004.
Rice à la Française, 1180.

Luncheon.
Lobster en Chevreuse, 362.
Breast of Veal à la Milanaise, 596.
Carrots and Cream, 927.
Spaghetti Napolitaine, 959.
Custard Pie, 1100.

Dinner.
Little Neck Clams, 300.
Chicken à la Créole, 65.
Radishes, 292.   Lyons Sausage, 286.
Bass à la Bordelaise, 341.
Broiled Sirloin Steak à la Moëlle, 493.
String Beans au Blanc, 947.
Salmi of Duck à la Chasseur, 828.
Celery, with gravy, 928.
Roast Saddle of Lamb, 664.
Escarole Salad, 1055.
Chocolate Pudding, 1146.
Coffee, 1349.

Thursday, February —.

Breakfast.
Omelet Espagnole, 472.
Broiled Perch, maître d'hôtel, 329.
Black Sausages, with mashed Potatoes, 719.
Stewed Tomatoes, 1027.
Whipped Cream à la Vanille, 1254.

Luncheon.
Fried Oysters, 380.
Broiled Chickens' Legs à la Diable, 766.
Spinach, with Eggs, 943.
Lamb's Tongue Salad, 1056.
Mince Pie, 1082.

Dinner.
Oysters, 298.
Consommé Dubourg, 101.
Olives.   Mortadella, 287.
Red-snapper, Caper sauce, 352-651.
Turban of Chicken à la Cleveland, 791.
Potatoes Duchesse, 1006.
Sweetbreads, Larded à la Cardinal, 602.
Brussels Sprouts, 922.
Roast Ptarmigan, with Watercress, 862.
Lettuce Salad, 1058.
Fruit Pudding, 1161.
Coffee, 1349.

WASHINGTON'S BIRTHDAY.

Friday, February —.

Breakfast.

Eggs à la Béchamel, 416.
Oysters en Brochette au Petit Salé, 385.
Minced Lamb à l'Anglaise, 688.
Potatoes, maître d'hôtel, 985.
French Pancake, with jelly, 1187.

Luncheon.

Crabs à la St. Jean, 371.
Stewed Veal à la Chasseur, 632.
Stuffed Egg-plant, 909.
Cauliflower Salad, 1040.
Coffee Eclairs, 1244.

Dinner.

Little Neck Clams, 300.
Cream Palestine, 74.
Tomatoes, 288.   Celery, 290.
Shad, with fine Herbs, 323.
Suprême of Chicken à la Bayard, 787.
Broiled Tomatoes, 1025.
Lamb Steak, with purée of Chestnuts, 716-131.
Stewed Mushrooms on Toast, 914.
Roast Squabs, 816.
Celery Salad, 1042.
Pie à la Martha Washington, 1105.
Coffee, 1349.

Saturday, February —.

Breakfast.

Omelet à la Vanderbilt, 471.
Tripe à la Bordelaise, 544.
Mutton Kidneys, with Bacon, 661.
Turnips, cream sauce, 967, 181.
Apples, with Rice, 1169.

Luncheon.

Stuffed Oysters à la Mali, 386.
Epigrammes of Lamb à la Chicorée, 690.
Fried Sweet Potatoes, 993.
String-Bean Salad, 1068.
Peach Tarts, 1106.

Dinner.

Oysters, 298.
Consommé au Sago, 104.
Thon, 282.   Radishes, 292.
Bass à la Bordelaise, 341.
Tenderloin of Beef Piqué, sauce Périgueux, 516, 191.
Stewed Tomatoes, 1027.
Sweetbread Croquettes, with Peas, 620.
Roast Teal Ducks, 859.
Tomato and Lettuce Salad, 1060.
Charlotte Panachée, 1300.
Coffee, 1349.

Sunday, February —.

Breakfast.

Poached Eggs on Toast, Anchovy butter, 404, 146.
Whitebait, 301.
Smoked Beef, with Cream, 486.
Potatoes à la Rice, 1007.
Preserved Raspberries, 1346.

Luncheon.

Broiled Spanish-mackerel, maître d'hôtel, 329.
Cucumber Salad, 289.
Beefsteak Pie à l'Américaine, 488.
Omelet au Kirsch, 476.

Dinner.

Oysters, 298.
Green Turtle, 16.
Olives.   Radishes, 292.
Small Bouchées à la Reine, 270.
Terrapin à la Baltimore, 396.
Mignon Filets, with Mushrooms, 514.
Fresh Green Peas à l'Anglaise, 978.
Fricassee of Chicken, with Curry, 792.
Lima Beans, 952.
Punch en Surprise, 1309.
Red-head Duck, 876.
Lettuce Salad, 1058.
Plum Pudding, 1163.
Gorgonzolla Cheese.
Coffee, 1349.

Monday, February —.

Breakfast.

Eggs, with Tarragon, 429.
Broiled Veal Kidneys à la Diable, 715.
Stewed Tomatoes, 1027.
Tripe à la Mode de Caën, 547.
Peach Marmalade, 1331.

Luncheon.

Stewed Oysters à la Pompadour, 384.
Mutton Chops, Soyer, 647.
Spaghetti, with black butter, 954, 159.
Anchovy Salad, 1037.
Hot Savarin, 1198.

Dinner.

Little Neck Clams, 300.
Purée of Lima Beans, 49.
Sardines, 283.   Celery, 290.
Sheep's-head à la Créole, 339.
Shoulder of Lamb à la Macédoine, 697.
Risotto, 1017.
Chicken Vol-au-Vent, with Mushrooms, 810.
Roast Loin of Pork, 751.
Barbe de Capucine Salad, 1038.
Meringues Glacées, 1301.
Coffee, 1349.

Tuesday, February —.

Breakfast.

Scrambled Eggs, with Mushrooms, 405.
Fish Balls, 347.
Minced Beef à l'Italienne, 500.
Oyster-plant, Cream sauce, 1020.
Rice à l'Airolo, 1171.

Luncheon.

Broiled Lobster, Ravigote sauce, 363.
Blanquette of Veal à l'Ancienne, 553.
Tomatoes à la Marseillaise, 1029.
Pineapple Pie, 1087.

Dinner.

Oysters, 298.
Chicken à la Turque, 69.
Cucumbers, 289.   Radishes, 292.
Fried Oyster Crabs, 375.
Stewed Antelope, sauce poivrade, 886.
Mushrooms, with Cream, 915.
Croquettes of Lamb à la Patti, 679.
Potatoes Bignon, 1001.
Teal Duck à l'Américaine, 840.
Doucette Salad, 1054.
Tapioca Pudding, 1141.
Roquefort Cheese.
Coffee, 1349.

Wednesday, February —.

Breakfast.

Omelet, with Peas, 459.
Broiled Ham, 753.
Calf's Liver à l'Alsacienne, 582.
Mashed Potatoes au Gratin, 998.
Wheat Cakes, 1184.

Luncheon.

Crabs à la St. Laurent, 372.
Sausages à la Gastronome, 740.
Broiled Tomatoes, 1025.
Potato Salad, 1073.
Boiled Apple Dumplings, 1127.

Dinner.

Little Neck Clams, 300.
Tomatoes and Rice, 57.
Olives.   Celery, 290.
Bluefish à l'Italienne, 337.
Tenderloin, Marinaded, Russian sauce, 511.
Beans Panachés, 950.
Lamb Chops à la Signora, 681.
Brussels Sprouts, 922.
Roast Chicken, 755.
Celery, Mayonnaise Salad, 1042.
Biscuits Tortoni, 1287.
Petites Bouchées à la Mme. Astor, 1238.
Coffee, 1349.

Thursday, February —.

Breakfast.

Kidney Omelet, 463.
Oysters à la Poulette, 383.
Hamburg Steak, Colbert sauce, 326, 190.
Stewed Sweet Corn, 964.
Crême en Mousse au Maraschino, 1257.

Luncheon.

Canapé Madison, 269.
Salmi of Duck à la Maréchale, 831.
Spinach à la Vieille Mode, 941.
Beef Salad, 1039.
Apple Tarts, 1120.

Dinner.

Oysters à l'Alexandre Dumas, 299.
Chicken à l'Hollandaise, 64.
Sardines, 283.   Radishes, 292.
Skate, with black butter, 325, 159.
Potatoes à la Windsor, 1008.
Saddle of Mutton à la Sevigné, 669.
Lima Beans, cream sauce, 952, 181.
Larded Sweetbreads au Salpicon, 605.
Fresh Asparagus, melted butter, 904, 155.
Roast Loin of Veal, 585.
Lettuce and Egg Salad, 1058.
Nelson Pudding, 1155.
Coffee, 1349.

Friday, March —.

Breakfast.

Eggs à la Post, 1359.
Picked-up Codfish, 346.
Pig's Feet à la St. Hubert, 727.
Potatoes, Hollandaise, 999.
Stewed Quinces, 1338.

Luncheon.

Scallops, poulette sauce 392, 598.
Veal Cutlets à la Maréchale, 562.
Potatoes, Julienne, 1013.
Lobster Salad à la Boardman, 1361.
Plum Pudding, 1163.

Dinner.

Clams, 300.
Purée of Green Peas, 49.
Olives.   Radishes, 292.
Bass à la Bordelaise, 341.
Hashed Turkey, with Cream, 804.
Lamb Chops à la Villeroi, 686.
Spinach au Croûtons, 943.
Roast Chicken, 755.
Celery Salad, 1041.
Baba, 1216.
Coffee, 1349.

Saturday, March —.

Breakfast.

Eggs à la Livingstone, 410.
Breaded Broiled Lamb Fries, Tomato sauce, 673.
Mignon Filets à la Parisienne, 514.
Potato Croquettes, 997.
Corn Fritters, 965.

Luncheon.

Stuffed Deviled Crabs, 370.
Stewed Mutton à la Parisienne, 708.
Broiled Chicken Livers au Petit Salé, 769.
Choux à la Crème, 1246.

Dinner.

Oysters, 298.
Ox-Tail à l'Ecossaise, 39.
Celery, 290.   Lyons Sausage, 286.
Perch aux Fines Herbes, 331.
Pork Chops, Apple sauce, 748.
Succotash, 1022.
Chicken Sauté à la Maryland, 785.
Green Peas à l'Anglaise, 978.
Roast Plovers, 865.
Dandelion Salad, 1049.
Charlotte Russe, 1261.
Coffee, 1349.

Sunday, March —.

Breakfast.

Eggs à la Suisse, 441.
Rice à l'Airolo, 1171.
Corned Beef Hash au Gratin, 529.
Sausages à l'Anglaise, 736.
Stewed Tomatoes, 1027.
Waffles and Sugar, 1196.

Luncheon.

Lobster à la Newburg, 359.
Stewed Veal, with Oyster-plant, 630.
Macédoine Salad, 1063.
Rice and Orange Pudding, 1130.

Dinner.

Oysters, 298.
Potage à la Dorsay, 96.
Celery, 290.   Radishes, 292.
Sole Joinville, 322.
Squabs en Crapaudine, 819.
Potatoes, Duchesse, 1006.
Antelope Steaks, purée of Chestnuts, 882.
Risotto, 1017.
Punch à la Cardinal, 1306.
Roast Tenderloin of Beef, 516.
Lettuce and Tomato Salad, 1060.
Omelet Soufflée, 474.
Camembert Cheese.
Coffee, 1349.

Monday, March —.

Breakfast.
Barley, with cream.
Fish Balls à la Mrs. Harrison, 347.
Mutton Kidneys à la Diable, 715.
Potatoes à l'Hollandaise, 999.
Watercress Salad, 1072.
Stewed Prunes, 1330.

Luncheon.
Oysters Fried à la Arthur Sullivan, 1360.
Game Pie à la Levi P. Morton, 1362.
Stewed Tomatoes, 1027.
Rhubarb Tarts, 1112.

Dinner.
Little Neck Clams, 300.
Printanier Chasseur, 52.
Olives.   Thon, 282.
Salmon en Papillotes, 302.
Sirloin Steak, with Marrow, 493.
Potatoes, Château, 1009.
Duck à la Rouennaise, 825.
Asparagus, Hollandaise, 904.
Roast Mutton, 585.
Romaine Salad, 1064.
Tutti Frutti à la Gen. Harrison, 1364.
Coffee, 1349.

Tuesday, March —.

Breakfast.
Eggs à la Duchesse, 449.
Broiled Sardines on Toast, 403.
Mignon Filets, Anchovy butter, 509, 146.
Broiled Sweet Potatoes, 983.
Whipped Cream à la Vanille, 1254.

Luncheon.
Stuffed Deviled Clams, 376.
Stewed Lamb, Louisianaise, 710.
Timbales à la Schultze, 263.
Cocoanut Pie, 1101.

Dinner.
Oysters à l'Alexandre Dumas, 299.
Giblet à l'Anglaise, 22.
Celery, 290.   Radishes, 292.
Broiled Shad, 326.
Cucumber Salad, 289.
Piloff of Chicken à la Turque, 782.
Potatoes en Surprise, 1005.
Spring Lamb Chops à la Soubise, 647, 250.
Stuffed Peppers, 975.
Roast Teal Duck, 859.
Chicory Salad, 1045.
Rice à la Condé, 1181.
Coffee, 1349.

Wednesday, March —.

Breakfast.
Eggs à la Paysanne, 433.
Chicken Hashed au Gratin, 805.
Black Sausage, with mashed potatoes, 719.
Carrots and Cream, 927.
Stewed Apricots, 1335.

Luncheon.
Oysters à la Villeroi, 381.
Mutton Kidneys en Brochette, with bacon, 661.
Chicory, with gravy, 933.
Calf's Liver Sauté à la Provençale, 581.
Onions, with cream, 968.
Chocolate Eclairs, 1243.

Dinner.
Clams, 300.
Consommé aux Quenelles, 129.
Sardines, 283.   Radishes, 292.
Bass à la Chambord, 343.
Civet of Antelope à la Française, 893.
Noix of Veal à la Bourgeoise, 590, 583.
Tomatoes à la Bock, 1026.
Roast Rice-birds, 877.
Lettuce, Mayonnaise salad, 1042.
Baba, crème à la vanille, 1218.
Coffee, 1349.

Thursday, March —.

Breakfast.

Omelet, with fine herbs, 451.
Boiled Codfish, oyster sauce, 352.
Mutton Chops à la Robinson, 682.
Potatoes, maître d'hôtel, 985.
Apple Fritters, 1191.

Luncheon.

Smelts, with white wine, 342.
Blanquette of Veal, with nouilles, 552.
Fried Egg-plant, 907.
Rum Cake, 1229.

Dinner.

Oysters, 298.
Purée of Tomato à l'Andalouse, 58.
Olives.   Radishes, 292.
Croquettes of Lobsters, sauce aurore, 365, 182.
Boiled Turkey, oyster sauce, 797.
Stuffed Tomatoes, 1023.
Roast Tenderloin of Beef à l'Hussarde, 519.
Potato Croquettes, 997.
Roast English Snipe, 868.
Dandelion Salad, 1049.
Peach Ice-cream, 1276.
Biscuits Ambroisienne, 1234.
Gruyère Cheese.
Coffee, 1349.

Friday, March —.

Breakfast.

Eggs, with brown butter, 414.
Broiled Shad, maître d'hôtel, 326.
Pig's Feet à la Boston, 730.
Saratoga Potatoes, 1011.
Buckwheat Cakes, 1183.

Luncheon.

Crabs à l'Anglaise, 373.
Epigramme of Lamb, Macédoine, 689.
Lima Beans, 952.
Cold Bass en Remoulade, 209.
Pineapple Fritters, 1191.

Dinner.

Little Neck Clams, 300.
Cream of Rice, 78.
Tomatoes, 288.   Celery, 290.
Codfish, egg sauce, 352, 161.
Salmi of Doe-birds à la Gastronome, 842.
String Beans, with butter, 948.
Veal Cutlets à la Philadelphie, 565.
Roast Leg of Lamb, 648.
Barbe de Capucine Salad, 1038.
Custard Pudding, 1154.
Coffee, 1349.

Saturday, March —.

Breakfast.

Omelet, with Sardines, 468.
Haddock, cream sauce, 352, 181.
Hamburg Steak, Russian sauce, 526.
Mashed Potatoes au Gratin, 998.
Brioche, 1201.

Luncheon.

Red-snapper à la maître d'hôtel, 329.
Fricandeau of Veal, with sorrel, 577.
Stewed Tomatoes, 1027.
Plum Tarts, 1110.

Dinner.

Oysters, 298.
Shin of Beef, liée, 29.
Radishes, 292.   Anchovies, 284.
Oyster Patties, 387.
Pigeon Cutlets, Victoria, 815.
Asparagus à la Tessinoise, 906.
Croustade of Kidneys à la Périgueux, 680, 191.
Roast Beef, 527.
Celery, Mayonnaise salad, 1042.
Charlotte Russe, 1261.
Coffee, 1349.

Sunday, March —.

Breakfast.

Eggs à l'Aurore, 444.
Fried Smelts, tartare sauce, 301, 207.
Broiled Calf's Liver and Bacon, 584.
Fried Potatoes, 993.
Stewed Apples, 1332.

Luncheon.

Lobster à l'Américaine, 357.
Irish Mutton Stew, 660.
Corn Stewed with butter, 964.
Deviled Lamb Fries, maitre d'hôtel, 672, 145.
Tomato Salad, 1070.
Caramel Pudding, 1166.

Dinner.

Oysters à l'Alexandre Dumas, 299.
Potage à la Montmorency, 97.
Olives.   Celery, 290.
Sheep's-head au Gratin, 319.
Broiled Tenderloin of Beef à la Chéron, 504.
Parisian Potatoes, 986.
Coquilles of Sweetbreads à la Dreux, 621.
Punch en Surprise, 1309.
Roast Chicken, 755.
Lettuce Salad, 1057.
Neapolitan Ice-cream, 1292.
Biscuits à la Richelieu, 1232.
Roquefort Cheese.
Coffee, 1349.

Monday, March —.

Breakfast.

Omelet Régence, 470.
Oysters en Brochette au Petit Salé, 385.
Smoked Beef, with cream, 486.
Potato Croquettes, 997.
Iced Timbale of Rice, 1175.

Luncheon.

Stuffed Oysters à la Mali, 386.
Lamb en Brochette à la Dumas, 674.
Stuffed Egg-plant, 909.
Chicken Croquettes, with peas, 276.
Pear Tarts, 1109.

Dinner.

Little Neck Clams, 300.
Sorrel Fermière, 81.
Celery, 290.   Sardines, 283.
Fresh Mackerel, with white wine. 342.
Curry of Lamb à l'Indienne, 677.
Fried Oyster-plant, 1021.
Chicken Sauté à la Bordelaise, 776.
Brussels Sprouts, 922.
Roast Leg of Lamb, 648.
Doucette Salad, 1054.
Sago Pudding, 1140.
Coffee, 1349.

Tuesday, March —.

Breakfast.

Eggs à la Turque, 439.
Broiled Perch, tomato sauce, 353, 205.
Hashed Lamb à la Polonaise, 700.
Saratoga Potatoes, 1011.
Stewed Peaches, 1334.

Luncheon.

Oysters à la Baltimore, 388.
Veal Cutlets à la Milanaise, 563.
Potatoes à la Rice, 1007.
Turban of Apples, 1174.

Dinner.

Oysters, 298.
Beef à l'Ecossaise, 5.
Tomatoes, 288.   Olives.
Red-snapper à l'Hollandaise, 317.
Balotine of Squab à l'Italienne, 818.
Shoulder of Lamb, jardinière, 696.
String Beans, 948.
Roast Plovers, 865.
Watercress Salad, 1072.
Almond Cake, 1224.
Coffee, 1349.

Wednesday, March —.

Breakfast.
Omelet Raspail, 467.
Broiled Spanish-mackerel, 329.
Sausages à l'Italienne, 737.
Mashed Potatoes, 998.
Milan Cake, 1228.

Luncheon.
Crabs à la St. Jean, 371.
Stewed Beef à la Turque, 542.
Saratoga Potatoes, 1011.
Stuffed Egg-plant, 909.
Apricot Pie, 1092.

Dinner.
Clams, 300.
Consommé au Semoule, 104.
Celery, 250.   Radishes, 292.
Salmon à la Créole, 339.
Chicken Fricassee à la Reine, 780.
Cauliflower, with butter, 925.
Fresh Artichokes à la Barigoul, 897.
Roast Snipe sur Canapé, 868.
Chicory Salad, 1045.
Maraschino Pudding, 1134.
Coffee, 1349.

Thursday, March —.

Breakfast.
Scrambled Eggs, with truffles, 407.
Cods' Tongues, black butter, 349.
Lamb en Brochette à la Dumas, 674.
Hashed Potatoes, 1002.
Crême en Mousse au Café, 1253.

Luncheon.
Broiled Pompano, maître d'hôtel, 329.
Calf's Head à la Cavour, 638.
Oyster-plant à la Poulette, 1019.
Tongue Salad, 1056.
Cherry Tarts, 1111.

Dinner.
Glen Cove Clams, 300.
Cream of Lentils à la Major-domo, 88.
Radishes, 292.   Olives.
Lobster Cutlets, sauce Colbert, 366, 190.
Broiled Tenderloin à la Florentine, 506.
Stewed Flageolets, 947.
Salmi of Duck, with olives, 827.
Brussels Sprouts, 923.
Roast Mutton, 585.
Lettuce, Mayonnaise salad, 1042, 1057.
Baked Apple Dumplings, 1122.
Gorgonzolla Cheese.
Coffee, 1349.

Friday, March —.

Breakfast.
Omelet à l'Espagnole, 472.
Scallops à la Poulette, 392, 598.
Chicken Livers, sautés au madère, 767.
Potatoes à l'Hanna, 1012.
Small Brioches, 1202.

Luncheon.
* Broiled Boned Smelts, tartare sauce, 353, 207.
Stewed Lamb, with Peas, 706.
String-Bean Salad, 1068.
Stewed Green-gages, 1336.

Dinner.
Blue Point Oysters, 298.
Frogs à l'Espagnole, 25.
Celery, 290.   Radishes, 292.
Lobster en Chevreuse, 362.
Brisotin of Veal, poivrade sauce, 554, 194.
Stewed Tomatoes, 1027.
Chicken Pot-pie, 757.
Roast Rhode Island Turkey, 800.
Dandelion Salad, 1049.
Orange Pudding, 1158.
Coffee, 1349.

Saturday, March —.

Breakfast.
Eggs à la Valencienne, 421.
Fried Sole, sauce tartare, 320, 207.
Amourettes of Lamb à la Diable, 672.
Potatoes à l'Anglaise, 988.
French Pancake, 1186.

Luncheon.
Oyster Patties, 387.
Chicken Croquettes à la Reine, 758.
French Peas.
Beef Salad, 1039.
Boiled Peach Dumplings, 1125.

Dinner.
Little Neck Clams, 300.
Ox-Tail à l'Anglaise, 40.
Olives.   Cucumbers, 289.
Bass à la Bordelaise, 341.
Salmi of Plover à la Moderne, 870.
Turnips, with gravy, 967.
Mignon Filets à la Bohémienne, 513.
Asparagus, Hollandaise, 904.
Roast Goose, 808.
Barbe de Capucine Salad, 1038.
Apple Pudding, 1152.
Coffee, 1349.

Sunday, March —.

Breakfast.
Omelet, with cheese, 469.
Picked-up Codfish, 346.
Minced Beef à la Catalan, 502.
Hashed Potatoes au Gratin, 1004.
Oatmeal, with cream.

Luncheon.
Canapé Lorenzo, 391.
Broiled Spring Chickens, 756.
Sweet Potatoes à l'Hollandaise, 999.
Russian Salad, 1065.
Chaussons, 1236.

Dinner.
Oysters à l'Alexandre Dumas, 299.
Purée Faubonne, 46.
Sardines, 283.   Celery, 290.
Shad, vert-pré, 328.
Shells of Sweetbreads à la Cardinal, 622.
Artichokes à la Florentine, 903.
Breast of Turkey à la Robinson, 807.
Cauliflower au Gratin, 926.
Punch à la Delmonico, 1303.
Roast Squab sur Canapé, 816.
Celery, Mayonnaise salad. 1042.
Raspberry Water-ice, 1281.
Lady-fingers, 1231.
Gorgonzolla Cheese.
Coffee, 1349.

Monday, March —.

Breakfast.
Eggs à la Meyerbeer, 437.
Aiguillettes of Bass, with White Wine, 342.
Chicken Livers en Brochette, with bacon, 769.
French Fried Potatoes, 993.
Stewed Apples, 1332.

Luncheon.
Welsh Rare-bit, Golden Buck, 295.
Shoulder of Lamb, purée Normande, 694.
Spinach au Croûtons, 940.
Herring Salad, 1074.
Rhubarb Pie, 1085.

Dinner.
Clams, 300.
Printanier Grenat, 51.
Olives.   Radishes, 292.
Codfish à l'Hollandaise, 317.
Mignon Filets à la Pompadour, 509.
French String Beans, 948.
Chicken Sauté à la Ch. C. Delmonico, 1355.
French Peas.
Roast Reed-birds, 877.
Doucette Salad, 1052.
Rice Pudding, 1143.
Coffee, 1349.

Tuesday, March —.

Breakfast.

Shrimp Omelet, 453.
Fish Balls, 347.
Hashed Beef au Gratin, 653.
Saratoga Potatoes, 1011.
Baked Apples, 1124.

Luncheon.

Oysters en Brochette au Petit Salé, 385.
Stewed Veal à la Grecque, 626.
Cauliflower Salad, 1040.
Gooseberry Tarts, 1114.

Dinner.

Blue Point Oysters, 298.
Consommé Napolitaine, 37.
Celery, 290. Lyons Sausage, 286.
Bass, Anchovy sauce, 352, 163.
Braised Beef à la Bignon, 484.
Sorrel, with Eggs, 974.
Pigeon Cutlets à la Victoria, 815.
Flageolets, 1365.
Roast Spring Lamb, 1361.
Escarole salad, 1055.
Baba au Rhum, 1217.
Imported Brie Cheese.
Coffee, 1349.

Wednesday, March —.

Breakfast.

Eggs au Miroir, 425.
Broiled Pickerel, maître d'hôtel, 329.
Calf's Liver à l'Alsacienne, 582.
Stewed Potatoes, 995.
Red Currant Jelly, 1326.

Luncheon.

Scallops Brestoise, 392.
Stewed Beef à la Dufour, 541.
Macaroni au Gratin, 955.
Apple Meringue Pie, 1103.

Dinner.

Little Neck Clams, 300.
Potage à la Windsor, 94.
Sardines, 283. Radishes, 292.
Broiled Shad Roe, 402.
Cucumber Salad, 289.
Suprême of Chicken à la Patti, 789.
String Beans Bretonne, 949.
Mignons of Lamb, sauce Béarnaise, 1360.
Spinach and Eggs, 940.
Roast English Snipe, 868.
Watercress Salad, 1072.
Meringues Panachées, 1302.
Coffee, 1349.

Thursday, March —.

Breakfast.

Kidney Omelet, 463.
Shad, maître d'hôtel, 326.
Veal Cutlets, Tomato sauce, 563.
Stewed Carrots, with Cream, 927.
Whipped Cream à la Vanille, 1254.

Luncheon.

Stuffed Deviled Crabs, 370.
Beef Tongue, Jardinière, 535.
Stewed Tomatoes, 1027.
Strawberry Tarts, 1117.

Dinner.

Rockaway Oysters, 298.
Sorrel, with Rice, 42.
Olives. Radishes, 292.
Cod's Tongues, black butter, 349.
Potato Croquettes, 997.
Balotine of Lamb, with Peas, 675.
Chicken Sauté à la Marengo, 771.
Stuffed Cucumbers, 937.
Roast Loin of Veal, 585.
Chicory Salad, 1046.
English Pudding, 1137.
Coffee, 1349.

Friday, March —.

Breakfast.
Omelet, with Asparagus-tops, 458.
Skate, with black butter, 325, 139.
Pig's Feet à la Poulette, 731.
Potatoes Julienne, 1013.
Preserved Green-gages, 1344.

Luncheon.
Broiled Spanish-mackerel, 329.
Broiled Philadelphia Spring Chickens, 756.
French Peas.
Tomato Salad, 1070.
Vermicelli Pudding, 1142.

Dinner.
Clams, 300.
Purée Soubise, with White Beans, 92.
Celery, 290.   Olives.
Perch à la Toulouse, 354.
Antelope Steak, Port Wine sauce, 891.
Stuffed Peppers, 975.
Fricandeau of Veal, with Spinach, 578.
Roast Squab, 816.
Lettuce and Egg Salad, 1058.
Macaroon Ice-cream, 1290.
Lady-fingers, 1231.
Domestic Brie Cheese.
Coffee, 1349.

Saturday, March —.

Breakfast.
Smoked Beef Omelet, 461.
Broiled Smelts, Béarnaise sauce, 353.
Lamb Steak à l'Américaine, 718.
Potatoes, maître d'hôtel, 985.
Apples and Rice, 1169.

Luncheon.
Matelote of Eels, 332.
Fried Sweet Potatoes, 993.
Corned Beef, with Kale Sprouts, 490.
Plum Pie, 1094.

Dinner.
Oysters, 298.
Consommé Dubourg, 101.
Radishes, 292.   Thon, 282.
Sheep's-head aux fines Herbes, 323.
Epigrammes of Lamb, Louisianaise, 691.
Stuffed Lettuce, 953.
Salmi of Ptarmigan à la Chasseur, 864.
Tomatoes à la Reine, 1024.
Roast Beef, 527.
Dandelion Salad, 1049.
Apricot Pudding, 1151.
Coffee, 1349.

Sunday, March —.

Breakfast.
Boiled Eggs.
Broiled Pompano, maître d'hôtel, 329.
Flat Sausages, with mashed Potatoes, 719.
Turnips and Gravy, 967.
Crème en Mousse au Kirsch, 1256.

Luncheon.
Broiled Shad, 326.
Cucumber Salad, 289.
Boiled Turkey, Celery sauce, 796.
Fried Sweet Potatoes, 993.
Frangipani Tarts, 1121.

Dinner.
Shrewsbury Oysters, 298.
Consommé Tapioca, 104.
Radishes, 292.   Lyons Sausage, 286.
Smelts à la Toulouse, 354.
Tenderloin of Beef, marinaded, Russian sauce, 511.
Succotash, 1022.
Saddle of Lamb à la Sévigné, 669.
Romaine Punch, 1304.
Roast Goose, 808.
Chicory Salad, 1045.
Iced Diplomatic Pudding, 1288.
Strachino Cheese.
Coffee, 1349.

Monday, March —.

Breakfast.
Omelet with Cèpes, 460.
Fish Balls, 347.
Minced Beef à la Catalan, 502.
Potatoes Gastronome, 1000.
Peach Marmalade, 1331.

Luncheon.
Oysters à la Poulette, 383.
Braised Calf's Liver, Bourgeoise, 583.
Fried Oyster-plant, 1021.
Timbales à la Schultze, 263.
Savarin, 1197.

Dinner.
Clams, 300.
Spaghetti, with Tomatoes, 56.
Tomatoes, 288.   Olives.
Salmon Croquettes, Cream sauce, 364, 181.
Croustade of Kidneys à la Périgueux, 680, 191.
Chicken Sauté, with Tarragon, 774.
Potatoes à l'Hanna, 1012.
Roast Mutton, 585.
Celery Salad, 1041.
Fruit Pudding, 1161.
Coffee, 1349.

Tuesday, March —.

Breakfast.
Scrambled Eggs, with Asparagus-tops, 406.
Broiled Sardines on toast, 403.
Lamb Chops, sauce Colbert, 647, 190.
Potatoes Lyonnaise, 991.
Maraschino Jelly, 1319.

Luncheon.
Stuffed Deviled Clams, 376.
Hamburg Steak, Poivrade sauce, 526, 194.
Broiled Tomatoes, 1025.
Iced Timbale of Rice, 1175.

Dinner.
Blue Point Oysters, 298.
Clear Green Turtle, 18
Radishes, 292.   Caviare, 281.
Red-snapper, Remoulade sauce, 309, 209.
Sirloin Steak à la Parisienne, 495.
Potatoes à la Windsor, 1008.
Broiled Sweetbreads, Colbert sauce, 617.
Brussels Sprouts, 922.
Roast Chicken, 755.
Watercress Salad, 1072.
Rum Cake, 1229.
Coffee, 1349.

Wednesday, March —.

Breakfast.
Omelet, with fine Herbs, 451.
Codfish, cream sauce, 352, 181.
Mashed Potatoes, 998.
Corned-beef Hash en bordure, 531.
Malaga Grapes.

Luncheon.
Stuffed Deviled Lobster, 367.
Grenadin of Veal, with mashed Peas, 586.
Sweet Potatoes soufflées, 1010.
Boiled Apple Dumplings, 1122.

Dinner.
Little Neck Clams, 300.
Brunoise, with Rice, 3.
Olives.   Lyons Sausage, 286.
Bass à la Chambord, 343.
Leg of Mutton à la Condé, 649.
Potato Croquettes, 997.
Chicken Livers, with Madeira Wine, 767.
Asparagus, sauce Hollandaise, 904.
Roast Beef, 527.
Tomato, Mayonnaise salad, 1071.
Iced Pound Cake, 1193.
Coffee, 1349.

Thursday, March —.

Breakfast.
Poached Eggs on toast, anchovy butter, 464.
Fried Whitebait, 301.
Tripe à la Bordelaise, 544.
Hashed Potatoes au Gratin, 1004.
Crême-en-mousse au maraschino, 1257.

Luncheon.
Crabs à la St. Jean, 371.
Hashed Turkey en bordure, 805.
Stewed Lima Beans, 952.
Pumpkin Pie, 1099.

Dinner.
Blue Point Oysters, 298.
Cream of Lima Beans, 75.
Celery, 290.   Thon, 282.
Salmon à l'Irlandaise, 307.
Shoulder of Lamb, Flamande, 699.
Risotto, 1017.
Sweetbreads, larded, with Mushrooms, 609.
Green Peas à l'Anglaise, 978.
Roast Red-head Ducks, 876.
Watercress Salad, 1072.
Charlotte Russe, 1261.
Stilton Cheese.
Coffee, 1349.

Friday, March —.

Breakfast.
Tomato Omelet, 456.
Shad, with Sorrel, 327.
Potatoes, maitre d'hôtel, 985.
Spaghetti au Gratin, 961.
Rice and Milk, 1177.

Luncheon.
Fish Balls, 347.
Stewed Beef à l'Egyptienne, 540.
Rice à la Ristori, 1016.
Lobster Salad, 1061.
Peach Tarts, 1106.

Dinner.
Little Neck Clams, 300.
Onion, 130.
Sardines, 283.   Olives.
Red-snapper, Egg sauce, 309, 161.
Mutton Chops, Napolitaine, 646.
Beans Panachés, 950.
Chicken Croquettes à l'Ecarlate, 760.
Cauliflower, Hollandaise, 925, 160.
Roast Corn Plovers, 865.
Chicory Salad, 1045.
Baba au Madère, 1217.
Coffee, 1349.

Saturday, March —.

Breakfast.
Eggs à la Tripe, 419.
Fried Sole, Colbert sauce, 320.
Hashed Mutton en bordure, 653.
Potatoes en paille, 1014.
Corn Fritters, 965.

Luncheon.
Broiled Veal Kidneys, with Bacon, 713.
Braised Beef en Daube, 483.
Stuffed Peppers, 975.
Allumettes, 1205.

Dinner.
Rockaway Oysters, 298.
Chiffonade, 14.
Anchovies, 284.   Tomatoes, 288.
Codfish, sauce Hollandaise, 352, 160.
Minced Veal à la Catalan, 575.
Chicory, Cream sauce, 932.
Broiled Sirloin à la Béarnaise, 492.
String Beans, 948.
Roast Leg of Mutton, 648.
Dandelion salad, 1049.
Chocolate Ice-cream, 1272.
Petites Bouchées à la Mme. Astor, 1238.
Coffee, 1349.

Sunday, March —.

Breakfast.

Omelet à la Vanderbilt, 471.
Boned Broiled Smelts, Béarnaise sauce, 353.
Tripe à la Lyonnaise, 548.
Fried Potatoes, 993.
Stewed Prunes à la Général Dufour, 1330.

Luncheon.

Cromesquis aux fines herbes, 268, 143.
Stewed Veal à la Marengo, 624.
Spaghetti Napolitaine, 959.
Chicken Salad, 1044.
Rice and Orange Pudding, 1130.

Dinner.

East River Oysters, 298.
Consommé Impérial, 111.
Radishes, 292.   Olives.
Shad with sorrel, 327.
Tenderloin of Beef, larded, with stuffed tomatoes, 516, 1023.
Suprême of Chicken à la Rothschild, 790.
Fresh Asparagus, 904.
Punch à la Lalla Rookh, 1308.
Roast English Snipe, 868.
Barbe de Capucine Salad, 1038.
Omelet Soufflée, 474.
Pont l'Evèque Cheese.
Coffee, 1349.

Monday, April —.

Breakfast.

Eggs à la Livingstone, 410.
Fillets of Sole à la Horly, 321.
Corned Beef Hash à la Zingara, 530.
Potatoes au Gratin, 1004.
Strawberries and Cream.

Luncheon.

Stuffed, Deviled Crabs, 370.
Blanquette of Veal à la Reine, 550.
Lamb Tongue Salad, 1056.
Cream au Cognac, 1258.

Dinner.

Clams, 300.
Pâté d'Italie, 103.
Sardines, 283   Olives.
Broiled Trout, maître d'hôtel, 314.
Sirloin Piqué à la Bordelaise, 491.
Spinach, with Eggs, 940.
Pigeon Cutlets à la Victoria, 815.
Succotash, 1022.
Roast Hindquarter of Spring Lamb, 1361.
Watercress Salad, 1072.
Baba, 1216.
Brie Cheese.
Coffee, 1349.

Tuesday, April —.

Breakfast.

Omelet, bonne femme, 466.
Broiled Beefsteak, 524.
Calf's Brains, black butter, 557.
Hashed Potatoes, 1002.
Brioches à la Condé, 1203.

Luncheon.

Scallops Brestoise, 392.
Mutton Stew, Fermière, 655.
Shrimp Salad, 1067.
Plum Pie, 1094.

Dinner.

Oysters, 298.
Mock Turtle, 17.
Thon, 282.   Celery, 290.
Bluefish à la Bordelaise, 341.
Mignons Filets à la Pompadour, 509.
Oyster-plant à la Poulette, 1019.
Antelope Steaks, Colbert sauce, 881.
String Beans, 948.
Roast Rhode Island Turkey, 800.
Chicory Salad, 1045.
Chocolate Ice-cream, 1272.
Sweet Almond Macaroons, 1210.
Coffee, 1349.

Wednesday, April —.

Breakfast.
Eggs, with black butter, 414.
Spring Lamb Chops, with Bacon, 647, 754.
Sausages, with White Wine, 735.
Saratoga Potatoes, 1011.
Waffles and Sugar, 1196.

Luncheon.
Smelts, sauce Béarnaise, 353.
Braised Beef à la Mode, 479.
Stewed Corn, 964.
Tomato Salad, 1070.
Coffee Eclairs, 1244.

Dinner.
Little Neck Clams, 300.
Purée Jackson, 43.
Lyons Sausage, 286.   Radishes, 292.
Kingfish, maître d'hôtel, 329.
Potatoes Hollandaise, 999.
Brisotin of Veal à l'Ecarlate, 555.
Spinach, with gravy, 943.
Broiled Turkey Legs à la Diable, 766.
Mushrooms on Toast, 914.
Roast Beef, 527.
Dandelion Salad, 1048.
Omelet Célestine, 477.
Coffee, 1349.

Thursday, April —.

Breakfast.
Omelet Raspail, 467.
Hashed Lamb à l'Anglaise, 688.
Broiled Calf's Liver, maître d'hôtel, 584, 145.
Stewed Tomatoes, 1027.
Rice Cake, 1222.

Luncheon.
Broiled Trout au Petit Salé. 314, 754.
Stewed Beef, Dufour, 541.
French Peas.
Croquettes of Sweetbreads, with Mushrooms, 620, 230.
Huckleberry Tarts, 1113.

Dinner.
Rockaway Oysters, 298.
Printanier Royale, 124.
Radishes, 292.   Celery, 290.
Shad, with fine Herbs, 315.
Fricandeau, with Sorrel, 577.
Piloff of Chicken à la Turque, 782.
Beans Panachés, 950.
Roast Squab, 816.
Barbe de Capucine Salad, 1038.
Peach Pudding à la Richelieu, 1150.
Swiss Cheese.
Coffee, 1349.

Friday, April —.

Breakfast.
Eggs au Miroir, 425.
Broiled Fresh Mackerel, 329.
Mutton Chops à la Provençale, 642.
Lima Beans, 952.
Galette, 1221.

Luncheon.
Frogs à la Poulette, 399.
Chicken Pot-pie, 757.
Risotto, 1017.
Lobster Salad, 1061.
French Pudding à la Delmonico, 1139.

Dinner.
Clams, 300.
Purée of Crécy, 47.
Tomatoes, 288.   Olives.
Bass à la Chambord, 343.
Porterhouse Steak à la Bordelaise, 491.
Stewed Oyster-plant, 1018.
Sweetbreads à la Financière, 603.
Fresh Peas, 978.
Roast Spring Chicken, 755.
Chicory Salad, 1046.
Kirsch Jelly, 1319.
Cheddar Cheese.
Coffee, 1349.

Saturday, April —.

Breakfast.
Omelet, with Chicken Livers, 464.
Broiled Smelts, Tartare sauce, 353, 207.
Pig's Feet, St. Hubert, 727.
Potato Croquettes, 997.
Stewed Apricots, 1335.

Luncheon.
Fried Whitebait, 301.
Braised Noix of Veal à la Providence, 590.
Spinach à l'Anglaise, 940.
Macédoine Salad, 1063.
Chocolate Eclairs, 1243.

Dinner.
Shrewsbury Oysters, 298.
Giblets, with Barley, 21.
Bologna Sausages, 286.   Radishes, 292.
Fresh Mackerel, Colbert, 329, 190.
Croustade of Chicken Livers, 763.
Turnips, with gravy, 967.
Lamb Sweetbreads en caisses, 274.
Artichokes Barigoul, 897.
Snipe sur Canapé, 868.
Doucette Salad, 1054.
Cocoanut Pudding, 1147.
Coffee, 1349.

Sunday, April —.

Breakfast.
Eggs, with Tarragon, 429.
Haddock, Cream sauce, 352, 181.
Calf's Liver Sauté à l'Italienne, 580.
Corn, stewed with butter, 964.
Cream Renversée, 1252.

Luncheon.
Sole au Gratin, 319.
Stewed Beef à la Dufour, 541.
Broiled Tomatoes, 1025.
Timbales à la Schultze, 263.
Fresh Strawberry Tarts, 1117.

Dinner.
Blue Point Oysters, 298.
Consommé Princesse, 113.
Olives.   Radishes, 292.
Stuffed Lobster, 367.
Saddle of Mutton, Londonderry sauce, 668.
Fried Oyster-plant, 1021.
Coquilles of Chicken, with Mushrooms, 271,
Fresh Asparagus, 904.   [230.
Punch au Kirsch, 1305.
Roast Teal Ducks, 859.
Celery, Mayonnaise Salad, 1042.
Rum Cake, 1229.
Gorgonzolla Cheese.
Coffee, 1349.

Monday, April —.

Breakfast.
Omelet, with fine Herbs, 451.
Hamburg Steak, Russian sauce, 526.
Kidneys, stewed with Madeira, 662.
Saratoga Potatoes, 1011.
Rice and Cream à la Croce, 1296.

Luncheon.
Gerthins Welsh Rarebit, 296.
Fish Balls, 347.
Hashed Turkey, with Cream, 804.
Russian Salad, 1065.
Custard Pie, 1100.

Dinner.
Little Neck Clams, 300.
Brunoise, with Sorrel, 4.
Radishes, 292.   Lyons Sausage, 286.
Shad, vert-pré, 328.
Sweetbreads à la Catalan, 616.
New String Beans au blanc, 947.
Balotine of Lamb au jus, 675.
French Peas.
Roast Goose, 808.
Watercress Salad, 1072.
Apple Fritters, 1191.
Coffee, 1349.

Tuesday, April —.

Breakfast.
Eggs à la Reine, 438.
Codfish Tongues, with black butter, 349.
Tripe à la Lyonnaise, 548.
Stewed Turnips, 967.
Brioche, 1201.

Luncheon.
Broiled Trout, maître d'hôtel, 314.
Cucumber Salad, 289.
Escalops of Veal à la Duxelle, 569.
Mashed Potatoes, 998.
Mille Feuilles, 1223.

Dinner.
East River Oysters, 298.
Ox-tail, with Barley, 38.
Olives. Radishes, 292.
Bouchées à la Reine, 270.
Beef Tongue à la Gendarme, 532.
Tomatoes à la Bock, 1026.
Haricot of Lamb à la Providence, 701.
Beans Panachés, 950.
Roast Squab, 816.
Lettuce Salad, 1057.
Charlotte Russe, 1261.
Coffee, 1349.

Wednesday, April —.

Breakfast.
Plain Omelet, 450.
Fish Balls, 347.
Mutton Chops, with Watercress, 647.
Julienne Potatoes, 1013.
Brioches Fluttes, 1204.

Luncheon.
Smelts, with White Wine, 342.
Hamburg Steak, Russian sauce, 526.
Cauliflower, Hollandaise, 925.
Madeleine, 1226.

Dinner.
Clams, 300.
Jardinière, 28.
Tomatoes, 288. Olives.
Bass en Matelote, 332.
Roast Ham, Champagne sauce, 723.
Stewed Corn, 964.
Antelope Chops, Port Wine sauce, 891.
Stuffed Green Peppers, 975.
Roast Beef, 527.
Barbe de Capúcine Salad, 1038.
Vanilla Ice-cream, 1271.
Petites Bouchées des Dames, 1237.
Coffee, 1349.

Thursday, April

Breakfast.
Eggs à l'Aurore, 444.
Broiled Salt Mackerel, 399.
Hashed Beef au Gratin, 529.
Fried Onions, 969.
Rice and Milk, 1177.

Luncheon.
Broiled Shad's Roe, with bacon, 402.
Lamb Steaks à l'Américaine, 718.
Potatoes au Gratin, 1004.
Home-made Cake, 1220.

Dinner.
Rockaway Oysters, 298.
Consommé Renaissance, 115.
Radishes, 292. Lyons Sausage, 286.
White Perch, Tartare sauce, 353, 207.
Curry of Lamb à l'Indienne, 677
Turnips, with gravy, 967.
Chicken Vol-au-vent à la Financière, 810.
Spring Lamb, Mint sauce, 1361, 169.
Dandelion Salad, 1049.
Apples Meringuées, 1248.
Imported Brie Cheese.
Coffee, 1349.

Friday, April —.

Breakfast.

Eggs à la Bennett, 447.
Picked-up Codfish, 346.
Sheep's Feet à la Poulette, 654.
Spaghetti à l'Italienne, 960.
Stewed Prunes, 1330.

Luncheon.

Cromesquis à la Reine, 765.
Trout, Ravigote butter, 147.
Minced Tenderloin a la Portugaise, 501.
Fried Egg-plant, 907.
Rhubarb Pie, 1085.

Dinner.

Olives.

Oysters, 298.
Gumbo of Frogs, 23.
Tomatoes, 288.
Bass à la Béarnaise, 353.
Sweetbreads au Salpicon, 605.
Pigeons en compote, 822.
Sorrel, with gravy, 974.
Roast Turkey, 800.
Chicory Salad, 1045.
Almond Cake, glacé, 1208.
Coffee. 1349.

Saturday, April —.

Breakfast.

Eggs à la Suisse, 441.
Broiled Boned Smelts, maitre d'hôtel, 355, 145.
Lamb Steak, 718.
Potatoes Sautées au beurre, 994.
Milan Cake, 1228.

Luncheon.

Stuffed Deviled Crabs, 370.
Veal Stew à la Marengo, 624.
Cauliflower au Gratin, 926.
Maraschino Jelly, 1319.

Dinner.

Little Neck Clams, 300.
Julienne, 27.
Sardines, 283.   Cucumbers, 289.
Red-snapper, Egg sauce, 352, 161.
Tenderloin of Beef à la Chéron, 504.
Oyster-plant à la Poulette, 1019.
Salmi of Snipe à la Moderne, 870.
Spinach, maitre d'hôtel, 942.
Roast Mutton, 585.
Escarole Salad, 1055.
Lemon Pudding, 1157.
Coffee, 1349.

Sunday, April —.

Breakfast.

Chicken Liver Omelet, 464.
Broiled Shad's Roe, maître d'hôtel, 402.
Sausages à l'Italienne, 737.
Fried Oyster-plant, 1021.
Crême en Mousse au Café, 1253.

Luncheon.

Long Island Smelts au Gratin, 355.
Tripe à la Bordelaise, 544.
Spaghetti Napolitaine, 959.
Timbales Lagardère, 809.
Pineapple Tarts, 1115.

Dinner.

Blue Point Oysters, 298.
Chicken à la Piémontaise, 63.
Celery, 290.   Radishes, 292.
Boiled Salmon, Oyster sauce, 303.
Escalops of Sweetbreads à la Richelieu, 574.
Stuffed Tomatoes, 1023.
Chicken Sauté à l'Hongroise, 772.
Green Peas à l'Anglaise, 978.
Romaine Punch, 1304.
Roast Grass Plover, 865.
Lettuce, Mayonnaise salad, 1042, 1057.
Strawberry Shortcake, 1214.
Strachino Cheese.
Coffee, 1349.

Monday, April —

Breakfast.
Scrambled Eggs, with chicory, 409.
Broiled Lamb Fries, Tomato sauce, 673.
Beefsteak, with watercress, 524.
Potatoes, maitre d'hôtel, 985.
Strawberries and Cream.

Luncheon.
Codfish à l'Hollandaise, 317.
Veal Cutlets, Pagasqui, 560.
Carrots and Cream, 927.
Cauliflower Salad, 1040.
Raspberry Tarts, 1118.

Dinner.
Little Neck Clams, 300.
 • Potage à la McDonald, 95.
Olives.
      Mortadella, 287.
Bluefish au Gratin, 319.
Turkey Legs à la Diable, 766.
Potatoes à l'Hollandaise, 999.
Lamb Chops, maison d'or, 683.
String Beans à l'Anglaise, 948.
Snipe sur Canapé, 868.
Chicory Salad, 1045.
Stewed Peaches, 1334.
Bitter Almond Macaroons, 1209.
Coffee, 1349.

Tuesday, April —.

Breakfast.
Omelet à l'Espagnole, 472.
Broiled Bluefish, maitre d'hôtel, 329.
Brochettes of Lamb à la Dumas, 674.
Potato Croquettes, 997.
Stewed Green-gages, 1336.

Luncheon.
• Oysters à la Baltimore, 388.
Beefsteak Pie à l'Américaine, 488.
Fried Egg-plant, 907.
Rum Omelet, 476.

Dinner.
Oysters, 298.
Consommé Pure, 100.
Anchovies, 284.   Radishes, 292.
Broiled Pompano, 329.
Potatoes, Windsor, 1008.
Chicken Croquettes, with mushrooms, 276.
Saddle of Venison, Currant Jelly sauce, 878.
Fresh Asparagus, 904.
Roast Leg of Mutton, 648.
Watercress Salad, 1072.
Cold Maraschino Pudding, 1134.
Coffee, 1349.

Wednesday, April —.

Breakfast.
Eggs à la Meyerbeer, 437.
Fried White Perch, Colbert sauce, 301, 190.
Broiled Calf's Liver and Bacon, 584.
Potatoes Lyonnaise, 991.
Sherry Wine Jelly, 1318.

Luncheon.
Canapé Lorenzo, 391.
Broiled Beefsteak, Marrow sauce, 493.
Spaghetti au Gratin, 961.
Suédoise Salad, 1069.
Strawberry Pie, 1095.

Dinner.
Massachusetts Bay Oysters, 298.
Mutton à l'Ecossaise, 31.
Radishes, 292.   Olives.
Fresh Mackerel, St. Nazaire, 329, 236.
Mignons Filets à la Lorillard, 1364.
Stuffed Tomatoes, 1023.
Suprême of Chicken à la Toulouse, 786.
New String Beans, 945.
Brochette of Reed-birds, with Bacon, 877, 754.
Barbe de Capucine Salad, 1038.
Coffee Ice-cream, 1273.
Galette, 1221.
Coffee, 1349.

Thursday, April —.

Breakfast.

Ham Omelet, 462.
Fried Whitebait, 301.
Minced Veal à la Catalan, 575.
Stewed Carrots and Cream, 927.
Strawberries and Cream.

Luncheon.

Scallops Brestoise, 392.
Pork and Beans, 752.
Crab Salad, 1047.
Rice Cake à la Mazzini, 1230.

Dinner.

Linn Haven Oysters, 298.
Consommé d'Orléans, 110.
Tomatoes, 288. Olives.
North River Shad, maître d'hôtel, 326.
Cucumber Salad, 289.
Haricot of Lamb à la Providence, 701.
Balotine of Squab à l'Italienne, 818.
Fresh Peas, 978.
Roast Beef, 527.
Dandelion Salad, with eggs, 1049.
Apples Meringuées, 1248.
Coffee, 1349.

Friday, April —.

Breakfast.

Lobster Omelet, 454.
Broiled Fresh Mackerel, maître d'hôtel, 329.
Lamb Mignons, Madeira sauce, 1360, 185.
Sweet Potatoes, stewed, 995.
Brioches Fluttes, 1204.

Luncheon.

Kingfish, with sorrel, 327.
Blanquette of Veal, with nouilles, 552.
Potatoes, Hollandaise, 999.
Lobster Salad, 1061.
Baked Apples, 1124.

Dinner.

Little Neck Clams, 300.
Cream of Asparagus, 70.
Celery, 290. Mortadella, 287.
Oyster Patties, 387.
Roast Ham, with sweet corn, 724.
Spinach, with eggs, 943.
Breast of Lamb, Jardinière, 702.
Brussels Sprouts, 922.
Roast Turkey, 800.
Doucette Salad, 1052.
Baba, with rum, 1217.
Coffee, 1349.

Saturday, April —.

Breakfast.

Eggs à la Tripe, 419.
Mutton Hash à la Zingara, 652.
Black Sausage, with mashed potatoes, 719.
Rice à la Croce, 1296.

Luncheon.

Lobster en Brochette, 361.
Porterhouse Steak, 524.
Carrots and Cream, 927.
Maccaroni Croquettes, 279.
Mille Feuilles, 1223.

Dinner.

Keyport Oysters, 298.
Chicken Hollandaise, 64.
Radishes, 292. Lyons Sausage, 286.
Fillets of Bass, with White Wine, 342.
Sweetbreads à la Montglas, 615.
String beans, 945.
Boiled Turkey, Oyster sauce, 797.
Stuffed Green Peppers, 975.
Roast Beef, 527.
Escarole Salad, 1055.
Nelson Pudding, 1155.
Coffee, 1349.

Sunday, April —.

Breakfast.
Omelet à la Vanderbilt, 471.
Boiled Skate, black butter, 325, 159.
Calf's Feet, sauce piquante, 599.
Stewed Potatoes, 995.
hipped Cream à la Vanille, 1254.

Luncheon.
Salmon, with Anchovy butter, 303, 146.
Braised Beef à l' Orsini, 481.
Spinach, with Eggs, 940.
Timbales à la Schultze, 263.
Mince Pie, 1082.

Dinner.
Mill Pond Oysters, 298.
Potage of Rice à la Maintenon, 98.
Radishes, 292.   Olives.
Broiled Trout, maître d'hôtel, 314.
Cucumber Salad, 289.
Breast of Lamb, Jardinière, 702.
Chicken Fricassé à la Reine, 780.
Fresh Green Peas, 978.
Punch à la Cardinal, 1306.
Snipe sur Canapé, 868.
Lettuce and Tomato Salad, 1060.
St. Honoré à la Rose Delmonico, 1212.
Roquefort Cheese.
Coffee, 1349.

Monday, April —.

Breakfast.
Oatmeal.
Eggs à l'Alsacienne, 443.
Broiled Veal Cutlets, sauce piquante, 564, 203.
Tripe à la Créole, 545.
Potatoes maître d'hôtel, 985.
Stewed Pears, 1333.

Luncheon.
Golden Buck, Welsh Rarebit, 295.
Beefsteak Pie, à l'Anglaise, 487.
Anchovy Salad, 1037.
Vermicelli Pudding, 1142.

Dinner.
Little Neck Clams, 300.
Consommé Patti, 126.
Tomatoes, 288.   Olives.
Lobster Croquettes, sauce Colbert, 365.
Saddle of Mutton, Poivrade sauce, 667.
Sorrel au gras, 974.
Salmi of Snipe à la Walter Scott, 856.
Roast Mushrooms on Toast, 916.
Roast Reed-birds, 877.
Tomato Salad, Mayonnaise, 1071.
Omelet Soufflée, 474.
Coffee, 1349.

Tuesday, April

Breakfast.
Omelet, with Green Peas, 459.
Lobster Cutlets, Victoria, 366.
Breaded Mutton Chops, Tomato sauce, 643, 205.
Fried Egg-plant, 907.
Apples, with Rice, Meringuées, 1169.

Luncheon.
Broiled Oysters on Toast, 382.
Mignons Filets, marinaded. Russian sauce, 511.
Potatoes en paille, 1014.
Stewed Artichoke Bottoms, 897.
Pear Pie, open, 1088.

Dinner.
Doxie Rockaway Oysters, 298.
Clear Green Turtle, 18.
Thon, 282.   Radishes, 292.
Shad, vert-pré, 328.
Curry of Lamb à la Créole, 678.
Balotine of Squab, à l'Italienne, 818.
Fresh Asparagus, Hollandaise, 904.
Roast Sirloin of Beef, 527.
Dandelion Salad, 1048.
Tutti Frutti, 1293.
English Cheese.
Coffee, 1349.

Wednesday, April —.

Breakfast.
Poached Eggs on Toast, 404.
Broiled Kingfish, maître d'hôtel, 329.
Stewed Chicken Livers, with Madeira 767.
Potatoes à la Rice, 1007.
Stewed Apples, 1332.

Luncheon.
Sheep's-head à la Créole, 339.
Calf's Head à la Cavour, 638.
French Peas.
Beef Salad, 1039.
Strawberry Tarts, 1117.

Dinner.
Cherry-stone Oysters, 298.
Menestra, 36.
Olives.   Caviare, 281.
Bass à la Chambord, 343.
Lamb Chops, maison d'or, 683.
Beans Panachés, 950.
Antelope Steak, purée of Chestnuts, 882.
Spinach, 940.
Roast Ptarmigan sur Canapé, 862.
Lettuce, Mayonnaise Salad, 1042.
Plum Pudding, 1163.
Coffee, 1349.

Thursday, April —.

Breakfast.
Sausage Omelet, 465.
Scallops, Tomato sauce, 392, 205.
Mignons Filets, with Anchovy butter, 509, 146.
Potato Croquettes, 997.
Strawberries and Cream.

Luncheon.
Broiled Trout, with fine Herbs, 315.
Chicken Croquettes à l'Ecarlate, 760.
Spaghetti, with Cream, 954.
Savarin, 1197.

Dinner.
Oak Island Oysters, 298.
Consommé Tapioca, 104.
Sardines, 283.   Radishes, 292.
Timbales à l'Ecossaise, 261.
Shoulder of Lamb, Rouennaise, 698.
Risotto, 1017.
Coquilles of Sweetbreads à la Reine, 623.
Roast Squabs, with Watercress, 816.
Barbe de Capucine Salad, 1038.
Banana Ice-cream, 1277.
Lady-fingers, 1231.
Coffee, 1349.

Friday, April—.

Breakfast.
Scrambled Eggs, with mushrooms, 407.
Oysters en brochette, with Bacon, 385.
Sausages à la Gastronome, 740.
Macaroni, with Cheese, 956.
Preserved Cherries, 1347.

Luncheon.
Lobster à la Diable, 364.
Stewed Mutton, Portugaise, 658.
Fried Oyster-plant, 1021.
Iced Timbale of Rice, 1175.

Dinner.
Shrewsbury Oysters, 298.
Cream of Artichokes, 72.
Radishes, 292.   Celery, 290.
Pompano au Gratin, 319.
Tenderloin Piqué à la Sevigné, 520.
Broiled Spring Chickens, 756.
Broiled Mushrooms, 916.
Roast Teal Ducks, 859.
Escarole Salad, 1055.
Apple Cake, 1211.
Coffee, 1349.

Saturday, April —.

Breakfast.
Eggs à la Provençale, 422.
Fried Frost-fish, 301.
Beefsteak à la Moëlle, 493.
Broiled Tomatoes, 1025.
French Pancake, with Jelly, 1187.

Luncheon.
Broiled Shad, maître d'hôtel, 326.
Blanquette of Veal, with Peas, 551.
Tomatoes à la Marseillaise, 1029.
Boiled Apple Dumplings, 1127.

Dinner.
Little Neck Clams, 300.
Purée Condé, 48.
Olives.   Thon, 282.
Smelts, Tartare sauce, 353, 207.
Amourettes of Lamb, Tomato sauce, 673.
String Beans, 948.
Salmi of Ptarmigan, Chasseur, 864.
Asparagus, sauce Hollandaise, 904.
Roast Loin of Veal, 585.
Watercress Salad, 1072.
Pudding à la U. S. Grant, 1159.
Coffee, 1349.

Sunday, April —.

Breakfast.
Kidney Omelet, 463.
Shad, White Wine sauce, 342.
Veal Cutlets à la Milanaise, 563.
Potato Croquettes, 997.
Crème en Mousse au Maraschino, 1257.

Luncheon.
Salmon à la Régence, 305.
Squabs à la Chipolata, 821.
Stewed Okras à la Créole, 1031.
Salad à l'Italienne, 1036.
Charlotte Russe, 1261.

Dinner.
Blue Point Oysters, 298.
Chicken à la Richmond, 62.
Radishes, 292.   Olives.
Timbales of Nouilles à la Genoise, 262.
Spring Lamb Chops, Colbert sauce, 647, 190.
Green Peas, 980.
Broiled Tenderloin à la Trianon, 507.
Asparagus à la Tessinoise, 906.
Champagne Punch, 1307.
Roast Capon, 755.
Lettuce, French dressing, 1070.
Strawberry Shortcake, 1214.
Gorgonzolla Cheese.
Coffee, 1349.

Monday, April —.

Breakfast.
Eggs à la Béchamel, 416.
Fish Balls, 347.
Brochettes of Lamb à la Dumas, 674.
Mashed Potatoes au Gratin, 1004.
Rice and Milk, 1177.

Luncheon.
Stuffed Oysters à la Mali, 386.
Roulade of Beef à l'Écarlate, 539.
Potatoes Hollandaise, 999.
Tongue Salad, 1056.
Cranberry Pie, 1095.

Dinner.
Prince's Bay Oysters, 298.
Paysanne, 53.
Radishes, 292.   Anchovies, 284.
Bass, sauce Hollandaise, 309, 160.
Calf's Brains, sauce Tartare, 559.
Stewed Corn, 964.
Boiled Leg of Mutton, Caper sauce, 651.
Spinach au Croûtons, 943.
Roast Ptarmigan, 862.
Dandelion Salad, 1049.
Baba, 1216.
Coffee, 1349.

Tuesday, April —.

Breakfast.
Omelet; with fine Herbs, 451.
Broiled Pickerel, butter sauce, 329, 155.
Hashed Chicken en Bordure, 805.
Stewed Beets, 911.
Corn Fritters, 965.

Luncheon.
Canapé Lorenzo, 391.
Minced Veal à la Catalan, 575.
Beans Panachés, 950.
Bermuda Potato Salad, 1073.
Allumettes, 1205.

Dinner.
Clams, 300.
Tomato à l'Andalouse, 58.
Olives.   Green Peppers.
Trout à la Chambord, 313.
Sirloin Piqué à la Duchesse, 516.
Stuffed Tomatoes à la Reine, 1024.
Stewed Antelope à la Française, 887.
Artichokes à la Duxelle, 898.
Roast Turkey, cranberry sauce, 800, 1329.
Chicory Salad, 1045.
Méringues Glacées, 1301.
Coffee, 1349.

Wednesday, May —.

Breakfast.
Eggs à la Bonne Femme, 432.
Porgies à la Horly, 321.
Pig's Feet, sauce Robert, 728.
Mashed Potatoes, à l'Hollandaise, 999.
Blackberries and Cream.

Luncheon.
Oysters en Brochette au Petit Salé, 385.
Stewed Lamb, with Flageolets, 707.
Tongue Salad, 1056.
Peach Tarts, 1106.

Dinner.
Rockaway Oysters, 298.
Cream of Barley, 77.
Olives.   Caviare, 281.
Bass en Matelote, 332.
Beef-tongue, Napolitaine, 534.
Artichokes, Barigoul, 897.
Squabs en Crapaudine, 819.
New String Beans, 948.
Roast Mutton, 585.
Dandelion Salad, 1049.
Cream Renversée, 1252.
Coffee, 1349.

Thursday, May —.

Breakfast.
Tomato Omelet, 456.
Broiled Kingfish, 329.
Lamb Chops au Petit Salé, 682, 754.
Potatoes Julienne, 1013.
Rice Cake, 1222.

Luncheon.
Stuffed Deviled Clams, 376.
Veal Cutlets en Papillotes, 566.
Stewed Tomatoes, 1027.
Herring Salad, 1074.
Mille Feuilles, 1223.

Dinner.
Little Neck Clams, 300.
Consommé Diplomate, 93.
Radishes, 292.   Olives.
Kennebec Salmon, Lobster sauce, 303, 158.
Tenderloin of Beef, Piqué à la Portugaise, 517.
Potatoes Duchesse, 1006.
Chicken Sauté à la Ranhofer, 1363.
Asparagus, sauce Hollandaise, 904.
Roast Ptarmigan, 862.
Romaine Salad, 1064.
Cabinet Pudding, 1164.
Coffee, 1349.

MENUS.

Friday, May —.

Breakfast.

Eggs à la Bourguignonne, 411.
Blackfish aux fines Herbes, 331.
Lamb Kidneys, with Bacon, 713.
Baked Potatoes.
Wheat Cakes, 1184.

Luncheon.

Sole au Gratin, 319.
Beefsteak Pie à l'Anglaise, 487.
Crab Salad, 1047.
French Pudding à la Delmonico, 1139.

Dinner.

Kirtig's Oysters, 298.
Busecca Milanaise, 7.
Sardines, 283. Radishes, 292.
Frogs à la Poulette, 399.
Brisotin of Veal, Poivrade sauce, 554, 194.
Stuffed Peppers, 975.
Chicken à la Maryland, 785.
Lima Beans, 952.
Roast Teal Ducks, with gravy, 859.
Chicory Salad, 1045.
Lemon Ice-cream, 1278.
Coffee, 1349.

Saturday, May —.

Breakfast.

Eggs à la Paysanne, 433.
Corned Beef Hash, 531.
Stewed Calf's Liver à l'Alsacienne, 582.
Sweet Potatoes Soufflées, 1010.
Stewed Apricots, 1335.

Luncheon.

Oysters, à la Mali, 386.
Ragout of Veal, Marengo, 624,
String Bean Salad, 1068.
Strawberry Pie, 1095.

Dinner.

Clams, 300.
Croute-au-Pot, 11.
Radishes, 292. Mortadella, 287.
Shad's Roe, with Bacon, 402.
Pigeon Cutlets, à la Victoria, 815.
Green Peas, with Cream, 980.
Brochette of Lamb, sauce Piquante, 674, 203.
Artichokes, Florentine, 903.
Roast Loin of Pork, 751.
Romaine Salad, 1064.
Charlottes Panachées, 1300.
Coffee, 1349.

Sunday, May —.

Breakfast.

Eggs à l'Impératrice, 440.
Broiled Spanish-mackerel, maître d'hôtel, 329.
Hashed Turkey en Bordure, 805.
Stewed Lima Beans, with Cream, 952.
Rice and Cream à la Croce, 1296.

Luncheon.

Canapé Lorenzo, 391.
Broiled Porterhouse Steak, Anchovy butter, 524, 146.
Potato Croquettes, 997.
Cauliflower Salad, 1040.
Strawberries and Cream.

Dinner.

Mill Pond Oysters, 298.
Purée Mongole, 50.
Olives. Radishes, 292.
Sole Normande, 318.
Turban of Chicken, à la Cleveland, 791.
Stuffed Tomatoes, 1023.
Lamb Chops à la Maintenon, 685.
Asparagus à la Vinaigrette, 905.
Punch à la Française, 1311.
Roast Grass Plovers, 865.
Chicory Salad, 1045.
Rum Cake, 1299.
Strawberry Ice-cream, 1274.
Strachino Cheese.
Coffee, 1349.

Monday, May —.

Breakfast.

Eggs à la Turque, 439.
Broiled Bluefish, 329.
Lamb Steak, sauce Piquante, 717.
Saratoga Potatoes, 1011.
Buckwheat Cakes, 1183.

Luncheon.

Coquilles of Chicken à l'Anglaise, 271.
Fricandeau à la Morlaisienne, 579.
Oyster-plant à la Poulette, 1019.
Madeleine, 1226.

Dinner.

Keyport Oysters, 298.
Consommé Célestine, 118.
Olives.   Anchovies, 284.
Broiled Lobster à la Diable, 364.
Sirloin Steak, with Marrow, 493.
Sorrel and Cream, 973.
Vol-au-Vent à la Financière, 810.
· Roast Leg of Mutton, 648.
Salad, Barbe de Capucine, 1038.
Pineapple Fritters, 1191.
Coffee, 1349.

Tuesday, May —.

Breakfast.

Omelet, with Sardines, 468.
Fried Whitebait, 301.
Veal Cutlets à la Pagasqui, 560.
Mashed Potatoes au Gratin, 998.
Brioche, 1201.

Luncheon.

Frogs broiled, 398.
Shoulder of Lamb, Jardinière, 696.
Fried Onions, 969.
Tomato, Mayonnaise salad, 1071.
Lemon Méringue Pie, 1102.

Dinner.

Little Neck Clams, 300.
Crabs, with Gumbo, 24.
Watercress, 1072.   Sardines, 283.
Bass á l'Italienne, 337.
Beef-tongue à la Gendarme, 532.
Lima Beans, 952.
Stewed Chicken, with fresh Tarragon, 774.
Asparagus, Hollandaise sauce, 904.
Roast Beef, 527.
Dandelion Salad, 1049.
Peach Pudding à la Richelieu, 1150.
Coffee, 1349.

Wednesday, May —.

Breakfast.

Eggs au Soleil, 415.
Broiled Oysters en Brochette, 385.
Pig's Feet à la Poulette, 731.
Potatoes en Paille, 1014.
Strawberries and Cream.

Luncheon.

Boiled Fresh Mackerel, maître d'hôtel, 329.
· Veal Cutlets à la Milanaise, 563.
Stewed Corn, 964.
Cherry Tarts, 1111.

Dinner.

Parker Bay Oysters, 298.
Chicken à la Créole, 65.
Anchovies, 284.   Radishes, 292.
Shad au Gratin, 319.
Fillet of Beef, larded à l'Egyptienne, 521.
Artichokes à la Vinaigrette, 902.
Croquettes of Game, sauce Périgueux, 833.
Roast Chicken, 755.
Watercress Salad, 1072.
Indian Pudding, 1145.
Rum Jelly, 1320.
Coffee, 1349.

MENUS.

Thursday, May —.

Breakfast.
Eggs à la Hyde, 448.
Fried Cod's Tongues, 350.
Pork Chops, Apple sauce, 748.
Hashed Potatoes, sautées, 1003.
Iced Timbale of Rice, 1175.

Luncheon.
Broiled Soft-shelled Crabs à la Diable, 369.
Tripe à la Mode de Caën, 547.
Potatoes Soufflées, 1010.
Salad Suèdoise, 1069.
Crême en Mousse au Curaçoa, 1259.

Dinner.
Oak Island Oysters, 298.
Consommé Vermicelli, 103.
Radishes, 292.   Olives.
Kingfish, Egg sauce, 329, 161.
Stewed Kidneys, with cêpes, 714.
Tomatoes à la Bock, 1026.
Sweetbreads à la Pompadour, 618.
Spinach, with Eggs, 940.
Broiled Snipe, with Bacon, 869, 754.
Lettuce Salad, 1057.
Strawberry Shortcake, 1214.
Coffee, 1349.

Friday, May —.

Breakfast.
Eggs à la Valencienne, 421.
Fresh Mackerel à l'Italienne, 337.
Escalops of Veal, with Spinach, 568, 939.
Fried Potatoes, 993.
Stewed Prunes à la Dufour, 1330.

Luncheon.
Mussels Marinière, 378.
Mutton Chops, Soyer with Potatoes, 647.
Green Peas, 978.
Lobster à la Plummer Salad, 1062.
Cocoanut Pudding, 1147.

Dinner.
Clams, 300.
Sorrel, with Asparagus-tops, 41.
Radishes, 292.   Lyons Sausage, 286.
Kennebec Salmon, Russian sauce, 303, 211.
Braised Beef à la Mode, 479.
Beans Panachés, 950.
Croustade of Chicken à la Dreux, 762.
Stuffed Tomatoes, 1023.
Saddle of Spring Lamb, 1361.
Dandelion à la Coutoise, 1051.
Almond Cake, 1224.
Coffee, 1349.

Saturday, May —.

Breakfast.
Omelet Raspail, 467.
Broiled Pickerel, Anchovy butter, 329, 146.
Corned Beef Hash au Gratin, 529.
Potato Balls, 996.
Milan Cake, 1228.

Luncheon.
Crabs à la St. Laurent, 372.
Calf's-head à la Vinaigrette, 640.
Stuffed Egg-plant, 909.
Maraschino Jelly, 1319.

Dinner.
Prince's Bay Oysters, 298.
Chicken, with Leeks, 68.
Tomatoes, 288.   Olives.
Shad's-roe on Toast, 400.
Potatoes, Hollandaise, 999.
Epigrammes of Lamb, Macédoine, 689.
Spaghetti à l'Italienne, 960.
Stuffed Pig's Feet, sauce Madère, 733.
Green Peas and Bacon, 981.
Roast Turkey, 800.
Chicory Salad, 1046.
Vanilla Ice-cream, 1271.
Lady-fingers, 1231.
Coffee, 1349.

Sunday, May —.

Breakfast.

Scrambled Eggs, with Truffles, 407.
Broiled Brook-trout, with Bacon, 314, 754.
Deviled Spring Lamb Chops, 647.
Potatoes à l'Italienne, 990.
Crême en Mousse au Café, 1253.

Luncheon.

Lobster à la Newburg, 359.
Broiled Spring Chicken, with Bacon, 756, 754.
Green Peas à la Bourgeoise, 979.
Salad à la Russe, 1065.
Pie à la Martha Washington, 1105.

Dinner.

East River Oysters, 298.
Cream of Artichokes, 72.
Radishes, 292.   Olives.
Bluefish, White Wine sauce, 342.
Mignons Filets à la Parisienne, 514.
Fresh Asparagus, 904.
Stewed Chicken à la Parmentier, 773.
Stuffed Lettuce, 953.
Punch à la Lorenzo Delmonico,' 1303.
Bay Plovers, Roasted, 865.
Lettuce Salad, 1058.
Diplomatic Pudding, glacé, 1288.
Fancy Almond Cakes, 1239.
Stilton Cheese.
Coffee, 1349.

Monday, May —.

Breakfast.

Omelet à l'Espagnole, 472.
Fish Balls, 347.
Fillet of Pork, sauce Robert, 741, 192.
Potatoes, Château, 1009.
Blackberries and Cream.

Luncheon.

Fried Soft-shelled Crabs, 368.
Hashed Mutton à la Zingara, 652.
String Beans, with cream, 946.
Charlotte au Café, 1262.

Dinner.

Little Neck Clams, 300.
Consommé Deslignac, 108.
Lyons Sausage, 286.   Radishes, 292.
Trout, Shrimp sauce, 311.
Stewed Chicken Livers au Madère, 767.
Lima Beans, 952.
Lamb Chops, Masséna, 687.
Stuffed Green Peppers, 975.
Squabs sur Canapé, 816.
Romaine Salad, 1064.
Bread Pudding, 1132.
Coffee, 1349.

Tuesday, May —.

Breakfast.

Eggs à la Duchesse, 449.
Shad's Roe, maître d'hôtel, 402.
Beefsteak, with Watercress, 524.
Potatoes à la Hanna, 1012.
French Pancake, 1186.

Luncheon.

Kingfish, sauce Ravigote, 329, 147.
Panpiette of Veal à la Faubonne, 592.
Spaghetti Napolitaine, 959.
Rum Omelet, 476.

Dinner.

Small Rockaway Oysters, 298.
Mock Turtle Soup, 17.
Olives.   Mortadella, 287.
Fried Sea Bass, sauce Tartare, 301, 207.
Ragout of Beef à la Dufour, 541.
Vol-au-Vent à la Reine, 812.
Cauliflower au Gratin, 926.
Leg of Lamb, roasted, 648.
Salad, Barbe de Capucine, 1038.
Strawberry and Vanilla Ice-cream, 1274, 1271.
Camembert Cheese.
Coffee, 1349.

Wednesday, May —.

Breakfast.
Oatmeal, with Cream.
Omelet, with Cheese, 469.
Broiled Porterhouse Steak au Cresson, 524.
Potatoes au Gratin, 1004.
Sherry Wine Jelly, 1318.

Luncheon.
Codfish, Shrimp sauce, 352, 178.
Chicken Hash à la Polonaise, 803.
Fried Sweet Potatoes, 993.
Sago Pudding, 1140.

Dinner.
Clams, 300.
Purée Crécy, 47.
Tomatoes, 288.   Radishes, 292.
Trout, Genoise sauce, 314, 187.
Braised Beef à la Flamande, 482.
Piloff of Chicken à la Créole, 783.
Fresh Mushrooms on Toast, 916.
Roast Capon, 755.
Dandelion Salad, 1049.
Peaches and Cream.
Sweet Almond Macaroons, 1210.
Coffee, 1349.

Thursday, May —.

Breakfast.
Eggs à la Bennett, 447.
Butterfish aux fines Herbes, 331.
Sausage à l'Anglaise, 736.
Potatoes, with Bacon, 989.
Stewed Prunes à la Dufour, 1330.

Luncheon.
Pompano, with White Wine, 342.
Spring Lamb Steaks, purée of peas, 716.
Fried Egg-plant, 907.
Macédoine Salad, 1063.
Rhubarb Pie, 1085.

Dinner.
Shrewsbury Oysters, 298.
Consommé Princesse, 113.
Watercress, 1072.   Olives.
Shad à la Vénitienne, 338.
Broiled Tenderloin of Beef à la Nivernaise, 505.
Spaghetti au Gratin, 961.
Turkey à l'Anglaise, 795.
Green Peas, 978.
Roast Pigeons, 816.
Doucette Salad, 1054.
Biscuits Glacés, 1286.
Coffee, 1349.

Friday, May —.

Breakfast.
Oatmeal and Cream.
Shrimp Omelet, 434.
Boiled Codfish, Egg sauce, 352, 161.
Corned-beef Hash, American style, 529.
Saratoga Potatoes, 1011.
Fresh Cherries.

Luncheon.
Shad's Roe, Béarnaise sauce, 402, 166.
Breast of Veal à la Milanaise, 596.
Crab Salad, 1047.
Baked Apples, 1124.

Dinner.
Linn Haven Oysters, 298.
Chicken à la Turque, 69.
Celery, 290.   Olives.
Kingfish an Gratin, 319.
Saddle of Mutton, currant jelly sauce, 666.
Potatoes à la Hanna, 1012.
Squabs en Compote, 822.
Baked Tomatoes, 1028.
Broiled Reed-birds, with Bacon, 877, 754.
Romaine Salad, 1064.
Baba au Rhum, 1217.
Coffee, 1349.

Saturday, May —.

Breakfast.

Eggs au Miroir, 425.
Fried Whitebait, 301.
Calf's Liver, Sauté à l'Alsacienne, 582.
Stewed Potatoes, 995.
Currant Jam.

Luncheon.

Broiled Soft-shelled Crabs à la Diable, 369.
Beefsteak Pie, 488.
Cauliflower au Gratin, 926.
Rhubarb Tarts, 1112.

Dinner.

Little Neck Clams, 300.
Cream of Asparagus, 70.
Caviare, 281. Radishes, 292.
Blackfish à la Joinville, 322.
Veal Cutlets, St. Cloud, 561.
String Beans, 948.
Chicken Fricassé à l'Américaine, 781.
Macaroni, with Cream, 954.
Hindquarter of Spring Lamb, Mint Sauce, 1361.
Watercress Salad, 1072. [1(9
Nelson Pudding, 1155.
Coffee, 1349.

Sunday, May —.

Breakfast.

Omelet à la Vanderbilt, 471.
Broiled Codfish, with Bacon, 310, 754.
Lamb Fries, Mustard Sauce, 673, 202.
Stewed Carrots à la Béchamel, 527, 154.
Rice and Cream à la Croce, 1296.

Luncheon.

Cream Cheese.
Scallops Brestoise, 392.
Brochette of Lamb, with Bacon, 674, 754.
Stewed Tomatoes, 1027.
Japanese Salad, 1075.
Apple Pie, 1083.

Dinner.

Blue Point Oysters, 298.
Consommé Masséna, 102.
Sardines, 283. Cucumber Salad, 289.
Radishes, 292.
Broiled Trout, with Bacon, 314, 754.
Tenderloin of Beef, Piqué à la Provençale, 518.
Stuffed Egg-plant, 909.
Coquilles of Sweetbreads aux Champignons, 623.
Champagne Punch, 1307.
Roast Rhode Island Turkey, 800.
Chicory Salad, 1045.
Strawberry Shortcake, 1214.
Imported Brie Cheese.
Coffee, 1349.

Monday, May —.

Breakfast.

Eggs à la Chipolata, 442.
Fried Sea-bass, 301.
Hashed Turkey en Bordure, 805.
Succotash, 1022.
Small Brioches, 1202.

Luncheon.

Stuffed Deviled Crabs, 370.
Stewed Mutton, Solferino, 656.
Herring Salad, 1074.
Vanilla Eclairs, 1245.

Dinner.

Little Neck Clams, 300.
Consommé aux Pâtes d'Italie, 103.
Olives. Lyons Sausage, 286.
Salmon, Genoise Sauce, 306.
Calf's-head en Tortue, 641.
Spinach, 940.
Mignons of Lamb à la Pompadour, 509.
Roast Ptarmigan, 862.
Dandelion Salad, 1048.
Stewed Prunes à la Général Dufour, 1330.
Pithiviers Cake, 1225.
Coffee, 1349.

MENUS.

Tuesday, May —.

Breakfast.

Smoked Beef Omelet, 461.
Skate, with black Butter, 325, 159.
Lamb Steak à l'Américaine, 718.
Potatoes, maître d'hôtel, 985.
Rice à l'Airolo, 1171.

Luncheon.

Oysters à la Baltimore, 388.
Veal Cutlets en Papillotes, 566.
String Beans, with Cream, 946.
Pumpkin Pie, 1099.

Dinner.

Small Rockaway Oysters, 298,
Purée Condé, 48.
Radishes, 292   Watercress.
Sole à la Toulouse, 354.
Broiled Tenderloin à la Béarnaise, 492.
Stuffed Lettuce, 953.
Croquettes of Sweetbreads, Cream Sauce, 620,
Asparagus a la Tessinoise, 906.   [181.
Squabs sur Canapé, 816.
Escarole Salad, 1055.
Charlottes Panachées, 1300.
Coffee, 1349.

Wednesday, May —.

Breakfast.

Boiled Eggs.
Broiled North River Shad, maître d'hôtel, 326.
Stewed Kidneys, with Mushrooms, 714.
Turnips and Cream, 967.
Stewed Peaches, 1334.

Luncheon.

Crabs à l'Anglaise, 373.
Stewed Beef à la Turque, 542.
Stuffed Peppers, 975.
Tomato Mayonnaise, 1071.
Strawberry Tarts, 1117.

Dinner.

Clams, 300.
Cream à l'Allemande, 84.
Tomatoes, 288.   Olives.
Lobster à la Bordelaise, 360.
Grenadins of Veal à l'Africaine, 589.
Succotash, 1022.
Chicken Sauté à la Regence, 777.
Spinach, with Croûtons, 943.
Roast Tenderloin of Beef au Jus, 516.
Watercress Salad, 1072.
Maraschino Pudding, 1134.
Coffee, 1349.

Thursday, May —.

Breakfast.

Omelet, with Cêpes, 460.
Chicken Halibut, Caper sauce, 309, 651.
Tripe à la Lyonnaise, 548.
Potatoes à la Rice, 1007.
Strawberries and Cream.

Luncheon.

Clams à la Marinière, 377.
Broiled Spring Chicken, 756.
Green Peas, with Cream, 980.
Savarin, 1197.

Dinner.

Linn Haven Oysters, 298.
Consommé Colbert, 120.
Caviare, 281.   Radishes, 292.
Trout a la Cambacères, 312.
Asparagus à la Vinaigrette, 905.
Lamb Chops, Soyer, 647.
• Suprême of Chicken à la Rothschild, 790.
Potato Croquettes, 997.
Roast Plover, 865.
Romaine Salad, 1064.
Vanilla Ice-cream, 1271.
Petites Bouchées des Dames, 1237.
Coffee, 1349.

Friday, May —.

Breakfast.

Scrambled Eggs, with Asparagus-tops, 406.
Broiled Pompano, 329.
Mutton Hash, 653.
Potatoes à la Lyonnaise, 991.
German Pancake, 1188.

Luncheon.

Scallops à la St. Jean, 371.
Porterhouse Steak au Cresson, 524.
Sweet Potatoes à l'Hollandaise, 999.
Lobster Salad, 1061.
Iced Timbale of Rice, 1175.

Dinner.

Little Neck Clams, 300.
Printanier Grénat, 51.
Olives.   Mortadella, 287.
Kingfish à la Vénitienne, 338.
Minced Veal à la Catalan, 575.
Fresh Mushrooms on Toast, 916.
Broiled Tenderloin à la Florentine, 506.
Roast Chicken, 755.
Dandelion Salad, 1049.
Orange Pudding, 1158.
Coffee, 1349.

Saturday, May —.

Breakfast.

Omelet à l'Espagnole, 472.
Fried Scallops, Tomato Sauce, 301, 205.
Mutton Chops, Bretonne, 644.
Hashed Potatoes and Cream, 1003.
Fritters à la Vanille, 1192.

Luncheon.

Mussels à la Poulette, 379.
Noix of Veal à la Bourgeoise, 590, 583.
Chicken Livers en Brochette au petit Salé, 769.
Potatoes Soufflées, 1010.
Boiled Apple Dumplings, 1127.

Dinner.

Keyport Oysters, 298.
Chicken Portugaise, 66.
Olives.   Lyons Sausage, 286.
Matelote of Eels à la Normande, 334.
Mignons Filets, with Marrow, 510.
Asparagus, sauce Hollandaise, 904.
Chicken Sauté à la Bohémienne, 778.
Stuffed Tomatoes, 1023.
Roast Loin of Spring Lamb, 1361.
Chicory Salad, 1045.
Cocoanut Pudding, 1147.
Coffee, 1349.

Sunday, May —.

Breakfast.

Poached Eggs on Toast, with Anchovy Butter, 404, 146.
Broiled Kingfish, maître d'hôtel, 329.
Hashed Chicken à la Crème, 804.
Crème Renversée, 1252.

Luncheon.

Lobster Cutlets, Victoria Sauce, 366.
Chops Soyer, with Potatoes, 647.
Stuffed Cucumbers, 937.
Chicken Salad, 1044.
Strawberries and Cream.

Dinner.

Little Neck Clams, 300.
Cream of Chicken, 82.
Sardines, 783.   Radishes, 292.
Salmon à la Régence, 305.
Roast Tenderloin, Piqué à la Duchesse, 516.
Risotto, 1017.
Chicken Fillets à la Patti, 789.
Artichokes, Florentine, 903.
Punch à la Cardinal, 1306.
Roast Ptarmigans, 862.
Lettuce, Mayonnaise, 1042.
St. Honoré à la Rose Delmonico, 1212.
Roquefort Cheese.
Coffee, 1349.

Monday, May —.

Breakfast.
Ham Omelet, 462.
Fish Balls, 347.
Calf's Liver and Bacon, 584.
Potatoes, maître d'hôtel, 985.
Sweet Potatoes, Sautées, 995.
Whipped Cream au Kirsch, 1256.

Luncheon.
Welsh Rarebit, Golden Buck, 295.
Ragout of Mutton aux Pommes, 659.
Spaghetti à l'Italienne, 960.
Frangipani Tarts, 1121.

Dinner.
Cherry Stone Oysters, 298.
Consommé Douglas, 114.
Tomatoes, 288.   Anchovies, 284.
North River Shad en Matelote, 332.
Sweetbreads, Soubise, 606.
Beans Panachés, 950.
Breast of Lamb, Jardinière, 702.
Roast Plovers, 865.
Escarole Salad, 1055.
Preserved Plums, 1343.
Coffee, 1349.

Tuesday, May —.

Breakfast.
Eggs à la Tripe, 419.
Fried Frostfish, 301.
Pig's Feet, Boston style, 730.
Potato Croquettes, 997.
Corn Fritters, 965.

Luncheon.
Shad's Roe, sauce Hollandaise, 402, 160.
Minced Beef à la Provençale, 500.
Stuffed Peppers, 975.
String Bean Salad, 1068.
Apple Méringue Pie, 1103.

Dinner.
Little Neck Clams, 300.
Mulligatawney à la Delmonico, 35.
Caviare, 281.   Radishes, 292.
Fresh Mackerel, Cream Sauce, 329, 181.
Lamb Chops à la Robinson, 682.
Sorrel, with Croûtons, 974.
Chicken Curry à l'Espagnole, 793.
Fresh Asparagus, 904.
Roast Snipe, 868.
Doucette Salad, 1054.
Fruit Pudding, 1161.
Coffee, 1349.

Wednesday, May —.

Breakfast.
Omelet à la Provençale, 457.
Fried Porgies, 301.
Broiled Deviled Mutton Kidneys, 715.
Fried Potatoes, 993.
Waffles with Sugar, 1196.

Luncheon.
Oysters à la Baltimore, 388.
Chicken Pot-pie, 757.
Macaroni au Gratin, 955.
Rice Pudding, 1143.

Dinner.
Massachusetts Bay Oysters, 298.
Chicken à la Richmond, 62.
Olives.   Lyons Sausage, 286.
Bass, Lobster Sauce, 352, 158.
Boiled Turkey, Egg Sauce, 798.
Spinach, maître d'hôtel, 942.
Sweetbreads aux Gourmets, 612.
Brussels Sprouts, 922.
Roast Fillet of Beef, 516.
Barbe de Capucine Salad, 1038.
Omelet Célestine, 477.
Coffee, 1349.

Thursday, May —.

Breakfast.

Eggs au Beurre noir, 414.
Spanish-mackerel, Vert-pré, 328.
Calf's Head à la Vinaigrette, 640.
Lima Beans and Cream, 952.
Blackberries and Cream.

Luncheon.

Broiled Trout, Butter sauce, 314.
Corned Beef with Kale-sprouts, 490.
Potatoes à l'Hollandaise, 999.
Herring Salad, 1074.
Baba au Rhum, 1217.

Dinner.

Small Rockaway Oysters, 298.
Consommé Suédoise, 122.
Mortedella, 287. Radishes, 292.
Kennebec Salmon à la Régence, 305.
Fillet of Beef, Broiled à la Trianon, 507.
Green Peas à l'Anglaise, 978.
Chicken Sauté à la Marengo, 771.
Stuffed Tomatoes, 1023.
Roast Hind Quarter of Spring Lamb, 1361.
Chicory Salad, 1045.
Blackberry Shortcake, 1215.
Coffee, 1349.

Friday, May —.

Breakfast.

Omelet aux Sardines, 468.
Broiled Bluefish, brown Butter, 329, 159.
Pig's Feet, St. Hubert, 727.
Spaghetti à la Italienne, 960.
Brioche, 1201.

Luncheon.

Crabs à la St. Jean, 371.
Stewed Mutton, Marseillaise, 657.
Salmon Salad, 1066.
Custard Pie, 1100.

Dinner.

East River Clams, 300.
Oyster Soup, 26.
Olives. Sardines, 283.
Bass à la Chambord, 343.
Escalops of Sweetbreads, Richelieu, 574.
Cauliflower au Gratin, 926.
Squabs en Crapaudine, 819.
String Beans, 948.
Roast Loin of Veal, 585.
Watercress Salad, 1072.
Omelet Soufflée, 474.
Coffee, 1349.

Saturday, June —.

Breakfast.

Eggs à la Bourguignonne, 411.
Haddock, Cream Sauce, 352, 181.
Lamb en Brochette, Colbert, 674, 190.
Fried French Potatoes, 993.
Rice Cake, 1222.

Luncheon.

Broiled Stuffed Deviled Crabs, 370.
Breaded Veal Cutlets, Tomato sauce, 563.
Macédoine Salad, 1063.
Mille Feuilles, 1223.

Dinner.

Ox-tail à l' Ecossaise, 39.
Tomatoes, 288. Olives.
Lobster à la Bordelaise, 360.
Tenderloin of Pork, Sauce piquante, 741, 203.
String Beans, 984.
Fried Chicken, Cream Sauce, 301, 181.
Stuffed Tomatoes, 1023.
Leg of Lamb, 648.
Lettuce Salad, 1057.
Tapioca Pudding, 1141.
Mazagran à la Gen. Bugeau, 1391.

Sunday, June —.

Breakfast.

Omelet with fresh Asparagus, 458.
Veal Kidneys, Broiled and Deviled, 715.
Broiled Ham, 753.
Fried Oyster-plant, 1021.
Fresh Cherries.

Luncheon.

Baked Bluefish, 319.
Hashed Chicken en Bordure, 805.
Stuffed Egg-plant, 909.
Timbales à la Schultze, 263.
Raspberry Pie, 1096.

Dinner.

Little Neck Clams, 300.
Cream of Cauliflower, 73.
Caviare, 281.   Radishes, 292.
Pompano, maître d'hôtel, 329.
Potatoes, Château, 1009.
Broiled Tenderloin à la Trianon, 507.
Broiled Tomatoes, 1025.
Shells of Sweetbreads à la Dreux, 621.
Punch à la Lalla Rookh, 1308.
Roast Turkey, Cranberry Sauce, 800, 1329.
Chicory Salad, 1045.
Cabinet Pudding à la Sadi-Carnot, 1164.
Swiss Cheese.
Coffee, 1349.

Monday, June —.

Breakfast.

Eggs au Soleil, 415.
Broiled Black Bass, 329.
Sausages, with White Wine, 735.
Hashed Potatoes, 1002.
Stewed Apricots, 1335.

Luncheon.

Stuffed Deviled Clams, 376.
Corned Beef Hash à la Polonaise, 528.
Oyster-plant à la Poulette, 1019.
Tomato, Mayonnaise Salad, 1071.
Blackberry Tarts, 1119.

Dinner.

Small Rockaway Oysters, 298.
Consommé Napolitaine, 127.
Anchovies, 284.   Radishes, 292.
Shad à l'Ecarlate, 326, 247.
Tenderloin Piqué à la Provençale, 518.
Potatoes en Paille, 1014.
Veal Cutlets à la Maréchale, 562.
Stuffed Lettuce, 953.
Roast Squabs, 816.
Doucette Salad, 1054.
Omelet au Kirsch, 476.
Coffee, 1349.

Tuesday, June —.

Breakfast.

Omelet, with Parsley, 451.
Broiled Bacon, 754.
Hashed Lamb à la Polonaise, 700.
Stewed Carrots and Cream, 927.
Cream Renversée, 1252.

Luncheon.

Broiled Trout à la maître d'hôtel, 314.
Vol-au-Vent à la Financière, 810.
Asparagus à la Tessinoise, 906.
Boiled Apricot Dumplings, 1126.

Dinner.

Massachusetts Bay Oysters, 298.
Mock Turtle, 17.
Lyons Sausage, 286.   Olives.
Bass en Matelote, 332.
Sweetbreads à la Duxelle, 608.
Chicken Sauté à l'Hongroise, 772.
Mushrooms on Toast, 914.
Roast Loin of Mutton, 585.
Escarole Salad, 1055.
Rum Cake, 1229.
Coffee, 1349.

Wednesday, June —.

Breakfast.
Fried Eggs, 412.
Broiled Kingfish, 329.
Minced Beef à la Provençale, 500.
Potatoes à la Hanna, 1012.
Buckwheat Cakes, 1183.

Luncheon.
Welsh Rarebit, Golden Buck, 295.
Shad's Roe, with Bacon, 402.
Stewed Mutton, with Oyster-plant, 703.
Tomatoes à la Marseillaise, 1029.
Rhubarb Pie, 1085.

Dinner.
Oysters, 298.
Cream of Sorrel, Fermière, 81.
Sardines, 283. Radishes, 292.
Salmon Croquettes, 364.
Broiled Tenderloin of Beef, Nivernaise, 505.
Turnips, with Gravy, 967.
Mutton Chops à la Clichy, 684.
Asparagus à la Vinaigrette, 905.
Roast Chicken, 755.
Watercress Salad, 1072.
Plombière a la Hamilton, 1370.
Coffee, 1349.

Thursday, June —.

Breakfast.
Omelet Régence, 470.
Picked-up Codfish, 346.
Lamb Steak, with Bacon, 716, 754.
Potato Balls, 996.
Brioches, 1201.

Luncheon.
Trout, Ravigote Sauce, 314, 147.
Tendron of Veal, Morlaisienne, 635.
Beef Salad, 1039.
Peach Pie, 1092.

Dinner.
Oak Island Oysters, 298.
Pot-au-Feu, 54.
Watercress, 1072. Anchovies, 284.
Crawfish à la Bordelaise, 360.
Sirloin à la Stanley, 491, 248.
String Beans à la Bretonne, 949.
Turban of Chicken à la Cleveland, 791.
Cauliflower au Gratin, 926.
Roast Plover, 865.
Romaine Salad, 1064.
Charlottes Panachées, 1300.
Coffee, 1349.

Friday, June —.

Breakfast.
Eggs à la Polonaise, 445.
Broiled Whitebait, 329.
Beef Tongue, sauce Piquante, 533.
Fried Sweet Potatoes, 993.
Kirsch Jelly, 1319.

Luncheon.
Stuffed Deviled Crabs, 370.
Beefsteak Pie à l'Américaine, 488.
Spinach, with Gravy, 943.
Shrimp Salad, 1067.
Frangipani Tarts, 1121.

Dinner.
Little Neck Clams, 300.
Bouille-à-Baisse, 1.
Celery, 290. Olives.
Bass, Egg Sauce, 352, 161.
Civet of Antelope à la Française, 887.
Spaghetti au Gratin, 961.
Lamb Chops, maison d'or, 961.
Green Peas, 978.
Roasted Squabs, 816.
Barbe de Capucine Salad, 1038.
Peach Pudding à la Richelieu, 1150.
Coffee, 1349.

Saturday, June —.

Breakfast.
Hominy and Cream, 1034.
Chicken Liver Omelet, 464.
Mutton Chops, with Bacon, 647, 754.
Saratoga Potatoes, 1011.
Rice à la Turque, 1178.

Luncheon
Frogs' Legs à la Geo. Merrill, 1372.
Stuffed Breast of Veal, Purée of Peas, 596, 49.
Asparagus à la Tessinoise, 906.
Cranberry Pie, 1104.

Dinner.
Little Neck Clams, 300.
Brunoise, with Rice, 3.
Radishes, 292.   Sardines, 283.
Salmon, Oyster Sauce, 303.
Tenderloin of Beef, larded à la Portugaise, 517.
Sorrel, with Eggs, 974.
Salmi of Ptarmigan à la Moderne, 870.
Lima Beans, 952.
Roast Leg of Spring Lamb, 648.
Lettuce Salad, 1058.
Apple Charlotte, 1167.
Coffee, 1349.

Sunday, June —.

Breakfast.
Scrambled Eggs, with Truffles, 407.
Fried Soles, Tartare Sauce, 320, 207.
Hashed Turkey à la Crême, 804.
Broiled Egg-plant, 908.
Stewed Prunes, 1330.

Luncheon.
Codfish à l'Hollandaise, 317.
Broiled Turkey Legs à la Diable, 766.
Okras, Sautés à la Créole, 1031.
Crab Salad, 1047.
Crême en Mousse au Cognac, 1258.

Dinner.
Little Neck Clams, 300.
Mulligatawney, 34.
Caviare, 28.   Radishes, 292.
Broiled Spanish-mackerel, maitre d'hôtel, 329.
Cucumber Salad, 289.
Curry of Lamb, with Asparagus-tops, 676.
Sweetbreads à la Catalan, 616.
Hashed Potatoes au Gratin, 1004.
Roman Punch, 1304.
Roast Tenderloin of Beef, 516.
Tomato, Mayonnaise Salad, 1071.
Strawberry Shortcake, 1214.
Camembert Cheese.
Mazagran à la Gen. Dufour, 1392.

Monday, June —.

Breakfast.
Omelet aux fines Herbes, 451.
Fish Balls, 347.
Brochette of Lamb à la Dumas, 674.
Succotash, 1022.
Milan Cake, 1228.

Luncheon.
Pickerel, with White Wine, 342.
Haricot of Lamb à la Providence, 701.
Stewed Corn, 964.
Herring Salad, 1074.
Maraschino Jelly, 1319.

Dinner.
East River Oysters, 298.
Consommé Rachel, 123.
Thon, 282.   Radishes, 292.
Broiled Pompano, 329.
Potatoes, Windsor, 1008.
Suprême of Chicken à la Bayard, 787.
Green Peas à l'Anglaise, 978.
Beefsteak à la Bordelaise, 491.
Fried Oyster-plant, 1021.
Roast Loin of Veal, 585.
Dandelion Salad, 1049.
Vermicelli Pudding, 1142.
Coffee, 1349.

Tuesday, June —.

Breakfast.
Eggs à la Livingstone, 410.
Broiled Mutton Kidneys, with Bacon, 661.
Potatoes, Saratoga, 1011.
Crême en Mousse au Café, 1253.

Luncheon.
Mussels à la Marinière, 378.
Hashed Turkey en Bordure, 805.
Fried Sweet Potatoes, 993.
Asparagus Salad, 905.
Raspberry Tarts, 1118.

Dinner.
Mill Pond Oysters, 298.
Mikado, 32.
Tomatoes, 288.   Radishes, 292.
Fresh Mackerel, St. Nazaire, 329, 236.
Tenderloin of Beef, Piqué à la Trianon, 507.
Stuffed Peppers, 975.
Sweetbreads à la Montglas, 615.
Roast Squab, 816.
Chicory Salad, 1045.
Baked Apple Dumplings, 1122.
Coffee, 1349.

Wednesday, June —.

Breakfast.
Tomato Omelet, 456.
Shad, maitre d'hôtel, 326.
Pig's Feet à la Boston, 730.
Potatoes Julienne, 1013.
Raspberries and Cream.

Luncheon.
Scallops Brestoise, 392.
Beefsteak Pie a l'Américaine, 488.
String Beans, 947.
Pineapple Pie, 1087.

Dinner.
Little Neck Clams, 300.
Beef à l'Anglaise, 5.
Lyons Sausage, 206.   Radishes, 292.
Bluefish à la Toulouse, 354.
Minced Beef à la Provençale, 500.
Fricassé of Chicken, with Curry, 792.
Asparagus, sauce Hollandaise, 904.
Roast Beef, 527.
Romaine Salad, 1064.
Peach Water-ice, 1284.
Biscuits à la Cuillère, 1231.
Coffee, 1349.

Thursday, June —.

Breakfast.
Omelet, with Peas, 459.
Porterhouse Steak, with Watercress, 524.
Potatoes, Lyonnaise, 991.
French Pancake, 1186.

Luncheon.
Shad, with Sorrel, 327.
Mutton Chops, Soyer, 647.
Stuffed Peppers, 975.
Jam Omelet, 475.

Dinner.
Parker Bay Oysters, 298.
Julienne, 27.
Watercress, 1072.   Anchovies, 284.
Clam Patties, 387.
Mignons Filets à la Bohémienne, 513.
Succotash, 1022.
Chicken à la Ranhofer, 1363.
Artichokes à la Florentine, 903.
Roast Reed-birds, 877.
Escarole Salad, 1055.
Riz au Lait d'Amandes, 1170.
Coffee, 1349.

Friday, June —.

Breakfast.
Lobster Omelet, 454.
Bluefish au Gratin, 319.
Minced Beef à la Catalan, 502.
Potatoes à la Rice, 1007.
Preserved Apples, 1342.

Luncheon.
Whitebait, 301.
Green Peas, 978.
Porterhouse Steak, Fried Onions, 524, 969.
Potato Salad, 1073.
Rice and Cream à la Croce, 1296.

Dinner.
Doxie Rockaway Oysters, 298.
Bisque of Crab, 9.
Thon, 282.   Radishes, 292.
Kingfish, with White Wine, 342.
Stewed Mutton, with Potatoes, 659.
Asparagus à la Tessinoise, 906.
Salmi of Pigeon à la Walter Scott, 856.
Roast Loin of Veal, 585.
Chicory Salad, 1045.
Pineapple Water-ice, 1283.
Sweet Almond Macaroons, 1210.
Coffee, 1349.

Saturday, June —.

Breakfast.
Omelet Espagnole, 472.
Skate, with black Butter, 325, 159.
Calf's Liver and Bacon, 584.
Broiled Potatoes, 983.
Fresh Grapes.

Luncheon.
Broiled Porgies à la Béarnaise, 353.
Sausages à la Gastronome, 740.
String Bean Salad, 1068.
Rhubarb Pie, 1085.

Dinner.
Linn Haven Oysters, 298.
Consommé à l'Africaine, 116.
Caviare, 28.   Celery, 290.
Lobster à la Newburg, 359.
Marinated Tenderloin of Beef, Russian Sauce, 511.
Mushrooms on Toast, 916.
Salmi of Duck, with Olives, 827.
Fried Egg-plant, 907.
Roast Spring Lamb, 1361.
Romaine Salad, 1064.
Cold Maraschino Pudding, 1134.
Coffee, 1349.

Sunday, June —.

Breakfast.
Eggs à l'Impératrice, 440.
Broiled Pompano, 327.
Hamburg Steak, Colbert, 526, 190.
Mashed Potatoes, 998.
Crème en Mousse au Café, 1253.

Luncheon.
Fresh Mackerel, fine Herbs, 331.
Stewed Veal, Marengo, 624.
Stuffed Lettuce, 953.
Tomato, Mayonnaise Salad, 1071.
Stewed Prunes à la Général Dufour, 1330.

Dinner.
Little Neck Clams, 300.
Mutton à l'Ecossaise, 31.
Radishes, 292.   Anchovies, 284.
Salmon, en Papillotes, 302.
Saddle of Mutton, Sevigné, 669.
Sweetbreads, with Asparagus-tops, 602, 676.
Punch à la Lorenzo Delmonico, 1303.
Roast Goose, 808.
Lettuce Salad, 1057.
Tutti-frutti, 1293.
Almond Biscuits, 1235.
Mazagran à la General Bugeau, 1391.

Monday, June —.

Breakfast.

Kidney Omelet, 463.
Hashed Beef à la Portugaise, 501.
Potatoes, Hollandaise, 999.
Fresh Red Currants.

Luncheon.

Soft Clams à la Newburg, 390.
Veal Cutlets à la Maréchale, 562.
String Beans, with Cream, 946.
Peach Pie, 1092.

Dinner.

Rockaway Oysters, 298.
Consommé d'Orléans, 110.
Mortadella, 287.   Radishes, 292.
Blackfish, Vert-pré, 328.
Potatoes, Duchesse, 1006.
Hashed Turkey, with Cream, 804.
Risotto, 1017.
Lamb Chops à la Masséna, 687.
Artichokes, Florentin, 903.
Roast Capon, 755.
Lettuce Salad, 1058.
Lemon Water-ice, 1279.
Coffee, 1349.

Tuesday, June —.

Breakfast.

Poached Eggs on Toast, Anchovy Butter, 404, 146.
Porgies, maître d'hôtel, 329.
Minced Tenderloin à l'Italienne, 500, 188.
Potatoes, Lyonnaise, 991.
Whipped Cream à la Vanille, 1254.

Luncheon.

Sheep's-head à la Créole, 339.
Mutton Steaks à la Colbert, 716, 190.
Spaghetti à l'Italienne, 960.
Red Currant Pie, 1090.

Dinner.

Clams, 300.
Consommé Paysanne, 53.
Tomatoes, 288.   Olives.
Frogs à la Bordelaise, 401, 243.
Croquettes of Lamb, Tomato Sauce, 679, 205.
Beans Panachés, 950.
Stewed Chicken à la Maryland, 785.
Cauliflower au Gratin, 926.
Roast Beef, 527.
Chicory Salad, 1045.
Strawberry and Vanilla Ice-cream, 1274, 1271.
Coffee, 1349.

Wednesday, June —.

Breakfast.

Cheese Omelet, 469.
Boiled Sea-bass, Tomato sauce, 352, 205.
Sausages à l'Anglaise, 736.
Oyster-plant Sauté au Beurre, 1018.
Rice and Apples, 1169.

Luncheon.

Broiled Brook-trout, 314.
Cucumber Salad, 289.
Stewed Mutton with Potatoes, 659.
Stuffed Peppers, 975.
Lamb-tongue Salad, 1056.
Raspberry Tarts, 1118.

Dinner.

Shrewsbury Oysters, 298.
Cream of Asparagus, 70.
Sardines, 283.   Celery, 290.
Porgies with fine Herbs, 315.
Tenderloin of Beef Marinated, sauce Poivrade, 511, 194.
Sorrel, with Eggs, 974.
Pigeon Cutlets à la Victoria, 815.
Brussels Sprouts, 922.
Roast Rhode Island Turkey, 800.
Doucette Salad, 1054.
Apricot Pudding, 1151.
Coffee, 1349.

Thursday, June —.

Breakfast.

Scrambled Eggs, with Mushrooms, 408.
Broiled, Deviled Soft-shelled Crabs, 370.
Stewed Mutton Kidneys, Madeira Wine, 662.
Fried Potatoes à la Française, 993.
Raspberries and Cream.

Luncheon.

Lobster à la Diable, 364.
Pork Chops, sauce Robert, 746.
Spaghetti au Gratin, 961.
Custard Pie, 1100.

Dinner.

Clams, 300.
Chicken à l'Hollandaise, 64.
Olives.   Celery, 290.
Pompano au Gratin, 319.
Broiled Sirloin, with Marrow, 493.
Spinach, maître d'hôtel, 942.
Duckling à l'Américaine, 823.
String Beans, with Cream, 946.
Roast Spring Lamb, 1361.
Lettuce Salad, 1057.
Méringues Glacées, 1301,
Coffee, 1349.

Friday, June —.

Breakfast.

Crawfish Omelet, 453.
Boiled Codfish, Cream sauce, 352, 181.
Corned Beef Hash à l'Américaine, 531.
Boiled Corn, 962.
Brioche Condé, 1203.

Luncheon.

Shad, maître d'hôtel, 326.
Stewed Lamb, with Lima Beans, 705.
Potatoes à la Hanna, 1012.
Lobster Salad, 1061.
Rice à la Bonne Femme, 1172.

Dinner.

East River Oysters, 298.
Chiffonade, 14.
Radishes, 292.   Mortadella, 287.
Broiled Sea-bass, sauce Tartare, 326, 207.
Piloff of Chicken à la Turque, 782.
Fresh Lima Beans, 952.
Veal Cutlets à la Philadelphia, 565.
Artichokes à la Vinaigrette, 902.
Reed-birds, with Bacon, 877, 754.
Romaine Salad, 1064.
Peaches and Cream.
Coffee, 1349.

Saturday, June —.

Breakfast.

Omelet, Bonne Femme, 466.
Fried Whitebait, 301.
Escalops of Veal à la Provençale, 573.
Broiled Tomatoes, 1025.
Peach Marmalade, 1331.

Luncheon.

Salmon Croquettes, 364.
Lamb en Brochette à la Colbert, 674, 190.
String Beans, Sautés au Beurre, 947.
Savarin, 1197.

Dinner.

Little Neck Clams, 300.
Consommé Printanier, 109.
nchovies, 284.   Radishes, 292.
Sheep's-head à la Chambord, 343.
Sirloin, Piqué à la Bernardi, 523.
Croquettes of Macaroni, 279.
Chicken Sauté à la Parmentier, 773.
Stuffed Tomatoes, 1023.
English Snipe sur Canapé, 868, 830.
Watercress Salad, 1072.
Sherry Wine Jelly, 1318.
Lady-fingers, 1231.
Coffee, 1349.

Sunday, June —.

Breakfast.

Eggs à l'Impératrice, 440.
Broiled Spanish-mackerel, 329.
Lamb Chops, Robinson, 682.
Hashed Potatoes, with Cream, 1003.
Fresh Cherries.

Luncheon.

Scallops Brestoise, 392.
Blanquette of Veal, with Nouilles, 552.
Green Peas, 978.
Chicken Salad, 1044.
Iced Timbale of Rice, 1175.

Dinner.

Blue Point Oysters, 298.
Cream of Cauliflower, 73.
Celery, 290.   Olives.
Bass, sauce Hollandaise, 352, 160.
Boiled Turkey, Celery sauce, 796.
Flageolets, 945.
Roast Tenderloin of Beef à la Hussard, 519.
Champagne Punch, 1307.
Roast Chicken, 755.
Tomato, Mayonnaise Salad, 1071.
Strawberry Ice-cream, 1274.
Almond Cake, 1224.
Neuchâtel Cheese.
Coffee, 1349.

Monday, June —.

Breakfast.

Omelet, with fine Herbs, 451.
Fish Balls, 347.
Broiled Pig's Feet, sauce Piquante, 729.
Turnips, with Gravy, 967.
Brioches Fluttes, 1204.

Luncheon.

Broiled, Deviled Soft-shelled Crabs, 369.
Beefsteak Pie à l'Anglaise, 487.
Anchovy Salad, 1037.
Fritters Soufflées, 1192.

Dinner.

Clams, 300.
Consommé Tapioca, 104.
Tomatoes, 288.   Olives.
Broiled Trout, sauce Béarnaise, 314, 166.
Potatoes à l'Hollandaise, 999.
Shoulder of Lamb à l'Africaine, 693.
Sweet Breads, Soubise, 606.
Spinach, with Gravy, 943.
Roast Beef, 527.
Chicory Salad, 1045.
Rice Pudding à l'Orange, 1130.
Coffee, 1349.

Tuesday, June —.

Breakfast.

Eggs en Filets, 423.
Broiled Shad's Roe, 402.
Hamburg Steak, Madeira Sauce, 526, 185.
Stewed Tomatoes, 1027.
Maraschino Cream, 1257.

Luncheon.

Codfish with black Butter, 352, 159.
Fricandeau of Veal, with Sorrel, 577.
Stuffed Egg-plant, 909.
Cauliflower au Gratin, 926.
Charlotte Russe, 1261.

Dinner.

Parker Bay Oysters, 298.
Clear Green Turtle, 18.
Radishes, 292.   Cucumbers, 289.
Broiled Fresh Mackerel, maître d'hôtel, 329.
Croustade of Kidneys, Périgueux, 680, 191.
Green Corn Sauté au Beurre, 964.
Broiled Tenderloin, with Watercress, 503.
Asparagus, Hollandaise sauce, 904.
Squabs on Toast, 816.
Macédoine Salad, 1063.
Banana Ice-cream, 1277.
Biscuits à la Livornaise, 1233.
Coffee, 1349.

Wednesday, June —.

Breakfast.

Omelet with Sausages, 465.
Halibut Steaks, Butter sauce, 310, 157.
Calf's Liver and Bacon, 584.
Lima Beans, 952.
Riz au Lait d'Amande, 1170.

Luncheon.

Canapé Lorenzo, 391.
Irish Mutton Stew, 660.
Risotto, 1017.
Baba au Madère, 1217.

Dinner.

Clams, 300.
Ox-tail with Barley, 38.
Tomatoes, 288.   Olives.
Bluefish au Gratin, 319.
Potatoes, Parisiennes, 986.
Tenderloin of Beef à la Nivernaise, 505.
Stuffed Peppers, 975.
Salmi of Snipe, maison d'or, 867.
Asparagus à la Tessinoise, 906.
Roast Loin of Mutton, 585.
Celery, Mayonnaise Salad, 1042.
Raspberry Water-ice, 1281.
Biscuits, Ambroisiennes, 1234.
Coffee, 1349.

Thursday, June —.

Breakfast.

Hominy and Cream.
Eggs à la Turque, 439.
Lamb Chops à la Diable, 672.
Potato Croquettes, 997.
Strawberries and Cream.

Luncheon.

Broiled, Deviled Soft-shelled Crabs, 369.
Breast of Turkey, à la Financière, 806, 246.
Salad à l'Italienne, 1036.
Pear Pie, 1084.

Dinner.

Doxie Rockaway Oysters, 298.
Purée Condé, 48.
Mortadella, 287.   Radishes 292.
Soles à la St. Nazaire, 323, 236.
Curry of Lamb à l'Indienne, 677.
Broiled Porterhouse Steak à la Bordelaise, 491.
Asparagus à la Vinaigrette, 905.
Roast Rhode Island Turkey, 800.
Lettuce and Tomato Salad, 1060.
Peach Pudding, 1150.
Imported Brie Cheese.
Coffee, 1349.

Friday, June —.

Breakfast.

Omelet aux Sardines, 468.
Broiled Kingfish, 329.
Sheep's Feet à la Poulette, 654.
Tomatoes à la Bock, 1026.
Small Brioches, 1202.

Luncheon.

Lobster à la Rushmore, 1358.
Cucumber Salad, 289.
Veal, Stewed, Marengo, 624.
Asparagus Salad, 905.
Choux à la Crème, 1246.

Dinner.

Small Prince's Bay Oysters, 298.
Chicken with Gumbo, 67.
Olives.   Lyons Sausage, 286.
Bluefish with fine Herbs, 331.
Potatoes, Châteaux, 1009.
Tenderloin of Beef, aux Gourmets, 508.
Green Peas, 978.
Fricassé of Chicken à la Reine, 780.
Boiled Green Corn, 962.
Roast English Snipe, 868.
Chicory Salad au Chapon, 1046.
Omelet au Kirsch, 470.
Coffee, 1349.

Saturday, June —.

Breakfast.

Eggs au Miroir, 425.
Picked-up Codfish, 346.
Lamb Fries, sauce Italienne, 673, 188.
Stewed Green Corn, 964.
Rice à l'Airolo, 1171.

Luncheon.

Fried Frogs, sauce Tartare, 400, 207.
Stewed Beef à l' Egyptienne, 540.
Spaghetti au Gratin, 961.
Russian Salad, 1065.
French Pudding, 1139.

Dinner.

Small Blue Point Oysters, 298.
Consommé Royal, 107.
Caviare, 281.   Cucumbers, 289.
Broiled Kingfish, maître d'hôtel, 329.
Potatoes, Duchesse, 1006.
Mutton Chops à la Provençale, 642.
Succotash, 1022.
Squabs en Compote, 822.
Green Peas, 978.
Roast Loin of Veal, 585.
Doucette and Egg Salad, 1054.
Apples, Meringués, 1248.
Coffee, 1349.

Sunday, June —.

Breakfast.

Omelet à la Vanderbilt, 471.
Broiled, Deviled Soft-shelled Crabs, 369.
Mutton Chops with Watercress, 643.
Sweet Potatoes, 982.
Stewed Pears, 1333.

Luncheon.

Broiled Lobster, sauce Ravigote, 363.
Calf's Head à la Cavour, 638.
Japanese Salad, 1075.
Water-melon à la José Paez, 1316.

Dinner.

Little Neck Clams, 300.
Cream of Lettuce, 87.
Olives.   Radishes, 292.
Spanish-mackerel, maître d'hôtel, 329.
Potatoes en Surprise, 1005.
Tenderloin of Beef à la Florentine, 506.
Broiled Tomatoes, 1025.
Coquilles of Sweetbreads, with Mushrooms, 621, 609.
Punch à la Française, 1311.
Roast Snipe on Toast, 868.
Romaine Salad, 1064.
Plum Pudding, Glacé à la Gladstone, 1289.
Biscuits Richelieu, 1232.
Camembert Cheese.
Coffee, 1349.

Monday, July —.

Breakfast.

Eggs à la Paysanne, 433.
Broiled Bacon, 754.
Lamb, Hashed à la Polonaise, 700.
Stewed Tomatoes, 1027.
Crème Renversée, 1252.

Luncheon.

Frogs' Legs à la Geo. Merrill, 1372.
Mutton Chops à la Robinson, 682.
Fried Sweet Potatoes, 993.
Beef Salad, 1039.
Blanc-mange à la J. Delmonico, 1270.

Dinner.

Small Rockaway Oysters, 298.
Consommé à l'Andalouse, 117.
Anchovies, 284.   Cucumbers, 289.
Bluefish à l'Icarienne, 336.
Curry of Lamb à l'Indienne, 677.
Spinach, maître d'hôtel, 942.
Chicken Croquettes à la Reine, 758.
Green Peas, 978.
Roast Woodcock, 871.
Escarole Salad, 1055.
Sago Pudding, 1140.
Coffee, 1349.

Tuesday, July —.

Breakfast.
Scrambled Eggs, with Cheese, 405.
Broiled Fresh Mackerel, 329.
Stewed Veal à la Chasseur, 632.
Stewed Bermuda Potatoes, 995.
Rice and Cream à la Croce, 1296.

Luncheon.
Clam Patties, 387.
Irish Mutton Stew, 660.
Baked Tomatoes, 1028.
Lobster Salad à la Boardman, 1368.
Musk-melons.

Dinner.
Linn Haven Oysters, 298.
Julienne, 27.
Lyons Sausage, 286. Radishes, 292.
Blackfish, Oyster sauce, 352.
Sweetbreads à la Godard, 614.
String Beans au Blanc, 947.
Chicken, Sauté à l'Hongroise, 772.
Asparagus, sauce Hollandaise, 904.
Reed-birds with Bacon, 877, 754.
Chicory Salad, 1045.
Apple Fritters, 1191.
Coffee, 1349.

Wednesday, July —.

Breakfast.
Oatmeal and Cream.
Ham Omelet, 462.
Porterhouse Steak, 524.
French Fried Potatoes, 993.
Brioche, 1201.

Luncheon.
Broiled, Deviled Soft-shelled Crabs, 369.
Veal Cutlets à la Philadelphia, 565.
Sweet Potatoes Soufflées, 1010.
Stuffed Peppers, 975.
Raspberry Tarts, 1118

Dinner.
Clams, 300.
Busecca à la Milanaise, 7.
Thon, 282. Celery, 290
Halibut, Cream sauce, 309, 181.
Tenderloin à la Hussard, 519.
Green Corn, 962.
Broiled Plovers, with Bacon, 866, 754.
Tomatoes à la Bock, 1026.
Roast Veal, 585.
Cauliflower Salad, 1040.
Charlotte Russe, 1261.
Coffee, 1349.

FOURTH OF JULY.

Thursday, July —.

Breakfast.

Eggs à la Bennett, 447.
Fish Balls à la Mrs. Harrison, 347.
Chicken Livers en Brochette, 769.
Tomatoes à la Marseillaise, 1029.
Raspberries and Cream.

Luncheon.

Toast, with fine Herbs, 315.
Cucumber Salad, 289.
Hashed Chicken with Cream, 804.
Salad Suédoise, 1069.
Pie à la Martha Washington, 1105.

Dinner.

Small Keyport Oysters, 298.
Cream of Asparagus, 70.
Olives.   Radishes, 292.
Sole au Gratin, 319.
Mignons Filets à la Bayard, 509, 231.
Green Peas, 978.
Spring Chicken à la Maryland, 785.
Asparagus à la Tessinoise, 906.
Oranges Glacées à la George Renauldt, 1297.
Doe-birds sur Canapé, 838.
Lettuce and Tomato Salad, 1060.
Tutti-frutti à la Gen. Harrison, 1371.
Small Méringues à la Ch. C. Delmonico, 1249.
Mazagran à la Gen. Dufour, 1392.

Friday, July —.

Breakfast.
Fresh Shrimp Omelet, 453.
Broiled Bluefish, 329.
Calf's Brains, with black Butter, 557.
Mashed Potatoes, 998.
Rice à la Française, 1180.

Luncheon.
Matelote of Eels, 332.
Stewed Lamb à la Française, 704.
Macaroni, Napolitaine, 957.
Salad Macédoine, 1063.
Peaches and Cream.

Dinner.
Purée Mongole, 50.
Tomatoes, 288.　　　　　　Olives.
Frogs à la Poulette, 399.
Tenderloin, Piqué à la Portugaise, 517.
Stuffed Egg-plant, 909.
Squabs en Crapaudine, 819.
Succotash, 1022.
Roast Saddle of Spring Lamb, 664.
Romaine Salad, 1064.
Lemon Water-ice, 1279.
Galette, 1221.
Coffee, 1349.

Saturday, July —.

Breakfast.
Eggs à l'Aurore, 444.
Lamb Steaks, sauce Piquante, 717.
Onions, with Cream, 968.
Fresh Plums.

Luncheon.
Kingfish, maître d'hôtel, 329.
Curry of Chicken à la Créole, 794.
Anchovy Salad, 1037.
Pineapple Tarts, 1115.

Dinner.
Croute-au-Pot, 11.
Cucumbers, 289.　　　　　Radishes, 292.
Porgies au Gratin, 319.
Broiled Sirloin aux Cépes, 496.
Flageolets, 1365.
Ducklings à l'Américaine, 823.
Stuffed Peppers, 975.
Roast Loin of Veal, 585.
Watercress Salad, 1072.
Apple Pudding à l'Helvétienne, 1152.
Roquefort Cheese.
Coffee, 1349.

Sunday, July —.

Breakfast.
Omelet with Asparagus-tops, 458.
Broiled Kingfish, 329.
Hashed Chicken à la Crême, 804.
Sweet Potatoes, Hollandaise, 999.
Milan Cake, 1228.

Luncheon.
Frogs' Legs à la Geo. Merrill, 1372.
Broiled Turkey Legs, Mustard sauce, 766, 202.
Broiled Potatoes, 983.
Lobster Salad à la Plummer, 1062.
Water-melon à la Romero, 1315.

Dinner.
Little Neck Clams, 300.
Chicken à la Créole, 65.
Radishes, 292.　　　　　　Olives.
Salmon à la Génoise, 306.
Broiled Lamb Chops, with Green Peas, 647, 977.
Tenderloin of Beef, Béarnaise, 503, 166.
Asparagus, Hollandaise, 904.
Punch au Kirsch, 1305.
Roast Woodcock, 871.
Lettuce, Mayonnaise Salad, 1057, 1042.
Plombiére à la Hamilton, 1370.
Coffee, 1349.

Monday, July —.

Breakfast.

Eggs à la Suisse, 441.
Mutton Chops, Anchovy Butter, 647, 146.
Potatoes, Lyonnaise, 991.
Breaded Pig's Feet, sauce Tartare, 727, 207.
Crême en Mousse au Café, 1253.

Luncheon.

Soft-shelled Clams à la Newburg, 389.
Leg of Mutton, Bretonne, 650.
Spinach with Eggs, 940.
Rhine Wine Jelly, 1324.

Dinner.

Consommé au Vermicelli, 103.
Cucumbers, 289.   Mortadella 287.
Lobster à la Newburg, 359.
Larded Sweetbreads, with Sorrel, 604.
Beef-tongue à la Milanaise, 538.
Green Peas, 978.
Roast Ptarmigan, 862.
Chicory Salad, 1045.
Baked Apple Dumplings, 1122.
Coffee, 1349.

Tuesday, July —.

Breakfast.

Ham and Eggs, 412, 753.
Escalops of Veal, Tomato sauce, 568, 205.
Potatoes à la Rice, 1007.
Rice à la Française, 1180.

Luncheon.

Musk-melon.
Scallops Brestoise, 392.
Lamb Croquettes à l'Italienne, 679, 188.
Hashed Potatoes au Gratin, 1004.
Green-gage Pie, 1093.

Dinner.

Clams, 300.
Crab with Gumbo, 24.
Caviare, 281.   Radishes, 292.
Shad with fine Herbs, 331.
Panpiette of Veal, Purée of Peas, 594, 49.
Stuffed Egg-plant, 909.
Chicken, Sauté with Tarragon, 774.
Celery, with Cream, 929.
Roast Beef, 527.
Escarole Salad, 1055.
Pineapple Water-ice, 1283.
Bitter Almond Macaroons, 1209.
Coffee, 1349.

Wednesday, July —.

Breakfast.

Boiled Eggs.
Bass, with White Wine, 342.
Minced Beef à la Portugaise, 501.
Potato Croquettes, 997.
Brioche, 1201.

Luncheon.

Mussels à la Marinière, 378.
Brochette of Lamb à la Dumas, 674.
Risotto, 1017.
Huckleberry Tarts, 1113.

Dinner.

Small Rockaway Oysters, 298.
Sorrel, with Asparagus-tops, 41.
Celery, 290.   Sardines, 283.
Sheep's-head à la Toulouse, 354.
Broiled Sirloin Steak à la Parisienne, 495.
Stuffed Tomatoes, 1023.
Sweetbreads aux Gourmets, 612.
Asparagus à la Vinaigrette, 905.
Roast Chicken, with Watercress, 755.
Lettuce Salad, 1057.
Brandy Jelly, 1321.
Pithiviers Cake, 1225.
Coffee, 1349.

Thursday, July —.

Breakfast.
Fresh Tomato Omelet, 456.
Broiled Kingfish, 329.
Lamb Chops, sauce Robert, 681, 192.
Stewed Turnips, 967.
Fresh Peaches and Cream.

Luncheon.
Stuffed Deviled Clams, 376.
Tripe à la Lyonnaise, 548.
Cauliflower au Gratin, 926.
Pumpkin Pie, 1099.

Dinner.
Clams, 300.
Chicken à la Piémontaise, 63.
Lyons Sausage, 286.   Radishes, 292.
Broiled Brook-trout, maître d'hôtel, 314.
Cucumber Salad, 289.
Chicken Sauté à la Parmentier, 773.
Green Peas, 978.
Braised Noix of Veal en Daube, 591.
Boiled Corn, 962.
Roast Turkey, 800.
Romaine Salad, 1064.
Maraschino Pudding, 1134.
Coffee, 1349.

Friday, July —.

Breakfast.
Scrambled Eggs, with Asparagus-tops, 406.
Boiled Skate, brown Butter, 325, 156.
Minced Veal à la Biscaënne, 576.
Hashed Potatoes, 1002.
Stewed Apricots, 1335.

Luncheon.
Fried Whitebait, 301.
Shoulder of Lamb, Macédoine, 697.
Macaroni Croquettes, 279.
Shrimp Salad, 1067.
Rice à l'Airolo, 1171.

Dinner.
Clam Chowder, 13.
Radishes, 292.   Olives.
Bass à la Chambord, 343.
Lamb Chops à la Villeroi, 686.
String Beans, 948.
Salmi of Plover, maison d'or, 867.
Fried Oyster-plant, 1021.
Roast Larded Tenderloin of Beef, 516.
Watercress Salad, 1072.
Macaroon Ice-cream, 1290.
Coffee, 1349.

Saturday, July —.

Breakfast.
Poached Eggs on Toast, 404.
Fried Porgies, 320.
Calf's Head à la Vinaigrette, 640.
Lima Beans, 952.
Fresh Cherries.

Luncheon.
Broiled Bluefish, maître d'hôtel, 329.
Veal, Stewed à la Marengo, 624.
Macédoine Salad, 1063.
Baked Apples, 1124.

Dinner.
Consommé Deslignac, 108.
Thon, 282.   Celery, 290.
Fried Soft-shelled Crabs, 368.
Broiled Spring Chickens, with Bacon, 756.
Green Peas, 978.
Coquilles of Sweetbreads à la Dreux, 621.
Roast Reed-birds, 877.
Celery Salad, 1041.
Baba, with Rum, 1217.
Coffee, 1349.

Sunday, July —.

Breakfast.

Omelet à la Régence, 470.
Broiled, Deviled Soft-shelled Crabs, 369.
Hashed Turkey en Bordure, 805.
Stewed Potatoes, 995.
Brioches Fluttes, 1204.

Luncheon.

Spanish-mackerel, Hollandaise, 317.
Coquilles of Chicken à l'Anglaise, 271.
Sweet Potatoes Soufflées, 1010.
Water-melon à la Seward, 1317.
Raspberry Pie, 1096.

Dinner.

Clams, 300.
Chicken à la Richmond, 62.
Olives. Radishes, 292.
Small Bouchées à la Reine, 270.
Frogs à l'Espagnole, 401.
Tenderloin Piqué à la Provençale, 518.
Stuffed Tomatoes, 1023.
Veal Cutlets à la Maréchale, 562.
Beans Panachées, 950.
Punch à la Cardinal, 1306.
Doe-birds à l'Américaine, 840.
Chicory Salad, 1046.
Plombière à la Kingman, 1294.
Mazagran à la Général Bugeau, 1384.

Monday, July —.

Breakfast.

Ham Omelet, with fine Herbs, 462, 451.
Kingfish, maître d'hôtel, 329.
Escalops of Veal à la Duxelle, 569.
Hashed Potatoes, with Cream, 1003.
Whipped Cream à la Vanille, 1254.

Luncheon.

Fish Balls, 347.
Braised Beef, Russian sauce, 485.
Boiled Corn, 962.
Lamb-tongue Salad, 1056.
Green-gage Tarts, 1107.

Dinner.

Purée Crécy, 47.
Celery, 290. Olives.
Broiled Deviled Lobster, 364.
Mignons Filets, with Marrow, 510.
Potatoes, Château, 1009.
Epigrammes of Lamb à la Chicorée, 690.
Roast Chicken, 755.
Escarole Salad, 1055.
Vermicelli Pudding, 1142.
Coffee, 1349.

Tuesday, July —.

Breakfast.

Eggs à la Tripe, 419.
Broiled Fresh Mackerel, 329.
Broiled Ham, 753.
Potato Croquettes, 997.
Fresh Apricots.

Luncheon.

Canapé Madison, 269.
Veal Cutlets à la Philadelphia, 565.
Chicken Salad, 1044.
Cocoanut Pie, 1101.

Dinner.

Westmoreland, 33.
Radishes, 292. Olives.
Frogs à la Poulette, 399.
Fricandeau of Veal à la Jardinière, 577, 1033.
Lamb Chops, maison d'or, 683.
Asparagus, with Cream sauce, 904, 181.
Roast Capon, 755.
Lettuce Salad, French Dressing, 1057, 1070.
Strawberry Water-ice, 1281.
Sweet Almond Macaroons, 1210.
Coffee, 1349.

Wednesday, July —.

Breakfast.
Shirred Eggs, with brown Butter, 414.
Broiled English Breakfast Bacon, 754.
Lamb Steak, with Green Peas, 716.
Green Corn Stewed with Butter, 964.
Apples and Rice Méringuées, 1169.

Luncheon.
Kingfish à l'Icarienne, 336.
Mutton Kidneys Sautés, with Madeira Wine, 662.
Sweet Potatoes à l'Hollandaise, 999.
Tomato, Mayonnaise Salad, 1071.
Crême en Mousse au Maraschino, 1257.

Dinner.
Little Neck Clams, 300.
Chicken à la Turque, 69.
Tomatoes, 288.   Celery, 29).
Lobster à la Bordelaise, 360.
Tendron of Veal, with Sorrel, 634.
Cromesquis of Chicken à la Reine, 765.
French Artichokes à la Vinaigrette, 902.
Roast Beef, 527.
Romaine Salad, 1064.
Charlotte Panachée, 1300.
Coffee, 1349.

Thursday, July —.

Breakfast.
Eggs à la Vanderbilt, 420.
Fried Porgies, Tartare sauce, 320, 207.
Tripe à la Bordelaise, 544.
Saratoga Potatoes, 1011.
Musk-melon.

Luncheon.
Haddock, Cream sauce, 352, 181.
Vol-au-Vent à la Finançière, 810.
Salad à l'Italienne, 1036.
Peaches and Cream.

Dinner.
Cream à la Palestine, 74.
Olives.   Bologna Sausage, 286.
Fresh Mackerel à la Colbert, 329, 190.
Sweetbreads with Mushrooms, 609.
Sorrel aux Croûtons, 974.
Chicken, Sauté à la Chasseur, 775.
Fresh Lima Beans, 952.
Roast English Snipe, 868.
Watercress Salad, 1072.
Iced Pudding Diplomate, 1288.
Coffee, 1349.

Friday, July —.

Breakfast.
Omelet with fine Herbs, 451.
Blackfish, brown Butter, 309, 156.
Hashed Beef à la Catalan, 502.
Tomatoes à la Bock, 1026.
Peach Marmalade, 1331.

Luncheon.
Fried Sea-bass, 320.
Mignons of Lamb, Béarnaise, 1360.
Crab Salad, 1047.
Rice and Cream à la Croce, 1296.

Dinner.
Purée Bretonne, 45.
Cucumbers, 289.   Anchovies, 284.
Salmon Cutlets, Victoria, 366.
Tenderloin, Piqué à la Portugaise, 517.
Spring Lamb Chops, with Bacon, 647, 754.
Brussels Sprouts, 922.
Asparagus à la Tessinoise, 906.
Roast Chicken, 755.
Doucette Salad, 1052.
Biscuits Glacés, 1286.
Allumettes, 1205.
Coffee, 1349.

Saturday, July —.

Breakfast.

Omelet, Bonne Femme, 466.
Fried Whitebait, 301.
Calf's Liver, Sauté à l'Alsacienne, 582.
Potatoes à la Rice, 1007.
Brioches à la Condé, 1203.

Luncheon.

Stuffed Deviled Clams, 376.
Boiled Turkey à l'Anglaise, 795.
Broiled Sweet Potatoes, 983.
Iced Timbale of Rice, 1175.

Dinner.

Consommé with Italian Paste, 103.
Caviare, 281.   Radishes, 292.
Kingfish with black Butter, 352, 159.
Braised Beef à la Flamande, 482.
Lamb Croquettes à la Soubise, 679, 250.
Stewed Fresh Tomatoes, 1027.
Broiled Squabs on Toast, with Bacon, 817.
Chicory Salad, 1045.
Almond Cake, Glacé, 1208.
Coffee, 1349.

Sunday, July —.

Breakfast.

Eggs à la Turque, 439.
Fish Balls à la Mrs. Harrison, 347.
Deviled Lamb Chops, with Bacon, 647, 754.
Succotash with Cream, 1022.
Fresh Plums.

Luncheon.

Broiled Pompano, maître d'hôtel, 329.
Cucumber Salad, 289.
Croustade of Chicken Livers au Madère, 763.
Lobster Salad à la Plummer, 1062.
Boiled Apple Dumplings, 1127.

Dinner.

Little Neck Clams, 300.
Consommé, Masséna, 102.
Mortadella, 287.   Olives.
Boiled Kennebec Salmon, Percillade sauce, 303, 165.
Potatoes, Windsor, 1008.
Broiled Tenderloin à la Chiron, 504.
Asparagus, sauce Hollandaise, 904.
Broiled Chicken with Bacon, 756.
Beans Panacheés, 950.
Punch Romaine, 1304.
Roast Woodcock on Toast, 871.
Escarole Salad, 1055.
Cabinet Pudding à la Sadi-Carnot, 1164.
Gorgonzolla Cheese.
Mazagran à la Général Dufour, 1392.

Monday, July —.

Breakfast.

Omelet Raspail, 467.
Fried Black-bass, Tomato sauce, 320, 205.
Hashed Lamb à la Zingara, 652.
Potatoes à la Hanna, 1012.
Crême en Mousse au Maraschino, 1257.

Luncheon.

Broiled, Deviled Soft-shelled Crabs on Toast, 369.
Stewed Veal, Marengo, 624.
Salad Suédoise, 1069.
Lemon Cream Pie, Méringué, 1102.

Dinner.

Oysters, 298.
Consommé Colbert, 120.
Radishes, 292.   Lyons Sausage, 286.
Lobster en Chevreuse, 362.
Cromesquis aux Truffles, 268.
Green Peas, 978.
Larded Sweetbreads au Salpicon, 605.
Broiled Tomatoes, 1025.
Roast Ducklings, 824.
Watercress Salad, 1072.
Vanilla Ice-cream, 1271.
Biscuits à la Richelieu, 1232.
Coffee, 1349.

Tuesday, July —.

Breakfast.
Eggs à la Finoise, 424.
Sole, with White Wine, 342.
Smoked Beef, with Cream, 486.
Potatoes en Paille, 1014.
Fresh Pears.

Luncheon.
Crawfish à la Bordelaise, 360.
Haricot of Lamb à la Providence, 701.
Fried Egg-plant, 907.
Baba au Rhum, 1217.

Dinner.
Clams, 300.
Brunoise with Rice, 3.
Watercress, 1072. Radishes, 292.
Matelote of Eels à la Parisienne, 333.
Minced Veal à la Biscaënne, 576.
Oyster-plant à la Poulette, 1019.
Fricassé of Chicken, with Curry, 792.
Succotash, 1022.
Roasted Larded Sirloin of Beef, 516.
Romaine Salad, 1064.
Farina Pudding, 1144.
Coffee, 1349.

Wednesday, July —.

Breakfast.
Omelet with Tarragon, 451.
Boiled Codfish, Egg sauce, 352, 161.
Broiled Lamb Kidneys, with Bacon, 713.
Roasted Tomatoes, 1028.
Corn Fritters, 965.

Luncheon.
Fried Soles, Tartare sauce, 320, 207.
Hashed Turkey en Bordure, 805.
Stewed Green Corn, 964.
Rice and Cream à la Croce, 1296.

Dinner.
Oysters, 298.
Printanier Chasseur, 52.
Tomatoes, 288. Olives.
Bass à la St. Nazaire, 341, 236.
Tenderloin of Beef à la Stanton, 1388.
Green Peas, 978.
Sweetbreads à la Godard, 614.
Brussels Sprouts, 922.
Roast Lamb, 1361.
Watercress Salad, 1072.
Chocolate Ice-cream, 1272.
Petites Bouchées des Dames, 1237.
Coffee, 1349.

Thursday, July —.

Breakfast.
Hominy and Cream, 1034.
Eggs à l'Impératrice, 440.
Minced Beef à la Catalan, 502.
Potato Croquettes, 997.
Raspberries and Cream.

Luncheon.
Fried Soft-shelled Crabs, 368.
Lamb Sweetbreads en Caisses, 274.
Tomatoes à la Marseillaise, 1029.
Plum Tarts, 1110.

Dinner.
Clams, 300.
Westmoreland, 33.
Lyons Sausage, 286. Radishes, 292.
Kingfish, Vert-pré, 328.
Stewed Lamb and Lima Beans, 705.
Turban of Chicken à la Cleveland, 791.
Beans Panachées, 950.
Roast Grass Plovers, 865.
Celery Salad, 1041.
Apple Pudding à l'Helvétienne, 1152.
Coffee, 1349.

Friday, July —.

Breakfast.

Omelet with fine Herbs, 451.
Broiled Bass, maître d'hôtel, 329.
Stewed Tripe à la Créole, 545.
Stewed Fresh Tomatoes, 1027.
Brioches Fluttes, 1204.

Luncheon.

Stuffed Deviled Lobsters, 367.
Sausages à la Gastronome, 740.
Salad Macédoine, 1063.
Jamaica Rum Jelly, 1320.

Dinner.

Oysters, 298.
Fish Chowder, 12.
Tomatoes, 288. Olives.
Fresh Mackerel à la Vénitienne, 338.
Tenderloin Marinated, Russian sauce, 511.
String Beans, 948.
Leg of Mutton à la Condé, 649.
Asparagus à la Vinaigrette, 905.
Reed-birds on Toast, 877.
Chicory Salad, 1045.
Charlotte Russe, 1261.
Coffee, 1349.

Saturday, July —.

Breakfast.

Eggs à la Béchamel, 416.
Porgies au Gratin, 356.
Sirloin Steak à la Bordelaise, 491.
Potatoes, maitre d'hôtel, 985.
Musk-melon.

Luncheon.

Frogs à la Poulette, 399.
Broiled Mutton Chops, Soyer, 647.
Fried Sweet Potatoes, 993.
Gooseberry Pie, 1091.

Dinner.

Oysters, 298.
Potage à la Montmorency, 97.
Sardines, 283. Celery, 290.
Timbales à l'Ecossaise, 261.
Mignons Filets à la Bohémienne, 513.
Stuffed Green Peppers, 975.
Breast of Lamb, Jardinière, 702.
Doe-birds à l'Américaine, 840.
Escarole Salad, 1055.
Bread Pudding, 1132.
Coffee, 1349.

Sunday, July —.

Breakfast.

Omelet Régence, 470.
Boiled Halibut, Egg sauce, 309, 161.
Hashed Chicken à la Béchamel, 802.
Broiled Tomatoes, 1025.
French Pancake, 1186.

Luncheon.

Canapé Lorenzo, 391.
Broiled, Deviled Chicken Legs, 766.
Oyster-plant, Poulette, 1019.
Japanese Salad, 1075.
Boiled Apple Dumplings, 1127.

Dinner.

Little Neck Clams, 300.
Cream of Chicken, 82.
Radishes, 292. Olives.
Sheep's-head à la Toulouse, 354.
Larded Tenderloin à la Financière, 516, 246.
Green Peas, 978.
Mutton Chops, Masséna, 687.
Tomatoes à la Bock, 1026.
Champagne Punch, 1307.
Roast Chicken, 755.
Lettuce and Egg Salad, 1058.
Tutti-frutti, 1293.
Petites Bouchées des Dames à la Mme. Astor, 1238.
Roquefort Cheese.
Coffee, 1349.

Monday, July —.

Breakfast.

Eggs à la Bourguignonne, 411.
Broiled Salt Mackerel, 329.
Minced Veal à la Catalan, 575.
Lima Beans Sautées, with Cream, 952.
Cream Renversée, 1252.

Luncheon.

Mussels, sauce Poulette, 379.
Stewed Lamb, with Flageolets, 707.
Herring Salad, 1074.
Raspberries and Cream.

Dinner.

Oysters, 298.
Purée Parmentier, 44.
Thon, 282.   Radishes, 292.
Bluefish au Gratin, 319.
Sweetbreads à la Financière, 603.
Spinach aux Croûtons, 940.
Chicken à la Maryland, 785.
Roasted Tomatoes, 1028.
Roast Beef, 527.
Romaine Salad, 1064.
Custard Pudding, 1154.
Coffee, 1349.

Tuesday, July —.

Breakfast.

Green Peas Omelet, 459.
Broiled Sardines on Toast, 403.
Hamburg Steak, Colbert, 526, 190.
Hashed Potatoes au Gratin, 1004.
Fresh Pears.

Luncheon.

Porgies, White Wine sauce, 342.
Chicken Pot-pie, 757.
Cauliflower Salad, 1040.
Rhubarb Tarts, 1112.

Dinner.

Clams, 300.
Chiffonade, 14.
Celery, 290.   Mortadella, 287.
Kennebec Salmon à la Créole, 339.
Braised Leg of Mutton à la Portugaise, 648.
Potato Croquettes, 997.
Croquettes of Sweetbreads, with Asparagus-tops, 620.
Fresh Broiled Mushrooms on Toast, 916.
Roast Ducklings, 824.
Tomato, Mayonnaise Salad, 1071.
Pineapple Water-ice, 1283.
Fancy Almond Cakes, 1239.
Coffee, 1349.

Wednesday, July —.

Breakfast.

Scrambled Eggs, with Fresh Mushrooms, 406.
Broiled Mackerel, maitre d'hôtel, 329.
Stewed Mutton Kidneys, with Madeira Wine, 662.
Stewed Turnips, 967.
Brioche, 1201.

Luncheon.

Lobster en Chevreuse, 362.
Haricot of Lamb à la Providence, 701.
Asparagus Salad, 905.
Pear Pie, 1084.

Dinner.

Little Neck Clams, 300.
Shin of Beef, Iiée, 29.
Radishes 292.   Olives.
Soles, with White Wine, 342.
Coquilles of Chicken à l'Anglaise, 271.
Sirloin Piqué, with Stuffed Tomatoes, 598, 1023.
Snipe sur Canapé, 868.
Celery Salad, 1041.
Chocolate Pudding, 1146.
Swiss Cheese.
Mazagran à la Général Bugeau, 1391.

Thursday, August —.

Breakfast.

Tomato Omelet, 456.
Tripe à la Lyonnaise, 548.
Brochette of Lamb à la Dumas, 674.
Sorrel au Gras, 974.
Peaches and Cream.

Luncheon.

Bluefish with White Wine, 342.
Ragout of Beef, Dufour, 541.
String Beans, 948.
Baba, 1216.

Dinner.

Clams 300.
Purée Condé, 48.
Radishes, 292. Sausage, 286.
Kennebec Salmon, à l'Hollandaise, 303, 160.
Saddle of Mutton, Londonderry sauce, 668.
Succotash, 1022.
Chicken Sauté à la Marengo, 771.
Stuffed Tomatoes, 1023.
Woodcock on Toast, 871.
Celery Salad, 1041.
Vanilla Ice-cream, 1271.
Coffee Eclairs, 1244.
Coffee, 1349.

Friday, August —.

Breakfast.

Omelet, Bonne Femme, 466.
Fried Soft-shelled Crabs, 368.
Hashed Beef à la Portugaise, 501.
Potatoes with Cream, 1003.
Rice à la Française, 1180.

Luncheon.

Matelote of Eels, 332.
Croquettes of Lamb à la Patti, 679.
Anchovy Salad, 1037.
Currant Tarts, 1114.

Dinner.

Oysters, 298.
Clam Chowder, 13.
Tomatoes, 288. Olives.
Crawfish à la Bordelaise, 360.
Calf's-head à la Cavour, 638.
Artichoke-bottoms, Florentine, 903.
Tenderloin of Beef à la Provençale, 518.
Asparagus à la Vinaigrette, 905.
Roast Turkey, Cranberry sauce, 800, 1329.
Chicory Salad, 1045.
Nelson Pudding, 1155.
Coffee, 1349.

Saturday, August —.

Breakfast.

Eggs au Beurre noir, 414.
Sole à la Horly, 321.
Broiled Lamb Fries à la Diable, 672.
Oyster-plant à la Poulette, 1019.
Whipped Cream à la Vanille, 1254.

Luncheon.

Frogs' Legs à la Geo. Merrill, 1372.
Escalops of Veal à la Duxelle, 569.
Fried Sweet Potatoes, 993.
Cranberry Pie, 1104.

Dinner.

Clams, 300.
Rice with Sorrel, 42.
Caviare, 281. Radishes, 292.
Kingfish with fine Herbs, 331.
Croquettes of Sweetbreads aux petits Pois, 620.
Chicken Fricassé à la Reine, 780.
Brussels Sprouts, 922.
Roast Beef, 527.
Tomato and Lettuce Salad, 1060.
Méringues Glacées, 1301.
Coffee, 1349.

Sunday, August —.

Breakfast.
Omelet Raspail, 467.
Broiled Sea-bass, 310.
Lamb Chops à la Robinson, 682.
Potatoes Soufflées, 1010.
Musk-melon.

Luncheon.
Broiled, Deviled Soft-shelled Crabs, 369.
Hamburg Steak, Russian sauce, 526.
Potatoes Hollandaise, 999.
Lobster Salad, 1061.
Crème en Mousse au Curaçoa, 1259.

Dinner.
Clams, 300.
Consommé Princesse, 113.
Radishes, 292.   Olives.
Fresh Mackerel en Papillotes, 330.
Roast Ham, Champagne sauce, 723.
Stewed Green Corn, 963.
Squabs en Compote, 822.
Beans Panachées, 950.
Romaine Punch, 1304.
English Snipe, 868.
Escarole Salad, 1055.
Pudding à la U. S. Grant, 1159.
Camembert Cheese.
Coffee, 1349.

Monday, August —.

Breakfast.
Eggs au Miroir, 425.
Fish Balls, 347.
Broiled Pork Tenderloin, Apple sauce, 741, 168.
Corn Sauté with Butter, 964.
Milan Cake, 1228.

Luncheon.
Mussels à la Marinière, 378.
Tendron of Veal à la Morlaisienne, 635.
Fried Oyster-plant, 1021.
Blackberry Tarts, 1119.

Dinner.
Little Neck Clams, 300
Giblets à l'Anglaise, 22.
Lyons Sausage, 286.   Celery, 290.
Pompano au Gratin, 319.
Curry of Lamb à l'Indienne, 677.
Chicken Vol-au-Vent à la Reine, 812.
Asparagus à la Tessinoise, 906.
Plovers sur Canapé, 865.
Lettuce Salad, 1057.
Omelet Soufflée, 474.
Coffee, 1349.

Tuesaay, August —.

Breakfast.
Omelet with Cheese, 469.
Broiled Kingfish, Anchovy Butter, 329, 146.
Sheep's Feet, maître d'hôtel, 654, 177.
Mashed Potatoes au Gratin, 998.
Fresh Pears.

Luncheon.
Scallops à la Poulette, 379.
Minced Tenderloin à la Portugaise, 501.
Fried Egg-plant, 907.
Rice à l'Airolo, 1171.

Dinner.
Clams, 300.
Cream of Green Peas, 76.
Caviare, 281.   Radishes, 292.
Sheep's-head à la Créole, 339.
Sweetbreads au Salpicon, 605.
Green Corn, 962.
Pork Chops, sauce Piquante, 745.
Stuffed Peppers, 975.
Roast Loin of Lamb, 585.
Romaine Salad, 1064.
Lemon Pudding. 1157.
Coffee, 1349.

Wednesday, August —.

Breakfast.

Eggs à la Valencienne, 421.
Fried Porgies, 320.
Lamb Steak, with Green Peas, 716.
Tomatoes à la Marseillaise, 1029.
Blackberries and Cream.

Luncheon.

Fried Whitebait, 301.
Stewed Veal à la Marengo, 624.
Fried Sweet Potatoes, 993.
Peach Marmalade, 1331.

Dinner.

Oysters, 298.
Consommé Tapioca, 104.
Olives.   Tomatoes, 288.
Spanish-mackerel à la Toulouse, 354.
Tenderloin of Beef à la Chéron, 504.
Asparagus à la Vinaigrette, 905.
Salmi of Snipe à la Moderne, 870.
Succotash, 1022.
Roast Veal, 585.
Watercress Salad, 1072.
Croustade of Rice, 1176.
Coffee, 1349.

Thursday, August —.

Breakfast.

Omelet with fine Herbs, 451.
Broiled Pompano, maître d'hôtel, 329.
Sausages, with White Wine sauce, 735.
Potatoes, Lyonnaise, 991.
Fresh Grapes.

Luncheon.

Weakfish à la Vénitienne, 338.
Tripe à la Bordelaise, 544.
Cauliflower Salad, 1040.
Iced Timbale of Rice, 1175.

Dinner.

Clams, 300.
Chicken à l'Okra, 67.
Radishes, 292.   Mortadella, 287.
Lobster Croquettes à la Victoria, 365, 208.
Escalops of Sweetbreads, Richelieu, 574.
Sorrel au Gras, 974.
Chicken, Sauté à l'Hongroise, 772.
Fresh Lima Beans, 952.
Roast Snipe on Toast, 868.
Celery Salad, 1041.
Rum Cake, 1229.
Coffee, 1349.

Friday, August —.

Breakfast.

Omelet Mexicaine, 473.
Fried Whitebait, 301.
Beefsteak and Watercress, 524.
Fried Sweet Potatoes, 993.
Fritters Soufflées, 1192.

Luncheon.

Broiled Sea-bass, 329.
Veal Cutlets Pagasqui, 560.
Stuffed Cabbage, 919.
Anchovy Salad, 1037.
Boiled Apple Dumplings, 1127.

Dinner.

Oysters, 298.
Cream of Celery à l'Espagnole, 86.
Olives.   Tomatoes, 288.
Fried Blackfish, 320.
Turkey Legs à la Diable, 766.
Corn, Stewed with Butter, 964.
Lamb Chops, maison d'or, 683.
Spaghetti Napolitaine, 959.
Squabs, with Watercress, 816.
Chicory Salad, 1045.
Peach Pie, 1092.
Coffee, 1349.

Saturday, August —.

Breakfast.
Ham Omelet, 462.
Lamb en Brochette à la Dumas, 674.
Macaroni, with Cream, 954.
Crême en Mousse au Maraschino, 1257.

Luncheon.
Fried Soft-shelled Crabs, 368.
Minced Beef à la Catalan, 502.
Stuffed Cucumbers, 937.
Sweet Potatoes, Soufflées, 1010.
Savarin à l'Anglaise, 1199.

Dinner.
Prince's Bay Oysters, 298.
Purée Faubonne, 46.
Olives.   Radishes, 292.
Codfish, nut-brown Butter, 352, 156.
Sweetbreads, with Mushrooms, 609.
Oyster-plant à la Poulette, 1019.
Saddle of Mutton, Sevigné, 669.
Roast Turkey, 800.
Romaine Salad, 1064.
Apple Charlotte, 1167.
Coffee, 1349.

Sunday, August —.

Breakfast.
Eggs à la Vanderbilt, 420.
Broiled Deviled Soft-shelled Crabs, 369.
Hashed Turkey en Bordure, 805.
Fried Oyster-plant, 1021.
Fresh Green-gages.

Luncheon.
Broiled Trout, maître d'hôtel, 314.
Cucumber Salad, 289.
Broiled Chicken Legs à la Diable, 766.
Mushrooms on Toast, 916.
Water-melon à la Romero, 1315.

Dinner.
Little Neck Clams, 300.
Consommé aux Quenelles, 129.
Radishes, 292.   Celery, 290.
Fried Frogs, 400.
Tenderloin of Beef, Larded à la Montglas, 516, 213.
Green Peas, Sautés au Beurre, 980.
Suprême of Chicken à la Toulouse, 786.
Brussels Sprouts, 922.
Kirsch Punch, 1305.
Roast Woodcock, 871.
Escarole Salad, 1055.
Strawberry Ice-cream, 1274.
Small Méringues à la Ch. C. Delmonico, 1249.
Strachino Cheese.
Coffee, 1349.

Monday, August —.

Breakfast.
Smoked Beef Omelet, 461.
Minced Veal à la Biscaënne, 576.
Stewed Lima Beans, 952.
Small Brioches, 1202.

Luncheon.
Stuffed Deviled Clams, 376.
Stewed Calf's Liver, sauce Piquante, 580, 203.
Stuffed Peppers, 975.
Herring Salad, 1074.
Choux à la Crême, 1246.

Dinner.
Oysters, 298.
Brunoise, with Sorrel, 4.
Olives.   Lyons Sausage, 286.
Broiled Deviled Lobsters, 364.
Haricot of Lamb à la Providence, 701.
Broiled Tenderloin Steak, Béarnaise, 492.
Green Peas, 978.
Plover, with Watercress, 865.
Lettuce Salad, 1058.
Orange Pudding, 1138.
Coffee, 1349.

Tuesday, August —.

Breakfast.
Eggs à la Bennett, 447.
Filet de Sole à la Joinville, 322.
Croquettes of Lamb, Russian sauce, 679, 211.
Potatoes en Julienne, 1013.
Raspberries and Cream.

Luncheon.
Broiled Fresh Mackerel aux fines Herbes, 331.
Blanquette of Veal, with Nouilles, 552.
Stuffed Lettuce, 953.
Pear Pie, 1084.

Dinner.
Clams, 300.
Ox-tail, with Barley, 38.
Olives.   Celery, 290.
Porgies, Lobster sauce, 353, 158.
Ballotin of Lamb à la Macédoine, 675. 1032.
Stuffed Tomatoes, 1023.
Beef-tongue à la Gendarme, 532.
Sorrel aux Croûtons, 974.
Roast Pigeons, 816.
Romaine Salad, 1064.
Omelet Soufflée, 474.
Coffee, 1349.

Wednesday, August —.

Breakfast.
Tomato Omelet à la Provençale, 457.
Broiled Porterhouse Steaks, 524.
Potatoes Château, 1009.
Sherry Wine Jelly, 1318.

Luncheon.
Fried Scallops, Tomato sauce, 392, 205.
Shoulder of Lamb, Rouennaise, 698.
Spinach, with Eggs, 940.
Raspberry Tarts, 1118.

Dinner.
Oysters, 298.
Consommé Garibaldi, 112.
Radishes, 292.   Mortadella, 287.
Sheep's-head, Oyster sauce, 352.
Sweetbreads à la Montglas, 615.
String Beans, 946.
Boiled Turkey, Celery sauce, 796.
Roast Mushrooms on Toast, 916.
Roast English Snipe, 868.
Watercress Salad, 1072.
Blackberry Shortcake, 1215.
Coffee, 1349.

Thursday, August —.

Breakfast.
Scrambled Eggs, with Asparagus-tops, 406.
Broiled Kingfish, maître d'hôtel, 329.
Calf's Feet à la Poulette, 598.
Tomatoes à la Bock, 1026.
Rice à la Condé, 1181.

Luncheon.
Lobster à la Rushmore, 1358.
Cucumber Salad, 289.
Salmi of Spring Duck à la Bourgeoise 829.
String Beans, 948.
French Pudding, 1139.

Dinner.
Little Neck Clams, 300.
Cream, Palestine, 74.
Olives.   Celery, 290.
Soles à la Joinville, 322.
Breast of Lamb à la Jardinière, 702.
Okras, Sautés à la Créole, 1031.
Chicken, Fricassé à la Reine, 780.
Fried Oyster-plant, 1021.
Roast Woodcock, 871.
Chicory Salad, 1045.
Pistache Ice-cream, 1275.
Lady-fingers, 1231.
Coffee, 1349.

Friday, August —.

Breakfast.

Omelet Mexicaine, 473.
Broiled Haddock à l'Hollandaise, 310, 160.
Tripe à la Lyonnaise, 548.
Potatoes, Duchesse, 1006.
Musk-melon.

Luncheon.

Weakfish, Italian sauce, 188.
Beefsteak Pie à l'Amèricaine, 488.
Lobster Salad, 1061.
Madeleine, 1226.

Dinner.

Oysters, 298.
Bouille-à-Baisse, 1.
Sardines, 283.   Radishes, 292.
Bass, with White Wine, 342.
Veal Cutlets à la Maréchale, 562.
Asparagus à l'Hollandaise, 904.
Salmi of Snipe à la Walter Scott, 856.
Boiled Corn, 962.
Roast Leg of Spring Lamb, 648.
Chicory Salad, 1046.
Rice Pudding à l'Orange, 1130.
Coffee, 1349.

Saturday, August —.

Breakfast.

Eggs au Parmesan, 431.
Blackfish au Gratin, 356.
Broiled Bacon, 754.
Breaded Veal Cutlets, Tomato sauce, 563.
Succotash, 1022.
Cream Renversée, 1252.

Luncheon.

Oysters à la Mali, 386.
Filet Mignon, Marinated, Russian sauce, 511.
Beans Panachées, 950.
Pumpkin Pie, 1099.

Dinner.

Small Rockaway Oysters, 298.
Purée Mongole, 50.
Celery, 290.   Lyons Sausage, 286.
Kingfish, Hollandaise sauce, 329, 160.
Mutton Chops à la Soubise, 647, 250.
Tomatoes à la Marseillaise, 1029.
Ballotin of Squab à l'Italienne, 818.
Oyster-plant à la Poulette, 1019.
Roast Saddle of Venison, Currant Jelly, 878.
Escarole Salad, 1055.
Rum Cake, 1229.
Coffee, 1349.

Sunday, August —.

Breakfast.

Eggs à la Meyerbeer, 437.
Broiled Spanish-mackerel, maître d'hôtel, 329.
Chicken Livers en Brochette, with Bacon, 769.
Saratoga Potatoes, 1011.
Peaches and Cream.

Luncheon.

Crawfish à la Bordelaise, 360.
Broiled Squab, with Bacon, 817.
Fried Sweet Potatoes, 993.
Timbales à la Schultze, 263.
Green-gage Tarts, 1107.

Dinner.

Little Neck Clams, 300.
Cream of Asparagus, 70.
Olives.   Radishes, 292.
Broiled Pompano, maître d'hôtel, 329.
Cucumber Salad, 289.
Lamb Chops à la Masséna, 687.
Brussels Sprouts, 922.
Tenderloin of Beef à la Florentine, 506.
Fresh Lima Beans, 952.
Oranges Glacées à la George Renauldt, 1297.
Roast Turkey, Cranberry sauce, 800, 1329.
Lettuce Salad, 1059.
Pineapple Fritters, 1191.
Mazagran à la Général Dufour, 1391.

Monday, August —.

Breakfast.
Fried Eggs, 412.
Fish Balls, 347.
Mutton Hash à la Zingara, 652.
Stewed Turnips, with Cream, 967.
Brioches, 1201.

Luncheon.
Frogs en Brochette, with Bacon, 398, 754.
Chicken Croquettes à l'Ecarlate, 760.
Spaghetti au Gratin, 961.
Anchovy Salad, 1037.
Charlotte Russe, 1261.

Dinner.
Oysters, 298.
Mutton, with Barley, 30.
Radishes, 292. Bologna Sausage, 286.
Fried Haddock, Tomato sauce, 320, 205.
Shoulder of Lamb, Rouennaise, 698.
Potato Croquettes, 997.
Coquilles of Sweetbreads à la Reine, 623.
Stewed Corn, 964.
Roast Plovers, 865.
Romaine Salad, 1064.
Peach Pudding à la Richelieu, 1150.
Coffee, 1349.

Tuesday, August —.

Breakfast.
Eggs à la Tripe, 419.
Kingfish au Gratin, 319.
Sausages à la l'Italienne, 737.
Potato Balls, 996.
Fresh Plums.

Luncheon.
Broiled Fresh Mackerel, maître d'hôtel, 329.
Stewed Mutton, Portugaise, 658.
Stuffed Cucumbers, 937.
Cauliflower au Gratin, 926.
Apple Pie, 1083.

Dinner.
Clams, 300.
Cream of Chicken, 82.
Olives. Radishes, 292.
Fried Porgies, Tartare sauce, 320, 207.
Tenderloin Piqué à la Sevigné, 520.
Oyster-plant à la Poulette, 1019.
Spring Chicken, Fricassé à l'Américaine, 781.
Green Peas, 978.
Roast Duck, Apple sauce, 824.
Lettuce Salad, 1058.
Lemon Water-ice, 1279.
Biscuits, Ambroisiennes, 1234.
Coffee, 1349.

Wednesday, August —.

Breakfast.
Scrambled Eggs, with Cheese, 405.
Lamb Fries, sauce Colbert, 673, 190.
Hamburg Steak, raw, 1359.
Fried Oyster-plant, 1021.
Iced Timbale of Rice, 1175.

Luncheon.
Pompano, White Wine sauce, 342.
Blanquette of Veal, with Peas, 551.
Broiled Sweet Potatoes, 983.
Musk-melon.

Dinner.
Oysters, 298.
Consommé Chatelaine, 128.
Tomatoes, 288. Sardines, 283.
Skate, with black Butter, 325, 159.
Veal Cutlets en Papillotes, 566.
Stuffed Egg-plant, 909.
Fillet of Chicken à la Rothschild, 790.
Asparagus à la Vinaigrette, 905.
Roast Sirloin of Beef, 516.
Watercress Salad, 1072.
Apples with Rice, 1169.
Coffee, 1349.

Thursday, August —

Breakfast.
Eggs en Filets, 423.
Sheep's-head à la Créole, 339.
Epigrammes of Lamb, with Watercress, 689.
Potatoes, Julienne, 1013.
Blackberries and Cream.

Luncheon.
Oysters à la Baltimore, 382.
Squabs en Compote, 822.
Green Peas, 978.
Macédoine Salad, 1063.
Gooseberry Tarts, 1114.

Dinner.
Clams, 300.
Paysanne, 53.
Radishes, 292. Olives.
Spanish-mackerel aux fines Herbes, 331.
Cucumber Salad, 289.
Boiled Leg of Mutton, Caper sauce, 651.
Stuffed Peppers, 975.
Broiled Tenderloin à la Trianon, 507.
Stewed Tomatoes, 1027.
Woodcock sur Canapé, 871.
Celery Salad, 1042.
Almond Cake, Glacé, 1208.
Coffee, 1349.

Friday, August —.

Breakfast.
Sardine Omelet, 468.
Broiled Fresh Mackerel, Anchovy Butter, 329, 146.
Stewed Mutton Kidneys, sauce Madère, 662.
Sweet Potatoes Soufflées, 1010.
Cream en Mousse au Café, 1253.

Luncheon.
Trout, maître d'hôtel, 314.
Roulade of Beef à l'Ecarlate, 539.
Boiled Onions, 968.
Crab Salad, 1047.
Apple Cake, 1211.

Dinner.
Oysters, 298.
Sorrel with Rice, 42.
Celery, 290. Mortadella, 287.
Whitebait, 301.
Mignons of Lamb à la Montebello, 1360, 249.
String Beans, 948.
Suprême of Chicken à la Patti, 789.
Fried Oyster-plant, 1021.
Roast English Snipe, 868.
Chicory Salad, 1045.
Vanilla Ice-Cream, 1271.
Sweet Macaroons, 1210.
Coffee, 1349.

Saturday, August —.

Breakfast.
Poached Eggs on Toast, 404.
Cold Bass, Ravigote sauce, 147.
Mutton Chops, Broiled, with Bacon, 647, 754.
Mashed Potatoes au Gratin, 998.
Kümmel Jelly, 1323.

Luncheon.
Oyster Patties, 387.
Beefsteak Pie à l'Anglaise, 487.
Spinach, with Eggs, 940.
Frangipani Tarts, 1121.

Dinner.
Keyport Oysters, 298.
Menestra, 36.
Radishes, 292. Bologna Sausage, 286.
Bluefish à l'Italienne, 337.
Sirloin Piqué à la Duchesse, 516.
Beans Panachées, 950.
Salmi of Doc birds à la Chasseur, 864.
Fried Egg-plant, 907.
Roast Chicken, 755.
Escarole Salad, 1055.
Baked Apple Dumplings, 1122.
Coffee, 1349.

Sunday, August —.

Breakfast.
Eggs à l'Impératrice, 440.
Hashed Turkey en Bordure, 805.
Broiled Fillets aux Pommes Parisienne, 515.
Tomatoes à la Bock, 1026.
Musk-melons.

Luncheon.
Crabs à la St. Laurent, 372.
Sirloin Steak à la Bordelaise, 491.
Fried Sweet Potatoes, 993.
Japanese Salad, 1075.
Stewed Prunes à la Général Dufour, 1330.

Dinner.
Clams, 300.
Consommé Douglas, 114.
Olives.   Celery, 290.
Frogs à la Bordelaise, 399, 186.
Escalops of Veal à la Duxelle, 569.
Stuffed Tomatoes, 1023.
Squabs en Crapaudine, 819.
Succotash, 1022.
Punch en Surprise, 1309.
Roast Turkey, 800.
Lettuce with Cream Salad, 1059.
Pudding Glacé à la Frankie Cleveland, 1291.
Camembert Cheese.
Coffee, 1349.

Monday, August —.

Breakfast.
Scrambled Eggs with Tomatoes, 406.
Fried Scallops, 301.
Flat Sausage and Mashed Potatoes, 719.
Fried Onions, 969.
Rice à la Française, 1180.

Luncheon.
Broiled, Deviled Soft-shelled Crabs, 369.
Veal Cutlets en Papillotes, 566.
Lima Beans, 952.
Anchovy Salad, 1037.
Sweet Omelet, 475.

Dinner.
Small Rockaway Oysters, 298.
Purée Jackson, 43.
Sardines, 283.   Radishes, 292.
Lobster Croquettes à la Victoria, 365, 208.
Tenderloin of Beef, Piqué à la Richelieu, 522.
Cauliflower, sauce Hollandaise, 925, 160.
Sweetbreads, with Asparagus-tops, 602.
Boiled Green Corn, 962.
Squabs sur Canapé, 816.
Romaine Salad, 1064.
Nelson Pudding, 1155.
Mazagran à la Général Bugeau, 1391.

Tuesday, August —.

Breakfast.
Omelet, with Peas, 459.
Boiled Halibut, Butter sauce, 309, 157.
Lamb Chops, with Bacon, 647, 754.
Potatoes, maître d'hôtel, 985.
Fresh Apricots.

Luncheon.
Kingfish, maître d'hôtel, 329.
Beefsteak Pie à l'Anglaise, 487.
Stewed Tomatoes, 1027.
Potato Salad, 1073.
Chocolate Eclairs, 1243.

Dinner.
Little Neck Clams, 300.
Chicken à la Piémontaise, 63.
Mortadella, 287.   Tomatoes, 288.
Codfish Steaks, black Butter, 310, 159.
Brisotin of Veal, Poivrade sauce, 554, 194.
Brussels Sprouts, 922.
Lamb Steak à l'Américaine, 718.
Asparagus, Cream sauce, 904, 181.
Roast Stuffed Goose, 808.
Tomato, Mayonnaise Salad, 1071.
Sago Pudding, 1140.
Coffee, 1349.

Wednesday, August —.

Breakfast.
Hominy, with Cream, 1034.
Kidney Omelet, 463.
Broiled Beefsteak à la Parisienne, 495.
Potatoes, Lyonnaise, 991.
Stewed Pears, 1333.

Luncheon.
Mussels à la Poulette, 379.
Leg of Mutton, Caper sauce, 651.
Baked Sweet Potatoes.
Fried Oyster-plant, 1021.
Rhubarb Pie, 1085.

Dinner.
Chicken with Gumbo, 67.
Celery, 290. Bologna Sausage, 286.
Pompano, with Sorrel, 327.
Corned Beef and Cabbage, 490.
Broiled Venison Steaks, Currant Jelly, 884.
Tomatoes à la Marseillaise, 1029.
Roast Plovers, 865.
Watercress Salad, 1072.
Maraschino Pudding, 1134.
Coffee, 1349.

Thursday, August —.

Breakfast.
Eggs à l'Aurore, 444.
Fried Porgies, 301.
Hashed Turkey en Bordure, 805.
Potatoes en Paille, 1014.
Peaches and Cream.

Luncheon.
Salmon en Papillotes, 302.
Braised Beef en Daube, 483.
Macaroni au Gratin, 955.
Chaussons, 1236.

Dinner.
Clams, 300.
Beef à l'Anglaise, 5.
Thon, 282. Tomatoes, 288.
Scallops, Brestoise, 392.
Sweetbreads à la Béarnaise, 610.
Green Peas à l'Anglaise, 978.
Lamb Chops, Maintenon, 685.
Spinach à la Vieille Mode, 941.
Roast Woodcock, 871.
Celery Salad, 1041.
Banana Ice-cream, 1277.
Pithiviers Cake, 1225.
Coffee, 1349.

Friday, August —.

Breakfast.
Omelet, with fine Herbs, 451.
Broiled Kingfish, maître d'hôtel, 329.
Lamb Steak, Piquante sauce, 717.
Stewed Green Corn, 964.
Brioches Fluttes, 1204.

Luncheon.
Stuffed Smelts, 355.
Stewed Veal à la Marengo, 624.
Sorrel au Gras, 974.
Custard Pudding, 1154.

Dinner.
Bisque of Lobster, 10.
Radishes, 292. Mortadella, 287.
Trout, Shrimp sauce, 311.
Sirloin Steak, with Marrow, 493.
Stuffed Tomatoes, 1023.
Vol-au-Vent à la Financière, 810.
Cauliflower à la Vinaigrette, 1040.
Roast Mutton, 585.
Chicory Salad, 1046.
Champagne Jelly, 1322.
Fancy Almond Cakes, 1239.
Coffee, 1349.

Saturday, August —.

Breakfast.
Eggs, with Tarragon, 429.
Broiled Ham, 753.
Mutton Hash au Gratin, 653.
Stewed Carrots, with Cream, 927.
Whipped Cream à la Vanille, 1254.

Luncheon.
Fried Whitebait, 301.
Hashed Chicken, with Cream, 804.
Asparagus à la Tessinoise, 906.
Baba au Rhum, 1217.

Dinner.
Shrewsbury Oysters, 298.
Cream of Artichokes, 72.
Olives.   Lyons Sausage, 286.
Weakfish, Hollandaise sauce, 160.
Beef-tongue à la Jardinière, 535.
Lima Beans, 912.
Chicken, Sauté with Tarragon, 774.
Stuffed Peppers, 975.
Roast Squab on Toast, 816.
Cauliflower Salad, 1040.
Parfait au Café, 1295.
Coffee, 1349.

Sunday, September —.

Breakfast.
Eggs à la Vanderbilt, 420.
Boned, Broiled Smelts, Béarnaise sauce, 353.
Small Mignons Filets, Madeira Wine sauce, 509.
185.
Lima Beans Stewed with Cream, 952.
Musk-melon.

Luncheon.
Broiled Trout, maître d'hôtel, 314.
Cucumber Salad, 289.
Chops Soyer, with Potato Croquettes, 647, 997.
Brussels Sprouts, 922.
Jelly à la Castellar, 1325.

Dinner.
Doxie Rockaway Oysters, 298.
Consommé Masséna, 102.
Radishes, 292.   Lyons Sausage, 286.
Spanish-mackerel aux fines Herbes, 331.
Fricandeau of Veal, with Sorrel, 577.
Croustade of Chicken à la Dreux, 762.
Cauliflower au Gratin, 926.
Punch à la Lalla Rookh, 1308.
Roast Woodcock, 871.
Escarole Salad, 1055.
St. Honoré à la Rose Delmonico, 1212.
Pont-de-Val Cheese.
Coffee, 1349.

Monday, September —.

Breakfast.
Tomato Omelet, 459.
Fried Soft-shelled Crabs, 368.
Pig's Feet, sauce Piquante, 729.
Potatoes, maître d'hôtel, 985.
Brioches à la Condé, 1203.

Luncheon.
Matelote of Eels, 332.
Breast of Veal, Milanaise, 596.
Celery, with Cream, 929.
Coffee éclairs, 1244.

Dinner.
East River Oysters, 298.
Julienne, 27.
Celery, 290.   Olives.
Sole au Gratin, 319.
Leg of Mutton, Bretonne, 650.
Fried Egg-plant, 907.
Chicken Croquettes, sauce Périgueux, 759.
Stuffed Tomatoes, 1023.
Brochette of Reed-birds, with Bacon, 877, 754.
Lettuce Salad, 1057.
Pineapple Water-ice, 1283.
Sponge Cake, 1195.
Coffee, 1349.

Tuesday, September —.

Breakfast.
Eggs à la Duchesse, 449.
Salmon Tails, Broiled, 308.
Calf's Liver Sauté à l'Italienne, 580.
Sorrel au Jus, 973.
Apples and Rice Méringuées, 1169.

Luncheon.
Frogs à la Poulette, 399.
Tripe à la Mode de Caën, 547.
Sweet Potatoes, Hollandaise, 999.
Plum Pie, 1094.

Dinner.
Clams, 300.
Clear Green Turtle, 18.
Radishes, 292. Mortadella, 287.
Chicken Halibut, Cream sauce, 309, 181.
Lamb's Kidneys, stewed with Cèpes, 714.
String Beans, 948.
Sweetbreads à la Pompadour, 618.
Broiled Mushrooms on Toast, 916.
Roast Lamb, Mint sauce, 1361, 169.
Romaine Salad, 1064.
Charlottes Panachées, 1300.
Coffee, 1349.

Wednesday, September —.

Breakfast.
Oatmeal.
Omelet, with Kidneys, 463.
Broiled Porterhouse Steak, 524.
Fried Onions, 969.
Fresh Pears.

Luncheon.
Oysters à la Mali, 386.
Hashed Mutton à la Zingara, 652.
Stuffed Egg-plant, 909.
Russian Salad, 1065.
Huckleberry Tarts, 1113.

Dinner.
Keyport Oysters, 298.
Consommé Célestine, 118.
Celery, 290. Bologna Sausage, 286.
Fresh Mackerel à la Vénitienne, 338.
Braised Beef, Flamande, 482.
Green Peas à la Française, 977.
Pillau of Chicken à la Créole, 783.
Sorrel, with Cream, 973.
Roast Plover and Watercress, 865.
Lettuce and Tomato Salad, 1060.
Apricot Pudding à la Richelieu, 1151.
Coffee, 1349.

Thursday, September —.

Breakfast.
Omelet, with Smoked Beef, 461.
Broiled Spanish-mackerel, 329.
Lamb Fries, Broiled à la Diable, 672.
Potatoes, Julienne, 1013.
Peaches and Cream.

Luncheon.
Blackfish, White Wine, 342.
Pigeon Cutlets à la Victoria, 815.
Spinach, with Croûtons, 940.
Savarin, 1197.

Dinner.
Clams, 300.
Mulligatawney, 34.
Radishes, 292. Caviare, 281.
Lobster à la Newburg, 359.
Larded Tenderloin of Beef à la Bernardi, 523.
Stuffed Tomatoes, 1023.
Vol-au-Vent à la Toulouse, 811.
Squabs sur Canapé, 816.
Celery Salad, Mayonnaise, 1042.
Vanilla Ice-cream, 1271.
Allumettes 1205.
Coffee, 1349.

Friday, September —.

Breakfast.

Eggs au Beurre noir, 414.
Fried Porgies, Tartare sauce, 320, 207.
Hashed Beef à la Catalan, 502.
Stewed Fresh Tomatoes, 1027.
Rice à la Bonne Femme, 1172.

Luncheon.

Picked-up Codfish, 346.
Chicken à la Maryland, 785.
Spaghetti à l'Italienne, 960.
Pineapple Pie, 1087.

Dinner.

Parker Bay Oysters, 298.
Cream of Celery, 71.
Olives.   Radishes, 292.
Scallops à la Poulette, 392, 379.
Chicken Livers Sautés, with Madeira, 767.
Artichokes, Barigoul, 896.
Lamb Chops à la Villeroi, 686.
Asparagus, sauce Hollandaise, 904.
Roast English Snipe, 868.
Chicory Salad, 1045.
English Pudding, 1137.
Coffee, 1349.

Saturday, September —.

Breakfast.

Omelet, with Green Peas, 459.
Broiled Ham, 753.
Tripe à la Créole, 545.
Sweet Potatoes Soufflées, 1010.
Baked Apples, 1124.

Luncheon.

Skate, with black Butter, 325, 159.
Mutton Chops à la Provençale, 642.
String Beans, with Cream, 946.
Potato Salad, 1073.
Sherry Wine Jelly, 1318.

Dinner.

Blue Point Oysters, 298.
A la Russe, 55.
Celery, 290.   Mortadella, 287.
Red-snapper, fine Herbs, 315.
Epigrammes of Lamb, with Asparagus-tops, 689.
Lima Beans, 952.
Croustade of Chicken Livers à la Dreux, 763.
Roast Turkey, 800.
Tomato, Mayonnaise Salad, 1071.
Baba au Madère, 1217.
Coffee, 1349.

Sunday, September —.

Breakfast.

Eggs à l'Aurore, 444.
Trout, maître d'hôtel, 314.
Hashed Chicken au Gratin, 805.
Potatoes en Paille, 1014.
Cream Renversée, 1252.

Luncheon.

Crabs à la St. Laurent, 372.
Calf's-head à la Cavour, 638.
Fried Sweet Potatoes, 993.
Timbales à la Schultze, 263.
Water-melon à la Seward, 1317.

Dinner.

Clams, 300.
Cream à l'Allemande, 84.
Celery, 290.   Olives.
Whitebait, 301.
Tenderloin Piqué à la Duchesse, 516.
Corn Sauté au Beurre, 964.
Salmi of Snipe à la Régence, 861.
Brussels Sprouts, 922.
Romaine Punch, 1304.
Roast Ducklings, 824.
Lettuce Salad, 1058.
Cocoanut Pudding, 1147.
Mazagran à la Général Dufour, 1392.

Monday, September —.

Breakfast.
Omelet, with fine Herbs, 451.
Broiled Sea-bass, maître d'hôtel, 329.
Minced Veal à la Biscaënne, 576.
Potatoes Sautées, 995.
Musk-melon.

Luncheon.
Fried Porgies, 320.
Stewed Lamb with Potatoes, 659.
Oyster-plant à la Poulette, 1019.
Rhubarb Tarts, 1112.

Dinner.
Linn Haven Oysters, 298.
Rice and Tomatoes, 57.
Anchovies, 284.   Radishes, 292.
Bluefish au Gratin, 319.
Mignons Filets à la Parisienne, 514.
Stuffed Cucumbers, 937.
Salmi of Duck, with Olives, 827.
Roast Mutton, 585.
Escarole Salad, 1055.
Lemon Water-ice, 1279.
Bitter Almond Macaroons, 1209.
Coffee, 1349.

Tuesday, September —.

Breakfast.
Scrambled Eggs, with Mushrooms, 406.
Codfish à l'Hollandaise, 352, 160.
Stewed Tripe à la Lyonnaise, 548.
Green Corn Sauté au Beurre, 964.
French Pancake, 1186.

Luncheon.
Oyster Patties, 387.
Hashed Turkey à la Polonaise, 803.
Onions, with Cream, 968.
Charlotte Russe, 1261.

Dinner.
Clams, 300.
Bisque of Lobster, 10.
Radishes, 292.   Olives.
Stuffed Deviled Crabs, 370.
Braised Beef à l'Orsini, 481.
Lima Beans, 952.
Chicken Sauté à la Bordelaise, 776.
Cauliflower au Gratin, 926.
Roast Loin of Veal, 585.
Lettuce Salad, 1057.
Omelet Célestine, 477.
Coffee, 1349.

Wednesday, September —.

Breakfast.
Omelet Raspail, 467.
Fried Smelts, Tomato sauce, 301, 205.
Beefsteak with Watercress, 524.
Saratoga Potatoes, 1011.
Preserved Strawberries, 1345.

Luncheon.
Stuffed Deviled Clams, 376.
Veal Cutlets à la Philadelphia, 565.
Sweet Potatoes, Hollandaise, 999.
Rice and Orange Pudding, 1130.

Dinner.
Small Rockaway Oysters, 298.
Consommé Impériale, 111.
Olives.   Celery, 290.
Edible Snails à la Bourguignonne, 393.
Broiled Sirloin Steaks à la Béarnaise, 492.
Beans Panachées, 950.
Vol-au-Vent à la Reine, 812.
Oyster-plant à la Poulette, 1019.
Roast Plovers, with Watercress, 865.
Romaine Salad, 1064.
Pudding à la Diaz, 1135.
Coffee, 1349.

Thursday, September —.

Breakfast.

Scrambled Eggs, with Truffles, 407.
Fried Porgies, 320.
Broiled Lamb Steak, Purée of Peas, 716.
Potatoes au Gratin, 1004.
Rice au Lait d'Amandes, 1170.

Luncheon.

Broiled Boned Smelts, Tartare sauce, 353, 207.
Stewed Beef à la Dufour, 541.
Broiled Mushroons on Toast, 916.
Apple Méringue Pie, 1103.

Dinner.

Oysters, 298.
Mikado, 32.
Celery, 290.   Radishes, 292.
Lobster en Chevreuse, 362.
Sweetbreads à la Colbert, 617.
Green Peas, 978.
Lamb Chops à la Clichy, 684.
Broiled Egg-plant, 908.
Roast Woodcock, 871.
Watercress Salad, 1072.
Baba, Crême de Vanille, 1218.
Coffee, 1349.

Friday, September —.

Breakfast.

Crab Omelet, 455.
Broiled Fresh Mackerel, maitre d'hôtel, 329.
Sausages à l'Italienne, 737.
Fried Oyster-plant, 1021.
Brioche, 1201.

Luncheon.

Mussels à la Marinière, 378.
Broiled Lamb Steaks à l'Américaine, 718.
Fried Sweet Potatoes, 993.
French Pancake à la Gelée, 1187.

Dinner.

Oysters, 298.
Cream of Sorrel, Fermière, 81.
Celery, 290.   Bologna Sausage, 286.
Pompano, Egg sauce, 309, 161.
Tenderloin of Beef à la Nivernaise, 505.
Stuffed Peppers, 975.
Chicken Croquettes, with Green Peas, 276.
Macaroni Napolitaine, 957.
Reed-birds, 877.
Tomato Salad, 1070.
Neapolitan Ice-cream, 1292.
Coffee, 1349.

Saturday, September —.

Breakfast.

Hominy and Cream, 1034.
Ham and Eggs, 412, 753.
Brochette of Lamb à la Dumas, 674.
Potatoes à la Hanna, 1012.
Fresh Pears.

Luncheon.

Oysters à la Baltimore, 388.
Breast of Veal, Milanaise, 596.
Sweet Potatoes, Hollandaise, 999.
Cocoanut Pie, 1101.

Dinner.

East River Oysters, 298.
Ox-tail à l'Anglaise, 40.
Lyons Sausage, 286.   Radishes, 292.
Salmon à la Créole, 339.
Saddle of Mutton, Currant Jelly, 666.
Stuffed Tomatoes, 1023.
Pigeons en Compote, 822.
Cardons à la Moëlle, 931.
Roast Beef, 527.
Chicory Salad, 1046.
Rice Pudding, 1143.
Coffee, 1349.

Sunday, September —.

Breakfast.
Omelet, with Truffles, 460.
Fried Whitebait, 301.
Chicken Livers Sautés au Madère, 767.
Fried Sweet Potatoes, 993.
Milan Cake, 1228.

Luncheon.
Welsh Rarebit, Golden Buck, 295.
Shoulder of Lamb, Macédoine, 697.
Macaroni, with Cheese, 954.
Salmon Salad, 1066.
Green-gage Pie, 1093.

Dinner.
Clams, 300.
Purée of Game à la Destaing, 89.
Olives.   Celery, 200.
Broiled Soft-shelled Crabs à la Diable, 369.
Veal Cutlets, St. Cloud, 561.
Artichokes, Vinaigrette, 902.
Chicken Fricassé à l'Américaine, 781.
Cauliflower, Hollandaise, 925, 160.
Punch à la Française, 1311.
Roast Woodcock, 871.
Lettuce and Tomato Salad, 1060.
Macédoine à la Cavour, 1298.
Gorgonzola Cheese.
Coffee, 1349.

Monday, September —.

Breakfast.
Eggs à la Bourguignonne, 411.
Fish Balls, 347.
Sausages, with White Wine, 735.
Hashed Potatoes, with Cream, 1003.
Baked Apples, 1124.

Luncheon.
Oysters à la Pompadour, 384.
Brochette of Lamb, with Bacon, 674, 754.
Macaroni à la Crême, 954.
Herring Salad, 1074.
Blackberry Tarts, 1119.

Dinner.
Small Blue Point Oysters, 298.
Printanier Colbert, 121.
Mortadella, 287.   Radishes, 292.
Fried Smelts, sauce Tartare, 301, 207.
Breast of Turkey, Celery Sauce, 806, 200.
String Beans, with Cream, 946.
Croquettes of Sweetbreads, Béarnaise, 619, 166.
Brussels Sprouts, 922.
Roast Grouse, 852.
Escarole Salad, 1055.
Indian Pudding, 1145.
Coffee, 1349.

Tuesday, September —.

Breakfast.
Tomato Omelet, 456.
Broiled Bluefish, 329.
Hashed Turkey en Bordure, 805.
Potatoes en Paille, 1014.
Stewed Rhubarb, 1112.

Luncheon.
Broiled Lobster à la Diable, 364.
Stewed Mutton, Solferino, 656.
Stuffed Peppers, 975.
French Pudding à la Delmonico, 1139.

Dinner.
Clams, 300.
Vermicelli, 103.
Olives.   Celery, 290.
Spanish-mackerel à la Toulouse, 354.
Calf's-head à la Vinaigrette, 640.
Stewed Corn, 964.
Coquilles of Chicken à l'Anglaise, 271.
Artichokes Sautés, 897.
Roast Beef, 527.
Lettuce Salad, 1057.
Rice à la Condé, 1181.
Coffee, 1349.

8

Wednesday, September —.

Breakfast.
Eggs au Miroir, 425.
Boiled Fresh Haddock, Cream sauce, 352, 181
Lamb Steak à l'Américaine, 718.
Stewed Turnips, with Cream, 967.
Musk-melon.

Luncheon.
Codfish, Hollandaise sauce, 352, 160
Veal Cutlets en Papillotes, 566.
Spaghetti au Gratin, 961.
Chocolate Eclairs, 1243.

Dinner.
Small Rockaway Oysters, 298.
Consommé Renaissance, 115.
Radishes, 292.   Anchovies, 284.
Broiled Soft-shelled Crabs à la Diable, 369.
Broiled Tenderloin à la Béarnaise, 492.
Potato Croquettes, 997.
Spring Lamb Chops à la Clichy, 684.
Green Peas, 978.
Roast Capon, 755.
Romaine Salad, 1064.
Rice, with Apples, 1169.
Coffee, 1349.

Thursday, September —.

Breakfast.
Oatmeal and Cream.
Kidney Omelet, 463.
Mutton Chops à la Provençale, 642.
Succotash, 1022.
Cream Renversée, 1252.

Luncheon.
Fried Sea-bass, 320.
Stewed Veal à la Marengo, 624.
Sweet Potatoes, Hollandaise, 999.
Mille-feuilles, 1223.

Dinner.
Prince's Bay Oysters, 298.
Consommé Patti, 126.
Mortadella, 287.   Celery, 290.
Kennebec Salmon, Cream sauce, 303, 181.
Grenadin of Veal à l'Africaine, 589.
Beans Panachées, 950.
Turban of Chicken à la Cleveland, 791.
Fried Oyster-plant, 1021.
Roast Snipe, 868.
Celery Salad, 1041.
Peach Ice-cream, 1276.
Vanilla Ice-cream, 1271.
Coffee, 1349.

Friday, September —.

Breakfast.
Omelet à l'Espagnole, 472.
Broiled Pompano, 329.
Pork Chops, sauce Robert, 746.
Broiled Sweet Potatoes, 983.
Corn Fritters, 965.

Luncheon.
Stuffed Deviled Clams, 376.
Tendron of Veal, Purée of Lentils, 633, 88.
Cauliflower au Gratin, 926.
Crab Salad, 1047.
Omelet au Kirsch, 476.

Dinner.
Clams, 300.
Fish Chowder, 12.
Cucumbers, 289.   Olives.
Fresh Mackerel en Papillotes, 330.
Cutlets of Venison, Port Wine sauce, 891.
Stuffed Tomatoes, 1023.
Suprême of Chicken à la Rothschild, 790.
Succotash, 1022.
Roast Loin of Veal, 585.
Chicory Salad, 1045.
Fruit Pudding, 1161.
Coffee, 1349.

MENUS.

Saturday, September —.

Breakfast.
Eggs à la Chipolata, 442.
Broiled Sardines on Toast, 403.
Hashed Mutton à la Zingara, 652.
Stewed Carrots, 927.
Preserved Cherries, 1347.

Luncheon.
Broiled Boned Smelts, à la Béarnaise, 353.
Braised Beef, Russian sauce, 485.
Lima Beans, 952.
Apricot Tarts, 1335.

Dinner.
Cherry Stone Oysters, 298.
Jardinière, 28.
Celery, 290.   Mortadella, 287.
Kennebec Salmon à l'Irlandaise, 307.
Minced Veal à la Catalan, 575.
Potatoes Hollandaise, 999.
Salmi of Snipe à la Florentine, 857.
Spinach, with Eggs, 940.
Roast Goose, Apple sauce, 808, 168.
Tomato Salad, 1070.
Charlotte Russe, 1261.
Coffee, 1349.

Sunday, September —.

Breakfast.
Hominy and Cream, 1034.
Boiled Eggs.
Broiled Deviled Soft-shelled Crabs, 369.
Lamb Chops, Breaded, 643.
Potatoes, maître d'hôtel, 985.
Brioche, 1201.

Luncheon.
Crabs à la St. Jean, 371.
Broiled Turkey Legs à la Diable, 766.
Stewed Green Corn, 964.
Japanese Salad, 1075.
Apple Fritters, 1191.

Dinner.
Little Neck Clams, 300.
Chicken à la Portugaise, 66.
Lyons Sausage, 286.   Radishes, 292.
Smelts à la Toulouse, 354.
Tenderloin of Beef à la Montglas, 503, 213.
Stuffed Tomatoes, 1023.
Chicken Sauté à la Bohémienne, 778.
Brussels Sprouts, 922.
Champagne Punch, 1307.
Reed-birds en Brochette au Petit Salé, 877, 754.
Escarole Salad, 1055.
Pudding à la U. S. Grant, 1159.
Mazagran à la Général Bugeau, 1391.

Monday, September —.

Breakfast.
Omelet, with fine Herbs, 451.
Fish Balls, 347.
Hashed Chicken à la Crème, 804.
French Fried Potatoes, 993.
Iced Timbale of Rice, 1175.

Luncheon.
Oysters à la Baltimore, 388.
Chops Soyer, Fried Potatoes, 647.
Sorrel au Gras, 974.
Rhubarb Tarts, 1112.

Dinner.
Doxie Rockaway Oysters, 298.
Cream of Cauliflower, 73.
Celery, 290.   Olives.
Weakfish au Gratin, 319.
Ballotin of Lamb, with Peas, 675.
Fried Egg-plant, 907.
Fillet of Chicken à la Patti, 789.
Tomatoes à la Bock, 1026.
Roast Beef, 527.
Lettuce Salad, 1058.
Méringues Panachées, 1302.
Coffee, 1349.

Tuesday, September —.

Breakfast.

Scrambled Eggs, with Asparagus-tops, 406.
Bass, sauce Mayonnaise, 352, 206.
Calf's Liver à l'Alsacienne, 582.
Stewed Lima Beans, 952.
Stewed Prunes, 1330.

Luncheon.

Scallops Brestoise, 392.
Curry of Lamb à l'Indienne, 677.
Sweet Potatoes Soufflées, 1010.
Gingerbread, 1213.

Dinner.

Massachusetts Bay Oysters, 298.
Consommé d'Orléans, 110.
Radishes, 292.   Lyons Sausage, 486.
Spanish-mackerel à l'Italienne, 337.
Sweetbreads à la Soubise, 606.
Succotash, 1022.
Broiled Venison Steaks, Currant Jelly sauce, 884.
Cêpes Bordelaise, 913.
Roast Chicken, with Watercress, 755.
Romaine Salad, 1064.
Cherry Water-ice, 1282.
Almond Cake, 1224.
Coffee, 1349.

Wednesday, September —.

Breakfast.

Poached Eggs on Toast, 404.
Oysters en Brochette, with Bacon, 385.
Minced Beef à la Catalan, 502.
Stewed Potatoes, 995.
Milan Cake, 1228.

Luncheon.

Codfish à la Provençale, 352, 642.
Hashed Chicken, with Cream, 804.
Herring Salad, 1074.
Kirsch Jelly, 1319.

Dinner.

Clams, 300.
Cream of Celery à l'Espagnole, 86.
Tomatoes, 288.   Olives.
Crawfish, Bordelaise, 360.
Lamb Chops à la Robinson, 682.
Corn, Stewed with Cream, 963.
Curry of Chicken à l'Espagnole, 793.
Oyster-plant à la Poulette, 1019.
Roast Partridges, 843.
Cauliflower Salad, 1040.
Nelson Pudding, 1155.
Coffee, 1349.

Thursday, September —.

Breakfast.

Scrambled Eggs, with Tomatoes, 406.
Fried Eels, 335.
Broiled Calf's Liver and Bacon, 584.
Potatoes à l'Hollandaise, 999.
Peaches and Cream.

Luncheon.

Frogs à la Poulette, 399.
Chicken Pot-pie, 757.
Mushrooms, Stewed with Cream, 915.
Gooseberry Pie, 1091.

Dinner.

East River Oysters, 298.
Ox-tail à l'Ecossaise, 39.
Celery, 290.   Mortadella, 287.
Haddock with White Wine, 342.
Boiled Turkey, Egg sauce, 798.
Fried Egg-plant, 907.
Sweetbreads à la Colbert, 617.
String Beans, 948.
Roast Woodcock, 871.
Watercress Salad, 1072.
Baked Apple Dumplings, 1122.
Coffee, 1349.

Friday, September —.

Breakfast.

Crab Omelet, 455.
Broiled Fresh Mackerel, maître d'hôtel, 329.
Tripe à la Poulette, 546.
Baked Sweet Potatoes.
Crême en Mousse au Café, 1253.

Luncheon.

Fried Soft-shelled Crabs, 368.
Corned Beef with Kale-sprouts, 490.
Lobster Salad, 1061.
Rum Omelet, 476.

Dinner.

Clams, 300.
Purée Faubonne, 46.
Olives.   Radishes, 292.
Sheep's-head, Egg sauce, 352, 161.
Pork Chops, Apple sauce, 748.
Beans Panachées, 950.
Chicken Croquettes à la Périgordine, 761.
Green Peas, 978.
Roast Leg of Mutton, 648.
Celery Salad, 1041.
Lemon Ice-cream, 1278.
Pithiviers Cake, 1225.
Coffee, 1349.

Saturday, September —.

Breakfast.

Eggs à la Tripe, 419.
Broiled Fresh Perch, 314.
Mutton Kidneys, Sautés à l'Italienne, 663.
Potatoes Duchesse, 1006.
French Pancake, 1186.

Luncheon.

Pompano, with Sorrel, 327.
Broiled Sirloin Steaks à la Bordelaise, 491.
Spaghetti à l'Italienne, 663.
Strawberry Tarts, 1117.

Dinner.

Little Neck Clams, 300.
Consommé à l'Anglaise, 119.
Tomatoes, 288.   Lyons Sausage, 286.
Porgies aux fines Herbes, 315.
Sweetbreads en Petites Caisses, 274.
Stuffed Egg-plant, 909.
Squabs en Crapaudine, 819.
Green Peas à la Française, 977.
Roast Saddle of Venison, 878.
Chicory Salad, 1045.
Indian Pudding, 1145.
Coffee, 1349.

Sunday, September —.

Breakfast.

Eggs à la Bennett, 447.
Broiled Spanish-mackerel, Anchovy Butter, 329, 146.
Hashed Lamb, à l'Anglaise, 688.
Potatoes Julienne, 1013.
Fresh Green-gages.

Luncheon.

Lobster à la Newburg, 359.
Breaded Veal Cutlets, Tomato sauce, 563.
Russian Salad, 1065.
Timbales à la Schultze, 263.
Rice and Cream à la Croce, 1296.

Dinner.

Small Blue Point Oysters, 298.
Purée à la Gentilhomme, 90.
Celery, 290.   Olives.
Sheep's-head à la Créole, 339.
Tenderloin of Beef à la Hussard, 519.
Sorrel au Gras, 974.
Chicken à la Ranhofer, 1363.
Cardons à la Moëlle, 931.
Punch à la Lorenzo Delmonico, 1303.
Woodcock sur Canapé, 871.
Escarole Salad, 1055.
Cabinet Pudding à la Sadi-Carnot, 1164.
Mazagran à la Général Dufour, 1392.

Monday, September —.

Breakfast.

Eggs au Soleil, 415.
Picked-up Codfish, 346.
Beefsteak with Watercress, 524.
Saratoga Potatoes, 1011.
Stewed Apples, 1332.

Luncheon.

Oyster Patties, 387.
Lamb Chops à la Robinson, 682.
Brussels Sprouts, 922.
Vanilla Eclairs, 1245.

Dinner.

Clams, 300.
Mock Turtle, 17.
Sardines, 283. Radishes, 292.
Bass à la Chambord, 343.
Chartreuse of Partridge, 849.
Curry of Chicken à la Créole, 794.
Beans, with Cream, 946.
Roast Loin of Lamb, 585.
Lettuce Salad, 1058.
Rhubarb Pie, 1085.
Apricot Water-ice, 1285.
Coffee, 1349.

Tuesday, October —.

Breakfast.

Eggs à la Pauvre Femme, 417.
Broiled Boned Smelts, Tartare sauce, 353, 207.
Sausages, with White Wine, 735.
Beet-roots, Sautés au Beurre, 911.
Brioches Fluttes, 1204.

Luncheon.

White Porgies, with Fine Herbs, 315.
Ragout of Veal à la Chasseur, 632.
Cauliflower à l'Hollandaise, 925, 160.
Mince Pie, 1082.

Dinner.

Oysters, 298.
Purée Mongole, 50.
Olives. Celery, 290.
Striped Bass, with White Wine, 342.
Brisotin of Veal à l'Ecarlate, 555.
Lima Beans, 952.
Lamb Sweetbreads en Caisses, 274.
Artichoke-bottoms, Florentine, 903.
Roast Grouse sur Canapé, 852.
Watercress Salad, 1072.
Peach Pudding, 1150.
Coffee, 1349.

Wednesday, October —.

Breakfast.

Omelet à la Provençale, 457.
Codfish à l'Hollandaise, 352, 160.
Corned Beef Hash à la Zingara, 530.
Saratoga Potatoes, 1011.
Fresh Pears.

Luncheon.

Crabs à la St. Laurent, 372.
Blanquette of Veal à la Reine, 550.
Fried Sweet Potatoes, 993.
Apple Cake, 1211.

Dinner.

Clams, 300.
Croûte-au-Pôt, 11.
Radishes, 292. Anchovies, 284.
Bluefish à la Vénitienne, 338.
Pigeon Cutlets à la Victoria, 815.
Brussels Sprouts, 922.
Filets Mignons à la Pompadour, 509.
Green Corn, 962.
Roast Saddle of Mutton, 664.
Celery Salad, 1041.
Lemon Pudding, 1157.
Coffee, 1349.

Thursday, October —.

Breakfast.
Barley, with Cream.
Eggs à la Turque, 439.
Broiled Sirloin Steak, with Watercress, 491.
Potatoes, Château, 1009.
Baked Apples, 1124.

Luncheon.
Soles à la Joinville, 322.
Hashed Chicken à la Royale, 801.
Macaroni au Gratin, 955.
Crême en Mousse au Café, 1253.

Dinner.
East River Oysters, 298.
Consommé Douglas, 114.
Celery, 290.   Sardines, 283.
Spanish-mackerel, with fine Herbs, 331.
Venison Steak, Colbert sauce, 881.
Stewed Tomatoes, 1027.
Sweetbreads à la Pompadour, 618.
Green Peas, 978.
Roast Red-head Ducks, 876.
Lettuce Salad, 1059.
Omelet Soufflées, 474.
Coffee, 1349.

Friday, October —.

Breakfast.
Oyster Omelet, 452.
Haddock, Cream sauce, 352, 181.
Pig's Feet à la St. Hubert, 727.
Mashed Potatoes au Gratin, 998.
Rice à la Française, 1180.

Luncheon.
Lobster à l'Américaine, 357.
Beef Braised à la Providence, 480.
Cauliflower au Gratin, 926.
Baked Apples, 1124.

Dinner.
Oak Island Oysters, 298.
Busecca à la Milanaise, 7.
Tomatoes, 288.   Olives.
Frogs à la Bordelaise, 398, 186.
Amourettes of Lamb à la Diable, 672.
Spaghetti à l'Italienne, 960.
Stewed Veal à la Chasseur, 632.
Celery, with Gravy, 928.
Roast Partridge sur Canapé, 843.
Escarole Salad, 1055.
Baba au Rhum, 1217.
Coffee, 1349.

Saturday, October —.

Breakfast.
Eggs à la Bourguignonne, 411.
Mutton Chops, with Watercress, 647.
Broiled Bacon, 754.
Potatoes à la Rice, 1007.
Apricot Preserves, 1340.

Luncheon.
Stuffed Oysters à la Mali, 386.
Chicken Pot-pie, 757.
Stuffed Cucumbers, 937.
Cherry Tarts, 1111.

Dinner.
Keyport Oysters, 298.
Purée Soubise of White Beans, 92.
Celery, 290.   Mortadella, 287.
Perch au Gratin, 356.
Double Porterhouse Steak à la Bordelaise, 52:, 491.
Fried Egg-plant, 907.
Salmi of Grouse à la Walter Scott, 856.
String Beans, 948.
Roast Lamb, Mint sauce, 1361, 169.
Lettuce Salad, 1057.
Pistache Ice-cream, 1275.
Small Méringues à la Ch. C. Delmonico, 1249.
Coffee, 1349.

Sunday, October —.

Breakfast.

Omelet à l'Espagnole, 472.
Broiled Kingfish, 329.
Hashed Turkey à la Crême, 804.
Succotash, 1022.
Whipped Cream à la Vanille, 1254.

Luncheon.

Terrapin à la Newburg, 396, 359.
Broiled Spring Chicken, with Bacon, 756.
Sweet Potatoes Soufflées, 1010.
Timbales à la Schultze, 263.
Water-melon à la Romero, 1315.

Dinner.

Clams, 300.
Consommé Renaissance, 115.
Olives.   Radishes, 292.
Red-snapper, Egg sauce, 352, 161.
Fricandeau of Veal, with Sorrel, 577.
Suprêmes of Chicken à la Bayard, 787.
Stuffed Tomatoes, 1023.
Punch à la Cardinal, 1306.
Roast Canvas-back Duck, 874.
Fried Hominy, 1035.
Celery Salad, Mayonnaise, 1042.
Plum Pudding, 1163.
English Cheese.
Coffee, 1349.

Monday, October —.

Breakfast.

Eggs au Gratin, 418.
Fish Balls, 347.
Stewed Kidneys, with Madeira, 662.
Potatoes, Julienne, 1013.
Preserved Cherries, 1347.

Luncheon.

Scallops, Brestoise, 392.
Hashed Turkey, with Cream, 804.
Macaroni au Gratin, 955.
Apricot Tarts, 1108.

Dinner.

Shrewsbury Oysters, 298.
Giblet, with Barley, 21.
Celery, 290.   Sardines, 283.
Sheep's-head, maître d'hôtel, 329.
Sweetbreads à la Catalan, 616.
Fried Oyster-plant, 1021.
Tenderloin of Beef aux Gourmets, 508.
French Peas.
Roast Pigeons, with Gravy, 816.
Barbe de Capucine Salad, 1038.
Turban of Apples, 1174.
Coffee, 1349.

Tuesday, October —.

Breakfast.

Omelet, with fine Herbs, 451.
Fried Whitebait, 301.
Andouillettes, Broiled, 742.
Hashed Potatoes au Gratin, 1004.
Rice, with Apples, Méringuées, 1169.

Luncheon.

Boned Boiled Smelts, sauce Béarnaise, 353.
Cromesquis à la Richelieu, 764.
Spinach, with Croûtons, 940.
Prunes à la Général Dufour, 1330.

Dinner.

Clams, 300.
Gumbo of Crabs, 24.
Radishes, 292.   Lyons Sausage, 286.
Bass en Matolote, 332.
Hashed Lamb à la Polonaise, 700.
Stewed Tomatoes, 1027.
Partridge, Celery sauce, 847.
Roast Beef, 527.
Russian Salad, 1065.
Fritters, Soufflées à la Vanille, 1192.
Coffee, 1349.

Wednesday, October —.

Breakfast.
Eggs à Reine, 438.
Black Basss, Caper sauce, 352, 651.
Stewed Calf's Liver à l'Italienne, 580.
Stewed Tomatoes, 1027.
Rice Cake, 1222.

Luncheon.
Canapé Madison, 269.
Broiled Lamb Steaks, Purée de Marrons, 716, 131.
Sweet Potatoes, Hollandaise, 999.
French Pudding à la Delmonico, 1139.

Dinner.
Small Rockaway Oysters, 298.
Consommé Dubourg, 101.
Olives.   Celery, 290.
Bluefish, Oyster sauce, 352.
Saddle of Venison, Londondery sauce, 878, 880.
Brussels Sprouts, 922.
Larded Fillet of Beef à la Sevigné, 520.
Beans Panachées, 950.
Roast Plover, 865.
Celery Salad, 1041.
Charlotte Russe, 1261.
Coffee, 1349.

Thursday, October —.

Breakfast.
Omelet, with fine Herbs, 451.
Broiled Deviled Soft-shelled Crabs, 369.
Hashed Beef au Gratin, 529.
Fried Oyster-plant, 1021.
Peach Marmalade, 1331.

Luncheon.
Broiled Bluefish, maitre d'hôtel, 329.
Tendron of Veal, Nantaise, 633.
Fried Potatoes, 993.
Herring Salad, 1074.
Savarin, 1197.

Dinner.
Clams, 300.
Ox-tail à l'Anglaise, 40.
Watercress, 1072.   Lyons Sausage, 286
Matelote of Eels, 332.
Roast Ham, Champagne sauce, 723.
Carrots à la Béchamel, 927, 154.
Venison Chops, Port Wine sauce, 891.
Sorrel au Gras, 974.
Roast Squabs on Toast, 816.
Chicory Salad, 1045.
English Pudding, 1137.
Coffee, 1349.

Friday, October —.

Breakfast.
Eggs à la Vanderbilt, 420.
Broiled Sardines on Toast, 403.
Lamb Chops à la Robinson, 682.
Sweet Potatoes, Broiled, 983.
Preserved Strawberries, 1345.

Luncheon.
Fillet of Soles, maître d'hôtel, 326.
Hamburg Steak, Russian sauce, 526.
Spaghetti Napolitaine, 959.
Lobster Salad, 1061.
Iced Timbale of Rice, 1175.

Dinner.
Linn Haven Oysters, 298.
Bisque of Crabs, 9.
Cucumbers, 289.   Olives.
Stuffed Deviled Lobster, 367.
Curry of Lamb à l'Indienne, 677.
Cèpes à la Bordelaise, 913.
Vol-au-Vent Financière, 810.
Flageolets, 1365.
Roast Grouse, 852.
Escarole Salad, 1055.
Omelet au Kirsch, 476.
Coffee, 1349.

Saturday, October —.

Breakfast.

Hominy and Cream, 1034.
Scrambled Eggs, with Ham, 408.
Broiled Porterhouse Steak, 524.
Lyonnaise Potatoes, 991.
Wheat Cakes, 1184.

Luncheon.

Codfish Tongues, Cream sauce, 349, 181.
Minced Tenderloin, Portugaise, 501.
Stuffed Peppers, 975.
Boiled Apple Dumplings, 1127.

Dinner.

Parker Bay Oysters, 298.
Consommé d'Orléans, 110.
Celery, 290.   Bologna Sausage, 286.
Broiled Deviled Soft-shelled Crabs, 369.
Sweetbreads au Salpicon, 605.
Tomatoes à la Marseillaise, 1029.
Squabs en Compote, 822.
Cauliflower, sauce Hollandaise, 925, 160.
Saddle of Venison, Currant Jelly, 878.
Lettuce Salad, 1057.
Méringues à l'Helvétienne, 1251.
Coffee, 1349.

Sunday, October —.

Breakfast.

Eggs, with Celery, 427.
Broiled Spanish-mackerel, maître d'hôtel, 329.
Mutton Kidneys, Sautés aux Champignons, 714.
Sweet Potatoes Soufflées, 1010.
Maraschino Cream, 1257.

Luncheon.

Mussels à la Marinière, 378.
Tripe à la Bordelaise, 544.
Broiled Grouse à la Pomeroy, 1390.
Cauliflower Salad, 1040.
German Pancake, with Apples, 1189.

Dinner.

Little Neck Clams, 300.
Westmoreland, 33.
Olives.   Radishes, 292.
Terrapin à la Maryland, 397.
Escalops of Sweetbreads, Richelieu, 574.
Green Peas, 978.
Chicken, Sauté à la Régence, 777.
Stuffed Egg-plant, 909.
Oranges Glacées à la George Renauldt, 1297.
Roast Red-head Duck, 876.
Celery Salad, 1041.
Pudding à la Diaz, 1135.
Camembert Cheese.
Coffee, 1349.

Monday, October —.

Breakfast.

Omelet aux Saucisses, 465.
Boiled Chicken Halibut, Cream sauce, 309, 181.
Beefsteak, with Watercress, 524.
Fried Saratoga Potatoes, 1011.
Fresh Grapes.

Luncheon.

Perch, Remoulade sauce, 314, 209.
Veal Cutlets, Pagasqui, 560.
Oyster-plant, Poulette, 1019.
Cranberry Tarts, 1116.

Dinner.

Shrewsbury Oysters, 298.
Spaghetti, with Tomatoes, 56.
Sardines, 283.   Celery, 290.
Fried Sea-bass, sauce Tartare, 320, 707.
Broiled Deviled Turkey Legs, 766.
Stewed Onions and Cream, 968.
Lamb Chops, maison d'or, 683.
Stuffed Tomatoes à la Reine, 1024.
Roast Snipe sur Canapé, 868.
Romaine Salad, 1064.
Bread Pudding, 1132.
Coffee, 1349.

Tuesday, October —.

Breakfast.
Scrambled Eggs, with Asparagus-tops, 406.
Fried Smelts, Tomato sauce, 301, 205.
Broiled Lamb Fries, 672.
Potato Croquettes, 997.
Corn Fritters, 965.

Luncheon.
Red-snapper, sauce Hollandaise, 352, 160.
Stewed Veal, Marengo, 624.
Spinach, with Eggs, 943.
Chaussons, 1236.

Dinner.
Parker Bay Oysters, 298.
Clear Green Turtle, 18.
Olives.   Watercress, 1072.
Salmon en Papillotes, 302.
Tenderloin of Beef à la Chéron, 504.
Stuffed Peppers, 975.
Suprême of Grouse à la Périgueux, 850.
Cardons, with Marrow, 931.
Roast Chicken au Jus, 755.
Lettuce and Tomato Salad, 1060.
Chocolate Ice-cream, 1272.
Lady-fingers, 1231.
Coffee, 1349.

Wednesday, October —.

Breakfast.
Omelet Raspail, 467.
Fried Scallops, Tartare sauce, 301, 207.
Broiled Calf's Liver and Bacon, 584.
Stewed Turnips, with Gravy, 967.
Fresh Pears.

Luncheon.
Smelts au Gratin, 356.
Broiled Squabs on Toast, 817.
Gumbo à l'Espagnole, 1030, 472.
Rice Pudding, with Pineapple, 1130.

Dinner.
Clams, 300.
Chicken à la Piémontaise, 63.
Radishes, 292.   Celery, 290.
Fresh Mackerel à la Béarnaise, 353.
Beef-tongue, with Spinach, 536.
Stewed Tomatoes, 1027.
Suprême of Chicken, Toulouse, 786.
Peas à l'Ancienne Mode, 976.
Roast Reed-birds, 877.
Macédoine Salad, 1063.
Omelet Soufflée, 474.
Coffee, 1349.

Thursday, October —.

Breakfast.
Eggs à la Meyerbeer, 437.
Baked Sea-bass, 319.
Minced Veal, Biscaënne, 576.
Potatoes, Duchesse, 1006.
Buckwheat Cakes, 1183.

Luncheon.
Lobster à la Bordelaise, 360.
Pork and Beans, 752.
Suédoise Salad, 1069.
Mille-feuilles, 1223.

Dinner.
Oysters, 298.
Cream of Sorrel, Fermière, 81.
Mortadella, 887.   Radishes, 292.
Clams, Marinière, 377.
Chicken Croquettes, with Green Peas, 758.
Stuffed Artichokes, 901.
Broiled Tenderloin à la Stanton, 1388.
Succotash, 1022.
Roast Grouse, 852.
Celery Salad, 1041.
Méringues à l'Helvétienne, 1251.
Coffee, 1349.

Friday, October —.

Breakfast.
Omelet à la Vanderbilt, 471.
Boiled Codfish, black Butter, 352, 159.
Brochette of Lamb à la Dumas, 674.
Green Corn, Sauté au Beurre, 964.
Preserved Peaches, 1340.

Luncheon.
Canapé Lorenzo, 391.
Minced Beef à la Portugaise, 501.
Fried Sweet Potatoes, 993.
Anchovy Salad, 1037.
Pumpkin Pie, 1099.

Dinner.
Clams, 300.
Oyster Soup, 26.
Olives.   Lyons Sausage, 286.
Pompano, maitre d'hôtel, 329.
Sweetbreads, with Spinach, 607.
Saddle of Venison, Currant Jelly, 878.
Stuffed Cucumbers, 937.
Roast Beef, 527.
Chicory Salad, 1046.
Rice au Lait d'Amande, 1170.
Coffee, 1349.

Saturday, October —.

Breakfast.
Omelet aux Cêpes, 460.
Picked-up Codfish, 346.
Mignons Filets, Madeira sauce, 509, 185.
Stewed Potatoes, Hollandaise, 999.
Stewed Apricots, 1335.

Luncheon.
Stuffed, Deviled Crabs, 370.
Blanquette of Veal à l'Ancienne, 553.
French Peas.
Hot Savarin, 1197.

Dinner.
Oysters, 298.
Brunoise, with Rice, 3.
Tomatoes, 288.   Mortadella, 287.
Sole à la Horly, 321.
Roast Ham, with Sweet Corn, 724.
String Beans, with Cream, 946.
Salmi of Duck à la Maréchale, 831.
Stuffed Tomatoes, 1023.
Roast Loin of Lamb, Mint sauce, 585, 169.
Escarole Salad, 1055.
Sago Pudding, 1140.
Coffee, 1349.

Sunday, October —.

Breakfast.
Eggs à la Livingstone, 410.
Broiled Fresh Mackerel, fines Herbes, 331.
Stewed Tripe à la Créole, 545.
Sweet Potatoes à l'Hollandaise, 999.
Cream Renversée, 1252.

Luncheon.
Terrapin à la Baltimore, 396.
Broiled Chicken Legs à la Diable, 766.
Cauliflower Salad, 1040.
Timbales Foies-Gras, Lagadère, 809.
Riz à la Bonne Femme, 1172.

Dinner.
Little Neck Clams, 300.
Consommé à l'Andalouse, 117.
Celery, 290.   Radishes, 292.
Broiled Spanish-mackerel, 329.
Cucumber Salad, 289.
Breast of Lamb à la Jardinière, 702.
Potatoes à la Hanna, 1012.
Tenderloin of Beef à la Bordelaise, 491.
Green Peas à la Crême, 980.
Champagne Punch, 1307.
Roast Partridge, Larded, 843.
Lettuce Salad, 1059.
St. Honoré à la Rose Delmonico, 1212.
Stilton Cheese.
Coffee, 1349.

Monday, October —.

Breakfast.

Omelet, with fresh Tomatoes, 456.
Fish Balls, 347.
Black Sausage, mashed Potatoes, 719.
Fried Egg-plant, 907.
Brioche, 1201.

Luncheon.

Broiled Salt Mackerel, 329.
Stuffed Onions, 970.
Shoulder of Lamb, Rouennaise, 698.
Fried Corn, 965.
Custard Pudding, 1154.

Dinner.

Rockaway Oysters, 298.
Consommé Sevigné, 106.
Olives.   Watercress, 1072.
Croquettes of Lobster, Tomato sauce, 365, 205.
Filets Mignons à la Brown, 1382.
Spinach, with Eggs, 940.
Boiled Turkey, Oyster sauce, 797.
Stuffed Green Peppers, 975.
Snipe sur Canapé, 868.
Romaine Salad, 1064.
Pineapple Fritters, 1191.
Coffee, 1349.

Tuesday, October —.

Breakfast.

Eggs à l'Alsacienne, 443.
Broiled Pompano, 329.
Breaded Veal Cutlets, Tomato sauce, 563.
Saratoga Potatoes, 1011.
Milan Cake, 1228.

Luncheon.

Spanish-mackerel à la Toulouse, 354.
Lamb Kidneys à la Colbert, 712.
Macaroni au Gratin, 955.
Peach Tarts, 1106.

Dinner.

East River Oysters, 298.
Printanier Grénat, 51.
Thon, 282.   Celery, 290.
Fried Porgies, Tartare sauce, 301, 207.
Croquettes of Lamb, à la Patti, 679.
Stewed Carrots, with Cream, 927.
Ballotin of Squab à l'Italienne, 818.
Mushrooms on Toast, 916.
Roast Reed-birds, 877.
Romaine Salad, 1064.
Apples with Rice à la Czar, 1173.
Coffee, 1349.

Wednesday, October —.

Breakfast.

Scrambled Eggs à la Chicorée, 409.
Codfish Tongues, brown Butter, 349.
Hashed Lamb à la Polonaise, 700.
Sorrel, with Gravy, 974.
Preserved Raspberries, 1346.

Luncheon.

Red-snapper, Egg sauce, 352, 161.
Curry of Chicken à l'Indienne, 792.
Fried Sweet Potatoes, 993.
Green-gage Pie, 1093.

Dinner.

Clams, 300.
Giblets à l'Anglaise, 22.
Radishes, 292.   Olives.
Salmon, Anchovy Butter, 303, 146.
Lamb Chops, maison d'or, 683.
Stewed Tomatoes, 1027.
Vension Steak, Londonderry sauce, 880.
Celery, with Cream, 929.
Roast Capon, 755.
Watercress Salad, 1072.
Omelet Célestine, 477.
Coffee, 1349.

Thursday, October —.

Breakfast.

Poached Eggs on Toast, 404.
Scallops, with White Wine, 342.
Minced Beef à la Provençale, 500.
Potatoes en Paille, 1014.
Apples Méringuées, 1248.

Luncheon.

Oysters à la Baltimore, 388.
Beefsteak Pie à l'Américaine, 488.
Salad Italienne, 1036.
Strawberry Tarts, 1117.

Dinner.

Massachusetts Bay Oysters, 298.
Consommé Royale, 107.
Celery, 290.   Sausage, 286.
Kingfish aux fines Herbes, 331.
Saddle of Mutton, Poivrade sauce, 667.
Green Peas à l'Anglaise, 978.
Croquettes of Sweetbreads, 620.
Brussels Sprouts, 922.
Roast Woodcock, 871.
Celery Salad, 1042.
Orange Water-ice, 1280.
Almond Biscuits, 1235.
Coffee, 1349.

Friday, October —.

Breakfast.

Cheese Omelet, 469.
Fried Soft-shelled Crabs, 368.
Sausage à l'Italienne, 737.
Potatoes, Sautées au Beurre, 994.
Stewed Prunes, 1330.

Luncheon.

Smelts à la Joinville, 322.
Stewed Mutton, Portugaise, 658.
Russian Salad, 1065.
Allumettes, 1205.

Dinner.

Clams, 300.
Pot-au-Feu, 54.
Radishes, 292   Olives.
Bass à la Chambord, 343.
Tenderloin, Piqué à la Sevigné, 520.
Succotash, 1022.
Veal Cutlets à la Milanaise, 563.
Asparagus-tops, Hollandaise, 904.
Roasted Plovers, 865.
Barbe de Capucine Salad, 1038.
Chocolate Pudding, 1146.
Coffee, 1349.

Saturday, October —.

Breakfast.

Fried Eggs, 412.
Boiled Halibut, sauce Hollandaise, 309, 160.
Broiled Deviled Beefsteak, 524.
Potatoes, Parisienne, 986.
Stewed Quinces, 1338.

Luncheon.

Oysters en Brochette, with Bacon, 385.
Blanquette of Veal, with Green Peas, 551.
Spinach aux Croûtons, 940.
Omelet au Rhum, 476.

Dinner.

Small Rockaway Oysters, 298.
Sorrel, with Rice, 42.
Lyons Sausage, 286.   Celery, 290.
Bluefish à l'Icarienne, 336.
Amourettes of Lamb, Tomato sauce, 673.
String Beans au Blanc, 947.
Beef-tongue à la Milanaise, 538.
Oyster-plant à la Poulette, 1019.
Roast Squabs, 816.
Celery Salad, 1041.
Baba, Cream à la Vanille, 1218.
Coffee, 1349.

Sunday, October —.

Breakfast.

Green Peas Omelet, 459.
Broiled White Perch, Anchovy Butter, 329, 146.
Hashed Turkey à la Béchamel, 802.
Broiled Tomatoes, 1025.
Baked Apples, 1124.

Luncheon.

Broiled Lobster à la Ravigote, 363.
Chicken Croquettes à l'Ecarlate, 760.
Fried Sweet Potatoes, 993.
Timbales à la Schultze, 263.
Peach Pie, 1092.

Dinner.

Little Neck Clams, 300.
Consommé Impérial, 111.
Olives. Radishes, 292.
Stuffed Deviled Crabs, 370.
Tenderloin of Beef, Piqué à la Bernardi, 523.
Brussels Sprouts, 922.
Sweetbreads, Larded à la Financière, 603.
Green Peas à l'Anglaise, 978.
Punch à la Française, 1311.
Roast Woodcock, 871.
Chicory Salad, 1045.
Vanilla Ice-cream, 1271.
Petites Bouchées à la Mme. Astor, 1238.
Camembert Cheese.
Coffee, 1349.

Monday, October —.

Breakfast.

Oatmeal and Cream.
Omelet aux Saucisses, 465.
Brochette of Lamb, Colbert, 674, 190.
Saratoga Potatoes, 1011.
Apple Fritters, 1191.

Luncheon.

Oysters à la Mali, 386.
Broiled Grouse à la Pomeroy, 1390.
Tomatoes à la Bock, 1026.
Crême en Mousse au Curaçoa, 1259.

Dinner.

Chincoteague Oysters, 298.
Purée Condé, 48.
Tomatoes, 288. Frizzled Celery, 291.
Frogs à l'Espagnole, 401.
Calf's-head en Tortue, 641.
Stewed Corn, 963.
Suprême of Chicken à la Patti, 789.
Cardons, with Marrow, 931.
Roast Beef, 527.
Escarole Salad, 1055.
Farina Pudding, 1144.
Coffee, 1349.

Tuesday, October —.

Breakfast.

Eggs à l'Aurore, 444.
Fish Balls, 347.
Veal Kidneys, Stewed à la Provençale, 615.
Lima Beans, with Cream, 952.
French Pancake, 1186.

Luncheon.

Soles au Gratin, 319.
Veal Cutlets à la Philadelphia, 565.
Croquettes of Macaroni, 279.
Lemon Pie, 1086.

Dinner.

East River Oysters, 298.
Gumbo, with Frogs, 23.
Radishes, 292. Caviare, 281.
Fried Black-bass, aux fines Herbes, 331.
Tenderloin, Piqué à la Duchesse, 516.
Fried Egg-plant, 907.
Civet of Venison à la Française, 807.
Cauliflower au Gratin, 926.
Broiled Grouse à l'Américaine, 844.
Lettuce Salad, 1057.
Savarin à l'Anglaise, 1199.
Coffee, 1349.

Wednesday, October —.

Breakfast.
Omelet, with Asparagus-tops, 458.
Boned Broiled Smelts, Béarnaise, 353.
Corned Beef Hash à l'Américaine, 529.
Stewed Carrots and Cream, 927.
Preserved Plums, 1343.

Luncheon.
Stuffed Deviled Lobster, 367.
Squabs à la Chipolata, 821.
Cauliflower, Vinaigrette, 1040.
Charlottes Panachées, 1300.

Dinner.
Oysters, 298.
Purée of Partridge à la Destaing, 89.
Celery, 290. Lyons Sausage, 286.
Broiled Spanish-mackerel, maître d'hôtel, 329.
Mutton Chops à la Robinson, 682.
Potato Croquettes, 997.
Sweetbreads à la Pompadour, 618.
Tomatoes à la Bock, 1026.
Roast Chicken, 755.
Watercress Salad, 1072.
Tapioca Pudding, 1141.
Coffee, 1349.

Thursday, October —.

Breakfast.
Eggs à la Bonne Femme, 432.
Fried Black-bass, 320.
Veal Cutlets à la Philadelphia, 565.
Fried Potatoes, 993.
Rice à la Française, 1180.

Luncheon.
Oysters à la Poulette, 383.
Lamb Chops à la Signora, 681.
Sweet Potatoes Soufflées, 1010.
Chicken Salad, 1044.
Madeleine Printanière, 1227.

Dinner.
Clams, 300.
Cream of Asparagus, 70.
Olives. Radishes, 292.
Pompano, maître d'hôtel, 329.
Boiled Turkey à la Baltimore, 799.
Stewed Lima Beans, 952.
Filets Mignons aux Gourmets, 508.
Spinach, with Gravy, 943.
Roast Canvas-back, Currant Jelly, 874, 1326.
Celery Salad, 1042.
Biscuits Tortoni, 1287.
Coffee, 1349.

Friday, November —.

Breakfast.
Tomato Omelet, 456.
Boiled Halibut, Lobster sauce, 309, 158
Lamb Chops, with Bacon, 647, 754.
Potatoes, Lyonnaise, 991.
Stewed Apples, 1332.

Luncheon.
Soft Clams à la Merrill, 389.
Beefsteak Pie à l'Anglaise, 487.
Lobster Salad, 1061.
Lemon Pudding, 1157.

Dinner.
Oysters, 298.
Printanier Chasseur, 52.
Lyons Sausage, 286. Celery, 290.
Pompano, with Sorrel, 327.
Brisotin of Veal, Poivrade sauce, 554, 194.
Oyster-plant, Poulette, 1019.
Chicken à la Maryland, 785.
Artichokes, Barigoul, 896.
Roast Quails on Toast, 834.
Watercress Salad, 1072.
Strawberry Ice-cream, 1274.
Lady-fingers, 1231.
Coffee, 1349.

Saturday, November —.

Breakfast.

Eggs à la Duchesse, 449.
Pig's Feet, Robert sauce, 728.
Corned Beef Hash à la Zingara, 530.
Fried Egg-plant, 907.
Pears and Grapes.

Luncheon.

Halibut Steaks, aux fines Herbes, 310, 331.
Stewed Lamb, with Flageolets, 707.
Fried Sweet Potatoes, 993.
Choux à la Crême, 1246.

Dinner.

Doxie Rockaway Oysters, 298.
Consommé à l'Anglaise, 119.
Olives.   Watercress, 1072.
Red-snapper à l'Icarienne, 336.
Beef-tongue à la Napolitaine, 534.
Lima Beans, 952.
Venison Steak, Purée of Chestnuts, 882.
Potatoes en Surprise, 1005.
Roast Veal, 585.
Tomato Salad, 288.
Rice Pudding, 1143.
Coffee, 1349.

Sunday, November —.

Breakfast.

Eggs à la Paysanne, 433.
Fresh Mackerel aux fines Herbes, 331.
Hashed Turkey en Bordure, 805.
Stewed Lima Beans, with Cream, 952.
Whipped Cream à la Vanille, 1254.

Luncheon.

Canapé Lorenzo, 391.
Broiled Squabs au Petit Salé, 817.
Stewed Carrots, 927.
Lobster Salad à la Plummer, 1062.
Pie à la Martha Washington, 1105.

Dinner.

Clams, 300.
Cream of Game, 83.
Celery, 290.   Radishes, 292.
Lobster à la Newburg, 359.
Sweetbreads à la Béarnaise, 610.
Green Peas à la Française, 977.
Lamb Chops, Maintenon, 685.
Cauliflower à l'Hollandaise, 925, 160.
Punch en Surprise, 1309.
Roast Partridges, with Watercress, 843.
Celery, Mayonnaise Salad, 1042.
Pudding à la U. S. Grant, 1159.
Neuchatel Cheese.
Coffee, 1349.

Monday, November —.

Breakfast.

Omelet, with Green Peas, 459.
Broiled Smelts, Tartare sauce, 353, 207.
Venison Steak, sauce Piquante, 879, 203.
Mashed Potatoes au Gratin, 998.
Brioches Fluttes, 1204.

Luncheon.

Scallops Brestoise, 392.
Fricandeau of Veal à la Morlaisienne, 579.
String-bean Salad, 1068.
Cranberry Pie, 1104.

Dinner.

Blue Point Oysters, 298.
Cream of Lima Beans, 75.
Olives.   Sardines, 283.
Broiled Frogs, maître d'hôtel, 398.
Sirloin Steak, with Marrow sauce, 493.
Stuffed Cucumbers, 937.
Chicken Vol-au-Vent à la Reine, 812.
Celery, with Gravy, 928.
Roast Grouse sur Canapé, 852.
Chicory Salad, 1045.
Vermicelli Pudding, 1142.
Coffee, 1349.

Tuesday, November —.

Breakfast.

Eggs au Soleil, 415.
Codfish à l'Hollandaise, 352. 160.
Stewed Calf's Liver à l'Alsacienne, 582.
Potatoes, maître d'hôtel, 985.
Rice à la Condé, 1181.

Luncheon.

Crabs à la St. Jean, 371.
Broiled Quails on Toast, 835.
Fried Egg-plant, 907.
Potato Salad, 1073.
French Pudding à la Delmonico, 1139

Dinner.

Mill Pond Oysters, 298.
Onion Soup, 130.
Frizzled Celery, 291.   Tomatoes, 288.
Matelote of Eels, 332.
Partridge, with Cabbage, 845.
Sweetbreads Larded à la Financière, 603.
Brussels Sprouts, 922.
Roast Lamb, 583.
Escarole Salad, 1055.
Omelet Soufflée, 474.
Coffee, 1349.

Wednesday, November —.

Breakfast.

Omelet, Vanderbilt, 471.
Broiled Sardines on Toast, 403.
Sausages Gastronome, 740.
Stewed Tomatoes, 1027.
Rhein-wine Jelly, 1324.

Luncheon.

Soles à la Horly, 321.
Civet of Venison à la Française, 887.
Lamb-tongue Salad, 1056.
Eclairs à la Vanille, 1245.

Dinner.

Oak Island Oysters, 298.
Mulligatawney à la Delmonico, 35.
Caviare, 281.   Radishes, 292.
Frogs à l'Espagnole, 401.
Fillet of Hare, sauce Poivrade, 895.
French Peas.
Chicken Croquettes à la Périgueux, 759.
Stuffed Egg-plant, 909.
Broiled Red-heads, Currant Jelly, 876, 1326.
Lettuce Salad, 1057.
Apple Pudding à l'Helvétienne, 1152.
Coffee, 1349.

Thursday, November —.

Breakfast.

Eggs à l'Aurore, 444.
Fish Balls, 347.
Calf's-head à la Vinaigrette, 640.
Hashed Potatoes, with Cream, 1003.
Peach Marmalade, 1331.

Luncheon.

Broiled Salmon Steaks, Anchovy Butter, 310, 146.
Tripe à la Créole, 545.
Spaghetti au Gratin, 961.
Hot Savarin, 1198.

Dinner.

Clams, 300.
Chicken à la Richmond, 62.
Celery, 290.   Lyons Sausage, 286.
Sheep's-head, with fine Herbs, 331.
Tenderloin of Beef, Piqué aux Cêpes, 496.
Succotash, 1022.
Sweetbreads à la Pompadour, 618.
Stuffed Peppers, 975.
Roast Quails, with Watercress, 834.
Celery Salad, 1041.
Pound Cake, Glacé, 1193.
Coffee, 1349.

Friday, November —.

Breakfast.
Omelet, Mexicaine, 473.
Fried Perch, 320.
Veal Cutlets, Pagasqui, 560.
Potatoes en Paille, 1014.
Buckwheat Cakes, 1183.

Luncheon.
Fillet of Sole à la Vénitienne, 338.
Shoulder of Lamb, Jardinière, 696.
Stuffed Lettuce, 953.
Iced Timbale of Rice, 1175.

Dinner.
Oysters, 298.
Clam Chowder, 13.
Radishes, 292.   Thon, 282.
Boiled Halibut, Shrimp sauce, 309, 178.
Beef-tongue à la Gendarme, 532.
Spinach, with Croûtons, 940.
Chicken, Sauté with Tarragon, 774.
Stewed Tomatoes, 1027.
Roast Woodcock, 871.
Tomato Salad, 1070.
Baked Apple Dumplings, 1122.
Coffee, 1349.

Saturday, November —.

Breakfast.
Eggs, with brown Butter, 414.
Fried Smelts, Tomato sauce, 301, 205.
Minced Veal à la Biscaënne, 576.
Potatoes, Duchesse, 1006.
Stewed Prunes à la Dufour, 1330.

Luncheon.
Red-snapper à l'Hollandaise, 317.
Gibelotte of Hare, 894.
Sorrel au Gras, 974.
Cherry Tarts, 1111.

Dinner.
Rockaway Oysters, 298.
Giblets, with Rice, 19.
Celery, 290.   Bologna Sausage, 286.
Broiled Salmon, maitre d'hôtel, 308.
Mignons Filets à la Béarnaise, 509, 166.
Succotash, 1022.
Game Croquettes, Madeira-wine sauce, 833, 185.
Tomatoes à la Bock, 1026.
Roast Quails, 834.
Escarole Salad, 1055.
Fritters Soufflées à la Vanille, 1192.
Coffee, 1349.

Sunday, November —.

Breakfast.
Omelet à la Vanderbilt, 471.
Picked-up Codfish, 346.
Corned Beef Hash au Gratin, 529.
Baked Potatoes.
Crême Renversée, 1252.

Luncheon.
Soft Clams à la Merrill, 389.
Stuffed Pig's Feet à la Périgueux, 732.
Lima Beans, 952.
Lobster Salad à la Plummer, 1062.
Charlotte Russe, 1261.

Dinner.
East River Oysters, 298.
Purée of Partridge à la Gentilhomme, 90.
Radishes, 292.   Olives.
Lobster à la Newburg, 359.
Epigrammes of Lamb, Macédoine, 689.
Suprême of Chicken à la Patti, 789.
Green Peas à l'Anglaise, 978.
Kirsch Punch, 1305.
Canvas-back Ducks, 874.
Lettuce Salad, 1058.
Plum Pudding, 1163.
English Cheese.
Coffee, 1349.

Monday, November —.

Breakfast.
Scrambled Eggs, with Asparagus-tops, 406.
Broiled Bluefish, 329.
Hashed Lamb à la Polonaise, 700.
Potatoes, Julienne, 1013.
Rice à l'Airolo, 1171.

Luncheon.
Oysters à la Mali, 386.
Chops, Soyer, 647.
Potatoes, Duchesse, 1006.
Carrots, with Cream, 927.
Pear Pie, 1084.

Dinner.
Clams, 300.
Croûte-au-Pot, 11.
Celery, 290.   Tomatoes, 288.
Smelts à la Toulouse, 354.
Civet of Rabbit à la Parisienne, 888.
Stuffed Peppers, 975.
Croustade of Chicken à la Dreux, 762.
Red-heads and Hominy, 876, 1035.
Celery Salad, 1042.
Baba au Madère, 1217.
Coffee, 1349.

Tuesday, November —.

Breakfast.
Sausage Omelet, 465.
Bass à la maitre d'hôtel, 326.
Mutton Chops, Breaded, 643.
Saratoga Potatoes, 1011.
Corn Fritters, 965.

Luncheon.
Broiled Oysters en Brochette au Petit Salé, 385.
Broiled Quails on Toast, 835.
Cauliflower Salad, 1040.
Rice and Cream à la Croce, 1296.

Dinner.
Oysters, 298.
Bisque of Crabs, 9.
Sardines, 283.   Radishes, 292.
Fresh Mackerel aux fines Herbes, 331.
Lamb Steak à l'Américaine, 718.
Celery à la Moëlle de Bœuf, 930.
Chicken, Sauté à la Marengo, 771.
Peas and Bacon, 981.
Grouse sur Canapé, 852.
Chicory Salad, 1046.
Diplomatic Pudding, 1129.
Coffee, 1349.

Wednesday, Novembver —.

Breakfast.
Eggs à la Bonne Femme, 432.
Hamburg Steak, Russian sauce, 526.
Broiled Bacon, 754.
Stewed Potatoes, 995.
Baked Apples, 1124.

Luncheon.
Crawfish à la Bordelaise, 360.
Salmi of Ducks, with Olives, 827.
Fried Sweet Potatoes, 993.
Tomato Salad, 1070.
French Pancake, with Jelly, 1187.

Dinner.
Small Rockaway Oysters, 298.
Consommé, Italian Paste, 103.
Celery, 290.   Caviare, 281.
Codfish Tongues, black Butter, 349.
Broiled Sirloin Steak à la Duchesse, 494.
Fried Oyster-plant, 1021.
Vol-au-Vent, Financière, 810.
Brussels Sprouts, 922.
Roast Woodcock, 871.
Lettuce Salad, 1057.
Caramel Pudding, 1166.
Coffee, 1349.

Thursday, November —.

Breakfast.
Cheese Omelet, 469.
Fried White Perch, Tartare sauce, 301, 207.
Beefsteak, with Watercress, 524.
Fried Sweet Potatoes, 993.
Pippin Apples and Grapes.

Luncheon.
Bluefish, Egg sauce, 352, 161.
Hashed Mutton à la Zingara, 652.
Corn, Stewed with Butter, 964.
Timbales à la Schultze, 263.
Lemon Cream Pie, Méringué, 1102.

Dinner.
Linn Haven Oysters, 298.
Tomatoes and Sago, 59.
Mortadella, 287.   Radishes, 292.
Crabs, St. Laurent, 372.
Braised Beef, Flamande, 482.
Pillau of Chicken à la Créole, 783.
Artichokes, Florentine, 903.
Roast Reed-birds, 877.
Escarole Salad, 1055.
Sweet Omelet, 475.
Coffee, 1349.

Friday, November —.

Breakfast.
Scrambled Eggs, with Tomatoes, 406.
Fillet of Soles à la Horly, 321.
Smoked Beef, with Cream, 486.
Potato Croquettes, 997.
Brioche, 1201.

Luncheon.
Frost Fish à la Toulouse, 354.
Stewed Veal à la Marengo, 624.
Fried Sweet Potatoes, 993.
Peach Tarts, 1106.

Dinner.
Clams, 300.
Cream of Artichokes, 72.
Radishes, 292.   Thon, 282.
Broiled Haddock, maître d'hôtel, 310.
Saddle of Venison, Currant-jelly sauce, 878.
Sorrel au Gras, 974.
Mutton Chops à la Robinson, 682.
Stuffed Peppers, 975.
Roast Partridge, 843.
Watercress Salad, 1072.
English Pudding, 1137.
Coffee, 1349.

Saturday, November —.

Breakfast.
Hominy, with Cream, 1034.
Ham Omelet, 462.
Stewed Chicken Livers à l'Italienne, 770.
Mashed Potatoes, 998.
Preserved Peaches, 1340.

Luncheon.
Oyster Crabs à la Poulette, 374.
Chicken Croquettes à la Reine, 758.
Succotash, 1022.
Macédoine Salad, 1063.
Stewed Prunes à la Général Dufour, 1330.

Dinner.
Clams, 300.
Busecca, 7.
Tomatoes, 288.   Mortadella, 287.
Pompano, with fine Herbs, 331.
Veal Chops, St. Cloud, 561.
Tomatoes à la Bock, 1026.
Breast of Turkey, Oyster sauce, 806, 173.
Spinach, with Eggs, 940.
Roast Beef, 527.
Watercress Salad, 1072.
Biscuits Glacés, 1286.
Coffee, 1349.

Sunday, November —.

Breakfast.
Scrambled Eggs, with Truffles, 407.
Broiled Salt Mackerel, 329.
Sausages à l'Italienne, 737.
Fried Potatoes, 993.
Whipped Cream au Maraschino, 1257.

Luncheon.
Lobster en Brochette, 361.
Broiled Squabs, with Bacon, 817.
Spaghetti au Gratin, 961.
Rhubarb Tarts, 1112.

Dinner.
Oysters, 298.
Cream of Asparagus, 70.
Celery, 290.   Olives.
Terrapin à la Maryland, 397.
Broiled Tenderloin à la Nivernaise, 505.
Broiled Tomatoes, 1025.
Sweetbreads Larded à la Bearnaise, 610.
Brussels Sprouts, 922.
Romaine Punch, 1304.
Roast Canvas-back Ducks, Currant Jelly, 874, 1326.
Celery Salad, 1042.
Tutti-frutti, 1293.
Méringues à la Ch. C. Delmonico, 1249.
Pont l'Evêque Cheese.
Coffee, 1349.

Monday, November —.

Breakfast.
Omelet, with Asparagus-tops, 458.
Fish Balls, 347.
Hashed Turkey en Bordure, 805.
Beet-roots à la Crême, 912.
Wheat Cakes, 1184.

Luncheon.
Broiled Fresh Mackerel, Anchovy Butter, 329, 146.
Veal Cutlets à la Maréchale, 562.
Potatoes, Château, 1009.
Anchovy Salad, 1037.
Vermicelli Pudding, 1142.

Dinner.
Prince's Bay Oysters, 298.
Purée of Crécy, 47.
Sardines, 283.   Radishes, 292.
Stuffed Deviled Lobster, 367.
Calf's-head en Tortue, 641.
String Beans, 948.
Tenderloin, Piqué à la Portugaise, 517.
Mashed Potatoes, 938.
Roast English Snipe, with Watercress, 868.
Tomato, Mayonnaise Salad, 1071.
Pineapple Pie, 1087.
Coffee, 1349.

Tuesday, November —.

Breakfast.
Poached Eggs on Toast, 404.
Fried Smelts, Tomato sauce, 301, 205.
Lamb Steak à l'Américaine, 718.
Potatoes au Gratin, 1004.
Small Brioches, 1202.

Luncheon.
Sheep's-head à la Créole, 339.
Beefsteak Pie à l'Anglaise, 487.
Macaroni au Gratin, 955.
Plum Pie, 1094.

Dinner.
Little Neck Clams, 300.
Purée Jackson, 43.
Olives.   Mortadella, 287.
Bass en Matelote, 332.
Broiled Tenderloin à la Béarnaise, 492.
Potatoes à la Windsor, 1008.
Suprême of Partridge à la Godard, 851.
French Peas.
Roast Lamb, Mint sauce, 585, 169.
Celery Salad, 1042.
Kümmel Jelly, 1323.
Sweet Almond Macaroons, 1210.
Coffee, 1349.

Wednesday, November —.

Breakfast.
Omelet, with fine Herbs, 451.
Fried Blackfish, 301.
Broiled Porterhouse Steak, 524.
Sorrel aux Croûtons, 974.
Preserved Pears, 1341.

Luncheon.
Oysters à la Villeroi, 381.
Brochette of Lamb, with Bacon, 674, 754.
Fried Sweet Potatoes, 993.
Beef Salad, 1039.
Pumpkin Pie, 1099.

Dinner.
Doxie Rockaway Oysters, 298.
Plain Consommé, 100.
Thon, 282.   Radishes, 292.
Halibut, with black Butter, 309, 159.
Chicken Croquettes, with Mushrooms, 276.
Venison Steak, Londonderry sauce, 880.
Stuffed Cucumbers, 937.
Roast Goose, Stuffed with Chestnuts, 808.
Chicory Salad, 1045.
Charlotte au Café, 1262.
Coffee, 1349.

Thursday, November —.

Breakfast.
Eggs à la Tripe, 419.
Broiled Deviled Soft-shelled Crabs, 369.
Mutton Kidneys, Sautés au Madère, 662.
Potatoes à la Rice, 1007.
Rice à la Française, 1180.

Luncheon.
Stewed Tripe à la Lyonnaise, 548.
Broiled Grouse on Toast, with Bacon, 854.
Spaghetti au Gratin, 961.
Peach Marmalade, 1331.

Dinner.
Blue Point Oysters, 298.
Gumbo, with Frogs, 23.
Celery, 290.   Sardines, 283.
Sole à la Joinville, 322.
Sweetbreads à la Duxelle, 608.
Potato Croquettes, 997.
Lamb Chops, maison d'or, 683.
String Beans, 948.
Roast Red-heads, 876.
Escarole Salad, 1055.
Orange Pudding, 1158.
Coffee, 1349.

Friday, November —.

Breakfast.
Sardine Omelet, 468.
Broiled Codfish à l'Hollandaise, 329, 160.
Tripe à la Lyonnaise, 548.
Broiled Sweet Potatoes, 983.
Jamaica-rum Jelly, 1320.

Luncheon.
Oyster Patties, 387.
Porterhouse Steak, with Watercress, 524.
Hashed Potatoes au Gratin, 1004.
Lobster Salad, 1061.
Iced Timbale of Rice, 1175.

Dinner.
Clams, 300.
Cream of Barley, 77.
Radishes, 292.   Mortadella, 287.
Haddock, Cream sauce, 352, 181.
Suprême of Partridge à la Rothschild, 790.
Stuffed Peppers, 975.
Ballotin of Lamb, with Peas, 675.
Roast Loin of Venison, Currant-jelly sauce, 878.
Lettuce Salad, 1059.
Omelet Célestine, 477.
Coffee, 1349.

Saturday, November —.

Breakfast.

Eggs à la Post, 1366.
Fresh Mackerel, maître d'hôtel, 329.
Broiled Lamb Fries à la Diable, 672.
Fritters Soufflées, 1192.

Luncheon.

Picked-up Codfish, 346.
Mignons Filets à la Brown, 1389.
Stuffed Lettuce, 953.
Boiled Apple Dumplings, 1127.

Dinner.

Prince's Bay Oysters, 298.
Consommé Suédoise, 122.
Anchovies, 284.   Celery, 290.
Red-snapper, Cream sauce, 352, 181.
Grenadins of Veal à l'Africaine, 589.
Stewed Corn, 964.
Chicken, Sauté à la Parmentier, 773.
Stuffed Tomatoes, 1023.
Roast Squabs, 816.
Watercress Salad, 1072.
Home-made Cake, 1220.
Coffee, 1349.

Sunday, November —.

Breakfast.

Omelet Raspail, 467.
Broiled Bluefish, maître d'hôtel, 329.
Venison Steak, Currant Jelly, 884.
Fried Potatoes, 993.
Crême en Mousse au Maraschino, 1257.

Luncheon.

Pompano, with White Wine, 342.
Broiled Chicken, with Bacon, 756.
Salad à l'Italienne, 1036.
Charlotte Russe, 1261.

Dinner.

Massachusetts Bay Oysters, 298.
Tomato à l'Andalouse, 58.
Lyons Sausage, 286.   Radishes, 292.
Lobster à la Newburg, 359.
Sweetbreads, Soubise, 606.
Artichoke-bottoms, Florentine, 903.
Civet of Rabbit à la Parisienne, 888.
String Beans, 948.
Punch à la Lorenzo Delmonio, 1303.
Canvas-back Ducks, Currant Jelly, 874, 1326.
Celery, Mayonnaise Salad, 1042.
Cabinet Pudding à la Sadi-Carnot, 1164.
Gorgonzolla Cheese.
Coffee, 1349.

Monday, November —.

Breakfast.

Eggs au Miroir, 425.
Porgies à l'Italienne, 337.
Lamb Chops, with Bacon, 647, 754.
Potatoes, Duchesse, 1006.
Rice au Lait d'Amandes, 1170.

Luncheon.

Stuffed, Deviled Crabs, 370.
Hashed Chicken à la Polonaise, 803.
Lobster Salad à la Plummer, 1062.
Cherry Pie, 1098.

Dinner.

Mill Pond Oysters, 298.
Purée Bretonne, 45.
Celery, 290.   Olives.
Broiled Salmon Tails, 308.
Double Porterhouse Steak, with Marrow, 525, 244.
Potatoes à la Parisienne, 986.
Chicken, Sauté à la Bohémienne, 778.
Brussels Sprouts, 922.
Roast Partridge, 843.
Watercress Salad, 1072.
Indian Pudding, 1145.
Coffee, 1349.

Tuesday, November —.

Breakfast.
Eggs à la Bennett, 447.
Oysters à la Arthur Sullivan, 1367.
Hashed Lamb à la Polonaise, 700.
Baked Potatoes.
Brioches Fluttes, 1204.

Luncheon.
Scallops, St. Jean, 371.
Sausages, Gastronome, 740.
Cauliflower au Gratin, 926.
Crême Renversée, 1252.

Dinner.
Clams, 300.
Consommé Tapioca, 104.
Tomatoes, 288.   Celery, 290.
Sheep's-head à la Créole, 339.
Sweetbreads, Piqués à la Financière, 603.
Fillet of Venison, Currant-jelly sauce, 884.
Spinach, with Gravy, 943.
Roast Lamb, 585.
Celery Salad, 1041.
Méringues Panachées, 1302.
Coffee, 1349.

Wednesday, November —.

Breakfast.
Plain Omelet, 450.
Broiled Haddock, Anchovy Butter, 310, 146.
Pig's Feet à la Boston, 730.
Stewed Potatoes, 995.
Waffles, with Sugar, 1196.

Luncheon.
Broiled Smelts, Béarnaise sauce, 353.
Beefsteak Pie à l'Américaine, 488.
Macaroni au Gratin, 955.
Mille-feuilles, 1223.

Dinner.
Small Rockaway Oysters, 298.
Cream of Game, 83.
Radishes, 288.   Olives.
Bass à la Chambord, 343.
Escalops of Veal à l'Italienne, 572.
Corn, Sauté with Butter, 964.
Squabs en Crapaudine, 819.
Stuffed Tomatoes, 1023.
Roast Grouse sur Canapé, 852.
Chicory Salad, 1045.
Fritters Soufflées à la Vanille, 1192.
Coffee, 1349.

THANKSGIVING DAY.

Thursday, November ―..

Breakfast.

Eggs à la Chipolata, 442.
Blackfish au Gratin, 356.
Calf's-head à la Cavour. 638.
Stewed Oyster-plant, 1018.
Preserved Green-gages, 1344.

Luncheon.

Fried Frogs, sauce Tartare, 400, 207.
Minced Beef à la Grecque, 500, 237.
Sweet Potatoes, Soufflées, 1010.
Pear Tarts, 1109.

Dinner.

Shrewsbury Oysters, 298.
Giblet à l'Ecossaise, 20.
Mortadella, 287. Celery, 290.
Codfish, Egg sauce, 352, 161.
Lamb Chops à la Robinson, 682.
Croquettes of Macaroni, 279.
Curry of Chicken à l'Éspagnole, 793.
Mushrooms on Toast, 916.
Punch en Surprise, 1309.
Roast Turkey, Cranberry sauce, 800, 1329.
Celery Salad, 1042.
Mince Pie, 1082.
Strachino Cheese.
Coffee, 1349.

Friday, November —.

Breakfast.
Crab Omelet, 455;
Fish Balls, 347.
Broiled Sheep's-feet, Tartare sauce, 654, 207.
Mashed Potatoes, 998.
Rice à la Condé, 1181.

Luncheon.
Soft Clams à la Merrill, 389.
Chicken Pot-pie, 757.
Broiled Egg-plant, 908.
French Pancake, 1186.

Dinner.
Kirtig's Oysters, 298.
Bouille-à-Baisse, 1.
Anchovies, 284.   Radishes, 292.
Red-snapper, with Cream, 352, 181.
Breast of Turkey à la Robinson, 807.
Fried Oyster-plant, 1021.
Sweetbreads à la Parisienne, 613.
French Peas.
Roast Plovers, 865.
Lettuce Salad, 1058.
Apricot Pudding à la Richelieu, 1151.
Coffee, 1349.

Saturday, November —.

Breakfast.
Eggs à la Bourguignonne, 411.
Picked-up Codfish, 346.
Minced Beef à la Provençale, 500.
Saratogo Potatoes, 1011.
Brioche, 1201.

Luncheon.
Lobster en Chevreuse, 362.
Corned Beef and Cabbage, 490.
Russian Salad, 1065.
Vanilla Eclairs, 1245.

Dinner.
Little Neck Clams, 300.
Frogs à l'Espagnole, 25.
Tomatoes, 288.   Olives.
Canapé Lorenzo, 391.
Suckling Pig, Apple sauce, 720.
Celery à la Bonne Femme, 928.
Chicken, Sauté with Tarragon, 774.
Stuffed Peppers, 975.
Woodcock sur Canapé, 871.
Celery, Mayonnaise Salad, 1042.
Omelet au Rhum, 476.
Coffee, 1349.

Sunday, December —.

Breakfast.
Eggs à la Turque, 439.
Boned, Broiled Smelts à la Béarnaise, 353.
Hashed Lamb à la Zingara, 652.
Turnips, with Gravy, 967.
Stewed Prunes, 1330.

Luncheon.
Terrapin à la Baltimore, 396.
Broiled Grouse à la Pomeroy, 1390.
Potato Croquettes, 997.
Timbales à l'Ecossaise, 261.
Crème en Mousse au Cognac, 1258.

Dinner.
Oysters, 298.
Sorrel, with Asparagus-tops, 41.
Celery, 290.   Radishes, 292.
Boiled Halibut, sauce Hollandaise, 309, 160.
Tenderloin, Piqué à la Provençale, 518.
Stewed Tomatoes, 1027.
Veal Cutlets à la Maréchale, 562.
Spinach à l'Anglaise, 940.
Oranges Glacées à la Geo. Renauldt, 1297.
Roast Quails, 834.
Lettuce Salad, 1057.
St. Honoré à la Rose Delmonico, 1212.
Swiss Cheese.
Coffee, 1349.

Monday, December —.

Breakfast.
Kidney Omelet, 463.
Broiled Ham, 753.
Tripe à la Créole, 545.
Potatoes à la Hanna, 1012.
Cream Renversée, 1252.

Luncheon.
Bass, Ravigote sauce, 352, 147.
Breaded Mutton Chops, Tomato sauce, 643, 205.
Fried Sweet Potatoes, 993.
Marcella-wine Jelly à la Castellar, 1325.

Dinner.
Clams, 300.
Paysanne, 53.
Lyons Sausage, 286.   Watercress, 1072.
Blackfish à la maître d'hôtel, 329.
Fried Chicken, Cream sauce, 301, 181.
Brussels Sprouts, 922.
Breast of Lamb à la Jardinière, 702.
Macaroni à l'Italienne, 956.
Roast Teal Ducks, with Hominy, 859, 1035.
Doucette Salad, 1052.
Rum Cake, 1229.
Coffee, 1349.

Tuesday, December —.

Breakfast.
Eggs en Panade, 436.
Codfish, Hollandaise sauce, 352, 160.
Veal Cutlets à la Philadelphia, 565.
Broiled Sweet Potatoes, 983.
Buckwheat Cakes, 1183.

Luncheon.
Crabs, St. Laurent, 372.
Beef-tongue, sauce Piquante, 533.
Lima Beans, 952.
Japanese Salad, 1075.
Strawberry Tarts, 1117.

Dinner.
Blue Point Oysters, 298.
Mikado, 32.
Radishes, 292.   Caviare, 281.
Red-snapper à la Bordelaise, 341.
Chicken, Sauté à la Marengo, 771.
Corn, Stewed with Butter, 964.
Coquilles of Sweetbreads à la Dreux, 621.
Brussels Sprouts, 922.
Roast Plover and Watercress, 865.
Barbe de Capucine Salad, 1038.
Apple Fritters, 1191.
Coffee, 1349.

Wednesday, December —.

Breakfast.
Omelet, with fine Herbs, 451.
Fried Scallops, Tomato sauce, 301, 205.
Lamb Steak, with Bacon, 716, 754.
Potatoes, maître d'hôtel, 985.
Brioche Condé, 1203.

Luncheon.
Fried Porgies, Egg sauce, 320, 161.
Tendron of Veal, Morlaisienne, 635.
Risotto à la Milanaise, 1017.
Charlotte Russe, 1261.

Dinner.
Rockaway Oysters, 298.
Chicken à la Piémontaise, 63.
Lyons Sausage, 286.   Olives.
Smelts à la Toulouse, 354.
Cromesquis of Chicken à la Reine, 765.
Stuffed Onions, 970.
Tenderloin, Piqué à la Portugaise, 517.
Cardons, with Marrow, 931.
Roast Grouse, with Watercress, 852.
Celery Salad, 1042.
Peach Pudding à la Richelieu, 1150.
Coffee, 1349.

Thursday, December —.

Breakfast.
Eggs à la Vanderbilt, 420.
Haddock, Cream sauce, 352, 181.
Broiled Pig's Feet à la Boston, 730.
Saratoga Potatoes, 1011.
German Pancake, 1188.

Luncheon.
Stuffed Deviled Lobster, 367.
Vol-au-Vent, Financière, 810.
Lamb-tongue Salad, 1056.
Apple Cake, 1211.

Dinner.
Clams, 300.
Cream of Lettuce, 87.
Sardines, 283.   Celery, 290.
Oysters en Petites Caisses, 275.
Sweetbreads à la Duxelle, 608.
Cauliflower, Hollandaise, 923, 160.
Squabs en Crapaudine, 819.
Stuffed Cucumbers, 937.
Roast Canvas-back Ducks, Currant Jelly, 874, 1326.
Chicory Salad, 1045.
Vanilla Ice-cream, 1271.
Biscuits à la Livornaise, 1233.
Coffee, 1349.

Friday, December —.

Breakfast.
Oyster Omelet, 452.
Broiled Salt Mackerel, 329.
Lamb Fries, Tomato sauce, 673.
Fried Potatoes, 993.
Preserved Raspberries, 1346.

Luncheon.
Pompano, with fine Herbs, 331.
Stewed Mutton, with Oyster-plant, 703.
Potatoes à l'Hollandaise, 999.
Apple Méringue Pie, 1103.

Dinner.
East River Oysters, 298.
Consommé au Spaghetti, 103.
Radishes, 292.   Celery, 290.
Perch au Gratin, 356.
Tenderloin, Piqué à la Duchesse, 516.
Cêpes à la Bordelaise, 913.
Lamb Chops à la Clichy, 684.
French Peas.
Partridge, Piqué sur Canapé, 843.
Escarole Salad, 1055.
Plum Pudding, 1163.
Coffee, 1349.

Saturday, December —.

Breakfast.
Barley and Cream.
Eggs à la Chipolata, 442.
Mutton Chops, Breaded, 643.
Lima Beans, with Cream, 952.
Malaga Grapes.

Luncheon.
Stuffed Oysters à la Mali, 386.
Breast of Veal à la Milanaise, 596.
Macédoine Salad, 1063.
Mince Pie, 1082.

Dinner.
Little Neck Clams, 300.
Purée of Partridge à la Destaing, 89.
Tomatoes, 292.   Olives.
Boiled Codfish, Oyster sauce, 352.
Salmi of Pigeons à la Moderne, 870.
Spinach au Gras, 943.
Fillet of Venison, Port-wine sauce, 891.
Succotash, 1022.
Roast Turkey, 800.
Lettuce Salad, 1058.
Almond Cake, Glacé, 1208.
Coffee, 1349.

Sunday, December —.

Breakfast.
Spanish Omelet, 472.
Fried Smelts, Tartare sauce, 301, 207.
Porterhouse Steak, 524.
Stewed Potatoes, 995.
Crême en Mousse au Café, 1253.

Luncheon.
Soft Clams à la Merrill, 389.
Breast of Turkey à la Robinson, 807.
Lobster Salad à la Plummer, 1062.
Pie à la Martha Washington, 1105.

Dinner.
Oysters, 298.
Cream of Celery, 71.
Radishes, 292.   Mortadella, 287.
Sheep's-head, maitre d'hôtel, 329.
Cucumber Salad, 289.
Chartreuse of Partridge, 849.
Stuffed Tomatoes, 1023.
Sweetbreads à la Montglas, 615.
String Beans, 948.
Punch à la Cardinal, 1306.
Saddle of Venison, with Currant Jelly, 878.
Celery Salad, 1041.
Neapolitan Ice-cream, 1292.
Petites Méringues à la Ch. C. Delmonico, 1249.
Camembert Cheese.
Coffee, 1349.

Monday, December —.

Breakfast.
Poached Eggs on Anchovy Toast, 404, 280.
Fish Balls, 347.
Beef-tongue, Piquante sauce, 533.
Mashed Potatoes au Gratin, 998.
Rice and Cream à la Croce, 1296.

Luncheon.
Oyster Patties, 387.
Salmi of Ducklings à l'Américaine, 826.
Sweet Potatoes Soufflées, 1010.
Cocoanut Pie, 1101.

Dinner.
Linn Haven Oysters, 298.
Consommé, Printanier Royale, 124.
Olives.   Watercress, 1072.
Bass aux fines Herbes, 331.
Civet of Rabbit à la Française, 887.
Artichokes, Florentine, 903.
Lamb Chops, maison d'or, 683.
Asparagus-tops à la Béchamel, 904, 154.
Roast Chicken, with Gravy, 755.
Doucette Salad, 1054.
Baked Apple Dumplings, 1192.
Coffee, 1349.

Tuesday, December —.

Breakfast.
Omelet, with Cheese, 469.
Cod's Tongues à la Poulette, 351.
Chicken Livers Sautés au Madère, 707.
Potato Croquettes, 997.
Preserved Egg-plums, 1343.

Luncheon.
Haddock, with White Wine, 342.
Veal Cutlets à la Milanaise, 563.
Crab Salad, 1047.
Savarin à l'Anglaise, 1199.

Dinner.
Shrewsbury Oysters, 298.
Clear Green Turtle, 18.
Radishes, 292.   Thon, 282.
Broiled Deviled Lobster, 364.
Calf's-head à la Vinaigrette, 640.
Spinach à la Vieille Mode, 941.
Suprême of Partridge à la Richelieu, 858.
Brussels Sprouts, 922.
Red-head Ducks, with Hominy, 876, 1035.
Lettuce Salad, 1057.
Pudding à la Porfirio Diaz, 1135.
Coffee, 1349.

Wednesday, December —.

Breakfast.
Scrambled Eggs, with Mushrooms, 405.
Oysters en Brochette au Petit Salé, 385.
Mutton Hash au Gratin, 653.
Stewed Corn, 964.
French Pancake, 1186.

Luncheon.
Matelote of Eels, 332.
Curry of Chicken à l'Indienne, 792.
Cauliflower, with Butter, 925.
Omelet Soufflée, 474.

Dinner.
Clams, 300.
Purée Parmentier, 44.
Watercress, 1072. Mortadella, 1087.
Frogs à l'Espagnole, 401.
Broiled Tenderloin à la Trianon, 507.
French Peas.
Sweetbreads à la Duxelle, 608.
Lima Beans, 952.
Roast Grouse sur Canapé, 852.
Doucette and Beet-root Salad, 1053.
Bread Pudding, 1132.
Coffee, 1349.

Thursday, December —.

Breakfast.
Omelet, with Peas, 459.
Broiled Sardines on Toast, 403.
Broiled Venison Steak, Currant Jelly, 884.
Potatoes, Hollandaise, 999.
Stewed Prunes à la Dufour, 1330.

Luncheon.
Flounders, maître d'hôtel, 329.
Beefsteak Pie à l'Américaine, 488.
Stuffed Cabbage, 919.
Green-gage Pie, 1093.

Dinner.
Doxie Rockaway Oysters, 298.
Consommé Impérial, 111.
Olives. Celery, 290.
Red-snapper à l'Icarienne, 336.
Croquettes of Lamb, Béarnaise sauce, 679, 166.
Turban of Chicken à la Cleveland, 791.
Peas, with Cream, 980.
Foies-Gras en Bellevue.
Woodcock sur Canapé, 871.
Celery, 1041.
Apple Charlotte, 1167.
Coffee, 1349.

Friday, December —.

Breakfast.
Lobster Omelet, 454.
Boiled Codfish, Hollandaise sauce, 352, 160.
Broiled Calf's Liver and Bacon, 584.
Fried Egg-plant, 907.
Brioches Fluttes, 1204.

Luncheon.
Oysters à la Baltimore, 388.
Sausages à l'Anglaise, 736.
Fried Sweet Potatoes, 993.
Custard Pie, 1100.

Dinner.
Clams, 300.
Chicken à la Turque, 69.
Radishes, 292. Lyons Sausage, 286.
Matelote of Eels, 332.
Ballotin of Squab à l'Italienne, 818.
Stuffed Egg-plant, 909.
Tenderloin, Marinated, Russian sauce, 511.
String Beans, 948.
Roast Veal, 585.
Chicory Salad, 1045.
Sago Pudding, 1140.
Coffee, 1349.

Saturday, December —.

Breakfast.

Hominy and Cream, 1034.
Ham and Eggs, 412, 753.
Broiled Deviled Mutton Kidneys, 715.
Fried Potatoes, 993.
Baked Apples, 1124.

Luncheon.

Mussels à la Marinière, 378.
Garnished Sourkrout, 924.
Beef Salad, 1039.
Jamaica-rum Jelly, 1320.
Gingerbread, 1213.

Dinner.

Cherry-stone Oysters, 398.
Menestra, 36.
Olives.   Tomatoes, 288.
Lobster Croquettes, sauce Aurore, 365, 182.
Mignons Filets, Bohémienne, 513.
Macaroni à l'Italienne, 956.
Chicken Vol-au-Vent, with Mushrooms, 812.
French Peas.
Roast Quails, 834.
Escarole Salad, 1055.
Baba au Madère, 1217.
Coffee, 1349.

Sunday, December —.

Breakfast.

Omelet Raspail, 467.
Halibut Steaks, maître d'hôtel, 310.
Minced Beef à l'Ecarlate, 500, 247.
Sweet Potatoes, Hollandaise, 999.
Apricot Preserves, 1340.

Luncheon.

Lobster à la Newburg, 359.
Broiled Chicken, with Bacon, 756.
Potatoes, Julienne, 1013.
Timbales à la Schultze, 263.
Apple Méringue Pie, 1103.

Dinner.

Blue Point Oysters, 298.
Consommé Duchesse, 125.
Celery, 290.   Radishes, 292.
Fillet of Sole au Gratin, 319.
Coquilles of Chicken à l'Anglaise, 271.
Tomatoes à la Bock, 1026.
Tenderloin, Piqué à la Parisienne, 516, 495.
Beans Panachées, 950.
Punch à la Lalla Rookh, 1308.
Roast Partridges, with Watercress, 843.
Lettuce Salad, 1057.
St. Honoré à la Rose Delmonico, 1212.
Roquefort Cheese.
Coffee, 1349.

Monday, December —.

Breakfast.

Eggs à la Bonne Femme, 432.
Fried Frost-fish, 301.
Mutton Chops, sauce Colbert, 647, 190.
Potatoes, Duchesse, 1006.
Whipped Cream à la Vanille, 1254.

Luncheon.

Stuffed Deviled Crabs, 370.
Minced Veal à la Biscaënne, 576.
Sorrel au Gras, 974.
Rhubarb Tarts, 1112.

Dinner.

Parker Bay Oysters, 298.
Jardinière, 28.
Olives.   Mortadella, 287.
Red-snapper à la Vénitienne, 338.
Sweetbreads au Salpicon, 605.
Stuffed Lettuce, 953.
Chicken à la Maryland, 785.
Stewed Tomatoes, 1027.
Roast Beef, 527.
Watercress Salad, 1072.
Raspberry Water-ice, 1281.
Fancy Almond Cakes, 1239.
Coffee, 1349.

Tuesday, December —.

Breakfast.
Oatmeal and Cream.
Sausage Omelet, 465.
Hamburg Steak, Russian sauce, 526.
Potatoes, Windsor, 1008.
Small Brioches, 1202.

Luncheon.
Oysters à la Pompadour, 384.
Stewed Veal, Marengo, 624.
Sweet Potatoes, Soufflées, 1010.
Pumpkin Pie, 1099.

Dinner.
Doxie Rockaway Oysters, 298.
Mock Turtle, 17.
Radishes, 292.   Thon, 282.
Smelts, Béarnaise, 353.
Saddle of Venison, Port Wine sauce, 878, 891.
Purée of Chestnuts, 131.
Sweetbreads, with Asparagus-tops, 607.
Lima Beans, 952.
Roast Ducklings, 824.
Celery Salad, 1042.
Pudding à la U. S. Grant, 1159.
Coffee, 1349.

Wednesday, December —.

Breakfast.
Eggs au Soleil, 415.
Fried Yellow Perch, 301.
Pig's Feet à la St. Hubert, 727.
Potato Croquettes, 997.
Apples and Rice, 1169.

Luncheon.
Black Bass, with White Wine, 342.
Sirloin Steak à la Bordelaise, 491.
Cauliflower au Gratin, 926.
Plum Pie, 1094.

Dinner.
Rockaway Oysters, 298.
Spaghetti, with Tomatoes, 56.
Celery, 290.   Caviare, 281.
Broiled Pompano, maître d'hôtel, 329.
Cucumber salad, 289.
Hashed Turkey à la Crème, 804.
Okras, Sautés à la Créole, 1031.
Lamb Chops à la Masséna, 687.
French Peas, with Lettuce, 977.
Roast Grouse, with Watercress, 852.
Chicory au Chapon-salad, 1046.
Méringues à l'Helvétienne, 1251.
Coffee, 1349.

Thursday, December —.

Breakfast.
Eggs à la Paysanne, 433.
Tripe à la Lyonnaise, 548.
Mignons Filets à la Provençale, 509, 518.
Hashed Potatoes au Gratin, 1004.
Wheat Cakes, 1184.

Luncheon.
Lobster Croquettes à la Victoria, 365, 208.
Stewed Beef à la Dufour, 541.
Timbales Lagardère, 809.
Boiled Apricot Dumplings, 1126.

Dinner.
Sound Oysters, 298.
Cream of Chicken, 82.
Radishes, 292.   Bologna Sausage, 286.
Frogs à la Poulette, 399.
Pillau of Chicken à la Turque, 782.
Stewed Corn, 963.
Broiled Partridge, with Bacon, 844, 754.
Spaghetti à l'Italienne, 960.
Roast Saddle of Mutton, 664.
Escarole Salad, 1055.
Cabinet Pudding à la Sadi-Carnot, 1164.
Coffee, 1349.

Friday, December —.

Breakfast.

Omelet Mexicaine, 473.
Fried Black-bass, 301.
Sausages à l'Anglaise, 736.
Saratoga Potatoes, 1011.
Peach Marmalade, 1331.

Luncheon.

Picked-up Codfish, 346.
Beefsteak Pie à l'Américaine, 488.
Lobster Salad, 1061.
Rice and Cream à la Croce, 1296.

Dinner.

Oak Island Oysters, 298.
Bisque of Clams, 8.
Sardines, 283.   Celery, 290.
Bouille-à-Baisse à la Marseillaise, 340.
Broiled Tenderloin à la Béarnaise, 492.
Tomatoes à la Reine, 1024.
Pigeon Cutlets à la Victoria, 815.
Fried Egg-plant, 907.
Roast Quails on Toast, 834.
Celery Salad, 1041.
Vanilla Ice-cream, 1271.
Petites Bouchées des Dames, 1237.
Coffee, 1349.

Saturday, December —.

Breakfast.

Eggs à la Valencienne, 421.
Broiled Sardines on Toast, 403.
Lamb Kidneys, Sautés à l'Italienne, 663.
Baked Potatoes.
Marcella-wine Jelly à la Castellar, 1325.

Luncheon.

Scallops à la Brestoise, 392.
Squabs à l'Américaine, 820.
Cauliflower au Gratin, 926.
Mince Pie, 1082.

Dinner.

Clams, 300.
Consommé Napolitaine, 127.
Radishes, 292.   Caviare, 281.
Haddock, Cream sauce, 352, 181.
Mignons Filets, with Marrow, 510.
Fried Egg-plant, 907.
Duck à la Rouennaise, 825.
Celery, with Cream, 929.
Roast Lamb, Mint sauce, 585, 169.
Chicory Salad, 1045.
Biscuits Tortoni, 1287.
Coffee, 1349.

Sunday, December —.

Breakfast.

Eggs à la Hyde, 448.
Fried Frogs' Legs, Tomato sauce, 400, 205.
Hashed Chicken, with Cream, 804.
Fried Oyster-plant, 1021.
Rice à la Condé, 1181.

Luncheon.

Stewed Terrapin à la Maryland, 397.
Broiled Red-head Ducks, Currant Jelly, 876, 1326.
Risotto à la Milanaise, 1017.
Japanese Salad, 1075.
Raspberry Tarts, 1118.

Dinner.

Small Rockaway Oysters, 298.
Chicken, with Leeks, 68.
Celery, 290.   Olives.
Stuffed Deviled Lobster, 367.
Salmi of Woodcock à la Gastronome, 842.
French Peas.
Sweetbreads à la Soubise, 606.
Tomatoes à la Bock, 1026.
Punch à la Lorenzo Delmonico, 1303.
Roast Grouse à la Sam Ward, 853.
Celery, Mayonnaise Salad, 1042.
Macédoine à la Cavour, 1298.
Biscuits Ambroisienne, 1234.
Camembert Cheese.
Coffee, 1349.

Monday, December —.

Breakfast.
Hominy, with Cream, 1034.
Eggs à l'Aurore, 444.
Broiled Venison Steaks, maître d'hôtel, 879, 145.
Fried Potatoes, 993.
Crême Renversée, 1252.

Luncheon.
Canapé Lorenzo, 391.
Mignons of Lamb à la Montebello, 1360, 249.
Brussels Sprouts, with Butter, 922.
Charlotte Russe, 1261.

Dinner.
Massachusetts Bay Oysters, 298.
Purée Faubonne, 46.
Celery, 290. Sardines, 283.
Red-snapper à la Bordelaise, 341.
Quails Braised, Celery sauce, 836.
Lamb Chops à la Maintenon, 685.
Cauliflower, Hollandaise, 925, 160.
Roast Plover sur Canapé, 865.
Doucette Salad, 1054.
Cocoanut Pudding, 1147.
Coffee, 1349.

Tuesday, December —.

Breakfast.
Smoked Beef Omelet, 461.
Stewed Oysters à la Baltimore, 388.
Broiled Lamb Chops, with Bacon, 647, 754.
Potatoes en Paille, 1014.
Preserved Strawberries, 1345.

Luncheon.
Scallops Brestoise, 392.
Soles à la Horly, 321.
Blanquette of Veal, with Nouilles, 552.
Oyster-plant à la Poulette, 1019.
Lobster Salad à la Plummer, 1062.
Rice and Cream à la Croce, 1296.

Dinner.
Chincoteague Oysters, 298.
Green Turtle, 16.
Anchovies, 284. Watercress, 1072.
Boned Deviled Smelts, sauce Tartare, 353, 207.
Boiled Turkey à l'Anglaise, 795.
French Peas.
Tenderloin à la Hussard, 519.
Stuffed Onions, 970.
Roast Saddle of Venison, 878.
Romaine Salad, 1064.
Omelet Soufflée, 474.
Coffee, 1349.

CHRISTMAS.

Wednesday, December —

Breakfast.

Eggs à l'Aurore, 444.
Broiled Salt Mackerel, 329.
Porterhouse Steak, 524.   Potatoes, Château, 1009.
Crème en Mousse au Maraschino, 1257.

Luncheon.

Lobster en Chevreuse, 362.
Chicken, Sauté with Tarragon, 774.
Broiled Sweet Potatoes, 983.
Pie à la Martha Washington, 1105.
Biscuits Glacés, 1286.

Dinner.

Small Rockaway Oysters, 298.
Consommé Printanier Royale, 124.
Celery, 290.   Radishes, 292.
Bouchées à la Reine, 270.
Terrapin à la Baltimore, 396.
Filets Mignons à la Bayard, 509, 231.
Stuffed Tomatoes, à la Reine, 1024.
Suprême of Partridge à la Périgueux, 850.
French Peas, with fresh Butter, 978.
Stuffed Deviled Lobster. 367.
Champagne Punch, 1307.
Canvas-back Ducks, with Currant Jelly, 874, 1326.
Lettuce and Egg Salad, 1058.
Nougat Pyramid, 1267.
Plombière à la Hamilton, 1370.
Petites Bouchées des Dames à la Mme. Astor, 1238.
Sweet Macaroons, 1210.
Lady-fingers, 1231.   Biscuits Richelieu, 1232.
Coffee, 1349.
Punch à la Czarina, 1312—to be served at 10 P. M.

Thursday, December —.

Breakfast.

Spanish Omelet, 472.
Fried Frost-fish, 301.
Hamburg Steak, Madeira sauce, 526, 185.
Potatoes, Lyonnaise, 991.
Prunes à la Général Dufour, 1330.

Luncheon.

Canapé Lorenzo, 391.
Broiled Calf's Liver and Bacon, 584.
Anchovy Salad, 1037.
Rice Pudding à l'Orange, 1130.

Dinner.

Mill Pond Oysters, 298.
Cream of Barley, 77.
Tomatoes, 288. Caviare, 281.
Stuffed Deviled Crabs, 370.
Croustade of Kidneys, with Mushrooms, 680.
Spinach, with Eggs, 940.
Broiled Tenderloin and Watercress, 503.
Stuffed Peppers, 975.
Roast Grouse, 852.
Escarole Salad, 1055.
Kirsch Omelet, 476.
Coffee, 1349.

Friday, December —.

Breakfast.

Scrambled Eggs, with Asparagus-tops, 406.
Cod's Tongues, black Butter, 349.
Hashed Turkey en Bordure, 805.
Broiled Sweet Potatoes, 983.
Baked Apples, 1124.

Luncheon.

Porgies, Tomato sauce, 301, 205.
Chicken Pot-pie, 757.
Russian Salad, 1065.
Madeleine, 1126.

Dinner.

Oysters, 298.
Consommé Chatelaine, 128.
Thon, 282. Celery, 290.
Red-snapper, Egg sauce, 352, 161.
Coquilles of Sweetbreads à la Dreux, 621.
Salmi of Reed-birds, maison d'or, 867.
Brussels Sprouts, 922.
Roast Chicken, 755.
Lettuce Salad, 1057.
Baba au Rhum, 1217.
Coffee, 1349.

Saturday, December —.

Breakfast.

Tomato Omelet à la Provençale, 457.
Fish Balls, 347.
Lamb en Brochette à la Dumas, 674.
Fried Potatoes, 993.
Brioche à la Condé, 1203.

Luncheon.

Stuffed Oysters à la Mali, 386.
Calf's-head à la Cavour, 638.
Stuffed Cabbage, 919.
Potato Salad, 1073.
Charlotte au Café, 1262.

Dinner.

Clams, 300.
Chicken à la Portugaise, 66.
Watercress, 1072. Sardines, 283.
Sheep's-head, maître d'hôtel, 329.
Salmi of Ducks, with Turnips, 826.
Spaghetti Napolitaine, 959.
Tenderloin, Piqué à la Florentine, 506.
Roast Red-heads, with Hominy, 876, 1035.
Celery Salad, 1042.
Plombière à la Kingman, 1294.
Coffee, 1349.

Sunday, December —.

Breakfast.

Eggs à la Bourguignonne, 411.
Broiled Frogs, maitre d'hôtel, 398.
Broiled Beefsteak à la Béarnaise, 492.
Stewed Tomatoes, 1027.
Buckwheat Cakes, 1183.

Luncheon.

Smelts, Toulouse, 354.
Blanquette of Veal, with Peas, 551.
Chicken Salad, 1044.
Mince Pie, 1082.

Dinner.

Blue Point Oysters, 298.
Cream of Asparagus, 70.
Radishes, 292.   Celery, 290.
Bass à la Chambord, 343.
Chicken Fricassé à la Reine, 780.
Brussels Sprouts, 922.
Broiled Tenderloin aux Gourmets, 508.
Stuffed Egg-plant, 909.
Punch en Surprise, 1309.
Roast Grouse à la Sam Ward, 853.
Chicory Salad, 1045.
Diplomatic Pudding, 1129.
Strachino Cheese.
Coffee, 1349.

Monday, December —.

Breakfast.

Omelet, with fine Herbs, 451.
Minced Beef à la Catalan, 502.
Sausages à l'Italienne, 737.
Potatoes, Julienne, 1013.
Apple Fritters, 1191.

Luncheon.

Clams à la Merrill, 389.
Stewed Lamb aux Flageolets, 707.
Oyster-plant, Poulette, 1019.
Rice and Apples à la Czar, 1173.

Dinner.

East River Oysters, 298.
Consommé Garibaldi, 112.
Olives.   Mortadella, 287.
Codfish, Oyster sauce, 352.
Leg of Mutton, Bretonne, 650.
Onions, with Cream, 968.
Squabs en Compote, 822.
Cauliflower au Gratin, 926.
Roast Beef, 527.
Escarole Salad, 1055.
Blanc-Manger à la J. Delmonico, 1270.
Coffee, 1349.

Tuesday, December —.

Breakfast.

Eggs à la Meyerbeer, 437.
Fried Soft-shelled Crabs, 368.
Tripe à la Lyonnaise, 548.
Saratoga Potatoes, 1011.
German Pancake, with Apples, 1189.

Luncheon.

Lobster à la Newburg, 359.
Breaded Veal Cutlets, Tomato sauce, 563.
French Peas.
Caviare on Toast, 281.
Cherry Tarts, 1111.

Dinner.

Small Rockaway Oysters, 298.
Bisque of Lobster, 10.
Celery, 290.   Radishes, 292.
Matelote of Bass, 332.
Salmi of Grouse à la Walter Scott, 856.
Tenderloin of Beef, Piqué à la Sévigné, 520.
Stewed Tomatoes, 1027.
Roast Partridge sur Canapé, 843.
Lettuce Salad, 1059.
Neapolitan Ice-cream, 1292.
Small Méringues à la Ch. C. Delmonico, 1249.
Coffee, 1349.

SOUPS.

1. Bouille-à-Baisse.—Chop two medium-sized, peeled, sound onions very fine, with one medium-sized, fine, fresh, green pepper, the same way, and put them in a pan on the hot range, with a gill of sweet oil. When well browned, moisten with three pints of hot white broth (No. 99). Cut three skinned, good-sized, sound, well-washed potatoes into quarters, also three fine, good-sized, sound, red, peeled tomatoes into rather small pieces; put all in the soup. Season with a pinch of salt (the equivalent of a tablespoonful) and half a pinch of pepper, and then boil well for fully one hour and a half, placing into it a strong bouquet (No. 254) at the beginning, also half a teaspoonful of powdered saffron, diluted in a little water; when nearly done, add one pound of boned codfish, cut into small pieces; boil again for three minutes, pour into a hot soup tureen, and serve with six slices of toasted bread.

2. Brunoise.—Pare and cut into small squares three medium-sized carrots, one turnip, half an onion, and two leeks; put these with two ounces of butter in a covered saucepan for a few moments; moisten with three pints of broth (No. 99), season with half a tablespoonful of salt, and a teaspoonful of pepper. Cook for three-quarters of an hour, and then add a handful of chiffonade (No. 132); when ready, serve with six slices of toasted bread.

3. Brunoise with Rice.—The same as for No. 2, adding half a cupful of uncooked rice about seventeen minutes before serving; taste to see if sufficiently seasoned, and serve.

4. Brunoise with Sorrel.—The same, adding two good handfuls of chopped sorrel about two minutes before serving.

5. Beef à l'Anglaise.—Cut up into small squares a quarter of a pound of raw, lean beef; brown them a little in a saucepan on the hot range, then moisten with three pints of broth (No. 99), add half a pint of printanier (No. 51), a handful of barley, and half a pinch each of salt and pepper. Boil thoroughly for half an hour, and a few moments before serving put in one medium-sized sliced tomato, taste to see if sufficiently seasoned, then pour the soup into a hot tureen, and send to the table.

6. Beef à l'Ecossaise, thickened.—Brown in a little fat, in a saucepan, a quarter of a pound of small squares of lean beef and a sliced onion, moisten with three pints of broth (No. 99), adding half a cup of oatmeal, a small glass of Madeira wine, half a tablespoonful of salt and a teaspoonful of pepper. Let cook for thirty minutes, then serve.

7. Buserca.—Brown in a saucepan one pint of raw printanier (No. 51), adding half a pint of chopped celery; let steam gently for about ten minutes, then moisten with three pints of white broth (No. 99) and a quarter of a pound of very finely shred tripe; season with half a tablespoonful of salt and a teaspoonful of pepper. Cook thoroughly for twenty-five minutes, and serve with a little grated cheese, separate.

8. Bisque of Clams.—Open twelve large clams, scald them whole in their own juice, and drain. Then pound them in a mortar, and put them back into a saucepan with the same water. Add one quart of white broth (No. 99), one bouquet (No. 254), half a pint of raw rice, a little pepper, but no salt; boil for forty-five minutes, then strain through a fine sieve, adding half a cupful of good cream. Let it heat, but not boil again, and serve with very small squares of fried bread.

9. Bisque of Crabs.—Boil four hard-shelled crabs in salted water for about fifteen minutes; wash and drain them well, and proceed as for No. 8.

10. Bisque of Lobster.—The same as for No. 8. Two pounds of lobster boiled in the shell will be sufficient; serve with small squares of boiled lobster claw, cut in dice.

11. Croûte-au-Pot.—Take two carrots cut in round slices, one turnip, cut the same, adding a few pieces of celery and half a quarter of chopped-up cabbage; stew them for ten minutes in a covered saucepan, with two ounces of butter; then moisten with three pints of white broth (No. 99), adding half a tablespoonful of salt and a teaspoonful of pepper. Boil well for thirty minutes, and serve with six pieces of dry toasted rolls.

12. Fish Chowder, Boston style.—Take a nice live codfish of about six pounds, cut the head off and remove all the bones, then cut the fish into square pieces, place them in a bowl, and add half a pinch of salt and a pint of cold water so as to have the flesh firm. Take the head and bones, place them in a saucepan with two quarts of white broth (No. 99) on the stove, and as soon as it comes to a boil, skim it well. Season with one pinch of salt and half a pinch of pepper. Let boil for twenty minutes. Peel and slice very fine one small, sound onion, place it in a saucepan with one ounce of butter, half an ounce of salt pork, cut in small dice-shaped pieces, let cook for five minutes, then add two tablespoonfuls of flour. Stir well together for three minutes on a brisk fire, being careful not to let it get brown. Strain the broth into a bowl, and when all strained in, add it to the flour, stirring well until all the broth is added. Let boil for ten minutes. Cut two good-sized, sound potatoes in small dice-shaped pieces, add them to the soup. Boil five minutes. Drain the codfish, wash it once more, and add it to the soup. Boil five minutes more; add half a pint of cold milk, being very careful not to allow to boil again; sprinkle a teaspoonful of chopped parsley over, and serve very hot.

13. Clam Chowder.—Wash six fine, medium-sized potatoes, peel and cut them into small dice-shaped pieces, wash again in fresh water, take them up with a skimmer; place them in a stewpan large enough to hold three quarts. Immediately add two quarts of cold water (not placing the pan on the fire until so mentioned). Peel one medium-sized, sound onion, chop it up very fine, and place it on a plate. Take a quarter of a bunch of well-washed parsley greens (suppressing the stalks), place it with the onions; wash well two branches of soup celery, chop it up very fine, place it with the parsley and onions, and add all these in the stewpan. Place the pan on a brisk fire. Season with a light pinch of salt, adding at the same time a light tablespoonful of good butter. Let all cook until the pototoes are nearly done; eighteen minutes will be sufficient. Cut out from a piece of fresh pork, *crosswise*, one slice a third of an inch thick, then cut it in pieces a third of an inch square, fry, and reduce it in a pan on the hot stove for four minutes. Add it to the broth, add also three-quarters of a teaspoonful of branch dry thyme. Lightly scald four fine, medium-sized tomatoes, peel and cut them into small pieces and add them to the preparation. Open and place in a bowl twenty-four medium-sized, fine, fresh clams; pour into another bowl half of their juice. Place the clams on a wooden board, cut each one into four equal pieces, and immediately plunge them into the pan with the rest; gently mix, so as to prevent burning at the bottom while boiling, for two minutes. Range the pan on the corner of the stove to keep warm. Season with a saltspoonful of black pepper, one tablespoonful of Worcestershire sauce, gently stir the whole with a wooden spoon; break in two pilot crackers in small pieces, stir a little again. Leave two minutes longer in the same position, but under no circumstances allow to boil. Pour it into a hot soup-tureen, and serve.

14. Chiffonade.—Wash well, drain, and chop up very fine one quart of sorrel with the green leaves of a lettuce-head. Brown in a saucepan, with two ounces of butter and a sliced onion, seasoning with half a tablespoonful of salt and a teaspoonful of pepper. Moisten with three pints of white broth (No. 99), add a handful of peas, the same of string beans and asparagus tops; boil for three-quarters of an hour with an ounce of butter; serve with six slices of toasted bread.

15. How to Prepare Green Turtle.—Select a medium-sized turtle, cut off the head, and let it bleed for twelve hours. Remove the bones by opening the sides; cut the carcass in pieces, and blanch them for three minutes in boiling water. Lift off the top shell and place it in a saucepan, covering it with white broth (No. 99), a handful of whole pepper, one dozen cloves, half a bunch of thyme, and six bay leaves (all the above spices and herbs carefully tied in a white cloth). Add a handful of salt, and cook for about one hour. Drain, remove the bones, cut the rest in dice-sized squares. Let the broth be reduced to three-fourths its quantity, then put in the white, lean meat, letting it cook for ten minutes, and then add the green part (the shell) of the turtle. Fill some medium-sized pots with this, and when cooled off pour hot lard over the tops. A good glassful of Madeira wine can be added to the broth, according to taste.

16. Green Turtle Soup.—Place a pint of green turtle, cut into pieces (No. 15) in a saucepan with two pints of broth (No. 99); add a bouquet

(No. 254), a glassful of Madeira wine, a little bit of red pepper, half a tablespoonful of salt, a little grated nutmeg, a teaspoonful of English sauce, and a cupful of Espagnole sauce (No. 151). Boil for twenty minutes, and serve with six slices of peeled lemon, after suppressing the bouquet.

17. Mock Turtle.—To be prepared as for green turtle (No. 16), substituting a pint of cooked calf's-head for the turtle.

18. Clear Green Turtle.—Proceed the same as for the green turtle (No. 16), omitting the Espagnole sauce, but adding two tablespoonfuls of dissolved corn-starch, also a quarter of a glassful more of Madeira wine before serving.

19. Giblets with Rice.—Take three chicken giblets and brown them in a saucepan, with half an ounce of fat and one sliced onion. Moisten with one quart of white broth (No. 99), adding one thinly sliced carrot, half a sliced turnip, a tablespoonful of well-washed rice, half a tablespoonful of salt, and a very little pepper. Boil for thirty minutes, and then put in one sliced tomato; cook for five minutes more, and serve, adding one teaspoonful of Parisian sauce.

20.—Giblets à l'Ecossaise.—The same as for No. 19, substituting half a cupful of oatmeal for rice ten minutes before serving.

21. Giblets with Barley.—The same as No. 19, substituting barley for rice forty minutes before serving.

22. Giblets à l'Anglaise.—Brown in a saucepan three minced giblets with a sliced onion; moisten with one quart of white broth (No. 99), adding a cupful of Espagnole sauce (No. 151)), a bouquet (No. 254), half a glassful of Madeira wine, a teaspoonful of Parisian sauce, and half a tablespoonful of salt and a teaspoonful of pepper. Cook thoroughly for about thirty minutes, and when done, serve with one chopped hard-boiled egg.

23. Gumbo with Frogs.—Brown in half an ounce of butter, in a saucepan, one chopped onion with about one ounce of raw ham cut into dice shape, half a green pepper cut in small dice, and half a tablespoonful of salt and a teaspoonful of pepper. Moisten with one quart of white broth (No. 99), or consommé (No. 100), add one tablespoonful of raw rice, six sliced gumbos, and one sliced tomato. Let all cook thoroughly for about twenty minutes; and five minutes before serving add a quarter of a pound of raw frogs cut up into small pieces.

24. Gumbo of Crabs.—The same as for No. 23; replacing the frogs by three well-washed, minced, soft-shelled crabs five minutes before serving.

25. Frogs à l'Espagnole.—The same as No. 23, adding one green pepper and two tomatoes (as green peppers and tomatoes must predominate when frogs are used instead of crabs), and omitting the gumbo.

26. Oysters.—Put thirty medium-sized oysters in their own water, with half a pint of water added, in a saucepan, with a tablespoonful of salt and half a teaspoonful of pepper, and one ounce of good butter. Let it boil once only; then serve, adding half a pint of cold milk.

SOUPS.

27. Julienne.—Cut into fine long shreds two carrots, half a turnip, two leaves of celery, one leek, an eighth of a cabbage, and half an onion; brown them in a saucepan with one ounce of butter; moisten with one quart of white broth (No. 99), or consommé (No. 100), and season with half a tablespoonful of salt and a teaspoonful of pepper. Cook for thirty minutes; add two tablespoonfuls of cooked green peas, and one tablespoonful of cooked string beans. Boil up again, and serve.

28. Jardinière.—The same as for No. 27, only the vegetables are cut larger, and omit the cabbage. When ready to serve, add a handful of chiffonade (No. 132) five minutes before serving.

29. Shin of Beef Liée.—Place ten pounds of leg of beef (shin) in a saucepan, with one gallon of cold water, on the fire. When it comes to a boil, thoroughly skim off all the scum. Add one good-sized carrot, one sound onion, six cloves, eighteen whole peppers, a well-garnished bouquet (No. 254), and two pinches of salt. Let all boil on a moderate fire for four hours. Place in a saucepan two ounces of butter, four tablespoonfuls of flour, mix well together, and place it also on a moderate fire, stirring it once in a while until it has obtained a light brown color, which will take six minutes. When the broth has boiled for four hours, strain either through a napkin or a sieve into a vessel and let cool for five minutes; then gradually add it to the flour, stirring until all is added; place it on the fire, and when it boils skim it once more, and let cook for ten minutes. Cut a piece of four ounces of the meat of the cooked shin of beef into small dice-shape pieces half an inch square, add them to the soup, let all boil ten minutes; squeeze in the juice of one medium-sized sound lemon, add a glassful of Madeira wine, and serve in hot tureen.

30. Mutton with Barley.—Cut in small squares a quarter of a pound of lean mutton, and brown them in saucepan, with a little fat, on the hot range, with half a chopped sound onion. Moisten with three pints of white broth (No. 99), and season with half a pinch of salt, and half a pinch of pepper; add half a pint of printanier (No. 51), a little cut-up celery, and a tablespoonful of well-washed barley. Boil well together for forty minutes; pour into a hot soup-tureen and serve.

31. Mutton à l'Ecossaise.—The same as for No. 30, substituting half a cupful of oatmeal for the barley ten minutes before serving.

32. Mikado.—Cut half of a small breast of chicken, a quarter of a pound of very lean veal, and a quarter of a pound of lean mutton, into small equal-sized dice-shaped pieces, and put them in a saucepan on the hot stove, with two ounces of good butter. Cook for five minutes, stirring with the spatula; then moisten with two quarts of broth (No. 99), adding a finely chopped medium-sized onion, the same of green pepper, two tablespoonfuls of diluted curry, and a bouquet (No. 254). Season with a tablespoonful of salt and a teaspoonful of pepper, and, after cooking for thirty minutes, add three tablespoonfuls of raw rice and cook again for thirty minutes. Remove the bouquet, skim thoroughly, and pour the soup into a hot soup-tureen to serve.

33. Westmoreland Soup.—Put into a saucepan one quart of broth

(No. 99), one quart of Espagnole sauce (No. 151), three tablespoonfuls of Parisian sauce, a little cayenne pepper (about the equivalent of a green pea), and a bouquet (No. 254); place the saucepan on the hot stove, and add two cooked and boned calf's feet, cut into small square pieces, and pour in a glassful of good Madeira wine. Cook for thirty minutes, remove the bouquet, and skim the fat from the surface; pour the soup into a hot tureen; add eighteen cooked chicken quenelles (No. 226), then send to the table.

34. Mulligatawney.—Cut a quarter of a medium-sized raw chicken in pieces, with half a green pepper, half an ounce of lean raw ham, and half a finely sliced onion. Brown the whole for five minutes in a saucepan; moisten with one quart of white broth (No. 99), adding a quarter of a pint of very finely cut printanier (No. 51), a teaspoonful of curry, and half a green apple cut into small pieces, one slice of egg-plant cut into small pieces, and a tablespoonful of uncooked rice. Season with half a tablespoonful of salt and a teaspoonful of pepper; boil for twenty-five minutes and serve.

35. Mulligatawney à la Delmonico.—The same as for No. 34, but instead of the printanier use two tablespoonfuls of rice, adding twelve medium-sized oysters two minutes before serving.

36. Menestra.—Cut up all together into fine pieces two carrots, half a turnip, two leeks, a quarter of a cabbage, half an onion, and one stalk of celery, and steam them in two ounces of butter for about ten minutes in a covered saucepan; moisten with three pints of white broth (No. 99), adding one tablespoonful of washed rice, a bouquet (No. 254), and half a tablespoonful of salt and a teaspoonful of pepper. Boil well for thirty minutes, and serve with two tablespoonfuls of grated cheese separately for each person.

37. Napolitaine.—Cut into small pieces a quarter of a raw chicken; brown them well in one ounce of butter, with an ounce of lean raw ham, half a green pepper, half a sliced onion, also one carrot cut in the same way. Steam for ten minutes in a saucepan, then moisten with three pints of white broth (No. 99); season with half a tablespoonful of salt and a teaspoonful of pepper, and add one tablespoonful of raw rice. Let it simmer until half cooked (about fifteen minutes), then throw in one ounce of pieces of macaroni and half a tomato. Boil again for ten minutes, and serve with two tablespoonfuls of grated cheese separately.

38. Ox-Tail with Barley.—Cut a small ox-tail into little pieces, wash well, drain them, then place in a saucepan with a quarter of an ounce of butter, fry for ten minutes on the hot stove. Moisten with three pints of consommé (No. 100); season with half a pinch of salt and half a pinch of pepper. Cook for one hour. Then add half a pint of printanier (No. 51), one tablespoonful of well-washed barley, and a teaspoonful of Parisian sauce. Cook for forty minutes, then skim the fat off, and a few moments before serving add one medium-sized, red, sliced tomato to the soup.

39. Ox-Tail à l'Ecossaise.—The same as for No. 38, substituting half a cupful of oatmeal for the barley ten minutes before serving.

40. Ox-Tail à l'Anglaise.—Cut a small ox-tail into pieces, and fry them the same as in No. 38. Moisten with a quart of consommé (No. 100), and one pint of Espagnole sauce (No. 151). Cook for one hour, then season with a pinch of pepper, add one tablespoonful of well-washed barley, one teaspoonful of Worcestershire sauce, half a glass of Madeira wine, and a bouquet (No. 254). Boil thoroughly for forty-five minutes, skim off the fat, then serve with six slices of lemon, and one chopped hard-boiled egg, and suppressing the bouquet.

41. Sorrel with Asparagus-tops.—Chop up fine one quart of well picked and washed sorrel; put it in a saucepan with two ounces of butter. Let it steam for ten minutes; then moisten with three pints of white broth (No. 99), adding half a cupful of asparagus-tops, and half a tablespoonful of salt and a teaspoonful of pepper. Cook together for twenty-five minutes, and when about serving thicken it with the yolk of one egg in half a cupful of cream. Serve with six sippets of toast.

42. Sorrel with Rice.—The same as for No. 41, using two tablespoonfuls of rice twenty minutes before serving, instead of the asparagus, and omitting the sippets of toast.

43. Purée Jackson.—Cut one pint of potatoes into pieces and cover them with one quart of white broth (No. 99) in a saucepan. Press the broth through a napkin, adding about two ounces of butter and a bouquet (No. 254.) Season with half a tablespoonful of salt and a teaspoonful of pepper, cook well for thirty minutes, then strain the soup, adding half a cupful of cream, and serve with six sippets of toast. Do not let it boil again after the cream has been added.

44. Purée Parmentier.—The same as for No. 43, adding one bunch of cut-up leeks fifteen minutes before serving.

45. Purée Bretonne.—The same as for No. 43, substituting one pint of dried white beans, previously soaked for four hours in cold water, for the potatoes.

46. Purée Faubonne.—The same as for No. 43, using one pint of lentils instead of potatoes. (Lentils must also be soaked for four hours before using.) Throw in two tablespoonfuls of cooked green peas and a pinch of chopped parsley one minute before serving.

47. Purée Crécy.—Steam four medium-sized finely chopped carrots for fifteen minutes in a saucepan, with two ounces of butter; then moisten with one quart of white broth (No. 99), adding half a cupful of raw rice, one bouquet (No. 254), and half a tablespoonful of salt and a teaspoonful of pepper. Cook thoroughly for thirty minutes, then strain through a fine colander. Finish with half a cupful of cream, and serve with two tablespoonfuls of croûtons (No. 133).

48. Purée Condé.—Place in a saucepan on the fire one pint of red beans, previously soaked for four hours in cold water. Moisten with one quart of white broth (No. 99), and add two ounces of blanched salt pork, one onion, one carrot, a bouquet (No. 254), and a teaspoonful of pepper. Cook thoroughly for one hour; then strain, add half a glassful of claret, and then serve with two tablespoonfuls of square croûtons of fried bread (No. 133).

49. Purée of Green Peas.—The same as for No. 48, using a pint of green peas instead of red beans, and adding half a cupful of cream in the place of claret, and one ounce of butter, one minute before serving.

50. Purée Mongole.—Boil in a saucepan half a cupful of dried peas in two gills of white broth (No. 99), for one hour; if fresh peas, half an hour will be sufficient. Cut up in julienne shape, one medium-sized sound carrot, one small turnip, and one leek; place them in a saucepan with half an ounce of butter on the hot stove, cover the pan, and let simmer for five minutes. Peel two good-sized ripe tomatoes, cut them into quarters, put them in a saucepan with a quarter of an ounce of butter; season with one pinch of salt and half a pinch of pepper, add one gill of white broth (No. 99). Let cook for twenty minutes on a brisk fire. Then strain the tomatoes through a fine sieve into a bowl, add them now to julienne, let all cook five minutes longer; strain the peas through the sieve into the julienne, let the whole come to a boil, and serve in a hot soup-tureen.

51. Printanier Grenat.—Cut into small pieces two carrots, half a turnip, half an onion, two leaves of celery, and two leeks; steam them well for ten minutes in a saucepan with one ounce of butter; then moisten with three pints of consommé (No. 100), adding two tablespoonfuls of rice, half a pinch each of salt and pepper. Cook thoroughly for thirty minutes and five minutes before serving put in one cut-up raw tomato.

52. Printanier Chasseur.—Proceed as for No. 51, only replacing the tomato with half the breast of a cooked grouse, partridge, or any other game, cut into small pieces, and twelve quenelles (No. 221).

53. Paysanne.—Cut in square-shaped pieces two carrots, half a turnip, an eighth of a cabbage, half an onion, one potato, and two leaves of celery. Steam them for ten minutes with two ounces of butter in a saucepan; then moisten with three pints of white broth (No. 99); season with half a tablespoonful of salt, and a teaspoonful of pepper. Cook for thirty minutes, and when serving add six thin slices of bread.

54. Pot-au-Feu.—Family Soup.—Thoroughly wash twice in cold water, either six pounds of brisket or eight pounds of shin of beef. Place it in the stock-pot, and entirely cover with cold water; place it on the fire, and be very careful, as soon as it comes to a boil, to thoroughly skim off all the scum. Add two medium-sized, sound, well-cleaned carrots, one turnip, one good-sized, well-peeled onion with six cloves stuck in it, and two leeks tied together. Season with two pinches of salt, and eighteen whole peppers; let boil for four hours. Strain either through a napkin or a sieve into a bowl; cut the carrots into round pieces, quarter of an inch thick, turnip the same, as also the leeks; add all these to the broth, and serve with six quarters of toasted rolls.

55. A la Russe.—Cut into pieces one ounce each of lean, raw ham, mutton, beef, and veal; brown them well in one ounce of butter with the half of a finely shred onion for five minutes. Moisten with one quart of white broth (No. 99), then throw in half a pint of prepared printanier as for No. 109, and a tablespoonful of raw rice. Boil thoroughly for thirty minutes, season with two teaspoonfuls of pepper, and five minutes before serving add a handful of chiffonade (No. 132).

56. Spaghetti with Tomatoes.—Pour into a saucepan one pint of white broth (No. 99), one pint of tomato sauce (No. 205), and season with half a pinch each of salt and pepper. Let it boil well for ten minutes; then throw in half a pint of cooked spaghetti—cut about three-quarters of an inch in length; cook again for five minutes, tossing them well meanwhile, and serve very hot.

57. Tomatoes with Rice.—The same as for No. 56, using three tablespoonfuls of raw rice twenty minutes before serving instead of the cooked spaghetti.

58. Tomatoes à l'Andalouse.—Boil together in a saucepan one pint of tomato sauce (No. 205), and three pints of consommé (No. 100). Add half a tablespoonful of salt and a teaspoonful of pepper; then put in two tablespoonfuls of tapioca, stirring it well all the time. Cook for fifteen minutes, and add twelve chicken quenelles (No. 226); then serve.

59. Tomato with Sago.—Boil for ten minutes in a saucepan one pint of tomato sauce (No. 205), and three pints of consommé (No. 100), seasoning with half a pinch each of salt and pepper; add two tablespoonfuls of sago, cook again for fifteen minutes, gently stirring, and serve.

60. Terrapin—how to prepare it.—Take live terrapin, and blanch them in boiling water for two minutes. Remove the skin from the feet, and put them back to cook with some salt in the saucepan until they feel soft to the touch; then put them aside to cool. Remove the carcass, cut it in medium-sized pieces, removing the entrails, being careful not to break the gall-bag. Put the pieces in a smaller saucepan, adding two teaspoonfuls of pepper, a little nutmeg, according to the quantity, a tablespoonful of salt, and a glassful of Madeira wine. Cook for five minutes, and put it away in the ice-box for further use.

61. Terrapin Soup.—Put in a saucepan one pint of Espagnole sauce (No. 151) and half a pint of consommé (No. 100). Add a good bouquet (No. 254), one tablespoonful of Parisian sauce, a very little red pepper, the same of nutmeg, and half a glassful of Madeira wine. Boil for twenty minutes, being careful to remove the fat, if any; add half a pint of terrapin prepared as above (No. 60), and boil for ten minutes longer. Then serve with six slices of lemon, always removing the bouquet.

62. Chicken à la Richmond.—Place a quarter of a medium-sized chicken, previously boned, into a saucepan with one ounce of butter or fat, one finely shred onion, and half a green pepper, also shred. Fry well together for ten minutes; then moisten with three pints of white broth (No. 99), adding a teaspoonful of powdered curry, diluted in two tablespoonfuls of broth, good bouquet (No. 254), a spoonful of Lima beans, two tablespoonfuls of fresh corn, and six cut-up gumbos, suppressing the stalks. Season with half a tablespoonful of salt, and a teaspoonful of pepper; cook thoroughly for thirty-five minutes; remove the bouquet and serve.

63. Chicken Piémontaise.—The same as No. 37, omitting the carrots and rice.

64. Chicken Hollandaise.—Cut one quarter of a medium-sized raw chicken into small pieces with half an onion; brown well together for ten minutes in a saucepan with an ounce of butter, and moisten with three pints of consommé (No. 100). Add three tablespoonfuls of raw rice, half a tablespoonful of salt, a very little red pepper, and a bouquet (No. 254). Boil thoroughly for twenty minutes; remove the bouquet, and serve.

65. Chicken à la Créole.—The same as for No. 64, adding half a chopped green pepper, one ounce of lean, raw ham, cut in small pieces. Five minutes before serving put one cut tomato in the soup.

66. Chicken à la Portugaise.—Prepare the chicken as for No. 64; add half a pint of cooked printanier (No. 51) cut very fine five minutes before serving.

67. Chicken à l'Okra.—The same as for No. 65, adding twelve raw okras cut in small pieces ten minutes before serving.

68. Chicken with Leeks.—Brown for ten minutes, in one ounce of butter in a saucepan, one quarter of a medium-sized chicken with half a cut-up small onion; moisten with three pints of consommé (No. 100), adding three leeks cut in pieces, a bouquet (No. 254), and half a tablespoonful of salt and a teaspoonful of pepper. Boil thoroughly for thirty minutes and serve, suppressing the bouquet.

69. Chicken à la Turque.—Brown in a saucepan a quarter of a raw chicken in one ounce of butter, with one ounce of raw ham and a sliced onion, moisten with a quart of consommé (No. 100), and half a pint of tomato sauce (No. 205), add two tablespoonfuls of raw rice, a bouquet (No. 254), half a tablespoonful of salt, half a cut-up green pepper, and one teaspoonful of diluted curry. Boil for thirty minutes and serve, removing the bouquet.

70. Cream of Asparagus.—Put two ounces of butter in a saucepan, adding three tablespoonfuls of flour; stir well, and moisten with three pints of white broth (No. 99). Put in the equivalent of half a bunch of asparagus; add a bouquet (No. 254), twelve whole peppers, and half a tablespoonful of salt. Boil thoroughly for thirty minutes; then strain through a fine sieve, add half a cupful of cream, and serve either with a handful of cooked asparagus tops or croûtons soufflés (No. 134).

71. Cream of Celery.—Heat half a pint of mirepoix (No. 138) in a saucepan with an ounce of butter, adding three tablespoonfuls of flour; moisten with three pints of white broth (No. 99), put in half a bunch of celery with a little nutmeg, and half a tablespoonful of salt; let boil well for forty-five minutes then strain through a sieve; add half a cupful of cream, and serve with two tablespoonfuls of croûtons (No. 133).

72. Cream of Artichokes.—Heat half a pint of mirepoix (No. 138) in a saucepan with one ounce of butter, adding three tablespoonfuls of flour, and half a tablespoonful of salt; moisten with three pints of white broth (No. 99), and put in two well-pared, fresh, or three canned, artichokes, and cook well for thirty minutes; strain through a sieve, stir in half a cupful of cream, and serve with a handful of croûtons soufflés (No. 134).

73. Cream of Cauliflower.—Proceed the same as for No. 72, omitting the mirepoix, and substituting half a medium-sized cauliflower instead of artichokes.

74. Cream Palestine.—Boil for about twenty-five minutes half a pound of Jerusalem artichokes; peel and mash them well, then put them in a saucepan with one ounce of butter, moistening with three pints of white broth (No. 99), and half a pint of mirepoix (No. 138). Add three tablespoonfuls of raw rice, and half a tablespoonful of salt. Cock thoroughly for thirty minutes; then strain through a sieve, and finish with half a cupful of cream, and a handful of croûtons soufflés (No. 134).

75. Cream of Lima Beans.—Put two ounces of butter in a saucepan with half a pint of mirepoix (No. 138), a tablespoonful of flour, and one pint of Lima beans, seasoning with half a tablespoonful of salt. Moisten with three pints of white broth (No. 99); cook for thirty minutes; then strain through a sieve, and serve with half a cupful of cream and a handful of croûtons soufflés (No. 134).

76. Cream of Dried Green Peas.—Soak one pint of dried peas for four hours; then cover them with three pints of white broth (No. 99), or water. Put them in a saucepan, adding a bouquet (No. 254), a good-sized piece of salt pork (about two ounces), one carrot, one onion, three cloves, and twelve whole peppers. Cook for forty-five minutes; then rub through a sieve, add two ounces of good butter, and half a cupful of cream, and serve with sippets of fried bread. Should water be used instead of broth, taste before serving to see if sufficiently seasoned.

77. Cream of Barley.—Moisten half a pint of well-washed barley with one quart of white broth (No. 99), adding a bouquet (No. 254), and one whole onion; boil in the saucepan on the stove for forty-five minutes, and season with half a tablespoonful of salt and a teaspoonful of pepper. Strain through a coarse colander, and removing the bouquet, serve with a thickening made of a cupful of cream and the yolks of two raw eggs, and a handful of sippets of bread fried in butter.

78. Cream of Rice.—Same as for No. 77, using rice instead of barley, and letting it cook thirty minutes.

79. Cream of Sorrel.—Steam three good handfuls of well-cleaned sorrel with one ounce of butter. After cooking ten minutes, rub through a sieve into a saucepan; add a quart of white broth (No. 99), and one pint of béchamel sauce (No. 154); season with half a tablespoonful of salt and a teaspoonful of pepper and let boil for fifteen minutes. Thicken the soup before serving with half a cupful of cream and the yolks of two raw eggs well beaten together, adding six slices of bread.

80. Cream of Sorrel and Rice.—The same as for No. 79, adding three tablespoonfuls of raw rice, and cooking for twenty minutes longer.

81. Cream of Sorrel, fermière.—Steam three good handfuls of well-cleaned sorrel with one ounce of butter for ten minutes, and then strain it as for the above. Moisten with three pints of broth (No. 99), adding one more ounce of butter, one sliced, raw potato, two leeks cut in small squares, half an onion, also cut, half a tablespoonful of salt, and a teaspoonful of pepper. Cook well for thirty minutes, and serve with six slices of bread, but add no thickening.

82. Cream of Chicken.—Pound half a boiled chicken in a mortar, then put it in a saucepan, and moisten with three pints of white broth (No. 99), adding one cupful of raw rice, one bouquet (No. 254), half a tablespoonful of salt, twelve whole peppers, and three cloves. Boil thoroughly for thirty minutes; then strain through a fine sieve; put in half a cupful of cream, and serve with two tablespoonfuls of small pieces of cooked chicken in the tureen, or croûtons soufflés instead of the chicken.

83. Cream of Game.—The same as for No. 82, using game instead of chicken; the same quantity of each being needed.

84. Cream à l'Allemande.—Heat half a pint of mirepoix (No. 138) in a saucepan with one ounce of butter, adding two tablespoonfuls of flour, and moistening with three pints of white broth (No. 99); season with half a tablespoonful of salt and three cloves. Boil for thirty minutes, then strain, and after adding an ounce of good butter, serve with two ounces of very finely cut noodles (No. 1182) which have been previously boiled in salted water.

85. Cream of Turnips.—Put three medium sized cut-up raw turnips in a saucepan with one ounce of butter; steam them for thirty minutes, then add one pint of good béchamel sauce (No. 154); rub through a sieve and moisten with one quart of white broth (No. 99); season with a tablespoonful of salt and a teaspoonful of pepper. Heat it while stirring continually, and serve with half a cupful of cream beaten with two egg yolks.

86. Cream of Celery à l'Espagnole.—Put two stalks of celery, cut into fine strips, in a covered saucepan, with one ounce of butter; add a pint of good broth (No. 99), with half a tablespoonful of salt and a teaspoonful of pepper. Boil for thirty minutes; then rub through a sieve, moisten with one quart of broth, and before serving thicken with two egg yolks diluted in half a cupful of cold consommé (No. 100). Add three tablespoonfuls of boiled rice, and, two minutes before serving, one ounce of butter. After the egg yolks have been added to the soup it should not be allowed to boil again.

87. Cream of Lettuce.—Wash thoroughly the green leaves of three good-sized heads of lettuce; drain and chop them up; place them in a saucepan with a quarter of a pound of butter, and cook for five minutes, stirring it lightly. Moisten with two quarts of white broth (No. 99); season with a tablespoonful of salt, a teaspoonful of pepper, and half a teaspoonful of grated nutmeg; add a bouquet (No. 254), and four ounces of well-cleaned, raw rice; cover the saucepan, and cook for forty-five minutes. Remove the bouquet and strain the soup through a fine sieve. Clean the saucepan well, replace the cream in it, and let it heat thoroughly, but do not let it boil, meanwhile stirring it gently with the spatula. Pour in a pint of sweet cream, stir a little more, and throw it into a hot soup tureen, serving it with croûtons soufflés (No. 134).

88. Cream of Lentils à la Major-domo.—Soak one pint of lentils for four hours in cold water; then put them on to boil in a saucepan, with two quarts of water, one carrot, one onion, two ounces of salt pork, six whole peppers, a bouquet (No. 254), and the bones of one partridge; also half a tablespoonful of salt. Cook for forty-five minutes, then rub through a sieve; cut half the breast of a partridge in slices, lay them in the soup-tureen with an ounce of butter, pour the purée over, and serve with a handful of fried sippets of bread, suppressing the bouquet.

89. Purée of Partridge à la Destaing.—Pound in a mortar the bones of a partridge, and half a pint of purée of chestnuts (No. 131). Put the whole into a saucepan, and moisten with three pints of white broth (No. 99), one ounce of butter, and half a tablespoonful of salt and a teaspoonful of pepper. Boil for forty-five minutes; then rub through a wire sieve, adding about an ounce more butter and three tablespoonfuls of cooked rice just before serving.

90. Purée of Partridge à la Gentilhomme.—Pound well the bones of one of any kind of game, place them in a saucepan, add half a pint of purée of lentils with three pints of white broth (No. 99), half a tablespoonful of salt and a teaspoonful of pepper, and one ounce of butter. Boil forty-five minutes, then rub through a fine sieve, stir well while on the fire, not letting it come to a boil, and finish with one ounce of fresh butter. Serve with twelve small game quenelles (No. 228).

91. Purée of Chestnuts à la Jardinière.—Place in a saucepan one pint of purée of chestnuts (No. 131), moisten it with one pint of white broth (No. 99) and a glassful of Madeira wine; boil for thirty minutes, then put in a quarter of a carrot, the same of turnip cut with a tin tube, a tablespoonful of asparagus-tops, six Brussels sprouts, and a piece of cut-up cauliflower the size of an egg. Boil all together for fifteen minutes, and serve after seasoning with half a tablespoonful of salt and a teaspoonful of pepper.

92. Purée of Beans Soubise.—After soaking a pint of white beans for four hours, cook them in a saucepan with one ounce of butter and two sliced onions, and moisten with three pints of white broth (No. 99); season with half a tablespoonful of salt and a teaspoonful of pepper. Boil for forty-five minutes; then rub through a fine sieve, and serve with a thickening of two egg yolks and half a cupful of cream. Add twelve quenelles to the soup (No. 231), and serve.

93. Potage à la Diplomate.—Blanch a beef palate for two minutes in boiling water, then scrape it well, drain, cook again for one hour, and then cut it up in dice shape. Place it in a stewpan with one pint of consommé (No. 100), half a glassful of Madeira wine, and half a pinch each of salt and pepper; pour the liquid over and cook for thirty minutes. Now prepare, in another saucepan, one quart of a stock such as clear green turtle (No. 18), add the beef palates, and twelve chicken quenelles or forcemeat balls (No. 226) and serve.

94. Potage à la Windsor.—Boil for one hour, in two quarts of white broth (No. 99) and one quart of water, three calf's feet; when done, bone and cut them into pieces (they are preferable if cold); moisten with three pints of their own broth, adding a bouquet (No. 254), half a glassful of

Madeira wine, half a tablespoonful of salt, and a very little cayenne pepper. Boil again for ten minutes, then strain through a fine sieve, darken the soup with a little essence of caramel, and when serving add twelve crawfish quenelles (No. 227).

95. Potage à la McDonald.—Pound a cooked calf's brain in a mortar; add two cooked onions, three raw egg yolks, and a teaspoonful of curry powder; rub well through a fine sieve, and when ready to serve pour it into three pints of white broth (No. 99) in the saucepan, adding a peeled and baked cucumber cut in slices. Then serve.

96. Potage à la D'Orsay.—Place in a saucepan a pint of béchamel (No. 154). One pint of white broth (No. 99), half a tablespoonful of salt and a teaspoonful of pepper, and let simmer on the corner of the fire for fifteen minutes. Add to this half a pint of cream of asparagus (No. 70) and one ounce of butter; when finished boiling, put in the tureen six soft-boiled and well-pared pigeon eggs, and the breast of one pigeon cut in julienne; pour the soup over, and serve.

97. Potage Montmorency.—Add to one quart of boiling consommé (No. 100), in a saucepan, half a cupful of noodles (No. 1182) previously blanched in salted water; thicken with the yolks of two beaten eggs, a tablespoonful of grated Parmesan cheese, half a cupful of cream, and one ounce of butter; pour into the tureen, adding either the minced leg or wing of a cooked chicken, and serve with three heads of baked lettuce cut in two, on a separate dish.

98. Potage of Rice à la Maintenon.—Take one quart of white broth No. 99), one pint of béchamel (No. 154), half a tablespoonful of salt and a teaspoonful of pepper, and add to it half a raw chicken; cook for twenty minutes in the saucepan on the fire, then take the chicken out and thicken the soup with the yolks of two beaten eggs, and a teaspoonful of powdered curry, mixed with half a cupful of cream; rub all through a fine sieve, and serve, adding two tablespoonfuls of boiled rice, and the breast of the half chicken previously cooked in the soup, and cut into small pieces.

99. Bouillon Blanc—White broth.—Place in a large stock-urn on a moderate fire a good heavy knuckle of a fine white veal with all the débris, or scraps of meat, including bones, remaining in the kitchen (but not of game); cover fully with cold water, adding a handful of salt; and as it comes to a boil, be very careful to skim all the scum off—no particle of scum should be left on—and then put in two large, sound, well-scraped carrots (whole), one whole, cleaned, sound turnip, one whole, peeled, large, sound onion, one well-cleaned parsley root, three thoroughly washed leeks, and a few leaves of cleaned celery. Boil very slowly for six hours on the corner of the range; keenly skim the grease off; then strain well through a wet cloth into a china bowl or a stone jar, and put it away in a cool place for general use.

100. Consommé pure—Consommé plain.—Chop up a shin of beef of twelve pounds, *using a machine if practicable;* put it in a large soup kettle with two sound, well-scraped, good-sized carrots, two peeled, sound onions, three well-washed and pared leeks, a few branches of celery, and one bunch of parsley roots, all well-scraped, washed, and shred, six cloves, eighteen whole peppers, a bay-leaf, and the whites of six raw eggs, including their shells. Mix all well together, and then moisten with two gallons of cold white broth (No. 99), one quart of cold water (all this should be done before the soup-kettle has been placed on the hot range). Stir thoroughly for two or three minutes without ceasing; and then place it on the hot range, add some débris of chicken if any at hand. Boil slowly for about four hours, skim the grease off thoroughly, and then strain through a wet cloth into a china bowl or stone jar, and put away in a cool place for general use. Should the white broth that you employ be hot, replace the cold water by a piece of ice well cracked, and the equivalent of a quart of water, adding it to the consommé very gradually at the beginning, but continually increasing, and stirring till all added. (Always taste if sufficiently seasoned before serving).

101. Consommé Dubourg.—Cut half a pint of royal (No. 107) into pieces; put three tablespoonfuls of cooked rice into a soup-tureen, and pour three pints of boiling consommé over it, and serve.

102. Consommé Massena.—Add half a glassful of Madeira wine and a bouquet (No. 254) to three pints of game-stock (No. 219), and boil well together for two hours. Have ready three tablespoonfuls of purée of chestnuts (No. 131), mixing in three egg yolks, adding a very little salt and the same of pepper. Take six small timbale-molds, butter them well, and fill them with the above preparation. Poach them for two minutes; take them out, and let them get cool before unmolding them. Put them in a soup-tureen and serve, adding the boiling game-stock.

103. Consommé aux Pâtes.—When one quart of consommé is boiling very hard, add three-quarters of a cupful of paste, such as vermicelli or any other Italian paste; let them cook for six minutes, stirring frequently; then serve. (Pastes such as macaroni, rice, spaghetti, noodles &c., must first be parboiled, and, when necessary, broken into pieces before being added to the soup.)

104. Consommé à la Semoule, or Tapioca.—Into one quart of boiling consommé (No. 100), sprinkle four tablespoonfuls of semolina, or tapioca, stirring constantly; boil thoroughly for ten minutes, and skim the surface just previous to serving.

105. Consommé Tapioca or Semoule à la Creme.—The same as for No. 104, adding to the tureen a thickening of two egg yolks with half a cupful of cream when ready to serve.

106. Consommé à la Sevigne.—With chicken forcemeat (No. 226) fill six very small timbale-molds; let them poach for two minutes in hot water, then set them aside to cool, turn them out, and put them into the tureen with two tablespoonfuls of cooked asparagus-tops, and two tablespoonfuls of cooked green peas; pour over it one quart of boiling consommé (No. 100), and serve.

107. Consommé Royal.—Take six egg yolks and two whole eggs, half a teaspoonful of nutmeg, half a tablespoonful of salt, and a scant teaspoonful of cayenne pepper; beat well together in a bowl, adding half a pint of cream; strain through a fine hair sieve and fill up six small timbale-molds, being careful that they are previously well buttered. Cook them in a stewpan with boiling water to half their height; then place them in the oven until they become firm, which will take about fifteen minutes; immediately after taking them from their moulds, cut them in slices, and add them to one quart of boiling consommé (No. 100) when ready to serve in a tureen.

108. Consommé Deslignac.—Make a royal consommé for three timbales (No. 107), but instead of cream use consommé; unmold, cut them dice-shaped, and put them in the tureen with half a cupful of cooked printanier (No. 109) and one quart of boiling hot consommé (No. 100); then serve.

109. Consommé Printanier.—Cut out, with a vegetable scoop, two carrots and one turnip; simmer them for twenty minutes in water and with a tablespoonful of salt, then drain and throw them into a quart of consommé (No. 100) in a saucepan with two tablespoonfuls of cooked green peas, and two tablespoonfuls of cooked string beans cut into small pieces. Add a handful of chiffonade (No. 132), cook five minutes more, and serve in a hot tureen.

110. Consommé à la D'Orleans.—Add a little crawfish butter (No. 150) to eight fish quenelles; fill six long-shaped quenelle molds with this and poach them in salted water for two minutes; drain, and after unmolding put them in a tureen with two tablespoonfuls of cooked green peas and as much boiled rice ; pour one quart of boiling consommé (No. 100) over it, and serve.

111. Consommé à l' Imperiale.—Place four tablespoonfuls of chicken forcemeat (No. 226) in a paper cornet; cut away the end of the cornet. Butter a pan, and with the contents of the cornet, make eighteen round quenelles; put on top of each quenelle a small slice of truffle; poach them for two minutes in white broth (No. 99); then drain through a sieve, and serve in the tureen, after pouring one quart of consommé (No. 100) over them and adding a tablespoonful of cooked green peas and six cock's combs.

112. Consommé Garibaldi.—Proceed the same as for No. 107; have two green timbales, two red ones; use a very little carmine Broton, then use two more plain timbales, and serve.

113. Consommé Princesse.—Wash well three tablespoonfuls of barley, drain, and place it in a saucepan with three pints of consommé (No. 100), and let boil for forty minutes. Add two tablespoonfuls of cooked breast of chicken cut in dice, two tablespoonfuls of cooked green peas, and serve in a hot tureen.

114. Consommé Douglas.—Pare and blanch for ten minutes half a root of celery as for a juliénne (No. 27); then place it in a saucepan, adding two tablespoonfuls of boiled rice, half an ounce of smoked, cooked tongue, and six mushrooms, both shred very small; pour one quart of hot consommé (No. 100) over it and serve.

115. Consommé Renaissance.—With two ounces of pâté-à-chou (No.

1240) make a handful of croûtons, the size of the little finger; cook them on a tin dish in the oven for ten minutes, and when done fill them inside with chicken forcemeat (No. 226) pressed through a cornet. Put them in a tureen with two tablespoonfuls of cooked peas, and two spoonfuls of sliced mushrooms; pour one quart of consommé (No. 100) over them, and serve.

116. Consommé à l'Africaine.—Cut one cooked artichoke bottom dice-shaped, also one slice of fried egg-plant cut in pieces; drain them on a cloth to remove all the fat, then add two tablespoonfuls of cooked rice, and a teaspoonful of powdered curry diluted in water; put these in a soup tureen with one quart of consommé (No. 100) poured over them, and serve.

117. Consommé à l'Andalouse.—Boil three tablespoonfuls of tapioca in one quart of consommé (No. 100); add half a pint of thin tomato sauce (No. 205), boil for ten minutes, and serve with twelve small quenelles of godiveau. (No. 221).

118. Consommé Celestine.—Make two light French pancakes (No. 1186) cover one with chicken forcemeat (No. 226), and sprinkle over it a little grated Parmesan cheese; then put the other one on top, and cut them in twelve slices with a tube, and serve in one quart of boiling consommé (No. 100) in a hot tureen.

119. Consommé à l'Anglaise.—Add half a cupful of minced cooked chicken, and three tablespoonfuls of cooked green peas to one quart of boiling consommé (No. 100), and serve in a hot tureen.

120. Consommé Colbert.—Add six poached eggs (No. 404) to one quart of boiling consommé (No. 100) before serving.

121. Consommé Printanier Colbert.—The same as for the above, adding half a pint of cooked printanier (No. 51).

122. Consommé Suèdoise.—Cut three rolls in halves, and take out the crumbs; make a preparation, cutting up together one carrot, half a turnip, one leaf of a white cabbage, two tablespoonfuls of peas, and one tablespoonful of string beans; add one ounce of butter, half a tablespoonful of salt, and very little pepper. Leave it very thick, and cook for twenty minutes in a saucepan, adding two tablespoonfuls of grated Parmesan cheese. Fill the rolls with this mixture, and sprinkle the tops with more cheese and a few drops of drawn butter; place them in the oven for two minutes, and serve with three pints of consommé (No. 100) in a hot soup-tureen.

123. Consommé Rachel.—Decorate the bottom and sides of twelve quenelle molds with sliced truffles, and the same of smoked cooked tongue, being careful to have them well buttered. Fill them with chicken forcemeat (No. 226); poach them in salted water for two minutes, unmold, and serve with one quart of boiling consommé (No. 100) in the hot tureen.

124. Consommé Printanier Royale.—Add to one quart of boiling consommé (No. 100) three royals (No. 107) cut into pieces, also half a pint of cooked printanier (No. 51), and serve.

125. Consommé Duchesse.—Butter and cover a tin plate with two ounces of pâté-à-chou (No. 1240), about the height of a quarter of an inch. Cook it in the oven for six minutes, then remove, and fill it with forcemeat (No. 226) pressed through a cornet; cut it with a paste cutter into twelve equal-sized pieces, put them in the tureen, pour one quart of boiling consommé (No. 100) over them, and serve.

126. Consommé Patti.—Cut half a breast of a cooked chicken into small pieces; put them in a tureen, adding two tablespoonfuls of boiled rice, two tablespoonfuls of cooked green peas, and one truffle cut dice-shaped. Pour one quart of boiling consommé (No. 100) over it, and serve with grated cheese separate.

127. Consommé Napolitaine.—Cut two ounces of cooked spaghetti into pieces, adding half an ounce of cut-up, cooked tongue, half an ounce of lean, cooked ham, and three mushrooms cut into small pieces. Pour all into a tureen with one quart of consommé (No. 100), and serve with grated cheese separate.

128. Consommé Chatelaine.—Take three molds. Add to the four whites of well-beaten eggs half a pint of purée of onions (Soubise No. 250), and a quarter of a pint of cream; beat well together with a very little grated nutmeg, and half a tablespoonful of salt. Fill the molds, previously well buttered; then poach them in water to half their height for six minutes, and unmold. Cut them into twelve pieces, and put them in the soup-tureen, adding two tablespoonfuls of cooked asparagus-tops, and the same quantity of green peas. Pour one quart of consommé (No. 100) over it, and serve very hot.

129. Consommé aux Quenelles.—Have ready eighteen small godiveau quenelles (No. 221). Arrange them in a well-buttered stewpan, being careful they do not touch each other; pour some salted water over them, and let them poach for two minutes. Drain on a perfectly dry sieve, and put them in the tureen with one quart of boiling consommé (No. 100), and serve.

130. Onion Soup.—Brown two onions in a saucepan with one ounce of butter, stir in a little flour, and moisten with three pints of white broth (No. 99); season with half a tablespoonful of salt and a teaspoonful of pepper, and cook for ten minutes. Place six pieces of toasted bread in a bowl; cover them with fine slices of Swiss cheese, pour the broth over them, add a few more slices of cheese on top, and put it in the oven five minutes before serving.

131. Pureé of Chestnuts.—Boil one pound of chestnuts for ten minutes; peel and skin them immediately, put them in a saucepan with one quart of white broth (No. 99), a tablespoonful of salt, and two teaspoonfuls of pepper and a quarter of a pound of butter. Let all boil well for thirty minutes; rub through a sieve, and use when needed.

132. Chiffonade for Soups.—Chop well together half a head of lettuce, half a handful of sorrel, a few branches of chervil, and a little parsley. Use it in soups five minutes before serving.

133. Croûtons for Soups.—Cut some dice-shaped pieces of bread, and fry them in a pan with clarified butter; when a rich golden color, drain, and add to the soup when needed.

133½. Croûtons for Garnishing.—Cut six rather thin slices out of an American loaf of bread; neatly pare, then cut them into heart-shaped croûtons. Lay them on a tin plate, drip a little clarified butter over them, place in the hot oven for four minutes, to let get a good golden color. Take from out the oven, and use when required.

134. Croûtons Soufflés.—Make some pâté-à-chou (No. 1240), spread it out to the thickness of macaroni, and cut with a knife the size of a pea. Put them in a sieve, sprinkle with flour, shake well, and fry in hot lard; when done, which will take five minutes, drain through a cloth, and serve with the soup when needed.

A pinch of salt represents 205 grains, or a tablespoonful.
Half a pinch of pepper represents 38 grains, or a teaspoonful.
A third of a pinch of nutmeg represents 13 grains, or half a teaspoonful.

STOCKS, SAUCES, FORCEMEATS, AND GARNISHINGS.

135. White-Roux.—Put in a saucepan two ounces of butter, and place it on the corner of the hot range, add to it two tablespoonfuls of flour; keep stirring constantly for seven minutes. Then let it cool, and when cold, use in various sauces, as directed.

136. Brown-Roux.—Place two ounces of good butter in a saucepan on the hot range; mix in two tablespoonfuls of flour, and cook rapidly for about seven minutes, or until it assumes a rich brown color. Let it thoroughly cool off, and then use in different sauces, as mentioned.

137. White Stock—for one gallon.—Reduce in saucepan on the hot range, one ounce of very good, finely shred, salt pork, previously well washed, and the same of beef suet. Add one carrot, one onion, a bouquet of aromatic herbs (No. 254), twelve whole peppers, and four cloves. Brown these well on a moderate fire for four minutes. Add four ounces of flour; stir well, and moisten with a glassful of white wine and three quarts of white broth (No. 99). Add one tablespoonful of salt, and stir until it comes to a boil; then let it cook thoroughly for one hour; strain through a fine sieve. This stock should be used without any further thickening.

138. Mirepoix.—Stew in a saucepan two ounces of fat, two carrots, one onion, one sprig of thyme, one bay-leaf, six whole peppers, three cloves, and, if handy, a ham bone cut into pieces. Add two sprigs of celery and half a bunch of parsley roots; cook for fifteen minutes, and use when directed in other recipes. Scraps of baked veal may also be added, if at hand.

139. Marinade Stock, cooked—for one gallon.—Stew together a finely sliced sound onion and four parsley roots, adding one pint of vinegar and four quarts of fresh water, also a quarter of a bunch of thyme, six bay-leaves, twenty-four whole peppers, and twelve cloves. Cook well for thirty minutes on a brisk fire, then place in a stone jar, and keep it in a cool place for general use.

140. Marinade Stock, raw—for six persons.—Finely slice one medium-sized, sound, peeled onion, place it in an earthen crock, with three slices of lemon, two bay-leaves, twelve whole peppers, four cloves, three whole mace, and three sprigs of parsley roots. Add to these two tablespoonfuls of sweet oil, a cupful of vinegar, and a pinch of salt. Place the meat or fish in this, and leave it to souse as long as necessary, or about six hours.

141. Meat Glaze—Glace de Viande.—As this meat glaze, when properly made, will keep in perfect condition for any length of time, I would advise that half a pint be made at a time, in the following manner. Place in a large saucepan ten quarts of white broth (No. 99), or nine quarts of consommé (No. 100), and reduce it on a moderate fire for fully four hours, at which time it should be reduced to half a pint. Transfer it in a stone jar or bowl; put a cover on, and keep in a cool place for general use.

142. Court Bouillon.—Cut up one good-sized, peeled and well-washed carrot, with a sound onion, and half a bunch of parsley roots, also cut up; brown them in a glassful of white or red wine, according to the fish; add to it any well-washed pieces of fish-heads and a pint of water. Season with half a pinch each of salt and pepper. Boil well for five minutes; let cool; strain through a napkin or a sieve into a jar, and use when needed. Always avoid straining anything acid into tin or copper vessels—to prevent blackening.

143. Cooked Fine Herbs.—Chop up one sound onion and two well-peeled shallots; brown them in a saucepan with one ounce of butter, for five minutes, then add double the quantity of finely minced mushrooms and a grain of garlic; season with half a tablespoonful of salt and a teaspoonful of pepper, and finish with a tablespoonful of chopped parsley. Cook ten minutes longer, and then let it cool.

144. Raw Fine Herbs.—Chop separately, half an onion, two shallots, two sprigs of parsley, four hairs of chives, and the same of chervil; mix thoroughly before using.

145. Butter, maître d'hôtel.—Put one ounce of good butter in a bowl with a teaspoonful of very finely chopped parsley, adding the juice of half a sound lemon. Mingle well with a very little nutmeg, and keep it in a cool place to use when needed.

146. Anchovy Butter.—To one ounce of good butter, add one teaspoonful of anchovy essence; mix well, and keep it on ice—for general use.

147. Butter à la Ravigote.—Pound together in a mortar one sprig of parsley, the same of tarragon, very little chives, the same of chervil, and

STOCKS, SAUCES, FORCEMEATS, GARNISHINGS. 171

one small, peeled shallot. Add half a teasponful of anchovy essence, one ounce of good butter, and half a drop of spinach-green. Rub through a fine sieve, and keep it in a cool place for general use.

148. Horseradish Butter.—Pound in a mortar one teaspoonful of grated horseradish with one ounce of good butter, and season with very little red pepper—third of a saltspoonful. Rub through a fine sieve, and keep it in a cool place. When this butter is added to other sauces, it should not boil again.

149. Lobster Butter.—Extract the coral from one cooked lobster (the eggs may be used instead); pound it in a mortar to a paste, mixing it with one ounce of good butter and a teaspoonful of mustard. Rub through a fine sieve, and keep in a cool place. The butter can also be used for coloring purposes.

150. Crawfish Butter.—Pick the meat from the tails of twelve boiled crawfish; dry the shells, and pound them all together in a mortar, adding one ounce of good butter; then place it in a saucepan on a moderate fire, stirring, until it clarifies, for about five minutes; then strain through a napkin, letting it drop into cold water. When it is congealed, take it out, and place it in a warm basin, stirring until it assumes the desired color. The same method can be used for lobsters and shrimps.

151. Sauce Espagnole—for one gallon.—Mix one pint of raw, strong mirepoix (No. 138) with two ounces of good fat (chicken's fat is preferable). Mix with the compound four ounces of flour, and moisten with one gallon of white broth (No. 99). Stir well, and then add, if handy, some baked veal and ham bones. Boil for three hours, and then remove the fat very carefully; rub the sauce through a very fine sieve, and keep it for many purposes in cooking.

152. Sauce Velouté.—Melt one ounce of good butter in a saucepan, adding two tablespoonfuls of flour, and stir well, not letting it get brown. Moisten with a pint and a half of good veal and chicken stock, the stronger the better. Throw in a garnished bouquet (No. 254), half a cupful of mushroom liquor, if at hand, six whole peppers, half a pinch of salt, and a very little nutmeg. Boil for twenty minutes, stirring continuously with a wooden spatula; then remove to the side of the fire, skim thoroughly, and let it continue simmering slowly for one hour. Then rub through a fine sieve. This sauce will make the foundation for any kind of good white stock.

153. Sauce Villeroi.—Strain and place in a saucepan with one ounce of butter, two tablespoonfuls of raw mirepoix (No. 138), adding two tablespoonfuls of flour. Cook, and mix well together for five minutes; moisten with three pints of white broth (No. 99), and season with half a tablespoonful of salt. Boil for one hour; then strain through a fine sieve and use when needed.

154. Béchamel Sauce.—Place in a saucepan two ounces of butter, add two tablespoonfuls of flour, and stir constantly for five minutes. Moisten with a pint and a half of boiling milk, being careful to pour it in gradually; then beat it well with a whisk. Add half a teaspoonful of grated nutmeg, a pinch of salt, a bouquet (No. 254), twelve whole peppers, and a little mushroom liquor, if at hand. Cook well for fifteen minutes, and when done rub through a fine sieve.

155. Melted Butter Sauce.—Put one ounce of good butter in a saucepan on a slow fire, stir, and when melted add the juice of half a lemon. Serve in a sauce bowl.

156. Nut-brown Butter Sauce.—Place one ounce of good butter in a frying-pan, let it heat until it assumes a nut-brown color, then add one drop of vinegar, and use when needed.

157. Black Butter Sauce.—Warm one ounce of good butter in the frying-pan until it becomes brown; add six parsley leaves, heat again for one minute, then throw in five drops of vinegar. Pour it into a sauce-bowl and serve.

158. Lobster Sauce.—Pour one pint of Hollandaise sauce (No. 160) into a saucepan; place it on the hot stove, but do not allow it to boil. Add the claw of a good-sized boiled lobster cut into lozenge-shaped pieces; heat well for five minutes, stirring it lightly, add a quarter of an ounce of lobster butter (No. 149), and serve when needed.

159. Drawn-Butter Sauce.—Put two ounces of butter in a saucepan, adding two tablespoonfuls of flour while stirring; moisten with one quart of water, and season with one tablespoonful of salt and half a teaspoonful of pepper. Let it simmer on the side of the stove for thirty minutes until it thickens; then add, little by little, half an ounce of butter, beating it continuously until it becomes perfectly white. Squeeze in the juice of a lemon; stir once more, strain through a hair sieve and serve.

160. Sauce Hollandaise.—Place one sound, sliced onion, six whole peppers and a bay-leaf in a saucepan with two ounces of good butter on the hot stove; stir in two tablespoonfuls of flour to thicken, then moisten with a pint and a half of either chicken or white broth (No. 99); mix well with a whisk or wooden spatula, being careful to remove any accumulated' fat. Add half a teaspoonful of grated nutmeg and half a tablespoonful of salt, and cook for twenty-five minutes. Beat the yolks of three eggs separately with the juice of half a medium-sized sound lemon. Pour them gradually into the sauce, being careful not to boil it again after they have been added. Rub through a hair sieve into a serving bowl, and finish with half an ounce of good butter, mixing it well, and serve.

161. Egg Sauce.—Use one pint of the Hollandaise sauce (No. 160), and when ready to serve sprinkle it with two chopped hard-boiled eggs and a teaspoonful of minced parsley.

162. Bread Sauce.—Crumble one and a half ounces of fresh bread crumbs, and place them in a saucepan with not quite half a cupful of cold water; add half an ounce of butter, half a tablespoonful of salt, and six whole peppers. Cook for five minutes; then pour in half a cupful of cream or milk. Cook again for five minutes, and serve in a sauce-bowl, removing the peppers.

163. Anchovy Sauce.—To three-quarters of a pint of drawn-butter sauce (No. 159), or Hollandaise sauce (No. 160), add one tablespoonful of anchovy essence; beat well together and serve.

164. Horseradish Sauce.—Add two tablespoonfuls of grated horseradish to three-quarters of a pint of béchamel sauce (No. 154); also half a pinch of powdered sugar, a third of a pinch of cayenne pepper, and half a pinch of salt. Boil for five minutes. Should the sauce be too thick add a little cream or milk, and three drops of vinegar in case the horseradish be fresh.

165. Sauce Percillade.—Pour half a cupful of sweet oil into an earthen bowl with the juice of half a lemon, half a tablespoonful of salt, and a scant teaspoonful of pepper. Beat well with a spoon or whisk, adding one teaspoonful of parsley, half the quantity of chervil, the same of tarragon and chives all chopped very fine together, and a teaspoonful of mustard. Mix the whole well before serving.

166. Sauce Béarnaise.—Chop very fine two medium-sized, sound, well-peeled shallots; place them in a small saucepan on the hot range, with two tablespoonfuls of either tarragon or chervil vinegar, and five whole crushed peppers. Reduce until nearly dry, then put away to cool. Mingle with it six fresh raw egg yolks, sharply stirring meanwhile, then gradually add one and a half ounce of good fresh butter; seasoning with half a tablespoonful of salt, half a teaspoonful of grated nutmeg, and twelve finely chopped sound tarragon leaves. Have a much wider pan on the fire with boiling water, place the small one containing the ingredients into the other, and see that the boiling water reaches up to half its height; thoroughly heat up, beating briskly with the whisk; when the sauce is firm add one teaspoonful of melted meat-glaze (No. 141), beat lightly for two seconds longer, then strain through an ordinary, clean kitchen towel, neatly arrange the sauce on a hot dish to be sent to the table; and dress over it any article required to be served.

167. Sauce Trianon.—The same as for Béarnaise sauce (No. 166), but pour the sauce over the article to be served, instead of under; finish with two medium-sized sliced truffles, nicely arranged on top.

168. Apple Sauce.—Core, peel and quarter four sour apples. Place them in a saucepan with half a glassful of water, half a tablespoonful of salt, and two ounces of sugar. Cover and cook for about twenty-five minutes, or until the apples are reduced to a marmalade; then strain through a colander, and add the third of a pinch of cinnamon, if necessary.

169. Mint Sauce.—Take one-quarter of a bunch of finely minced mint-leaves, moistening with half a cupful of water and half a cupful of broth (No. 99), or consommé (No. 100); add four tablespoonfuls of vinegar, a tablespoonful of salt, and half an ounce of sugar; stir well and serve in a sauce-bowl.

170. Green Sauce.—Pound in a mortar one sprig of parsley and three hairs of chervil; add three medium-sized vinegar-pickles, half a small, white onion, one anchovy, and a teaspoonful of capers. Mix these with soaked bread the size of an egg, and pound all well together. When the preparation is reduced to a paste, rub it through a fine sieve, put it in a bowl and stir well, adding half a cupful of sweet oil, two tablespoonfuls of vinegar, half a teaspoonful of pepper, and half a tablespoonful of salt. This sauce must be consistent and of a green color.

171. Suprême Sauce.—Clean thoroughly the carcass of one raw chicken and place it in a saucepan, covering it with water; cook quickly, and at the first boil take it off, drain and wash the carcass well. Put it back into a very clean saucepan, covering it with one quart of white broth (No. 99), adding a bouquet (No. 254) and half a tablespoonful of salt. Cook for forty-five minutes; have two tablespoonfuls of white roux (No. 135) separate; pour the broth over it, continuing to stir; reduce to half, and strain through a fine Chinese strainer. Add half a cupful of good cream and an ounce of fresh butter, and finish with the juice of half a lemon.

172. Tarragon Sauce.—Put half a pint sauce velouté (No. 152) to boil in a saucepan on the hot stove. Add half a cupful of white broth (No. 99) and two sprigs of tarragon. Season with a very little salt, and cook for ten minutes. Cut up very fine, and add to the sauce when serving twelve blanched tarragon leaves.

173. Oyster Sauce.—Open eighteen medium-sized, fine Shrewsbury oysters and put them in a saucepan with one ounce of good butter, placing the pan on the stove. Cook for four minutes; remove half the liquid from the pan and add a pint of hot Allemande sauce (No. 210). Then with the spatula mix lightly together without allowing it to boil, and serve.

174. Indian Sauce.—Brown in a saucepan one sliced onion, one ounce of raw lean ham, one sprig of thyme, and twelve whole peppers, with one ounce of butter. Add a teaspoonful of powdered curry diluted in a pint of sauce velouté (No. 152); boil for ten minutes. Then strain through a Chinese strainer into another saucepan, being careful to pour in half a cupful of cream, the juice of half a lemon and two egg yolks. Then serve.

175. Sauce Normande, for Fish.—To a pint of sauce velouté (No. 152) add two tablespoonfuls of mushroom liquor. Reduce the sauce for ten minutes, and place in it two tablespoonfuls of fish-stock (No. 214). Let it just boil again, then add two egg yolks and the juice of half a lemon; strain through a fine sieve and stir in half an ounce of fresh butter. This sauce should be consistent.

175½. Normande, garnishing for Meat.—Neatly peel and wash well twelve celery knobs, drain, and then place six of them in a saucepan with one tablespoonful of butter, one pinch of salt, half a pinch of pepper, and a gill of white broth (No. 99), and cook for twenty minutes on a moderate fire; then mash them as you would potatoes; when thoroughly mashed place them in a warm place for further action. Take the other six celery knobs, cut out very carefully the centres with the aid of a vegetable scoop, leaving about half an inch uncut at the bottom to prevent burning. Season with one pinch of salt only, evenly divided. Stuff them with the above farce; then place them in a saucepan with half a medium-sized, sound, scraped and sliced carrot, half a peeled and sliced onion, and a tablespoonful of butter. Cook three minutes on a moderate fire. Add a wineglassful of good cider and a gill of white broth (No. 99). Cook again for twenty minutes. Arrange the remaining mashed celery in the centre of the hot serving dish, place the meat over it, nicely surround the dish with the six stuffed celery knobs, strain the gravy over, arranging a small piece of cooked cauliflower on top of each, and serve very hot.

176. **Sauce à la Toulouse.**—To a pint of Hollandaise sauce (No. 160) add two tablespoonfuls of white wine, one sliced truffle, and six minced mushrooms. Heat well without boiling, and when serving add a little meat-glaze (No. 141).

177. **Sauce maître d'hôtel, liée.**—Add to half a pint of warm Hollandaise sauce (No. 160), a teaspoonful of chopped parsley, half an ounce of butter, a scant teaspoonful of pepper, and half a teaspoonful of nutmeg; then serve.

178. **Shrimp Sauce.**—Place half an ounce of shrimp butter (No. 150) in half a pint of Hollandaise sauce (No. 160); stir well on the fire for five minutes, and when ready to serve add twelve picked shrimp tails and the juice of half a lemon. Heat without boiling, and serve.

179. **Sauce à la Venitienne.**—Reduce for four minutes one tablespoonful of tarragon-vinegar and chervil-vinegar with six whole peppers, one ounce of lean cooked ham cut into small dice, six parsley roots, one sprig of thyme, and one bay-leaf. Then strain through a napkin into a bowl; moisten with half a pint of sauce velouté (No. 152), and finish the sauce with twelve leaves of finely cut tarragon, two drops of spinach green, and a teaspoonful of chopped parsley.

180. **Sauce à la Matelote.**—Reduce for five minutes one glassful of good red wine with a bouquet (No. 254) and a small glassful of mushroom liquor; then add half a pint of velouté (No. 152) and boil for five minutes. Strain, and then add the third of a tablespoonful of salt and a scant teaspoonful of pepper, and throw in twelve small, cooked, glazed onions (No. 972), four mushrooms cut into quarters, and one ounce of cooked salt pork cut in dice. Cook again for five minutes, and serve.

181. **Cream Sauce.**—Take half a pint of béchamel sauce (No. 154); add half an ounce of butter, and beat them together carefully, adding half a cupful of sweet cream. Then serve.

182. **Sauce à l'Aurore.**—To half a pint of hot, highly seasoned béchamel sauce (No. 154) in a saucepan add a small glassful of mushroom liquor, half an ounce of butter, and three tablespoonfuls of very red tomato sauce (No. 205). Stir well on the fire for five minutes, then add square cuts of six whole mushrooms, and serve.

183. **Sauce à la Duchesse.**—Cut up in small dice-shaped pieces half an ounce of cooked ham and two truffles, place these in a saucepan on the fire, with half a wine-glassful of white wine; let reduce for three minutes on a brisk fire. Add one gill of good tomato sauce (No. 205). Boil for one minute with a tablespoonful of glace de viande (No. 141). Add half a pint of Allemande sauce (No. 210). Toss well while heating, but do not allow to boil again, and serve very hot.

184. Sauce Princesse.—Take eighteen chicken quenelles, two truffles cut in slices, and one blanched chicken liver cut in dice shape; place all in a saucepan on the fire with half a glassful of white wine, and let reduce for three minutes; then add one tablespoonful of glace de viande (No. 141), let come to a boil; add half a pint of good Allemande sauce (No. 210). Toss well together, but do not allow to boil, and serve very hot.

185. Sauce Demi-Glace, or Madeira.—Add one small glassful of mushroom liquor to one pint of good Espagnole sauce (No. 151); also a small glassful of Madeira wine, a bouquet (No. 254), and a scant teaspoonful of pepper. Remove the fat carefully and cook for thirty minutes, leaving the sauce in a rather liquid state; then strain and use when needed. This takes the place of all Madeira sauces.

186. Sauce Bordelaise.—Chop up two shallots very fine; put them with half a glassful of red wine in a saucepan on the fire, reduce to half, and then add three-quarters of a pint of good Espagnole sauce (No. 151) and a scant teaspoonful of red pepper. Cook for twenty minutes, and before serving place eighteen round slices of blanched marron in the sauce.

187. Sauce à la Génoise.—Strain about two tablespoonfuls of cooked mirepoix (No. 138), and moisten it with half a glassful of red wine; reduce to half on the hot stove, then add half a pint of Espagnole (No. 151), two tablespoonfuls of white broth (No. 99), and a scant tablespoonful of pepper. Cook for ten minutes, then strain through a sieve; put in half an ounce of good butter and a teaspoonful of anchovy sauce (No. 163), and serve.

188. Sauce Italienne.—Brown two medium-sized, fine, peeled, and chopped-up shallots in a saucepan with a quarter of an ounce of butter, adding half an ounce of cooked, lean ham cut into small dice shape, four minced mushrooms, one finely minced truffle, and a glassful of Madeira wine. Let all cook together for five minutes; then add half a pint of Espagnole sauce (No. 151); let it then come to a boil, and serve very hot.

189. Sauce Duxelle.—Reduce half a pint of Madeira sauce (No. 185) with half a glassful of white wine; add to it twelve very finely chopped mushrooms, two shallots also chopped up and browned in a very little butter for five minutes, and half an ounce of chopped, cooked beef-tongue. Boil again for five minutes and serve.

190. Sauce Colbert.—Put in a saucepan half a pint of very thick Madeira sauce (No. 185); add to it very gradually one ounce of good, fresh butter, also two tablespoonfuls of meat-glaze (No. 141). Mix well together without boiling; then squeeze in the juice of half a sound lemon, and add one teaspoonful of chopped parsley when serving.

191. Sauce Perigueux.—Chop up very fine two fine truffles; place them in a sautoire with a glassful of Madeira wine. Reduce on the hot stove for five minutes. Add half a pint of Espagnole sauce (No. 151). Just allow to come to a boil, and serve very hot.

192. Sauce Robert.—Slice half an onion and fry it in a saucepan with half an ounce of butter and a teaspoonful of sugar until it is of a golden

STOCKS, SAUCES, FORCEMEATS, GARNISHINGS. 177

color, or about five minutes; then moisten with half a glassful of white wine and half a pint of Espagnole sauce (No. 151). Boil for ten minutes; then add a teaspoonful of dry English mustard, diluted in cold broth or gravy; stir carefully, and finally rub through a hair sieve and serve.

193. Sauce Salmi.—Place in a saucepan two tablespoonfuls of fumet of game (No. 213) with a half pint of Madeira sauce (No.' 185); add two or three livers of any kind of game at hand, cut into small dice-shape pieces. Cook together on a moderate fire for ten minutes; then strain through a colander; mix in the zest of a sound lemon just before serving.

194. Sauce Poivrade.—Fry in half an ounce of butter half an onion and half a carrot, cut up, a sprig of thyme, one bay-leaf, six whole peppers, three cloves, a quarter of a bunch of parsley-roots, and half an ounce of raw ham cut in pieces. Cook it together for five minutes, then moisten with two tablespoonfuls of vinegar, and a pint of Espagnole sauce (No. 151). Boil thoroughly for twenty minutes, then strain through a colander, being careful to remove every particle of grease.

195. Sauce Napolitaine.—Reduce in a saucepan two tablespoonfuls of raw mirepoix (No. 138) with half an ounce of butter; after five minutes moisten with a small glassful of Madeira wine, half a pint of Espagnole sauce (No. 151), two tablespoonfuls of tomato sauce (No. 205), and two tablespoonfuls of fumet of game (No. 218), if any on hand. Reduce for ten minutes, and rub through a sieve.

196. Sauce Hachée.—Chop up very fine two shallots and fry them lightly in a saucepan with half an ounce of butter; add a tablespoonful of capers and three small chopped vinegar-pickles, also a teaspoonful of vinegar. Reduce the sauce for ten minutes; then moisten with half a pint of Espagnole sauce (151), adding a tablespoonful of cooked fine herbs (No. 143). Cook again for ten minutes, and serve.

197. Sauce Chasseur.—Reduce in a saucepan half a pint of Espagnole sauce (No. 151) with two tablespoonfuls of fumet of game (No. 218); after five minutes thicken it with two tablespoonfuls of hare's blood—the blood of any other kind of game will answer—mixed with six drops of vinegar. Do not let it boil after the blood is added to the sauce.

198. Sauce Diable.—Pour a pint of Espagnole sauce (No. 151) into a saucepan with a teaspoonful of dry mustard, diluted in two teaspoonfuls of Parisian sauce, adding a third of a saltspoonful of red pepper. Mix well together. Cook for five minutes and serve.

199. Crapaudine Sauce.—Place half a pint of light piquante sauce (No. 203) in a saucepan on the fire, add four chopped mushrooms, and a teaspoonful of dry mustard, diluted in two teaspoonfuls of tarragon-vinegar. Boil for five minutes and serve.

200. Celery Sauce.—Clean well, nicely pare, and cut into dice-shaped pieces, and then wash thoroughly in fresh water three roots of fine celery, using only the white parts. Lift them out with the hand, so that the sand and dirt remain at the bottom of the pan, and place them in a saucepan. Cover them with fresh water, adding two pinches of salt and half an ounce of butter. Put on the lid, and cook on the hot stove for twenty-five minutes. Drain, and place the celery in the saucepan again with a pint of hot Allemande sauce (No. 210); toss well for just a little while, and serve.

201. Vinaigrette Sauce.—Chop up together very fine one shallot, two branches of parsley, the same of chervil and chives, and when very fine place them in a sauce-bowl with a tablespoonful of salt, a teaspoonful of pepper, and three tablespoonfuls of vinegar. Stir all well together; then add four tablespoonfuls of good oil, mix well again, and serve.

202. Mustard Sauce.—Dilute in a saucepan one tablespoonful of ground English mustard with a tablespoonful of tarragon-vinegar, and half the same quantity of Parisian sauce; strain into this a pint of Espagnole sauce (No. 151), and place the pan on the hot stove. Beat continually until thoroughly heated, then add a teaspoonful of chopped parsley. This sauce must not be allowed to boil.

203. Sauce Piquante.—Place one onion chopped up very fine in a saucepan with half a cupful of vinegar; reduce until almost dry, and then add one pint of Espagnole sauce (No. 151), one tablespoonful of capers, three small gherkins and three mushrooms, all finely chopped up together. Cook for ten minutes; season with the third of a tablespoonful of salt, and a scant teaspoonful of pepper, and serve.

204. Champagne Sauce.—Place two cloves, six whole peppers, one bay-leaf, half a tablespoonful of powdered sugar in a saucepan with a good glassful of champagne; place it on the fire, and reduce for five minutes. Then moisten with three-quarters of a pint of Espagnole sauce (No. 151), and cook for fifteen minutes longer; strain through a Chinese strainer, and serve.

205. Tomato Sauce.—Place two tablespoonfuls of raw mirepoix (No. 138) in a saucepan with one ounce of butter; cook on a moderate fire for five minutes, then add two tablespoonfuls of flour, brown all well. Select one quart of well-washed, ripe, sound, fresh tomatoes, cut them into quarters, and plunge them into the saucepan with the rest, stirring briskly with a wooden spoon until they boil. Season with a good pinch of salt, half a pinch of pepper, and half a teaspoonful of powdered sugar. Boil the whole for forty-five minutes, then strain through a sieve into a vessel, and use when needed. This sauce can also be made with canned tomatoes, in which case cook them for only thirty minutes.

206. Sauce Mayonnaise.—Place two fresh egg yolks into an earthen bowl, with half a teaspoonful of ground English mustard, half a pinch of salt, half a saltspoonful of red pepper; sharply stir with a wooden spoon for two or three minutes without ceasing. Pour in, drop by drop, one and a half cupfuls of the best olive oil. Should it become too thick, add, drop by drop, the equivalent of a teaspoonful of very good vinegar, stirring vigorously with the wooden spoon meanwhile. Taste, and if found a little too acid, gradually add a tablespoonful of oil, stirring continually until all added. The whole operation to prepare the above sauce will take from ten to twelve minutes. To avoid spoiling the sauce, the sweet oil should always be kept in a place of moderate temperature, say, from 70° to 75° Fahrenheit.

207. Sauce Tartare.—Chop up one shallot exceedingly fine, with half a tablespoonful of chervil, and the same of tarragon, and twelve capers chopped exceedingly fine. Place these in an earthen bowl with half a teaspoonful of ground English mustard, two raw egg yolks, a teaspoonful of vinegar (a small drop at a time), half a pinch of salt, and a third of a pinch of pepper. Pour in very lightly, while continuing to stir, a cupful of good olive oil, and if too thick, add a little more vinegar. Taste it to find whether the seasoning is correct; if too salt, add a little more mustard and oil.

208. Victoria Sauce.—Pound one tablespoonful of lobster coral very fine with half an ounce of fresh butter. Then lay it aside. In three-quarters of a pint of Allemande sauce (No. 210), place half a glassful of white wine and six chopped mushrooms; let it warm thoroughly, without boiling, in a saucepan, and then mix in the lobster coral. Stir well, and serve. A few sliced truffles can be used, according to the quality of the dinner.

209. Remoulade Sauce.—Chop up very fine twelve capers, one shallot, three small vinegar-pickles, and add one-half a tablespoonful of chives, with one tablespoonful of parsley. Place them in a bowl with a whole raw egg, a teaspoonful of ground English mustard, half a pinch of salt, and half a pinch of pepper. Incorporate well together, adding four tablespoonfuls of oil and four of vinegar, but keep the sauce sufficiently liquid. Serve when required.

210. Sauce Allemande.—Melt two ounces of butter in a saucepan on a slow fire, with three tablespoonfuls of flour to thicken. Stir well, not letting it brown; then moisten with one pint of white broth (No. 99), beating constantly, and cook for ten minutes. Dilute three egg yolks separately in a bowl; pour the sauce over the eggs, a very little at a time; strain through a Chinese strainer, and finish with half an ounce of good butter and the juce of half a lemon, taking care that it does not boil a second time.

211. Prussian Sauce.—Add to three-quarters of a pint of hot béchamel sauce (No. 154), a teaspoonful of powdered sugar, a scant teaspoonful of red pepper, three tablespoonfuls of grated horseradish, and two tablespoonfuls of cold cream. Let it boil for four minutes, meanwhile stirring it well, and use when needed.

212. Sauce Chambord.—Place one truffle and three mushrooms, sliced very thin, in half a pint of Espagnole sauce (No. 151), adding three tablespoonfuls of Court bouillon (No. 142), six fish quenelles (No. 227), and twelve medium-sized, whole, blanched oysters. Cook slowly for five minutes, and serve.

213. Sauce Montglas.—Cut very carefully into small julienne-shaped pieces one ounce of cooked smoked beef tongue, one ounce of cooked chicken, two truffles, and four mushrooms. Place all in a saucepan, with half a wineglassful of good Madeira wine; place the pan on a brisk fire, and let reduce for three minutes. Then add half a pint of Espagnole sauce (No. 151), and one gill of good tomato sauce (No. 205). Let all cook for five minutes longer, and serve very hot.

214. Cuisson de Poisson — Fish Broth. For One Gallon.—Fill a saucepan with three quarts of water, a good handful of salt, half a glassful of vinegar, one carrot, and one onion (both sliced), half a handful of whole peppers, one bunch of parsley-roots, three sprigs of thyme, and three bay-leaves. Cook on a moderate fire for fifteen minutes. Cool, and use when needed for various methods of cooking fish.

215. Duxelle.—Reduce half a pint of cooked, fine herbs (No. 143) in a saucepan, with a quarter of a pint of Madeira sauce (No. 185), on a moderate stove for about ten minutes, when it will then be of a proper consistency and ready to serve.

216. Clear Gravy — For One Gallon.—Place two carrots and one onion cut in slices in a saucepan, with two ounces of uncooked, sliced, salt pork, one sprig of thyme, two bay-leaves, and half a bunch of parsley-roots. Add any scraps of meat, such as shin-bone of veal or beef, or chicken giblets, and a handful of salt; cover well, as it should not color, and moisten with one and a half gallons of water. Cook thoroughly for an hour and a half, then press through a napkin; place it in a stone jar, and use it after carefully removing all the fat.

217. Chicken Essence.—Press one quart of chicken broth through a napkin, and then reduce it in a saucepan until there remains only one-half a pint, and use when needed.

218. Fumet of Game.—Pare and slice one sound carrot and half a medium-sized onion; place them with half a sprig of thyme, one bay-leaf, a small piece of raw, lean ham, also cut up, and the carcass of any kind of raw game in a covered saucepan. Let them brown well; add a glassful of Madeira wine, let it come to a boil; then moisten with one quart of white broth (No. 99), or consommé (No. 100); add a pinch of salt, twelve whole peppers. Cook well for forty-five minutes, then press through a napkin.

219. Game Stock.—Place in a saucepan two game carcasses and one pint of mirepoix (No. 138); cover them with water, adding a pinch of salt. Cook for twenty minutes, and use when needed.

220. Sausage Forcemeat.—Cut up one pound of fresh pork into small pieces, season it with one pinch of salt, a saltspoonful of pepper, half a saltspoonful of grated nutmeg, and the same quantity of powdered thyme, and chop all up very fine. A quarter of a pound of lean, raw meat can be added if desired. Use when needed.

221. Godiveaux Forcemeat.—Remove the stringy tissue from half a pound of veal suet, pound it in a mortar; take the same quantity of lean veal, chopped in the machine, a quarter of a pound of very consistent pâte-à-chou (No. 1240), omitting the eggs, and pound all together. Season highly with a tablespoonful of salt, a teaspoonful of pepper, and half a teaspoonful of nutmeg. Add four raw egg yolks and two whole ones, and when well incorporated strain through a sieve, and put it on ice to be used when required in other recipes. Poach it for three minutes before serving.

This recipe can be prepared with poultry or game instead of veal.

222. Lobster Forcemeat—Fry an onion, chopped very fine, in one ounce of good butter until it is of a golden brown color, adding one tablespoonful of flour to make a roux (No. 135). Moisten with half a pint of white stock (No. 137), stirring well and constantly until the sauce hardens. Season with half a tablespoonful of salt, a scant teaspoonful of white pepper, the same of cayenne, one tablespoonful of English sauce, half a teaspoonful of mustard, a crushed grain of garlic, and one teaspoonful of chopped parsley. Stir well, adding two pounds of cooked lobster, cut up very fine, with twelve mushrooms, also chopped. Cook for thirty minutes in a saucepan, then put it back off the hot fire; add four egg yolks, stir again for a moment, cool, and serve when required.

223. Crab Forcemeat.—The same as for No. 222, using twelve crabs in the place of lobster.

224. Clam Forcemeat.—Proceed the same as for No. 222, seasoning it more highly, and having twenty-four clams blanched and minced exceedingly fine, so that they will better incorporate in the forcemeat.

225. Chicken Forcemeat à la Crême.—Cut two raw chicken breasts in slices, pound them well in a mortar, adding the whites of three eggs; bruise well together, and season with half a tablespoonful of salt, a scant teaspoonful of pepper, and a teaspoonful of nutmeg. Add three tablespoonfuls of very fresh cream, strain through a sieve, cool on the ice, and use when required.

226. Chicken Forcemeat.—Cut in large pieces two raw chicken breasts, pound them in a mortar, adding the same quantity of bread soaked in milk, a teaspoonful of fresh butter and four egg yolks, seasoning with half a tablespoonful of salt, a scant teaspoonful of pepper, and a teaspoonful of nutmeg. Mix all together; strain, and put it in a bowl with three tablespoonfuls of velouté sauce (No. 152).

227. Forcemeat Quenelles of Fish.—Select one pound of firm fish (bass is preferable), remove the skin and take out the bones. Pound it well in a mortar, adding the whites of three eggs a little at a time. When well pounded add half a pint of cream, half a tablespoonful of salt, and a little white pepper and nutmeg. Mix well, and use when needed.

228. Partridge Forcemeat.—Cut two breasts of partridges into large pieces, pound them well in a mortar, gradually adding the same quantity of bread soaked in milk, four egg yolks, one after another, and a teaspoonful of butter. Season with half a pinch of salt, the third of a pinch of pepper, and the same quantity of grated nutmeg; thoroughly pound all together, then rub through a sieve. If not sufficiently consistent, add one more egg yolk.

When game other than partridge is used add two pounded truffles, and use when required.

229. American Forcemeat.—Place on the fire in a saucepan for five minutes two very finely chopped onions with an ounce of butter. Soak in water for fifteen minutes the crumbs of a loaf of bread; press out all the water either with the hands or through a cloth, put the crumbs in a bowl with three whole raw eggs, a tablespoonful of salt, two teaspoonfuls of pepper, a tablespoonful of sage, a large half teaspoonful of nutmeg, three skinned sausages, and a pinch of chopped parsley. Add the cooked onions, and mix well together; use the forcemeat when needed in other recipes.

230. Mushroom Garnishing.—Mince finely twelve mushrooms and place them in a saucepan with half a pint of Madeira sauce (No. 185). Cook for five minutes, and serve.

231. Garnishing Bayard.—Cut into very thin round slices with a tube one good-sized truffle, one ounce of cooked smoked beef-tongue, three mushrooms, and two artichoke bottoms. Place all in a saucepan on the fire with half a wine-glassful of Madeira wine. Reduce to one-half, which will take about five minutes. Then add half a pint of Espagnole sauce (No. 151), and cook for fifteen minutes. Surround the dish with croûtons of bread (No. 133) covered with thin slices of paté-de-foie-gras.

232. Garnishing à la Chipolata—for one gallon.—Fry a quarter of a pound of salt pork, cut dice-shaped, for two minutes in a saucepan; then add half a pint of carrots cut tubular shaped, half a pint of onions browned and glazed in the oven (No. 972), one pint of blanched and peeled chestnuts, half a pint of mushrooms, and six small sausages cut in pieces. Add two quarts of Espagnole sauce (No. 151), half a pint of tomato sauce (No. 205), a tablespoonful of salt, and a large teaspoonful of pepper. Cook for thirty minutes, and use when needed.

233. Garnishing Vanderbilt.—Peel one green pepper; chop it very fine, and place it in a stewpan with one tomato cut into small pieces. Add an ounce of butter and eighteen canned, picked, and chopped-up shrimps; season with a third of a tablespoonful of salt and a scant teaspoonful of pepper. Cook for ten minutes, and use for garnishing.

234. Garnishing Valencienne.—Cut in long shreds one truffle, three mushrooms, and a very little cooked tongue, adding three tablespoonfuls of cooked rice; put all together in a stewpan with three tablespoonfuls of tomato sauce (No. 205), a third of a tablespoonful of salt, a scant teaspoonful of pepper, and one tablespoonful of grated cheese. Boil for five minutes, and serve when needed.

235. Garnishing Régence.—Take one pint of hot Allemande sauce (No. 210), add to it six mushrooms cut into large pieces, two truffles, six quenelles, either of godiveau (No. 221) or chicken, according to the usage, pieces of sweetbreads, six cocks combs (if handy) and six kidneys. This garnishing must be poached, before adding it to the sauce, in half a glassful of white wine, seasoned with a little salt and pepper. Let cook for six minutes, and add it to the sauce; warm it for three minutes, and serve. The same for fish, omitting the sweetbreads.

236. Garnishing à la St. Nazaire.—Add three tablespoonfuls of court bouillon (No. 142) to a small glassful of white wine, also one tablespoonful of cooked fine herbs (No. 143); add half a pint of Allemande sauce (No. 210), and a third of a pinch each of salt and pepper; pour the sauce over the fish to be served, and garnish with six very small, hot, stuffed clams (No. 376).

237. Garnishing à la Grecque—for roast or broiled meats.—Cut off both ends from twelve medium-sized whole okras, parboil them in boiling water for five minutes, drain, and put them into any kind of meat-juice or Madeira sauce (No. 185). Cook for ten minutes, and serve arranged in clusters with a quarter of a pint of Béarnaise sauce (No. 166).

238. Godard Garnishing.—Take six godiveau quenelles (No. 221) two truffles cut dice-shaped, six cocks' combs, six cocks' kidneys, and three mushrooms cut into square pieces; add half a glassful of Madeira wine, a pinch of salt, and half a pinch of pepper. Cook in a saucepan for five minutes, then add a pint of Madeira sauce (No. 185); boil again for five minutes, and serve when needed.

239. Tortue Garnishing.—Boil three chicken livers in water for three minutes, let them get cool, then cut them up into three pieces each, put them in a saucepan with six stoned and blanched olives, two truffles, four mushrooms, and a throat sweetbread, all cut dice-shaped; add a glassful of Madeira wine, half a pinch of salt, and the third of a pinch each of pepper and nutmeg. Let cook for five minutes, then put in half a pint of Madeira sauce (No. 185), and cook for five minutes longer. Serve with six bread croûtons (No. 133) and six fried eggs (No. 413) as garnishing.

240. Garnishing Parisienne.—Put in a saucepan half a glassful of Madeira wine, six sliced mushrooms, three sliced truffles, and let cook for four minutes. Add half a pint of Madeira sauce (No. 185), cook again for five minutes, then serve.

241. Garnishing Gourmet.—Take a cooked artichoke bottom, either fresh or conserved, and cut it into six pieces; place them in a saucepan with four mushrooms, two truffles, and a piece of cooked palate, all cut dice-shaped; add half a glassful of Madeira wine, and let cook five minutes; pour in half a pint of Madeira sauce (No. 185), cook again for five minutes, and serve.

242. Garnishing Cêpes.—Cut four cêpes into pieces; cook them in a sautoire for three minutes with a tablespoonful of olive oil, half a tablespoonful of salt, a teaspoonful of pepper, and half a clove of crushed garlic. Moisten with half a pint of Espagnole sauce (No. 151), and serve.

243. Bordelaise Garnishing, for tenderloins and steaks.—Place a peeled shallot chopped very fine in a sautoire with half a glassful of red wine, and cook for five minutes; add half a pint of Espagnole sauce (No. 151), a small pinch of red pepper, and cook for five minutes longer. Serve it poured over the fillets or steaks, placing on each one six slices of beef marrow, previously parboiled for one-half a minute.

244. Marrow Garnishing.—Open two fine marrow bones by setting them upright on the table, the narrow part on top, and with a sharp blow of the hatchet cleaving them in two, striking on one side only. Remove the marrow, put it into fresh salted water, and let it remain in for one hour. Then take it up, drain, and cut it into slices. Heat half a pint of

Madeira sauce (No. 185), add the pieces of marrow, and let it boil up once with a few drops of tarragon-vinegar. Serve with the slices of marrow on top.

245. Garnishing à la Patti.—Wash well two ounces of rice; drain, dry, and then put it in a saucepan with a pint of good white broth (No. 99). Pound the wing of a cooked chicken in a mortar and add it to the rice; season with a tablespoonful of salt and a teaspoonful of white pepper. Cook on a moderate fire for thirty minutes; strain through a fine sieve, return it to the saucepan with half an ounce of good butter and three tablespoonfuls of sweet cream, and heat slowly on the stove without boiling. Dress this garnishing in an artistic crown-shape around the hot serving dish; arrange the suprêmes in the centre, and decorate the garnishing with thin slices of truffles; with a light hair-brush drip a little meat-glaze (No. 141) over it and serve.

Suprêmes of partridges, quails, cotelettes of squabs, or sweetbreads à la Patti, are all to be served this way.

246. Garnishing Financière.—Cut a blanched, throat sweetbread into dice-sized pieces, put it in a saucepan with two truffles, six mushrooms, twelve stoned olives, six godiveau quenelles (No. 221), and two blanched chicken livers cut in pieces. Moisten with half a glassful of sherry or Madeira wine, and season with half a pinch each of salt and pepper, and a quarter of a pinch of nutmeg; add a pint of Madeira sauce (No. 185), cook again for ten minutes, skim off the fat, and serve when required.

247. Garnishing Ecarlate.—Cook in a saucepan half a pint of tomato sauce (No. 205) with half a pint of Espagnole sauce (No. 151), and a little cooked, smoked beef-tongue, chopped very fine; let cook for six minutes, then serve.

248. Garnishing à la Stanley.—Pour a pint of very hot Russian sauce (No. 211) upon the hot serving-dish. Lay the mignons filets, or any other meat, including broiled fillets, sirloin steaks, etc., on top, and garnish with six fried bananas cut in halves, and send to the table immediately.

249. Garnishing à la Montebello.—Place a pint of tomato sauce (No. 205) in a saucepan; add a pint of Béarnaise sauce (No. 166) and three good-sized, nicely sliced truffles; heat well by means of the Bain-Marie, without boiling, and serve.

250. Garnishing Soubise.—Cut up three medium-sized, white onions, and place them in a saucepan with an ounce of butter, half a cupful of white broth (No. 99), a tablespoonful of salt, and a small saltspoonful of white pepper. Cover the saucepan and cook for twenty minutes, stirring frequently. Add one pint of béchamel sauce (No. 154), and boil again for five minutes. Strain the sauce through a tammy, return it to the saucepan, season it a little more, if necessary, adding a little grated nutmeg and a little warm milk, in case it should be too thick; warm it well again, and serve.

251. Garnishing Milanaise.—Cut into julienne-shaped pieces two medium-sized truffles, six mushrooms, and the same quantity of smoked, cooked tongue, and place them in a saucepan with a pint of cooked rice, half a pint of tomato sauce (No. 205), half a pint of Madeira sauce (No. 185), a tablespoonful of salt, very little pepper, and three tablespoonfuls of grated cheese, either Parmesan or Swiss. Cook for ten minutes and serve.

252. Garnishing Rouennaise.—Cut three medium-sized turnips into six pieces, clove-of-garlic-shaped, pare them nicely and put them in a sautoire with one ounce of butter, sprinkling over them a little powdered sugar. Put the lid on tightly and cook in the oven for ten minutes, shaking it by the handle frequently. Moisten with a pint of Espagnole sauce (No. 151); add a pinch each of salt and pepper; cook again for twenty minutes, skim off the fat, and serve.

253. Garnishing Robinson.—Cut the gall away carefully from twelve chicken livers, wash clean and wipe them well, and then fry them with an ounce of butter in a frying-pan. Season them with a tablespoonful of salt and two teaspoonfuls of pepper, and after cooking three minutes, put them in a saucepan, with a pint of Madeira sauce (No. 185); boil for five minutes and serve.

254. A Bouquet.—how to prepare.—Take four branches of well-washed parsley-stalks—if the branches be small, take six—one branch of soup-celery, well washed; one blade of bay-leaf, one sprig of thyme, and two cloves, placed in the centre of the parsley, so as to prevent cloves, thyme, and bay-leaf from dropping out of the bouquet while cooking; fold it well, and tightly tie with a string, and use when required in various recipes.

A pinch of salt represents 205 grains, or a tablespoonful.

Half a pinch of pepper represents 38 grains, or a teaspoonful.

A third of a pinch of nutmeg represents 13 grains, or half a teaspoonful.

HORS D'OEUVRES.

255. Salpicon Royal.—Cut a blanched throat sweetbread (No. 601) into small pieces, and put them into a saucepan, with half an ounce of good butter, six mushrooms, and one truffle, all nicely cut into dice-shape. Thicken with half a pint of good béchamel sauce (No. 154), or Allemande sauce (No. 210), and let cook on a slow fire for five minutes, gently tossing meanwhile. Finish by adding half an ounce of crawfish-butter (No. 150); stir well, and it will then be ready to use for the desired garnishing.

256. Salpicon à la Financière.—Take either the leg or the breast of a roasted chicken. Cut it into dice-shaped pieces, and put them into a saucepan with half an ounce of good butter, adding four mushrooms, one truffle, half an ounce of cooked, smoked beef-tongue, all cut in dice-shaped pieces, and twelve small godiveau quenelles (No. 221); thicken with half a pint of Madeira sauce (No. 185), and let cook for five minutes. It will then be ready for any garnishing desired.

257. Salpicon au Chasseur.—Cut the breast of a fine cooked partridge into dice-shaped pieces, and put them into a saucepan on the hot range, with half an ounce of butter, half a glassful of good sherry wine, three blanched chicken livers, one truffle, four mushrooms, and half an ounce of cooked, smoked beef-tongue, all cut into dice. Thicken with half a pint of hot salmi sauce (No. 193), and let all cook for five minutes, and use it for any garnishing desired.

258. Salpicon of Lobster, Crawfish, or Shrimps.—Put a pint of good béchamel (No. 154) into a saucepan, with four mushrooms, one truffle, and the meat from the claw of a cooked lobster, cutting them all into dice-shaped pieces. Thicken well and let cook for five minutes, and serve. If a lobster cannot be obtained, the meat of three cooked crawfish, or of six prawns or shrimps, may be used instead.

259. Salpicon à la Montglas.—Mince, as for a julienne, four mushrooms, one truffle, the breast of a small cooked chicken, or of any game, and half an ounce of cooked ham, or the same quantity of cooked, smoked beef-tongue. Put all into a saucepan, adding a gill of well reduced Madeira sauce (No. 185) and a gill of tomato sauce (No. 205); let cook for five minutes ; then use when needed.

260. Salpicon, Sauce Madère.—Place half an ounce of good butter in a saucepan, adding half a glassful of sherry wine, a blanched throat sweetbread (No. 601) nicely cut into dice-shaped pieces, four mushrooms, one truffle, and an ounce of cooked, smoked beef-tongue, all cut the same as the sweetbread. Let cook for five minutes, then add half a pint of Madeira sauce (No. 185), and let cook again for five minutes. It will now be ready to use for the desired garnishing.

261. Timbales à l'Ecossaise.— Butter well six small timbale-molds, and line them with cuts of plain, unsweetened pancake (No. 1186). Take a preparation of purée of chicken (No. 226), and the same quantity of raw forcemeat (No. 220), add to it a reduced salpicon (No. 256), and with this fill the molds. Cover with small round pieces of the pancake. Then steam them in a moderate oven for eight minutes. Unmold, dress them on a hot dish, pour a gill of hot Madeira sauce (No. 185) over, and serve.

262. Timbales de Nouilles à la Genoise.—Sprinkle the insides of six well-buttered timbale-molds with grated, fresh bread-crumbs; line them with thin foundation paste (No. 1078), and fill with finely shred, boiled nouilles (No. 1182), adding an ounce of good butter, and seasoning with half a pinch each of salt and pepper, and the third of a pinch of nutmeg; also half an ounce of grated Parmesan cheese. Thicken with a gill of strong Madeira sauce (No. 185). Cover the molds with pieces of the foundation paste, and put them into a brisk oven for six minutes. Unmold, and arrange them on a hot dish containing a gill of hot Madeira sauce (No. 185), and with the timbales on top.

263. Timbales Russe à la Schultze.—Prepare six light timbales as for No. 262, one and a quarter inches high by two and a quarter inches in diameter. Arrange them on a dessert dish with a folded napkin, and lay them in a cool place until needed. Put into a china bowl half of a fine, well-cleaned, sound Camembert cheese, mash it thoroughly with a fork, and drop on to it very gradually one and a half ponies of old brandy. Cut into small pieces two medium-sized, cooked, throat sweetbreads (No. 601), and add them to the cheese, mixing well together. Season with half a teaspoonful of salt, a saltspoonful of pepper, and the same quantity of grated nutmeg, stirring well for a minute longer. Then add four medium-sized, chopped truffles, and mix again. Divide the above preparation equally, into the six timbales, cover each with a thin slice of truffle, previously dipped in brandy, and send to the table.

264. Croustade á la Régence.—Spread out a quarter of a pound of pâté-à-foucer (No. 1078) an eighth of an inch thick. Clean well six tartlet moulds; line them with the paste, then fill them with cracker-dust; cover them with a buttered paper, place them in the hot oven on a tin plate, and bake for ten or twelve minutes. Take from out the oven and let cool. Remove all the cracker-dust, and they will be ready for use. Fill them with a pint of hot régence (No. 235), evenly divided; dress on a hot dish with a folded napkin, and send to the table.

265. Croustades de Riz à la Victoria.—Wash thoroughly and boil in a saucepan one quart of rice with two quarts of broth and one ounce of butter. Keep it as dry as possible so that it remains firm, and add to it half an ounce of grated Parmesan cheese, half a pinch of pepper, and a third of a pinch of nutmeg. Mix well with a wooden spoon; then put it in a buttered sautoire, spreading it an inch and three-quarters thick, and cover with a buttered paper. Leave it to cool with a weight pressed down on the top. Then cut it out with a No. 8 paste-cutter into six croustades (being careful to dip the cutter in warm water each time it is used), and with a No. 4 paste-cutter make a mark on the surface of each without cutting. Dip the pieces in beaten egg, roll them in bread-crumbs (No. 301), and repeat this. Then fry them in very hot fat for five minutes; drain, empty them with a vegetable spoon, and fill the insides with a pint of hot salpicon of shrimps (No. 258), mushrooms, and cream sauce (No. 181). Put the covers on top, and serve the same as the croustades à la régence (No. 264).

266. Small Hot Patties à l'Anglaise.—Line with fine pâté-à-foucer (No. 1078) six small, hot patty-molds, fluted, and provided with hinges. Pinch the tops and fill them with common flour. Bake in a moderate oven for fifteen minutes; empty them, and leave them to dry at the oven door for five minutes. Fill them with a pint of hot salpicon royal (No. 255), place a slice of truffle on the top of each instead of a cover, and serve on a hot dish with a folded napkin.

267. Ortolan Patties.—Make six patties the same as for the above, (No. 266), only use them when cold. Place at the bottom of each a tablespoonful of salpicon royal (No. 255), and then place in each patty two well-picked, fine, fat, raw, seasoned reed-birds, covered with a slice of thin lard; lay them on a small roasting-pan, place in a moderate oven and roast for fifteen minutes. Remove from the oven, take off the lard from the birds, moisten each patty with two tablespoonfuls of good, hot, Madeira sauce (No. 185), and serve on a hot dish with a folded napkin over it.

268. Cromesquis aux Truffles.—Bone a cooked chicken, hash the meat very fine, and put it in a sautoire with a pint of very strong velouté sauce (No. 152), adding two well-hashed truffles, and seasoning with a good pinch of salt, half a pinch of pepper, and the third of a pinch of nutmeg. Let cook for ten minutes, stirring occasionally, then transfer it to a flat tin plate and let it cool. Spread it out an inch thick; then divide it into six parts, and wrap each one in a veal udder, or a piece of crepinette well rolled around. Immerse them in flour batter (No. 1185), and plunge them into boiling fat for five minutes, or until they are slightly browned. Drain on a cloth, and serve on a hot dish with a folded napkin, decorating with fried parsley.

All cromesquis are made the same way, only serving with different garnishing or sauces.

269. Canapé Madison.—Prepare six medium-sized slices of bread, all the same shape. Toast them to a good golden color and lay them on a dish. Cover each toast with a very thin slice of lean, cooked ham; spread a little mustard over; then cover with a layer of garnishing à la provençale (No. 642), dredge grated Parmesan cheese on top, and strew a little fresh bread-crumbs over all. Place them in the hot oven and bake for ten minutes; remove, dress them on a hot dish with a folded napkin, and send to the table.

270. Small Bouchées à la Reine.—Roll three-quarters of a pound of feuilletage paste (No. 1076) to a quarter of an inch thick; let it rest for ten minutes in a cold place, then cut six rounds out of the paste with a No. 4 channeled paste-cutter. Lay them on a borderless, buttered tin baking-dish, slightly apart from each other; cover with beaten egg, and make a mark on the surface of each with a paste-cutter, No. 2, being careful to dip the cutter each time in hot water, so that the marked outline may remain perfect. Put them in a brisk oven for twelve minutes; then lift the covers with a knife, and fill each one with a white salpicon royal (No. 256) made of truffles, mushrooms, and finely shred chicken. Set the covers on, and serve on a hot dish with a folded napkin.

All bouchées are made the same way, adding different garnishings according to taste.

271. Coquilles of Chicken à l'Anglaise.—Fill six table-shells with a thick chicken and truffle salpicon (No. 256); besprinkle the tops with grated, fresh bread-crumbs, spread a little clarified butter over each, and lay them on a very even baking-dish. Place them in a very hot oven for about six minutes, or until they are of a golden brown color, then serve the same as for the above.

272. Coquilles of Oysters au Gratin.—Blanch twenty-four medium-sized oysters in their own liquor for five minutes; add half a pinch of pepper and half an ounce of butter; then drain them, keeping the liquor for further use. Add to the oysters half a pint of velouté sauce (No.

152), mixed with three tablespoonfuls of the oyster liquor; keep it thick, and be very careful not to break the oysters. Fill six table-shells with this preparation, sprinkle with grated, fresh bread-crumbs and a very little clarified butter, and brown well in the oven for six minutes. Dress on a hot dish with a folded napkin, and serve.

273. Oysters in Shells à l'Anglaise.—Select eighteen large oysters. Put three into each of six table-shells and season with a pinch of pepper, besprinkle with slightly fried bread-crumbs, and lay them on a flat roasting-pan. Place them in a very brisk oven for about four minutes, or until the oysters raise; then serve on a dish with a folded napkin.

274. Lamb Sweetbreads en Petites Caisses.—Blanch, pare, and clean six small lamb sweetbreads as for No. 601. Lay them aside to cool, then lard them with either fresh fat pork or truffles. Place them in a well-buttered sautoire, adding a gill of chicken broth or a gill of Madeira wine. Cover with a buttered paper, and let cook to a golden color in the oven for ten minutes. Then lay them on a dish. Put half a gill of cooked fine herbs (No. 143) and a gill of well-reduced Espagnole sauce (No. 151) into the sautoire, letting it cook for five minutes. Take six small boxes of buttered paper and pour a little of the gravy at the bottom of each; cover with sweetbreads, and place them on a baking-dish; keep them for five minutes in an open oven, then serve on a folded napkin.

275. Oysters en Petites Caisses.—Open and blanch for five minutes twenty-four medium-sized oysters in a sautoire with half a glassful of white wine and half an ounce of butter. Season with half a pinch of pepper and a third of a pinch of nutmeg. Let cook for five minutes; then add one pint of well-reduced velouté sauce (No. 152), and let cook for another five minutes, adding half an ounce of crawfish butter (No. 150), and stirring it occasionally. Fill six buttered paper boxes with four oysters each, and the garnishing equally divided. Sprinkle over a little fresh bread-crumbs, and arrange them on a tin roasting-pan. Spread a very little butter over each patty, and put them in a moderate oven for five minutes. Have a hot dish ready, with a folded napkin nicely arranged on it; dress the patties over, and serve.

276. Chicken Croquettes with Truffles.—Bone and cut up a medium-sized, cooked chicken into small, square pieces; put them in a sautoire with two truffles cut the same way, adding half a pint of strong velouté (No. 152), and let cook for ten minutes. Then incorporate therein half a glassful of Madeira wine, four egg yolks, a pinch of salt, half a pinch of pepper, and the third of a pinch of nutmeg. Stir briskly, then put it away to cool in a flat dish. Now divide the mixture into six even parts; lay them on a cold table, besprinkle with fresh bread-crumbs, and roll them into oblong shapes. Dip each one into a beaten egg, and roll again in fresh bread-crumbs. Fry to a nice color in hot fat for four minutes. Drain thoroughly, and serve on a hot dish with a folded napkin, decorating with a little green parsley.

All chicken croquettes are prepared the same way, only served with different garnishings and sauces, or by omitting the truffles and substituting six hashed mushrooms. Sweetbread croquettes are prepared the same, only substituting four blanched sweetbreads (No. 601) for the chicken.

277. Croquettes of Game.—To be made exactly like the chicken croquettes (No. 276), adding six hashed mushrooms and half a gill of cold fumet de gibier (No. 218).

278. Croquettes of Foie-gras.—Mix half an ounce of cooked, smoked beef-tongue with half a pint of dry salpicon of foie-gras. Put it into a saucepan with a gill of béchamel (No. 154), half a glassful of Madeira or sherry wine, and a tablespoonful of meat-glaze (No. 141). Reduce for ten minutes, stirring well, then transfer to a cold, flat dish, cover with buttered paper, and put aside to cool. Divide the preparation into six parts—each one shaped like a pear—roll them in fresh bread-crumbs, dip in beaten egg, and put a slice of truffle on the top of each. Again roll in bread-crumbs, and fry in boiling fat for four minutes. Remove them, drain well, and serve on a hot dish with a folded napkin. Any desired garnishing may be added.

279. Croquettes of Macaroni.—Boil a quarter of a pound of Italian macaroni in salted water for twenty-five minutes. Drain, and put it in a saucepan with a good ounce of butter, half an ounce of Parmesan cheese, and a quarter of an ounce of cooked, smoked tongue cut into small pieces, and one truffle cut the same. Toss all together, then change it to a well-buttered sautoire, spreading the preparation one inch thick on the bottom. Cover with a buttered paper, press it well down, and put away to cool. Cut the preparation with a plain paste-cutter into six parts; roll each one in grated Parmesan cheese, dip in beaten egg, and roll in grated, fresh, white bread-crumbs. Fry in very hot fat for four minutes, drain well, and serve on a hot dish with a folded napkin.

280. Anchovies on Toast.—Prepare with American bread six dry toasts, spread over them a little anchovy butter (No. 146), and cover each with four half anchovies. Place the toasts on a tin baking-sheet in the oven for one minute. Arrange them on a dish with a folded napkin, and serve.

281. Caviare on Toast.—Prepare six toasts of American bread. Put half the contents of a small box of Russian caviare into a sautoire; add two tablespoonfuls of cream, and heat one and a half minutes on the stove, stirring it carefully meanwhile; pour this over the toasts, and serve on a dish with a folded napkin.

282. Thon Mariné.—Fold a napkin on a radish-dish, and dress on it the desired quantity of Thon Mariné—*pickled tunny*. Decorate with a little fresh parsley, and serve as a *hors-d'œuvre*.

283. Sardines à l'Huile.—Lift the sardines carefully out of the box to avoid breaking them, and lay them on a plate; neatly pare off the loose skin, then dress on a radish-dish, and decorate with parsley.

284. Anchovies à l'Huile.—Take a pint bottle of boned anchovies, drain them on a cloth, then dress them artistically on a radish-dish. Decorate with a hashed, hard-boiled egg and some chopped parsley.

285. **Norwegian Anchovies.**—These are considered far superior to the bottled anchovies. On taking them out of the keg they should be placed in cold, fresh water for two hours, then drained, and with the hand split in two along the backbone. Lay them in a small bowl and cover with sweet oil, and use as desired.

286. **Saucisson de Lyon.**—Procure a medium-sized, fine saucisson de Lyon, cut twelve very thin slices from it, dress nicely upon a radish-dish, and place a few parsley-leaves in the centre.

287. **Mortadella.**—To be served the same as the above (No. 286).

288. **Tomatoes, side dish.**—Take six fine, firm, red tomatoes, wipe well, then plunge them into boiling water for one minute, drain and peel them. Put them in a cool place, and when thoroughly cold, cut them into slices, arrange them on a radish-dish, sprinkle a little salt, pepper, and vinegar over.

289. **Cucumbers, side dish.**—Take two medium-sized, fine cucumbers, peel neatly, and cut them in thin slices. Place in a bowl with a good pinch of salt, and put them in a cold place for two hours. Then drain the liquid off, and season with half a pinch of pepper, a tablespoonful of vinegar, and the same quantity of oil. Dress nicely in a radish-dish.

290. **Celery, in glass.**—Procure a bunch of fine, white Kalamazoo celery, pare off the green stalks, and trim the roots neatly. Be careful to save the clear, white hearts. Cut each plant lengthwise into four equal branches. Wash them well in cold water, and put them into clean water with a piece of ice until ready to serve; then arrange them nicely in a celery glass, or dress on a china radish-dish, with a few pieces of ice in the centre.

291. **Celery, frizzled.**—Another and economical way to prepare celery for a side dish to decorate the table. Take only one large head of fine celery. Pare off the green stalks, and cut off the root (reserving it for a delicious and wholesome salad). Cut the stalk lengthwise into four equal branches. Wash them well in cold water, then cut each one into pieces about as long as one's finger; by so doing, all the branches will be separated. With the aid of a small, keen knife pare the thin sides a little, making five or six slits in each piece, starting from the top, downwards, leaving half to three-quarters of an inch uncut; place them in cold water with plenty of ice, leaving them in for two hours. Lift it from the ice-water, artistically dress on a round glass dish, and send to the table. Celery arranged and served in this way makes a beautiful effect on the table, but requires a little patience in its preparation.

292. **Radishes, how to prepare.**—If the radishes be quite large, take three bunches—if small, four bunches—being careful to select them round, firm, and the reddest procurable. Pare off all the leaves and stems except the two prettiest on each radish. Cut away the roots, and also a little of the peel around the roots. With a small, sharp knife divide the remaining peel into five or six equal-sized leaves, beginning at the root end, and cutting toward the green stems, but being careful to

avoid detaching the leaves. They can be formed into any desired design by cutting them with care. Place them in cold water until required. When serving, arrange the radishes artistically on a flat saucer, the radishes meeting toward the centre, the green leaves lying outward. Serve with chopped ice over them.

293. Remarks Regarding Radishes.—The following incident happened in my presence over twenty-five years ago. One evening, dinner was served to a party of prominent gentlemen in Lyons, France, among whom were Alexander Dumas, père, the great novelist, and Berger, the famous billiard player. While the waiter was in the act of handing the radishes to M. Dumas, he saw a change come over him; anger was depicted in his face, and he thoroughly expected to see the radishes, radish-dish, etc., flung full at him. He stood amazed, not daring to question the distinguished guest. When his anger subsided, he amiably explained that the cause of his sudden ill-temper was offering to him radishes peeled, and deprived of their green stalks; he asserted that the healthiest and best parts had been removed. After inquiries of more experienced co-laborers, the waiter thoroughly agreed with M. Dumas, and experience has taught him the correctness of his judgment.

Radishes are a luxurious and healthful adjunct to the dinner-table, and can be procured almost the whole year; but in the spring the markets are more plentifully supplied, and that is the most wholesome season to partake of them.

294. Welsh Rarebit.—Take one pound of American cheese; cut up in small pieces. Place them in a sautoire, adding half a glassful of good ale. Season with half a saltspoonful of red pepper. Stir it continually with a wooden spoon until the mass is well melted, which will take about ten minutes. Have six nice, fresh, large pieces of toast; arrange them on a very hot dish, and distribute the preparation equally over, serving the rarebit very hot.

295. Golden Buck.—Proceed as for the above (No. 294), and when ready to serve, dress a poached egg (No. 404) on each piece of toast, and serve very hot.

296. Gherkin Buck.—Prepared the same as Golden Buck (No. 295), only adding to each toast a slice of broiled bacon (No. 754), and sending to the table very hot.

297. Welsh Rarebit au Gratin.—Prepare six toasts of American bread; broil them lightly, remove, and cover each with a slice of Swiss cheese a little less than half an inch thick; lay them in a roasting-pan, sprinkling a very little pepper over. Put in the oven for ten minutes. Arrange the toasts on a very hot dish, and send to the table.

A pinch of salt represents 205 grains, or a tablespoonful.

Half a pinch of pepper represents 38 grains, or a teaspoonful.

A third of a pinch of nutmeg represents 13 grains, or half a teaspoonful.

FISH.

298. How to Serve Oysters for Private Families.—Oysters should be kept in a very cold place before they are opened, and well washed before using, otherwise their appearance will be destroyed. They should, according to the French custom, be opened on the deep shell, so as to better preserve the liquor, then laid on finely chopped ice for a short time —too long destroys their flavor. While they should be kept as cold as possible, they should never be allowed to freeze, therefore they must only be opened shortly before they are needed; for once frozen, they quickly turn sour. The proper way to open them is to place the deep shell in the palm of the left hand, and break them on one side. The Boston stabbing-knife is preferable for this, but if there be none handy use a small block that the oyster can fit into, and stab it on the edge; or even a chopping-block and chopping-knife may be employed in case of necessity. Serve six oysters for each person, nicely arranged on oyster-plates with quarters of lemon.

299. Oysters à l'Alexandre Dumas.—Place in a sauce-bowl a heaped teaspoonful of salt, three-quarters of a teaspoonful of very finely crushed white pepper, one medium-sized, fine, sound, well-peeled, and very finely chopped shallot, one heaped teaspoonful of very finely chopped chives, and half a teaspoonful of parsley, also very finely chopped up. Mix lightly together, then pour in a light teaspoonful of olive oil, six drops of Tabasco sauce, one saltspoonful of Worcestershire sauce, and lastly one light gill, or five and a half tablespoonfuls, of good vinegar. Mix it thoroughly with a spoon; send to the table, and with a teaspoon pour a little of the sauce over each oyster just before eating them.

300. How to serve Clams.—Clams should be served on deep plates, covered previously with finely chopped ice. To have them sweet and fresh, they should be kept as cold as possible. Serve six on each plate with quarters of lemon.

301. To prepare Breaded Fish.—1. After the fish is pared, cleaned, and dried, dip it first in milk, then in flour, and fry in very hot fat.

2. Take very clean fish, dip it in beaten egg, then in freshly grated bread-crumbs, and fry in very hot fat.

3. For certain fish, like whitebait, immerse them in milk, then in flour mixed with pulverized crackers, shake well in a colander, and throw into very hot fat. Oysters are breaded the same way, but should be flattened before frying.

4. For croustades of rice or potatoes, dip in beaten egg and roll in fresh bread-crumbs; repeat three times before frying.

302. Salmon, en Papillotes.—Procure two pounds of very fresh salmon and cut it into six even slices. Season these with a good pinch of salt and a pinch of pepper. Roll them well. Cut out six heart-shaped pieces of paper, oil them nicely, and have twelve thin slices of cooked ham (No. 753), then proceed to prepare them exactly as for mackerel en papillote (No. 330).

303. Salmon, oyster sauce.—Place two pounds of very fresh salmon in a fish-kettle, completely cover with cold water, season with a handful of salt, add one medium-sized, sliced onion, half a wine-glassful of white vinegar, eight whole peppers, two cloves, and two parsley-roots. Range the kettle on a brisk fire. Five minutes after coming to a boil the salmon will be sufficiently cooked. Remove from the kettle, drain it well; dress on a hot dish with a folded napkin, nicely decorate with parsley-greens all around the salmon, and serve with a pint of hot oyster sauce (No. 173) separately.

The necessary time to cook the above to perfection, from beginning to end, will be thirty-five minutes.

304. Salmon Colbert.—Proceed as for the above, and serve with three-quarters of a pint of Colbert sauce (No. 190), also four plain boiled potatoes served separately, and cut in quarters (No. 982).

305. Salmon à la Régence.—Take a fine but very small salmon, fill it with fish forcemeat (No. 227), and put it on a grate in the fish-kettle with half a bunch of parsley-roots, three sprigs of celery, three sliced onions, six cloves, and half a handful of whole pepper. Moisten with half a bottle of white wine, season with a pinch of salt, and cover with a thin *barde* of raw salt pork. Add a little mushroom-liquor, if any on hand, and place it in a moderate oven for one and a half to two hours; then lift it from the kettle, removing the pork and herbs. Slide the fish on to a hot dish, strain the broth into a sautoire, reduce it to one-half, and add to the garnish with a régence garnishing (No. 235); glaze the top of the fish with just a little crawfish butter (No. 150) mixed with very little white glaze (No. 141), and serve with the sauce in a sauce-bowl.

306. Salmon à la Genoise.—To be prepared the same as salmon Colbert (No. 304), garnishing with four clusters of mushrooms—four mushrooms on each cluster—and six cooked crawfish instead of the boiled potatoes. Serve with half a pint of Genoise sauce (No. 187) separate.

307. Salmon, rolled à l'Irlandaise.—Bone three pounds of salmon. Parboil it. -Besprinkle the sides and insides with a pinch of salt, half a pinch of pepper, and the same of nutmeg; also twelve chopped oysters, one tablespoonful of parsley, and half a cupful of bread-crumbs. Roll it together, then put it in a deep pan with one ounce of butter. Bake in a hot oven for twenty-five minutes and serve on a dish, pouring its own gravy over.

308. Broiled Salmon-tail.—Take three pounds of the tail part of a salmon. Steep it for five or six hours in a marinade composed of three tablespoonfuls of olive oil in a dish with a quarter of a bunch of parsley-roots, two bay-leaves, and a sprig of thyme. Take out the salmon and broil for ten minutes on one side and five minutes on the other (skin side). Dress on a hot dish, and serve with two ounces of melted butter (No. 155), flavored with a light teaspoonful of finely chopped chervil, half a teaspoonful of chives, and the juice of half a medium-sized, sound lemon.

309. Boiled Halibut.—Put a piece of halibut weighing two pounds in a saucepan, and cover it with fresh water ; add one sliced onion, half a sliced carrot, and a bouquet (No. 254). Season with a handful of salt and two tablespoonfuls of vinegar. Put on the lid and let cook gently, but no more than five minutes after boiling-point ; then lift up the fish alone, drain well ; dress it on a hot dish, and serve with any desired sauce.

310. Halibut Steaks, maître d'hôtel.—Wipe well a two-pound piece of fresh halibut, lay it on a dish, and season it with a pinch of salt, a pinch of pepper, and two tablespoonfuls of sweet oil. Roll it well and lay it on a double broiler ; then place it on a brisk fire, and broil for eight minutes on each side. Dress the fish on a hot dish, pour a gill of maître d'hôtel sauce (No. 145) over, decorate with parsley-greens, and serve.

311. Trout, shrimp sauce.—Clean, wash, and dry six fine trout, weighing about a quarter of a pound each. Place them on a grate in the fish-kettle, with a pinch of salt, adding one sliced carrot, one sprig of thyme, and two bay-leaves. Moisten with half a glassful of white wine and half a pint of water. Put it on the stove, and let it simmer gently for five minutes after boiling-point; then drain, and serve on a dish garnished with parsley. Send it to the table with half a pint of shrimp sauce (No. 178) in a separate bowl, also four plain, boiled potatoes, cut in quarters, à l'Anglaise (No. 988). Keep the fish-stock for further use.

312. Trout à la Cambaceres.—Cook six trout as for the above (No. 311); when cooked, then place on a hot dish. Put in a saucepan two minced truffles, six mushrooms, also minced, and half a pint of Espagnole sauce No. 151), also twelve olives and three tablespoonfuls of tomato sauce No. 205). Let cook for ten minutes, then skim off the fat very carefully, and pour the sauce over the trout before serving.

313. Trout à la Chambord.—Clean, wash, and dry three fine trout of half a pound each. Stuff them with fish forcemeat (No. 227), and place them in a deep baking-dish, buttering it well with about half an ounce of butter. Add half a glassful of white wine, a bouquet (No. 254), half a pinch of salt, and half a pinch of pepper. Cook for fifteen minutes in the oven, being very careful to baste it frequently. Take the juice from under the fish, and put it in a saucepan with half a pint of good Espagnole sauce (No. 151). Reduce, and skim off the fat. Add one truffle and four mushrooms, all well-sliced, also twelve blanched oysters. Dress the trout on a hot dish, pour the sauce over, and decorate the fish with six fish quenelles (No. 227).

314. Broiled Trout, maître d'hôtel.—Procure six fine trout, of a quarter of a pound each ; clean and wash well, drain them in a napkin, and make three incisions on each side. Place them on a dish with one teaspoonful of oil, a pinch of salt, and half a pinch of pepper ; roll gently and put them on the broiler. Cook for four minutes on each side, then lay them on a dish, pour a gill of maître d'hôtel sauce (No. 177) over, and serve with six slices of lemon, or with any other sauce desired.

315. Trout, with fine herbs.—Clean, wash, and dry six fine trout, of a quarter of a pound each. Put them on a buttered dish, adding half a glassful of white wine and one finely chopped shallot. Let cook for ten minutes, then put the gravy in a saucepan, with two tablespoonfuls of cooked herbs (No. 143), moistening with half a pint of Allemande sauce (No. 210). Reduce the gravy to one-half, and pour it over the trout with the juice of half a sound lemon, and serve.

316. Trout en Papillotes.—Take six trout, of a quarter of a pound each, and stuff them with fish forcemeat (No. 227). Oil as many pieces of paper as there are fish; put a *barde* of salt pork on either end of each piece of paper, lay a trout on top, add a little salt and pepper, then fold the paper and tie it securely with string. Cook in a baking-dish in a rather slow oven for about twenty minutes, and serve them in their envelopes, after removing the strings, with any sauces desired.

317. Sole à l'Hollandaise.—Skin and bone well three medium-sized soles; put the fillets in a stewpan, and cover them with salted water, adding a few drops of vinegar. Cook for about six minutes. Then take them off, drain well, and arrange them on a dish. Pour one ounce of melted butter over, with the juice of half a lemon; garnish with green parsley, and serve with twelve pieces of potatoes à l'Anglaise (No. 988) separate.

318. Soles Normande.—Take the fillets from three fine soles, as for the above; fold them in two, and lay them in a buttered, flat saucepan, with half a glassful of white wine, three tablespoonfuls of mushroom liquor, and half a pinch each of salt and pepper. Cover and cook for six minutes; then lift them up, drain, and arrange them on a dish. Reduce the gravy to one-half, add twelve blanched oysters, and six sliced mushrooms, moistening with half a pint of Allemande sauce (No. 210). Thicken the sauce well with a tablespoonful of good butter, tossing well till dissolved, and add the juice of half a lemon. Garnish the sides of the dish with the oysters and mushrooms, and pour the sauce over the fish. Decorate with three small, cooked crawfish, three fried smelts, and three small, round croquettes of potatoes (No. 997).

319. Soles au Gratin.—Proceed as for No. 318. Put three tablespoonfuls of cooked, fine herbs (No. 143) in the bottom of a deep baking-dish, fold the fillets in two, and place them in, crown-shaped. Season with half a pinch each of salt and pepper, then moisten with half a glassful of white wine, and bake for five minutes. Take out the dish, decorate it with twelve mushroom buttons, adding half a pint of good Espagnole sauce (No. 151). Sprinkle over with fresh bread-crumbs, pour on a few drops of melted butter, and bake once more for three minutes, then press the juice of half a lemon over the fillets, add half a pinch of chopped parsley, and serve. (All fish au gratin are prepared the same way.)

320. Fried Soles, sauce Colbert.—Select six small soles, cut off their heads, and make an incision down the backbone. Season with one pinch of salt, half a pinch of pepper, and the juice of half a lemon; roll in fresh bread-crumbs and beaten eggs, then flatten them well, and leave them to drip for a few minutes; fry them for three minutes in very hot fat; drain, add another half a pinch of salt, and arrange them on a dish on a folded napkin. Garnish with a quarter of a bunch of fried parsley, and serve with half a pint of Colbert sauce (No. 190) separate.

321. Fried Soles à la Horly.—Fry twelve fillets of sole as for No. 320, and serve with half a pint of tomato sauce (No. 205) separate.

322. Fillets of Sole, Joinville.—Take the fillets of three soles, fold them, and lay them crown-shaped in a buttered, flat stewpan, moistening with half a glassful of white wine, and three tablespoonfuls of mushroom liquor. Season with half a pinch each of salt and pepper, and cook on a moderate fire for six minutes. Arrange the fillets on a dish, and put it on the side of the stove; reduce the gravy to half, adding one cooked lobster claw, one truffle, and three mushrooms, all cut julienne-shaped. Add half a pint of Allemande sauce (No. 210); stir it well, and pour it over the soles before serving, inserting a piece of truffle and a mushroom button on each fillet, also in every one stick a picked shrimp, with its head erect, if at hand, and then serve.

323. Sole, with fine herbs.—Proceed as for sole Joinville (No. 322), but replace the truffles and lobster claw by two tablespoonfuls of cooked, fine herbs (No. 143), half a pinch of chopped parsley, and the same of chervil and chives. Garnish with six heart-shaped croûtons (No. 133), and serve.

324. Sole Dieppoise.—Lift the fillets from three medium-sized soles, put them in a buttered stewpan, with one very finely chopped shallot, moistening with half a glassful of white wine, and three tablespoonfuls of mushroom liquor. Cook for six minutes, then lay them on a dish, reduce the gravy to half, adding twelve cooked mussels, six mushroom buttons, and half a pint of good Allemande sauce (No. 210). Thicken it well with a tablespoonful of butter, tossing till well dissolved, and throw it over the fillets with the juice of half a lemon. Serve with six croûtons of fried bread (No. 133) around the dish.

325. Skate or Raie au Naturel.—Pare and cut off the fins from half a skate weighing four pounds the half; divide it into six square pieces, wash them well, being very careful to scrape it with a sharp knife, so as to remove the mucus adhering to it. Put the pieces into a saucepan in which are already placed one sliced carrot, one onion, half a bunch of parsley-roots, one sprig of thyme, two bay-leaves, half a handful of whole peppers, plenty of salt—at least a handful—and half a cupful of vinegar. Cover it well with water, boil on a moderate fire for forty-five minutes, then take it off and lift up the pieces of skate with a skimmer; lay them on a table, and remove the skin from both sides; place them on a deep dish, and strain the stock slowly over, and use, whenever needed, with any kind of sauce desired.

326. Shad, broiled maître d'hôtel.—Pare and cut a small shad in two, scale it and remove the backbone; lay it on a dish, sprinkling it over with a pinch of salt, and baste with one tablespoonful of oil. Leave it for a few moments, then broil it on a slow fire in a double broiler for about fifteen minutes on the flesh side, and for one minute on the skin side, leaving the roe in the inside. Put it on a hot dish, spread a gill of good maître d'hôtel sauce (No. 177) over, and serve with six slices of lemon.

327. Shad, with Sorrel.—Select a small, fine shad, pare and scale it, then let it steep as long as possible in a marinade composed of one tablespoonful of oil, half a sliced lemon, a quarter of a bunch of parsley-roots, and half a sliced onion. When ready, place it in a buttered stewpan, with half a glassful of white wine, three tablespoonfuls of mushroom liquor, also a good bouquet (No. 254). Take two handfuls of picked and washed sorrel, mince it very fine, then put it in the stewpan with the fish, adding a good pinch of salt and half a pinch of pepper; cover it, and let it cook as long as possible on a slow fire—at least two hours; then arrange the shad on a dish. Add one tablespoonful of white roux (No. 135) to the juice, thicken well, and pour the sauce over the fish when serving, with some more of its own gravy in a sauce-bowl.

328. Shad vert-pré.—Pare and scale a small, fine shad, put it on a deep baking-dish, well buttered, and season with one pinch of salt and half a pinch of pepper, adding two finely chopped shallots and half a glassful of white wine. Cover with a piece of buttered paper, and cook in a moderate oven for twenty-five minutes. When done, put the juice in a saucepan, with half a pint of Allemande sauce (No. 210), a pinch of finely chopped chervil, and a little spinach green (Breton essence, a saltspoonful). Let cook again for three minutes, then pour a little of it, through a Chinese strainer, on the fish, and serve the rest in a separate sauce-bowl.

329. Broiled Fresh Mackerel, maître d'hôtel.—Pare and split two good-sized, fresh mackerel through the back, remove the spine, score them slightly, and rub them with one tablespoonful of sweet oil; season with a pinch of salt and half a pinch of pepper, then broil them on a brisk fire for ten minutes on the split side, and one minute on the skin side. Lay them on a dish, pour a gill of maître d'hôtel butter (No. 145) over, and serve with a few parsley-greens and six slices of lemon.

Broiled Spanish-mackerel are prepared in the same way.

330. Mackerel en Papillotes.—Oil three sheets of white paper a little larger than the length of the fish. Cut six thin slices of cooked, lean ham; lay one slice on each piece of paper, and on top a tablespoonful of cooked fine herbs (No. 143). Select three mackerel; make four or five incisions on each side; season with a good pinch of salt and a pinch of pepper, divided evenly on both sides of the fish, then roll them lightly, and lay the mackerel on top of the fine herbs; spread a tablespoonful more herbs over each mackerel, and cover with a slice of ham. Then lift up the other side of the paper and twist the edges together with the fingers, or a simpler way is to fold them the same as trout (No. 316). When ready, put them in a baking-sheet, place them in a moderate oven, and let bake for fifteen minutes. Have a hot dish ready, and after taking them from the oven, use a cake-turner to lift the fish up gently, and dress them on the dish, leaving the paper undisturbed, then serve.

331. Fresh Mackerel aux Fines Herbes.—Choose two fine, fresh mackerel, make six small incisions on both sides, and place them in a buttered baking-dish, with half a glassful of white wine, three tablespoonfuls of mushroom liquor, a finely chopped shallot, and half a pinch of salt, with the third of a pinch of pepper. Cover with a piece of buttered paper, and bake in a moderate oven for fifteen minutes, then place the fish on a dish. Pour the gravy into a stewpan, adding two tablespoonfuls of cooked fine herbs (No. 143), a pint of Allemande sauce (No. 210), and a pinch of chopped parsley. Thicken well with a tablespoonful of butter; stir well until dissolved, and pour it over the mackerel when serving. (All mackerel can be prepared the same way, only adding different sauces to the gravy.)

332. Matelote of Eels.—Pare and then cut one and a half pounds of eels into pieces two inches in length. When well washed, put them in a stewpan with one tablespoonful of butter; fry them for two minutes; add a glassful of red wine, a third of a pinch of nutmeg, half a pinch of salt, and a third of a pinch of pepper, also a bouquet (No. 254), a glassful of fish-stock (No. 214), or white broth (No. 99), and three tablespoonfuls of mushroom liquor. Add six small, glazed onions (No. 972), and six mushroom buttons. Cook for thirty minutes, then put in a tablespoonful of white roux (No. 135); stir well while cooking five minutes longer, and serve with six heart-shaped croûtons (No. 133).

333. Matelote of Eels à la Parisienne.—Proceed the same as for the above (No. 332), only lift out the fish when cooked; reduce the sauce to half, adding three tablespoonfuls of Espagnole (No. 151), six mushroom buttons, six glazed onions (No. 972), and six fish quenelles (No. 227). Stir well while cooking two minutes longer, and serve with six fried pieces of bread garnished with Soubise (No. 250).

334. Matelote of Eels à la Normande.—Cut one and a half pounds of eels into pieces, put them in a saucepan with a tablespoonful of butter; fry two minutes; add a glassful of white wine, and three tablespoonfuls of mushroom liquor. Season well with half a pinch each of salt and pepper, and a third of a pinch of nutmeg. Cook for ten minutes, then add half a pint of good velouté (No. 152), six mushrooms, twelve blanched oysters, six fish quenelles (No. 227), and six small, cooked crawfish tails. Cook again for five minutes, and when ready to serve, beat in three egg yolks, but do not boil again, and garnish with six fried croûtons (No. 133).

335. Blanched Eels.—Select a pound and a half of well-skinned eels, cut them into pieces and tie them in rings; put them with cold water in a saucepan, with a good pinch of salt and a little vinegar, a sprig of thyme, two bay-leaves, twelve whole peppers, a quarter of a bunch of parsley-roots, one onion, and one carrot. Place them on a slow fire, and take them off before they boil; lay them in an earthen jar with the water they were boiled in. (These can be used for frying or boiling, according to need).

336. Bluefish à l'Icarienne.—Scale and score two pounds of bluefish, place it on a well-buttered baking-dish, moistening with three tablespoonfuls of mushroom liquor and half a glassful of white wine. Season with half a pinch of salt and a third of a pinch of pepper, then cover with a buttered paper, and put to cook in a moderately heated oven for fifteen minutes; lift it out, lay it on a dish, and put the gravy into a stewpan, adding three tablespoonfuls of tomato sauce (No. 205) and half an ounce of finely minced, cooked, smoked beef-tongue. Boil for two minutes again, and throw the whole over the fish when serving. Garnish with six small, cooked crawfish, if any on hand.

337. Bluefish à l'Italienne.—Score and scale two pounds of bluefish; place it in a buttered pan, with half a glassful of white wine, three tablespoonfuls of mushroom liquor, half of a very finely chopped onion, and six chopped-up mushrooms. Season with a pinch of salt and half a pinch of pepper. Cover the fish with a buttered paper, and cook in a moderate oven for fifteen minutes; take the fish out, lay it on a serving dish, and put the juice in a stewpan, adding a gill of Espagnole sauce (No. 151), with a small glassful of white wine; reduce for two minutes, then pour it over the fish, with one pinch of finely chopped parsley, and serve with six heart-shaped pieces of croûton (No. 133).

338. Bluefish à la Venitienne.—Prepare the fish as for the above (No. 337), adding to it one tomato cut in pieces, half a pint of Espagnole sauce (No. 151) and six whole mushrooms. Besprinkle lightly with fresh bread-crumbs, and throw over all a few drops of clarified butter; put it in the oven for eight minutes, and serve with half a pinch of chopped parsley.

339. Sheep's-head à la Créole.—Put one chopped onion and one very finely chopped green pepper—the seed extracted—in a stewpan; brown them in a half gill of oil for five minutes, then add one tomato, cut in pieces, four sliced mushrooms, a good bouquet (No. 254), and a clove of garlic. Season well with a pinch of salt and half a pinch of pepper, then moisten with half a pint of Espagnole sauce (No. 151). Cut a fish weighing three pounds in six slices, lay them flat in the stewpan, with three tablespoonfuls of mushroom liquor (if any handy), and let cook for one hour on a very slow fire. When ready to serve, sprinkle over with a pinch of chopped parsley, and decorate with six pieces of heart-shaped croûton (No. 133). (All fish à la Créole are prepared the same way, the time allowed for cooking depending on the firmness of the fish. The fish can be left whole instead of dividing in slices, if desired.)

340. Bouille-à-Baisse, à la Marseillaise.—Brown two sliced onions in a gill of oil for five minutes in a saucepan, then moisten with one quart of fish-stock (No. 214), adding a bouquet (No. 254), three cloves of garlic, bruised and minced exceedingly fine. Dilute a third of a pinch of powdered Spanish saffron in water, and add it to the gravy. Take one small eel, one very small bass, the same of sole, one raw lobster—in fact, all the firm fish ready at hand—cut them in slices, season with a pinch of salt and the third of a saltspoonful of cayenne pepper, and put them all together on a slow fire. Let cook for twenty minutes, and when ready, serve in a deep dish, on which you previously arrange six pieces of toast from a French loaf of bread.

N. B.—The above should be served exceedingly hot.

341. Bass à la Bordelaise.—Cut a deep incision down the back of a three-pound sea-bass, put it in a baking-dish with half a glassful of red wine, half a pinch of salt, and a third of a pinch of pepper. Besprinkle with a finely chopped shallot, cover with a buttered paper, and cook in a moderate oven for fifteen minutes. Lay the bass on a dish, put the juice in a saucepan with a gill of good Espagnole (No. 151), four finely shred mushrooms, and a thin slice of finely chopped garlic; finish cooking for five minutes more, then pour it over the fish. Decorate with six cooked crawfish or shrimps, and serve very hot.

342. Bass, with White Wine.—Lay a three-pound, well-cleaned bass on a well-buttered baking-dish; season with half a pinch of salt and a third of a pinch of pepper; moisten with half a glassful of white wine and three tablespoonfuls of mushroom liquor. Cover with a heavy piece of buttered paper, and cook in a moderate oven for fifteen minutes, then lay the fish on a dish; put the juice in a saucepan, with half a pint of good Allemande (No. 210), thicken well with a tablespoonful of butter till well dissolved, and throw it over the bass, serving with six heart-shaped croûtons (No. 133).

343. Bass à la Chambord.—Lift the middle skin from the back of a three-pound bass, leaving the head and tail covered; lard the fish nicely with a very small larding needle, and then lay it on a buttered, deep baking-pan, adding to it half a glassful of white wine, and half a carrot, and half an onion, both sliced, also a bouquet (No. 254). Season with a pinch of salt and half a pinch of pepper, then cover with a buttered paper; cook it in the oven for thirty minutes, being very careful to baste it frequently, then lift out the fish and lay it on a dish. Strain the gravy into a saucepan, with half a pint of Chambord garnishing (No. 212), moistened with half a pint of Espagnole (No. 151); reduce for five minutes. Decorate the dish with clusters of the garnishing, and three decorated fish quenelles (No. 227) to separate them, also three small, cooked crawfish, and serve.

344. Salt Cod à la Biscaënne.—Take two pounds of boneless cod, and soak it in plenty of cold water for twenty-four hours, changing the water as often as possible. Place it in a saucepan with plenty of fresh water, then let simmer on a slow fire till boiling; take it off, and drain it well; return it to the pan with fresh water, and let come to a boil again, then scale it by separating the bones. Fry together in a saucepan two chopped onions and one green pepper in a gill of oil. Let cook for five minutes, then add one good-sized tomato, cut in pieces, one clove of bruised garlic, and one Chili pepper. Moisten the fish with three pints of broth, add a bouquet (No. 254), three tablespoonfuls of tomato sauce (No. 205), and a pint of Parisian potatoes (No. 986). Let cook for forty-five minutes, then add the codfish; boil again for five minutes more. Dress it on a hot dish, and serve with a teaspoonful of chopped parsley sprinkled over.

345. Codfish, bonne femme.—Have two pounds of cooked, soaked, boneless cod; prepare it the same as for the above (No. 344), then put it in a saucepan, moistening with half a pint of béchamel (No. 154), and half a pint of Allemande (No. 210). Add three sliced potatoes, and three hard-boiled eggs, cut in thin slices, and half a pinch of pepper. (If too thick, put in a little milk.) Cook for about five minutes longer, then serve with a teaspoonful of chopped parsley.

346. Picked-up Codfish.—The same as for the above, only all the materials should be shred smaller, and add three tablespoonfuls of cream.

347. Fish Balls.—Place in a large pan, with plenty of fresh water, three pounds of boneless codfish, and let soak for twelve hours. Drain, and place it in a saucepan on the hot range, with plenty of cold water, and as soon as it begins to boil, drain all the water through a colander. Carefully pick out all the bones from the cod, and return it to the saucepan, adding five medium-sized, well-washed, and peeled sliced potatoes, one gill of cold water or broth, and cook on a moderate fire for twenty minutes, then add half an ounce of butter. Take from off the fire. Season with one pinch of white pepper, then, with the aid of a potato-masher or a pounder, mash all well together right in the pan. Transfer it to a dish, and let cool. Make up small fish balls two inches in diameter by one inch thick, lightly sprinkle them with a very little flour. Heat in a frying-pan one gill of clarified butter; when very hot, put in the fish balls and fry for three minutes on each side, so as to have them of a good brown color. Gently lift them from the pan with a skimmer, dress on a hot dish with a folded napkin, crown-shaped, one overlapping another. Decorate the centre of the dish with parsley-greens, and serve.

Fish Balls à la Mrs. Benjamin Harrison.—To be prepared exactly the same as above (No. 347), dressing them on six dry toasts, placing one poached egg (No. 404) on top of each fish ball, and decorating the dish with six slices of broiled bacon, and serve hot.

348. How to Blanch Codfish-tongues.—Procure eighteen fine, fresh codfish-tongues, wash them thoroughly in cold water, then drain, and place them in a saucepan on the hot stove: cover with fresh water, and season with a handful of salt, six cloves, twelve whole peppers, one sliced onion, a bouquet (No. 254), and half a sliced lemon. Let them come to a boil, then transfer them with the water and garnishings to a stone jar, and use when needed.

349. Codfish-tongues au beurre noir.—Take eighteen blanched codfish-tongues, as for No. 348, heat them in a saucepan with half a gill of their own juice, but do not let them boil; drain well, then dress them on a hot dish, pour a pint of black butter (No. 159) over, and decorate each side of the dish with a few sprigs of parsley, then send to the table.

350. Fried Codfish-tongues.—Take eighteen fine, fresh codfish-tongues, wash them well, drain them in a napkin, dip them in cold milk, and roll them, one by one, in flour. Put one gill of clarified butter in the frying-pan, heat it well, then gently lay in the tongues separately, and let cook for three minutes. Turn them on the other side, using a fork, and cook for three minutes more. Lift them up carefully with a skimmer, and put them on a cloth to drain. Season with one pinch of salt and half a pinch of pepper; dress them on a hot dish with a folded napkin, and decorate with sprigs of parsley. Serve a gill of hot tomato sauce (No. 205) in a separate bowl.

351. Codfish-tongues à la poulette.—Take eighteen blanched tongues, as for No. 348, put them in a saucepan on the stove, adding a pint of sauce Hollandaise (No. 160), half a gill of their own stock, and a teaspoonful of chopped parsley. Heat well for five minutes without boiling, then pour the whole into a deep, hot dish, sprinkle a little chopped parsley over them, and serve.

352. Boiled Codfish, Oyster Sauce.—Cover a three-pound fresh codfish with well-salted fish-stock (No. 214), and let cook thirty minutes without boiling ; then take it out and drain it well. Lay it on a dish, and garnish with a few branches of parsley-greens, and twelve pieces of potato à l'Anglaise (No. 988). Serve with three-quarters of a pint of oyster sauce (No. 173) separately. (All codfish with different sauces are prepared the same way.)

353. Broiled Boned Smelts à la Béarnaise.—Split twelve good-sized or eighteen medium-sized smelts up the back, remove the backbone, rub them with one tablespoonful of oil, and season with half a pinch of salt and a third of a pinch of pepper. Broil them in a double broiler for two minutes on each side; pour a little more than a gill of good Béarnaise sauce (No. 166) on a dish, arrange the smelts carefully on top, and serve, finishing with a very little demi-glace sauce (No. 181) around the dish.

354. Smelts à la Toulouse.—Take twelve large or eighteen medium-sized smelts, bone them as for the above, and then close them up again. Put them in a stewpan, with half a glassful of white wine and three tablespoonfuls of mushroom liquor; season with half a pinch of salt and the third of a pinch of pepper, and cook on a moderate fire for six minutes. Arrange the smelts on a dish, add to the sauce twelve mushroom buttons, two sliced truffles, six fish quenelles (No. 227), and moisten with half a pint of Allemande sauce (No. 210). Thicken with a tablespoonful of butter sufficiently, and throw the sauce over the smelts. Neatly dress the garnishing around the dish, and serve with six heart-shaped croûtons (No. 133). (Smelts are all prepared the same way, only adding different garnishings.)

355. Stuffed Smelts.—Cut off the fins, wash, and dry well with a towel, eighteen fine, fresh, medium-sized, Long Island smelts ; remove the eggs without splitting the stomachs open, then fill them with a fish forcemeat (No. 227), using a paper cornet for the purpose. Lay the smelts on a well-buttered silver baking-dish (if possible), and cover them with a pint of sauce Italienne (No. 188). Put them in a hot oven and let bake for eight minutes ; remove them, squeeze the juice of a good lemon over, and lay the silver dish on top of another to avoid soiling the table-cloth; then serve.

356. Smelts au Gratin.—Clean eighteen smelts, wipe them very dry, and put them on a baking-dish with two tablespoonfuls of cooked fine herbs (No. 143), half a glassful of white wine, half a pinch of salt, and a third of a pinch of pepper. Cover with six whole mushrooms and half a pint of Espagnole sauce (No. 151). Besprinkle lightly with fresh breadcrumbs and six drops of melted butter; place it in a hot oven for ten minutes, and serve with the juice of half a lemon, also a teaspoonful of chopped parsley sprinkled over. (The smelts can be boned if so desired).

357. Lobster à l'Américaine.—Split two fine, good-sized, freshly boiled lobsters; remove all the meat carefully, then cut it up into pieces one inch in length. Have a pan on the hot range with half a gill of good olive oil, and when the oil is very hot add the pieces of lobster. Chop very fine one medium-sized, peeled onion, one fine, sound, green pepper, and half a clove of peeled, very sound garlic; add all to the lobster, and let cook for five minutes, gently mixing meanwhile. Season with a pinch of salt and half a saltspoonful of red pepper, adding also half a wine-glassful of good white wine. Reduce for two minutes, then add one gill of tomato sauce (No. 205) and one medium-sized, sound, red, peeled tomato, cut into small dice-shaped pieces. Cook for ten minutes longer, gently shuffling meanwhile. Pour the whole into a very hot, deep dish, or in a hot tureen, and serve.

358. Lobster with Curry.—Pick out all the meat from two good-sized, fine, freshly boiled, and split lobsters. Cut the meat up in one-inch-length equal pieces. Have a saucepan on the hot range with an ounce of very good butter; add the lobster to it, and let cook for five minutes. Season with one pinch of salt and half a pinch of pepper. Place in a bowl one tablespoonful of Indian curry, with half a wine-glassful of good white wine, mix well together, then pour it into the lobster. Cook for two minutes. Add two gills of hot Allemande sauce (No. 210), shuffle briskly for one minute longer. Make a border of fresh-boiled rice all around the hot dish; dress the lobster right in the centre of the dish, and serve hot.

359. Lobster à la Newburg.—Split two good-sized, fine, freshly boiled lobsters. Pick all the meat out from the shells, then cut it into one-inch-length equal pieces. Place it in a saucepan on the hot range with one ounce of very good, fresh butter. Season with one pinch of salt and half a saltspoonful of red pepper, adding two medium-sized, sound truffles cut into small dice-shaped pieces. Cook for five minutes; then add a wine-glassful of good Madeira wine. Reduce to one-half, which will take three minutes. Have three egg yolks in a bowl with half a pint of sweet cream, beat well together, and add it to the lobster. Gently shuffle for two minutes longer, or until it thickens well. Pour it into a hot tureen, and serve hot.

360. Lobster à la Bordelaise.—Add to one glassful of red wine in a stewpan one chopped shallot, and half of a small carrot cut into exceedingly small pieces. Boil for five minutes, and then put in pieces of boiled lobster, the same quantity as for the above—about a pound and a half—a pinch of salt, a third of a pinch of pepper and a very little nutmeg, also half a pint of velouté (No. 152). Stew well together for five minutes, then serve.

861. Lobster en Brochette au Petit Salé.—Take one and a half pounds of fresh, shelled, boiled lobster, cut it into two-inch-square, even pieces, lay them in a bowl, then season with a good pinch of salt, a pinch of pepper, the third of a pinch of nutmeg, and a tablespoonful of Parisian sauce, and mix all well together. Have six silver skewers, arrange in the centre of one a piece of lobster, then a mushroom, another piece of lobster and another mushroom; continue the same for the other skewers, then place them on the broiler and broil for eight minutes, turning them over carefully once in a while. Remove them from the broiler, dress them on a hot dish, pour a gill of maître d'hôtel butter (No. 145) over, decorate with six slices of broiled bacon (No. 754), and serve very hot.

362. Lobster en Chevreuse.—To two finely chopped shallots in a stewpan add one glassful of Madeira wine, one ounce of butter, and a pound and a half of pieces of boiled lobster; moisten with one pint of velouté (No. 152), and season with a pinch of salt, half a pinch of pepper, and a very little nutmeg. Let boil for ten minutes, and with this preparation fill six table-shells, or, better still, six small St. Jacques-shells; on top of each lay three slices of truffle and one tablespoonful of good béchamel (No. 154). Put one drop of clarified butter over each, and place them in the oven for five minutes. Serve very hot on a folded napkin.

363. Broiled Lobster à la Ravigote.—Cut three small, raw lobsters into two equal parts, taking out the gravel from the head, season with one pinch of salt and half a pinch of pepper, and rub with a very little oil, then broil the pieces for ten minutes. Take them from the fire, and remove the meat from the head of the lobsters and put it in a salad-bowl with half a pint of ravigote butter (No. 147), and mix well together ; take the meat from the balance of the lobster, dip it in the sauce, and return it to its shell; warm again for two minutes in the oven, then serve on a folded napkin, garnishing the shells with parsley-greens, and serving the sauce in a sauce-bowl.

364. Broiled Lobster.—Select three medium-sized, good, live lobsters, split them in halves, and take out the stony pouch and intestines ; glaze them slightly with sweet oil, and season them with half a pinch of salt and half a pinch of pepper, and then broil them for seven minutes on each side. Place them on a dish, moisten with a gill of good maître d'hôtel (No. 145), then serve.

365. Lobster Croquettes.—Make some lobster forcemeat (No. 222); form it into the shape of six pears with the hand, roll them in breadcrumbs (No. 301), and fry in very hot fat for three minutes ; drain well, then serve on a folded napkin, garnishing with parsley-greens, and add any sauce required in a sauce-bowl.

Salmon croquettes to be prepared the same way, substituting minced, boiled salmon for the lobster forcemeat.

366. Lobster Cutlets, Victoria.—The same as for the above, only giving them the shape of a chop, and when serving stick a lobster leg in the point of each one.

367. Stuffed Lobster.—Fill six empty lobster-tails with forcemeat (No. 222), roll them in bread-crumbs, put them on a baking-dish, smoothing the surface with the blade of a knife; place them in a baking-pan. Pour a little clarified butter over, and brown gently in the oven for six minutes, and serve on a folded napkin with a garnishing of parsley-greens.

368. Fried Soft-shelled Crabs.—Procure six good-sized, live, soft-shelled crabs, cleanse and wash them thoroughly, and dip each one in flour, then in beaten egg, and finally in rasped bread-crumbs or pulverized crackers, using them very lightly. Fry in very hot fat for five minutes, drain, season with one pinch of salt, evenly divided, and serve on a hot dish with a folded napkin with fried parsley around.

369. Broiled Soft-shelled Crabs.—Have six good-sized, fresh, soft-shelled crabs, cleanse and wash them well, then drain them, oil them slightly, and season with a pinch of salt and half a pinch of pepper. Put them on the broiler, and broil for five minutes on each side. Have six pieces of toast ready, lay a crab on top of each, slightly glaze them with a little maître d'hôtel butter (No. 145), and serve. This makes a delicious dish, but must be served very hot.

370. Hard-shelled Crabs à la Diable.—Fill six thoroughly cleaned crab-shells with some crab forcemeat (No. 223), flatten them with the hand, besprinkle with fresh bread-crumbs, smooth the surface with the blade of a knife, moistening the top with a very little clarified butter. Place them on a baking-pan, and bake a little brown for six minutes. Serve on a hot dish with a folded napkin decorated with parsley-greens.

371. Crabs à la St. Jean.—Add double the quantity of onions to some crab forcemeat (No. 223), also garlic, parsley, and chervil (let the crabs be in as large pieces as possible). Then, as for No. 362, fill six St. Jacques-shells, besprinkle with fresh bread-crumbs, smooth the surface with the blade of a knife, moisten slightly with clarified butter, and bake in a brisk oven for six minutes. Serve on a hot dish with a folded napkin decorated with parsley-greens.

372. Crabs à la St. Laurent.—Reduce half a pint of good velouté (No. 152) with half a glassful of white wine, season with one pinch of salt, half a pinch of pepper, and a very little cayenne pepper, adding three tablespoonfuls of grated Parmesan cheese. Take three-quarters of a pound of shelled crabs, put them in the saucepan, and boil them for ten minutes; then lift from the fire and let cool. Prepare six squares of toasted bread, and with a knife spread some of the mixture smoothly over each slice, sprinkle well with grated cheese, and moisten slightly with clarified butter; place them on a baking-dish; bake in a very hot oven for three minutes, and serve on a hot dish with a folded napkin, garnished with parsley-greens.

373. Crabs à l'Anglaise.—Pick twelve boiled, hard-shelled crabs in as large pieces as possible; mix them in a salad-bowl with half a cupful of the white of celery or finely shred lettuce leaves, one pinch of salt, half a pinch of pepper, one tablespoonful of olive oil, and one and a half tablespoonfuls of vinegar. Refill six well-cleaned shells with the salad, and on each one lay a good teaspoonful of mayonnaise sauce (No. 206), sprinkled over with one hard-boiled, finely chopped egg, the yolk and white separated, some crab or lobster coral, and a teaspoonful of chopped parsley, every article to be used separately, so they have each a different color. Serve on a dish with a folded napkin.

374. Oyster-crabs à la Poulette.—Take one and a half pints of oyster-crabs, and proceed the same as for oysters à la poulette (No. 383).

375. Fried Oyster-crabs.—Wash well, and dry one and a half pints of oyster-crabs, dip them in flour, then in cold milk, and finally in cracker-dust; shake them well in a colander, and fry in hot fat for three minutes; serve in shells made of foundation paste, or short paste for tarts (No. 1078), garnishing with parsley-leaves, and sprinkling a very little salt on top.

376. Stuffed Clams.—Refill six good-sized, very clean clam-shells with clam forcemeat (No. 223), and prepare them the same as stuffed crabs (No. 370).

377. Clams à la Marinière.—Open and remove thirty-six small clams from their shells; put them in a stewpan with two ounces of fresh butter, one pinch of chives, and one pinch of finely chopped chervil; add half a cupful of water, so they will not be too salty, with half a pinch of pepper, and two tablespoonfuls of fresh bread-crumbs. Boil for two minutes, and serve with the juice of half a lemon.

378. Mussels à la Marinière.—Steam in a stewpan thirty-six mussels for ten minutes, and proceed as for No. 377, leaving a mussel in each half shell.

379. Mussels à la Poulette.—Steam in a stewpan thirty-six mussels for ten minutes, and proceed the same as oysters à la poulette (No. 383), leaving a mussel in each half shell.

380. Fried Oysters.—Procure twenty-four large freshly opened oysters, or thirty-six of medium size, dip each one separately in flour, then in beaten egg, and lastly in powdered cracker-dust. Fry in very hot fat for four minutes, drain well, and serve on a hot dish with a folded napkin, sprinkling over a very little salt, and garnishing with fried parsley-leaves.

381. Oysters à la Villeroi.—Blanch twenty-four large oysters in their own juice for two minutes, then drain them; take some chicken forcemeat (No. 226), spread it over both sides of the oysters, dip in egg and fresh bread-crumbs, then fry in hot lard for three minutes, and serve with fried parsley.

382. Broiled Oysters.—Dip twenty-four large and freshly opened oysters in half bread-crumbs and half cracker-dust; flatten them with the hand, and broil them on a well-greased broiler for two minutes on each side, then salt them slightly, and serve on six pieces of toast; lightly glaze them with maître d'hôtel sauce on top (No. 177).

383. Oysters à la Poulette.—Put thirty-six freshly opened oysters in a saucepan with a little of their own juice, one ounce of butter, half a pinch of salt, and the same of pepper; parboil for three minutes, adding half a pint of Hollandaise sauce (No. 160), stew well together for two minutes again, but do not let boil, and add one teaspoonful of chopped parsley and the juice of half a lemon. Stir slightly, and serve.

384. Oysters à la Pompadour.—Proceed the same as for No. 383, suppressing the parsley, and adding two chopped truffles.

385. Oysters en Brochette au Petit Salé.—Place twenty-four freshly opened oysters in a stewpan with their own juice; season with a very little salt, half a pinch of pepper; parboil for two minutes. Take six skewers and pass them through the oysters, separating each one by a small square of cooked bacon—that is, alternating each oyster with a piece of the bacon—besprinkle with grated, fresh bread-crumbs, and broil for one and a half minutes on each side. Serve with half a gill of maître d'hôtel sauce (No. 177) poured over, and a bunch of parsley-leaves spread on both sides of the dish.

386. Oysters à la Mall.—Chop an onion very fine; place it in a stewpan with one ounce of butter, and let it get a good golden color, then add a tablespoonful of cooked, finely minced spinach, also a small glassful of white wine. Have eighteen medium-sized oysters chopped exceedingly small, and seasoned with a pinch of salt, and the same of pepper; place these in the stewpan, and let cook for fifteen minutes. Put in one whole egg, also a bruised clove of garlic; stir; then take six large, clean oyster-shells; fill the bottoms with a bed of three parboiled oysters, cover them with the spinach mixture, and besprinkle with fresh bread-crumbs. Flatten the tops with the blade of a knife, pour a very little clarified butter over, and put them for three minutes in the oven. Serve on a folded napkin, garnishing with parsley-leaves.

387. Oyster Patties.—Take twenty-four medium-sized oysters (the least salted oysters are better for this purpose), put them in a stewpan with their own liquor, and add half a pinch of pepper. Cover, and let cook for two minutes; then take half the liquor out, and add to the oysters three-quarters of a pint of béchamel sauce (No. 154), and a very little grated nutmeg; simmer for two minutes, but do not let boil. Take six hot patties (No. 266), fill them up with four oysters each, pour the sauce over, and place the covers on top. Serve on a dish with a folded napkin.

388. Stewed Oysters à la Baltimore.—Open neatly thirty-six medium-sized, fresh Rockaway oysters; place them in a saucepan without their juice, adding one ounce of good butter; cover the pan, put it on the stove, and let cook for two minutes, then add a small glassful of good Madeira wine (about a cocktail glass) and a very little cayenne pepper. Cook together for two minutes longer, then add one gill of Espagnole sauce (No. 151) and one gill of demi-glace (No. 185). Stir thoroughly until boiling, and just before serving squeeze in the juice of a good lemon, add half an ounce of good butter, also a teaspoonful of finely chopped parsley, and serve immediately in a hot tureen.

389. Soft Clams à la George Merrill.—Have thirty-six fresh and rather small soft clams, throw away all the hard part, keeping nothing but the body. Place them in a stewpan with two ounces of butter, half a pinch of pepper, a finely chopped shallot, and half a glassful of Madeira wine. Let cook on the hot stove for seven minutes, then add a gill of Espagnole sauce (No. 151), a pinch of chopped parsley, the juice of a medium-sized, good lemon, and half an ounce of good butter, shuffling the whole well for three minutes longer, without letting it boil, then pour the clams into a hot tureen, and serve.

390. Soft Clams à la Newburg.—Procure forty-two very fresh, soft clams, so that no sand should adhere to them after they are opened; lay them carefully in the palm of the left hand, and with the fingers of the right remove the body gently, but nothing else, being very careful not to break it, and throw away all that remains. When they are all prepared, place them in a stewpan with an ounce of good butter, half a pinch of white pepper, a wine-glassful of good Madeira wine, and two finely hashed, medium-sized truffles. Put on the cover, and let cook gently for eight minutes. Break three egg yolks into a bowl, add a pint of sweet cream; beat well for three minutes, then pour it over the clams; turn well the handle of the saucepan for two or three minutes, very gently shuffling the clams, but it must not boil again or the clams will break, and be very careful not to use either a spoon or fork. Pour them into a hot tureen, and send to the table at once.

391. Canapé Lorenzo.—Cut out from an American bread six slices, the width of the bread, one-quarter of an inch in thickness; neatly pare off the crust, fry them in a sautoire with half an ounce of butter, so as to have them of a light brown color. Boil eighteen hard-shelled crabs in salted water for twelve minutes, remove them, and let cool until they can be handled with bare hands; then remove the upper shell, and with the aid of a pointed knife pick out all the meat; crack both claws, pick the meat out also; place the meat on a plate, season with a tablespoonful of salt and a saltspoonful of red pepper. Place one ounce of butter in a saucepan with half a medium-sized, sound, peeled, and very finely chopped-up onion. Cook on a moderate fire for two minutes, being very careful not to let get brown. Add two tablespoonfuls of flour, stirring constantly for two minutes; then add one gill of broth, stir well again for five minutes while slowly cooking. Add now the crab-meat, and cook for fifteen minutes more, lightly stirring with a wooden spoon once in a while. Transfer it into a vessel, and let cool for fifteen minutes. Place a tablespoonful of good butter in a sautoire on a hot stove, mix in well together one tablespoonful of flour, and cook very slowly for three minutes. Add two ounces of grated Parmesan cheese, and the same quantity of grated Swiss cheese; stir all well together. Then place in a vessel and let cool. Place a layer of crab forcemeat on each toast a quarter of an inch thick. Divide the prepared cheese, etc., into six equal parts, giving them a ball-shaped form two inches in diameter. Arrange them over the layer of the crab forcemeat right in the centre. Place them on a silver dish, and bake in a brisk oven for five minutes. Then take out from the oven, and send to the table in the same dish.

392. Scallops Brestoise.—Blanch in one ounce of butter for ten minutes, and then drain, one pint of scallops; chop up two onions, and put them in a saucepan with an ounce of butter; when brown add one tablespoonful of flour, stirring carefully, and moisten with half a pint of the scallop liquor; if none, white broth (No. 99) will answer. Let reduce while stirring, then season with a good pinch of salt, and half a pinch of white pepper, also a very little cayenne pepper; add the chopped scallops, four egg yolks, and a bruised clove of garlic, also half a cupful of fresh bread-crumbs, and a tablespoonful of chopped parsley. Stir well for two minutes, then put it in a dish and lay aside to cool. Fill six scallop-shells, or St. Jacques-shells with this, besprinkle the tops with fresh bread-crumbs, moisten slightly with clarified butter, and lay them on a baking-sheet; brown them nicely in the oven for five minutes, and serve on a hot dish with a folded napkin garnished with parsley-leaves.

393. Edible Snails à la Bourguignonne.—Have some fine Bourgogne snails; disgorge them well with a little salt for two or three days, then wash them several times in cold water, strain, and place them in a stew-pan, covering them with water. Add a bouquet (No. 254), some cloves and whole pepper tied in a cloth, and sufficient salt; cook until the snails fall from their shells, and then empty them, clipping off their tails; clean the shells well. Mix together some good butter, shallots, parsley, and chervil, the whole chopped very fine; put it in a bowl with as much fresh bread-crumbs, and a small glassful of white wine; season to taste with salt and pepper, and knead well. Fill each shell with a little of this mixture, replace the snails, and finish filling with more of the kneaded butter; spread bread-crumbs over, and lay them on a baking-dish, the opened part on the top. Brown in the oven for four minutes, and serve on a dish with a folded napkin.

394. Edible Snails à l'Italienne.—Prepare the snails as for the above, leaving them in their shells; drain, and put them in a saucepan with white wine and a little strong Espagnole sauce (No. 151), a few chopped, fried onions and finely minced mushrooms. Season well with a pinch of salt, cook for a few minutes, and serve.

395. Edible Snails à la Provençale.—Prepare the snails as for No. 393; fry a little chopped onion with oil, add the snails taken from the shells, a little white wine, two cloves of chopped garlic, a little fresh bread-crumbs, and chopped parsley. Cook, add the juice of a lemon; then serve.

396. Terrapin à la Baltimore.—Prepare two medium-sized terrapins as for No. 60, make half a pint of mirepoix (No. 138), add to it a tablespoonful of flour, let cook for fifteen minutes, then moisten with half a glassful of Madeira wine, and a cupful of strong broth. Stir well, and constantly, then season with half a pinch of salt, and a very little cayenne pepper; reduce to half. Cut the terrapin into small pieces, throwing the ends of the claws away; put them in a stewpan, straining the sauce over, and finish with an ounce of fresh butter, also the juice of a lemon.

397. Terrapin à la Maryland.—Carefully cut up two terrapins as described in No. 60; place them in a saucepan with half a wine-glass of good Madeira wine, half a pinch of salt, and a very little cayenne pepper, also an ounce of good butter. Mix well a cupful of good, sweet cream with the yolks of three boiled eggs, and add it to the terrapin, briskly shuffling constantly, while thoroughly heating, but without letting it come to a boil. Pour into a hot tureen, and serve very hot.

Terrapin à la Newburg is prepared exactly the same as above (No. 397), only substituting two raw egg yolks for the three boiled egg yolks, and adding two sound, sliced truffles while heating.

398. Broiled Frogs.—Select eighteen good-sized, fine, fresh frogs pare off the feet neatly, then lay the frogs on a dish, and pour two tablespoonfuls of sweet oil over, season with a pinch of salt and a pinch of pepper, and squeeze in the juice of a fresh lemon. Roll them around several times in their seasoning, then place them nicely on the broiler, and broil them for four minutes on each side. Take them off, and dress them on a hot dish, pouring a gill of maître d'hôtel butter (No. 145) over, and send to the table immediately.

399 Frogs à la Poulette.—Procure eighteen pieces of medium-sized, fine, fresh frogs; pare off the claws, then place the frogs in a sautoire with two ounces of butter, seasoning with a pinch of salt and a pinch of pepper. Add half a glassful of white wine, cover, and let cook on a brisk stove for five minutes, then add a pint of Hollandaise sauce (No. 160), and two teaspoonfuls of finely chopped parsley, and a little lemon juice; mix well for two minutes, but do not let it boil again; then serve the frogs on a very hot dish.

400. Fried Frogs.—Select eighteen fine, fresh, medium-sized frogs; trim off the claws neatly, and put the frogs in a bowl. Marinade them with a tablespoonful of vinegar, the same of sweet oil, a pinch of salt and a pinch of pepper; mix well together in the bowl, then immerse them in frying batter (No. 1185). Plunge the frogs into very hot fat, one by one, and let fry for five minutes; then drain, and dress them on a hot dish with a folded napkin, decorating with a little parsley-greens. Serve with any desired sauce.

401. Frogs à l'Espagnole.—Trim nicely eighteen fine, fresh, medium-sized frogs' feet; lay the frogs in a sautoire on the hot stove with two ounces of good butter, season with a pinch of salt and half a pinch of pepper, and add half a glassful of white wine. Let cook for five minutes, then put in it half an empty green pepper and two freshly peeled tomatoes, all cut up into small pieces; cook for ten minutes longer, then dress the frogs on a hot dish, and send to the table.

402. Broiled Shad's Roe, with Bacon.—Procure six pieces of fresh shad's roe, wipe them thoroughly with a towel, then lay them on a dish, and season with a good pinch of salt and two tablespoonfuls of sweet oil. Roll them gently to avoid breaking, then arrange them on a broiler, and broil them for six minutes on each side. Take them off the fire, lay them on a hot dish, and pour a gill of maître d'hôtel butter (No. 145) over;

decorate with six slices of broiled bacon (No. 754), and six quarters of lemon ; then send to the table.

403. Broiled Sardines on Toast.—Select twelve good-sized, fine, and firm sardines ; arrange them in a double broiler, and broil for two minutes on each side on a very brisk fire. Place six fresh, dry toasts on a hot dish, lay the sardines over, being careful not to break them, pour half a gill of maitre d'hôtel butter (No. 145) over, decorate with six quarters of lemon, and serve.

A pinch of salt represents 205 grains, or a tablespoonful.
Half a pinch of pepper represents 38 grains, or a teaspoonful.
A third of a pinch of nutmeg represents 13 grains, or half a teaspoonful.

EGGS.

404. Poached.—Boil in a deep saucepan three quarts of water with a heavy pinch of salt and three drops of vinegar. Have easily at hand twelve fresh eggs. When, and only when, the water boils, rapidly but carefully crack six of them, one by one. As success to have them in proper shape and cooked to perfection depends upon how they are handled, special care should be taken to crack them as rapidly as possible, carefully avoiding to break the yolks, and dropping each one right on the spot where the water bubbles, and as near the boiling-point as possible. Poach for one minute and a quarter from the time that the water boils after the eggs were put in. Lift them up with a skimmer, lay them on the freshly prepared toasts, or use for any other desired purpose; and repeat the same with the other six. If handled strictly as above described you will have them to perfection, and no necessity of trimming any superfluous adherings; serve when required.

405. Scrambled Eggs.—Melt three ounces of butter in a saucepan, break into it twelve fresh eggs ; season with a pinch of salt, half a pinch of pepper, and a third of a pinch of grated nutmeg. Mix thoroughly without stopping for three minutes, using a spatula, and having the pan on a very hot stove. Turn into a warm tureen, add a little verjuice or lemon juice, and send to the table very hot.

406. Scrambled Eggs with Asparagus-tops.—To be prepared exactly the same as for No. 405. After the eggs have been well mixed with butter in the pan, there is added a quarter of a bunch of freshly boiled asparagus-tops.

407. Scrambled Eggs with Truffles.—Place in a saucepan four good-sized, sliced truffles with a glassful of Madeira wine. Reduce to about half, which will take two minutes ; add a tablespoonful of butter ; season with one pinch of salt and half a pinch of pepper. Crack into the saucepan twelve eggs, mix all well together with the spatula for three minutes on a very hot stove without stopping. Turn into a hot tureen and serve.

408. Scrambled Eggs with Smoked Beef.—Fry in a sautoire for one minute two ounces of finely minced smoked beef. Scramble twelve eggs as for No. 405, mixing with the above prepared beef. Any kind of garnishing may be added to the scrambled eggs.

409. Scrambled Eggs with Chicory.—Blanch for fifteen minutes a good-sized head of chicory; drain it and cut it into one-inch lengths. Put these in a saucepan on the hot stove with an ounce of butter and one minced onion, fry, and then moisten with half a pint of broth (No. 99), adding a pinch of salt and half a pinch of pepper. Let cook until all the liquid is evaporated (which will take from twenty to twenty-two minutes). Break twelve eggs into a saucepan, add the chicory and another ounce of butter, then scramble with a spatula all together for four minutes, and serve with heart-shaped bread croûtons (No. 133) around the dish.

410. Eggs à la Livingstone.—Cover six pieces of cut toast with pâté-de-foie-gras, lay them on a dish, and pour twelve scrambled eggs over (No. 405), add two tablespoonfuls of demi-glace around the dish and serve (No. 185).

411. Eggs à la Bourguignonne.—Place in a saucepan one tablespoonful of meat-glaze with one pint of broth (No. 99), or consommé (No. 100). Boil, then crack into it two fresh eggs, and poach for one and a quarter minutes. Carefully lift up with a skimmer, and gently lay them on a hot silver dish. Repeat the same operation with ten more, two at a time ; when all on the dish, sprinkle over them an ounce of grated Parmesan cheese. Place in the hot oven to brown for one minute. Reduce the gravy in which they were poached to one-half, then carefully pour the sauce around the eggs, but not over them, and serve hot.

412. Fried Eggs.—Place in a frying-pan on the hot range three tablespoonfuls of very good sweet oil, heat it well, then carefully break into it one fresh egg, being careful not to break the yolk, and with the aid of a table knife fold the white right over the yolk, cook for a quarter of a minute, turn it over with a cake-turner; cook for a quarter of a minute on the other side, lift it up with the cake-turner, dress on a hot dish with a folded napkin. Proceed precisely the same way with eleven more, and then they will be ready to serve for any purpose desired.

N. B.—Mix one pinch of salt, and half a pinch of white pepper, and as soon as the eggs are dressed on the dish season each one evenly with it ; taking special care to cook them separately, and no more than a quarter of a minute on each side.

413. Fried Eggs for Garnishing.—Pour half a gill of sweet oil into the frying-pan; when the oil is hot break in one egg, carefully closing up the white part with a skimmer, so as to have it firm, and in a single form. Only one at the time should be cooked, and two minutes will be sufficient.

414. Eggs au Beurre Noir.—Put one ounce of butter in a frying-pan on the hot stove, let heat well, but not brown; break gently into a dish twelve very fresh eggs, slide them carefully into the pan, then season with a pinch of salt and half a pinch of white pepper; let cook slowly for three minutes. Have ready a hot, flat dish, slide the eggs gently onto it, without turning them over, and be careful to avoid breaking them; lay the dish containing the eggs in a warm place. Put two ounces of butter in the same pan, place it on the hot stove, and let the butter get a good brown color for three minutes, then drop in two teaspoonfuls of vinegar. Pour this over the eggs, and send them to the table.

415. Eggs au Soleil.—Put two tablespoonfuls of lard in a frying-pan on the hot stove, break in twelve fresh eggs, dropping them in carefully, one by one; let them cook for two minutes, then with a skimmer take each one up separately and lay it carefully on a dry cloth. Have some fritter-batter (No. 1190) ready, cut a piece of half-cooked bacon into small, square pieces of about an inch, and add them to the batter, then dip in the eggs, one after the other, taking up with each one a piece of the bacon, and with the fingers drop them into very hot grease, and cook to a good golden color for two minutes. Lift them up with the skimmer, lay them on a dry cloth to drain; sprinkle over half a pinch of salt, dress on a hot dish with a folded napkin, and serve.

416. Eggs à la Béchamel.—Pour one pint of béchamel (No. 154) into a saucepan, and put it on the hot stove. Cut twelve hard-boiled eggs in halves, add them to the hot béchamel; season with half a pinch of white pepper, and let heat thoroughly for three minutes, but be careful not to let it boil. Add one ounce of butter and a saltspoonful of grated nutmeg, then pour it on a hot serving-dish, and serve with six heart-shaped croûtons (No. 133).

417. Eggs à la Pauvre Femme.—Heat half an ounce of butter in a dish on the hot stove, then break into it twelve fresh eggs, and sprinkle over two ounces of fresh bread-crumbs. Set the dish in the hot oven, and let bake for two minutes; then pour over the eggs half a pint of well-reduced Espagnole sauce (No. 151), add three ounces of cooked, tender ham, or cooked kidneys cut up finely, and then send to the table.

418. Eggs au Gratin.—Knead well together in a bowl, one tablespoonful of bread-crumbs two ounces of butter, three chopped anchovies, a pinch of parsley, a pinch of chervil, one chopped shallot, three raw egg yolks, a good pinch of salt, half a pinch of white pepper, and a pinch of grated nutmeg. When ready, put these ingredients into a silver baking-dish (by preference) with one ounce of butter at the bottom. Place it on a slow fire for two minutes, then break over it six eggs, which will be plenty; cook for five minutes in the hot oven, remove, lay the dish on top of another, and serve immediately.

419. Eggs à la Tripe.—Fry two medium-sized, sound, sliced onions in a frying-pan with two ounces of butter, but do not brown them; mix in half a spoonful of flour, and a large cupful of sweet cream; season with a pinch of salt, half a pinch of white pepper, and the third of a pinch of grated nutmeg. Cook for eight minutes, stirring constantly with the spatula; then add twelve sliced, hard-boiled eggs, and heat together thoroughly for two minutes without letting it boil again ; pour on a hot dish and serve.

420. Eggs à la Vanderbilt.—Place one ounce of good butter on a silver dish, set it on the hot stove, and break in twelve fresh eggs, being careful not to disturb the yolks; season with a light pinch of salt and the third of a pinch of pepper; then let cook slowly for four minutes. Pour over the eggs a pint of hot Vanderbilt garnishing as for the omelet (No. 471), and serve immediately.

421. Eggs à la Valencienne.—Put into a saucepan half a pint of hot, boiled rice, half a pint of hot tomato sauce (No. 205), two good-sized mushrooms, cut julienne-shaped, one truffle cut the same, and two tablespoonfuls of grated Parmesan cheese; season with half a pinch of salt, half a pinch of pepper, and the third of a pinch of grated nutmeg, and let cook on the hot stove for five minutes, stirring it lightly with the spatula. Leave the pan on the corner of the stove to keep warm, while putting half an ounce of good butter on a silver dish, and when placed on the hot stove, crack in twelve fresh eggs, being careful not to break the yolks; season with half a pinch of salt and the third of a pinch of pepper, then let cook for two minutes. Dress the prepared garnishing in four dome-shaped heaps—one at each end of the dish, and one at each side—and send to the table at once.

422. Eggs à la Provençale.—Pour two tablespoonfuls of oil into a small frying-pan, and set it on the fire. When well heated, break one egg into a bowl, season with a pinch of salt and half a pinch of pepper (divided up for the twelve eggs), then drop it into the oil; baste the egg with a spoon, turn it over, and when a good color on both sides, drain it on a wire sieve. Cook the twelve eggs separately (each one will take two minutes), then pare them nicely, and serve crown-shaped on a dish, putting a piece of fried bread between every other one. Pour over half a pint of reduced Espagnole (No. 151), to which has been added the zest of a lemon, and six sliced mushrooms, and serve very hot.

423. Eggs en Filets.—Mix in a dish that can be put in the oven (a silver one by preference) twelve raw egg yolks, with a spoonful of brandy and a pinch of salt. Cook them for five minutes in a hot oven, then let them cool; cut the preparation into twelve thin fillets or slices, and steep each one in a light pancake batter (No. 1186). Fry them in very hot fat for about two minutes, then lift up with a skimmer, lay them on a napkin to drain, and serve on a folded napkin laid on a hot dish and garnished with fried parsley.

424. Eggs à la Finoise.—Pour a pint of good tomato sauce (No. 205) into a saucepan on the hot stove, add two cut-up, peeled, sweet peppers, fry for two minutes in a tablespoonful of butter, a teaspoonful of chopped chives, and reduce it gradually to about half the quantity, which will take ten minutes. Poach six very fresh eggs, as for No. 404, pare their edges neatly. Place six freshly prepared hot toasts on a warm serving-dish, arrange the eggs carefully on top, and pour the above sauce over all, then send them to the table at once.

425. Eggs au Miroir.—Lightly butter a silver dish large enough to hold twelve eggs, one beside another; carefully break into it twelve eggs, taking care to keep the yolks intact. Evenly sprinkle over them half a pinch of salt. Cook for one minute on the hot stove; then place them in the oven for one and a half minutes. Take out, and place the dish on another, and serve.

426. Eggs with Fresh Mushrooms.—Peel, wash, and drain a quarter of a pound of fine, fresh mushrooms. Place them in a saucepan, with a tablespoonful of very good butter. Season with half a pinch of salt and a third of a pinch of white pepper, squeezing in first two drops of lemon juice. Cover the saucepan, and cook for ten minutes on a moderate fire. Add a quarter of a glassful of good Madeira wine; reduce to one-half, which will take two minutes; add now a gill of béchamel sauce (No. 154), and let come to a boil again. Prepare twelve fresh-poached eggs, as in No. 404; pour the sauce on a hot serving-dish, keeping the mushrooms in the saucepan. Neatly lay the eggs over the sauce around the dish, and dress the mushrooms right in the centre, and serve very hot.

427. Eggs with Celery.—Boil for fifteen minutes, in a quart of white broth (No. 99), two heads of well-washed and neatly pared, sound celery. Remove it from the broth; then cut it up in one-inch-length pieces, and return it to the pan with the broth in which it was first boiled, leaving it on the hot stove. Season with one pinch of salt and the third of a pinch of white pepper. Reduce to three-quarters (which will require ten minutes). Add a gill of hot béchamel sauce (No. 154), let come to a boil. Poach twelve fresh eggs exactly as in No. 404, neatly arrange them on a hot dish, crown-like. Pour the celery sauce right in the centre, and serve very hot.

428. Eggs with Truffles.—Peel three medium-sized, sound truffles. Cut them into thin slices, place in a saucepan with a glassful of Madeira wine; reduce to one-half on a moderate fire. Season with one pinch of salt and the third of a pinch of white pepper; add one gill of béchamel sauce (No. 154); let come to a boil. Prepare twelve heart-shaped croûtons (No. 133); dip the thin parts first into the sauce half an inch in depth, then into fresh, finely chopped-up parsley up to the same depth. Gently dress (arrange) them on the hot serving-dish in star-shape, so that the decorated ends of the croûtons will just reach up to the edge of the dish equally all around. Prepare twelve poached eggs exactly the same as in No. 404; dress an egg on each croûton. Gently pour the above prepared sauce right in the centre of the dish, being careful not to pour any over the eggs. Evenly slice one good-sized, sound truffle into twelve equal slices; dip them in a little hot broth for two seconds; lay one slice on top of each egg, and immediately send to the table.

429. Eggs with Tarragon.—Blanch for one minute in a sautoire a quarter of a bunch of tarragon-leaves, drain, and chop them up very fine. Break twelve eggs into a bowl, add the tarragon, season with a pinch of salt and half a pinch of pepper, and beat well for four minutes; meanwhile adding half a cupful of sweet cream. Then make an omelet, as for

No. 450, and roll it on a hot serving dish. Prepare a little roux with flour and butter (No. 135), moisten with half a pint of strong broth and a glassful of white wine; skim off any fat that may accumulate on top, and let it cook slowly for ten minutes. Strain through a fine sieve and pour it around the omelet; then serve.

430. Eggs with Livers.—Remove the gall carefully from about a pint of chicken livers, wash them well, drain, and slice them into small pieces. Place them in a sautoire with one ounce of butter, range the pan on the hot stove, then season with one pinch of salt and half a pinch of pepper; toss the contents gently for two minutes; then add a pinch of chopped parsley, one pinch of chervil, and three well-minced mushrooms, and moisten with half a pint of Madeira sauce (No. 185), and let cook for five minutes; make an omelet of twelve eggs, as for No. 450, and when ready to finish, pour the livers in the centre, reserving two tablespoonfuls of it for further action; close the sides up carefully, cook two seconds longer, then gently turn it on a hot dish, and, with a spoon, pour all the sauce around the omelet. Dress the livers that were reserved, at both ends of the omelet, equally divided, and serve.

431. Eggs au Parmesan.—Beat twelve eggs in a saucepan, with two tablespoonfuls of grated Parmesan cheese, a pinch of pepper, but no salt; stir them well with a whip, and make of this six small omelets, as for No. 450. As soon as they are sufficiently firm, lay them on a dish. Besprinkle the tops with a little grated Parmesan cheese, roll, and trim them nicely, sprinkle more cheese over the tops, wipe off the sides of the dish, and put them in a hot oven for five minutes. Remove from the oven, pour around the omelets one gill of hot Madeira sauce (No. 185); and serve very hot.

432. Eggs à la Bonne Femme.—Slice two large, sound onions, and fry them in two ounces of butter, in a saucepan, stirring frequently, so that they do not burn; when done, dredge in a good pinch of flour, moistening with half a pint of cream or milk, and season with a pinch of salt, half a pinch of pepper, and a saltspoonful of nutmeg. Break six eggs, froth the whites, mix the yolks with the onions, and afterward the beaten whites, stirring well. Lay two pieces of white paper on the bottom of a baking-tin, butter them thoroughly, lay the eggs on top, and set it in the oven for about fifteen minutes. When done, turn them on to a hot dish, remove the papers, add two tablespoonfuls of Espagnole sauce (No. 151) to the eggs, and serve.

433. Eggs à la Paysanne.—Put half a pint of cream into a dish, on the fire, and when it boils, break in twelve fresh eggs, season with a pinch of salt and twelve whole peppers; let cook for two minutes, and then set it in the oven for three minutes, so that the eggs get a good golden color, taking care that they do not harden. Remove from the oven, place the dish on another, and serve.

434. Eggs à la Régence.—Shred an ounce and a half of salt pork into fine pieces (ham will answer the same purpose), also one onion cut into small squares, and six medium-sized mushrooms, all of equal size; moisten with a spoonful of good gravy, and cook for five minutes. When done, reduce with a tablespoonful of mushroom essence (liquor). Break twelve fresh eggs in a dish, with an ounce of melted butter on the bottom, and set it in a moderate oven for five minutes; pour the garnishing over, drip off the fat, wipe the sides of the dish, and add six drops of strong tarragon-vinegar. Remove from the oven, place the dish on another, and serve.

485. Eggs with Melted Cheese.—Grate two ounces of Parmesan cheese on a dish; set it on a slow fire, adding half a glassful of white wine, a pinch of chopped parsley, a pinch of chopped chives, half a pinch of pepper, and a saltspoonful of grated nutmeg, also two ounces of good butter. Stir thoroughly while cooking, and as the cheese melts, break in twelve eggs; cook for five minutes longer, then surround the dish with heart-shaped croûtons (No. 133), set it on another dish, and serve very hot.

486. Eggs en Panade.—Cut out twelve round pieces of bread-crumbs, each one measuring two inches in diameter, and place them in a pie-plate, spreading a little butter over each; brown them in the hot oven for one minute. Break twelve eggs in a bowl, add one pinch of chopped parsley, half a pinch of chives, two tablespoonfuls of thick, sweet cream, one ounce of butter, a pinch of salt, and a very little white pepper. Beat sharply all together for four minutes. Add the twelve pieces of browned bread to the beaten eggs, mix them well together. Place in a frying-pan on the hot range one ounce of clarified butter, heat thoroughly, then fry one egged bread at a time for one and a half minutes on each side. Dress, with the aid of a cake-turner on å hot dish with a folded napkin; keep in a warm place. Repeat the same process with the others, and serve.

487. Eggs à la Meyerbeer.—Butter a silver dish and break into it twelve fresh eggs; or, if desired, use six small silver dishes, breaking two eggs into each one; then cook them on the stove for two minutes. Cut six mutton kidneys in halves, broil or stew them according to taste, then add them to the eggs, and serve with half a pint of hot Périgueux sauce (No. 191) thrown over.

488. Eggs à la Reine.—Prepare twelve eggs as for the above (No. 437), cook them for two minutes. Make a garnishing of one ounce of cooked chicken-breast, one finely shred, medium-sized truffle, and six minced mushrooms. Moisten with half a pint of good Allemande sauce (No. 210), heat it up well, but do not let it boil; then pour over the eggs and serve immediately.

489. Eggs à la Turque.—Cook twelve eggs the same as for No. 437, and pour over them six chicken livers, tossed gently but rapidly in a saucepan on a brisk fire with one ounce of butter for three minutes, and then with a spoon remove all the butter from the saucepan. Season with a pinch of salt, and half a pinch of white pepper, adding half a glassful of good Madeira wine. Reduce it to one half, then add one gill of hot Madeira sauce (No. 185), heat up a little, and then pour the sauce over the eggs and serve.

440. Eggs à l'Impératrice.—Cook twelve eggs exactly as in No. 437, arranging six small slices of pâté-de-foie-gras, one on top of each egg, and serving very hot.

441. Eggs à la Suisse.—Fry twelve eggs as for No. 437; after cooking for two minutes, cover with half a pint of hot tomato sauce (No. 205), and add three cooked sausages, cut in two, also a little grated cheese, then send to the table.

442. Eggs à la Chipolata.—Prepare twelve eggs as for No. 437, and cover them with a pint of hot Chipolata garnishing (No. 232), and serve very hot.

443. Eggs à l'Alsacienne.—Fry twelve eggs as for No. 437, only putting them on a long dish. Add one chopped onion to four ounces of finely minced calf's liver, quickly toss them on a brisk fire for about eight minutes, then pour in about six to eight drops of vinegar, a pinch of salt, and a little pepper to season. Garnish both ends of the dish with this, then serve.

444. Eggs à l'Aurore.—Boil twelve eggs until hard, then let them cool; shell them, and separate the yolks from the whites, putting the former into a mortar, adding one ounce of fresh butter, a pinch of salt, half a pinch of nutmeg, the same of ground spice, and three raw egg yolks; pound all well together. Mince the whites, and put them in a sautoire with a pint of well reduced béchamel (No. 154), cook without boiling, although letting them attain a good consistency; place them on the dish used for serving, lay the pounded yolks on top, and garnish with twelve square sippets of bread dipped in beaten egg, and put in the oven to brown for about four minutes; then serve.

445. Eggs à la Polonaise.—Cut twelve hard-boiled eggs in halves, separate the whites from the yolks, and pound the latter in a mortar, adding about one ounce of butter, a pinch of salt, half a pinch of ground spice, a saltspoonful of grated nutmeg, and five raw yolks; when well blended, without any lumps, strew half a tablespoonful of very finely chopped parsley over, and add the whites of the five eggs well beaten. Garnish the bottom of a baking-dish with this preparation, laying it in about a finger thick; also fill the whites with a part of it, making them have the appearance of whole eggs. Arrange them tastefully on top, and set the dish in the oven; brown slightly for about five minutes, remove it from the oven, lay the dish on top of another, wipe the sides carefully, and serve immediately.

446. Eggs à la Sauce Robert.—Peel two medium-sized onions, and remove the hearts, cut them in slices (the hearts), and put them with a tablespoonful of butter in a saucepan on a brisk fire, and brown them well. Moisten with a cupful of lean broth, season with a pinch of salt and half a pinch of pepper, cook, and let the sauce reduce for about ten minutes. When ready to serve, cut eight hard-boiled eggs into slices, mix them in the preparation, and let heat together without boiling for two minutes; finish with a teaspoonful of diluted mustard, and then serve.

447. Eggs à la Bennett.—Cut twelve hard-boiled eggs lengthwise, remove the yolks, and place them in a bowl with two ounces of good butter, a teaspoonful of anchovy essence, and a pinch of chopped chives. Beat well together, and fill the whites with it, besprinkle with breadcrumbs, and pour over a few drops of clarified butter; put them in the oven for three minutes on a buttered dish, and serve with half a pint of hot Madeira sauce (No. 185) thrown over.

448. Eggs à la Hyde.—Boil six fresh eggs for seven minutes, then lay them in cold water for five minutes to cool them off; shell them, and put them on a plate. Hash fine half a small canful of mushrooms with two branches of parsley and one medium-sized, sound shallot. Put in a saucepan on the hot stove one ounce of good butter, and when melted add the prepared mushrooms, and let cook rather slowly for fifteen minutes, stirring it occasionally. Add half a pint of Madeira sauce (No. 185), season with a pinch of salt and a light pinch of pepper, then cook again slowly for ten minutes. Strain the whole through a fine sieve into another saucepan, and set it aside to keep warm; cut the six hard-boiled eggs into halves, remove the entire yolks, and mash them thoroughly in a bowl, adding half an ounce of good, fresh butter and half a pint of sweet cream. Season with a light pinch of salt, half a pinch of pepper, and half a teaspoonful of grated nutmeg; mix well together, and with this fill the twelve pieces of egg-white. Lay them on a lightly buttered dish, pour the sauce over, and put them in the oven for eight minutes before sending to the table.

449. Eggs à la Ducheese.—Place a quarter of a pound of powdered sugar in a saucepan, adding half a pint of water, a small piece of lemon peel, and a short stick of cinnamon. Boil until the sugar is reduced to a syrup, then remove the lemon peel and cinnamon, and add half a teaspoonful of orange-flower water. Beat together, then strain twelve egg yolks with a pint of milk or cream, add this to the syrup with a very little salt, then transfer the whole to a silver baking-dish, place it on the hot stove, and let cook for ten minutes, stirring briskly, and when it forms a cream, squeeze in the juice of a fine, sound lemon; remove from the fire, lay the dish on another, and send to the table.

450. Plain Omelet.—Crack into a bowl twelve fresh eggs, season them with a pinch of salt and half a pinch of white pepper, beat them well until the whites and yolks are thoroughly mixed, or for fully four minutes. Place in a No. 8 frying-pan two tablespoonfuls of clarified butter; heat it well on the hot range, and when it crackles pour in the eggs, and with a fork stir all well for two minutes, then let rest for half a minute. Fold up with the fork—the side nearest the handle first—to the centre of the omelet, then the opposite side, so that both sides will meet right in the centre; let rest for half a minute longer; have a hot dish in the left hand, take hold of the handle of the pan with the right, bring both dish and pan to a triangular shape, and with a rapid movement turn the pan right over the centre of the dish, and send to the table. (The omelet should be made on a very brisk range, without taking the lid off the stove.)

Should the pan be smaller than the above-mentioned No. 8 it will require three minutes' stirring, one minute to rest, and half a minute to rest after having been folded.

When making an omelet for one person, for instance, use three fresh eggs, seasoned with half a teaspoonful of salt, and half a saltspoonful of white pepper. Thoroughly heat in a small frying-pan half a teaspoonful of clarified butter; after sharply beating the eggs in the bowl, pour into the pan, and gently mix for one minute on a very brisk range, let rest for a quarter of a minute, fold one side up, rest a quarter of a minute more, then turn on a small hot dish, and serve.

451. Omelet with Fine Herbs.—Break twelve fresh eggs into a bowl, add a pinch of finely chopped parsley, half a pinch of chopped tarragon, and half a pinch of chives; also, if desired, half a cupful of sweet cream. Beat the whole thoroughly without stopping for four minutes; melt one ounce of good butter in a frying-pan on the hot stove; when it is melted, and begins to crackle, pour in the eggs, and mix them gently with a fork, while they cook for three minutes; let them rest for one minute, then bring the sides towards the centre, turn it on a hot dish, and serve.

452. Oyster Omelet.—Blanch eighteen oysters to boiling-point in their own water; drain, and return them to the saucepan, moistening with half a pint of good Allemande (No. 210); season with half a pinch of salt. Make a plain omelet with twelve eggs as for No. 450, bring the sides toward the centre, and fill it with the oyster preparation. Turn it on a hot dish, pour the rest of the sauce around, and serve very hot.

453. Crawfish Omelet.—Stew twelve crawfish tails in a sautoire on the hot stove with half an ounce of butter, letting them cook for five minutes. Break twelve eggs into a bowl, add half a cupful of sweet cream, and a pinch of finely chopped parsley ; season with a pinch of salt and half a pinch of pepper, then sharply beat for four minutes. Make an omelet as in No. 450, fold up the side opposite the handle of the pan, place the crawfish right in the centre, fold up the other side, turn it on a hot dish, and serve.

454. Lobster Omelet.—Take six ounces of boiled lobster meat, and cut it into small pieces ; put them into a sautoire with half a glassful of white wine and a quarter of an ounce of butter. Moisten with a quarter of a pint of strong, hot béchamel (No. 154), and let cook for five minutes. Make an omelet with twelve eggs as for No. 450, and with a skimmer place the stewed lobster in the middle, fold the opposite side, pour in the garnishing, fold the other side up, turn it on a hot dish, pour the sauce around it, and serve.

455. Crab Omelet.—Proceed exactly the same as for the above (No. 454), substituting six ounces of crab meat cut into small pieces for the lobster.

456. Tomato Omelet.—Break twelve fresh eggs in a bowl, season them with a pinch of salt and half a pinch of pepper, and beat thoroughly for four minutes. Place two ounces of butter in a frying-pan on the hot stove, let it heat well without browning, then pour into it half a pint of freshly cooked stewed tomatoes, suppressing all the liquid. Cook for two minutes, then throw the beaten eggs over, and with a fork mix the whole gently for three minutes; let rest for one minute longer. Bring up the two opposite sides, turn it carefully on a hot dish, and serve.

457. Tomato Omelet à la Provençale.—Peel a medium-sized, sound onion, then chop it fine; place it in a sautoire on the hot stove with one ounce of butter, and let get a good golden color, adding half a pint of stewed tomatoes (No. 1027), or two good-sized, peeled, raw tomatoes cut into small slices, a crushed clove of garlic, and season (should the tomatoes be fresh) with a pinch of salt and half a pinch of pepper, adding a teaspoonful of chopped parsley; let the whole cook together for ten minutes; then proceed as for the tomato omelet (No. 456).

458. Asparagus-top Omelet.—Put a quarter of a bunch of boiled asparagus-tops into a bowl, pour twelve beaten eggs over, season with a pinch of salt and half a pinch of pepper, mix lightly again, and make an omelet exactly as for No. 450.

459. Omelet, with Green Peas.—Break twelve eggs into a bowl, adding half a pint of boiled green peas, a pinch each of salt and pepper, beat well for four minutes, and make into an omelet as for No. 450.

460. Omelet au Cèpes.—Fry six cèpes, cut into small pieces, in half an ounce of butter for two minutes. Beat twelve eggs in a bowl, season with a pinch of salt and half a pinch of pepper, pour them over the cèpes, and make an omelet as for No. 450.

461. Smoked Beef Omelet.—Fry two ounces of finely mixed, smoked beef in a frying-pan, with half an ounce of butter, add twelve well-beaten eggs, and make an omelet as for No. 450.

462. Ham Omelet.—Cut about two ounces of lean ham into small, square pieces, fry them for two minutes with an ounce of butter in a frying-pan, and throw over twelve well beaten eggs; with this make an omelet as for No. 450.

463. Kidney Omelet.—Stew on the hot stove three minced kidneys, with a quarter of a pint of Madeira wine sauce (No. 185), let cook for three minutes. Make a plain omelet with twelve eggs as for No. 450, fold the opposite side up, put the kidneys in the centre, fold the other side up, and turn on a dish, and pour the sauce around; then serve.

464. Chicken Liver Omelet.—The same as for the above (No. 463), substituting six minced chicken livers for the kidneys.

465. Sausage Omelet.—Skin three raw sausages, then put them in a saucepan with a quarter of an ounce of butter; set it on the hot fire for five minutes, and stir well until they cook. Make a plain omelet with twelve eggs, as for No. 450, fold the opposite side, lay the sausages in the centre, fold the other side up, and serve with a quarter of a pint of hot Madeira sauce (No. 185), poured around the omelet.

466. Omelet Bonne Femme.—Cut one ounce of salt pork into small square pieces, also two tablespoonfuls of crust from off a fresh loaf of bread cut the same way; fry them together in a frying-pan with an ounce of butter for about two minutes, adding a boiled potato cut into small squares, a pinch of chopped parsley, half a pinch of chopped chives, half a pinch of salt, and the same quantity of pepper. Beat twelve eggs for four minutes in a bowl, pour them into the pan, and make an omelet as for No. 450; turn on a hot dish, and serve.

467. Omelet Raspail.—Chop one raw onion very fine, and put it in a saucepan with an ounce of butter. Take one ounce of small squares of salt pork, cook them slightly, adding an ounce of scraps of very finely minced, cooked roast beef, the same of ham, two finely chopped mushrooms, and a pinch of chopped parsley. Stir in well a tablespoonful of tomato sauce (No. 205) and a tablespoonful of grated bread-crumbs; season with a pinch of pepper and the third of a pinch of salt. Make a plain omelet with twelve eggs as for No. 450, fold up the opposite side, fill it with the preparation, fold the other side up, turn it on a hot dish, and serve.

468. Sardine Omelet.—Thoroughly skin eight fine sardines, place six of them in a frying-pan with an ounce of butter, cook for two minutes. Beat well twelve eggs in a bowl. Season with one pinch of salt and half a pinch of pepper, add them to the sardines in the pan; make an omelet as in No. 450, fold the opposite end up, place the two remaining sardines right in the centre, fold the other end up, turn it on a hot dish, and send to the table.

469. Cheese Omelet.—Put one ounce of butter in a frying-pan, heat it on the hot stove. Break twelve eggs into a bowl, beat them thoroughly for four minutes, adding two tablespoonfuls of grated Swiss cheese, half a pinch of salt, and half a pinch of pepper. Pour the whole into the frying-pan, and make an omelet as for No. 450; turn it on a hot dish, and besprinkle the top lightly with a very little Parmesan cheese; place in the oven for two seconds, then serve.

470. Omelet Régence.—Make an omelet with twelve eggs as for No. 450, and when nearly cooked, fold up the opposite side, then fill the centre with a quarter of a pint of hot Régence garnishing (No. 434), fold the other side up; turn on a hot dish, pour the sauce around, and serve hot.

471. Omelet à la Vanderbilt.—Take two fine, sound, green peppers, plunge them into hot fat for half a minute, then take them up and lay them on a dry cloth; skin them neatly, remove all the seeds from the insides, and when emptied cut them into small slices. Put these into a saucepan on the hot stove with two medium-sized fresh, sound, sliced tomatoes, twelve nicely shelled shrimps, and three tablespoonfuls of Madeira wine sauce (No. 185), then season with half a pinch of salt and a third of a pinch of pepper; cook slowly for fifteen minutes. Break twelve fresh eggs into a bowl, season them with half a pinch of salt and a third of a pinch of pepper, and beat well for five minutes. Put two ounces of good butter in a frying-pan, place it on the hot stove, and when the butter is melted drop in the eggs, and with a spoon or fork mix briskly for two minutes. Fold the opposite side up with a skimmer, lift up the thick part of the prepared sauce, and place it in the centre of the omelet, fold the other side either with a knife or fork, and let it cook for two minutes longer, then turn on a hot dish; pour the rest of the sauce in the saucepan around the omelet, and send to the table very hot.

472. Omelet à l'Espagnole.—Put in a stewpan on the stove one finely shred onion, one ounce of butter, a chopped green pepper, six minced mushrooms, and one large, finely cut-up tomato; season with half a pinch of pepper and one pinch of salt, adding a spoonful of tomato sauce (No. 205); let cook for fifteen minutes. Make a plain omelet with twelve eggs, as for No. 450, fold the opposite side, and put more than half of the stew inside of it, say three-quarters; fold the other side up, and turn it on a long dish, then pour the rest of the sauce around, and serve.

473. Omelet Mexicaine.—Have a pint of velouté sauce (No. 152) in a saucepan, place it on a moderate fire, add a piece of lobster butter (No. 149) about the size of an egg, twenty-four shelled and cooked shrimps, and season with half a pinch of salt and a very little pepper. Let cook for three minutes, stirring it lightly, then add half of a good-sized, empty and peeled green pepper, finely hashed; cook for two minutes longer, then let rest on the corner of the stove. Make an omelet with twelve eggs, as for No. 450, fold up the opposite side, pour half of the preparation in the centre, fold the other end up, turn the omelet on a hot dish, and garnish both sides with the rest of the shrimps, pouring the balance around the dish; then send to the table.

474. Omelet Soufflée, for Six Persons.—Have a deep, cold, silver dish ready, fifteen inches long by eleven wide. Put into a vessel four ounces of powdered sugar. Break twelve fresh eggs, drop the whites into a copper basin, and the yolks of five into the vessel containing the sugar, reserving the other seven yolks for other purposes. Add to the vessel containing the sugar and yolks a light teaspoonful of vanilla essence: now with the wooden spatula, begin to beat the yolks with the sugar as briskly as you possibly can for fifteen minutes. Lay it aside. Then with the aid of a pastry wire-whip, beat up to a very stiff froth the twelve egg whites in the copper basin, which will take from twelve to fifteen minutes. Remove the pastry wire-whip; take a skimmer in the right hand, and with the left take hold of the vessel containing the preparation of the yolks and sugar. Gradually pour it over the whites, and with the skimmer gently mix the whole together for two minutes. The preparation will now be of a light, firm consistency. Now, with the aid again of the skimmer, take up the preparation and drop it down in the centre of the cold dish, ready as above mentioned, taking special care to pile it as high as possible, so as to have it of a perfect dome-shape; a few incisions can be made all around, according to taste; immediately place it in a moderate oven to bake for fifteen minutes. Take it out of the oven, and, in order to avoid burning or soiling the table-cloth, lay the dish containing the omelet on another cold one, liberally sprinkle powdered sugar over it, and immediately send to the table.

N. B.—Special care should be taken when piling the preparation into the cold, silver dish; and the making of the incisions should be done as rapidly as possible, so that success will be certain. When desired, the vanilla essence can be substituted with the same quantity of orange-flower water.

475. Sweet Omelet.—Beat and sweeten with one ounce of sugar twelve eggs; make an omelet as for No. 450, using one ounce of fresh butter; turn it on a dish, and dredge another ounce of sugar over, then glaze it with a hot shovel or salamander, and serve very warm.

476. Omelet au Kirsch, or Rum.—Make a sweet omelet with twelve eggs as for the above (No. 475); when completed and glazed, throw around it a glassful of kirsch, and set the omelet on fire; serve it while burning. Rum omelet is prepared exactly the same way, substituting rum for kirsch.

477. Omelet Célestine.—Pulverize six macaroons, put them in a bowl, adding three tablespoonfuls of apple jelly (No. 1327) and one spoonful of whipped cream (No. 1254); mix well with the spatula. Make a sweet omelet as for No. 475, with twelve eggs; fold the opposite side up, pour the mixture into the centre, fold the other end up, turn it on a hot dish, and sprinkle the top with three tablespoonfuls of powdered sugar; glaze the omelet with a hot shovel or salamander, and decorate it with three lady-fingers (No. 1231) cut in two, also a cupful of whipped cream (No. 1254), the latter poured into a paper-funnel, and piped over in any design the fancy may dictate.

A pinch of salt represents 205 grains, or a tablespoonful.
Half a pinch of pepper represents 38 grains, or a teaspoonful.
A third of a pinch of nutmeg represents 13 grains, or half a teaspoonful.

BEEF.

478. Braised Beef à la Morlaisienne.—Procure a rump-piece of beef weighing three pounds, lard it with four large pieces of salt pork, seasoned with a pinch of chopped parsley and a crushed garlic. Lay the beef in a saucepan, with pieces of salt pork or fat at the bottom, add one sliced onion, the round slices of one carrot, one sprig of thyme, and a bay-leaf ; season with a pinch of salt and half a pinch of pepper, then cover, and brown it well on both sides for ten minutes. Moisten with half a pint of white broth (No. 99) and half a pint of Espagnole sauce (No. 151), then cook for one hour. When finished, lay it on a dish, garnishing with six stuffed cabbages (No. 919). Skim off the fat, strain the gravy, and pour the sauce over, or else serve it in a separate sauce-bowl.

479. Braised Beef à la Mode.—Lard and prepare a piece of beef weighing three pounds as for the above (No. 478). Let it marinate for twelve hours in the juice of half a lemon, with one good pinch of salt, the same quantity of pepper, one sprig of thyme, two bay-leaves, and half a bunch of parsley-roots. Put the meat in a saucepan with half an ounce of butter, and let both sides brown well for ten minutes; take it out and lay it on a dish, then add to the gravy about two tablespoonfuls of flour, stirring it well, and moisten with one quart of broth (No. 99), mingling it carefully while the sauce is boiling. Replace the beef in the saucepan with two sliced carrots and twelve small glazed onions (No. 972), and cook for one hour, adding a strong bouquet (No. 254), a glassful of claret wine, if desired, and a little crushed garlic, also half a pinch of salt, and the third of a pinch of pepper. Serve on a hot dish, skim the fat off the gravy, straining it over. Arrange the carrots and onions in clusters around the dish, and serve.

All braised beef to be prepared exactly the same, only adding different garnishings.

480. Braised Beef à la Providence.—Braise a piece of beef of three pounds, as for No. 479, adding a quarter of a cooked cauliflower, half a cupful of flageolet-beans, and a cupful of cooked carrots cut with a vegetable-scoop five minutes before serving. Place the vegetables with the skimmed gravy in a pan, reduce for five minutes. Dress the beef on a hot dish, arrange the vegetables in four heaps, one at each end of the dish and one on each side of it. Pour the gravy over the beef, and serve.

481. Braised Beef à l'Orsini.—Braise a piece of beef as for No. 479, serve it on a dish garnished with rice, prepared as follows: with some cold risotto (No. 1017) form six balls the size of an egg; roll them in bread crumbs, then dip them in beaten eggs, lard them with half-inch slices of cooked, smoked tongue, and fry in hot fat for three minutes. Serve these round the beef, with its own gravy well skimmed and strained over.

482. Braised Beef à la Flamande.—Prepare the beef as for No. 479, and serve it decorated with clusters of a quarter of a cooked, red cabbage, two cooked carrots, and two turnips, all sliced. (Red cabbage, carrots, and turnips should always be cooked separately).

483. Braised Beef en Daube.—Add to a piece of braised beef, as for No. 479, one ounce of salt pork cut into small square pieces, the round slices of two carrots, and twelve glazed onions (No. 972), also one cut-up turnip. Put all these ingredients in the saucepan with the beef, three-quarters of an hour before serving.

484. Braised Beef à la Bignon.—Braise a piece of beef as for No. 479. Take six large potatoes and pare them as round as possible, scoop out the insides with a Parisian potato-spoon, being careful not to break them, parboil them slightly for three minutes on a quick fire, and then fill them with any kind of forcemeat handy; place them in the oven with two tablespoonfuls of clarified butter, and bake well for twenty minutes. Serve them around the beef, three on each side of the dish.

485. Braised Beef, Russian Sauce.—Cook a piece of braised beef as for No. 479, and serve it with a little of the gravy on the dish, and half a pint of Russian sauce (No. 211) separate.

486. Smoked Beef à la Crême.—Take one pound of very finely minced smoked beef, put it in a stewpan with half an ounce of butter, cook for two minutes, and moisten slightly with half a cupful of cream, adding two tablespoonfuls of béchamel (No. 154), and serve as soon as it boils. (Do not salt it).

487. Beefsteak Pie à l'Anglaise.—Slice two pounds of lean beef in half-inch-square slices, add two sliced onions, and stew together in a sauce-pan with one ounce of butter for ten minutes, stir in two tablespoonfuls of flour, and mix well; moisten with one quart of water or white broth (No. 99), still stirring. Season with a pinch each of salt and pepper, and add a bouquet (No. 254); let cook for twenty minutes, take out the bouquet, and fill a deep dish with the above preparation. Cut two hard-boiled eggs in slices, and lay them on top, cover with pie-crust (No. 1077), glaze the surface with egg yolk, and bake a light brown color for about eight minutes in the oven; then serve.

488. Beefsteak Pie à l'Américaine.—Proceed the same as for No. 487, but using in place of the eggs one pint of potatoes cut with a vegetable-scoop, also one ounce of lard, cut in small pieces, and cooking them with the beef the same length of time.

489. Corned Beef with Spinach.—Take three pounds of rump or brisket of corned beef, and put it into a saucepan, covering it with fresh water; boil briskly for an hour and a half, and serve with boiled spinach à l'Anglaise (No. 940).

490. Corned Beef with Kale-sprouts.—The same as for the above, only adding two quarts of kale-sprouts, half an hour before the beef is cooked, then arrange the cooked kale-sprouts on a dish, and put the corned beef over, and serve.

491. Sirloin Steak, or Entrecôte à la Bordelaise.—Procure two sirloin steaks of one pound each; season them with one pinch of salt and half a pinch of pepper. Baste on both sides with half a tablespoonful of oil, and put them on a broiler over a bright charcoal fire; broil them for six minutes on each side, and then place them on a hot serving-dish. Pour a pint of Bordelaise sauce (No. 186) over the steaks, being careful to have the rounds of marrow on top of the steaks unbroken, and serve very hot. (Broiled sirloin steaks are all to be prepared as above, only adding different sauces or garnishings).

492. Sirloin Steak à la Béarnaise.—Prepare and broil two sirloin steaks as for No. 491, and when cooked, pour over half a pint of Béarnaise sauce (No. 166), and serve.

493. Sirloin Steak à la Moëlle.—Broil two sirloin steaks as for No. 491, take half a pint of Madeira sauce (No. 185), and to it add six drops of tarragon-vinegar, also the marrow of one marrow-bone cut in round slices. Boil once only, then pour the sauce over the steaks, and serve very hot.

494. Sirloin Steak Larded à la Duchesse.—Procure a piece of four pounds of tender sirloin, pare and trim it nicely, taking out the bones; lard it over the top with a small larding-needle, and season with half a pinch of salt and a third of a pinch of pepper. Line a baking-dish with some pork-skin, one medium-sized, sliced carrot, half a bunch of well-cleaned and pared parsley-roots, one peeled, sound, sliced onion, one sprig of thyme, and a bay-leaf. Place the sirloin on top, and put it in the oven to roast for thirty minutes. Take from out the oven, dress on a hot dish, leave it at the oven door ; add half a pint of white broth (No. 99) or consommé (No. 100) to the gravy, boil it for two minutes, skim the fat off, strain the gravy into a sauce-bowl, and serve separate.

495. Sirloin Steaks à la Parisienne.—Broil two sirloin steaks as for No. 491, and serve surrounded with one pint of cooked Parisian potatoes (No. 986), and half a gill of maître d'hôtel butter (No. 145).

496. Sirloin Steaks aux Cêpes.—Lay two broiled sirloin steaks, as for No. 491, on a hot dish ; cut six medium-sized cêpes into quarter pieces, put them in a frying-pan with one tablespoonful of oil, and fry for two minutes with one finely chopped shallot and a quarter of a clove of crushed garlic. Add these ingredients to half a pint of Madeira sauce (No. 185), and boil for two minutes longer, then pour over the steaks, besprinkle with a teaspoonful of chopped parsley, and serve.

497. Sirloin Steak, with Green Peppers.—Dish two broiled sirloin steaks (No. 491), and pour over them a sauce made as follows : empty three green peppers, mince them very fine, suppressing the seeds, and put them in a stewpan with a tablespoonful of oil. Cook for about three minutes, moistening with half a pint of Madeira sauce (No. 185); cook for five minutes longer, then pour the sauce over the steaks, and serve.

498. Sirloin Piqué à la Bordelaise.—Proceed the same as for No. 491, adding a pint of Bordelaise sauce (No. 186) separately.

499. Sirloin Piqué, Marrow sauce.—The same as for No. 491, only serving with a pint of hot marrow garnishing (No. 244) separately.

500. Minced Beef à la Provençale.—Cut into small slices a piece of beef weighing one pound and a half, put them in a saucepan with two tablespoonfuls of oil and two medium-sized, chopped onions; brown them together for five minutes, then add two tablespoonfuls of flour, and cover with a pint and a half of white broth (No. 99). Stir well and put in two cut-up tomatoes, two crushed cloves of garlic, and six finely shred mushrooms ; season with a good pinch of salt and a pinch of pepper; place the lid on the pan. Let cook for twenty minutes, then dress on a hot dish. Arrange six heart-shaped croûtons (No. 133) around the dish, and serve.

501. Minced Beef à la Portugaise.—The same as for the above, only leaving out the mushrooms, and garnishing with six timbales prepared as follows : thoroughly clean the interiors of six small timbale-molds, then butter them well inside. Fill them up half their height with hot, boiled rice, well pressed down, so that when unmolding they will hold perfectly firm. Place them in the hot oven for two minutes. Unmold and arrange them around the dish at equal distances ; dress six small, hot, roasted tomatoes (No. 1028), one on top of each column of rice, and then serve.

502. Minced Beef à la Catalan.—Proceed as for No. 500, browning the meat in oil, and adding two very finely chopped shallots, one onion, and a green pepper cut into pieces. When well browned, after five minutes, put in a pint of Espagnole sauce (No. 151), half a pinch of salt, and the same of pepper. Cook again for fifteen minutes and serve, with a teaspoonful of chopped parsley strewn over.

503. Broiled Tenderloin of Beef.—Procure two and a half pounds of tenderloin of beef; pare, cut it into three equal parts, flatten a little, then place them on a dish, and besprinkle with a pinch of salt, and the same of pepper. Baste them with one teaspoonful of sweet oil; roll them well, and put them on the broiler on a moderate fire; let cook for five minutes on each side; then place them on a hot dish, and use any kind of sauce or garnishing desired.

All broiled tenderloins are prepared the same way.

504. Broiled Tenderloin à la Chéron.—Broil three tenderloin steaks, as for No. 503; lay them on a dish on the top of a gill of hot Béarnaise sauce (No. 166), place on each steak one hot artichoke-bottom filled with hot Macédoine (No. 1032), pour just a little meat-glaze (No. 141) over, and serve.

505. Tenderloin à la Nivernaise.—Broil three tenderloin steaks, as for No. 503; put them on a hot dish, with half a pint of garnishing of mushroom sauce (No. 230); lay six poached eggs (No. 404) on top, and serve.

506. Tenderloin à la Florentin.—Prepare three fillets the same as for No. 503; pour a gill of hot Madeira sauce (No. 185) over the steaks, and garnish with three hot artichokes à la Florentin (No. 903), and serve.

507. Tenderloin à la Trianon.—Broil three fillets, as for No. 503; pour half a pint of Béarnaise sauce (No. 166) over, and garnish with four slices of truffles on each; also a little meat-glaze (No. 141), and serve.

508. Broiled Tenderloin aux Gourmets.—Have three tenderloin steaks prepared as for No. 503; when taken from the broiler, place them on a warm dish, and have already prepared the following garnishing: put in a saucepan one pint of Madeira sauce (No. 185); add to it two truffles cut into square pieces, four mushrooms, an artichoke-bottom, and a small blanched sweetbread, either from the throat or heart, all well minced together. Cook for ten minutes; then pour this over the hot serving-dish. Dress the fillets over, and serve.

509. Mignons Filets à la Pompadour.—After procuring two and a half pounds of fine, tender fillet of beef, pare it nicely all around; then cut it into six equal, small fillets. Flatten them slightly and equally. Place on a dish, season with a pinch of salt and half a pinch of pepper, evenly divided. Place them in a pan on the hot range, with half a gill of clarified butter, and cook them for four minutes on each side. Prepare a pint of Béarnaise sauce, as in No. 166. Dress three-quarters of it on a hot dish (reserving the other quarter for further action). Lay six round-shaped pieces of bread-croûtons, lightly fried in butter, over the Béarnaise sauce; dress the six fillets, one on top of each croûton; arrange them six warm artichoke-bottoms right in the centre of the fillets. Fill up the artichokes with a tablespoonful of hot Jardinière (No. 1033). Evenly divide the remaining quarter of a pint of hot Béarnaise sauce over the Jardinière. Cut into six even slices one good-sized, sound truffle; place one slice on the top of each, right in the centre of the Béarnaise sauce, and send to the table as hot as possible.

510. Mignons Filets à la Moëlle.—Prepare and fry six small fillets as for the above (No. 509) for three minutes on both sides; lay them on a dish, adding one pint of hot Madeira sauce (No. 185) with six drops of tarragon-vinegar and eighteen round slices of marrow. Let boil once only; then pour the sauce around the dish, dressing the marrow on top of the fillet, and serve.

511. Mignons Filets, Marinated, Russian Sauce.—Trim nicely and lard six fillets of beef—tail ends weighing each a quarter of a pound—steep them in a cooked marinade (No. 139) for twelve hours; then drain, and cook them in a sautoire, with one ounce of clarified butter, for three minutes on each side, and serve with one pint of Russian sauce (No. 211) on the dish, and the fillets on top.

512. Mignons Filets à la Bernardi.—Prepare six small fillets, as directed for No. 509; cook them for three minutes on each side; then lay them on a dish and pour over half a pint of hot Madeira sauce (No. 185). Serve with six small croûstades (No. 264), garnished with Macédoine (No. 1032), and six large game quenelles (No. 228).

513. Mignons Filets à la Bohémienne.—Lay on a dish six small fillets prepared the same as for No. 509. Pour over them half a pint of hot Madeira sauce (No. 185). Make six small croûstades (No. 264), fill them with a cooked macaroni à la crême (No. 954) cut into small pieces; also two tablespoonfuls of grated cheese. Cover them with a round slice of cooked smoked tongue, and garnish the steaks with these.

514. Mignons Filets à la Parisienne.—Pare nicely six small fillets; cook three minutes, as directed in No. 509; put half a pint of Madeira sauce (No. 185) in a saucepan, with two truffles and six mushrooms, all cut in slices. Let cook for ten minutes. Nicely arrange six small, round croûtons on the hot dish; dress the fillets over them, and pour the sauce around, but not over them; then serve.

515. Mignons Filets aux Pommes-de-terre Parisiennes.—When cooked the same as the above, for three minutes, pour over the fillets placed on a dish half a gill of good maître d'hôtel butter (No. 145) thickened with some meat-glaze (No. 141), and garnish with half a pint of Parisian potatoes (No. 986.)

516. Tenderloin Piqué à la Duchesse.—Procure four pounds of tenderloin; pare it well, and lard it, using a fine needle. Line the bottom of a roasting-pan with some pork-skin, one sliced onion, one sliced carrot, and half a bunch of well-washed parsley-roots. Place the tenderloin on top; add a pinch of salt, and roast it in a brisk oven for thirty-five minutes, basting it occasionally with its own juice. Dish it up, skim the fat off the gravy, then strain it over the fillet, and pour half a pint of good Madeira sauce (No. 185) over, and garnish with six potatoes Duchesse (No. 1006).

517. Tenderloin Piqué à la Portugaise.—Roast four pounds of tenderloin as in No. 516, lay it on a hot dish, arrange six stuffed tomatoes (No. 1023) around the tenderloin at equal distances. Put in a saucepan half a pint of tomato sauce (No. 205), and one gill of demi-glace (No.

185). Let boil for one minute, then pour it into a sauce-bowl and serve separate.

518. Roast four pounds of tenderloin as for No. 516, slice half a pint of cêpes, and add them to half a pint of Madeira sauce (No. 185) with one crushed clove of garlic. Pour the sauce onto a dish, lay the tenderloin on top, and decorate with some twisted anchovies, and twelve stoned olives laid one on each one; then serve.

519. Roast Tenderloin à la Hussard.—Procure four pounds of fillet of beef, pare it nicely, and season with one pinch each of salt and pepper; butter the surface lightly, and lay it in a roasting-pan, and put it to cook for ten minutes in a brisk oven, then set it aside to cool, and afterwards lay on it some very fine chicken forcemeat (No. 226), besprinkle with fresh bread-crumbs, and baste with three tablespoonfuls of clarified butter. Roast it again for thirty-five minutes, and serve with three-quarters of a pint of the following Hussard garnishing on the dish.

Put in a saucepan on the hot stove half a pint of Madeira sauce (No. 185), a gill of tomato sauce (No. 205), six good-sized, sound mushrooms, cut into small pieces, twelve godiveau quenelles (No. 221), and three ounces of cooked, smoked beef-tongue, cut in round pieces. Let all cook together for five minutes, and use when required.

520. Tenderloin Piqué à la Sevigne.—Roast a piece of tenderloin as for No. 519; when done and laid on a dish, pour over it half a pint of good Madeira sauce (No. 185), and decorate with six small bouchées filled with spinach (No. 588).

521. Tenderloin Piqué à l'Egyptienne.—Roast a piece of tenderloin as for No. 519, lay it on a dish, pouring over it half a pint of good Madeira sauce (No. 185). Garnish one side of the dish with three roots of boiled celery—the white part only—and the other side with eighteen cooked gumbos (No. 1030), then serve.

522. Tenderloin Piqué à la Richelieu.—Exactly the same as for No. 519, only adding one pint of hot Richelieu sauce under the fillet (No. 539), and serve.

523. Tenderloin Piqué à la Bernardi.—Take a four-pound piece of tenderloin, lard it—using a small larding needle—with very thin pieces of fresh ham and truffles, all cut the same size; put it into the oven to roast for thirty-five minutes, and then lay it on a dish, trimming the fillets carefully, the larded part being on the top. Pour over half a pint of good, hot Madeira sauce (No. 185), and garnish with three artichoke-bottoms, filled with hot Macédoine (No. 1032), three bouchées filled with spinach (No. 588), and three large game quenelles (No. 228). Arrange these to represent one single bouquet, and serve.

524. Porterhouse Steak.—Procure two porterhouse steaks of one and a half pounds each—see that they are cut from the short loin—flatten them well, pare and trim, and season with one pinch of salt and half a pinch of pepper. Put them on a dish with half a tablespoonful of oil: roll well, and put them on a moderate fire to broil seven minutes on each side. Lay them on a warm dish, pour one gill of maître d'hôtel butter (No. 145) over, and serve with a little watercress around the dish.

525. Double Porterhouse Steak.—Have a fine porterhouse steak of three pounds, and proceed as for No. 524. Broil on a rather slow charcoal fire, if possible, ten minutes on each side, then serve as for the above.

526. Hamburg Steak, Russian Sauce.—Take two pounds of lean beef—the hip part is preferable—remove all the fat, and put it in a Salisbury chopping machine; then lay it in a bowl, adding a very finely chopped shallot, one raw egg for each pound of beef, a good pinch of salt, half a pinch of pepper, and a third of a pinch of grated nutmeg. Mix well together, then form it into six flat balls the size of a small fillet. Roll them in fresh bread-crumbs, and fry them in the pan with two tablespoonfuls of clarified butter for two minutes on each side, turning them frequently and keeping them rare. Serve with half a pint of Russian sauce (No. 211) or any other desired.

527. Roast Beef.—In order to have a fine piece of beef cooked to perfection, and at the same time have it retain all its juices, purchase, from a first-class butcher only, a three-rib piece near the short loin part. Saw off the spine, also the bones of the three ribs to one inch from the meat, so as to have it as nearly a round shape as possible. Season with one and a quarter pinches of salt, divided equally all over, tie it together, and place it lengthwise in a roasting-pan. Pour a tablespoonful and a half of water into the pan so as to prevent its burning, then a few very small bits of butter can be distributed on top of the beef, if so desired. Set it in a rather moderate oven, and let roast for one hour and ten minutes, taking care to baste frequently with its own gravy. Remove it from the oven, untie, and dress it on a very hot dish, skim the fat from the gravy, and pour in two tablespoonfuls of broth, heat up a little, strain the gravy into a sauce-bowl, and send to the table.

The parings from the beef can be utilized for soup-stock; nothing need be wasted.

528. Corned Beef Hash à la Polonaise.—Brown in a saucepan two onions, with one ounce of butter; add one pound of cooked, well-chopped corned beef, and one pint of hashed potatoes. Moisten with a gill of broth, and a gill of Espagnole (No. 151). Season with half a pinch of pepper and a third of a pinch of nutmeg; stir well and let cook for fifteen minutes, then serve with six poached eggs on top (No. 404), and sprinkle over with a pinch of chopped parsley.

529. Corned Beef Hash au Gratin.—Make a hash as for the above, (No. 528), put it in a lightly buttered baking-dish, and besprinkle with rasped bread-crumbs. Moisten slightly with about one teaspoonful of clarified butter, and bake in the oven for fifteen minutes, or until it obtains a good brown color; then serve.

530. Corned Beef Hash à la Zingara.—The same as for No. 528, adding to the hash two good-sized, freshly peeled, and cut-up tomatoes (or half a pint of canned), one bruised clove of garlic, and one pinch of chopped parsley. Let all cook together for fifteen minutes, then serve.

531. Corned Beef Hash en Bordure.—Form a border around a baking-dish with mashed potatoes (No. 998), set it for two minutes in the oven, then fill the centre with hot corned beef hash (No. 528). Besprinkle the top with one pinch of chopped parsley, and serve.

532. Beef-Tongue à la Gendarme.—Boil a fresh beef-tongue in the soup-stock for one hour and a half. Skin it, then place it on a dish, adding one pint of Gendarme garnishing, made by pouring a pint of Madeira sauce (No. 185) into a saucepan. Put it on the hot stove, and add twelve small godiveau quenelles (No. 221). Cut up six small, sound pickles, four mushrooms, and two ounces of smoked beef-tongue; add these to the sauce, and let cook for five minutes, stirring it lightly, then serve.

533. Beef-Tongue, Sauce Piquante.—The same as for the above, No. 532. When the tongue is ready, decorate it with pickles, and serve with a pint of sauce piquante (No. 203) separate, instead of the other garnishing.

534. Beef-Tongue, Napolitaine.—The same as for No. 532, adding one pint of hot Napolitaine garnishing (No. 195), instead of the other garnishing.

535. Beef-Tongue à la Jardinière.—The same as for No. 532, adding one pint of hot Jardiniére (No. 1033), in place of the other garnishing.

536. Beef-Tongue, with Spinach.—The same as for No. 532, substituting one pint of spinach with gravy (No. 943) for the other garnishing.

537. Beef-Tongue, au Risotto.—The same as for No. 532, only adding one pint of hot Risotto (No. 1017) for the other garnishing.

538. Beef-Tongue à la Milanaise.—The same as for No. 532, only substituting one pint of Milanaise garnishing (No. 251) for the other.

539. Roulade of Beef à l'Ecarlate.—Procure six pounds of fine brisket of prime beef; roll it up as close as possible, so as to have it very firm, then firmly tie it around. Put in a saucepan one sound, peeled onion, one well-washed and scraped, sound carrot, both cut into slices, one sprig of thyme, one bay-leaf, three cloves, and a few shreds of larding-pork. Place the roulade over all. Season with two pinches of salt and one pinch of pepper. Cover the pan very tightly to prevent steam from escaping. Should the lid be loose, place a weight on top of it. Place it on a moderate fire, and let gently simmer for twenty minutes in all. Remove the lid, add two glasses of white wine, and one gill of broth (No. 99). Cover very tightly again, place in the hot oven, and let braise for fully two hours. Remove from the oven, untie, dress on a hot dish. Skim the fat off the gravy, strain the gravy into a sautoire, and reduce it on the hot range to one-half. Cut up an ounce of cooked, smoked beef-tongue into cock's-comb shape, one good-sized, sound, sliced truffle, six godiveau quenelles (No. 221), and six mushrooms. Place all these in a sautoire on the fire, with half a wine-glassful of Madeira wine, letting boil for one minute. Strain the reduced gravy of the roulade over this; add half a gill of tomato sauce (No. 205), and half a gill of Espagnole sauce (No. 151). Cook again for five minutes, then pour it into a sauce-bowl and send to the table separate, very hot.

540. Stewed Beef à l'Egyptienne.—Cut two pounds of beef into small, square pieces, brown them in a stewpan with one ounce of butter, adding two onions, cut into square pieces. When well browned, for about ten minutes, add two tablespoonfuls of flour; stir briskly with a pint and a half of white broth (No. 99), also one gill of tomato sauce (No. 205). Season with one good pinch of salt and half a pinch of pepper. put in a bouquet (No. 254), one clove of crushed garlic, and let cook for twenty-five minutes. Dish up the beef with a bunch of eighteen cooked gumbos (No. 1030), also three stalks of white, cooked celery.

541. Stewed Beef à la Dufour.—Prepare two pounds of small, square cuts of beef, brown them with two onions cut in square pieces, adding two tablespooufuls of flour, cooking for six minutes. Stir well, and moisten with one quart of broth (No. 99), and one gill of tomato sauce (No. 205.) Put in also one pint of raw potatoes, cut in quarters, and let cook thoroughly for twenty-five minutes, with a bouquet (No. 254), a good pinch of salt and half a pinch of pepper, also one crushed garlic; then serve.

542. Stewed Beef à la Turque.—Cook the beef as directed in No. 541, substituting a good teaspoonful of curry, and serve with six timbales filled with cooked rice (No. 501). Unmold them, and use them instead of the potatoes.

543. Stewed Beef à la Marseillaise.—Proceed the same as for No. 541, omitting the potatoes, but adding two tomatoes cut in pieces, six chopped mushrooms, and two crushed cloves of garlic, all cooked six minutes with the beef. Serve with a teaspoonful of chopped parsley strewn over.

544. Tripe à la Bordelaise.—Take a pound and a half of lozenge-shaped pieces of tripe, cut into twelve parts. Marinate them for two hours in one tablespoonful of oil, with a pinch of salt, half a pinch of pepper, one bay-leaf, one sprig of thyme, six whole peppers, the juice of one sound lemon, and one crushed clove of garlic. Drain, roll them in flour, then in beaten egg, and finally in fresh bread-crumbs. Fry in one ounce of clarified butter in a pan for five minutes on each side, and serve with a gill of maître d'hôtel butter (No. 145), adding to it a teaspoonful of meat-glaze (No. 141).

545. Tripe à la Créole.—Cut a pound and a half of tripe into small pieces, fry them in a pan with two ounces of butter, one chopped onion, and half a green pepper, also chopped. Brown them slightly for six minutes, then transfer them to a saucepan with one cut-up tomato and half a pint of Espagnole sauce (No. 151). Season with one pinch of salt and half a pinch of pepper, adding a bouquet (No. 254), also a crushed clove of garlic. Cook for ten minutes and serve with one teaspoonful of chopped parsley.

546. Tripe à la Pleoutte.—Shred one and a half pounds of tripe, brown it slightly for three minutes in a pan, with an ounce of butter, one pinch of salt, and half a pinch of pepper; then transfer it to a saucepan, with half a pint of good Allemande sauce (No. 210). Let cook five minutes longer, then squeeze in the juice of half a lemon, besprinkle with a pinch of chopped parsley, and serve.

547. Tripe à la Mode de Caën.—Take one raw, double tripe, one ox-foot, three calf's feet, all well-washed and cleansed several times in fresh water, cutting them in pieces two inches long by one square. Have an earthen pot, or a saucepan, put pieces of feet at the bottom, cover over with tripe, then a layer of sliced carrots and onions, and continue the same until the vessel is full, carefully seasoning each layer. Tie in a cloth a sprig of thyme, two bay-leaves, twelve whole peppers, and six cloves; put this in the middle of the pot, throw over a bottleful of cider or white wine, and a little brandy (say one pony); lay on the top the stalks of some green leeks, parsley-roots, and cabbage leaves; cover, and fasten it down with paste, so that the steam cannot escape, and leave it for about ten hours in a very slow oven. Take it from the oven and serve when required.

548. Tripe à la Lyonnaise.—Cut up a pound and a half of double tripe, also two onions, and brown them in the pan with one ounce of clarified butter until they assume a fine golden color. Drain them, put them back on the fire, add one tablespoonful of vinegar and a gill of good Espagnole (No. 157). Stew for two minutes longer, and serve with a pinch of chopped parsley sprinkled over.

A pinch of salt represents 205 grains, or a tablespoonful.
Half a pinch of pepper represents 38 grains, or a teaspoonful.
A third of a pinch of nutmeg represents 13 grains, or half a teaspoonful.

VEAL.

549. Blanquette of Veal.—Cut into two-inch-square pieces two and a half pounds of breast of veal. Soak it in fresh water for one hour; drain it well, then lay it in a saucepan; cover with fresh water; boil, and be very careful to skim off all the scum. Add a well-garnished bouquet (No. 254), six small, well-peeled, sound, white onions, two good pinches of salt and a pinch of white pepper. Cook for forty minutes. Melt about an ounce and a half of butter in another saucepan, add to it three table-spoonfuls of flour, stir well for three minutes; moisten with a pint of broth from the veal; boil for five minutes. Set it on the side of the stove. Beat up in a bowl three egg yolks, with the juice of a medium-sized, sound lemon and a very little grated nutmeg. Take the preparation in the saucepan, gradually add it to the egg yolks, &c., briskly mix with a wooden spoon meanwhile until all added. Throw this over the veal, lightly toss the whole, but be careful not to allow to boil again;

then serve. All blanquettes are prepared the same way, adding different garnishings.

550. Blanquette of Veal à la Reine.—The same as for No. 549, adding six chopped mushrooms, and twelve godiveau quenelles (No. 221) two minutes before serving.

551. Blanquette of Veal with Peas.—The same as for No. 549, adding one pint of cooked, green, or canned blanched peas two minutes before serving.

552. Blanquette of Veal with Nouilles.—The same as for No. 549, adding a quarter of a pound of cooked nouilles (No. 1182) around the serving-dish as a border.

553. Blanquette of Veal à l'Ancienne.—The same as for No. 549, adding one ounce of salt pork cut into small pieces, and cooked with the meat from the commencement, and six sliced mushrooms two minutes before serving.

554. Brisotin of Veal.—Cut up six pieces of lean veal about a quarter of an inch thick, and of the length of the hand. Flatten them, and season with one pinch of salt and half a pinch of pepper. Lard the centres, using a small larding needle, with strips of larding-pork. Lay any kind of forcemeat at hand on them, roll well, and tie with a string. Put them into a deep sautoire with a very little fat, one sliced carrot, and one medium-sized, sliced onion. Cover the whole with a piece of buttered paper; set it on the fire, and let it take a good golden color for about five minutes. Moisten with half a pint of white broth (No. 99), then put the saucepan in the oven, and cook slowly for twenty minutes, basting it occasionally, and serve.

Brisotins are all prepared the same way, adding different garnishings.

555. Brisotin of Veal à l'Ecarlate.—The same as for No. 554, adding half a pint of hot écarlate sauce (No. 539).

556. Brisotin of Veal, Nantaise.—The same as for No. 554, placing six stuffed lettuce-heads (No. 953) around the dish, and pouring one gill of hot Madeira sauce (No. 185) over it.

557. Calf's Brains with Black Butter.—Place three fine, fresh calf's brains in cold water, and then peel off the skins. Wash again in cold water; neatly drain; put them in a sautoire and cover with fresh water. Add two pinches of salt, half a cupful of vinegar, one medium-sized, sliced carrot, one sprig of thyme, one bay-leaf, and twelve whole peppers. Boil for five minutes, drain well, and cut each brain in two. Dress them on a dish, and serve with a gill of very hot black butter (No. 159).

Calf's brain is always prepared as above, adding any desired sauce.

558. Calf's Brains à la Vinaigrette.—Exactly the same as for No. 557, serving on a folded napkin on a dish, garnishing with a few green parsley-leaves, and a gill of vinaigrette sauce (No. 201), separately.

559. Fried Calf's Brains, Tartare Sauce.—Proceed as in No. 557, then dry the brains well in a napkin; bread them à l'Anglaise (No. 301), and fry in hot grease for five minutes. Serve with half a pint of tartare sauce (No. 207), separately.

560. Veal Cutlets à la Pagasqui.—Chop well two or three times in the machine two pounds of lean veal, from the hip if possible; place the meat in a bowl with two ounces of finely chopped, raw veal-suet. Season with one good pinch of salt, half a pinch of pepper, and the third of a pinch of nutmeg. Add half a cupful of good cream, one chopped shallot and two raw eggs. Mix well together. Shape six pieces like chops, sprinkle them with bread-crumbs, and fry in a stewpan with two ounces of clarified butter for four minutes on each side. Serve with a gill of any kind of sauce.

561. Veal Cutlets à la St. Cloud.—Lard thoroughly six veal cutlets with two small truffles, cut julienne-shape, one ounce of cooked beef-tongue, and one ounce of larding-pork, both cut the same. Place them in a sautoire with a pinch of salt, one sliced carrot, and one sliced onion, and let them brown for ten minutes, being careful to keep the lid on the pan. Moisten with half a pint of broth, and put them in the oven to finish cooking for at least fifteen minutes. Serve with a hot salpicon sauce, the chicken cut in large pieces (No. 256), pouring the sauce on the dish, and lay the chops on top.

562. Veal Cutlets à la Maréchale.—Pare nicely six veal cutlets; season them with a tablespoonful of salt and a teaspoonful of pepper. Cook in a sautoire with two ounces of butter for five minutes on each side. Moisten with half a pint of Espagnole sauce (No. 151), adding four sliced mushrooms, twelve small godiveau quenelles (No. 221), and three chicken livers, blanched and cut into pieces. Cook for five minutes longer, and serve with six croûtons (No. 133).

563. Veal Cutlets à la Milanaise.—Pare nicely and season well with a tablespoonful of salt and a teaspoonful of pepper six veal cutlets. Dip them in beaten egg, then in grated Parmesan cheese, and finally in fresh bread-crumbs. Flatten them, and cook them in a sautoire with six ounces of clarified butter for five minutes on each side, and serve with half a pint of garnishing Milanaise (No. 251).

To prepare breaded veal cutlets with tomato sauce, bread six cutlets as for the above, omit the cheese, cook them as described, and serve with half a pint of tomato sauce (No. 205).

564. Broiled Veal Cutlets.—Cut six even veal cutlets from a fine piece of the loin of white veal, pare them and flatten them slightly; lay them on a dish, and season with a tablespoonful of salt, a teaspoonful of pepper, and one tablespoonful of sweet oil. Turn the cutlets around several times; then put them on the broiler to broil for eight minutes on each side. Remove them from the fire; arrange them on a hot dish, spread a little maître d'hôtel (No. 145) over them, and send to the table.

565. Veal Cutlets à la Philadelphia.—Pare and brown in a sautoire with two ounces of butter six veal cutlets. Season them with a pinch of salt and half a pinch of pepper, turning them carefully at times. Add two onions cut in thick slices, and place the lid on the sautoire. Stir the onions occasionally, and when of a golden brown color, moisten with half a pint of Espagnole sauce (No. 151). Cook for fifteen minutes, and serve with one teaspoonful of chopped parsley.

566. Veal Cutlets en Papillotes.—Pare nicely six veal cutlets; put them in a sautoire with one ounce of butter, and season with a tablespoonful of salt and a teaspoonful of pepper. Add half a chopped onion, and brown slightly. Cook for eight minutes with four finely chopped mushrooms, moistening with a gill of Espagnole sauce (No. 151). Cook for four minutes longer. Then take out the cutlets, drain them, and put them to cool. Add to the gravy a teaspoonful of chopped parsley and two tablespoonfuls of fresh bread-crumbs. Now take six pieces of oiled white paper cut heart-shaped, put a thin slice of cooked ham on one side of the paper; then lay on the ham a little of the stock, and on top of it a cutlet, and another layer of the stock, and over all a thin slice of cooked ham. Cover with the second part of the paper, close it by folding the two edges firmly together, and proceed the same with the other cutlets. Bake for a short time (at most five minutes) in the oven, rather slowly, and then serve.

567. Curry of Veal à l'Indienne.—Cut into pieces and blanch in salted water two pounds of any kind of lean, raw veal. Drain and wash them well. Put the pieces into a saucepan, and cover them with warm water; seasoning with two pinches of salt and one pinch of pepper, adding also a bouquet (No. 254), and six small whole onions. Cook for twenty-five minutes. Then make a gill of roux blanc (No. 135), in a saucepan, moistening it with the liquor from the veal; stir it well, and then add a tablespoonful of diluted curry-powder and three raw egg yolks, beating up as they are put in. Dress the veal on a hot dish; immediately strain the roux over it (as it must not cook again). Neatly arrange half a pint of hot, plain, boiled rice all around the dish, then serve.

568. Escalops of Veal, plain.—Pare and cut two pounds of veal (from the hip is preferable) into six even steak-form slices. Season with one pinch of salt and half a pinch of pepper. Then brown them in a sautoire on a very hot range, with one ounce of butter, for five minutes on each side; dress on a hot dish, and serve with any kind of sauce or garnishing desired.

569. Escalops of Veal à la Duxelle.—Prepare six escalops as for No. 568, adding a chopped shallot, six mushrooms shred as finely as possible, one crushed clove of garlic, and a teaspoonful of chopped parsley. Moisten with a gill of Espagnole sauce (No. 151), and half a glassful of white wine. Cook for five minutes longer, pour them on a hot dish, place the escalops over, and then serve.

570. Escalops of Veal with Stuffed Peppers.—Proceed exactly as for No. 568, adding the juice of half a medium-sized, sound lemon, and a gill of hot Madeira sauce (No. 185). Cook for three minutes longer, and decorate the dish with six stuffed green-peppers (No. 975) three minutes before serving.

571. Escalops of Veal à la Chicorée.—Prepare and proceed precisely the same as for No. 568. Cook for eight minutes. Then dress half a pint of chicorée au jus (No. 934) on the hot dish, and send to the table.

572. Escalops of Veal à l'Italienne.—The same as for No. 568, adding one medium-sized, chopped onion, six chopped mushrooms, one teaspoonful of parsley, and a crushed clove of garlic. Moisten with half a glassful of white wine, and cook for five minutes with a gill of Espagnole sauce (No. 151), and serve.

573. Escalops of Veal à la Provençale.—Prepare as for No. 568, replacing the butter by the same quantity of oil. Season well, and when browned on both sides add one shallot or a finely chopped onion. Let them color, and then moisten with a gill of broth. Add two tablespoonfuls of Espagnole sauce, (No. 151), three chopped cêpes, two crushed cloves of garlic, and a teaspoonful of parsley. Boil once, and then serve with six croûtons of fried bread (No. 133).

574. Escalops of Sweetbreads à la Richelieu.—Take four blanched sweetbreads (No. 601); cut them into slices, and stew them in a saucepan, with an ounce of butter and half a glassful of white wine. Season with a tablespoonful of salt, a teaspoonful of pepper, and half a teaspoonful of nutmeg. Cook for six minutes, then moisten with a gill of thick Allemande sauce (No. 210), and add two sliced truffles and four sliced mushrooms. Fill six scallop-shells with the preparation; sprinkle the tops with fresh bread-crumbs; pour a few drops of clarified butter over all, and brown slightly in the oven for five minutes. Serve on a dish with a folded napkin.

575. Minced Veal à la Catalan.—Mince two pounds of lean veal, and brown it in a saucepan with three tablespoonfuls of sweet oil, one onion cut in quarters, and half a minced green-pepper. When a fine color, add two tablespoonfuls of flour, and mix thoroughly. Moisten with one pint of white broth (No. 99), and season with a heaped tablespoonful of salt, a teaspoonful of pepper; stir briskly, and add a bouquet (No. 254), three cloves of crushed garlic, and a gill of tomato sauce (No. 205). Cook well for twenty-five minutes; then serve, sprinkling a little chopped parsley over it.

576. Minced Veal à la Biscaënne.—Proceed as for No. 575, adding one pint of potatoes Parisiennes (No. 986), and two cut-up tomatoes, fifteen minutes before serving.

577. Fricandeau with Sorrel.—Cut a slice of three pounds from a leg of veal; remove the sinews, and lard the surface with a medium-sized larding needle. Place it in a sautoire in which there are already pieces of pork-skin, one sliced onion, one sliced carrot, and a bouquet (No. 254). Season with a tablespoonful of salt, cover with a buttered paper, and let it color slightly for five minutes on the stove. Then moisten with half a pint of white broth (No. 99), and cook one hour, basting it occasionally. Serve with half a pint of purée of sorrel (No. 974) on the dish, placing the veal on top.

All fricandeaus are prepared in the same way.

578. Fricandeau with Spinach.—The same as for No. 577, adding half a pint of hot spinach au gras (No. 943) instead of the sorrel.

579. Fricandeau à la Morlaisienne.—The same as for No. 577, serving it with a gill of hot Madeira sauce (No. 185), and garnishing with six small stuffed cabbages around the dish (No. 919).

580. Calf's Liver Stewed à l'Italienne.—Cut two pounds of fresh calf's liver into small pieces. Put them with one ounce of clarified butter into a pan on the hot range, with one peeled and finely chopped, sound onion, and a clove of crushed garlic. Season with one pinch of salt and half a pinch of pepper. Cook well for five minutes, shuffling the pan well meanwhile, then moisten with half a glassful of white wine and a gill of Espagnole sauce (No. 151). Add six chopped mushrooms, and cook once more for three minutes. Serve with a teaspoonful of finely chopped parsley.

581. Calf's Liver Sauté à la Provençale.—Proceed as for No. 580, adding two crushed cloves of garlic. Squeeze in the juice of half a lemon. Serve with a tablespoonful of chopped parsley.

582. Calf's Liver à l'Alsacienne.—Cut two pounds of calf's liver into square pieces, and put them in a sautoire with one ounce of clarified butter. Season with a tablespoonful of salt and a teaspoonful of pepper, and add two medium-sized, sliced onions. When well stewed for six minutes, pour in a teaspoonful of vinegar, and two tablespoonfuls of Espagnole sauce (No. 151), and let it just come to a boil. ̄Serve with a little chopped parsley.

583. Calf's Liver Braised à la Bourgeoise.—Place a small calf's liver, larded thoroughly with pieces of larding pork, previously seasoned with a pinch of chopped parsley and a hashed clove of garlic, in a saucepan on the fire, with two tablespoonfuls of clarified butter, one sprig of thyme, two bay-leaves, half a sliced carrot, and half a sliced onion. Turn the liver over and moisten it with one gill of Espagnole sauce (No. 151), and a gill of white broth (No. 99). Season with a pinch of salt and half a pinch of pepper, and cook for forty-five minutes. Strain the sauce into another saucepan (meanwhile keeping the liver in a warm place), adding to the gravy two medium-sized, sound, well-scraped, sliced, raw carrots, and two ounces of salt pork cut into shreds. Stew well together for twenty-five minutes, and pour the garnishing over the liver just before serving, decorating with six small onions around the dish.

584. Calf's Liver Broiled with Bacon.—Take a nice, tender, fresh calf's liver weighing a pound and a half ; pare and trim off the hard portions; cut it into six equal-sized slices, and put them on a dish. Season with a tablespoonful of salt, a teaspoonful of pepper, and one tablespoonful of sweet oil; mix well together. Broil for four minutes on each side. Arrange the slices on a hot serving-dish, and decorate with six thin and crisp slices of broiled bacon (No. 754). Spread a gill of maître d'hôtel butter (No. 145) over, and serve very hot.

585. Loin of Veal, Roasted.—Saw from a fine, white, fresh, and fat loin of veal with the kidney, the spine, and whatever hip-bone remains. Season the loin with a tablespoonful and a half of salt, and one heaped teaspoonful of pepper and roll the flank part neatly over the kidney, and tie it with a string.

Have ready a lightly buttered roasting-pan. Lay in it the loin; pour in half a glassful of water, and distribute a few bits of butter over the meat. Then cover its entire length with a piece of well-buttered paper. Place the pan in a moderate oven, and roast it for one hour and three-quarters, meanwhile basting it frequently with its own gravy. Take it out of the oven, untie it, and place it on a hot serving-dish. Add three tablespoonfuls of broth to the gravy in the pan, skim off the fat and reduce it to the consistency of a demi-glace sauce; then strain it through a colander, either over the roast or into a separate sauce-bowl, and send it to the table immediately.

Loin of lamb, roasted, is to be prepared exactly as above described, letting it cook fifty minutes instead of an hour and three-quarters.

Loin of mutton is also to be roasted and served in the same way, but one hour's cooking will be sufficient.

586. Grenadins of Veal, Purée of Peas.—Cut into six pieces two pounds of lean veal from off the leg; extract the sinews, and lard the veal nicely on one side, using a needle for the purpose. Lay the pieces in a sautoire, with one carrot, one onion, and some scraps of pork, and let them brown together for six minutes. Season with a tablespoonful of salt, and moisten with a gill of white broth (No. 99). Put the sautoire into the oven, covering it with a piece of buttered paper. After thirty minutes, or when of a good color, remove, and serve with half a pint of hot purée of peas (No. 49) on the dish, the grenadins on top, and the gravy strained over all.

587. Grenadins of Veal à la Chipolata.—The same as for No. 586, only adding half a pint of hot chipolata garnishing (No. 232) instead of the peas.

588. Grenadins of Veal à la Sevigné.—The same as for No. 586, only decorating the dish with six bouchées Sevigné, made by preparing six small bouchées (No. 270), and filling them with very finely chopped spinach au jus (No 943). Lay the covers on and serve very hot without any other garnishing.

589. Grenadins of Veal à l'Africaine.—Prepare the same as for No. 586, serving very hot, with three small, stuffed egg-plants (No. 909), and eighteen medium-sized, cooked gumbos (No. 1030).

590. Braised Noix of Veal à la Providence.—Lard thoroughly a knuckle of veal of three pounds, braise it nicely in a saucepan with an ounce of fresh salt pork, one tablespoonful of salt, and a teaspoonful of pepper. Cook for fifteen minutes, stirring occasionally, and moistening with half a pint of white broth (No. 99), and half a pint of Espagnole sauce (No. 151.) Add one pint of raw Jardinière (No. 1033) and a cupful of flageolets. Cook for forty-five minutes all together. Transfer the knuckle to a hot dish, pour the garnishing over, and serve.

591. Braised Noix of Veal en Daube.—Proceed the same as for braised beef en Daube (No. 483).

592. Panplette of Veal à la Faubonne.—Cut two pounds of veal off the leg into six thin slices. Pare them to the size of the hand, and season with a tablespoonful of salt and a teaspoonful of pepper. Fill them with any kind of forcemeat, roll, and tie together with string. Put them in a sautoire with small scraps of pork, adding half a sliced carrot and half a sliced onion. Cover with a *barde* of larding pork on top, and brown for ten minutes. Moisten with a gill of white broth (No. 99); cover with buttered paper, and put in the oven to finish cooking for twenty-five minutes. Serve with half a pint of purée of lentils (No. 46), mixed with two tablespoonfuls of cream, and a teaspoonful of chopped parsley.

593. Panpiette of Veal à l'Ecarlate.—The same as for No. 592, pouring half a pint of hot Ecarlate sauce (No. 247) over the panpiettes.

594. Panpiette of Veal, Purée of Chestnuts.—The same as for No. 592, adding half a pint of hot purée of chestnuts (No. 131).

595. Panpiette of Veal, Sauce Duxelle.—The same as for No. 592, putting half a pint of hot Duxelle sauce (No. 189) on the dish, and arranging the panpiettes over it.

596. Breast of Veal à la Milanaise.—Bone a breast of veal of two and a half pounds; season with one tablespoonful of salt and a teaspoonful of pepper. Stuff it in the usual way with forcemeat (No. 229). Roll and tie it, making a few incisions in the skin, and put it in a saucepan, with one sliced carrot and one sliced onion. Braise it for one hour and a half in the oven, basting it occasionally with its own gravy. Serve with half a pint of hot Milanaise garnishing (No. 251) on the dish, placing the meat on top, and straining the gravy over it.

597. Calf's Feet, Naturel. Split each of three calf's feet in two; remove the large bone, and put them in fresh water for one hour. Wash thoroughly, drain, and place them in a saucepan, with two tablespoonfuls of flour and three quarts of cold water. Stir well; add a gill of vinegar, one onion, one carrot (all cut in shreds), twelve whole peppers, a handful of salt, and a bouquet (No. 254), and cook briskly for one hour and a half. Drain well, and serve with any kind of sauce required.

598. Calf's Feet à la Poulette.—The same as for No. 597, adding half a pint of hot poulette sauce, made by putting one pint of hot Allemande sauce (No. 210) into a saucepan, with one ounce of fresh butter, adding the juice of half a medium-sized lemon, and a teaspoonful of chopped parsley. Heat well on the hot stove until thoroughly melted and mixed, but do not let it boil. Keep the sauce warm, and serve for all sauce poulettes.

599. Calf's Feet, Sauce Piquante.—Same as for No. 597, adding half a pint of hot piquante sauce (No. 203).

600. Calf's Feet, Sauce Remoulade.—Same as for No. 597, adding half a pint of hot Remoulade sauce (No. 209).

601. How to Blanch Sweetbreads.—Clean and neatly trim three pairs of fine sweetbreads. Soak them for three hours in three different fresh waters, one hour in each water, with one pinch of salt in each water. Drain, place in cold water, and blanch them until they come to a boil. Then drain, and freshen them in cold water. Cover with a napkin, lay them aside in a cool place, and they will now be ready for general use.

When they are to be used in molds, they should be gently pressed down with a pound weight.

602. Sweetbreads, Braised.—Take six blanched heart-sweetbreads as above, lard the upper parts slightly, and put them in a sautoire with some slices of pork-skin. Add half a sliced carrot, half a sliced onion, and a bouquet (No. 254). Sprinkle over them a pinch of salt, and cover them with a buttered paper. Reduce to a golden color, and moisten with half a pint of strong white broth (No. 99). Cook it in the oven for forty minutes, basting occasionally with the gravy, lifting the buttered paper, and replacing it each time in the same position. The sweetbreads will now be ready to serve with any kind of sauce or garnishing desired. Always place the sauce or garnishing on a hot serving-dish, and lay the sweetbreads over it, then send to the table.

603. Sweetbreads Braised à la Financière.—Prepare six sweetbreads, as in No. 602, and serve with half a pint of hot Financière sauce (No, 246).

604. Sweetbreads Braised with Sorrel.—The same as for No. 602, adding half a pint of hot purée of sorrel (No. 974).

605. Sweetbreads Braised au Salpicon.—The same as for No. 602, adding half a pint of hot salpicon (No. 256).

606. Sweetbreads à la Soubise.—The same as for No. 602, adding half a pint of hot soubise (No. 250).

607. Sweetbreads Braised, with Spinach.—The same as for No. 602, adding half a pint of hot spinach (No. 943).

608. Sweetbreads à la Sauce Duxelle.—The same as for No 602, adding half a pint of hot duxelle sauce (No. 189).

609. Sweetbreads Braised, with Mushroom Sauce.—The same as for No. 602, adding half a pint of hot mushroom sauce (No. 230).

610. Sweetbreads Braised à la Sauce Béarnaise.—The same as for No. 602, adding half a pint of hot Béarnaise sauce (No. 166).

611. Sweetbreads Braised aux Cêpes.—The same as for No. 602, adding half a pint of hot cêpes.

612. Sweetbreads Braised aux Gourmets.—The same as for No. 602, adding half a pint of hot gourmet garnishing (No. 241).

613. Sweetbreads Braised à la Parisienne.—The same as for No. 602, adding half a pint of hot Parisienne garnishing (No. 240).

614. Sweetbreads Braised à la Godard.—The same as for No. 602, adding half a pint of hot Godard garnishing (No. 238).

615. Sweetbreads Braised à la Montglas.—Place six braised sweetbreads, prepared as for No. 602, in six small, buttered paper-boxes, having cooked fine herbs (No. 143) strewn around the bottom. Heat in the oven for five minutes ; then pour one tablespoonful of hot montglas sauce (No. 213) over each. Serve on a dish with a folded napkin.

616. Stewed Sweetbreads à la Catalan.—Cut four blanched sweetbreads (No. 601) into slices; put them in a sautoire with half a gill of sweet oil, one tablespoonful of salt, a teaspoonful of pepper, two well-hashed shallots, and half a sliced green pepper. Reduce to a good golden color for about six minutes, and add two peeled tomatoes cut into pieces, one gill of Espagnole sauce (No. 151), and a crushed clove of garlic. Cook for ten minutes; arrange on a hot dish, and serve.

617. Sweetbreads Broiled à la Colbert.—Cut in two each of three fine blanched sweetbreads as in No. 601. Season them with one pinch of salt and half a pinch of pepper, and pour one tablespoonful of sweet oil over them; mix them in well, and then broil them on a brisk fire for five minutes on each side. Dress on a hot dish, and serve with half a pint of hot Colbert sauce (No. 190).

618. Sweetbreads Braised à la Pompadour.—Braise the sweetbreads exactly as for No. 602. Serve with half a pint of hot Béarnaise sauce (No. 166), two truffles cut in small square pieces; arrange six artichoke-bottoms on the sauce, place a sweetbread on each artichoke, with a thin slice of truffle on top of each, and serve.

619. Sweetbread Croquettes, Périgueux Sauce.—Prepare six sweetbread croquettes (No. 276), and serve them on a dish with a folded napkin. Serve half a pint of Périgueux sauce (No. 191), separate.

620. Sweetbread Croquettes with Peas.—The same as for No. 619, adding half a pint of cooked peas, with a gill of Madeira sauce (No. 185), cooked together for two minutes. Pour it on the dish; place the croquettes over it, and serve.

621. Coquilles of Sweetbreads à la Dreux.—Cut four blanched sweetbreads (No. 601) into small slices, and stew them in a saucepan with half an ounce of good butter, half a glassful of white wine, and three tablespoonfuls of mushroom liquor. Reduce them for ten minutes, then add a gill of velouté sauce (No. 152), six minced mushrooms, and two truffles cut the same. Season with half a tablespoonful of salt, a scant teaspoonful of pepper, and half a teaspoonful of nutmeg, and finish by adding two tablespoonfuls of good cream, or half an ounce of good butter. Fill six silver table-shells with this; sprinkle them with fresh bread-crumbs; pour a few drops of clarified butter over them, and put them in the baking oven. Brown slightly for six minutes longer, and serve on a hot dish with a folded napkin.

622. Coquilles of Sweetbreads à la Cardinal.—The same as for No. 621, but instead of truffles use one ounce of smoked beef-tongue, and the same quantity of tomato sauce (No. 205), instead of the cream.

623. Coquilles of Sweetbreads à la Reine.—Cut four blanched sweetbreads (No. 601) in slices, and fry them in half an ounce of butter, half a glassful of white wine, and three tablespoonfuls of mushroom liquor. Season with half a tablespoonful of salt, a scant teaspoonful of pepper, and half a teaspoonful of nutmeg. Reduce for ten minutes, and moisten with one gill of Allemande sauce (No. 210), adding six sliced mushrooms, two sliced truffles, and twelve small quenelles of godiveau (No. 221). Finish the same as for No. 621.

624. Veal Stew, Marengo.—Cut three pounds of lean veal into pieces, and reduce them in a stewpan with one gill of oil, a cut-up onion or two shallots, and two ounces of salt pork, also cut up. Toss them occasionally, and when well browned after ten minutes, strew in two tablespoonfuls of flour, stirring well again. Moisten with one quart of white broth (No. 99), and one gill of tomato sauce (No. 205); season with a good tablespoonful of salt and a teaspoonful of pepper, adding a crushed clove of garlic, and a bouquet (No. 254). Cook for forty minutes, and serve with six croûtons (No. 133) around the dish, and a little chopped parsley sprinkled over it.

625. Veal Stew à la Provençale.—Cut three pounds of lean veal from the breast or shoulder into pieces, and place them in a stewpan with one ounce of butter, two tablespoonfuls of sweet oil, and one chopped onion. Cook them for ten minutes, stirring occasionally; add two tablespoonfuls of flour, stir again, and moisten with one quart of white broth (No. 99). Season with a heaped tablespoonful of salt and a teaspoonful of pepper, and add six minced mushrooms, three crushed cloves of garlic, and a bouquet (No. 254). Cook for forty minutes, and serve on a hot dish, sprinkling a little chopped parsley over it.

626. Veal Stew à la Grecque.—Place two pounds of lean veal cut in pieces in a stewpan, with two ounces of butter and one cut-up onion, and reduce for ten minutes, adding two tablespoonfuls of flour. Moisten with one quart of white broth (No. 99), and one gill of tomato sauce (No. 205). Add a heaped tablespoonful of salt, a teaspoonful of pepper, and half a teaspoonful of nutmeg, a bouquet (No. 254), three white roots of table-celery, cut in two, and eighteen raw okras, pared whole. Cook for thirty minutes, and serve with the dish nicely decorated with the garnishing.

627. Veal, Stewed à la Portugaise.—The same as for No. 626, substituting three stuffed tomatoes (No. 987), or plain, roasted tomatoes, and three timbales of cooked rice (No. 501) for the other garnishing.

628. Veal, Stewed à la Solferino.—Reduce three pounds of pieces of veal cut from the breast or shoulder, in one ounce of butter, with six small onions. When cooked for ten minutes, add two tablespoonfuls of flour. Moisten with one quart of white broth (No. 99), and one gill of tomato sauce (No. 205), seasoning with one heaped tablespoonful of salt, and one teaspoonful of pepper. Stir well together until it reaches boiling-point; then add two carrots, and two turnips cut out with a vegetable-scoop, and a bouquet (No. 254). Cook again for forty minutes, and serve.

Any kind of vegetables in season can be added.

629. Veal, Stewed à la Bourgeoise.—Reduce in one ounce of butter three pounds of lean veal cut in pieces, with six small onions. After cooking ten minutes add two tablespoonfuls of flour, and moisten with one quart of white broth (No. 99). Stir well, and season with one heaped tablespoonful of salt, one teaspoonful of pepper, and half a glassful of red wine. Add two carrots cut in square pieces, one ounce of salt pork also cut in pieces, and a bouquet (No. 254). Cook for forty minutes longer, remove the bouquet, and serve.

630. Veal, Stewed with Oyster-plant.—The same as for No. 629, substituting for the garnishing one bunch of well-cleaned, raw oyster-plant cut into pieces, forty minutes before serving.

631. Veal, Stewed with Peas.—The same as for No. 629, substituting one pint of fresh peas for the oyster-plant thirty minutes before serving. Should green peas be out of season, use one pint of canned peas five minutes before serving.

632. Veal, Stewed à la Chasseur.—The same as for No. 629, substituting for the garnishing twelve minced mushrooms, sixteen quenelles de godiveau (No. 221), and one clove of garlic three minutes before serving. Serve with six croûtons (No. 133) around the dish.

633. Tendron of Veal à la Nantaise.—Pare nicely three pounds of the breast of veal; make a few incisions on the top, and tie it firmly together. Lay it in a deep sautoire with a piece of pork-skin cut up, a carrot, and a cut-up onion. Cover with a buttered paper, and when it begins to color after five minutes, moisten it slightly with a pint of water or broth. Baste as frequently as possible, and let it cook one hour. Then put it on a dish, strain the sauce over it, garnish with six stuffed lettuce-heads (No. 953). Decorate with a tablespoonful of croûtons all around the dish, and serve.

634. Tendron of Veal with Sorrel.—The same as for No. 633, substituting one pint of cooked, hot sorrel (No. 974) on the dish, for the other garnishing.

635. Tendron of Veal à la Morlaisienne.—The same as for No. 633, substituting six small stuffed cabbages (No. 919) for the other garnishing.

636. Tendron of Veal à la Chipolata.—The same as for No. 633, pouring one pint of hot chipolata (No. 232) on the dish, and placing the tendron on top.

637. Calf's Head, plain.—Plunge a fine, fresh, white calf's head into hot water for one minute, lift it up, sharply rub it all over with a coarse towel, so as to remove all the remaining hairs. Carefully cut the flesh, starting from the centre of the head, right down to the nostrils. Then, with a very keen knife, bone it from the top to the base on both sides. Place in a saucepan two tablespoonfuls of flour, one gill of vinegar, one medium-sized, well-cleaned, sliced carrot, one sound peeled onion, eighteen whole peppers, and two pinches of salt. Pour in very gradually two quarts of cold water—briskly stirring meanwhile until all added. Cut up half of the head into six equal pieces; add them to the broth, as also the other whole half. Let all cook together on a moderate fire for one hour and a half. Lift up the pieces and half the head, place the six pieces on a dry napkin. Have ready a hot dish with a folded napkin over it, neatly dress the six pieces on it, decorate with parsley-greens, and serve with any desired sauce. Place the remaining whole half in a stone jar, strain the broth over it, and keep in a cool place for any purpose required.

For calf's brains, see No. 557.

638. Calf's Head à la Cavour.—Take half a boiled calf's head as for No. 637. Before serving pour a gill of hot tomato sauce (No. 205) over it, and surround it with twenty-four stoned and blanched olives, arranged in clusters, and six sippets of fried bread (No. 133).

639. Calf's Head à la Poulette.—The same as for No. 637, pouring half a pint of hot poulette sauce (No. 598) over it, and sprinkling it with half a tablespoonful of parsley.

640. Calf's Head à la Vinaigrette.—The same as for No. 637, laying a folded napkin on the dish, and arranging thereon the half of the head. Serve with parsley-leaves around the dish, and one pint of vinaigrette (No. 201), separately.

641. Calf's Head en Tortue.—Prepare and cut into six equal pieces, as for No. 637, half a calf's head. Place them on a hot dish, pour over it half a pint of hot tortue garnishing (No. 239), decorate with three pieces of heart-shaped, fried croûtons (No. 133), a little fried parsley, and send to the table very hot.

A pinch of salt represents 205 grains, or a tablespoonful.
Half a pinch of pepper represents 38 grains, or a teaspoonful.
A third of a pinch of nutmeg represents 13 grains, or half a teaspoonful.

MUTTON—LAMB.

642. Mutton Chops à la Provençale.—Flatten and pare neatly six fine, thick mutton chops, season them with a pinch of salt and half a pinch of pepper, oil them slightly with sweet oil, and then either broil or cook them in a sautoire for two minutes on one side only, and lay them aside to get cold. The chops should always be cooked for two minutes as above mentioned, after the garnishing has been prepared.

Garnishing à la Provençale.—Peel two small, sound, white onions, mince them very fine, place them in a pan with boiling water for five minutes to prevent them from getting brown, drain well, place them in a sautoire with one ounce of good butter, and cook for five minutes. Add a dash of white wine, a thin slice of garlic crushed with a spoon, half a spoonful of grated Parmesan cheese, and one gill of good béchamel sauce (No. 154). Season with half a pinch of salt and half a pinch of pepper. Stir all well until it comes to a boil, then put it away to cool. Divide the garnishing over the cooked side of the six chops about a quarter of an inch in thickness; besprinkle with fresh bread-crumbs mixed with a little grated Parmesan cheese. Carefully place the chops in a well-buttered pan, and pour a little clarified butter over them. Place in a very hot oven for five minutes, or until of a good color, and serve with half a pint of hot velouté (No. 152).

643. Mutton Chops, Breaded.—Flatten six fine, thick mutton chops, pare nicely, and season with one tablespoonful of salt and a teaspoonful of pepper. Dip them in beaten egg, roll in fresh bread-crumbs, and place in a sautoire with one ounce of clarified butter. Cook four minutes on each side, and serve with half a pint of any hot sauce or garnishing desired.

644. Mutton Chops, Bretonne.—Pare six nice mutton chops, season with a tablespoonful of salt and a teaspoonful of pepper, and pour a few drops of oil over each. Broil four minutes on each side. Arrange them on a dish, and serve with half a pint of purée of white beans (No. 92), mingled with two tablespoonfuls of good, hot meat-glaze (No. 141).

645. Mutton Chops à l'Africaine.—Broil six mutton chops as for No. 644, and serve with three stuffed egg-plants for garnishing (No. 909), and twelve sliced okras in clusters, in place of the other garnishing.

646. Mutton Chops à la Napolitaine.—The same as for No. 644, but substituting for the garnishing half a pint of hot Napolitaine (No. 195).

647. Chops Soyer, with Potatoes.—Take five pounds of saddle of mutton, cut and saw it into six pieces crosswise. Flatten, pare, and trim. Season with one tablespoonful of salt and a teaspoonful of pepper. Broil them for six minutes on each side, then place them on a hot dish, and serve with a garnishing of one pint, or the equivalent, of fried potatoes (No. 993) around the dish.

648. Leg of Mutton à la Portugaise.—Take a medium-sized leg of mutton, cut off the shank-bone, trim well, and make an incision on the first joint. Season with two pinches of salt and half a pinch of pepper, rub half an ounce of butter over it, and roast for one hour in a pan, basting occasionally with the gravy, and turning it once in a while. Remove from the oven; dress on a hot dish, and serve with three stuffed tomatoes (No. 1023), and three timbales of cooked rice (No. 501), straining the gravy over.

Plain roast leg of mutton is prepared the same, only served without any other garnishing than its own gravy.

649. Leg of Mutton à la Condé.—Roast a leg of mutton the same as for No. 648, and serve it with half a pint of cooked red beans (No. 951) added to the gravy, either on the same dish as the leg, or in a separate bowl.

650. Leg of Mutton, Bretonne.—Proceed the same as for No. 648, but using half a pint of cooked white beans instead of the other garnishing, and adding one teaspoonful of chopped parsley, also one hashed and browned onion.

651. Leg of Mutton, Caper Sauce.—Pare a nice leg of mutton as for No. 648, put it on to boil in a stock-pot, filled with slightly salted cold water, add a bouquet (No. 254), and one cut-up carrot. Boil one hour and a quarter, and serve with half a pint of hot caper sauce, made by putting a pint of hot Hollandaise sauce (No. 160) into a saucepan with a light handful of capers, and heating thoroughly for five minutes without boiling.

652. Mutton Hash à la Zingara.—Chop up two onions, and fry them in a saucepan with one ounce of butter for three minutes, adding one and a half pounds of cooked and hashed mutton, also one-fourth the quantity of hashed potatoes. Season with a good tablespoonful of salt, the same of pepper and half a saltspoonful of nutmeg. Also put in two cut-up, raw tomatoes, a tablespoonful of chopped parsley, and a crushed clove of garlic. Add a gill of Espagnole sauce (No. 151), and a gill of broth (No. 99). Mix all together, and cook twenty minutes, then serve with a pinch of chopped parsley sprinkled over the dish.

653. Mutton Hash au Gratin.—Proceed as for No. 652, omitting the tomatoes and garlic. Place the hash on a baking-dish, sprinkle a little fresh bread-crumbs over, spread a very little butter on top, and put into the oven until of a good golden color, for which it will require from eight to ten minutes.

654. Lamb's Feet à la Poulette.—The same as directed for calf's feet (No. 598), adding half a pint of hot poulette sauce (No. 598).

655. Mutton Stew, Fermière.—Put into a saucepan three pounds of breast or shoulder of mutton cut into square pieces, with one ounce of butter, and six small onions.. Cook for ten minutes, or until of a good golden color. Add three tablespoonfuls of flour, mix well together, and moisten with three pints of light white broth or water, stirring continually while boiling. Season with a good tablespoonful of salt a teaspoonful of pepper, and half a teaspoonful of nutmeg, adding two carrots and two turnips, cut in square pieces, a bouquet (No. 254), and one crushed clove of garlic. Cook on a moderate fire for thirty minutes ; put in half a pint of lima beans, and let the whole cook again for fifteen minutes. Skim off the fat well, remove the bouquet and serve.

656. Mutton Stew, Solferino.—Proceed as directed for No. 655, adding half a pint of carrots and a like quantity of turnips, both cut with a vegetable-spoon ; cook these thirty minutes with the stew, and ten minutes before serving add half a pint of stewed tomatoes (No. 1027) instead of the lima beans.

657. Mutton Stew à la Marseillaise.—The same as for No. 655, but instead of the other garnishings, add one pint of stewed tomatoes (No. 1027), four cloves of crushed garlic, two chopped onions, and twelve minced mushrooms. Let cook for thirty minutes, and serve with chopped parsley sprinkled over.

658. Mutton Stew, Portugaise.—Proceed the same as for No. 655, replacing the garnishing with three stuffed tomatoes (No. 1023), and three timbales of cooked rice (No. 501), nicely arranged around the dish.

659. Mutton Stew with Potatoes.—Exactly the same as for No. 655, replacing the garnishing with one pint of potatoes cut in quarters, (paring the edges a little), also six small onions. Let cook thirty minutes, and serve.

660. Irish Mutton Stew.—Cut in square pieces three pounds of mutton; wash well, drain, and put them in a saucepan, covering with fresh water. Let them come to a boil; then remove into another pan. Clean the pieces well again, return them to the saucepan and cover them with boiling water. Place on the fire, seasoning with two tablespoonfuls of salt, a teaspoonful of pepper, and half a teaspoonful of nutmeg. Add two carrots, two turnips, all cut up, six small onions, and a bouquet (No. 254). Let cook for twenty-five minutes, then add half a pint of potatoes cut in quarters. Dilute half a cupful of flour with half a pint of water, strain it into the stew, stirring thoroughly, and cook again for twenty-five minutes. Remove the bouquet, thoroughly skimming it before serving.

661. Mutton Kidneys en Brochette au Petit Salé—Split twelve mutton kidneys in two, but do not separate the parts; remove the skin, place them in a deep plate, and season with a tablespoonful of salt, and a teaspoonful of pepper, adding two tablespoonfuls of sweet oil. Roll them well. Take six skewers, put a skewer through the two kidneys in the centre, and repeat the same for the others. Broil four minutes on each side. Arrange on a hot dish, pour a gill of maître d'hôtel butter (No. 145) over, and cover with six slices of broiled bacon (No. 754.)

662. Mutton Kidneys Sautés, Madeira Sauce.—Pare well twelve mutton kidneys and cut them into slices. Put into a frying-pan, with one ounce of butter, a tablespoonful of salt, and a teaspoonful of pepper. Toss them well for six minutes. Add half a pint of Madeira wine sauce (No. 185), squeeze in the juice of half a lemon, add another small piece of fresh butter, toss well again without boiling, and serve.

663. Mutton Kidneys Sautés à l'Italienne.—Proceed as for No. 662, adding one gill of cooked fine herbs (No. 143); toss well for one minute, being careful not to let it boil. Avoid boiling any kidneys when being prepared in this way. All stewed mutton kidneys are prepared the same, adding either six minced mushrooms one minute before serving, or if truffles are preferred, add three medium-sized, minced truffles.

664. Saddle of Mutton, Roasted, Plain.—Pare and trim a fine saddle of mutton, weighing about six pounds (if possible). Lift off the upper skin, make one slight incision in the middle, also three on each side; tie it firmly together with three strings, so that it retains its shape, season it with a good pinch of salt, and it will then be ready to roast. Place the saddle in a roasting-pan, adding a gill of cold water; put it in a moderate oven, and let cook for forty-five minutes. Baste it frequently with its own gravy, and serve on a very hot dish. Skim off all the fat, strain the gravy into a sauce-bowl, and serve separately.

N. B.—Should the saddle be of heavier weight, say twelve to fourteen pounds, one hour and a quarter will be necessary to cook it.

665. Saddle of Mutton, Sauce Colbert.—Proceed exactly the same as for No. 664, serving half a pint of Colbert sauce (No. 190) in a bowl.

666. Saddle of Mutton, Currant Jelly.—Same as directed for No. 664 serving with half a pint of hot jelly sauce (No. 884), or with a little currant jelly, separately.

667. Saddle of Mutton, Sauce Poivrade.—Proceed the same as for No. 664, serving with half a pint of poivrade sauce, separately (No. 194).

668. Saddle of Mutton, Londonderry Sauce. — The same as for No. 664, serving with half a pint of hot Londonderry sauce (No. 880).

669. Saddle of Mutton à la Sevigné—Exactly the same as for No. 664, only serving with six boucheés à la Sevigné (No. 588).

670. Saddle of Mutton à la Duchesse.—Proceed as for No. 664, serving with six potatoes Duchesse (No. 1006).

671. Saddle of Mutton with Potatoes.—Served exactly the same as for No. 664, only adding one pint of potatoes château (No. 1009).

672. Lamb Fries à la Diable.—Skin well six medium-sized lamb fries; cut each into three slices and put them into a bowl. Season with a tablespoonful of salt, a very little cayenne pepper, the juice of half a lemon, one tablespoonful of sweet oil, and a teaspoonful of ground mustard diluted in a tablespoonful of Parisian sauce. Mix all well together, roll them in flour, and broil five minutes on each side. Arrange them on a hot dish garnished with six slices of lemon, and serve with a hot sauce à la Diable (No. 198), separately.

Lamb chops can be prepared the same way. Lamb fries, as above prepared, should be immediately served as soon as cooked.

673. Lamb Fries, Tomato Sauce.—Same as for No. 672, only dipping the slices in beaten egg instead of mustard, and then in rasped bread-crust. Fry them in hot fat for six minutes, and serve on a hot dish on a folded napkin, with half a pint of hot tomato sauce (No. 205), separately.

Lamb fries with Tartare sauce are prepared the same way, only serving with half a pint of Tartare sauce (No. 207), in a separate bowl.

674. Brochette of Lamb à la Dumas.—Take a raw leg of lamb weighing about three pounds; remove the bone and pare off the skin. Then cut into six square pieces of equal size. Put them in a vessel with two very finely chopped shallots, one teaspoonful of chopped chives, one teaspoonful of parsley, and a crushed clove of garlic. Add the juice of half a lemon, a tablespoonful of salt, a teaspoonful of pepper, and half a teaspoonful of nutmeg. Let them steep for about two hours, stirring at times; then take the pieces out, run a skewer through the centre of the six pieces, interlarding them with pieces of salt pork; dip them in bread-crumbs and broil for four minutes on each side. Serve with half a pint of hot Colbert sauce (No. 190), poured on the serving-dish, and place the brochettes over, arranging them nicely.

675. Ballotin of Lamb with Peas.—Bone a shoulder of spring lamb weighing about two and a half pounds. Let the end bone remain for a handle. Season with half a tablespoonful of salt, and the same quantity of pepper. Sew it up with a needle, fasten it firmly, and boil two or three minutes in the stock-pot. After letting it cool, lard the top with a larding needle as for a fricandeau, and place it in a saucepan with a piece of lard-skin, a carrot and an onion cut in slices. Brown slightly for six minutes; then moisten with a pint of broth (No. 99) and half a pint of Espagnole sauce (No. 157); cook in the oven forty-five minutes, take it out, and strain the sauce over a pint of hot, boiled, green peas (No. 978). Cook two minutes longer. Place the garnishing on a hot dish; remove the strings of the ballotin; lay it on the top of the garnishing, and serve.

676. Curry of Lamb, with Asparagus-tops.—Have three pounds of shoulder of lamb cut into pieces about two inches square. Wash well in fresh water, drain, put into a saucepan, and cover with fresh water. Let it come to a boil, then strain through a colander, and wash again in water. Place the pieces in a saucepan, covering them with boiling water;

season with two tablespoonfuls of salt, one teaspoonful of pepper, six small onions, and a bouquet (No. 254). Put the lid on, and cook forty minutes. Then strain off the liquor into another saucepan containing half a pint of roux blanc (No. 135), stirring well until it boils, and then let it stand on the corner of the stove. Break into a separate bowl four egg yolks with the juice of half a lemon, beaten well together. Add this to the sauce, dropping it in little by little, and stirring continually. Pour all over the lamb, and add one pint of cooked asparagus-tops, but be careful not to let it boil again. Serve with a border of hot, boiled rice all around the dish.

677. Curry of Lamb à l'Indienne—Proceed exactly as for No. 676, only adding three tablespoonfuls of curry diluted in half a cupful of water. Instead of the asparagus-tops, use a border of hot, cooked rice, carefully arranged around the dish. Lay the curry of lamb on top and serve.

678. Curry of Lamb à la Créole.—The same as for No. 676, adding, ten minutes before serving, one gill of tomatoes cut in pieces, and a green pepper cut into small pieces, serving with a border of hot, cooked rice around the dish.

679. Croquettes of Lamb à la Patti.—Prepare six lamb croquettes as for No. 276, adding half a pint of Patti garnishing (No. 245) laid on the dish, and arranging the croquettes on top. Pour over it a little meat-glaze (No. 141).

680. Croustades of Kidneys, with Mushrooms.—Prepare six croustades (No. 264), and fill them with kidneys sautés au Madère (No. 662).

681. Lamb Chops à la Signora.—Pare six fine lamb chops, and split them through the centre. Fill the insides with a very fine salpicon (No. 256); season with a pinch of salt and half a pinch of pepper. Close together, and dip in beaten egg, then in fresh bread-crumbs. Fry them for four minutes on each side in two ounces of clarified butter in a sautoire, and serve with a gill of hot Montglas sauce (No. 213) after arranging a curled paper at the end of each chop.

682. Lamb Chops à la Robinson.—Pare six lamb chops, flatten nicely, and season with one pinch of salt and half a pinch of pepper. Place them in a sautoire with one ounce of butter, and fry for three minutes on each side. Serve with a pint of hot Robinson garnishing (No. 253) on the dish, and arrange the chops nicely over it, or any other garnishing desired.

683. Lamb Chops, Maison d'Or.—Pare neatly six lamb chops, make an incision in each one, and insert therein a slice of truffle. Season with a pinch of salt and half a pinch of pepper. Dip the chops in beaten egg and then in fresh bread-crumbs. Fry them in a sautoire with two ounces of clarified butter for four minutes on each side, and serve with six heart-shaped pieces of fried bread, each one covered with some pâté-de-foie-gras, and a gill of hot Madeira wine sauce (No. 185). Arrange a curled paper on the end of each chop.

684. Lamb Chops à la Clichy.—Pare nicely and flatten six lamb chops;

season with one pinch of salt and half a pinch of pepper. Fry slightly in a sautoire with one ounce of butter for one minute on each side; then let them cool. Cover the surfaces with chicken forcemeat (No. 226), and wrap them in crepinette (a skin found in the stomach of the pig); dip in beaten egg, then in fresh bread-crumbs, and cook in a sautoire, with two ounces of butter for four miuutes on each side. Arrange a nice paper curl at each end of the chops, and serve with half a pint of hot champagne sauce (No. 204) on the dish, and the chops over it.

685. Lamb Chops à la Maintenon.—Take six well-pared and flattened lamb chops. Season with a pinch of salt and half a pinch of pepper; put into a sautoire with one ounce of butter, and fry on one side only for one minute. Cover the cooked side with a mellow chicken croquette preparation (No. 276), also a little chicken forcemeat (No. 226) on top. Besprinkle with one very finely chopped truffle. Place the chops on a well-buttered baking-pan, and put them in a slow oven to cook for four minutes. Put a curled paper on the end of each chop, and serve with half a pint of hot, clear velouté (No. 152) on the dish, and the chops laid over it.

686. Lamb Chops à la Villeroi.—Pare neatly six chops, flatten them well, and season with a pinch of salt and half a pinch of pepper. Make an incision in each chop, and garnish the inside with a slice of truffle, previously dipped in demi-glace (No. 185); then dip the chops in beaten egg, roll them in fresh bread-crumbs, and put into a sautoire with two ounces of butter, and fry four minutes on each side. Pour half a pint of hot Perigueux sauce (No. 191) on the dish, arrange the chops over, with curled paper on the ends, and serve.

687. Lamb Chops à la Masséna.—Trim neatly, flatten, and season with half a pinch each of salt and pepper, six lamb chops. Put them into a sautoire with one ounce of butter, and fry on one side only for one minute. Let them cool, and then fill the cooked centres with a little pâté-de-foie-gras. Take six pieces of fried bread the size of the chop, cut out the middles with a bread-cutter, fill in the space with pâté-de-foie-gras, and lay it on the cooked side of the chops. Garnish all around with chicken forcemeat à la crême (No. 225), forced through a paper cornet. Place them on a buttered baking-sheet, and put them into a slow oven. Cook for seven minutes. Prepare a pint of hot Madeira sauce (No. 185), pour it on a hot dish, arrange the chops nicely on top, with curled papers on the ends, and serve.

688. Minced Lamb à l'Anglaise.—Chop two onions fine, and fry in a saucepan with two ounces of butter for five minutes. Add two table-spoonfuls of flour, stirring well for two minutes. Moisten with a pint of broth (No. 99), and two tablespoonfuls of Parisian sauce, a bouquet (No. 254), and season with a tablespoonful of salt, a teaspoonful of pepper, and half a teaspoonful of nutmeg. Stir until it comes to a boil. Then cut two pounds of cooked lamb in small pieces, either from the shoulder or leg, mince finely, and add to the sauce. Cook twenty-five minutes, and serve with chopped parsley sprinkled over.

689. Epigrammes of Lamb, Macédoine.—Take two breasts of lamb, tie them and put them on to boil in the soup-stock for forty-five minutes. Drain them well, then extract all the bones, and press down with a heavy weight on top. When thoroughly cold, cut each breast into three heart-shaped pieces, dip them in oil or fat, seasoning with a tablespoonful of salt and a teaspoonful of pepper. Roll in fresh bread-crumbs, and broil on a slow fire for four minutes on each side. Take six broiled, breaded lamb chops, prepared and cooked exactly the same, and serve with half a pint of hot Macédoine (No. 1032) or any other garnishing that may be required, arranging the breasts and chops over the garnishing.

690. Epigrammes of Lamb à la Chicorée.—Proceed exactly the same as for No. 689, only adding half a pint of hot chicory with a little gravy (No. 934), instead of the other garnishing, and serve the same.

691. Epigrammes of Lamb à la Louisiannaise.—The same as for No. 689, only serving with one pint of fried sweet potatoes (No. 993) around the dish, and a gill of hot Madeira wine sauce (No. 185).

692. Epigrammes of Lamb à la Soubise.—The same as for No. 689, serving with half a pint of hot Soubise (No. 250) and basting with a little meat-glaze (No. 141).

693. Shoulder of Lamb à l'Africaine.—Take a shoulder of lamb of about three pounds, season with one pinch of salt and one pinch of pepper, and tie it up well. Place in a saucepan with one sliced onion, and one sliced carrot, and brown for six minutes. Moisten with one pint of broth (No. 99), and a pint of Espagnole sauce (No. 151). Let cook for forty-five minutes. Skim all the fat from the gravy, and remove the shoulder to a hot dish and untie it. Garnish the dish with three stuffed egg-plants (No. 909), and half a pint of cooked gumbo (No. 1030). Strain the gravy over the shoulder, and serve.

694. Shoulder of Lamb, Purée Normande.—Proceed exactly the same as for No. 693, only substituting one pint of hot Normande (No. 175) for the other garnishing.

695. Shoulder of Lamb, with Stuffed Tomatoes.—The same as for No. 693, placing six stuffed tomatoes (No. 1023) around the dish before serving.

696. Shoulder of Lamb, Jardinière.—Proceed as directed in No. 693, only serving with one pint of hot Jardinière (No. 1033).

697. Shoulder of Lamb, Stuffed à la Macédoine.—Prepare a shoulder the same as for No. 693, but before tying it, fill the interior with American forcemeat (No. 229); let cook the same, and serve with one pint of hot Macédoine (No. 1032).

698. Shoulder of Lamb à la Rouennaise.—Braise a shoulder of lamb as for No. 693, cut three medium-sized turnips the shape of a large clove of garlic, and put them in a sautoire, with an ounce of butter, and a teaspoonful of powdered sugar on top. Place it in the oven, and leave it in until they become thoroughly brown, tossing the pan frequently to prevent burning. Pour the gravy from the meat over the turnips, dish up the shoulder, arrange the turnips around and serve.

699. Shoulder of Lamb à la Flamande.—The same as for No. 693, serving for garnishing half a pint of cooked carrots, half a pint of cooked turnips, and half a pint of cooked red cabbage, nicely arranged in clusters around the dish.

700. Hashed Lamb à la Polonaise.—Fry two chopped onions in a saucepan with an ounce of butter; add half a pound of cooked, hashed lamb to one pint of cooked, hashed potatoes (No. 1002). Season with a good tablespoonful of salt, a teaspoonful of pepper, and half a teaspoonful of nutmeg. Moisten with half a pint of broth, and cook for ten minutes. Place the hash on a hot dish, and arrange six poached eggs (No. 404) on top. Serve with chopped parsley sprinkled over.

701. Haricot or Ragout of Lamb à la Providence.—Take a fine breast or a shoulder of lamb weighing about three pounds, cut it into equal square pieces, and fry them in a saucepan with an ounce of butter or fat. Add six small, sound, peeled onions, and when browned, after about ten minutes, dredge in three tablespoonfuls of flour, stirring well for two minutes. Moisten with three pints of water or white broth; stir well, adding two pinches of salt, one pinch of pepper, two crushed cloves of sound garlic, and a bouquet (No. 254). Let cook for forty-five minutes. Two minutes after it begins to boil, thoroughly skim off the scum on the surface. Remove the bouquet and pour the ragout on a hot dish. Arrange half a pint of flageolets, plunged for half a minute into boiling water and well drained, or cooked lima beans, on one side of the dish, and the same quantity of cooked carrots, cut in quarters, on the other, and then serve.

702. Breast of Lamb, Jardinière.—Boil three medium-sized breasts of lamb for fifty minutes in the stock-pot, then the bones will be detached. Take them out, put the meat under a heavy weight, and let it thoroughly cool; then pare neatly. Cut each breast in two, and place on a dish. Season them with a good tablespoonful of salt, a teaspoonful of pepper, and immerse them in two tablespoonfuls of oil. Roll them in fresh bread-crumbs, and broil them for four minutes on each side. Serve them with one pint of hot Jardinière garnishing (No. 1033) on the dish, and the breasts nicely arranged over it.

703. Stewed Lamb and Oyster-plant.—As directed for ragout of lamb (No. 701); substituting for garnishing one bunch of thoroughly scraped and well-washed oyster-plant, cut into medium-sized pieces, and cooked with the stew.

704. Stewed Lamb à la Francaise.—The same as for No. 701; adding half a pint of carrots, half a pint of turnips, cooked with the lamb, and half an hour before serving putting in a pint of pared, small, whole, raw potatoes.

705. Stewed Lamb and Lima Beans.—Proceed as directed for No. 701, replacing the garnishing by one pint of cooked lima beans, added five minutes before serving.

706. Stewed Lamb, with Peas.—The same as for No. 701, only substituting for the garnishing one pint of green peas half an hour before the stew is ready or, if canned peas, five minutes before serving.

707. Stewed Lamb and Flageolets.—Proceed as directed for No. 701, only using instead of the garnishing a pint of well-soaked and drained flageolets, five minutes before serving.

708. Stewed Lamb à la Parisienne.—The same as for No. 701, using a garnishing of one pint of raw Parisian potatoes (No. 986) half an hour before serving.

709. Stewed Lamb and String Beans.—The same as for No. 701, only substituting for garnishing, one pint of pared and cleaned string-beans half an hour before serving.

710. Stewed Lamb Louisiannaise.—Proceed exactly as for No. 701, substituting for garnishing one pint of fried sweet potatoes, when serving, all around the dish.

711. Stewed Lamb à la Créole.—The same as for No. 701, adding for garnishing two cut-up tomatoes, one cut-up green pepper, and one chopped onion. Serve with a bouquet of cooked rice for a garnishing around the dish.

712. Lamb's Kidneys, Colbert Sauce.—Split open twelve kidneys, skin them well, and place on a dish with a tablespoonful of sweet oil. Season with a tablespoonful of salt, a teaspoonful of pepper, and half a teaspoonful of nutmeg. Take six silver skewers (if none on hand, use wooden ones), run each skewer through the centre of two kidneys (which should never become detached), roll them in fresh bread-crumbs, and put them to broil on a moderate fire for four minutes on each side. Place them on a very hot dish on which has been previously poured a pint of hot Colbert sauce (No. 190), and send to the table very hot.

713. Lamb's Kidneys, with Bacon.—Proceed as for No. 712, but do not roll them in bread-crumbs, and serve them with six slices of broiled bacon (No. 754) and a gill of maître d'hôtel butter (No. 145).

714. Stewed Kidneys with Cêpes.—Pare, trim, and skin well twelve kidneys. Cut them into slices, and cook for five minutes in a frying-pan with an ounce of clarified butter, a tablespoonful of salt, and a teaspoonful of pepper. Brown well ; then add half a pint of Espagnole sauce (No. 151), also four cêpes cut into pieces. Warm without boiling, add the juice of half a lemon, and a teaspoonful of chopped parsley, and serve.

All stewed kidneys are prepared the same way, with any other garnishing required.

715. Lamb's Kidneys à la Diable.—Skin and pare well twelve kidneys, split them in two without separating the parts, and run the skewers through as for No. 712. Broil them slightly for one minute on each side. Mix together in a dish one teaspoonful of English mustard with two tablespoonfuls of Parisian sauce, the third of a teaspoonful of cayenne pepper, a teaspoonful of salt, and a like quantity of mignonette pepper. Roll the kidneys well in this, then in bread-crumbs, and finish by broiling them once more for three minutes on each side. Serve with a gill of maître d'hôtel butter (No. 145) poured over the kidneys.

716. Lamb Steak with Purée of Peas.—Cut and saw off six small steaks from a tender leg of lamb ; pare and trim them nicely, flatten, and season with a good tablespoonful of salt sprinkled over, and a teaspoonful of pepper. Put a tablespoonful of sweet oil on a dish, roll the steaks well in it, then broil them for five minutes on each side. Place on a hot serving-dish half a pint of hot purée of peas (No. 49); arrange the steaks over, and serve.

The steaks can be served with any other garnishing required.

717. Lamb Steak, Sauce Piquante.—The same as for No. 716, serving for garnishing half a pint of hot piquante sauce (No. 203).

718. Lamb Steak à l'Américaine.—Proceed as for No. 716, and serve the lamb steaks with six small pieces of fried hominy (No. 1035), also one gill of hot Madeira sauce (No. 185) on the dish, and the steaks arranged over, with six slices of broiled bacon over them.

A pinch of salt represents 205 grains, or a tablespoonful.
Half a pinch of pepper represents 38 grains, or a teaspoonful.
A third of a pinch of nutmeg represents 13 grains, or half a teaspoonful.

PORK.

719. Black Sausage, Mashed Potatoes.—Take six black sausages (or blood pudding); make four light incisions on each side of them with a knife, then broil them for five minutes on each side. Neatly arrange a pint of mashed potatoes (No. 998) on a hot dish; nicely dress the sausages over, and serve. They also may be baked in a pan in the hot oven for ten minutes.

720. Suckling Pig, Apple Sauce.—Thoroughly clean the interior of a small, tender, suckling pig (reserving the liver); drain it well. Season the interior with two pinches of salt, one good pinch of pepper, and the third of a pinch of grated nutmeg. Chop up the liver very fine, and fry it in a saucepan, with half an ounce of butter, for five minutes. Stuff it with American forcemeat (No. 229), then sew up the aperture with a kitchen-needle. Have a roasting-pan ready, sprinkle into it half a cupful of cold water, then lay in the pig, so that it rests on its four legs. Completely cover all around with a buttered paper, then put it into a moderate oven, and let cook for two hours; baste it frequently, while cooking, with its own gravy. Remove it to a hot dish, untie, skim the fat from the gravy, and strain the lean part of it over the pig. Serve with a pint of hot apple sauce (No. 168) in a separate bowl.

721. Boiled Ham, plain.—Select a nice, small, lean ham of about seven pounds, and steep it in cold water during a whole night; take it out, lay it on a board or table, dry it thoroughly in a cloth, then put it in a saucepan and cover it with cold water. Let it boil for two hours, then remove it from its stock, lift off the upper skin, trim it neatly, and ornament artistically the large end bone with a pretty paper ruffle, then serve it with any kind of sauce required for garnishing.

722. Cold Boiled Ham, for family use.—Proceed the same as for No. 721, but let the ham be thoroughly cooled off before serving.

723. Roast Ham, Champagne Sauce.—Boil a ham exactly as directed for No. 721, making a few lengthwise incisions on the surface. Sprinkle the top with a little powdered sugar; arrange it in a roasting-pan, then place it in a slow oven for fifteen minutes. Serve with half a pint of champagne sauce (No. 204).

724. Roast Ham, with Corn à la Crême.—The same as for No. 723, serving with it one pint of hot corn à la crême (No. 963).

725. Roast Ham, with Spinach.—Proceed as for No. 723, only serving with one pint of cooked hot spinach au jus (No. 943).

726. Pig's Cheek, with Spinach.—Take two lean, smoked pig's cheeks; let them soak in cold water over night, then drain them well, and put them in a saucepan, covering them with cold water. Let cook for one hour and three-quarters; then lay them on a dish, drain well again, and lift off the rind and skin which adheres to the tongue, then remove the bones, and place the cheeks on a hot serving-dish. Garnish with one pint of hot spinach au jus (No. 943); arrange the cheeks nicely on top, and serve.

727. Pig's Feet à la St. Hubert.—Split three good-sized, boiled pig's feet in two, place them on a deep dish, season with a pinch of salt, half a pinch of pepper, and one tablespoonful of oil. Roll them well together, and lay them in fresh bread-crumbs. Put them to broil for four minutes on each side, and then serve with half a pint of hot piquante sauce (No. 203), to which has been added a teaspoonful of diluted mustard. Pour the sauce on the dish, and arrange the feet nicely upon it.

728. Pig's Feet, Sauce Robert.—Exactly the same as for No. 727, serving with half a pint of hot Robert sauce (No. 192).

729. Pig's Feet, Sauce Piquante.—The same as for No. 727, serving with half a pint of hot piquante sauce (No. 203), omitting the mustard.

730. Pig's Feet, New York Style.—The same as for No. 727, serving them on six pieces of toast, with a gill of maître d'hôtel butter (No. 145) over the feet.

Boston Style.—Dip them in frying batter, then fry in a pan with two ounces of butter on a moderate fire for ten minutes. Dress them on a hot dish with a folded napkin, and serve with any sauce desired separately.

731. Pig's Feet à la Poulette.—Put three boiled pig's feet, cut in two, into a saucepan with half an ounce of butter, let simmer for five minutes, add a pint of poulette sauce (No. 598); heat without boiling for five minutes, then serve with a little chopped parsley sprinkled over.

732. Stuffed Pig's Feet à la Périgueux.—To one and a half pounds of boned turkey forcemeat (No. 813) add two minced truffles and half a glassful of Madeira wine; mix well together in a bowl. Spread six pieces of crépinette a skin found in the stomach of the pig), the size of the hand, on the table. Lay on each one a piece of forcemeat the size of an egg; spread it well, and lay one-half of a boned pig's foot on top (No. 734). Cover with another light layer of forcemeat, and finish each with three thin slices of truffles. Cover the crépinettes so that they get the form of envelopes; fold them up, and dip one after the other in beaten egg, then in fresh bread-crumbs, and cook in a sautoire with two ounces of clarified butter. Place a heavy weight on top of the feet, let cook on a slow fire for twelve minutes on each side, and serve with half a pint of hot Périgueux sauce (No. 191) on the dish, and the pig's feet on top.

733. Stuffed Pig's Feet, Madeira Sauce.—Exactly the same as for the above, only serving with half a pint of hot Madeira sauce (No. 185) in place of the other.

734. Boned Pig's Feet.—Take three boiled feet, cut them in two, put them into boiling water for four minutes, then take them out. Drain well, bone them, then put the flesh into a dry, clean cloth, and wipe them thoroughly.

735. Sausages, with White Wine.—Brown a very finely chopped onion in a sautoire with one ounce of butter. Moisten with half a glassful of white wine, and add two country sausages; prick them slightly with a fork, then cover the pan, and let cook for five minutes. Put in half a pint of Espagnole sauce (No. 151), cook again for five minutes, and serve with a little chopped parsley sprinkled over.

736. Sausages à l'Anglaise.—Place twelve country sausages on a baking-tin; prick them a little, and separate them by twelve slices of bread cut the same height as the sausages. Bake in the oven for twelve minutes, baste them occasionally with their own juice, and serve with half a pint of hot Madeira sauce (No. 185) in a separate bowl.

737. Sausages à l'Italienne.—The same as for No. 735, adding six minced mushrooms to the sauce five minutes before serving.

738. Sausages à la Bourguignonne.—Take twelve country sausages, prick them with a fork, and place them in a baking-dish. Put them in the oven, and let cook for ten minutes; garnish a hot dish with a pint of hot purée of red beans (No. 951); and arrange the sausages on top, then serve.

739. Sausages, with Cabbage.—Procure a medium-sized white cabbage; remove all the green leaves, and cut it into four square parts, suppressing the centre stalks.. Wash thoroughly in cold water, then drain well in a cloth; when finished cut them into small pieces, and put them into boiling, salted water for five minutes. Remove into cold water to let it cool off moderately; take it out, drain in a colander, and put the cabbage into a saucepan with a gill of fat from the soup-stock, or an ounce of butter. Season with a good pinch of salt and half a pinch of pepper, also a whole medium-sized onion, and a carrot cut into four pieces. Put on the lid of the saucepan, remove to a moderate fire, and let cook for thirty minutes. Take twelve country sausages, prick them with a fork, add them to the cabbage, and let all cook together for twelve minutes. Dress the cabbage on a hot dish, and decorate with the sausages and carrots on top. Serve very hot.

740. Sausages au Gastronome.—Prick twelve nice, lean sausages with a fork; put them in a tin baking-dish, and cook them for six minutes in the oven. Add two raw eggs to a pint and a half of mashed potatoes, with three tablespoonfuls of grated Parmesan or Swiss cheese, mix well together, and lay it on a baking-dish. Place the sausages on top, put it in the oven, and let cook for six minutes. When finished take them out, and serve on a dish with half a gill of demi-glace (No. 185) thrown over.

741. Pork Tenderloin.—Procure three good-sized pork tenderloins, pare them neatly, remove the sinews, and cut each fillet lengthwise in two without detaching; place in a sautoire with a tablespoonful of butter. Season them one hour before cooking with two pinches of salt and one pinch of pepper, and let them cook on the stove for six minutes on each side. Arrange them on a hot serving-dish, and skim the fat from the surface of the gravy. Add to the lean part half a cupful of broth (No. 99), letting it come to a boil, and mixing well with a spoon. Strain the gravy over the fillets, and serve. Any sauce or garnishing desired may be added to the tenderloins.

742. Pork Andouillettes.—Procure one and a half pounds of andouillettes; cut them into six pieces, and make four slight incisions on each side. Place them in a tin baking-dish, and put them in the oven to cook for eight minutes. Remove them to a hot serving-dish, previously placing thereon a pint of mashed potatoes, or a pint of hot purée of peas, and place the andouillettes, nicely arranged, on top.

743. Pork Chops, Plain.—Take six thick pork chops, pare and flatten them nicely, then season with a pinch of salt and a pinch of pepper one hour before using them. Put them in a sautoire with one ounce of butter, and let cook on the stove for six minutes on each side. Arrange the chops on a hot dish, skim off the fat from the gravy, and add half a cupful of broth to the lean part. Let come to a boil, strain over the chops, and serve.

744. Pork Chops, Broiled.—These are to be prepared exactly the same as for No. 743, only to the seasoning add one tablespoonful of sweet oil, and roll in the chops well. Put them to broil for six minutes on each side, then arrange them on a hot dish, and serve with a gill of hot maître d'hôtel butter (No. 145), well spread over the chops.

745. Pork Chops, Piquante Sauce.—Proceed exactly as for No. 743, serving with half a pint of hot piquante sauce over the chops (No. 203).

746. Pork Chops, Sauce Robert.—Same as for No. 743, sending them to the table with half a pint of hot Robert sauce (No. 192) poured over the chops.

747. Pork Chops à la Diable.—The same as for No. 743, but serving with half a pint of sauce à la Diable (No. 198) over the chops.

748. Pork Chops, Apple Sauce.—Proceed as for No. 743, serving with one pint of hot apple sauce (No. 168) in a separate bowl.

749. Pork Chops à la Purée de Pois.—The same as for No. 743, pouring half a pint of hot purée of peas on the dish, and placing the chops over.

PORK.

750. Pork Chops with Purée of Potatoes.—Exactly the same as for No. 743, serving with a pint of purée of hot potatoes (No. 998) on the dish, and the chops nicely arranged over.

751. Roasted Fresh Pork.—Take three pounds of fresh loin of pork; season two hours before needed with two good pinches of salt and one good pinch of pepper, well distributed. Put it into a roasting-pan with half a cupful of water, place it in the oven, and let roast for fully one and a half hours, being careful to baste it frequently with its own gravy. Remove it to a hot dish, skim the fat from the gravy, strain the lean part over the roast, and serve.

752. Pork and Beans.—Take a pint of white dry beans, soak them in fresh water for six hours, then drain through a colander. Place them in a saucepan, or preferably an earthen dish ; season with one small pinch of salt, half a pinch of pepper, one tablespoonful of either syrup or brown sugar, and one medium-sized carrot cut in two. Take a pound and a half of freshened salt pork (previously well-washed in fresh water), make four incisions on each side, and place it in the vessel with the beans ; cover with the lid, and let cook all together, either on the stove or in the oven, for two hours and a half. If it should get too dry, moisten with a little broth. It will now be ready to serve. Place the garnishing on a hot dish, and arrange the pork on top ; the whole can be returned again to the oven with a little powdered sugar sprinkled over the top, leaving it in five minutes to give it a golden color; then serve.

753. How to Prepare Ham for Broiling and Frying.—Procure a fine, sound, smoked ham, weighing about twelve to thirteen pounds, selecting it as lean as possible. With a sharp knife, begin cutting it carefully at the end of the shank bone, between the bone and the string used for hanging purposes, coming down on to the knuckle ; follow the edge of the bone, until the small edge-bone is fully reached, then make a straight cross-cut from the bone, so as to separate it entirely. When this is accomplished, put the bone part aside for soup, garnishing, scrambled eggs, sauces, or any other needful purposes. Keep the ham hung up in a dry place in a moderate temperature.

For broiling and frying.—Cut from the boneless part the necessary number of slices desired to be used each time, as thin as possible, always beginning from the side of the edge-bone. Pare off the skin neatly from the slices, and arrange them on the broiler, then broil them for two minutes on each side; take from off the fire, dress them on a hot dish, and send to the table.

By preparing the ham as described in the above, it will always be crisp and enjoyable. When frying, four minutes will be sufficient in very hot fat.

754. How to Prepare English Breakfast Bacon.—Procure a fine, fresh English breakfast bacon, and with a keen knife cut the under bones off; pare both edges neatly, also the end (the opposite side to the string which hangs it up). With the use of the same sharp knife, cut the necessary number of slices desired for immediate use, and no more. Thin slices are always preferable, so that the bacon, whether broiled or fried, will be crispy and tasty. When cutting off the slices be careful to avoid detaching them from the skin, also cut them crosswise, but never lengthwise. Arrange the slices on the broiler, and broil on a moderate fire for two minutes on each side; dress the crispy slices on a hot dish, and serve immediately.

Four minutes will suffice for frying. See that the bacon is kept hanging by the string in a dry, cool place, but never put it on the ice.

A pinch of salt represents 205 grains, or a tablespoonful.

Half a pinch of pepper represents 38 grains, or a teaspoonful.

A third of a pinch of nutmeg represents 13 grains, or half a teaspoonful.

POULTRY.

755. Chicken Roasted, Plain.—Singe, draw, wipe nicely, and truss a fine large chicken weighing three pounds. Cover it with a thin slice of salt fat pork, and place it in a roasting-pan with two tablespoonfuls of broth. Spread a very little butter over the breast, sprinkle on half a pinch of salt, and put it in the oven to cook for fifty minutes. Baste it frequently, and arrange it on a hot dish, untie, and decorate with a little watercress. Strain the gravy into a sauce-bowl, and send it to the table.

756. Chicken Broiled with Bacon.—Procure two very fine, tender, spring chickens, singe, draw, wipe neatly, and cut the heads off, then split them without separating. Place them on a dish, season with one pinch of salt, half a pinch of pepper, and one tablespoonful of sweet oil; turn them well in the seasoning. Put them to broil for nine minutes on each side. Prepare six small toasts on a hot dish, arrange the two broiled chickens over, spread half a gill of maître d'hôtel butter on top (No. 145), and decorate with six thin slices of broiled bacon (No. 754); then serve.

757. Chicken Pot-pie.—Take one fine Philadelphia chicken, from three and a half to four pounds, singe, draw, wipe well, and cut it into twelve even pieces. Put these in a saucepan, and cover them with cold water; leave them in for thirty minutes, then wash well, drain, and return them to the saucepan. Cover again with fresh water, season with two pinches of salt, one pinch of pepper, and a third of a pinch of nutmeg; add a bouquet (No. 254), six small onions, and four ounces of salt pork cut into square pieces. Cook for three-quarters of an hour, taking care to skim well, then add one pint of raw potatoes, Parisiennes (No. 986), and three tablespoonfuls of flour diluted with a cupful of cold water. Stir until it boils, then let cook for ten minutes. Remove the bouquet and transfer the whole to a deep earthen baking-dish; moisten the edges slightly with water, and cover the top with a good pie-crust (No. 1078). Egg the surface;

make a few transverse lines on the paste with a fork, and cut a hole in the centre. Bake it in a brisk oven for fifteen minutes, then send to the table.

758. Chicken Croquettes à la Reine.—Make a croquette preparation as for No. 276, with chicken and mushrooms; roll it into six cork-shaped croquettes, dip each one separately in beaten egg, then in fresh or rasped bread-crumbs, fry them in very hot fat for four minutes, then drain them thoroughly, and place them on a hot dish over a folded napkin. Serve with half a pint of hot sauce à la Reine (No. 623) separately.

759. Chicken Croquettes à la Périgueux.—The same as for No. 758, serving with half a pint of hot Périgueux sauce (No. 191) separately.

760. Chicken Croquettes à l'Ecarlate.—Exactly the same as for No. 758, serving with half a pint of hot sauce Ecarlate (No. 247) separately.

761. Chicken Croquettes à la Périgourdin.—Prepare some forcemeat as for croquettes (No. 276), composed of chicken, mushrooms, two truffles cut into small square pieces, and bits of cooked smoked tongue, about one ounce. Fry them for four minutes, then serve the six croquettes with half a pint of hot Madeira sauce (No. 185). Add to it one chopped truffle and six chopped mushrooms; let cook five minutes, and serve in a separate bowl.

762. Croustade of Chicken à la Dreux.—Make six croustades (No. 264), each one four inches and a half long by three inches in diameter. Take three-quarters of a pound of white, boned, cooked chicken meat, cut in half-inch pieces; add to them half a pint of Duxelle sauce (No. 189), half a glassful of Madeira wine, and let cook together for four minutes. Fill the six croustades with this, arrange them nicely on a hot dish over a folded napkin, and serve.

763. Croustade of Chicken Livers, au Madère.—Prepare six croustades as for No. 762, fill them with chicken livers stewed in Madeira wine sauce (No. 767).

764. Cromesquis of Chicken à la Richelieu.—Make six cromesquis as for No. 268, and serve on a hot dish with a folded napkin, decorating with a little parsley-greens, and serving a pint of hot Richelieu sauce (No. 574) separately.

765. Cromesquis of Chicken à la Reine.—Exactly the same as for No. 764, serving with half a pint of hot sauce à la Reine No. 623) separately, and garnishing the dish with parsley-greens.

766. Chicken Legs à la Diable.—Detach the legs from three medium-sized chickens; singe them slightly with a little alcohol lighted on a plate, then put them into the soup-pot and let boil for ten minutes. Remove them to a dish, cool them off thoroughly, then season with a good pinch of salt, half a pinch of pepper, and a very little cayenne pepper; add also two tablespoonfuls of Parisian sauce and half a teaspoonful of ground English mustard. Now roll them well together, and pass one after another into fresh bread-crumbs; put them to broil on a moderate fire for four minutes on each side, then arrange them on a hot serving-dish. Pour over one gill of hot sauce à la Diable (No. 198), sprinkle a little chopped parsley on top, and serve very hot. The legs can be served with any sauce or garnishing required.

Turkeys' legs are prepared exactly the same way, only they should be broiled six minutes on each side instead of four, and served with any desired sauce or garnishing.

767. Chicken Livers Stewed in Madeira Wine.—Cut away the gall from a pint of chicken livers, dry them well with a cloth, then fry them in a sautoire with one ounce of butter, on a brisk fire, for five minutes. Season with a pinch of salt, and half a pinch of pepper, add half a glass of Madeira wine, reduce for one minute, then moisten slightly with about half a pint of Espagnole sauce (No. 151). Cook again for three minutes, then add half an ounce of good butter, and the juice of half a lemon, tossing well without letting it boil; pour the whole on a hot serving-dish, and serve with six heart-shaped croûtons (No. 133).

768. Chicken Livers with Mushrooms.—Proceed the same as for No. 767, only adding six minced mushrooms three minutes before serving.

769. Chicken Livers en Brochette with Bacon.—Procure eighteen fresh chicken livers; cut away the gall, dry them well with a clean cloth, season with half a pinch each of salt and pepper, and cut each liver in two. Now prepare six slices of lean bacon (No. 754), broil them for one minute, then cut each slice into six pieces. Take six silver skewers, run a skewer through the centre of the liver, the same with a piece of bacon, and continue the same process until the six skewers are each one filled with a piece of liver and a piece of bacon. Roll them on a dish with one tablespoonful of good oil, dip them in fresh bread-crumbs, and put them on a moderate fire to broil for five minutes on each side. Arrange them on a hot dish, pour half a gill of maître d'hôtel butter (No. 145) over, and serve with a little watercress around the dish.

770. Chicken Livers Sautés à l'Italienne.—Proceed exactly as for No. 767, only adding half a gill of cooked fine herbs (No. 143) five minutes before serving.

771. Chicken Sauté à la Marengo.—Singe, draw, and cut into six pieces two small, tender chickens, each weighing a pound and a quarter. Lay them in an oiled sautoire, and brown slightly on both sides for five minutes, seasoning with a good pinch of salt and half a pinch of pepper; when a golden color, moisten with half a pint of Espagnole (No. 151), and half a cupful of mushroom liquor. Add twelve mushroom-buttons, and two truffles cut in thin slices, also half a glassful of Madeira wine. Let cook for twenty minutes, then serve with six fried eggs, as in No. 413, and six heart-shaped croûtons (No. 133). Adjust paper ruffles on the ends of the wings and legs of the chickens, and dress them nicely on the dish, decorating the borders with the fried eggs and sippets of bread, then serve.

772. Chicken Sauté à l'Hongroise.—Singe, draw, and cut into twelve pieces, two chickens of a pound and a quarter each; put them in a sautoire with an ounce of clarified butter, adding one finely chopped onion, half a pinch of salt, and half a pinch of pepper. Let cook slowly, without browning, for five minutes on each side, then moisten with half a pint of béchamel (No. 154), and half a cupful of cream. Let cook again for twenty minutes, skim the fat off, and serve with six pieces of fried bread croûtons (No. 133) around the dish.

773. Chicken Sauté à la Parmentier.—Singe, draw, and cut two chickens of a pound and a quarter each into twelve pieces; put them in a sautoire with one ounce of butter, season with a pinch of salt and half a pinch of pepper, and let cook on the stove for five minutes on each side, turning the pieces over with a fork. Moisten with half a pint of Espagnole sauce (No. 151), half a cupful of mushroom liquor, and add the juice of half a lemon. Let cook again for twenty minutes, then dress on a hot serving-dish, and decorate it with half a pint of potatoes château (No. 1009) in clusters.

774. Chicken Sauté with Tarragon.—Have two nice, tender young chickens of a pound and a quarter each; singe, draw, and cut each one into six pieces, and when well dried put them in a sautoire with one ounce of butter; season with a pinch of salt, and half a pinch of pepper, and let cook on a brisk stove for five minutes on each side. Moisten with half a pint of Espagnole sauce (No. 151), half a cupful of mushroom liquor, and half a glassful of sherry wine, and add a quarter of a bunch of well-washed, green tarragon-leaves. Let cook for twenty minutes, then dress nicely on a hot serving-dish, and decorate with six heart-shaped croûtons (No. 133).

775. Chicken Sauté à la Chasseur.—Prepare two chickens exactly as for the above (No. 774), moistening with half a pint of Espagnole sauce (No. 151), and half a cupful of mushroom liquor; add six finely minced mushrooms, half a glassful of sherry or Madeira wine, the zest of half a sound lemon, and one chopped shallot. Let cook for twenty minutes, and serve with six pieces of fried bread, cut heart-shaped, croûtons (No. 133).

776. Chicken Sauté à la Bordelaise.—Singe, draw, and cut up two chickens, each weighing a pound and a quarter, into twelve pieces; put them in a sautoire with two tablespoonfuls of oil and one chopped shallot. Let brown well for five minutes, then moisten with half a glassful of white wine, adding three artichoke-bottoms, each one cut into four pieces. Season with a pinch of salt, and half a pinch of pepper, then put the lid on and let simmer slowly for fifteen minutes; when ready to serve, add a little meat-glaze, a teaspoonful (No. 141), the juice of half a lemon, and a teaspoonful of chopped parsley. Dish up the pieces, crown-shaped, with paper ruffles nicely arranged, and garnish with the artichoke-bottoms in clusters, and twelve cooked potatoes château (No. 1009).

777. Chicken Sauté à la Régence.—Singe, draw, and dry well two tender chickens of a pound and a quarter each; cut them into twelve pieces, and put them in a sautoire with one ounce of butter. Season with a good pinch of salt and half a pinch of pepper, add half a glassful of Madeira wine, reduce for one minute, then put the lid on, and let simmer for six minutes. Moisten with half a pint of velouté (No. 152), and half a cupful of mushroom liquor. Let cook for ten minutes, then put in two truffles cut into small pieces, six mushrooms, a small sweetbread, and one ounce of cooked, smoked beef-tongue, all finely chopped. Finish cooking for ten minutes longer, then take from off the fire and incorporate therein two raw egg yolks diluted in the juice of half a lemon; while adding the egg yolks gently shuffle the pan, thicken well the sauce, then serve with paper ruffles neatly arranged at the ends of the wings and legs of the chickens.

778. Chicken Sauté à la Bohémienne.—Prepare two chickens as for the above (No. 777); put them in a sautoire with one ounce of butter, seasoning with a good pinch of salt and half a pinch of pepper. Cook on a brisk fire for six minutes, turning the pieces of chicken frequently with a fork; moisten with half a wine-glassful of Madeira wine, reduce for one minute, then add half a pint of Espagnole sauce (No. 151). Cook for ten minutes; add half a pint of cooked macaroni cut in small pieces. Cook again for ten minutes. Nicely arrange the chicken on a hot dish, pour the gravy over, and fill six bouchées (No. 270) with the macaroni taken from the stew, also a little grated Parmesan cheese sprinkled over. Garnish the dish all around with the bouchées, adjust paper ruffles at the end of the chicken legs, and serve hot.

779. Chicken Boiled à la Providence.—Singe, draw, and wipe well two chickens of a pound and a quarter each; truss them from the wing to the leg with a needle, and boil them in good broth for three-quarters of an hour. Prepare a pint of Allemande sauce (No. 210) with the broth of the chickens, adding a gill of small cuts of boiled carrots, the same of cooked Lima beans or flageolets, and let all cook together for three minutes. Dish up the chickens, untruss them, and pour the sauce over, arranging the vegetables on each side. Serve with chopped parsley strewn over.

780. Chicken Fricassé à la Reine.—Cut up two fine, tender, raw chickens into twelve even pieces. Place them in a large sautoire, with one quart of cold water, on a brisk fire; as soon as it comes to a boil, thoroughly skim. Season with one and a half pinches of salt, half a pinch of pepper, two cloves, and one bay-leaf, also a light bouquet (No. 254). Let boil slowly for twenty-five minutes. Place in another saucepan one and a half ounces of butter, which you melt on the hot range, add to it three tablespoonfuls of flour, thoroughly mix with a wooden spoon, while slowly cooking without browning, as the above, under no circumstances, should be allowed to get brown. Strain the broth into a bowl through a sieve. Return the pieces of chicken to the sautoire (but only the chicken), leaving it at the oven door till further action. Now add, little by little, the broth to the flour, being careful to stir continually until all added. Let boil for two minutes. Have three egg yolks in a bowl with a tablespoonful of good butter, half a gill of cold milk, and just a little cayenne pepper—*no more than a third of a saltspoonful*—squeezing in also the juice of half a medium-sized sound lemon. Mix all well together; and then add it to the sauce; stirring continually till all added. Heat up well, but do not allow to boil. Strain it through a sieve over the chicken. Mix well together, adding two truffles, and four mushrooms cut into small dice-shaped pieces. Dress the whole on a hot dish, arrange paper ruffles at the end of the legs, and serve with heart-shaped croûtons (No. 133) around the dish.

781. Chicken Fricassé à l'Américaine.—Boil two chickens as for No. 779; cut them into twelve pieces, and put them into a sautoire with eight minced mushrooms, an ounce of cooked salt pork cut into small squares, and half a pint of Allemande sauce (No. 210). Warm thoroughly without boiling, and serve with six heart-shaped pieces of fried bread (No. 133).

782. Pillau of Chicken à la Turque.—Take a fine tender chicken weighing two pounds, singe, draw, and wipe it well, then cut it into twelve even pieces. Brown them in a stewpan with an ounce of butter, one chopped onion, and one chopped green pepper. Let cook for six minutes, stirring lightly with a wooden spoon, then moisten with a pint of good broth (No. 99), and a gill of tomato sauce (No. 205). Add two ounces of dried mushrooms which have been soaking in water for several hours, or twelve canned mushrooms; season with a good pinch of salt, half a pinch of pepper, and half a teaspoonful of diluted saffron. Now add half a pint of well-washed, raw rice (if using Italian rice, only pick it) and three tablespoonfuls of grated Parmesan cheese; cook for twenty minutes longer, dress neatly on a hot dish, and serve.

783. Chicken Pillau à la Créole.—Exactly the same as for No. 782, adding three medium-sized, cut-up, fresh tomatoes, or half a pint of canned tomatoes with the other garnishings.

784. Chicken with Rice.—Singe, draw, and wipe well a tender fowl of three pounds; truss it from the wing to the leg, then put it into a saucepan covering it with water; add two pinches of salt, half a pinch of pepper, one carrot cut into four pieces, one whole onion stuck with three cloves, and a bouquet (No. 254). Cook for about twenty-five minutes, or until half done, then add half a pint of well-picked, raw rice; cook again for twenty minutes, and when finished, dish up the chicken, suppressing the bouquet, onion, and carrot; arrange the rice nicely around it, and serve.

785. Chicken à la Maryland.—Procure two small, tender spring chickens, leave the half of one aside for other use, and detach the legs and the wings; lay them on a plate, season with a good pinch of salt and half a pinch of pepper, then dip them in beaten egg, and afterward roll them in fresh bread-crumbs. Place them in a buttered pan, pour an ounce of clarified butter over, and roast in the oven for eighteen minutes. Pour half a pint of cream sauce (No. 181) onto a hot serving-dish, arrange the chicken nicely on top, and decorate with six thin slices of broiled bacon (No. 754), also six small corn-fritters (No. 965). Serve as hot as possible.

786. Suprême of Chicken à la Toulouse.—Singe, draw, and wipe neatly three fine, tender spring chickens. Remove the skin from the breasts. Make an incision on top of the breast-bone from end to end, then with a small sharp knife, carefully cut off the entire breast on each side, including the small wing-bone, which should not be separated from the breast, and seeing that the entire breasts are cleverly cut away, without a particle of it on the carcasses.

Under each breast will be found a small fillet, which you carefully remove, and place on a dish for further action. With a small sharp knife make an incision in each breast—at their thinner side—three inches in length by one inch in depth. Season the inside of each breast with a pinch of salt and half a pinch of pepper, equally divided. Stuff the breasts with two ounces of chicken forcemeat (No. 226), mixed with two fine, sound truffles finely sliced, and four mushrooms, also finely sliced. Butter well *a well-tinned* copper sautoire. Gently lay in the six breasts; then take each small fillet, press gently with the fingers, and give each a boatlike shape. Make six slanting, small incisions on top of each, insert in each incision a small slice of truffle, cut with a tube half an inch in diameter. Slightly wet the top of each breast with water; carefully arrange one fillet on top of each breast lengthwise. Sprinkle a little clarified butter over all with a feather brush. Pour into the pan, *but not over the suprême*, a quarter of a glassful of Madeira wine and two tablespoonfuls of mushroom liquor; tightly cover the pan with the lid, then place in the hot oven for ten minutes. Pour on a hot serving-dish one pint of hot Toulouse garnishing (No. 176). Remove the suprêmes from the oven, neatly dress them over the garnishing, adjust paper ruffles on each wing-bone, and immediately send to the table.

787. Suprême of Chicken à la Bayard.—Proceed as for No. 786, only serving with one pint of garnishing Bayard (No. 231).

788. Suprême of Chicken à la Reine.—Exactly the same as for No. 786, only substituting one pint of hot sauce à la reine (No. 780) for the other garnishing.

789. Suprême of Chicken à la Patti.—Prepare the suprême the same as for No. 786, then have a purée of rice with cream à la Patti (No. 245), garnish the dish with this, and lay the suprême on top. Decorate the rice with two thinly sliced truffles, pour a gill of good sauce Périgueux (No. 191) over, and serve with paper ruffles.

790. Suprême of Chicken à la Rothschild.—Have six chicken suprêmes prepared exactly the same as in No. 786, but stuffing them with purée of chestnuts instead of the chicken forcemeat. Mince very fine two sound truffles, then mix them with a pint of hot purée of chestnuts (No. 131); then arrange the purée on a hot dish, place six round-shaped croûtons (No. 133), instead of heart-shaped, nicely dress the suprêmes over the croûtons, decorate the top of each suprême, *right in the centre*, with one mushroom-head.

791. Turban of Chicken à la Cleveland.—Select two very tender chickens, singe, draw, and wipe them well; bone them and cut them into quarters, then put them into a sautoire with one ounce of butter, a good pinch of salt and half a pinch of pepper; add half a glassful of Madeira wine, and let parboil very slowly for ten minutes. Take half a pint of chicken forcemeat (No. 226), add to it one chopped truffle, three chopped mushrooms, and half an ounce of cooked minced tongue. Stir well together; put this forcemeat on a silver dish, lay the pieces of chicken on top, crown-shaped, and decorate with twelve whole mushrooms and two thinly sliced truffles. To the gravy in which the chickens were cooked add half a pint of Espagnole sauce (No. 151), a teaspoonful of chopped chives, and a small pat of fresh butter. Pour this immediately over the chickens, put the dish in the oven, and let cook very slowly for ten minutes. Squeeze the juice of half a lemon over, and serve with six heart-shaped pieces of fried bread (No. 133).

792. Chicken Curry à l'Indienne.—Take a good, tender three-pound chicken, singe, draw neatly, and cut it into square pieces. Put them in cold water for five minutes, wash them well, then drain, and put them in a saucepan, covering it to the surface with hot water; season with two good pinches of salt, one pinch of pepper, and the third of a pinch of nutmeg. Add a bouquet (No. 254), and six small onions; let cook on a moderate stove for forty-five minutes, skimming it well. Take another saucepan, in it place one and a half gills of white roux (No. 135), moisten it with all of the broth from the chicken, and mix well together. Prepare a tablespoonful of diluted curry with four egg yolks, and the juice of half a lemon, beat all this well together, pour it into the sauce a little at a time, stirring continually and not allowing it to boil. Pour the sauce over the chicken, which remains in the saucepan, and dress immediately on a hot dish, decorated with boiled rice all around as a border, and serve.

793. Chicken Curry à l'Espagnole.—The same as for No. 792, adding two cut-up tomatoes and one green pepper, cooking them ten minutes with the chicken.

794. Chicken Curry à la Créole.—The same as for No. 792, adding one green pepper cut very fine, also one chopped onion, and half a clove of garlic, cooking them twenty minutes with the chicken.

795. Boiled Turkey à l'Anglaise.—Take a very fine, tender turkey of about five pounds, singe, draw, and truss well with a needle from the wing to the leg. Put it into the soup-pot, and let cook for one hour; remove to a hot serving-dish. Decorate the dish with a pint of cooked spinach à l'Anglaise (No. 940), and six slices of hot, cooked, lean ham. Serve with half a cupful of hot broth poured over the turkey so as to keep it moist.

796. Boiled Turkey, Celery Sauce.—Exactly the same as for No. 795, substituting for garnishing one pint of hot celery sauce (No. 200), served separately.

797. Boiled Turkey, Oyster Sauce.—Proceed as for No. 795, serving with one pint of hot oyster sauce (No. 173), separately.

798. Boiled Turkey, Egg Sauce.—The same as for No. 795, serving with one pint of hot egg sauce (No. 161), separately.

799. Boiled Turkey à la Baltimore.—Serve a boiled turkey as for No. 795, garnishing it with half a head of cooked and hot cauliflower, one good-sized cooked carrot, cut in slices, and six cooked small onions, all neatly arranged around the dish, with half a pint of hot Allemande sauce (No. 210), served separately.

800. Roast Turkey, Stuffed with Chestnuts.—Singe, draw, wash well, and neatly dry a fine, tender turkey, weighing five to six pounds; fill the inside with the chestnut stuffing described below, then nicely truss the turkey from the wing to the leg; season with a heavy pinch of salt, well sprinkled over. Cover the breast with thin slices of larding pork. Put it to roast in a roasting-pan in a moderate oven for one hour and a half, basting it occasionally with its own gravy. Take from out the oven, untruss, dress it on a hot dish, skim the fat off the gravy, add a gill of broth (No. 99) or consommé (No. 100) to the gravy, let it just come to a boil, strain into a bowl, and send to the table separately.

Plain roast turkey is prepared the same, suppressing the stuffing, and roasting it only one hour and fifteen minutes.

Chestnut Stuffing.—Peel a good-sized, sound shallot, chop it up very fine, place in a saucepan on the hot range with one tablespoonful of butter, and let heat for three minutes without browning, then add a quarter of a pound of sausage meat. Cook five minutes longer, then add ten finely chopped mushrooms, twelve well-pounded, cooked, peeled chestnuts; mix all well together. Season with one pinch of salt, half a pinch of pepper, half a saltspoonful of powdered thyme, and a teaspoonful of finely chopped parsley. Let just come to a boil, then add half an ounce of fresh bread-crumbs, and twenty-four whole cooked and shelled French chestnuts; mix all well together, being careful not to break the chestnuts. Let cool off, and then stuff the turkey with it.

801. Hashed Turkey à la Royale.—Take a pound and a half of dice-shaped pieces of cooked turkey; place them in a saucepan with a pint of béchamel (No. 154), three tablespoonfuls of mushroom liquor, and two truffles cut in square pieces. Season with one pinch of salt, half a pinch of pepper, and the third of a pinch of nutmeg. Let all heat together for ten minutes, then serve with six heart-shaped pieces of bread (No. 133), lightly covered with pâté-de-foie-gras neatly arranged around the dish.

802. Hashed Turkey à la Béchamel.—The same as for No. 801, omitting the truffle and bread croûtons, and serving with chopped parsley strewn over.

803. Hashed Turkey à la Polonaise.—The same as for No. 801, only serving with six poached eggs (No. 404), and six heart-shaped croûtons (No. 133), instead of the truffles and pâte-de-foie-gras.

804. Hashed Turkey à la Crême.—Exactly the same as for No. 801, substituting one pint of cold, fresh cream, and a tablespoonful of fresh butter for the béchamel, also omitting the truffles and pâté-de-foie-gras; reducing the cream with the hash to one half, which will take from four to five minutes. Pour on a hot dish and serve.

805. Hashed Turkey en Bordure.—Decorate the border of a baking-dish with a potato croquette preparation (No. 997), place it in the oven for six minutes, then fill the centre with hashed turkey à la béchamel (No. 802), and put it in the oven again for five minutes before serving.

806. Turkey Breasts à la Chipolata.—Singe, draw, and wipe neatly a fine young turkey of six pounds. Detach the two legs entirely from the turkey. Place in a saucepan any piece of pork-skin that is on hand, adding one cut-up carrot, one onion, also cut up, and a bouquet (No. 254).

Lay the breasts of the turkey over the garnishing, season with one pinch of salt and half a pinch of pepper, then put on the lid and let get a golden color for about ten minutes. Moisten with one pint of broth (No. 99), and put it into the oven without the lid, letting it cook for forty minutes, basting it frequently with its own gravy. Arrange on a hot dish, and serve with a pint of hot chipolata (No. 232). The stock remaining in the pan can be used for preparing Espagnole sauce.

807. Turkey Breasts à la Robinson.—Proceed exactly as for No. 806, but after cooking for twenty minutes, take it off and place it in another saucepan. Baste it with its own gravy, adding half a pint of Espagnole sauce (No. 151). Blanch half a pint of chicken or turkey livers, cut them into two or three pieces according to their size, and put them with the turkey, adding half a glassful of Madeira wine. Let cook for twenty minute more, and serve with the livers around the breasts, and the gravy thrown over.

808. Roast Goose, Stuffed with Chestnuts, Apple Sauce.—Have a fine, tender goose of four pounds, singe, draw, wash well, and thoroughly wipe the interior with a cloth; then fill it with some stuffing as for the turkey (No. 800). Close both ends, truss well, sprinkle a pinch of salt over, envelop in buttered paper and put it into a roasting-pan. Cook it for one hour and a half in a moderate oven, basting it occasionally with the dripping. Remove from the oven, dress on a hot serving-dish, untruss, skim off the fat from the gravy, add to it a gill of white broth (No. 99), let come to a boil, then strain the gravy into a sauce-bowl and serve separately.

809. Timbale of Foie-Gras Lagardère.—Butter lightly six timbale molds; decorate the inside according to taste with pieces of truffle and smoked beef-tongue; fill them half full with cream forcemeat (No. 225), leaving an empty space in the centre, filling this in with a reduced salpicon (No. 256). Cover the salpicon with a very little pâté-de-foie-gras, and finish filling with the cream forcemeat. Put the molds in a sautoire holding hot water to half their height; boil gently, and then place them in a slow oven for ten minutes. Unmold on a hot dish, and serve with half a pint of hot sauce Périgueux (No. 191) separately. Place on top of each timbale a small, round croquette of foie-gras, then serve.

810. Vol-au-Vent à la Financière.—Fill six vol-au-vents made with feuilletage paste (No. 1076) with a quart of financière garnishing (No. 246), and serve them on a dish with a folded napkin.

811. Vol-au-Vent à la Toulouse.—Fill six vol-au-vents (No. 1076) with a quart of hot Toulouse garnishing (No. 196), and serve the same as for the above.

812. Vol-au-Vent à la Reine.—Fill six vol-au-vents (No. 1076) with a quart of hot Reine garnishing (No. 623), and serve as for No. 810.

813. Boned Turkey à la Prosperity of America.—Procure a fine, tender, young Rhode Island turkey, weighing eight pounds. Singe, draw, and neatly wipe the interior. Make an incision right along the back. Begin boning from the neck down toward the breast, on both sides, being very careful not to make any holes in the skin, as it should remain perfectly intact. Make an incision from the first joint, then bone both legs. Cut away also, very carefully, the two wing bones. Season the inside with one pinch of salt and half a pinch of pepper, evenly divided. Place it on a dish, and lay it in the ice-box until needed. Take two pounds of lean, raw veal, three pounds of fresh pork, and half a pound of larding pork, all cut up into small dice-shaped pieces. Season with two pinches of salt, one pinch of white pepper, the third of a saltspoonful of grated nutmeg, and the same quantity of thyme. Mix all well together. Place all in the chopping machine, and chop it exceedingly fine, repeating the process, if necessary, until it is chopped to perfection. Should there be any sinews among the ingredients, remove them all. Place on a cold dish, and put away in the ice-box to cool until the following is prepared. Have ready a quarter of a pound of the end (red) part of a cooked smoked beef-tongue, eighteen medium-sized, sound truffles, both tongue and truffles cut in dice-shaped pieces half an inch square. Take the forcemeat from the ice-box, and thoroughly mix the tongue and truffles with it, pouring in also a wine-glassful of Madeira wine. Half a cup of well-peeled pistache can be added, if at hand. Take the turkey from the ice-box, spread it on a clean table (skin-side downward). Then, with a keen knife, cut away even slices from the breasts, arrange them on the thin, so that the turkey should have an equal thickness all over. Place the forcemeat right in the centre of the turkey, column shaped, leaving a clear space of two inches at each end, and of four inches at each side. Spread on a table a strong, clean napkin, sprinkling over it a little cold water. Fold up first both ends of the turkey, then both sides, so that the four ends should be enveloped; gently lift, and lay it right in the centre of the napkin. Roll it carefully in the napkin. Tightly tie one end first, then the other, as firmly as possible, taking in the slack of the napkin. Place it in a large saucepan on the hot range, with the carcass, and whatever bones and débris pertain to it, completely cover with cold water, place the lid on, and when coming to a boil thoroughly skim it, then add one medium-sized, sound, scraped carrot, and one well-peeled onion with three cloves stuck in. Season with one pinch of salt, and then let boil on a moderate fire for fully two and a half hours. Remove the galantine with a skimmer; let cool enough so that it can be easily handled. Cut the strings at both ends; roll it over again as before, and tightly tie both ends exactly as before. Lay it in a flat tin pan, placing on top of it a board the size of the boned turkey, and on top of it a weight of seven pounds, leaving the weight on until the galantine is thoroughly cold, which will take a whole night; but avoid placing it in the ice-box until thoroughly cold. Two days after the preparation it will be ready for use; keeping it in the ice-box in the same napkin in which it was cooked.

814. Jelly for Boned Turkey.—Strain the broth in which the galantine was cooked into another saucepan, thoroughly skim all the fat off, add one ounce of clarified gelatine. Boil for five minutes. Crack into another saucepan the whites of two raw eggs, and the shells as well, squeeze in the juice of half a sound lemon, adding half a glassful of Madeira wine, and a small piece of ice, the size of an egg, finely cracked. Beat all sharply together with a wire whip. Place the broth on the table at hand near the eggs, &c., and with a soup-ladle in the left hand, a wire whip in the right, add a ladleful of broth, little by little, to the eggs, carefully and sharply stirring with the whip until all the broth has been added. Place it then on a very moderate fire, and let gently come to a boil. Immediately strain through a flannel bag or a napkin into a clean bowl and let cool, and it will be ready for use.

815. Pigeon Cutlets à la Victoria.—Singe, draw, and bone three fine pigeons, leaving on the legs; cut them in two, and stuff lightly with chicken forcemeat (No. 226), immerse then in beaten egg and fresh bread-crumbs, then cook in a sautoire with half an ounce of clarified butter, for four minutes on each side, and serve with half a pint of hot Victoria sauce (No. 208) on the warm dish, and the cutlets on top, with paper ruffles nicely arranged.

816. Squabs Roasted Plain.—Singe, draw, cut off the necks, wipe neatly, and truss six fine, small squabs; put them in a roasting-pan with half a pinch of salt, evenly divided, and a very little butter spread over. Put the pan into a brisk oven to cook for twelve minutes; then remove from the oven, untruss, and dress them on a hot dish, on which you previously have placed six small canapés, prepared as in No. 832, one on each canapé; neatly decorate the dish with fresh watercress; skim the fat from off the gravy, add to it a gill of white broth (No. 99); let it just come to a boil, strain it into a sauce-bowl, and send to the table separately.

817. Squabs Broiled on Toast, with Bacon.—Singe, draw, cut the necks off, and wipe nicely three very good-sized squabs; split them without detaching the parts, then lay them on a dish, and season with a pinch of salt, half a pinch of pepper, and a tablespoonful of sweet oil; roll them in well, and put them to broil for six minutes on each side. Prepare a dish with six toasts, arrange the squabs over, and spread a gill of maître d'hôtel butter (No. 145) on top. Decorate the dish with six slices of broiled bacon (No. 754), and serve.

818. Ballotin of Squab à l'Italienne.—Singe, draw, and bone six tender squabs; stuff them with a good chicken forcemeat (No. 226), and leave on one leg, to decorate later with a ruffle. Form them into a circle, arranging each squab so it assumes a round shape; place them in a buttered sautoire; season with a good pinch of salt and half a pinch of pepper, and cover with a piece of buttered paper. Put it in the oven for fifteen minutes, and when cooked serve with half a pint of hot Italian sauce (No. 188), the squabs laid on top, with a paper ruffle fastened on to each leg.

819. Squabs à la Crapaudine.—Singe, draw, then split six squabs through the back without entirely dividing the parts; break the bones of the legs and wings, flatten them well, and lay them on a dish to season with a good pinch of salt, one pinch of pepper, and two tablespoonfuls of oil, roll them in well, then dip them in fresh bread-crumbs, and broil them slowly for seven minutes on each side. Arrange them on a hot dish, and serve with half a pint of hot Robert sauce (No. 192), to which add three chopped mushrooms. Serve the sauce on a dish, and the squabs on top.

820. Squabs à l'Américaine.—Singe, draw, and truss nicely six fine, fat squabs; stuff them with American forcemeat (No. 229), and place them in a roasting-pan with a pinch of salt, evenly distributed, and half an ounce of butter well spread over the squabs. Place them in the hot oven, and roast for eighteen minutes. Take from out the oven, dress them on a hot dish; untruss; skim the fat off the gravy, add to it one gill of broth (No. 99), let come to a boil, strain into a sauce-bowl, decorate the dish with a little fresh watercress. Arrange a slice of broiled bacon (No. 754) over each bird, and send to the table.

821. Squabs à la Chipolata.—Prepare and roast six squabs same as for No. 816, and serve them with a pint of hot chipolata garnishing (No. 232) on a hot dish, and the squabs arranged over.

822. Squabs en Compote.—Singe, draw, and truss with their legs thrust inside, six fine, fat squabs; lay them in a saucepan with half an ounce of butter, one cut-up onion, and one carrot cut the same. Season with a pinch of salt, then put the lid on the pan, and cook on a good fire for ten minutes. Put in a saucepan six small glazed onions (No. 967), one medium-sized carrot, cut with a vegetable-scoop (blanching the latter for two minutes), one ounce of salt pork cut into small pieces, and six cut-up mushrooms; moisten them with a pint of Espagnole sauce (No. 151), and let cook together for thirty minutes. Transfer the squabs to this preparation, and let cook again for five minutes; dress the garnishing on a hot dish, arrange the squabs on top, and serve.

823. Roast Duck à l'Américaine.—Select a fine young duck, weighing three and a half pounds; singe, draw, and wipe it well, then stuff it with American forcemeat (No. 229), and place it in a roasting-pan with half an ounce of butter, and besprinkle with a pinch of salt, then roast it in the oven for forty minutes, basting it occasionally. Lay it on a dish, untruss, skim the fat off, add a gill of white broth (No. 99), let it come to a boil, then strain the lean part of the gravy over, and garnish with six pieces of fried hominy (No. 1035).

824. Roast Duck, Apple Sauce.—Have a fine, tender duckling of three and a half pounds; singe, draw, wipe neatly, and truss. Place it in a roasting-pan, spread half an ounce of butter over, and a pinch of salt. Place it in a brisk oven, and let cook for thirty minutes, not failing to baste it occasionally with its own gravy. Dress it on a hot dish, untie the string, skim the fat off the gravy, add a gill of broth (No. 99), let it come to a boil, then strain the lean part over the duck, decorate with a little watercress, and serve with half a pint of hot apple sauce separately (No. 168).

825. Duckling à la Rouennaise.—Take two fine ducklings of one and a half pounds each, singe, draw, and truss them with the legs thrust inside; lay them in a roasting-pan, and cover them with half an ounce of butter, seasoning with a pinch of salt ; put them in the oven for ten minutes. Cut four medium-sized turnips into small dice-shaped pieces, put them in a saucepan with half an ounce of butter and half a teaspoonful of powdered sugar ; let cook for ten minutes, then moisten with a pint of Espagnole sauce (No. 151). Lay the ducks in the saucepan with the turnips, and let cook again all together for twenty-five minutes ; arrange the ducks on a hot dish, untruss, and decorate the dish with the turnips. Pour the sauce over all, and serve.

826. Salmi of Duck à l'Américaine.—Procure two fine ducks ; singe, draw, wipe neatly, and cut off the wings, legs, and breasts ; put the two carcasses in a saucepan, sprinkle a little salt over, and put it in the oven to cook for six minutes ; remove them, and hash them up. Put them back into a saucepan with a pint of white broth (No. 99), and a small bouquet (No. 254), and let cook on a moderate fire for fifteen minutes. Put an ounce of butter in a sautoire, lay in the wings, legs, and breasts, then season with a pinch of salt and half a pinch of pepper ; cook on a very brisk fire for three minutes on each side, then add half a glassful of Madeira wine, half a pint of Espagnole sauce (No. 151), and the zest of a lemon ; strain the gravy of the carcasses over, and let all cook again for fifteen minutes. Dress nicely on a hot dish, and decorate with six heart-shaped croûtons of fried hominy, and serve (No. 1035).

827. Salmi of Duck, with Olives.—Prepare the salmi of ducks as for the above (No. 826), adding half a pint of parboiled and stoned olives to the sauce. Use six heart-shaped fried croûtons of bread (No. 133) instead of the hominy, and serve.

828. Salmi of Duck à la Chasseur.—Make a salmi the same as for No. 826, adding twelve sliced mushrooms, and serve with six heart-shaped croûtons (No. 133).

829. Salmi of Duck à la Bourgeoise.—Prepare two fine ducks as for No. 826, and add twelve glazed onions (No. 967), and two raw carrots cut clove-garlic-shaped, letting them cook in salted water for ten minutes previous to adding them to the salmi, also half an ounce of salt pork, cut in square pieces, and let cook together with the ducks for fifteen minutes more ; then serve.

830. Salmi of Duck à la Montglas.—Singe, draw, and wipe two fine, tender ducks ; cut away the wings, legs, and breasts, then put the carcasses in a roasting-pan ; sprinkle a little salt over, spread on each bird a very little butter, and place them in the oven for six minutes ; remove them, and hash them up. Lay them in a saucepan, moistened with a pint of white broth (No. 99) ; add a small bouquet (No. 254), and let cook on the stove for fifteen minutes. Put an ounce of butter in a sautoire, add the wings, legs, and breasts, previously laid aside ; season with a pinch of salt, half a pinch of pepper, and the third of a pinch of nutmeg, and let cook on a brisk fire for three minutes on each side. Add half a glassful of good sherry, half a pint of Espagnole sauce (No. 151), half a pint of tomato sauce (No. 205), two thin slices of smoked beef-tongue cut into Julienne-shaped pieces, two cut-up truffles, six fine mushrooms, also cut up ;

then strain the gravy of the carcasses over this ; let cook all together for fifteen minutes more, then artistically dress the salmi on a hot dish, decorate with six heart-shaped bread croûtons (No. 133), adjust paper ruffles to the end of the wings and legs, and serve.

831. Salmi of Duck à la Maréchale.—Proceed exactly the same as for "Salmi à l'Américaine" (No. 826), adding twelve small godiveau quenelles (No 221), and twelve mushrooms cut in two. Let heat well for five minutes, then serve with six fried bread croûtons (No. 133).

A pinch of salt represents 205 grains, or a tablespoonful.
Half a pinch of pepper represents 38 grains, or a teaspoonful.
A third of a pinch of nutmeg represents 13 grains, or half a teaspoonful.

GAME.

832. Canapés for Game.—Cut out the desired number of canapés from a loaf of American bread (a stale one is preferable) one and a half inches thick. Trim neatly, pare off the crusts; then cut out a piece in the centre of each, from end to end, so that the cavity will hold the bird easily when sending to the table. Spread a little butter over them, place on a tin plate; then brown in the hot oven until they obtain a good golden color. Remove from out the oven, arrange them on a hot dish, and they will be ready to serve.

833. Croquettes of Game à la Périgueux.—Make six game croquettes exactly the same as the chicken croquettes (No. 758)—the mushrooms can be omitted—and serve with half a pint of hot sauce périgueux (No. 191), separately.

834. Quails Roasted, Plain.—Pick six fine, tender, fat quails, singe, draw, and wipe them well; truss them, laying a thin layer of lard on the breasts. Put them in a roasting-pan, spreading a very little butter on top of each quail; then pour half a cupful of water in the pan. Season with a pinch of salt, and let cook in the oven for eighteen minutes. Place on a hot dish six heart-shaped pieces of toast; untruss the quails, and arrange them on top, decorating with a little watercress. Strain the gravy into a sauce-bowl, and serve it separately.

835. Quails Broiled with Bacon.—Have six fine fat quails. Singe, draw, and wipe them well. Split them through the back without separating the parts, and break the two leg bones. Put them on a dish; season with a pinch of salt, half a pinch of pepper, and a tablespoonful of sweet oil, mixing them in well, and put them to broil on a moderate fire for six minutes on each side. Arrange six toasts on a hot dish, lay the quails on top, and pour a gill of maître d'hôtel butter (No. 145) over, decorating with six slices of broiled bacon (No. 754), and serve.

836. Braised Quails, Celery Sauce.—Take six nice fat quails, singe, draw, and wipe them well. Truss, and cover the breasts with a thin layer of lard. Place them in a sautoire with a piece of pork rind, half a carrot, and half an onion, both cut-up, and let them get a good golden color on the fire. Moisten with half a cupful of water, then put them in the oven, and let cook for twenty minutes. Serve with a pint of celery sauce (No. 200), and a little meat-glaze (No. 141) thrown over.

837. Quails à la Financière.—Braise six quails the same as for the above (No. 836), and serve them with a pint of hot financière garnishing (No. 246) in place of the celery sauce.

838. Doe-birds, Roasted, Plain.—Singe, draw, and truss six fine, fat doe-birds. Put them in a roasting-pan with half a cupful of water, seasoning with a pinch of salt. Spread a very little butter over the birds, and put them in a hot oven for twelve minutes. Dress them on a hot dish with six small canapés (No. 832). Decorate the dish with a little watercress, and serve.

839. Broiled Doe-birds.—Singe, draw, and wipe well six fine doe-birds; split them through the back without detaching the parts, and lay them on a dish. Season with a good pinch of salt, half a pinch of pepper, and one tablespoonful of oil. Roll them in well, and broil for four minutes on each side. Prepare a hot dish with six toasts; arrange the doe-birds on top, and serve with a gill of maître d'hôtel butter (No. 145) well spread over. Decorate the dish with a little watercress.

840. Roasted Doe-birds à l'Américaine.—Proceed exactly as for No. 838, replacing the canapés of bread with six canapés of fried hominy (No. 1035), or corn fritters, arranging six slices of broiled bacon over each bird, and serve the same.

841. Roasted Doe-birds à l'Africaine.—Exactly as for No. 838, only serving with six stuffed egg-plants (No. 909) instead of the canapés.

842. Salmi of Doe-birds à la Gastronome.—Make a salmi as for salmi of snipe (No. 870), and serve with six small potato croquettes (No. 997).

843. Roast Partridge, Bread Sauce.—Singe, draw, and wipe two fine, young partridges; truss them neatly, and cover the breasts with a layer of thin lard, tying it twice around. Lay them on a roasting-pan, spreading a little butter over each, and moistening with half a cupful of water. Put the pan in a brisk oven for twenty-five minutes, basting the birds occasionally. Dress each one on a bread canapé (No. 832), removing the strings. Decorate the dish with a little watercress. Strain the gravy into a sauce-bowl, and serve it separately; also serving half a pint of hot bread-sauce (No. 162) in another bowl.

844. Partridge Broiled à l'Américaine.—Singe, draw, and wipe neatly three tender partridges; cut them in halves, lay them on a dish, and season with a good pinch of salt, half a pinch of pepper, and a tablespoonful of oil. Roll them in well, then put them to broil for seven minutes on each side. Prepare six slices of fried hominy (No. 1035). Arrange them on a hot dish; place the partridges over, and pour a gill of maître d'hôtel butter on top (No. 145). Place six slices of broiled bacon (No. 754) over the birds, and serve.

845. Partridge and Cabbage.—Select a fine, tender cabbage, clean it thoroughly, cut it into four parts; wash well in cold water, remove the root, and put into salted boiling water for five minutes. Remove, and drain well, then return it to the saucepan with one carrot cut in four pieces, one whole onion stuck with four cloves, a quarter of a pound of salt pork, in one piece, a bouquet (No. 254), one pint of white broth (No. 99), and one pint of lean stock. Season with a good pinch of salt and a pinch of pepper. Take (in preference) two old partridges; singe, draw, and wipe them well; truss them with their wings turned inside, and put them on a roasting-pan with half a pinch of salt, and a little butter well spread over their breasts, and put them to roast for six minutes. Make a hollow space in the centre of the cabbage, place therein the two partridges and cover them over, laying a piece of buttered paper on top to prevent the air from escaping; put the lid on and cook in the oven for one hour. Now lift off the lid, remove the paper, skim off any fat adhering to the surface, and dress the cabbage neatly on a hot dish; untruss, and arrange the partridges, decorating the dish artistically with the carrots and salt pork, cut into six slices. Take away the onion and bouquet, and serve.

846. Partridge à la Financière.—Singe, draw, wipe, and truss two partridges with their wings inside. Lay a piece of pork-rind in a saucepan, adding one carrot and one onion, both cut in slices, two bay-leaves, one sprig of thyme, and the two partridges. Season with one pinch of salt and half a pinch of pepper. When they have assumed a good golden color on the hot stove, moisten with half a pint of white broth (No. 99), then put the saucepan in the oven and let cook for twenty minutes. Dress them on a serving-dish, untruss, pour half a pint of hot sauce financière (No. 246) over, and serve. The gravy from the partridges can be utilized for making the financière sauce.

847. Partridge Braised with Celery Sauce.—Proceed exactly the same as for the above (No. 846), replacing the financière by a pint of hot celery sauce (No. 200).

848. Partridge Sauté à la Chasseur.—Singe, draw, and wipe two fine, tender partridges, cut them into twelve pieces, and place them in a sautoire with an ounce of butter, seasoning well with a good pinch of salt and half a pinch of pepper. Brown well for three minutes on each side; then add a finely chopped shallot, half a glassful of Madeira wine, half a pint of Espagnole sauce (No. 151), and twelve whole mushrooms. Finish cooking for fifteen minutes, then serve with six bread croûtons (No. 133) around the dish.

849. Chartreuse of Partridge.—Prepare the partridges as for No. 845. Take a Charlotte-mold, which will hold three pints; butter lightly, and decorate with small pieces of cooked carrot and turnip, cut very evenly with a vegetable-tube. When ready, fill the bottom with a layer of cooked cabbage; cut the partridges into pieces, put a layer of them on the cabbage, covering the hollow spaces with more cabbage; lay on top six slices of salt pork, add the rest of the partridges, and finish by covering the surface with cabbage, pressing it down carefully. Place the mold on a tin baking-dish, and put it in a moderate oven for fifteen minutes, leaving the oven-door open during the whole time. Have a hot dish ready, turn the mold upside down on it, and draw off carefully. Serve with a little demi-glace (No. 185).

850. Suprême of Partridge, Sauce Périgueux.—Singe, draw, wipe neatly, and remove the skin from the breasts of three partridges. Make an incision on top of each breast-bone, from end to end, then with a keen knife carefully cut off the entire breast on both sides of the partridges, including the small wing-bone, which should not be separated from the breasts, and seeing that the entire breasts are cleverly cut away, without leaving a particle of it on the carcasses. Under each breast will be found a small fillet, which you carefully remove, and place on a dish for further action. With a small, sharp knife, make an incision in each breast, at their thinner side, three inches in length by one inch in depth. Season the inside of each breast with a pinch of salt, and half a pinch of pepper, equally divided. Stuff the breasts with two ounces of chicken forcemeat (No. 226), mixed with two fine, sound, finely sliced truffles, and four finely sliced mushrooms. Butter well a *well-tinned* copper sautoire; gently lay in the six breasts; take each small fillet, press them gently with the fingers, giving them a boatlike form. Make six slanting, small incisions on top of each, insert in each incision a small slice of truffle, cut with a tube half an inch in diameter. Lightly wet the top of each breast with water, then neatly lay one fillet on top of each breast lengthwise. Sprinkle a little clarified butter over all with a feather brush. Pour into the pan (not over the suprêmes) a quarter of a glassful of Madeira wine and two tablespoonfuls of mushroom liquor, tightly cover the pan with a lid, then place in the hot oven for ten minutes. Pour on a hot dish one pint of hot Toulouse garnishing (No. 176). Remove the suprêmes from the oven, neatly dress them over the garnishing, adjust paper ruffles on each wing bone, and immediately send to the table.

851. Suprême of Partridge à la Godard.—The same as for the above (No. 850), but serving with half a pint of Allemande sauce (No. 210), adding two sliced truffles, six sliced mushrooms, six blanched cock's combs, and six blanched cock's kidneys, in place of the Périgueux sauce. Heat up well on the corner of the stove for four minutes, but do not allow it to boil, and pour the garnishing over the hot dish, dressing the suprêmes over it; serve very hot.

852. Grouse, Roasted Plain.—Singe, draw, wipe, and truss two fine fat grouse. Place them in a roasting-pan with half a cupful of water, spread a little butter over each, and season with a pinch of salt. Put them into a brisk oven, and let cook for eighteen minutes, taking care to baste frequently with their own gravy; then untruss. Have a hot serving-dish ready; place two bread canapés (No. 832) on it; arrange the grouse over, and decorate the dish with a little watercress. Strain the gravy into a sauce-bowl, and serve it separately.

853. Grouse, Roasted à la Sam Ward.—Take two fine fat grouse; pick, singe, draw, and dry them well; then truss them nicely. Place them in a roasting-pan, putting inside of each bird a piece of broiled toast four inches long and two wide. Drip in on each toast, with a spoon, a small glassful of good Madeira wine or sherry; season the grouse with a pinch of salt; spread a little butter over. Put them in a brisk oven, and let cook for eighteen minutes, taking care to baste them frequently. Lay them on a hot dish, untruss, strain the gravy over, and decorate with a little watercress. Serve with a little red currant jelly separately.

854. Grouse, Broiled with Bacon.—Singe, draw, and wipe nicely two fat grouse. Split them in two through the back without separating the parts; lay them on a dish, and season with a pinch of salt, half a pinch of pepper, and a tablespoonful of sweet oil. Roll them in well; then put them to broil on a brisk fire for seven minutes on each side. Prepare a hot dish with six small toasts, arrange the grouse over, spread a gill of maître d'hôtel butter (No. 145) on top, and garnish with six thin slices of broiled bacon (No. 754), then serve.

855. Salmi of Grouse à la Parisienne.—Singe, draw, wipe, and truss two fine fat grouse; season with a pinch of salt, spread a few small bits of butter on the birds, then place them in a roasting-pan, and put them in a brisk oven to cook for eight minutes. Untruss and cut away the wings, legs, and breasts. Put an ounce of good butter into a saucepan with half a medium-sized carrot, cut in very small pieces, half an onion cut the same, a sprig of thyme, two bay-leaves, and six whole peppers. Reduce to a good golden color for about five minutes, then hash the bodies of the two grouse, and add them to the other ingredients. Moisten with a pint of Espagnole sauce (No. 151), half a glassful of good sherry wine, half a cupful of mushroom liquor, and the zest of a lemon; season with half a pinch of salt, half a pinch of pepper, and a third of a pinch of nutmeg; let cook for twenty minutes. Now put the wings, legs, and breasts into a separate saucepan, and strain the above sauce over the parts, adding six minced mushrooms and two minced truffles. Let cook for three minutes, then dress neatly on a hot dish, and serve with six croûtons (No. 133) on top, and paper ruffles nicely arranged.

856. Salmi of Grouse à la Walter Scott.—Proceed exactly the same as for the above (No. 855), omitting the mushrooms and truffles, and serving with half a pint of bread sauce (No. 162) separately.

857. Salmi of Grouse à la Florentine.—The same as for No. 855, only serving the salmi with a garnishing of six hot artichokes à la Florentine (No. 903) in place of the other garnishing.

858. Suprême of Grouse à la Richelieu.—Proceed the same as for the suprême of partridge (No. 850), but substituting tongue for truffles, and serving with a gill of hot sauce Périgueux (No. 191), mingled with a gill of tomato sauce (No. 205), boiled together for three minutes.

859. Teal Duck, Roasted Plain.—Pick, singe, draw, wipe, and truss three fine teal ducks; place them in a roasting-pan. Season with a pinch of salt; put them in a brisk oven to roast for fourteen minutes, then untruss. Arrange on a hot serving-dish, and decorate with six slices of fried hominy (No. 1035) and a little watercress.

860. Teal Duck, Broiled.—Have three fine, fat teal ducks; pick, singe, and dry them neatly; cut the heads off, and split the birds in two without separating the parts. Lay them on a dish, and season them with a pinch of salt, half a pinch of pepper, and a tablespoonful of sweet oil. Roll them in well, and put them to broil on a moderate fire for seven minutes on each side. Have a hot dish with six toasts ready, lay the ducks on top, spread a gill of maître d'hôtel butter (No. 145) over, decorate with a little watercress, and serve.

861. Salmi of Teal Duck à la Régence.—Prepare the salmi of teal duck as for the salmi of duck á l'Américaine (No. 826), adding half a pint of hot Régence garnishing (No. 235) four minutes before serving.

862. Ptarmigan, Roasted Plain.—Proceed exactly the same as for roasted teal ducks, No. 859.

863. Ptarmigan, Broiled Plain.—Prepared the same as for teal ducks broiled, No. 860.

864. Salmi of Ptarmigan à la Chasseur.—To be prepared exactly as salmi of duck á l'Américaine (No. 826), adding twelve mushrooms, cut in two, four minutes before serving, and decorating with six heart-shaped croûtons (No. 133).

865. Plovers, Roasted Plain.—Pick, singe, draw, and wipe neatly six fine, fat, tender plovers; pick out the eyes, truss the legs together, skewer the head under one leg, and lay a thin slice of larding pork on each bird; tie securely, then place them in a roasting-pan. Season with a pinch of salt evenly divided over each; spread also a very little butter over. Put them in the hot oven, and roast for ten minutes. Remove from the oven, arrange six small canapés (No. 832) on a hot dish, dress the birds on the canapés, decorate with a little watercress, and serve.

866. Plovers Broiled.—Pick, singe, draw, and wipe six fine, fat plovers; pick out the eyes, split them through the back without separating the parts, and place them on a dish. Season with one pinch of salt, half a pinch of pepper, and a tablespoonful of sweet oil. Roll them in well, and put them on a broiler to cook for four minutes on each side. Dress them on a hot dish with six pieces of toast, spread a gill of maître d'hôtel butter (No. 145) over, decorate with a little watercress, and serve.

867. Salmi of Plover à la Maison d'Or.—Proceed exactly the same as for salmi of woodcock (No. 873), adding, on the serving-dish, six heart-shaped bread croûtons (No. 133), covered with pâté-de-foie-gras.

868. English Snipe, Roasted.—Procure six fine English snipe; pick, singe, draw, and wipe them (reserve the hearts and livers for further use); pick out the eyes, remove the skin from the heads, truss the legs, skewer them with the bills; tie a thin slice of larding pork around each bird, and put them in a roasting-pan, sprinkling a pinch of salt over. Set them in the oven to roast for eight minutes. Hash up very fine the hearts and livers, with a teaspoonful of chives and a teaspoonful of good butter, seasoning with half a pinch of salt and the third of a pinch of pepper. Cover six bread canapés (No. 832) with this, sprinkling a little fresh bread-crumbs on top. Spread a very little butter over all, and put them on a tin plate in the oven for two minutes. Arrange the canapés on a hot dish, dress the snipe nicely over, decorate with a little watercress, and strain the gravy into a sauce-bowl, serving it separately.

869. English Snipe, Broiled.—Pick, singe, draw, and dry well six fine English snipe; remove the skin from the heads, split them in two without detaching the parts, and put them on a dish. Season with a pinch of salt, half a pinch of pepper, and a tablespoonful of oil. Roll them in well, then put them to broil (with the bills stuck into the breasts), and let them cook for four minutes on each side. Prepare a hot dish with six toasts, arrange the snipe over, spread a gill of maitre d'hôtel butter (No. 145) on top, decorate the dish with a little watercress, and serve.

870. Salmi of Snipe à la Moderne.—Singe, draw, and neatly wipe six fine, fat snipe. Chop off the legs, and then stuff the inside with a little game forcemeat (No. 228) through a paper cornet; fill the cavity of the eyes with a little more of the game forcemeat (No. 228), and covering each eye right over the game forcemeat with a small bit of truffle, cut with a tube. Insert the bills in the breasts, and then lay them on a roasting-pan, with a little butter; place in the hot oven to roast for six minutes. Take from out the oven, lay each one on a square piece of bread, fried in a little clarified butter, pour one pint of hot salmi sauce (No. 193) over, to which have been added twelve whole mushrooms, and serve.

871. Woodcock, Roasted Plain.—Procure six fine, fat woodcocks, pick, singe, and draw them, putting the hearts and livers on a plate for further use. Take out the eyes, and remove the skin from the heads; truss up the feet, skewer them with the bill, and tie a *barde* of fat pork around the breasts; then chop up all the hearts and livers very fine, with one teaspoonful of chives, half a pinch of salt, a third of a pinch of pepper, and a teaspoonful of butter. Prepare six bread canapés (No. 832), two and a half inches long, by one and a half wide; fry them for two minutes in very hot fat, drain them thoroughly, and cover each canapé with some of the above mixture, spreading a little fresh bread-crumbs and a very little butter over; place them in a small baking-pan and lay aside. Now put the woodcocks in a roasting-pan with a little butter well spread over the birds, and roast them in a brisk oven for ten minutes. Two minutes before they are done, put the canapés in the oven, then take both out, and lay the canapés on a hot dish; untie the birds, and arrange them over the canapés, decorating the dish with a little watercress. Strain the gravy into a sauce-bowl, and serve it separately.

872. Woodcock, Broiled with Bacon.—Pick, singe, draw, pick out the eyes, and remove the skin from the heads of six fine woodcocks; wipe them neatly, and split them through the back without separating the parts. Put them on a dish to season with a pinch of salt, half a pinch of pepper, and one tablespoonful of sweet oil. Roll them in well, then put them on to broil with the bills stuck into the breasts. Let broil for four minutes on each side, then arrange them on a dish with six pieces of heart-shaped fried bread, covered with the hashed hearts and livers as in No. 871, spread a gill of maître-d'hôtel butter (No. 145) over, and decorate with six slices of broiled bacon (No. 754), then serve.

873. Salmi of Woodcock à la Chasseur.—Pick, singe, draw, pick out the eyes, and remove the skin from the heads of six fine woodcocks; wipe them neatly, and put them in a roasting-pan with half a pinch of salt. Cook for four minutes in the oven; then cut off the legs and necks, but preserve the heads. Put an ounce of butter into a saucepan, with half a raw carrot and half a raw onion, all cut in pieces, a small bouquet (No. 254), and six whole peppers. Cook for five minutes on the stove, then moisten with half a pint of Espagnole sauce (No. 151), half a glassful of sherry wine, and three tablespoonfuls of mushroom liquor. Season with half a pinch of salt and half a pinch of pepper, and let cook for fifteen minutes more. Stick a good-sized, fine mushroom in the bill of each head, run the bill into the breast of each woodcock, and put them in a sautoire; strain the sauce over, add twelve mushrooms cut in two, and the zest of one lemon. Let cook for six minutes more, then arrange nicely on a dish, decorating it with six bread croûtons (No. 133); pour the sauce over, and serve.

874. Canvas-back Ducks, Roasted.—Procure two fine, fat canvas-back ducks, pick, singe, draw well, and wipe neatly; throw a light pinch of salt inside, run in the head from the end of the neck to the back, truss nicely, and place in a roasting-pan. Sprinkle a little salt over, put them in a brisk oven, and let cook for eighteen minutes; arrange on a very hot dish, untruss, throw two tablespoonfuls of white broth (No. 99) into each duck, and serve with six slices of fried hominy (No. 1035), and currant jelly.

875. Canvas-back Ducks, Broiled.—Take two fine, fat canvas-back ducks; pick, singe, draw, and wipe them thoroughly. Split them through the back without detaching them, and lay them on a dish to season with a good pinch of salt, half a pinch of pepper, and a tablespoonful of oil. Roll them in well, and put them to broil for seven minutes on each side. Dress them on a hot dish, spread a gill of maître-d'hôtel butter over (No. 145), decorate with a little watercress, and serve.

876. Red-head Ducks, roasted—Broiled.—Red-head ducks roasted are prepared exactly the same as canvas-back ducks roasted (No. 874).

Red-head ducks broiled are prepared exactly the same as for canvas-back ducks broiled (No. 875).

877. Reed-birds, Roasted.—Procure twelve freshly killed, fine, fat reed-birds; cut off their legs and wings, pick the eyes out, and remove the skin from the heads, clean and wipe them neatly, and with a skewer remove the gizzards from the sides, then cover their breasts lightly with thin slices of bacon; arrange them on three kidney-skewers, four on each, and lay them in a roasting-pan; season with a pinch of salt, spread a very little butter over, and set them in the oven to roast for seven minutes; remove them to a hot dish with six hot toasts; garnish with watercress and send to the table immediately.

878. Saddle of Venison, Jelly Sauce.—Procure a saddle of a small venison, weighing about five pounds; pare it neatly, remove the sinews from the surface, and lard it with a larding-needle as finely as possible; tie it three times around. Put into the roasting-pan one sliced onion and one sliced carrot; lay in the saddle, seasoning with one pinch of salt; spread half an ounce of butter over, and put it in a brisk oven to roast for forty minutes, basting it frequently with its own gravy. Untie before lifting it from the pan, arrange neatly on a hot dish; pour into the pan half a glassful of Madeira wine and a gill of white broth (No. 99); let come to a boil on the stove. Skim the fat off the gravy, straining the lean part over the saddle. Serve with half a pint of hot currant-jelly sauce (No. 884) separately.

All saddles of venison are prepared the same way, only with different sauces and garnishings.

879. Venison Steak, Broiled.—Procure from a freshly killed deer a fine leg of about five pounds weight; remove the noix, cut it into six steaks; pare and flatten them nicely. Put them on a plate to season with a good pinch of salt, a pinch of pepper, the third of a pinch of nutmeg, and one tablespoonful of oil. Roll them in well, and put them to broil for five minutes on each side. Dress on a hot dish, and spread a gill of maître-d'hôtel butter (No. 145) over; decorate the dish with a little watercress, and serve.

All venison steaks are prepared the same way, only served with different sauces and garnishings.

880. Venison Steak, Londonderry Sauce.—To be prepared the same as for the above (No. 879). Cut into Julienne-shaped pieces half an ounce of citron, also the zest of half a small, sound lemon cut in the same way. Place them in a saucepan with a glassful of good port wine; cook for two or three minutes at most. Add now a gill of currant jelly, stir all well together until the jelly is thoroughly dissolved, add just a little Cayenne pepper, but no more than the equivalent of the third of a saltspoonful. Allow to come to a boil. Pour the sauce on the hot serving-dish, place the steaks one overlapping another, and serve very hot.

881. Venison Steak, Colbert Sauce.—Proceed the same as for No. 879, serving with half a pint of hot Colbert sauce (No. 190).

882. Venison Steak, Purée of Chestnuts.—The same as for No. 879, serving with half a pint of purée of chestnuts (No. 131).

883. Venison Steak, Mashed Potatoes.—The same as for No. 879, serving with a pint of mashed potatoes and a little gravy (No. 998).

884. Venison Steaks, Currant-Jelly Sauce.—The same as in No. 879, serving with the following sauce: put in a saucepan on a hot range a wine-glassful of good port wine, let it come to a boil; then add half a pint of currant jelly (No. 1326), thoroughly stir until the jelly is well dissolved, pour in a gill of sauce Espagnole (No. 151); let again come to a boil, then pour the sauce on a hot dish; dress the steaks over it, one overlapping another, and send to the table hot.

885. Venison Chops, Chestnut Purée.—Have six fine venison chops;

pare, flatten a little, and place them on a plate with a good pinch of salt, half a pinch of pepper, and a tablespoonful of oil. Roll them in well, and put them to broil for four minutes on each side ; arrange half a pint of hot purée of chestnuts (No. 131) on a dish. Place the chops over, and serve with a good gravy thrown over all.

886. Civet of Venison, Poivrade Sauce.—Procure two and a half pounds of venison, the lower part if possible (for the lean parts are preferable), cut it into small square pieces, and lay them in an earthen jar, with one sliced onion, half a bunch of parsley-roots, a sprig of thyme, two bay-leaves, twelve whole peppers, two pinches of salt, half a pinch of pepper, and half a glassful of vinegar. Let them marinate for twelve hours. Drain off the juice, and put the venison in a sautoire with an ounce of clarified butter ; let cook for ten minutes, then add three tablespoonfuls of flour, stirring well. Moisten with one and a half pints of broth (No. 99), also the marinade-liquor (or juice), well strained. Season with a pinch of salt and half a pinch of pepper, and let cook again for forty minutes. Arrange the civet nicely on a hot dish, sprinkle a little chopped parsley over, and serve.

887. Civet of Venison à la Française.—Prepare the venison exactly the same as for No. 886, and after marinating it twelve hours, drain it well from the marinade-juice, and place it in a saucepan with an ounce of clarified butter, and let brown for ten minutes on a moderate fire ; then add three tablespoonfuls of flour, constantly stirring while adding it. Moisten with one and a half glassfuls of red wine, also a pint of hot white broth (No. 99). Season with half a pinch of salt and half a pinch of pepper, then stir well again until boiling, and add twelve well-peeled, small, sound onions, and one ounce of salt pork cut into small, square pieces, also a bouquet (No. 254). Let cook all together for forty minutes ; and four minutes before serving add twelve whole mushrooms. Dress on a hot dish, suppress the bouquet, decorate with bread croûtons as in No 133, all round the dish, and serve.

888. Civet of Venison à la Parisienne.—The same as for the above (No. 887), omitting the salt pork, and substituting for it eighteen small mushrooms instead of twelve.

889. Venison Pie à l'Américaine.—Have three pounds of venison cut into small, square pieces (the parings are preferable) ; place them in a saucepan with an ounce of butter, and brown them well for six minutes, then add one tablespoonful of flour ; stir well, and moisten with a quart of white broth (No. 99) ; throw in six small, glazed, white onions, a bouquet (No. 254), two pinches of salt, one pinch of pepper, and the third of a pinch of nutmeg. Let cook on the stove for forty-five minutes with the lid on, and when done, lay the stew into a deep dish ; cover with a good pie-crust (No. 1077), carefully wetting the edges ; egg the surface with beaten egg, make two incisions on each side and a small hole in the centre, then bake in the oven for forty minutes. Prepare a dish with a folded napkin, lay upon this the dish containing the pie, and serve.

890. Antelope Steak, Russian Sauce.—Prepared exactly the same as

Venison steak (No. 879), and served with half a pint of hot Russian sauce (No. 211) on the dish, and the steak over it.

891. Antelope Chops, Port Wine Sauce.—Broil six fine antelope chops exactly the same as in No. 885. Heat a glassful of port wine in a saucepan, add two cloves, one bay-leaf, eighteen whole peppers, a gill of currant jelly (No. 1326), thoroughly stir until the jelly is completely dissolved, then thicken with half a gill of sauce Espagnole (No. 151), lightly heat again ; then strain on a hot serving-dish, neatly dress the chops over it, and send to the table very hot.

892. Hare, Roasted, Stuffed.—Procure two fine hares, cut them in half, that is, separating the fore-quarters from the hind-quarters. Bone the saddles down to the legs, but not the legs ; place them on a deep earthen dish, pour in a wine-glassful of white wine, adding one medium-sized, sound, sliced lemon, one peeled and sliced onion, one sprig of thyme ; seasoning with a pinch and a half of salt, a pinch of pepper, and two cloves. Roll the saddles well several times in the seasoning, and put aside to steep for at least twelve hours.

Stuffing.—Place in a saucepan on the hot range half a good-sized, sound, chopped onion with a tablespoonful of butter ; cook for one minute, then add two ounces of sausage-meat, six chopped mushrooms, a teaspoonful of chopped parsley, season with half a pinch of salt and the third of a pinch of pepper. Cook all together for six minutes. Let cool, until needed.

Peel four fine, sound apples, cut each into six equal parts, remove the cores ; place them in a pan on the fire with half a glassful of white wine or good cider. Boil for four minutes, then place this with the above forcemeat, and mix all well together.

Take the marinated hares, stuff the saddles (which were boned) with the above stuffing evenly, give them a nice round shape, and tie so as to hold them firm ; arrange a piece of larding pork over each saddle, then lay them in a roasting-pan, with one carrot and one onion cut into slices and placed at the bottom of the pan ; pour one pint of white broth (No. 99) right over the hares. Place in the hot oven, and roast for forty-five minutes, taking care to baste frequently with its own gravy. Remove from the oven, untie, dress on a hot dish, strain the gravy over the saddles, nicely decorate the dish with heart-shaped croûtons (No. 133) all around, and serve.

The fore-quarters can be utilized for Civet, etc., as desired.

893. Civet of Hare à la Française.—Remove the entire skin from a good-sized, tender hare, neatly draw it, preserving the blood, if there is any, and also the liver, the gall being carefully removed. Place the blood and liver on the same dish, and proceed to cut the hare into twelve pieces. Put them into a stone jar, seasoning with one and a half good pinches of salt, a good pinch of pepper, a third of a pinch of nutmeg, one sliced onion, one sprig of thyme, two bay-leaves, and half a glassful of white wine. Mix all well together, and steep well for six hours. Lift out the pieces of hare, and put them in a saucepan with one ounce of butter, adding twelve glazed, small onions, and one ounce of salt pork, cut into small pieces ; let cook on a brisk fire for ten minutes, then add three tablespoonfuls of flour, stir well, and moisten with a glassful of red wine, also half a pint of white broth (No. 99). Stir until it boils, then season again with half a pinch of salt and half a pinch of pepper ; cook for one hour longer, and fifteen minutes before it is done put in the blood, heart, and liver, finely chopped and all well mixed together. Serve on a dish with six croûtons (No. 133).

894. Gibelotte of Hare.—Proceed exactly the same as for the above (No. 893), replacing the glassful of red wine by a full pint of white broth (No. 99), and adding twelve whole mushrooms four minutes before serving.

895. Fillets of Hare, Sauce Poivrade.—Have two fine English or American hares ; clean them neatly as for No. 893, cut them off from the end of the rack, remove the skin from the fillets, and lard the surface with a small needle. Put them on a dish, and season with a pinch and a half of salt, half a pinch of pepper, and the third of a pinch of nutmeg ; add one onion, and one carrot cut in pieces, also three tablespoonfuls of white wine. Let all souse together for two hours, then transfer the whole to a roasting-pan, with any scraps of pork-rind, one sliced carrot, and a sliced onion at the bottom of the pan ; put it in the oven, and let cook for thirty minutes. Place the fillets on a dish, add to the pan one gill of hot broth (No. 99), let come to a boil, and then strain the gravy over, and serve with half a pint of poivrade sauce (No. 194) separately.

A pinch of salt represents 205 grains, or a tablespoonful.
Half a pinch of pepper represents 38 grains, or a teaspoonful.
A third of a pinch of nutmeg represents 13 grains, or half a teaspoonful.

VEGETABLES.

896. Artichokes à la Barigoul—Lean.—Take three large, fine, sound French artichokes, parboil them for three minutes, drain, and pare the tips as well as the bottoms. Remove the chokes with a vegetable-scoop. Place them in a saucepan, with a medium-sized, sliced carrot, one sound, sliced onion, and a tablespoonful of good butter. Season the artichokes with a pinch of salt only. Cut up very fine one peeled, sound shallot, and place it in a separate pan with a tablespoonful of butter, and cook it for three minutes, being careful not to let it get brown. Add ten chopped mushrooms, a tablespoonful of chopped parsley, and a teaspoonful of finely chopped chervil. Season with a pinch of salt and half a pinch of pepper. Cook for five minutes, stirring occasionally meanwhile. Then stuff the artichokes with the preparation, placing on top of each, one whole mushroom. Place them in the hot oven, with a wine-glassful of white wine and a gill of white broth (No. 99); put the lid on the pan, and cook for forty minutes. Remove, and dress them on a hot dish. Add a gill of good Allemande sauce (No. 210) to the sauce of the artichokes, heat up a little, but do not boil; strain it into a bowl, and serve separately.

The Same, Fat.—Pare the tips, as also the bottoms, of three fine, fresh, large French artichokes. Remove the chokes with a vegetable-scoop. Place them in a saucepan with half an ounce of butter, one sliced carrot, two cloves, one bay-leaf, and one sprig of thyme. Cut up very fine one sound, peeled shallot, place it in a saucepan, with one medium-sized green pepper cut up in small dice-shaped pieces, and a tablespoonful of sweet oil. Cook three minutes. Add a quarter of an ounce of minced cooked ham, eight chopped mushrooms, and one tablespoonful of well-cleaned rice. Let cook for three minutes. Season with a pinch of salt and half a pinch of pepper; add a glassful of white wine, cook for five minutes longer. Add half a gill of tomato sauce (No. 205), and let cook for five minutes more. Stuff the artichokes with the above; arrange a thin slice of larding pork on top of each, place them on the hot stove, with half a glassful of white wine; boil for two minutes, then add half a gill of white broth (No. 99); cover the pan, place in the hot oven, and let cook for forty minutes. Remove from the oven; dress the artichokes on a hot dish, add a gill of Madeira sauce (No. 185) to the gravy. Reduce it for three minutes; strain it into a bowl, and serve separately, very hot.

897. Artichokes Sautés.—Cut six fine, solid, green artichokes into quarters, and remove the choke entirely. Trim the leaves neatly, and parboil them for five minutes in salted and acidulated water. Remove, and drain them thoroughly. Lay them in a sautoire; season with a pinch of salt, a pinch of pepper, and add two ounces of good butter. Cover the pan with the lid, and set to cook in a moderate oven for twenty-five minutes. Take it out, place the artichokes in a deep dish, and serve with any desired sauce.

898. Artichokes à la Duxelle.—Chop up finely, and brown for ten minutes in an ounce of butter, six mushrooms, two fine, sound shallots, a quarter of a bunch of parsley, and a clove of garlic. Pare six small or three large artichokes; remove the choke with a spoon, and fry the tops of the leaves in boiling fat for two minutes, being careful to fry only the leaves. Place them in a sautoire, covering each artichoke with a thin slice of salt pork, and laying a buttered paper on top. Moisten with half a pint of hot consommé (No. 100) and half a glassful of white wine. Then place them in a moderate oven to braise for thirty-five minutes. When done, put the prepared gravy into a gill of Italian sauce (No. 188); place the artichokes in a hot dish, pour the sauce over them, and serve.

899. Fried Artichokes.—Take three fine, large French artichokes; remove the first three or four rows of leaves; cut each artichoke into six pieces; remove the choke with a spoon; pare the tips of the remaining leaves, and lay the pieces in a bowl, with two tablespoonfuls of oil, a good pinch of salt, half a pinch of pepper, a third of a pinch of nutmeg, and a tablespoonful of vinegar. 'Stir all well together. Make a batter as for

No. 1186, dip the artichokes in it, and mix well. Have some fat boiling in a deep pan; lift up the pieces with a skimmer and lay them in one by one, putting in as many as the pan will hold. Stir well, detach those pieces which adhere to the others, and after twelve minutes, or when they are of a golden color, take them out with a strainer. Throw a good handful of parsley-greens into the pan, and as the fat ceases to crackle, after three minutes, take it up; drain through a napkin sprinkled with a little salt. Pile the artichokes on a dish, dome-shaped, garnish with fried parsley, and serve.

900. Artichokes, with Sauce.—Trim neatly six small raw artichokes; pare the under parts, lay them in a saucepan, and cover them partially with boiling water, adding a handful of salt and one tablespoonful of vinegar. Let them cook for about forty minutes, then draw out a leaf, and if it detaches easily, the artichokes are sufficiently done. Take them from the water, and put them to drain upside down. Arrange them on a dish with a folded napkin, and serve. Artichokes prepared in this way can be eaten with white, blonde, Hollandaise, or any kind of sauce. To keep the artichokes green, tie a piece of charred wood about the size of an egg in a linen cloth, and pour over it the water to be used for boiling the artichokes.

901. Stuffed Artichokes à la Barigoul.—Pare three fine, large, French artichokes; cut the under leaves straight, then parboil them sufficiently to remove the choke. After laying them in cold water for five minutes, and draining them thoroughly, fill the empty space with a forcemeat made of half an ounce of hashed salt pork, six minced mushrooms, a teaspoonful of chopped parsley, and two hashed shallots, and seasoning with half a pinch of pepper and a third of a pinch of nutmeg, mixing all well together. Tie them up with a string. Heat three tablespoonfuls of olive oil in a pan, and in it brown well the artichokes for three minutes on each side. Place them in a sautoire, and put on top of each artichoke a small slice of fresh pork or veal, or some butter, adding a glassful of broth (No. 99). Cook them in the oven for forty minutes, place the artichokes in a hot dish, pour the sauce over and serve.

902. Artichokes à la Vinaigrette.—Prepare and cook three large or six small, fine artichokes the same as for No. 900. The large ones are to be eaten boiled, cooled, and served with the following sauce in a saucebowl: pound the yolk of a hard-boiled egg in a bowl, dilute it with two spoonfuls of vinegar, season with a pinch of salt, and half a pinch of pepper, a finely chopped shallot, and three tablespoonfuls of good oil. Mix well together, and serve.

The small artichokes may be served in the same way, or they can be eaten raw (as they frequently are in Europe), with the choke removed. Dress the artichokes on a dish with a folded napkin, and serve the sauce in a separate bowl.

903. Artichokes à la Florentine.—Fill six parboiled fresh or conserved artichoke-bottoms with a preparation made of fresh sliced mushrooms, if at hand, a small, cooked cauliflower, weighing half a pound when pared, and stewed in half a pint of béchamel (No. 154), with two tablespoonfuls of grated cheese, seasoned with half a pinch of pepper, and the third of a pinch of nutmeg. Sprinkle with fresh bread-crumbs, and pour over them a little clarified butter; brown in the oven for ten minutes; place the artichokes in a hot dish, pour a gill of hot Madeira sauce (No. 185) over them, and serve.

904. Asparagus, Sauce Hollandaise.—Scrape nicely and wash carefully two bunches of fine asparagus; tie them into six equal bunches, arranging the heads all one way, and chop off the ends evenly. Boil them until they are done in salted water, or from twenty to twenty-two minutes; lift them out, drain them thoroughly on a cloth, and lay them nicely on a dish with a folded napkin. Untie, and serve with half a pint of hot Hollandaise sauce (No. 160), in a separate bowl.

Asparagus with drawn butter is prepared in exactly the same way, and is served with a gill of drawn butter (No. 157).

905. Asparagus à la Vinaigrette.—Prepare two bunches of sound asparagus as in No. 904, and serve with half a pint of sauce vinaigrette (No. 902), after the asparagus has been thoroughly cooled. Asparagus can be served in this way either hot or cold.

906. Asparagus à la Tessinoise.—Boil for only twelve minutes two bunches of fine fresh asparagus as for No. 904, place them on a dish in layers, with grated Swiss or Parmesan cheese between. Lightly brown a third of a medium-sized, sound, chopped onion in one ounce of butter, and pour over the whole; sprinkle the top with a little cheese and fresh bread-crumbs, and cook in a moderate oven for fifteen minutes.

Take out of the oven, and send to the table in the same dish.

907. Fried Egg-plant.—Peel one medium-sized egg-plant, cut it into six round slices, about half an inch in thickness, and season with half a teaspoonful of salt and a teaspoonful of pepper. Dip the pieces in beaten egg and in fresh bread-crumbs, and fry them in hot fat for five minutes. Remove, salt slightly again, and drain them well; serve on a hot dish over a folded napkin.

908. Broiled Egg-plant.—Peel neatly a sound, medium-sized egg-plant, and cut it into six even slices half an inch thick, in such a way that one egg-plant will be sufficient. Place the slices in a dish; season them with a pinch of salt and half a pinch of pepper, and throw over them a tablespoonful of sweet oil. Mix well together; then arrange the slices on the broiler, and broil them for five minutes on each side. Remove them from the fire, place them in a hot dish, spread a gill of maître d'hôtel (No. 145) over them, and send them to the table.

909. Stuffed Egg-plant.—Cut a good-sized egg-plant into six parts, so that the peel remains intact on one side. Make four incisions inside of each piece, and fry them for one minute in boiling fat; dig out the fleshy part of the egg-plant with a potato-scoop, and fill it with any forcemeat at hand. Sprinkle the top with bread-crumbs and a little clarified butter; brown well in the oven for ten minutes, and serve.

910. Beet-roots, Boiled Plain.—Wash a quart of sound, young beet-roots thoroughly in cold water. Place them in a saucepan, covering them with cold water; season with a handful of salt and two tablespoonfuls of vinegar; put on the lid and cook for one hour and ten minutes. Take them from the fire; lift them from the water, and peel them while they are warm. When done, put them in a stone jar; strain over them the liquor in which they were boiled; spread two tablespoonfuls of powdered sugar on top; cover them, and put them away in a cool place for use when required.

Beet-roots are generally served as a salad, a hors-d'œuvre, or a garnishing for salad.

911. Beet-roots Sautées au Beurre.—With the same quantity of beet-roots proceed as in No. 910; when cooked and peeled, cut them up in clove-shaped pieces; then put them in a sautoire with one ounce of butter, seasoning with a pinch of pepper, and sprinkling a very little powdered sugar over them. Let them cook on the stove for six minutes, carefully tossing them from time to time; then arrange them in a hot vegetable-dish, and serve.

912. Beet-roots Sautées à la Crême.—Proceed the same as in No. 911, adding half a pint of hot béchamel (No. 154) three minutes before serving.

913. Mushrooms Sautées à la Bordelaise.—Select a pound of the largest, driest, thickest, and firmest mushrooms procurable; pare neatly, wash them well, drain, and cut lozenge-shaped. Place them in an earthen dish, sprinkle them with a tablespoonful of good oil, a pinch of salt, and twelve whole peppers, and leave them in the marinade for two hours. Take them out and stew them for six minutes; when done, place them on the serving-dish, and cover them with the following sauce: Place in a sautoire three tablespoonfuls of oil, a teaspoonful of parsley, the same of chives, and a clove of crushed garlic, all well chopped. Heat for five minutes; then add them to the mushrooms, which are ready to serve.

914. Mushrooms Sautés on Toast.—Choose a pound of fine, sound, large, fresh mushrooms, neatly pare off the ends, clean, and wash them well. Drain, and place them in a sautoire with an ounce of good butter. Season with a pinch of salt and half a pinch of pepper. Cover, and let them cook for ten minutes, tossing them well meanwhile. Squeeze in the juice of half a medium-sized sound lemon; add a pinch of chopped parsley, nicely sprinkled over. Place six pieces of toasted bread on a hot dish, dress the mushrooms over the toasts, and serve.

915. Mushrooms Sautés à la Crême.—Prepare a pound of fine, fresh mushrooms exactly the same as above (No. 914), and if very large cut them in two. Place them in a sautoire with an ounce of good butter. Season with a pinch of salt and half a pinch of pepper, then put the lid on, and cook on a moderate fire for six minutes; then add two tablespoonfuls of velouté sauce (No. 152), and half a cupful of sweet cream. Cook again for four minutes, and serve them in a very hot dish with six heart-shaped bread croûtons (No. 133) around it.

916. Mushrooms Broiled on Toast.—Pare neatly, wash well, and dry thoroughly one pound of fine, large mushrooms. Lay them on a dish, season with a pinch of salt, half a pinch of pepper, and a tablespoonful of sweet oil. Roll them in well; then put them on to broil for four minutes on each side; arrange them on a hot dish with six slices of toast; pour a gill of maltre d'hôtel butter (No. 145) over the mushrooms, and serve.

917. Blanched Cabbage.—Pare off the outer leaves from a medium-sized cabbage; cut it into four square pieces, wash thoroughly, dry, and put it in a saucepan covering it with salted hot water. Cook for ten minutes, drain, and put it into cold water to cool off; remove from the water, and drain again.

All cabbages are blanched before using them, with the exception of stuffed cabbage, which must be left whole.

918. Cabbage with Cream.—Drain, and let cool a well-blanched cabbage (No. 917); chop it up, and place it in a saucepan with two ounces of butter, seasoning with a good pinch of salt, half a pinch of pepper, and the third of a pinch of grated nutmeg; add a tablespoonful of flour, stir well, and moisten with a cupful of cream. Reduce until the cabbage and gravy are well incorporated, which will take about forty-five minutes. Arrange on a hot dish, and serve.

919. Stuffed Cabbage.—Cut out the root and heart from a medium-sized cabbage-head, and pick off several of the outer leaves; parboil the rest as for No. 917. After removing it from the fire, open the leaves carefully, so as not to break them; then season the cabbage with a pinch of salt and half a pinch of pepper, and fill the inside of the leaves with a good sausage forcemeat (No. 220). Close them up, and tie the cabbage so that none of the stuffing escapes; then lay it in a sautoire containing one cut-up carrot, one cut-up onion, a piece of lard skin, and half a pint of white broth (No. 99). Cover with a little fat from the soup-stock; lay a buttered paper on top, and let cook for one hour in the oven, basting it occasionally with its own juice; untie, and serve with half a pint of Madeira sauce (No. 185).

920. Cabbage for Garnishing.—Prepare a cabbage exactly the same as for No. 919; divide it into six parts, stuff each one with sausage forcemeat (No. 220), wrap them up, and tie, rolling them well. Put them in a sautoire garnished the same as for the stuffed cabbage, and cook for forty minutes in the oven; untie, and serve when needed.

921. Pork and Cabbage.—Pare neatly, and divide a medium-sized cabbage into four pieces; wash them well, parboil for ten minutes, and then put them into any kind of vessel with a pound of salt pork, well washed, three cervelas, a branch of celery, one onion, two large carrots, a blade each of bay-leaf and thyme, half a pinch of pepper, but no salt, and cover with a buttered paper. Let simmer on a gentle fire for one hour and a half; then place the cabbage in a dish, using a skimmer; also the pork and sausages, laying them on top; decorate the dish with the rest of the vegetables, and serve.

922. Brussels Sprouts, Sautés au Beurre.—Pare neatly, and pick off the outer dead leaves of one pound of imported Brussels sprouts, or one and a half pounds of domestic sprouts; wash them thoroughly, drain, and cook them in boiling salted water for seven minutes. Drain, and let cool in cold water; drain them once more, then throw the sprouts into a sautoire containing two ounces of butter. Season with half a pinch each of salt and pepper, adding a teaspoonful of chopped parsley; cook slightly for five minutes; then serve.

923. Brussels Sprouts, Sautés à la Crême.—Pare, pick, and blanch one pound of sprouts as in No. 922. When well drained, put them in a sautoire with two tablespoonfuls of velouté (No. 152); season with half a pinch of salt, and the third of a pinch each of pepper and nutmeg. Add half a cupful of sweet cream. Let them heat, but not boil, for five minutes, tossing them frequently; dress on a hot dish, and serve.

924. Sourkrout.—After washing three pints of imported sourkrout in several waters, drain it well, and put it in a saucepan with a large piece of well-washed salt pork, three cervelas, two carrots, two whole onions, half a cupful of roast meat-fat, six juniper berries, a glassful of good white wine, and a pint of white broth (No. 99). Let it cook slowly for three hours; then drain the sourkrout, dish it up with the pork on top, which can either be served in one piece, or divided into six slices, arranging the cervelas around, nicely dressed.

925. Cauliflower, Boiled with Butter.—Take one large or two small cauliflowers; pare, pick, and examine them well to see if anything adheres which should be removed; wash them thoroughly in fresh water, and then put in a saucepan, covering with cold water; season with a handful of salt and half a pinch of pepper, and add an ounce of kneaded butter. After cooking about thirty minutes, drain them through a colander, and lay them on a dish, pouring over them a sauce made of one ounce of good butter, a third of a pinch of salt, the same of pepper, and a tablespoonful of vinegar, then serve.

Cauliflowers prepared the same way can be served with a white sauce or Hollandaise sauce. They are also eaten as a salad when cold.

926. Cauliflower au Gratin.—Pare, pick, cook, and drain one large or two medium-sized cauliflowers as for No. 925. Cut off the roots; then place them on a buttered baking-dish, covering them with a pint of good béchamel (No. 154), to which three tablespoonfuls of grated Parmesan cheese have been added. Sprinkle the top with three more tablespoonfuls of grated cheese and a little fresh bread-crumbs. Place the dish in the oven and let it get a golden brown color. It will require about twenty minutes' cooking, but care must be taken to turn the dish frequently, so that the cauliflower will be equally well browned all over.

927. Carrots Sautées à la Crême.—Pare\off the ends of six good-sized carrots, scrape them neatly, wash thoroughly, and cut them in rounds half an inch thick. Cook them in white broth (No. 99), (salted water will answer as well); cover the saucepan, and let them cook for thirty minutes. Remove, drain, and place them in a sautoire, with three tablespoonfuls of béchamel (No. 154), and a cupful of cream or milk. Season with a pinch of salt, half a pinch of pepper, and the third of a pinch of nutmeg. After ten minutes, place them in a hot dish, sprinkle a good pinch of chopped parsley over, and serve.

928. Celery, with Gravy à la Bonne Femme.—Procure two bunches of fine Kalamazoo celery. If there should be four heads in each bunch, reserve two for table celery, as hors-d'œuvres. Pare the outer branches, and clean thoroughly, cutting off the hard and green leaves. Cut them into equal lengths, and blanch them in boiling water for five minutes; drain, and add half a pint of broth (No. 99) to the water. Put the celery into a gill of white roux (No. 135) in a sautoire, and season with a pinch of salt, twelve whole peppers, and a third of a pinch of nutmeg. When the celery is sufficiently cooked, or after twenty-five minutes, finish the sauce with a gill of clear gravy or half an ounce of butter. Place the celery in a hot dish, pour the sauce over and serve.

929. Celery with Cream.—Pare nicely four heads of fine celery, and cut it into pieces two inches in length; wash thoroughly; remove from the water with the hands, and lay it on a napkin. By so doing no sand will adhere to the celery. Blanch it in boiling salted water for five minutes; remove, drain, and put it in a sautoire with two ounces of butter and one tablespoonful of fecula; stir all well together, and moisten with half a pint of consommé (No. 100). Cook and reduce the whole for twenty minutes; when done, thicken with two beaten egg yolks diluted in three tablespoonfuls of cream, and add the third of a pinch of grated nutmeg. Serve garnished with six croûtons (No. 133).

930. Celery à la Moëlle de Bœuf.—Take six heads of fine celery, cut off the green leaves, pare neatly, wash thoroughly, drain, and tie each head near the end where the green part has been cut away. Blanch them in salted boiling water for ten minutes, then remove, drain, and put them in a sautoire, with a pint of Madeira sauce (No. 185). Cook for fifteen minutes. Arrange the heads on a hot dish; remove the strings, and add to the sauce in the sautoire eighteen slices of marrow half an inch thick. Cook for one minute, being careful not to break the pieces of marrow; pour the sauce over the celery, and serve.

931. Cardons à la Moëlle.—Prepared exactly the same as in No. 930.

932. Chicory, with Cream or White Sauce.—Clean and pick three large heads of chicory; throw away all the outer green leaves; wash them in two waters, drain, and blanch them in boiling, salted water. Remove them after ten minutes, and cool them in fresh water. Take them out, and press out the water thoroughly; then chop up the chicory, and place it with four ounces of butter in a saucepan, and cook a quarter of an hour, or until dry. Pour over it two glassfuls of cream or milk, a very little at a time, reduce, and grate in a third of a pinch of nutmeg; add a pinch of salt and half a pinch of pepper; stir well together, leave it on for five minutes, and serve with six heart-shaped croûtons (No. 133) around the dish.

933. Chicory, with Gravy.—Take six large, fine, fresh heads of chicory, pare any outer leaves that may be damaged, leaving the root intact; wash well in two waters, remove, and put them to blanch for ten minutes in salted boiling water. Take them out, put them back into cold water, and let them cool off thoroughly. Drain neatly, and cut them in halves. Put a piece of lard skin at the bottom of a sautoire, add one carrot, one onion, both cut up, and a bouquet (No. 254). Place the chicory on top, season with half a pinch of salt, half a pinch of pepper, and a third of a pinch of nutmeg, and cover with a buttered paper. Place the sautoire on the stove, and when the chicory is a golden color (not letting it take longer than ten minutes), moisten with half a pint of white broth (No. 99). Put it in the oven for thirty minutes; arrange the chicory on a hot dish, strain the sauce over, and serve.

934. Chicory for Garnishing.—Prepare exactly as for No. 933, using it when needed.

935. Cucumbers à la Poulette.—Peel three fine, large cucumbers, blanch them in salted boiling water for five minutes, drain, and cut them into pieces one inch thick. Place them in a sautoire with one ounce of butter, strew over them a pinch of very fine flour, stir well, and moisten with half a pint of white broth (No. 99), seasoning with half a pinch of salt, and the same of pepper. Stir well until it boils, and reduce the whole for fifteen minutes, adding a teaspoonful of chopped parsley, a third of a pinch of nutmeg, two beaten egg yolks, and two tablespoonfuls of sweet cream. Cook again, without letting it come to a boil, for three minutes, and serve.

936. Cucumbers à la Béchamel.—Peel, pare nicely, and blanch six small, fine cucumbers in salted boiling water for five minutes. Remove, drain, and place them in a sautoire with half a pint of good béchamel sauce (No. 154), half an ounce of butter, the third of a pinch of nutmeg, and three tablespoonfuls of milk. Cook all together for fifteen minutes, and pour the whole on a hot dish, and serve.

937. Stuffed Cucumbers.—Peel six small cucumbers, pare them carefully and shapely; cut off the lower ends, and with a vegetable-spoon empty them, after extracting all the seeds. Place them in slightly acidulated water; rinse them well, and parboil them in boiling water for three minutes. Remove them, and put in cold water to cool. Drain them, and fill the insides with a cooked forcemeat made of the breasts of chickens (No. 226). Line a sautoire with slices of pork-skin; add the cucumbers, season with a pinch of salt and half a pinch of pepper, a bouquet (No. 254), a glassful of white wine, two cloves, and a spoonful of dripping from any kind of roast. Cover with a piece of buttered paper, and place it in a slow oven to cook gently for twenty minutes. When done, transfer them carefully to a hot dish; free them entirely from any fat, pour half a pint of Madeira sauce (No. 185) over them, and serve.

938. Stewed Cucumbers for Garnishing.—Peel and slice three large, fine cucumbers; marinate them with a pinch of salt, half a pinch of pepper, a tablespoonful of vinegar, and one sliced onion. Leave them in for one hour; strain, and put the whole into a saucepan with a pint of Espagnole sauce (No. 151). Cook for twenty minutes; strain through a fine sieve, and use for any garnishing required.

939. Spinach Blanched au Naturel.—Take a peck of fresh, sound spinach, cut off the stalks, pare neatly, wash it twice in plenty of water, lifting it out with the hands. Place it in boiling salted water, and boil it for fifteen minutes. Remove, and drain it thoroughly; place it in cold water again, and let it cool. Lift and drain, pressing it well; lay it on a wooden board, and hash it very fine.

940. Spinach à l'Anglaise.—Proceed exactly the same as for No. 939, but the spinach must not be hashed; when well drained put it into a saucepan with one ounce of butter; mix well for five minutes, and it will be ready for any use desired.

941. Spinach à la Vieille Mode.—After the spinach is blanched and well chopped, as for No. 939, put it in a saucepan with an ounce of butter and the third of a pinch of grated nutmeg. Stir with a wooden spoon, and cook for five minutes, adding an ounce of butter kneaded with two tablespoonfuls of flour, two tablespoonfuls of powdered sugar, and half a pint of milk. Stir frequently, and cook for ten minutes; then serve, garnished with six sippets of bread fried in butter.

942. Spinach à la Maître d'Hôtel.—After blanching the spinach as for No. 939, and chopping it very fine, put it dry into a saucepan. Place it to simmer on a moderate fire, seasoning with a pinch of salt, half a pinch of pepper, and the third of a pinch of grated nutmeg. When warm, add an ounce and a half of butter; stir well, and let it heat for fifteen minutes. Lay it on a hot dish, and decorate it with six bread croûtons (No. 133); then serve.

943. Spinach, with Gravy.—When the spinach is blanched and well drained (No. 939), put it in a saucepan with half a cupful of veal-stock (either the reduced gravy of a fricandeau, or a glaze), cook for ten minutes, and when ready to serve, add a good ounce of butter; melt well together, and serve with six pieces of fried bread.

944. Spinach, with Sugar.—Season the blanched spinach (No. 939) with a very little salt, three lumps of sugar, a little crushed lemon-peel, and two pulverized macaroons. Cook slowly all together for ten minutes, and serve surrounded by six lady-fingers (No. 1231).

945. String Beans, Blanched.—Take two quarts of fresh, tender string beans; break off the tops and bottoms carefully; string both sides, and pare both edges neatly; wash them well in cold water, lift them, and drain. Place them in boiling salted water, and cook for twenty-five minutes. Drain again, and return them to cold water, letting them get thoroughly cool. Lift them out, and dry. They are now ready to use when required, for salads or any other purpose.

946. String Beans, with Cream.—Place the blanched beans (No. 945) in a saucepan with an ounce of butter, and cook on the stove for five minutes, tossing them well. Season with half a pinch of salt, the same of pepper, and add half a bunch of chives and two sprigs of parsley tied together. Pour in half a cupful of fresh cream or milk, diluted with two egg yolks. Heat well, without boiling, for five minutes. Then serve as a *hors-d'œuvre* or *entremet*. Sugar may be added with advantage, if desired.

947. String Beans au Blanc.—String the fresh string beans (No. 945); if too large, cut them lengthwise, and cook them in water with salt and butter; drain, and place them in a saucepan with one ounce of butter; add a teaspoonful of parsley and the same of chopped chives. Cook for five minutes, and when done, thicken the gravy with half a cupful of cream, two egg yolks, and the juice of a lemon. Mix well together for two minutes, and serve.

948. String Beans à l'Anglaise.—Blanch and cook the beans as for No. 945, keep them warm, and of a light green color; place them in a hot dish, pour over them a gill of good melted butter, sprinkle a little chopped parsley on top, and serve very hot.

949. String Beans à la Bretonne.—Cut a medium-sized onion in dice-shaped pieces, and place them in a saucepan with an ounce and a half of butter; let it get a good golden color on the stove for five minutes; then add a tablespoonful of flour. Stir well, and moisten it with a pint of white broth (No. 99). Stir well again, until it comes to a boil; season with half a pinch each of salt and pepper. Add the cooked string beans, with a clove of crushed garlic, to the sauce; cook for ten minutes; place in a hot dish; sprinkle a teaspoonful of chopped parsley over it, and serve.

950. Beans Panachées.—Place half a pint of cooked string beans (No. 945) and the same quantity of flageolets or Lima beans in a sautoire with an ounce and a half of good butter; season with half a pinch each of salt and pepper; toss them well while cooking for five minutes. Place them in a hot dish; sprinkle a light pinch of chopped parsley over them, and send to the table.

951. Red Beans à la Bourguignonne.—Take a quart of sound red beans; pick out all the small stones that are likely to be mixed with them; wash them thoroughly, lay them in plenty of cold water, and let them soak for six hours. Drain, and put them in a saucepan, covering them with fresh water, adding an ounce of butter, a bouquet (No. 254), and a medium-sized onion with two cloves stuck in. Boil for twenty minutes, stirring in a good glassful of red wine; season with a pinch of salt and half a pinch of pepper, and let it cook again for forty-five minutes. Remove, take out the bouquet and onion, and place the beans in a hot, deep dish; decorate with six small glazed onions (No. 972) around the dish, and serve.

Dried red beans, white beans, Lima beans, split dried peas, lentils, or any other kind of dried beans, should always be soaked six hours in fresh water before using them.

952. Fresh Lima Beans.—Take a quart of fresh, shelled Lima beans, or three quarts of unshelled; parboil them in salted water for about twenty minutes, then take them from the fire, drain, and let cool in fresh water. Drain again, and place them in a sautoire with an ounce and a half of good butter, seasoning with half a pinch each of salt and pepper, and the third of a pinch of nutmeg. Cook for five minutes, tossing well; then moisten with two tablespoonfuls of cream, adding a pinch of chopped parsley; mix well together, and serve.

953. Stuffed Lettuce.—Pick, clean, pare nicely, and wash thoroughly six lettuce-heads; parboil them for five minutes, drain them well, and fill the insides with godiveau (No. 221) or sausage forcemeat (No. 220). Tie each head, and put them in a sautoire, laying them down carefully, and adding a gill of Madeira sauce (No. 185), and a gill of white broth (No. 99). Season with half a pinch each of salt and pepper, cover with buttered paper, and cook in the oven for fifteen minutes. Arrange on a hot dish, untie, pour the sauce over, and serve.

954. Macaroni à la Crème.—Boil for three-quarters of an hour three-quarters of a pound of Italian macaroni in plenty of salted water, adding a small piece of butter (half an ounce), and an onion stuck with two cloves. Drain well, and put it back into a saucepan with a third of a pound of butter, a third of a pound of grated Swiss cheese, the same quantity of grated Parmesan cheese, a third of a pinch of nutmeg, and a pinch of pepper. Moisten with half a pint of white broth (No. 99) and four tablespoonfuls of cream. Cook all together for five minutes, stirring well, and when the macaroni becomes ropy, dish it up, and serve.

955. Macaroni au Gratin.—After the macaroni is prepared as for No. 954, place it in a baking-dish, sprinkle over it a little bread-crumbs and grated cheese; pour over it a little clarified butter, and place it in the baking oven for ten minutes, or until it assumes a golden color; then serve.

956. Macaroni à l'Italienne.—Prepare three-quarters of a pound of sound Italian macaroni as for No. 954; place it in a saucepan with a gill of tomato sauce (No. 205), a gill of Madeira sauce (No. 185), and a quarter of a pound of grated Parmesan cheese; season with half a pinch of pepper and the third of a pinch of nutmeg; then let cook slowly for ten minutes, tossing frequently. Arrange on a hot dish, and serve with some grated cheese, separately.

957. Macaroni à la Napolitaine.—Boil the macaroni in salt and water as for No. 954; drain, place it in a saucepan, and add half a pint of good Espagnole sauce (No. 151), half a pint of tomato sauce (No. 205), a quarter of a pound of grated cheese, two truffles, six mushrooms, and half an ounce of cooked, smoked beef-tongue, all cut up in dice-shaped pieces. Cook together on a brisk stove for ten minutes, tossing them well meanwhile, and serve.

958. Macaroni à la Milanaise.—Prepare exactly the same as for No. 957, cutting the truffles, mushrooms, and beef-tongue julienne-shaped.

959. Spaghetti à la Napolitaine.—Boil three-quarters of a pound of sound, fine spaghetti as for the macaroni in No. 954; drain, and put it back into a saucepan with half a pint of tomato sauce (No. 205), half a pint of Espagnole (No. 151), six mushrooms, two truffles, and a small piece of cooked, smoked, red beef-tongue, all cut up dice-shaped. Season with half a pinch of pepper and the third of a pinch of nutmeg, adding a quarter of a pound of grated Parmesan cheese. Cook for ten minutes, tossing well, and serve with a little cheese, separately.

960. Spaghetti à l'Italienne.—Place the spaghetti in a saucepan as for No. 959; add a pint of tomato sauce (No. 205), and a quarter of a pound of grated Parmesan cheese; season with half a pinch of pepper and a third of a pinch of nutmeg, and cook for ten minutes, tossing well, and serving as in No. 959.

961. Spaghetti au Gratin.—Prepare three-quarters of a pound of boiled spaghetti as in No. 959, place it in a saucepan, moistening with half a pint of Allemande sauce (No. 210), and half a pint of béchamel sauce (No. 154). Season with one pinch of pepper, and the third of a pinch of nutmeg, adding a quarter of a pound of grated cheese. Toss well, put it in a baking-dish, sprinkle the top with grated cheese and fresh bread-crumbs; pour over it a very little clarified butter, and place it in the oven. When of a fine golden color, after about fifteen minutes, take from the oven, and serve.

962. Boiled Green Corn.—Pare off the outer leaves and silk of six young and tender ears of corn, and place them in a saucepan, covering them with water. Add half a cupful of milk, half an ounce of butter, and a handful of salt. Cook for twenty minutes, and serve on a folded napkin.

963. Corn Sauté à la Crême.—Take six ears of cooked green corn, prepared as for No. 962, drain, cut off the corn from the cobs with a sharp knife, being very careful that none of the cob adheres to the corn. Place it in a sautoire with a gill of hot béchamel sauce (No. 154), half a cupful of cream, and half an ounce of butter; season with half a pinch each of salt and pepper, and the third of a pinch of nutmeg. Cook gently on the stove for five minutes, place in a hot dish, and serve.

964. Corn Sauté au Beurre.—Proceed as for No. 963, adding one ounce of butter, but suppressing the other ingredients. Season the same, but cook only for eight minutes, tossing it well. Place in a hot dish, and serve.

965. Corn Fritters.—Prepare four young, tender, good-sized, fresh ears of green corn exactly as for No. 963; after draining it carefully, place it in a china bowl; season with a pinch of salt and half a pinch of pepper, and add two fresh eggs, a quarter of a pound of well-sifted flour, and half a pint of cold milk. Do not beat the mixture, but stir it vigorously with a wooden spoon for five minutes, and it will be sufficiently firm. Butter well a frying-pan, take a kitchen ladle that contains the equivalent of a gill, and with this put the preparation into the pan in twelve parts; be careful they do not touch one another, and let them get a good golden color on each side for four minutes. Dress them on a folded napkin, and serve.

966. Barley Fritters.—The same as in No. 965, substituting boiled barley for corn.

967. Glazed Turnips, with Gravy.—Pare, and cut pear-shaped, twelve equal-sized, small white turnips; parboil them for five minutes, and drain them when done. Butter the bottom of a sautoire capable of holding them, one beside the other, and let them get a golden color, adding half a pint of powdered sugar. Moisten with half a pint of white broth (No. 99), half a pinch of salt, and add a very small stick of cinnamon. Cover with a buttered paper cut the shape of the sautoire, and place it in the oven to cook for twenty minutes. When the turnips are cooked, lift off the paper. Place the turnips on a hot dish, and reduce the gravy to a glaze for six minutes. Arrange them nicely on a dish, pour half a gill of good broth (No. 99) into the saucepan to loosen the glaze, remove the cinnamon, and throw the sauce over the turnips.

968. Onions, with Cream.—Peel twelve medium-sized, sound onions; pare the roots without cutting them, and place them in a saucepan; cover with salted water, add a bouquet (No. 254), and cook for forty-five minutes. Lift them from the saucepan, and lay them on a dish; cover them with half a pint of cream sauce (No. 181), mixed with two tablespoonfuls of the broth they were cooked in, and serve.

969. Fried Onions.—Peel, pare, and slice round-shaped, four medium-sized onions. Lay them first in milk, then in flour, and fry them in very hot fat for eight minutes. Lift them up and lay them on a cloth to dry. Serve on a dish with a folded napkin, with a little fried parsley.

970. Stuffed Onions.—Peel six medium-sized Spanish onions; empty out the centres with a vegetable-scoop; parboil them for three minutes, and turn them upside down on a cloth to drain. Fill the insides with sausage forcemeat (No. 220). Line the bottom of a sautoire with a piece of lard skin, and one carrot and one onion, both cut up; lay the onions on top, and moisten with half a pint of broth (No. 99). Cover with a buttered paper; then put it in the oven to glaze for forty minutes, taking care to baste frequently. Place them in a hot dish; strain the gravy over them, and serve.

971. Minced Onions.—Peel and pare three medium-sized onions; cut them in two, and mince them into fine slices. Place them in a sautoire, with half an ounce of butter, and let them get a good golden color on the stove for ten minutes, tossing them briskly. Place them in a bowl, and use when required.

972. Glazed Onions for Garnishing.—Select one quart of small onions; peel the sides only, and pare the roots neatly, being careful not to cut them. Place them in a sautoire with half an ounce of clarified butter, and sprinkle them with half a pinch of powdered sugar. Glaze them in a slow oven for fifteen minutes; place them in a stone jar, and use for garnishing when required.

973. Sorrel au Maigre.—Pick off the stems from half a peck of sorrel; wash it in several waters, drain, and chop up with a head of well-cleansed lettuce. Add half a bunch of chervil, and chop all together very fine. Place all in a saucepan, stir well together on the hot stove for three minutes, and then place it in the oven until the vegetables are well dissolved; then add an ounce and a half of butter, and stir again for about ten minutes, or until the sorrel is reduced to a pulp. Season with a pinch of salt and half a pinch of pepper, and pour into it a thickening of two egg yolks and half a cupful of cream; stir well, without boiling, and serve.

974. Sorrel au Gras.—Dissolve the same quantity of sorrel as in No.

973, adding enough butter to form it into a perfect pulp (one ounce and a half will answer); stir it until it begins to bubble; then moisten it with half a pint of gravy or good stock, roast-beef gravy, or reduced broth. Cook it for five minutes, and use this purée as a sauce for various meats.

975. Stuffed Peppers.—Fry for one minute only, six medium-sized green peppers in very hot fat; drain and skin them properly, and cut a round piece off the bottom to use for a cover. Remove the insides, and fill them with a good sausage forcemeat (No. 220); put on the round cover previously cut off, and lay them on an oiled baking-tin. Moisten the peppers lightly with sweet oil, and place them in a slow oven to cook for fifteen minutes; then arrange them on a hot dish, and serve with a gill of demi-glace sauce (No. 185).

976. Green Peas à l'Ancienne Mode.—Take three quarts of unshelled, young, tender green peas; shell them carefully, and keep them wrapped up in a wet napkin until needed. Clean, drain, and tie up a lettuce-head; put it in a saucepan with the peas; season with a pinch of salt; cover with a glassful of water, and add a quarter of a pound of very good butter. After cooking for a quarter of an hour, remove the lettuce, and when ready to serve, thicken the peas with three spoonfuls of cream, diluted with one egg yolk, adding half a pinch of white pepper, and a spoonful of powdered sugar. Let all thicken together for five minutes, and serve immediately in a tureen.

977. Green Peas à la Française.—Shell carefully three quarts of fine, young, tender, fresh green peas, and place them in a saucepan with one ounce of butter and half a cupful of water. Knead together with a wooden spoon; strain off the water, and add a bouquet (No. 254), one small onion, a well-cleansed lettuce-heart, half a pinch of salt, and a teaspoonful of powdered sugar. Cover the saucepan, and cook very slowly for half an hour; remove the bouquet and onion; lay the lettuce upon a dish, incorporate into the peas half an ounce of fresh butter, and cook until it thickens, which will require at least five minutes. Pour the peas dome-formed over the lettuce, and send to the table.

978. Green Peas à l'Anglaise.—Procure the same quantity of green peas as for No. 977; put them in a saucepan, and cover them with boiling water. Add a handful of salt, and boil quickly, without covering, for fifteen minutes. Skim the water as soon as the scum rises. When done, strain them through a colander, return them to the saucepan, and toss them well, adding an ounce and a half of fresh butter. Dish them in a vegetable-dish, place another half ounce of butter in the middle, and serve.

979. Green Peas à la Bourgeoise.—Shell three quarts of tender green peas; put them in a saucepan, and toss the peas quickly in a gill of light roux (No. 135); moisten with a pint of boiling water, adding half a pinch each of salt and pepper, a bouquet (No. 254), and a raw lettuce-heart. Reduce it for twenty minutes, or until all the juice has evaporated; then add two raw egg yolks well beaten, with three tablespoonfuls of sweet cream. Stir quickly for four minutes, without allowing it to boil, and then serve, removing the bouquet.

980. Green Peas, with Cream.—Put one ounce of butter in a saucepan with one tablespoonful of flour kneaded well together. Dissolve it; then add the shelled peas as for No. 977, a bouquet (No. 254), a quarter of a bunch of chives, a pinch of salt, and half a pinch of pepper. Cook in their own juice for twenty minutes, then take the saucepan from off the fire. Pour the gravy from the peas into another vessel, add to it half a cupful of cream and a teaspoonful of powdered sugar; pour this sauce over the peas, and heat up once again without boiling, for two minutes, before serving.

981. Green Peas, with Bacon.—Brown in a saucepan half an ounce of butter with two ounces of small, dice-shaped pieces of bacon, and when of a good golden color, take them out, and put a spoonful of flour into the fat to make a roux. Moisten with a pint of white broth (No. 99); replace the bacon, add the raw shelled peas, as for No. 977, one whole onion, a bouquet (No. 254), and half a pinch of pepper. Cover, and let cook on the corner of the stove for thirty minutes; place in a hot, deep dish, and serve.

982. Potatoes, Boiled Plain.—Take twelve medium-sized, fine, sound potatoes; wash them thoroughly, peel off a piece of the skin, about half an inch wide, around each potato, to ensure mealiness, and lay them in a saucepan, covering them with cold water, and adding half a handful of salt; place the lid on, and cook for forty-five minutes. Drain, lay a napkin on a hot dish, in which you envelop the potatoes, and serve.

983. Broiled Potatoes.—Peel six medium-sized, sound, cooked potatoes; cut them in halves; lay them on a dish, and season them with a pinch of salt. Pour two tablespoonfuls of melted butter over them, and roll them well in it. Arrange them on a double broiler, and broil them on a moderate fire for three minutes on each side. Place them in a hot dish, with a folded napkin, and serve.

984. Potatoes à la Génevroise—Peel, wash, and drain four medium-sized, sound potatoes; cut them into julienne-shaped pieces, and wash and drain them again. Season with a pinch of salt and half a pinch of pepper. Butter lightly six tartlet-molds with clarified butter; cover the bottoms with grated Parmesan cheese; arrange a layer of potatoes on top, sprinkle more cheese over them, and continue until all are filled, finishing by sprinkling cheese over the surface and dropping a little clarified butter over all. Set them on a very hot stove for two minutes; then place in a hot oven, and bake them for twenty-five minutes. Unmold, and place them in a hot dish, with a folded napkin, and serve.

985. Potatoes, Maître d'Hôtel.—Take eight medium-sized potatoes, boiled as for No. 982; peel them, cut them into slices, and place them in a saucepan, with an ounce of butter and a pinch of chopped parsley, and season with half a pinch each of salt and pepper, the third of a pinch of nutmeg, and the juice of half a lemon. Warm all together, toss well, and add half a cupful of cream; heat slightly once more, and serve.

986. Potatoes, Parisienne.—Take six good-sized, well-cleansed potatoes; with a round vegetable-spoon cut out the Parisian potatoes; then put them in fresh water; wash well, and drain. Melt an ounce of butter in a sautoire, throw in the potatoes, and season with half a pinch of salt. Place the sautoire in the oven; cook for twenty minutes, and serve on a hot dish with a folded napkin.

987. Potatoes à l'Anglaise à Crû.—Wash well six medium-sized, sound potatoes; cut them into quarters, pare them neatly, clove-garlic-shaped; wash again, drain, and place them in a saucepan. Cover with water, throw in a heavy pinch of salt, put the lid on, and cook for twenty minutes. Drain, and put them in a saucepan, with an ounce of butter, a pinch of chopped parsley, heat slowly for five minutes, toss gently, and serve.

988. Potatoes à l'Anglaise.—Wash well six good-sized potatoes; boil them in salted water for forty-five minutes; peel, and cut them each into quarters. Melt an ounce of butter in a saucepan; add the sliced potatoes, half a pinch of salt, and the third of a pinch of pepper. Cook them on a very slow fire for five minutes, tossing them well, and serve on a very hot dish, sprinkling a little chopped parsley over them.

989. Potatoes, with Bacon.—Cut one ounce of bacon or pork into small pieces; put them in a saucepan, with half an ounce of butter; cook for five minutes; add a spoonful of flour; stir, and brown well for four minutes. Moisten with a pint of white broth (No. 99), and cook for five minutes longer. Put in eight well-peeled, washed, and sliced raw potatoes; season with half a pinch of pepper and the third of a pinch of nutmeg; lay the lid on, and cook for twenty-five minutes. Then skim off the fat, and serve in a hot, deep dish.

990. Potatoes à l'Italienne.—Boil eight medium-sized potatoes in boiling water, as for No. 982 ; peel, put them in a saucepan, and mash them. Add a piece of butter of one ounce, and a piece of fresh bread the size of a French roll, suppressing the crust, and soaking it in milk. Add two more tablespoonfuls of milk, in order to form a pliable paste, three fresh egg yolks, and the whites of the three beaten to a froth ; season with half a pinch of salt, half a pinch of pepper, and the third of a pinch of nutmeg. Mix well together, and pile it high on a baking-dish ; pour over it a little melted butter; sprinkle a little Parmesan cheese over; place it in the oven, and after ten minutes, when of a good golden color, serve.

991. Potatoes à la Lyonnaise.—Cut eight potatoes, boiled, as for No. 982, into round slices ; lay them in a frying-pan with an ounce and a half of butter, and the round slices of a previously fried onion, and season with half a pinch each of salt and pepper. Cook well together for six minutes, until well browned ; toss them well, and serve with a pinch of chopped parsley sprinkled over the whole.

992. Stuffed Potatoes.—Wash and peel about six large potatoes ; cut them, lengthwise, in two, and scoop out the centres carefully with a knife or spoon. Fill the cavities with a sausage forcemeat (No. 220), letting it bulge out a little on the top ; butter a baking-pan, arrange the potatoes on it, and cook in a slow oven for half an hour, or until nicely browned, then serve.

993. Fried Potatoes.—Peel and wash six large potatoes, cut them up into fine slices, a quarter of an inch in thickness; plunge them into very hot, clarified beef suet or fat, and cook slowly. When they are soft, lift them out with a skimmer (it generally takes ten minutes to cook them); heat the fat again to boiling-point, and put the potatoes back. Smooth them down with a skimmer, and after two minutes they will swell up considerably; lift them out with the skimmer, drain, sprinkle a pinch of salt over, and serve on a hot dish with a folded napkin. These potatoes answer for garnishing chops and other meats.

994. Potatoes Sautées au Beurre.—Peel and clean eighteen small, round, raw potatoes, new ones if possible; place two ounces of butter in a saucepan; place it on a hot fire, adding the potatoes; cook them until they are a golden color, which will take fifteen minutes, then drain. Sprinkle over them a pinch of table-salt, and arrange them on a dish without any further seasoning than a little chopped parsley; then serve.

995. Potatoes Sautées.—Take eight good-sized boiled and peeled potatoes (No. 982); cut them in slices a quarter of an inch in thickness; place them in a frying-pan with an ounce and a half of good butter. Season with a pinch of salt and half a pinch of pepper; toss well for eight minutes, dress on a very hot dish, and serve with a little parsley sprinkled over.

996. Potato Balls.—Peel, clean neatly, and boil in salted water for thirty minutes, eight good-sized, sound, round, yellow potatoes; drain and return them to the same pan, and mash them well, adding two egg yolks, and the whites beaten to a froth, three tablespoonfuls of cream, a teaspoonful of chopped parsley, very little chives, half a pinch of salt, and the third of a pinch of nutmeg. Mix well together for two minutes, and dip about half a tablespoonful at a time into frying batter (No. 1185). Slide them into very hot fat, and leave them in for three minutes; this swells them, and forms them into a species of fritters. Place in a very hot dish with a folded napkin, and serve.

997. Potato Croquettes and Quenelles.—Peel, wash, and drain nicely eight medium-sized mealy potatoes; cut them in quarters, put them in a saucepan, cover them with water, add a pinch of salt, cook for thirty minutes, and drain. Lay them in a mortar with an ounce of fresh butter, pound them well, and add three raw egg yolks. Season with half a pinch each of salt and pepper and the third of a pinch of nutmeg; mix well, and then divide into twelve parts, shaping each one like a cork, or any other shape desired. Dip them separately into beaten egg, and roll them in fresh bread-crumbs; fry a golden color for three minutes, and serve on a dish with a folded napkin.

998. Mashed Potatoes.—Peel, wash, drain, and cut into quarters eight good-sized potatoes; put them in a sautoire, cover with water, add a good pinch of salt, and boil for thirty minutes. Drain, rub them through a purée strainer, and put them in a saucepan with an ounce of butter, and half a pinch each of salt and white pepper. Stir well, adding half a cupful of hot milk, until it becomes of a good consistency. Serve, garnished with six pieces of bread fried in butter.

999. Potatoes à l'Hollandaise.—After boiling eight good-sized potatoes as for No. 982, peel, and cut them into quarters ; put them in a sautoire with an ounce of butter and half a pinch of chopped parsley ; season with half a pinch each of salt and pepper, toss them gently, and warm them slightly for five minutes. Place in a hot dish, and serve.

Sweet potatoes à l'Hollandaise are prepared the same way.

1000. Potatoes à la Gastronome.—Peel, clean, and with a No. 3 tube cut twelve medium-sized potatoes into inch-and-a-half-long pieces. Place them in a saucepan ; cover with water, add a pinch of salt, and cook for twenty-five minutes. Drain, and place them in a hot dish ; pour a gill of hot Périgueux sauce (No. 191) over them, and serve.

1001. Potatoes à la Bignon.—Prepare twelve potatoes as for No. 982; empty them with a potato-scoop, leaving the bottoms uncut : blanch them in boiling water for two minutes ; drain, and fill them with sausage forcemeat (No. 220). Lay them in a buttered sautoire ; place it in the oven, and cook for twenty minutes. Use for any garnishing desired.

1002. Hashed Potatoes, Sautées.—Hash eight medium-sized, cold, boiled potatoes ; place an ounce and a half of good butter in a frying-pan, add the potatoes, season with half a pinch each of salt and pepper, and toss them well in the pan for two minutes. Give them the shape of an omelet, and let them take a golden color, which will require five minutes. With a spoon take up all the butter which lies at the bottom of the pan ; slide the potatoes carefully on a hot dish, and serve.

1003. Hashed Potatoes, with Cream.—Hash eight cold, boiled potatoes, and place them in a sautoire ; add half a cupful of cream and half an ounce of butter ; season with half a pinch each of salt and pepper, and the third of a pinch of nutmeg ; stir well with a wooden spoon for five minutes, until well heated, and serve.

1004. Hashed Potatoes, with Cream au Gratin.—Prepare the potatoes as for No. 1003 ; place them in a dish (a silver dish preferred); sprinkle over them two tablespoonfuls of grated Parmesan cheese, and two tablespoonfuls of fresh bread-crumbs ; spread well over them a piece of butter the size of a nut ; then place the dish in the oven. After ten minutes, when a good golden color, serve.

1005. Potatoes en Surprise.—Prepare some potatoes as for croquettes (No. 997); form them into twelve balls the size of a good-sized egg ; scoop out the centres, and fill in with a salpicon (No. 256). Close the opening with a little more potato ; dip them in beaten egg, then in fresh bread-crumbs, and fry them in very hot fat for three minutes. Lift, drain, and serve them on a hot dish with a folded napkin.

1006. Potatoes à la Duchesse.—Place some croquette preparation (No. 997) in a bag, and squeeze it upon a buttered baking-sheet, forming it into any shape required, and with a light hair brush cover the surface with a beaten egg. Brown lightly in the oven for eight minutes, and serve for various garnishings.

Balls can also be formed about the size of an egg; spread a little flour on the table; place the balls on top, and flatten them, shaping them nicely; cover the surface with a beaten egg; brown lightly in the oven on a buttered baking-sheet for eight minutes, and serve.

1007. Potatoes à la Rice.—Peel, wash, and drain eight medium-sized potatoes. Cut them into half-an-inch-square pieces; place them in a frying-pan with an ounce and a half of butter; season with a pinch of salt, toss well, and let them get a golden color (fifteen minutes will suffice). Drain the butter from the bottom of the pan, and place the potatoes in a hot dish; sprinkle a pinch of chopped parsley over, and serve.

1008. Potatoes à la Windsor.—Peel, and clean nicely, twelve large potatoes; cut them into balls with a Parisian potato-scoop, then place them in a saucepan, covering them with water containing a pinch of salt. Cook for fifteen minutes; then strain them and place them in another saucepan with an ounce of fresh butter and a pinch of chopped parsley. Warm them well for five minutes, and add the juice of half a lemon before serving.

1009. Potatoes, Château.—Cut six medium-sized potatoes into quarters, and pare them like cloves of garlic; wash them well, and drain. Fry them slowly in moderately heated fat for ten minutes; lift, drain thoroughly, and put them in a sautoire with half an ounce of butter. Season with half a pinch of salt, heat well for two minutes, and serve.

1010. Potatoes, Soufflées.—Peel eight good, mealy potatoes, and cut them into even pieces a quarter of an inch in thickness, shaping them as oval as possible. Fry them in moderately heated fat for eight minutes; then lift them out, and lay them aside for a few moments; plunge them into boiling hot fat, and the potatoes will swell considerably. Drain, and serve them on a dish with a folded napkin.

Sweet potatoes soufflées are prepared the same way.

N. B.—When cutting the potatoes for a soufflée, a continuous, sharp, and rapid cut should be made, so as to have them to perfection.

1011. Potatoes, Saratoga.—Peel and clean six medium-sized potatoes; cut them with a sharp Saratoga potato-knife into thin slices; place them in cold water, wash thoroughly, drain, and plunge them into very hot fat for eight minutes. Take them out, drain thoroughly, and sprinkle over them half a pinch of salt. Serve them on a dish with a folded napkin.

1012. Potatoes à la Hanna.—Peel, wash, and drain six medium-sized potatoes; cut them into as thin slices as possible; then wash them well again. Take a flat mold large enough to contain the potatoes, butter it well; put in a layer of potatoes, then a very light layer of grated cheese; season with a very little salt, and the same of pepper. Cover with another layer of potatoes, season again the same as before (the whole not to exceed half a pinch of each); then spread half an ounce of butter over them. Place the mold in the oven, and cook for thirty minutes; remove, turn it upside down on a hot dish, unmold, and serve.

1013. Potatoes, Julienne.—Peel and clean six medium-sized potatoes; cut them into square pieces two inches long by the third of an inch wide;

wash well, and drain; place them in very hot fat for six minutes, then lift them out, and lay them on a cloth to drain. Sprinkle half a pinch of salt over, and serve them on a dish with a folded napkin.

1014. Potatoes en Paille (Straw).—Prepare the same as in No. 1013, cutting a little thinner.

1015. Rice, Plain Boiled.—Clean and wash neatly a quarter of a pound of Italian rice ; place it in a saucepan with a pint and a half of cold water and a pinch of salt ; put the lid on, and boil for twenty-two minutes. Pour through a colander, being careful to let it drain thoroughly without crushing the rice, otherwise it will be spoiled. When well dried, return it to the saucepan, put the lid on, and leave it on the corner of the stove to dry gradually for five or six minutes. It will now be ready to use as required.

1016. Rice à la Ristori.—Wash well and drain a quarter of a pound of good Italian rice; shred two ounces of bacon into small pieces, and place them in a saucepan with a medium-sized, chopped-up, raw cabbage, letting them steam for thirty minutes. Add a pinch of salt, half a pinch of pepper, and a teaspoonful of chopped parsley ; put in the rice, and moisten with half a pint of white broth (No. 99). Cook for fully a quarter of an hour longer, and serve with grated Parmesan cheese sprinkled over it.

1017. Risotto à la Milanaise.—Chop rather fine one good-sized, very sound, peeled onion. Melt two ounces of very good butter in a saucepan on a very brisk fire ; add the onions, brown them for six or seven minutes, or until they have obtained a good golden color ; then add ten ounces of well-picked Italian rice (a heaped cupful), with two good-sized chopped truffles ; stir well with the spatula without ceasing for one and a half minutes, then add one quart of boiling and strained white broth (No. 99), lightly stir once only, and cook for fourteen minutes. Add six fine chopped mushrooms, and little by little, at intervals, another quart of boiling white broth—stirring almost constantly with the wooden spatula while cooking, very rapidly, for ten minutes more. Season with a heavy half-teaspoonful of salt, a light saltspoonful of white pepper, adding one and a half ounces of grated Swiss cheese, and a heaped teaspoonful of Spanish branch saffron, diluted in two tablespoonfuls of hot white broth, and strained. Cook for three or four minutes longer, stirring continually meanwhile ; then pour it into a hot soup-tureen, and send to the table with a little grated Swiss cheese, separate. A little beef-marrow can be added to advantage, by making a small cavity in the centre, while yet in the pan, one minute before the time to serve, and plunging into it one tablespoonful of marrow.

1018. Oyster-plant Sauté au Beurre.—Scrape nicely a large bunch of fine oyster-plant; plunge it into cold water containing two tablespoonfuls of vinegar, so as to prevent it from turning black. Take it from the water, drain, and cut it into two-inch-long pieces. Place them in a saucepan, with two tablespoonfuls of vinegar and two tablespoonfuls of flour; mix well; cover with plenty of cold water and a handful of salt; put the lid on, and let them boil slowly for forty minutes. Then drain, and return them to a sautoire, with an ounce and a half of the best butter procurable; season with half a pinch of pepper, the juice of half a lemon, and a teaspoonful of chopped parsley. Heat well for five minutes, tossing occasionally; then place them in a hot, deep dish, and serve.

1019. Oyster-plant à la Poulette.—Scrape nicely a good-sized bunch of fine, fresh oyster-plant; plunge it at once into acidulated water, and when well washed, drain, and cut it into two-inch pieces. Place them in a saucepan, and boil them in plenty of water, adding two pinches of salt, two tablespoonfuls of vinegar, and the same quantity of diluted flour. After forty minutes, or as soon as they bend to the finger, they are done. Lift them out, drain them well, and serve with a pint of hot poulette sauce (No. 598) poured over them.

1020. Oyster-plant Santé à la Crême.—To be cooked the same as for No. 1019; but after draining them, place them in a sautoire with a gill of béchamel sauce (No. 154) and a gill of sweet cream. Season with half a pinch of salt, a quarter of a pinch of pepper, and the third of a pinch of nutmeg. Let all heat well together for five minutes, stirring lightly with a wooden spoon, and serve in a hot, deep dish.

1021. Fried Oyster-plant.—Cook a good bunch of oyster-plant as for No. 1019, and, when done, put it in a dish, and season with half a pinch each of salt and pepper, and a tablespoonful of vinegar. Dip it well in a good fritter batter (No. 1190), and fry it in very hot fat for five minutes, separating the pieces with a spoon. Lift them up with a skimmer, drain on a cloth, sprinkle a very little salt over them, and serve on a folded napkin, decorating with a little fried parsley.

1022. Succotash.—Place six medium-sized, freshly cooked, and scraped ears of green corn (a can of canned corn will answer the purpose) in a saucepan, with half a pint of boiled Lima beans, adding a good-sized piece of butter weighing about an ounce, a pinch of salt, half a pinch of pepper, the third of a pinch of grated nutmeg, and half a pint of milk. Heat it well for five minutes, add two tablespoonfuls of good, hot béchamel (No. 154); stir thoroughly, and serve.

1023. Stuffed Tomatoes.—Wash and dry well six fine, sound red tomatoes. Cut the top of each up, without detaching, so that it will serve as a cover. Scoop out the inside of each with a vegetable-scoop; and place on a plate for further action. Season the inside of the six emptied tomatoes with one pinch of salt and half a pinch of pepper, equally divided. Chop very fine one medium-sized, sound, peeled onion; place it in a saucepan with half an ounce of butter; and cook for three minutes on a brisk fire, being careful not to let get brown. Add six chopped mushrooms and one ounce of sausage-meat. Season with one pinch of salt and half a pinch of pepper; cook for three minutes, stirring once in a while. Add now the tomatoes which were scooped out, with half a cupful of fresh bread-crumbs and a teaspoonful of fresh chopped parsley. Mix well together, and cook for two minutes longer, or until it comes to a boil; then place in a bowl to cool. Stuff the emptied tomatoes with the above preparation, close down the covers, gently lay them on a tin plate (dish), cover them with a buttered paper, and cook in a moderate oven for eighteen minutes, and serve.

Stuffed tomatoes are served as a garnishing in various ways.

For egg-plants, the same stuffing is used, but instead of tomatoes, use the scooped out egg-plant.

Green peppers the same, using half a very finely chopped-up green pepper in place of the tomatoes.

1024. Stuffed Tomatoes à la Reine.—Prepare six tomatoes exactly the same as in No. 1023, substituting chicken forcemeat (No. 226) for the sausage meat, and pouring a gill of hot Madeira sauce (No. 185) on a hot dish, and dressing the tomatoes over.

1025. Broiled Tomatoes.—Take six good-sized, firm, red, fresh tomatoes; pare the underparts in case anything adheres, wipe them nicely, and slit them in halves. Lay them on a dish; season with a good pinch of salt, half a pinch of pepper, and a tablespoonful of sweet oil; mix well together; keep the tomatoes in as good shape as when cut, then arrange them in a double broiler. Put them on a moderate fire, and cook for eight minutes on each side. Place in a hot dish; spread a gill of maître d'hôtel butter (No. 145) over them, and serve.

1026. Tomatoes à la Bock.—Wipe neatly and peel eight fine, sound, fresh tomatoes; cut each one into six equal-sized pieces, and place them in a saucepan with two ounces of fresh butter, seasoning with a pinch of salt, half a pinch of pepper, and the third of a pinch of nutmeg. Cover the pan, and place it on the hot stove to cook for fifteen minutes. Take from off the fire, pour the tomatoes into a deep, hot vegetable-dish, and send them to the table very hot.

1027. Stewed Tomatoes.—Plunge six good-sized, fresh, sound tomatoes into boiling water for half a minute; drain, nicely peel them, cut each one into six pieces; put them into a saucepan with an ounce and a half of good butter, season with half a pinch each of salt and pepper, and the third of a pinch of nutmeg. Cook slowly for twenty minutes, and add a very little powdered sugar (half a teaspoonful will be sufficient). Stir well, and cook for two minutes longer; then place in a hot, deep dish, and serve.

1028. Roasted Tomatoes.—Plunge in boiling water for half a minute six good-sized red, sound tomatoes; drain, and peel them neatly, then cut away the tops without detaching them entirely, and remove the seeds with a teaspoon. Divide an ounce of good butter into six equal parts, and put a piece into each tomato, seasoning with a light saltspoonful of salt, and half the quantity of pepper. Close the tops, and lay them in a buttered baking-dish, moistening each tomato with a very little sweet oil. Put them in a hot oven, and bake for twelve minutes. Remove, and with a cake-turner dress them on a hot dish, and serve.

1029. Tomatoes à la Marseillaise.—Take six good-sized, firm, red tomatoes; wipe, and cut them in halves through the sides. Place half a gill of sweet oil in a frying-pan; let it heat well; lay in it the tomatoes on the sides which were cut, and cook briskly for one minute. Butter well a tin baking-dish, and lay the tomatoes in this on the uncooked side, and season with half a pinch each of salt and pepper. Make a stuffing with one shallot, finely chopped, two cloves of crushed garlic, two hard-boiled egg yolks, a teaspoonful of chopped chives, the same of parsley, two medium-sized, finely chopped anchovies, and an ounce of butter. Mix well together in a bowl, and cover the tops of the tomatoes with the stuffing, dividing it equally. Sprinkle a little fresh bread-crumbs over them; drip three or four drops of clarified butter over each tomato; then place them in a very hot oven for eight minutes. Place them neatly on a hot dish, and serve.

1030. Okras, Plain Boiled.—Take twenty-four medium-sized, sound okras, and wash them well in cold water. Drain thoroughly, and pare both ends. Have a saucepan containing salted boiling water, into which plunge the okras, and let them cook for fifteen minutes. Lift them out with a skimmer, and lay them on a cloth to drain. Use the boiled okras for sautéing, salad, or any other purpose desired.

1031. Okras, Sautés à la Créole.—Prepare twenty-four okras as for No. 1030. Place in a sautoire one ounce of good butter, one medium-sized minced onion, and a medium-sized, minced green pepper. Place on the stove for six minutes, until it is of a golden color, and add two raw, peeled tomatoes cut into pieces, three tablespoonfuls of Espagnole (No. 151), a pinch of salt, the third of a pinch of pepper, and one crushed clove of garlic. Add the okras, put the lid on, and cook slowly for fifteen minutes. Place in a hot, deep dish, sprinkle over them a teaspoonful of chopped parsley, and serve.

1032. Macédoine of Vegetables.—Cut a small, raw carrot with a vegetable-scoop; put it into salted boiling water, and cook for fifteen minutes; repeat with a small, raw turnip, cooking each separately; drain, and place them in a saucepan with half a gill of cooked peas, the same quantity of cooked half-inch lengths of string beans, two tablespoonfuls of cooked flageolets, and a small piece of cauliflower, if at hand. Moisten with half a pint of hot béchamel (No. 154), and season with half a pinch each of salt and pepper, and the third of a pinch of nutmeg. Let it simmer well for ten minutes, and use when required.

1033. Jardinière of Vegetables.—Prepare exactly as in No. 1032, substituting half a pint of hot Madeira sauce (No. 185) for the béchamel.

1034. Boiled Hominy.—Wash a quart of very white hominy in fresh water; drain, put in a saucepan with a quart of cold water, and place it on the fire, adding a pinch of salt. Boil for thirty minutes, stirring it well, and serve.

1035. Fried Hominy.—After preparing the hominy as for No. 1034, put it to cool, and cut it into six slices. Dip each slice in beaten egg, roll them in fresh bread-crumbs, and fry in very hot fat until of a good golden color, for four minutes. Serve on a folded napkin, or use for garnishing when required.

A pinch of salt represents 205 grains, or a tablespoonful.

Half a pinch of pepper represents 38 grains, or a teaspoonful.

A third of a pinch of nutmeg represents 13 grains, or half a teaspoonful.

SALADS.

1036. Salad à l'Italienne.—Pare well a good-sized carrot and a good-sized turnip; cut them with a vegetable-scoop, and cook them in separate salted waters; the carrot fifteen minutes, and the turnip ten. Drain, let cool, then place them in a salad-bowl, dome-shaped. Cut two good-sized truffles into julienne-shaped pieces; keep them apart, and cut up six mushrooms the same way, also the breast of a cooked, medium-sized chicken, cut likewise. Cover the vegetables with a cluster of the truffles, the same of the mushrooms, and repeat with the chicken, keeping each article separate; form a small cavity in the centre of the dome, pour into it a teaspoonful of anchovy sauce, a tablespoonful of vinegar, one tablespoonful of sweet oil, a pinch of salt, and half a pinch of pepper. Cover the cavity with a piece of cooked cauliflower, or Brussels-sprouts, or in default of both, cooked asparagus-tops will answer the purpose; send to the table, and mix well before serving it to the guests.

1037. Anchovy Salad.—Have eighteen bottled anchovies (or the same quantity of Norwegian anchovies if possible), soak them in cold water for two hours, so they are thoroughly unsalted, then drain them in a cloth, and remove the bones. Clean and pare a small head of lettuce, cut it into small pieces, and put it in a salad-bowl, covering it with two tablespoonfuls of Tartare sauce (No. 207). Decorate with the anchovies, two hard-boiled eggs cut in quarters, twelve capers, six stoned olives, and a small, cooked, sliced beet-root; season with half a pinch of pepper and one tablespoonful of vinegar. When ready to serve mix well together.

1038. Barbe de Capucine.—Take two bunches of clear, white, fresh barbe de capucine; clean, and wipe them carefully and thoroughly, but do not wash the salad, as it loses its taste, and renders it too soft to use; cut it into three shreds, and place it in a salad-bowl. Mix well, in a wooden salad-spoon, two spoonfuls of vinegar, half a pinch of salt, and the third of a pinch of pepper, and pour it over the salad, then add one spoonful of oil, mix well, and serve immediately.

1039. Beef Salad.—Take one pound of lean, boiled, cold beef, the rump-part in preference; suppress all the fat, then cut it into pieces an inch and a half in length, as thinly as possible. Place the pieces in a bowl, season with a pinch of salt, half a pinch of pepper, and two medium-sized, cooked, and sliced potatoes, also a pinch of parsley, two tablespoonfuls of vinegar, and the same of sweet oil. Mix all well together, then arrange in a serving salad-bowl; decorate with six medium-sized pickles or beets, and serve.

1040. Cauliflower Salad.—Take a medium-sized head of cooked cauliflower; pare off the root, and detach it into equal-sized flowerets; place these in a salad-bowl, seasoning with a pinch of salt, half a pinch of pepper, and sprinkle over a pinch of chopped parsley; add three tablespoonfuls of vinegar, two of good oil, and mix all well together with a wooden spoon, then serve.

1041. Celery Salad.—If the heads of celery be large and white, use two; if they should be small, use three. Pare off the green stalks, trim the roots nicely, and cut it into short shreds; wash thoroughly in cold water, lift it up with the hands, and drain in a cloth. When well drained, place the celery in a salad-bowl, and season with a pinch of salt, half a pinch of pepper, and one and a half wooden salad-spoonfuls of vinegar, also the same quantity of oil. Mix well, and serve.

1042. Celery Salad, Mayonnaise Dressing.—Prepare the celery exactly the same as for No. 1041; and when in the salad-bowl, season with half a pinch of salt, half a pinch of pepper, and three tablespoonfuls of mayonnaise dressing (No. 206). Mix well just before serving.

1043. Chapon, for Chicory and Escarole Salad.—Cut a thin crust, off a French loaf of bread, two inches long by one inch square, sprinkle over it a very little salt, then take a good-sized clove of sound garlic; rub it over both sides of the bread-crust, reject the peel which adheres, and lay the crust at the bottom of the salad-bowl; place the salad over, and mix thoroughly together, serving immediately.

1044. Chicken Salad.—Take a young, tender chicken of two and a half pounds; boil it in the soup-stock for one hour, or should it be a fowl, it will take from half to three-quarters of an hour longer; when cooked, let it get thoroughly cold. Bone the chicken, cut it up into small pieces, and put them into a deep dish; season with a pinch of salt, half a pinch of pepper, one tablespoonful of vinegar, and six leaves of chopped lettuce, or a few leaves of the white of celery in preference, cut up. Mix well, place it in a salad-bowl, and cover with half a cupful of mayonnaise dressing (No. 206); decorate the top with a chopped, hard-boiled egg, a tablespoonful of capers, twelve stoned olives, quarters of two hard-boiled eggs, and six small, white lettuce leaves around the dish, then serve.

1045. Chicory Salad, Plain.—Procure two medium-sized heads of white, fine, fresh chicory; pare off the green leaves, and cut away the root. Wash thoroughly, drain well in a salad-shaker or a linen napkin, then place it in a salad-bowl; season with half a pinch of salt and the third of a pinch of pepper, diluted in a salad-spoonful of vinegar, and add one and a half salad-spoonfuls of sweet oil. Mix thoroughly together, and send to the table.

1046. Chicory Salad au Chapon.—Prepare the salad exactly the same as for the above (No. 1045), only adding a chapon (No. 1043).

1047. Crab Salad.—Take twelve hard-shelled, live crabs; boil them in salted water, with half a cupful of vinegar, for twenty minutes; then drain and shell them. Pare off the gills; put a finger in the centre, to prevent the sand getting in the cavity; wash thoroughly and quickly under the faucet, then pick the meat from the shell; put it in a salad-bowl and proceed the same as for the salmon salad (No. 1066).

1048. Dandelion Salad, Plain.—Procure a quart of very fresh, white dandelion; pare the roots and stale leaves, if any; then wash thoroughly in two different waters; drain nicely on a cloth, and place it in a salad-bowl. Dilute a pinch of salt and half a pinch of pepper in a salad-spoonful of vinegar, adding one and a half spoonfuls of sweet oil; mix thoroughly together, and serve.

1049. Dandelion Salad, with Eggs.—Proceed the same as for the above (No. 1048), only adding, when serving, two hard-boiled eggs cut in quarters.

1050. Dandelion and Beet-root Salad.—Take half the quantity of dandelion salad as for the plain (No. 1048); put it in a salad-bowl, adding two medium-sized, cooked beet-roots (No. 919); cut into thin slices, and season it exactly the same as for No. 1049.

1051. Dandelion à la Contoise.—Pare and clean a quart of fine white dandelion; wash well in two different waters; then drain in a cloth, and place it in a salad-bowl. Season with a third of a pinch of salt and half a pinch of pepper; cut two ounces of bacon in dice-shaped pieces, put them in a frying-pan, place it on the stove, and let them get a good golden color, for about five minutes; put them into the salad; then place two tablespoonfuls of vinegar in the pan, and let it heat for half a minute; pour it over all, mix well together and serve.

1052. Doucette Salad, Plain.—Take a quart of very fresh doucette, pare off the outer stale leaves, if any; also the roots, and wash well in two waters; drain in a napkin, and then place it in a serving salad-bowl. Season with one pinch of salt, and a half pinch of pepper diluted in a wooden salad-spoonful of vinegar; also with one and a half spoonfuls of sweet oil. Mix well together when ready to serve, but not before.

1053. Doucette Salad, with Beet-roots.—Use a pint of doucette only, and three medium-sized cooked beet-roots, cut in slices; place them all in a salad-bowl, and season the same as for the above (No. 1052).

1054. Doucette Salad, with Hard-boiled Eggs.—Proceed the same as for doucette salad (No. 1052), only when ready to serve, decorate with two hard-boiled eggs cut into quarters.

1055. Escarole Salad.—Have two heads of fine, white escarole; pare off the green leaves and cores. If the escarole be tolerably clean, wipe it carefully without washing it, as it should not be washed unless plenty of earth adheres to it. Place it in a salad-bowl, and season with half a pinch of salt and the third of a pinch of pepper, mixed in a wooden salad-spoonful of tarragon-vinegar, adding one and a half spoonfuls of oil. Mix well just before serving.

1056. Lamb-tongue Salad.—Have six cooked, pickled lamb's tongues; pare them neatly, and cut them into very thin slices; lay them in a dish, adding two cooked and sliced potatoes, a pinch of salt, half a pinch of pepper, two tablespoonfuls of vinegar, and the same quantity of sweet oil. Mix the whole well together, then dress it in a bowl, sprinkle a little chopped parsley over, and decorate with a few small lettuce-leaves. Send to the table.

1057. Lettuce Salad, Plain.—Take two fine, white heads of lettuce; pare off the outer green leaves and stems; cut the leaves in two, wash well in cold water, drain thoroughly in a wire basket, then place it in a salad-bowl, with the hearts on top. Mix half a pinch of salt and the third of a pinch of pepper in one salad-spoonful of vinegar, adding one and a half salad-spoonfuls of good sweet oil; pour this seasoning over the lettuce, mix all well together, and send to the table.

Lettuce salad should never be dressed longer than five minutes before the time to serve it.

1058. Lettuce Salad with Hard-boiled Eggs.—Dress a lettuce salad the same as for the above (No. 1057), and just before serving add two hard-boiled eggs cut in quarters.

1059. Lettuce Salad with Cream.—Prepare a lettuce salad the same as for No. 1057, substituting three tablespoonfuls of sweet cream for the oil.

1060. Lettuce and Tomato Salad.—Take a white head of lettuce, pare off the outer green leaves and core, wash, drain in a wire basket, then cut the leaves in two, and put them in a bowl. Have two fine, firm, peeled red tomatoes, prepared as for No. 1070, cut them into thin slices, and place them over the lettuce, seasoning as follows: Mix a pinch of salt and half a pinch of pepper in a wooden salad-spoonful of vinegar; add a spoonful and a half of oil, mix well, and serve.

1061. Lobster Salad.—Take three pounds of boiled lobster; shell, and cut the meat into small pieces; lay them in a deep dish, seasoning with a pinch of salt, half a pinch of pepper, and a tablespoonful of vinegar, adding a few branches of the white of celery, likewise cut up. Mix well together, then transfer it to a salad-bowl, and pour over half a cupful of good mayonnaise dressing (No. 206), decorate with two hard-boiled eggs cut into quarters, six leaves of lettuce, twelve stoned olives, a tablespoonful of capers, and a little of the lobster coral, hashed well. Decorate nicely, according to taste, and serve.

1062. Lobster Salad à la Plummer.—Take two fine, freshly boiled, medium-sized lobsters; cut them in two, and pick out all the meat from the shell, carefully abstracting the gall. Cut the meat into small, equal-sized, square pieces, and place them in a salad-bowl; shell three hard-boiled eggs, lay them on a plate, and with a knife chop them up as thoroughly as hashed potatoes; then add this to the lobster, also two finely chopped shallots, two teaspoonfuls of freshly chopped chives, and one and a half teaspoonfuls of finely chopped parsley. Take half a head of good and well-cleaned lettuce, chop it up very fine, add it to the lobster; then season with a pinch and a half of salt, a light pinch of fresh and finely crushed white pepper—two tablespoonfuls of vinegar, two tablespoonfuls of good sweet oil, and three tablespoonfuls of mayonnaise sauce (No. 206). Gently but thoroughly mix the whole together, then wipe well the edges of the salad-bowl with a napkin, and send this delicious salad to the table.

1063. Salad Macédoine.—Have a medium-sized carrot and turnip; peel, and wash them well, then cut them with a vegetable-scoop; put them into separate boiling salted waters, and cook the carrot fifteen minutes, and the turnip ten. Drain, and let thoroughly cool; place them in a salad-bowl with three tablespoonfuls of cooked peas, the same quantity of string beans cut into small pieces, a pinch of salt, half a pinch of pepper, two tablespoonfuls of sweet oil, and one and a half tablespoonfuls of vinegar. Mix all thoroughly together. If there be any cooked cauliflower on hand, use it for decorating the bowl, or a few asparagus-tops or Brussels-sprouts will answer. Send to the table at once.

1064. Romaine Salad.—Take two good-sized hearts of fine romaine; remove the outer greens; wipe, washing it carefully. Drain, then place it in a salad-bowl, sprinkling over a teaspoonful of chopped chives, half a teaspoonful of chopped chervil, the same of tarragon, and season with one pinch of salt, and half a pinch of pepper, diluted in a wooden salad-spoonful of vinegar, and one and a half spoonfuls of sweet oil. Mix thoroughly together, and serve immediately.

1065. Russian Salad.—Cut up separately, in small dice-shaped pieces, one ounce of cooked roast beef, same of cooked ham, same of cooked beef-tongue, same of cooked chicken, same of lean leg of cooked mutton, and two truffles cut into very small dice-shaped pieces. Put them in a salad-bowl, separating each kind by six boned anchovies; then pour a tablespoonful of Tartare sauce (No. 207) in the centre, covering the sauce with two chopped leaves of lettuce. Send it as it is to the table; for it should be mixed together just before serving only.

1066. Salmon Salad.—Procure a piece of good salmon, plunge it into cold, salted water; add half a cupful of vinegar, one sliced carrot, one sliced onion, a bouquet (No. 254), and let cook for thirty minutes; drain, put aside to cool; then pare off the skin, and bone the salmon completely. When done, tear or break it into small pieces. Place these in a bowl, seasoning with a pinch of salt, a pinch of pepper, three tablespoonfuls of vinegar, two tablespoonfuls of sweet oil, and a pinch of chopped parsley. Mix all well together; then decorate the salad-bowl with six small lettuce-leaves, six stoned olives, twelve capers, and two hard-boiled eggs cut in quarters. Send to the table.

1067. Shrimp Salad.—Have a quart, or two pint boxes, of boiled and skinned shrimps, and proceed the same as for lobster salad (No. 1061).

1068. String-bean Salad.—Take a quart of cooked string beans, and prepare it exactly the same as the cauliflower salad (No. 1040).

1069. Suédoise Salad.—Cut two ounces of cooked beef-tongue into small pieces; cut two cooked potatoes the same; also half a peeled apple, half a cooked beet-root, and half a cooked carrot. Place these in a bowl, adding the fillets of a boned herring cut in small pieces, and season with half a pinch each of salt and pepper, a teaspoonful of diluted mustard, one tablespoonful of vinegar, and one and a half tablespoonfuls of oil. Mix all well together, then transfer to a serving salad-bowl, sprinkle over a pinch of chopped parsley, and serve.

1070. Tomato Salad, French Dressing.—Take six fine, firm, red tomatoes; wipe them neatly, and plunge them into boiling water for one minute; drain in a cloth, remove the skins, pare off the stem side, let get cool, and then cut them into very thin slices; or, if preferred, into quarters, keeping them in a bowl, so that the juice be not wasted. Season with a pinch of salt, half a pinch of pepper, a wooden salad-spoonful of vinegar, and the same quantity of oil. Mix thoroughly together, and serve as cold as possible. A teaspoonful of chopped chives may be added, if desired, which will give a delicious flavor.

1071. Tomato Salad, Mayonnaise Dressing.—Prepare six tomatoes, the same as for the above (No. 1070), and when sliced, or quartered, in the salad-bowl, season with a pinch of salt, half a pinch of pepper, and two good tablespoonfuls of mayonnaise dressing (No. 206); mix well, and serve very cold.

1072. Watercress Salad.—Procure three bunches of sound, fresh watercress; clean, and pare off the stalks, wash well, then dry in a cloth, place it in a salad-bowl, seasoning with half a pinch of salt, just a little pepper, and two wooden salad-spoonfuls of vinegar; mix well, and serve. Watercress salad does not require any oil.

1073. Potato Salad.—Peel ten medium-sized, sound, freshly cooked potatoes; cut them into small slices, lay them in a salad-bowl, and add a finely chopped onion and a teaspoonful of chopped parsley. Season with a pinch and a half of salt, one pinch of pepper, half a gill of vinegar, and three tablespoonfuls of sweet oil, then mix thoroughly and gently with a spoon and fork, without breaking the potatoes. Wipe the bowl neatly with a napkin, and send the salad to the table.

1074. Herring Salad.—Take three medium-sized smoked herrings, lay them on the corner of the stove for half a minute on each side, then tear off the skin, cut off the heads, and split them in two; remove the bones, and cut them up into small square pieces. Place them in a salad-bowl with half a hashed onion, two hard-boiled eggs, cut in pieces, a cold boiled potato cut the same, and a teaspoonful of chopped parsley. Season with half a pinch of salt, one pinch of pepper, three tablespoonfuls of vinegar, and two of oil. Mix well together, and decorate with a small, cooked beet-root cut in slices, also twelve capers; then serve.

1075. Japanese Salad.—Mince three medium-sized truffles very fine, also two large, cold, boiled potatoes; put the whole into a bowl, and season with half a pinch each of salt and pepper, and the third of a pinch of nutmeg; pour half a glassful of champagne over all, and let rest for two hours, then add eighteen whole cooked mussels (No. 379), a teaspoonful of chopped chives, and the same quantity of chopped parsley. Mix all well together, then dress the salad into a bowl, decorating it with six small, white lettuce-leaves and six fillets of anchovies; then serve.

A pinch of salt represents 205 grains, or a tablespoonful.
Half a pinch of pepper represents 38 grains, or a teaspoonful.
A third of a pinch of nutmeg represents 13 grains, or half a teaspoonful.

DESSERTS:

PASTRY, JELLIES, ICES, PRESERVES, ETC.

1076. Feuilletage, or Puff Paste.—Have ready one pound of flour, one pound of fresh butter, one pint of ice-water, and a saltspoonful of salt. If the butter be salted instead of fresh, no salt is necessary, but wash the butter well before using it. Put the flour on the table, make a hollow space in the centre, then put in it one ounce of the butter, adding the pint of ice-water and the salt, and mix the whole well together, incorporating it gradually. Put it aside in a cool place for five minutes. Have ready the remaining fifteen ounces of butter, which must be very firm; sprinkle the space of a square foot of the table with a very little flour, place the dough on it, then lengthen and widen with a wooden roller to the thickness of half an inch, and lay the fifteen ounces of butter in one lump in the centre. Fold over the four edges so as to enclose it, then flatten again lightly with the roller until it forms a piece two inches thick, and then put it away to cool for ten minutes. Roll it again lengthwise, fold it in four, and let it rest for another five minutes; then repeat the same twice more, rolling it each time in a contrary direction. After five minutes it will be ready for use. This feuilletage, or puff paste, if put away carefully in a cool place, will keep for three days, and can be used for the following purposes: vol-au-vents of chickens, oysters, clams, shrimps, lobsters, codfish, crabs, and crawfish; also for making chicken patties, bouchées à la reine, all kinds of tarts, allumettes, mille-feuilles, chaussons, turnovers, petits pâtés à la religieuse, etc., etc.

1077. Paste for Pies.—Sift on a table one pound of flour; make a hollow space in the centre, pour into it a pint of cold water, two ounces of butter, and half a saltspoonful of salt; then, with the hand, knead the ingredients well together for two minutes, and gradually and slowly incorporate the flour with the rest for four minutes. Lay the paste on a dish, and put it to rest in a cool place for three minutes. Have ready six ounces of well-washed butter in one lump, as for feuilletage (No. 1076); return the paste to the table, flatten it slightly, then put the lump of butter in the centre, fold over the edges, so as to enclose the butter, then roll it out lengthwise with the pastry roller, and refold the paste into three folds. Let it rest again in a cool place for three minutes, then roll it again, fold it as before, and set it in the ice-box for five minutes; the paste will now be ready to use, and by keeping it in the ice-box it will remain in good condition for three days.

1078. Pâte-à-Foucer, Foundation Paste.—Sift one pound of flour on the table, make a hollow in the centre, and pour into it half a pound of well-washed butter, a saltspoonful of salt, and a gill of cold water. Knead well the salt, butter, and water, using the hand, for two minutes, then incorporate the flour gradually, which will take three minutes more, and knead sharply with the hands. Detach it from the table, and roll it into a ball, then press it again on the table in different directions for two minutes; remove again from the table. Flour the table slightly, lay the paste over, and with the fingers of the right hand press down the paste in the centre, and with the left bring up the edges all around to the centre, repeat this three times, and when finished the paste must have its original shape; lay it on a dish, cover with a towel, and set it in a cool place to rest for twenty minutes.

1079. How to Make a Pastry-bag, for General Use.—Cut a piece of white duck-cloth as follows: twenty-four inches wide at the top, twenty inches deep, and three inches at the lower end. Fold, and sew up lengthwise, so as to make a perfect cornet-bag. Hem the top and the bottom, and the pastry bag will then be ready for use.

The accompanying design will show how it should be made.

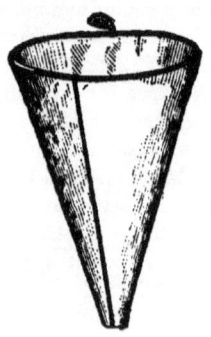

PASTRY-BAG.

This pastry-bag is essential and useful for kitchen and pastry use, being both facile and economical, but care must be taken to wash it thoroughly, and immediately after using it, and to let it dry perfectly, otherwise it will soon become useless.

1080. How to Clean and Prepare Sultana Currants and Raisins for Pastry.—To avoid the trouble of preparing them each time they are needed, it were better to clean many at a time, for they will keep in perfect condition for five or six months, if put away in a well-closed tin box. Procure ten pounds of currants or Sultana raisins, lay them on a table, and should they be damp, dredge a little flour over to prevent them adhering to the hands. Rub them thoroughly, then take a wire sieve, No. 3 (or as fine a one as will prevent them passing through), place the

DESSERTS.

currants on it, and shake them well for two or three minutes, so that they be perfectly free from flour and stalks. Lay the sieve containing the currants in a large dish-pan, filling it to the level of the sieve with hot water, then, with a skimmer, stir them, so that they get washed thoroughly for at least five minutes. Lift up the sieve, and let them drain in the same for three minutes. Cover an iron oven-pan with a sheet of brown paper, pour the currants on it, spreading them out evenly, and set it in a very slow oven for ten minutes; remove, and lay them aside in the warmest spot on the kitchen shelf, and leave them to dry thoroughly for at least two days. If in the country, the pan can be left out in the sun during the day. When dry, lay them on the table, and should any more foreign matter be found among them, pick it out carefully with the fingers, and examine them well to see whether they be free of stones, stalks, stems, sand, &c. When finished, put them away in a closed tin box, and they will then be ready for use.

1081. How to Clean Malaga Raisins.—Have as many Malaga raisins as deemed necessary, but it were better to purchase five pounds at a time. Lay the raisins on a table, have a bowl of cold water on the right hand, and the raisins in front; pick off the dry stalks adhering to them, then, either using a small knife or the fingers, pick out the seeds, taking care to wet the fingers in the bowl of water, so as to prevent them sticking while seeding them. Close up again, giving them their original form; when finished, put them in a tin can, cover well, and place in a moderate temperature for use when required. Raisins prepared in this way will surely keep six months.

1082. Mince Pie.—Put into a vessel two ounces of currants, prepared as for No. 1080, two ounces of Sultana, and three ounces of Malaga raisins, as for No. 1081, one ounce of finely chopped citron, two ounces of well-chopped, cold, boiled beef, and two ounces of beef-suet, also chopped very fine. Mix the whole well together for five minutes, then add one ounce of powdered sugar, a saltspoonful of salt, one drachm of ground allspice, half a drachm of ground cloves, half a drachm of ground cinnamon, and mix together for one minute. Peel, core, and chop up very fine three large, sound apples, add them to the preparation, then pour in half a gill each of brandy and sherry wine, mixing again for three minutes. Take half a pound of pie-paste as for No. 1077, cut out a piece of three ounces, roll it round-shaped, ten inches in diameter, and lightly butter a pie-plate nine and a half inches in diameter, Arrange the paste over, and pour the preparation in the centre, flattening it evenly, and leaving an inch space clear around the edge of the plate; take the remaining five ounces of paste, roll it out round-shaped, the same as before, fold it in two, and, with a knife, make incisions in the centre, of half an inch each. Moisten lightly the edge of the plate with a little beaten egg, then cover with the paste, pressing down with the hand all around the edge, so as to inclose the preparation entirely, then moisten the surface slightly with the beaten egg. Place in a moderate oven, and let bake for fifty minutes; remove it to the oven-door, sprinkle plenty of powdered sugar over, return it to the oven, closing the door for two minutes, so that the sugar melts entirely, then slide it carefully onto a dessert-dish, and serve either hot or cold.

1083. Apple Pie.—Peel, core, and slice four medium-sized, fine, sound apples; put them into a vessel, and add three ounces of powdered sugar and a saltspoonful of ground cinnamon. Have a plate covered as for the above (No 1082); arrange the apples on top, cover, and finish exactly the same as for the mince pie. Serve cold.

1084. Pear Pie.—Peel and slice six medium-sized, fine, sound, pears; put them into a vessel with three ounces of powdered sugar; put this over a lined plate, and proceed exactly the same as for mince pie (No. 1082).

1085. Rhubarb Pie.—Pare off the leaves, and peel the stalks neatly from two bunches of fine rhubarb, cut them into small pieces about half an inch long, and put them in a vessel with three ounces of powdered sugar; mix well; lay them on the pie-plate, cover, and bake the same as for mince pie (No. 1082).

1086. Lemon Pie.—Take one and a half pounds of apple sauce (No. 1328), put it in a vessel, adding one ounce of powdered sugar, and one ounce of corn-starch; grate in the peel of a medium-sized lemon, squeezing in the juice of two others, and mix the whole well together with a spatula for three minutes. Pour the preparation over a lined plate, as for mince pie (No. 1082), cover, and finish exactly the same.

1087. Pineapple Pie.—Procure a medium-sized, fine, sound, pineapple; pare, peel, and slice it into fine slices, laying them in a vessel, and mixing in three ounces of powdered sugar. Have a pie-plate lined with paste, as for mince pie (No. 1082), spread over one tablespoonful of apple sauce (No. 1328); arrange the pineapple nicely on top, then take three ounces of pie-paste, roll it out lengthwise, two feet long, and fold it carefully in two, so as to make a long narrow strip; roll it slightly again until about thirty inches long by one wide, paring off both sides evenly, so as to have it exactly the one inch in width. Moisten the edge of the pie-plate with beaten egg, and arrange the strip around, fastening the two ends together, one over the other; glaze the surface of the strip with beaten egg, then place the pie in a moderate oven, and let bake for fifty minutes. Remove to the door, dredge the pie well with powdered sugar, return to the oven for two minutes to allow the sugar to melt, then spread evenly over the top two ounces of apple jelly (No. 1327), and send to the table.

1088. Pear Pie, Open.—Peel and slice six medium-sized fine and sound pears; place them in a vessel with three ounces of powdered sugar, mix well, and proceed exactly the same as for pineapple pie (No. 1087).

1089. Huckleberry Pie.—Put in a vessel one pint and a half of well-picked and cleaned huckleberries, add two ounces of powdered sugar, mix well, and proceed the same as for pineapple pie (No. 1087).

1090. Fresh Currant Pie.—Put in a vessel a pint and a half of well-picked and cleaned currants, with four ounces of powdered sugar, and proceed exactly the same as for pineapple pie (No. 1087).

1091. Gooseberry Pie.—To be prepared the same as the above (No.

1090), only using one pint and a half of gooseberries instead of the currants.

1092. Peach Pie.—Wipe neatly and slice eight fine, sound, medium-sized peaches; put them in a vessel with three ounces of powdered sugar, and proceed exactly the same as for pineapple pie (No. 1087).

1093. Green-gage Pie.—Select one dozen ripe, sound, green-gages; cut them in two, remove the stones, and put them in a vessel with three ounces of powdered sugar. Finish the same as for pineapple pie (No. 1087).

1094. Plum Pie.—To be prepared as for the above (No. 1093), substituting one dozen plums for the green-gages.

1095. Strawberry Pie.—Have a pie-plate lined as for pineapple pie (No. 1087), lay in three-quarters of a pound of apple sauce (No. 1328), arrange the strip around, then place it in the oven for thirty minutes only; remove to the oven door, dredge profusely the strip with powdered sugar, return to the oven, close the door, and leave it for two minutes to let the sugar melt. Take it out, and let it get thoroughly cold, then, with a spoon, remove half of the apple sauce, and fill the interior with a pint and a half of well-picked and cleaned strawberries, mixed with two ounces of powdered sugar. Spread two ounces of apple jelly (No. 1327) evenly over the strawberries, and serve.

1096. Raspberry Pie.—Have the pie prepared exactly the same as for strawberry pie (No. 1095), and fill it with a pint and a half of well-picked and cleaned raspberries mixed with two ounces of powdered sugar, and spread evenly over the top two ounces of apple jelly (No. 1327); then serve.

1097. Blackberry Pie.—Blackberry pie is to be prepared exactly the same as strawberry pie (No. 1095), only substituting a pint and a half of well-picked and cleaned blackberries for the strawberries.

1098. Cherry Pie.—Procure two pounds of fine, sound cherries; pick off the stalks, then stone them with the hands, and place them in a vessel with four ounces of powdered sugar, mixing well. Have ready a lined pie-plate, fill it with the cherries, arrange the strip around, and proceed the same as for pineapple pie (No. 1087), then serve.

1099. Pumpkin Pie.—Have a deep pie-plate, one and a half inches deep by nine and a half wide; line it with four ounces of pie-paste (No. 1077). Cut a two-pound piece off a sound pumpkin, peel it well with a knife, remove the seeds and soft parts, then cut it into twelve pieces; place them in a saucepan with three quarts of cold water, leave the pan on the hot stove, and let cook for twenty-five minutes. Take from the fire, put the pumpkin in a drainer, leaving it for one hour, then press out the water thoroughly with the hand, and rub it through a sieve into another vessel. Add two ounces of powdered sugar, and break in three whole eggs; add a saltspoonful of ground cloves, a saltspoonful of ground allspice, half a saltspoonful of salt, and the same quantity of cinnamon; mix all together for two minutes, and pour in half a pint of cold milk, mixing well again for one minute, then strain through a sieve into another vessel, and use the preparation to fill up the pie-plate, then lay it carefully in a moderate oven, and let bake for thirty minutes. Take it from the oven, put aside to cool, and cut it into six equal parts; dress them on a dessert dish with a folded napkin, sprinkle liberally with powdered sugar, and serve.

1100. Custard Pie.—Put four ounces of powdered sugar into a vessel; break in five whole eggs, and with a pastry whip beat together for three minutes. Add one quart of cold milk, and flavor with a teaspoonful of lemon essence; mixing well together for two minutes longer; strain through a sieve into another vessel. Have a deep pie-plate lined exactly the same as for pumpkin pie (No. 1099), and fill it with the above preparation. Place it in a moderate oven, and let bake for thirty minutes, then remove, and let get thoroughly cold; cut the pie into six equal pieces, and with the blade of a knife dress them onto a dessert-dish with a folded napkin, and serve.

1101. Cocoanut Pie.—Prepare and proceed exactly the same as for custard pie (No. 1100), and when filled, before placing it in the oven, spread evenly over six ounces of dried cocoanut; baking and serving it exactly the same.

1102. Lemon Cream Pie, Méringué.—Boil one pint of water in a saucepan; put in another vessel four ounces of powdered sugar, mix in one ounce of corn-starch, grate in the rind of a sound lemon, squeezing in the juice, and mingle well together with the spatula for one minute. Break in two whole eggs, beat all together for one minute, and add it to the boiling water in the pan, stirring sharply with a wire whip until it comes to a boil; then take from off the fire. Have ready a lined, flat pie-plate as for mince pie (No. 1082), put it in the oven, and let it bake for ten minutes, so that the crust gets a good golden color. Remove from the oven, and pour the preparation into it, then let it get thoroughly cold. Beat in a copper basin three egg whites to a stiff froth, using a wire pastry-whip; mix in three ounces of powdered sugar, and with a spoon lay half of it over the pie, using a knife to flatten it evenly on the top and sides. Slide down a fancy tube (No. 3) into a pastry-bag (No. 1079), and pour the rest of the froth into it, then decorate the top of the pie artistically, laying it in any fanciful design. Sprinkle plenty of sugar over, place it in a slow oven for ten minutes to let get a pale brown color, then remove it, put it away to cool, slide it carefully onto a dessert-dish, and send to the table.

1103. Apple Pie, Méringué.—Butter and line a pie-plate as for mince pie (No. 1082); put in a vessel one pound of apple sauce (No. 1328), one ounce of powdered sugar, and one ounce of corn-starch. Mix well for one minute, then grate in the rind of a sound lemon, squeezing in the juice as well; add half a saltspoonful of grated nutmeg, and mix the whole well together for two minutes, then with this fill the pie-plate. Place it in the oven, and let bake for twenty minutes; remove, let get thoroughly cold, and finish the same as for lemon pie, méringué (No. 1102), serving it as for the above.

DESSERTS.

1104. Cranberry Pie.—Put one quart of fresh cranberries in a saucepan with a gill of cold water and three ounces of powdered sugar; place on a hot stove, stir lightly with the spatula, and let cook for fifteen minutes. Remove from the fire, and rub through a sieve into a vessel, then pour it into a lined pie-plate, the same as for mince pie (No. 1082). Place it in the oven, and let bake for twenty minutes, then take it out, and let cool thoroughly, and finish by decorating it exactly the same as for lemon cream pie, méringué (No. 1102); return it to the oven for ten minutes, then serve as for the lemon pie.

1105. Pie à la Martha Washington.—Peel four ounces of almonds; put them in a mortar with two ounces of powdered sugar, then pound them thoroughly, adding gradually one raw egg. When well pounded, add two ounces more of powdered sugar, two ounces of melted fresh butter, half a gill of rum, half a saltspoonful of ground cinnamon, six drops of orange-flower water, and break in another whole egg. Pound the whole briskly for five minutes, then add two ounces of well-pounded macaroons (No. 1210), and mix again for two minutes more. Line a pie-plate as for mince pie (No. 1082), pour all the preparation over, cover, and bake exactly the same as for the mince pie; when arranged on a dessert-dish, decorate the top and sides artistically with two ounces of candied cherries, three ounces of pear, one of angelica, two of apricot, and two of pineapple, all the fruits being candied, then send to the table.

1106. Peach Tarts.—Take half a pound of feuilletage (No. 1076), roll it out twelve inches long by eight wide, then with a paste-cutter (No. 7) cut out six pieces, and arrange them neatly on six scalloped tart-molds, each three and a half inches wide. Take each separate mold in the hand, and with the thumb press the paste gently at the bottom and sides, so to give it the perfect shape of the mold, but avoid pressing the paste on the edge, so that in baking it will swell and raise beautifully. Divide three ounces of apple marmalade (No. 1332) into six equal parts, and fill the bottom of the tarts with it, then wipe six good-sized, solid, fine peaches, peel and cut them into six quartered pieces; arrange them nicely over the marmalade in the tarts, then distribute two ounces of powdered sugar evenly over all; lay them on a baking-sheet, put them in a moderate oven for twenty minutes, draw them to the door, and sprinkle the edges lightly with powdered sugar; then leave them in the closed oven for two minutes to allow the sugar to melt thoroughly. Remove them from the fire, put to cool for twenty minutes, and then spread evenly over the peaches one and a half ounces of apple jelly (No. 1327). Dress the tarts on a dessert-dish with a folded napkin, and serve.

1107. Green-gage Tarts.—Procure twelve ripe green-gages, wipe well, cut them in quarters, remove the stones, and proceed to prepare them exactly the same as for the above peach tarts (No. 1106).

1108. Apricot Tarts.—Prepare and proceed exactly the same as for peach tarts (No 1106), using ten apricots instead of the peaches, and serving the same.

1109. Pear Tarts.—Are to be prepared precisely the same as peach tarts (No. 1106), only substituting six sound, sliced pears for the peaches.

1110. Plum Tarts.—Have twelve good, ripe plums; wipe and quarter them; remove the stones, and prepare them exactly the same as for peach tarts (No. 1106).

1111. Cherry Tarts.—Have a pound of picked and stoned cherries; divide them evenly into six tarts, prepared as for peach tarts (No. 1106), and finishing them the same.

1112. Rhubarb Tarts.—Take six medium-sized rhubarb stalks, pare off the green parts, and peel them well. Then cut them into small pieces half an inch long; put them into a saucepan, on a very slow fire; cover, and let cook slowly for fifteen minutes; then remove, and add three ounces of powdered sugar; mix well for one minute, then transfer to another vessel, and set aside in a cool place for at least an hour and a half. Divide the rhubarb into six tarts, as for peach tarts (No. 1106); finish, and serve exactly the same.

1113. Huckleberry Tarts.—Put in a vessel one pint of well-picked and cleaned, sound huckleberries; mix in two ounces of powdered sugar, and with it fill evenly six tarts; cook and serve the same as for peach tarts (No. 1106).

1114. Gooseberry and Currant Tarts.—Are to be prepared precisely the same as for the above (No. 1113); using either one pint of gooseberries or currants instead of the huckleberries.

1115. Pineapple Tarts.—Choose a small, sound pineapple, cut it in two, roll a towel round one-half and lay it in the ice-box for further use. Pare and peal neatly the other half; then cut it into small and very thin slices; lay them in a vessel with two ounces of powdered sugar, mixing lightly for one minute. Arrange the slices carefully over the marmalade in the six tarts, prepared as for peach tarts (No. 1106); then finish, and serve exactly the same.

1116. Cranberry Tarts.—Have six tart-molds lined as for peach tarts (No. 1106); divide into them twelve ounces of cranberry sauce (No. 1329), then cook, and serve the same.

1117. Strawberry Tarts.—Line six tart-molds as for peach tarts (No. 1106), divide into them evenly eight ounces of apple marmalade (No. 1332); lay them on a baking-sheet, and put them in a moderate oven for twenty minutes; remove them to the door; sprinkling the edges liberally with powdered sugar, return them to the oven, and close the door for two minutes, so that the sugar melts thoroughly; lift them out, put them to cool for twenty minutes, then take out half the marmalade. Pick and wash neatly a pint of ripe and sound strawberries; put them in a vessel with two ounces of powdered sugar; mix well for one minute, then divide them equally into the six tarts; spread over one and a half ounces of apple jelly (No. 1327); dress them on a dessert-dish with a folded napkin, and serve.

1118. Raspberry Tarts.—Prepare and proceed precisely the same as for strawberry tarts (No. 1117), only substituting a pint of raspberries for the strawberries.

1119. Blackberry Tarts.—Are to be prepared exactly the same as strawberry tarts (No. 1117), using one pint of the smallest sized blackberries instead of the strawberries, and serving the same.

1120. Apple Tarts.—Take four ounces of pie-paste (No. 1077), and with it line six oval, channeled tart-molds, four inches long, three inches wide, and one deep. Have three ounces of apple marmalade, and divide it evenly at the bottom of the molds; then peel, core, and cut four sound, medium-sized apples into quarters, and put them in a saucepan, with a pint of cold water; place the lid on, and let cook on the hot stove for ten minutes; remove, and pour into a drainer; let drain thoroughly; then put to cool for thirty minutes. Cut the quartered apples each into three lengthwise slices; arrange them nicely over the marmalade, dredging equally over them two ounces of powdered sugar; lay them on a baking-sheet, and bake for twenty-five minutes in a moderate oven; leave to cool for twenty minutes; then spread evenly over them two ounces of apple jelly (No. 1327); dress them onto a dessert-dish with a folded napkin, and serve.

1121. Frangipani Tarts.—Peel three ounces of shelled almonds, as for No. 1207; put them in a mortar, and pound them thoroughly with three ounces of powdered sugar, adding one whole raw egg. When a fine paste, mix in two ounces of melted fresh butter, half a spoonful of ground cinnamon, six drops of orange-flower water, one more egg, and half a gill of rum. Stir well together for ten minutes with the powder. Have ready six tart-molds, lined as for peach tarts (No. 1106); then fill them with the above preparation; lay them on a baking-sheet, put them in a moderate oven for thirty-five minutes; when done, put them to cool for twenty minutes; then glaze the surface with a glace à l'eau and rum (No. 1197). Dress on a hot dessert-dish, with a folded napkin, and send to the table.

1122. Baked Apple Dumplings.—Sift one pound of flour on the table, make a hollow in the centre, laying in it half a pound of butter, mingling it slightly with the flour for five minutes ; when done, make another hollow in the centre, pour into it half a pint of cold water and two ounces of powdered sugar. Mix all together gradually for five minutes longer; it will then be a firm dough. Roll it together with the hands, and put it in a cool place for five minutes. Peel and core six medium-sized pippin apples, sprinkle the table lightly with flour, lay the butter on it, roll it out twelve inches long by eight wide, and about the thickness of a silver dollar, then cut it into six equal-sized, square pieces. Arrange the apples upwards in the middle of each square piece ; mix together two ounces of granulated sugar with one teaspoonful of ground cinnamon, and fill the cavities of the apples with this. Break one egg into a bowl, beat it well, adding two tablespoonfuls of cold milk, mix well, and with a pastry hair-brush moisten the edges of the pieces of dough, and fold them firmly so that the apples are entirely enclosed. Lay them on a baking-pan, and with the rest of the beaten egg brush over the surface and sides of the dumplings. Place them in a moderate oven for thirty minutes, and after they are a nice light golden color, remove, and dress them on a dessert-dish, leaving them to rest in the open oven for twenty minutes, then pour the following sauce over before serving : put into a saucepan one pint of water, six ounces of granulated sugar, one bay-leaf, six cloves, and an inch-long stick of cinnamon. Place the pan on the hot stove, and let boil for five minutes ; dilute half an ounce of corn-starch in a bowl with half a gill of cold water, add it to the sauce, mix well, and let cook for two minutes longer, stirring briskly with a spatula. Remove from the fire, and immediately add half a pint of good claret ; stir again, and when ready to serve, strain the sauce through a sieve over the dumplings. Hard sauce, as in the following number, may be substituted if desired, or both.

1123. Hard Sauce.—Put in a bowl two ounces of very good fresh butter with four ounces of powdered sugar, then with a spatula, beat together sharply for twenty minutes ; add half a saltspoonful of powdered mace, beat briskly for five minutes longer, then arrange it tastefully on a dessert-dish, and place it in the ice-box for two hours before serving.

1124. Baked Apples.—Core with an apple-corer six fine, sound Newtown apples, lay them in a tin pan. Put in a plate two ounces of granulated sugar with a saltspoonful of cinnamon, mix well, and with this fill the holes in the apples ; add half a pint of cold water, and place the pan in a moderate oven to let bake for twenty-five minutes ; remove, and dress them on a dessert-dish, pouring over the juice remaining in the pan, and serve either hot or cold.

1125. Boiled Peach Dumplings.—Put in a vessel half a pound of well-sifted flour, mixed with half an ounce of baking-powder ; make a hollow in the centre, and pour into it a gill of lukewarm milk, half an ounce of butter, half a saltspoonful of salt, and break in one whole egg. Mix these ingredients well for two minutes, then incorporate the flour gradually. Lay the paste on a lightly floured board or table, roll it into a square a quarter of an inch thick, then with a plain paste-cutter (No. 7) cut out six pieces, putting in the middle of each piece two ounces of stewed peaches (No. 1334), fold up the edges all round, so as to enclose the peaches entirely, then have six small pieces of thick white cloth, eight inches square, butter and flour them well, then arrange the dumplings in them ; tie them firmly, leaving an empty space of an inch to allow the dumplings to swell, and plunge them in a large saucepan, holding a gallon of boiling water, and let them boil for twenty minutes ; remove from the fire, and lift them out with a fork ; let drain for two minutes, then cut the strings and remove the cloths. Dress the dumplings on a hot dessert-dish, pour over a hot wine sauce as for No. 1122, and serve.

1126. Boiled Apricot Dumplings.—Prepare and proceed exactly the same as for boiled peach dumplings (No. 1125), only substituting twelve ounces of stewed apricots (No. 1335) for the peaches, and serve with a rum sauce (No. 1162), instead of wine sauce.

1127. Boiled Apple Dumplings.—Prepare and proceed precisely as for boiled peach dumplings (No. 1125), only using twelve ounces of stewed apples (No. 1332) for the peaches, and pouring the sauce (No. 1128) over, instead of the wine sauce.

1128. Apricot Sauce.—Put four ounces of apricot marmalade (No. 1335) into a saucepan with one ounce of fresh butter and a gill of water; set it on the hot stove and stir briskly with the spatula until it comes to a boil, then take from off the fire, and add immediately a gill of good brandy, mixing again with the spatula for one minute more, then pour the sauce over the boiled apple dumplings, and serve.

1129. Diplomatic Pudding, Punch Sauce.—Pare off, remove the skin and strings from four ounces of veal-suet and three ounces of beef-marrow, lay them in a saucepan with two ounces of finely chopped plums and three ounces of flour. Place the saucepan on a slow fire, and stir well with the spatula for six minutes; add three egg yolks and one whole egg, half a gill of sweet cream, half a gill of maraschino, a saltspoonful of salt, and half a saltspoonful of grated nutmeg. Stir all together thoroughly for six minutes, not letting it boil, then take it off the fire, and lay the pan in a cool place, adding one ounce of whole pistache, also two ounces of macaroons pounded in a mortar, half an ounce of angelica, and half an ounce of candied cherries, all well chopped. Mix well for one minute; peel, core, and chop up three medium-sized apples, add them to the preparation with two ounces of powdered sugar, and a tablespoonful of vanilla flavoring; then stir all together for twelve or fifteen minutes. Butter and flour neatly a cloth, arrange it in a deep vessel, and pour the preparation into it; lift up the four corners, close them together, and tie firmly with a string, leaving an empty space, about the eighth of the contents, to allow it to swell. Have a saucepan half full of boiling water ready to plunge the pudding into, then let boil for three full hours; the pudding will constantly float, therefore turn it every hour, when it will be thoroughly cooked. Remove it, let drain for two minutes, untie, lift it from the cloth, and dress it on a hot dessert-dish. Have ready the following sauce: put in a saucepan half a gill of rum, three ounces of powdered sugar, the grated rind of half an orange, and a teaspoonful of vanilla flavoring. Put it on the stove, and as soon as the liquid catches a light flame, put on the lid and let all infuse for one minute. Take from off the fire, and immediately squeeze in the juice of one orange; strain through a sieve over the pudding, and serve very hot.

1130. Rice Pudding with Orange.—Clean half a pound of fine rice; wash it in lukewarm water, then drain in a colander; put three pints of milk into a saucepan, place it on the hot stove, and when near a boil, drop in the rice. Let cook slowly for twelve minutes, stirring it frequently from the bottom with a spatula; remove it from the fire, and add one ounce of fresh butter, three ounces of powdered sugar, and the grated rind of a medium-sized orange. Mix well for two minutes, then add three ounces of well-skinned and stringed marrow, finely chopped, two ounces of dried and cleaned currants (No. 1080), two ounces of bitter almond macaroons (No. 1209), one ounce of finely shred candied orange-peel, three egg yolks, one whole one, half a gill of brandy, and half a saltspoonful of salt; mix well together for ten minutes. Have a buttered and floured cloth, arrange it in a deep vessel, and pour the preparation into it; lift up the four corners, tie it firmly, being careful to leave an empty space of about an eighth of the contents.

Place a deep saucepan on the stove, half filled with boiling water; plunge the pudding in, and let cook for one hour and a half, turning it over a couple of times; remove, drain for one minute, untie, and lift from the cloth. Dress on a dessert-dish, and serve with the following sauce (No. 1131).

1131. Sauce à l'Anglaise à l'Orange.—Put in a saucepan four egg yolks with four ounces of powdered sugar, and stir with a spatula until it becomes a whitish color. Add two gills of sweet cream, little by little, beating continually, then grate in the rind of an orange. Place the pan on a slow stove, and stir well for four minutes, being careful not to let it boil; take it off, strain through a sieve over the pudding, and serve very hot.

1132. Bread Pudding, Cream Sauce.—Take a deep, oval dish as for a pot-pie, and large enough to hold three pints. Pare off the crust of half a loaf of stale American bread, and cut it into slices the third of an inch thick; butter them well with melted butter, and with them line the dish. Put in a vessel six ounces of currants, prepared as for No. 1080, two whole eggs, a pint of cold milk, four ounces of powdered sugar, and grate in the rind of a medium-sized lemon, adding its juice. Mix well together with a spatula for two minutes, then pour it into the lined dish, and place it in a moderate oven to cook for thirty minutes. Take it from the oven, lay it on another dish, and serve very hot.

1133. Cream Sauce.—Put a pint of milk to boil in a saucepan on the stove. Break into a vessel two whole raw eggs, add one ounce of flour, half an ounce of corn-starch, and three ounces of powdered sugar, beating the whole well together with a spatula for three minutes. If the milk be boiling, add it gradually to the preparation, stirring continually for two minutes, return the whole to the saucepan, place it on the stove, and stir briskly till it comes to a boil, then remove, and add immediately a teaspoonful of vanilla flavoring. Strain the sauce through a sieve into a sauce-bowl, and serve.

1134. Cold Maraschino Pudding.—Put in a copper basin a quarter of a pound of powdered sugar, two whole raw eggs, and grate in the rind of a quarter of a medium-sized lemon, and with a pastry whip beat the whole sharply for two minutes ; put the basin on a very moderate fire, then beat it vigorously for five minutes more. Remove it from the fire, lay the basin on a table, continue beating slowly for two minutes longer, then give the whip a sharp shake, so that all that adheres to it falls into the basin. Now add a quarter of a pound of flour, and with a wooden spoon mix slowly and carefully the whole for two minutes. Cover a pastry baking-pan with a sheet of brown paper, pour the paste over it, spread out to the thickness of half an inch ; put it into a moderate oven, and let bake for fifteen minutes, then take it out, let cool for another fifteen minutes, and remove from the pan. Place it on a table upside down, remove the paper, and with a knife cut it into small, square, dice-shaped pieces, mixing with them one ounce of dried currants, as for No. 1080, and one ounce of finely chopped candied citron.

Butter and sugar well six small pudding-molds, each capable of containing one and a half gills. Fill them equally with the above preparation, then put in a vessel four ounces of powdered sugar with two raw eggs; beat well with a pastry-whip for two minutes, then add a pint of cold milk, mixing again for one minute, strain through a sieve into another vessel, add half a teaspoonful of lemon essence, and stir lightly for one minute more. Pour this slowly over the puddings, a little each time, so as to give the necessary opportunity for it to absorb; lay them on a tin pan, filled to half the height of the molds with warm but not boiling water, then place in a moderate oven to steam for thirty minutes; remove them from the pan, and lay them in a cool place for one hour, afterwards leaving them in the ice-box until ready to serve. Take a pint of whipped cream, as for No. 1254, put it in a vessel, mixing in for two minutes half a gill of good maraschino, and leave it in the ice-box until ready; then prepare a cold dessert-dish. Run a thin knife down each pudding separately, from top to bottom, pass it carefully around the mold, so as to detach them easily. Pour the maraschino sauce over, and send to the table immediately.

1135. Cold Pudding à la Porfirio Diaz.—Prepare six small puddings exactly the same as for No. 1134, only substituting sauce à la Diaz (No. 1136) for the maraschino sauce.

1136. Sauce à la Diaz.—Put into a saucepan half a pint of Jamaica rum, three ounces of granulated sugar, half a split vanilla-bean, grate in the rind of a medium-sized orange, and add a gill of Marcella wine. Place the pan on the stove, and as soon as the liquid catches fire put on the cover, and let boil for one minute only. Set the pan on one side to allow it to infuse for five minutes, then strain through a fine sieve into a bowl, transfer it to a jar, cover tightly, and let cool off thoroughly. When ready to serve, pour the sauce over the puddings, distributing it evenly, and then send to the table.

1137. English Pudding, Baked.—Put in a saucepan two gills of sweet cream, three ounces of powdered sugar, and the peel of half a medium-sized lemon; place the pan on the stove, and, with a spatula, stir, and let boil for three minutes and take off the fire. Have ten ounces of stale French bread, pare off the crust and cut it into small, dice-shaped pieces; add them to the preparation, mixing lightly; put on the lid, and let the bread soak for ten minutes. Chop up very fine one ounce of candied citron; mix it with four ounces of dried currants, prepared as for No. 1080, four ounces of melted butter, four ounces of melted and strained beef-marrow, and a saltspoonful of salt. With the hand stir thoroughly for two minutes. Pour this preparation in with the soaked bread, and mix gently, either with the hand or a spatula, for ten minutes; meanwhile breaking in three eggs, one by one at a minute's interval, and adding a gill of Madeira wine and half a gill of cognac. Butter, and sprinkle well with bread-crumbs a two-quart pudding-mold; pour in all the preparation, lay it on a baking-pan, and place it in a slow oven to bake for one and a half hours. Remove, and with the aid of a towel turn it onto a hot dessert-dish, serving it with a hot Sabayon sauce au madère (No. 1138).

1138. Sabayon Sauce au Madère.—Put in a saucepan four egg yolks and an ounce and a half of powdered sugar; place it on a hot stove, and with a wire whip stir well for two minutes. Drop in gradually two gills of Madeira wine; stir continually for two minutes; take from the fire, and strain through a fine sieve over the pudding.

1139. French Pudding à la Delmonico.—Line the insides of six oval, channeled, deep tart-molds, each holding one and a half gills, with four ounces of pie-paste (No. 1077). Prepare a cake exactly as for Maraschino pudding (No. 1134), and when cooked and on the table, remove the paper, and break up the cake in small pieces, into a vessel. Moisten with two gills of cold milk and two eggs, and mix well with the spatula for two minutes; add two ounces of dried currants (No. 1080). Mix in a saucer a saltspoonful of cinnamon, with one of allspice and one of cloves, all ground, and add it to the preparation in the bowl; stir well for three minutes; then, with a wooden spoon, fill up the molds, and lay them on a baking-pan. Put it into a moderate oven for ten minutes; then remove, cool off, and unmold; lay them on a table, and pour over each pudding a teaspoonful of rum, and with a light pastry-brush glaze the surface with glace à l'eau (No. 1197). Dress them on a dessert-dish, and serve.

1140. Sago Pudding.—Boil in a saucepan one quart of milk; add a quarter of a pound of sago, and, with a pastry wire-whip, stir briskly and continually for fifteen minutes. Take from off the fire; let cool; then add four ounces of powdered sugar, mixing well again for one minute. Break in four eggs, and flavor with a teaspoonful of vanilla essence; then mix well for two minutes longer. Butter and sugar well six small pudding-molds, the same size as for maraschino pudding (No. 1134), and, with a ladle, fill up the molds with the sago; place them in a tin pan, filling it to half the height of the molds with warm but not boiling water. Then put in the oven and let steam for thirty-five minutes. Remove; take the molds from the pan with a towel, and with a thin knife detach them properly. Then turn them on a hot dessert-dish, serving them with a sauce à la crême (No. 1133).

1141. Tapioca Pudding.—The same as for the above, using tapioca.
1142. Vermicelli Pudding.—The same, using vermicelli.
1143. Rice Pudding.—The same, using rice.
1144. Farina Pudding.—The same, using farina.
1145. Indian Pudding.—The same, using corn-meal.

1146. Chocolate Pudding.—Put in a saucepan five ounces of fresh butter, five ounces of powdered sugar, five ounces of finely cut cocoa, and five egg yolks; place the pan on the hot stove, and with a pastry-whip stir briskly for five minutes, then take from off the fire. Beat up in a copper basin the whites of the five eggs to a firm froth, and add them to the preparation in the saucepan, mixing all well together for two minutes.

Butter and sugar well six small pudding-molds as for No. 1134, and fill them with the preparation, then place them in a tin pan, filling the pan to half the height of the molds with warm but not boiling water. Put in the oven for thirty minutes, then take out, turn them on a hot dessert-dish, and serve with a sauce à la crême (No. 1133) poured over.

1147. Cocoanut Pudding.—Butter and sugar well six small pudding-molds as for No. 1134; distribute evenly in them half a pound of dried cocoanut. Put into a vessel four ounces of powdered sugar, break in three whole eggs, mix well for two minutes with the wire whip, then add one and a half pints of cold milk; flavor with a teaspoonful of vanilla flavoring, then mix two minutes longer. Strain through a sieve into another vessel, and with it fill up the molds; arrange them on a tin pan, fill to half their height with warm but not boiling water, then put in the oven and let steam for thirty-five minutes. Take from the oven, turn on a hot dessert-dish, and serve with a sauce à la crême (No. 1133), flavored with half a gill of brandy.

1148. Pineapple Pudding à la Richelieu.—Boil in a saucepan two gills of milk, adding two ounces of fresh butter; let melt well. Have half a pound of flour and the spatula ready. Drop the flour in, and stir immediately with the spatula as briskly as possible for two minutes; remove from off the fire, add three egg yolks, and stir again vigorously for two minutes more, drop in three ounces of powdered sugar, continue stirring for one minute, then pour in a gill of cold milk, mixing well. Beat to a stiff froth the whites of the three eggs, and add them gradually to the preparation, mixing slowly for two minutes. Butter and sugar a mold holding three pints; put a layer of the preparation half an inch thick at the bottom, cover with two ounces of fine slices of stewed pineapple, then another layer of the preparation, again the same quantity of pineapple, and repeat twice more. Place the mold in a tin pan, fill it to half the height of the mold with warm water, and set it in the oven to steam for one hour. Remove, and with a towel turn it on a hot dessert-dish, and serve with a sauce-bowl of sauce au Kirsch (No. 1149).

1149. Sauce au Kirsch.—Pour in a saucepan one pint of cold water and half a pound of granulated sugar; place it on a hot stove. Dilute an ounce of corn-starch in a cup with a gill of cold water, and when the water in the saucepan is boiling, add it to it, stirring well for two minutes with the pastry-whip. Take off from the fire, then add immediately half a gill of kirsch, and mix again for one minute; strain through a fine sieve into a sauce-bowl, and serve very hot with the pudding.

1150. Peach Pudding à la Richelieu.—Prepare and proceed exactly the same as for the above, No. 1148, only instead of using pineapple, have eight peeled and finely sliced peaches, either fresh or preserved. Steam, arrange on the dish, and serve precisely the same, with the sauce au kirsch (No. 1149).

1151. Apricot Pudding à la Richelieu.—The same as for the pineapple pudding (No. 1148), but using twelve sound, peeled, and finely sliced apricots instead of the pineapples, and then serve the pudding and sauce exactly the same.

1152. Apple Pudding à l'Helvétienne.—Prepare a pudding-paste exactly the same as for pinapple pudding (No. 1148); when ready, peel, core, and slice finely five medium-sized, sound apples; put them into a vessel, mix with them one ounce of powdered sugar and a teaspoonful of powdered cinnamon, and add this to the paste, and with a spatula mix thoroughly all together for three minutes. Butter and sugar well a three-pint mold, pour in the preparation, and lay the mold in a tin pan, filled to half the height of the mold with warm water; place in the oven, and let steam for one hour; take it from the oven, and with a towel turn it on a hot dessert-dish, and serve with the following sauce (No. 1153) in a sauce-bowl.

1153. Sauce Chaufausen.—Put half a pint of cold water in a sauce-pan, with three ounces of powdered sugar, six cloves, a bay-leaf, and a piece of cinnamon about an inch long. Put the pan on the fire, and let it boil for five minutes; then dilute an ounce of corn-starch with a gill of cold water; add it to the contents of the pan, and with a whip stir briskly for two minutes. Add one pint of Chaufausen wine, still stirring for one minute longer, then take from off the fire, strain through a sieve into a sauce-bowl, and serve.

1154. Custard Pudding.—Put into a vessel a quarter of a pound of powdered sugar, break in five whole eggs, and with the pastry-whip mix well for two minutes; add a quart of good, cold milk, and flavor with a teaspoonful of lemon essence; mix well together for one minute. Butter and sugar well six small pudding-molds, as for maraschino pudding (No. 1134); strain the preparation into another bowl, and then pour it into the molds; arrange them on a tin pan filled to half the height of the molds with warm but not boiling water; then place them in a moderate oven to steam for forty minutes. Remove from the oven, and with a towel turn them on a hot dessert-dish, serving with a sauce à la crème. (No. 1133).

1155. Nelson Pudding.—Butter and sugar well six small pudding-molds, as for maraschino pudding (No. 1134). Prepare twelve lady-fingers (No. 1231), cut them in two, paring them neatly and carefully, so as to be able to line the molds evenly, then cut the parings into small pieces. Mix in a plate three ounces of candied cherries with two ounces of well-chopped citron; cover the bottom of the molds with two ounces of this, then a layer of the lady-fingers; spread half of the remaining fruit on top, and fill in with the rest of the cake, finishing with the balance of the fruit; then pour over the following custard: put into a vessel four ounces of powdered sugar three whole eggs, and beat briskly with a pastry-whip for two minutes, then add a pint of cold milk, flavor with a teaspoonful of lemon essence, mix for one minute longer, then strain through a sieve into another vessel, and with a ladle divide it evenly over the six puddings. Set the molds in a tin pan, filling it to half their height with warm water, and place it in a moderate oven to steam for thirty-five minutes; take out from the oven, turn them on a hot dessert-dish, and serve with a Daniel Webster sauce (No. 1156).

1156. Daniel Webster Sauce.—Put into a saucepan four ounces of apricot marmalade (No. 1335), with half a gill of cold water; place it on the fire, and stir until boiling; then take it off, and add immediately half a pint of Saint Angelos Tokay wine, stirring thoroughly for one minute. Strain through a sieve over the puddings, and serve.

1157. Lemon Pudding, Cream Sauce.— Put in a saucepan six ounces of fresh butter, six ounces of powdered sugar, six egg yolks, and the grated peel of a medium-sized, sound lemon, squeezing in the juice as well. Set the pan on the hot stove, and with a wire pastry-whip stir sharply for at least five minutes. Remove from the fire and lay it on a table; beat in a copper basin the six egg-whites to a stiff froth, and add them to the other preparation, beating with the whip thoroughly but not briskly for ten minutes. Butter and sugar well six pudding-molds as for No. 1134, fill them with the preparation, steam them in a tin pan, and serve exactly the same as for custard pudding (No. 1154).

1158. Orange Pudding.—Proceed and prepare the same as for lemon pudding (No. 1157), only substituting an orange for the lemon, and serving with the following sauce: put in a saucepan two ounces of powdered sugar, half an ounce of flour, and break in three eggs, adding a teaspoonful of corn-starch, and then with the pastry-whip beating all together for three minutes. Mix in three gills of boiling milk, place it on the stove, and stir well until boiling; then remove, and add immediately a gill of sherry wine, mixing well for a minute longer, then strain through a sieve over the puddings. Send to the table hot.

1159. Pudding à la U. S. Grant.—Cut into small pieces six biscuits à la cuillère (No. 1231); put them into a vessel with three ounces of candied cherries cut in two, three ounces of preserved quinces cut into very fine pieces, two ounces of dried currants (No. 1080), three ounces of powdered sugar, and two ounces of finely chopped candied apricots; break in three whole eggs, and pour over half a pint of cold milk, and with the spatula mix well together for two minutes. Peel, core, and chop up three medium-sized, fine, sound apples; add them to the other ingredients, and mix lightly for one minute. Butter and sugar well around the inside of a three-pint pudding-mold, pour in the preparation, lay the mold in a tin pan, filling it to half the height of the mold with warm water; put it in a moderate oven, and let steam for one hour, then remove, and with a towel turn it on a hot dessert-dish, serving with the following sauce (No. 1160), in a sauce-bowl.

1160. Sauce for U. S. Grant Pudding.—Put five ounces of peach marmalade (No. 1331) into a saucepan with one ounce of quince jelly and one ounce of fresh butter ; place the pan on the stove, and stir with the spatula, letting it boil for one minute ; take from off the fire, add immediately a pint of champagne, then return to the stove, and stir well, heating it thoroughly, but not allowing it to boil. Remove, and strain through a sieve into a sauce-bowl, and send to the table very hot with the pudding.

1161. Fruit Pudding, Rum Sauce.—Butter well a pudding-mold four inches high, containing one quart, line the interior with half a pound of dumpling-batter (No. 1125). Put into a vessel four ounces of stoned cherries, three ounces of stoned plums, and three ounces of stoned apricots; sift four ounces of powdered sugar over, mix well, and pour it into the mold. Have half a pint of water in a saucepan with six ounces of granulated sugar, place it on the stove, and let boil for five minutes, then fill up the mold with this syrup, and lay it in a baking-pan in a very hot oven for thirty minutes. Remove, and keep it in a warm place.

1162. Rum Sauce.—Put in a saucepan half a pint of water with four ounces of granulated sugar, and place it on the stove, adding a teaspoonful of caramel (No. 1252); when boiling add half an ounce of corn-starch, diluted in two tablespoonfuls of cold water, stir well with a spatula, and let cook for two minutes. Remove from the fire, and add immediately half a gill of Jamaica rum, mixing well, then strain it through a fine sieve into a bowl. Lay a dessert-dish over the mold, turn the pudding onto it, pour the sauce over, and serve.

1163. Plum Pudding.—Remove the skin and strings from six ounces of fresh beef-marrow; chop it up very fine, and place it in a basin; pick and wash, as for No. 1080, three ounces of dried currants, three ounces of dried Sultanas (No. 1080), and mix them well together with the marrow; add three ounces of Malaga raisins (No. 1081), three-quarters of a pound of crumbled bread-crumbs, half a gill of Madeira wine, half a gill of brandy, half a gill of rum, the grated rind of half a lemon, two ounces of candied citron, shred very fine, two ounces of powdered sugar, a saltspoonful of salt, and two whole eggs. Moisten the whole with a gill of cold milk, add a saltspoonful each of allspice, ground clove, and cinnamon, and half the quantity of grated nutmeg; knead well with the hands, so that the ingredients are thoroughly incorporated, which will take ten minutes. Boil some water in a saucepan capable of holding the pudding; butter and flour a cloth, lay it on a large colander, which will answer for a hollow mold; pour the mixture into it, then hold the four corners together, and tie it firmly, allowing sufficient space for it to swell. Plunge the pudding into the boiling water, and let cook, leaving it half covered; the water must boil steadily for five hours; every hour turn it over, and then make the following sauce: put into a saucepan one ounce of fresh butter, two drachms of flour, and three drops of lemon juice, the finely sliced rind of a quarter of a lemon, half a saltspoonful of salt, and half an ounce of powdered sugar. Moisten with a gill of port wine, then place the pan on the stove, and with a spatula stir well, until it comes to a boil. Remove from the fire, and strain through a fine sieve into a bowl. When ready to serve, drain the plum pudding for one moment, untie, and open the cloth; serve it immediately, pouring some of the sauce over.

1164. Cabinet Pudding à la Sadi-Carnot.—Butter and sugar a pudding-mold of the capacity of three pints. Have ready four ounces of Malaga raisins, prepared as for No. 1081, three ounces of Sultana, three ounces of currants, as for No. 1080, three ounces of finely chopped candied citron, and three ounces of candied cherries, cut in two. Mix well together, then with four ounces of the fruit cover the bottom of the mold, put on top a layer of biscuits à la cuillère (No. 1231), or slices of sponge cake, four more ounces of fruit, another layer of cake, and repeat twice more, and the mold will then be full. Put into a vessel a pint and a half of cold milk, six ounces of powdered sugar, three raw, fresh eggs, and a teaspoonful of lemon essence, and with a pastry-whip beat well for two minutes. Strain into another vessel, then pour it slowly and carefully over the cake in the mold, so that it will be thoroughly impregnated. Lay the mold in a square tin pan, filling it to half its height with hot water, then place in a moderate oven for one hour. Remove it from the pan, lay a dessert-dish over the mold, unmold, and decorate the top with fanciful designs of red-currant jelly (No. 1326); serve it hot with a sauce-bowlful of the following sauce (No. 1165).

1165. Sauce à la Sadi-Carnot.—Put in a saucepan two ounces of fresh butter, stir in one ounce of flour, and moisten slowly with a gill of cold water, turning continually; add two ounces of powdered sugar, place the pan on the stove, add half a pint of Château-Lagrange wine, and a teaspoonful of vanilla flavoring. Stir well, and let boil for one minute, then remove, and strain it through a sieve into another saucepan; replace the pan on the corner of the stove so as to keep it hot, then take one ounce of citron, slice it as fine as possible, also one ounce of finely minced pistache; add them to the other ingredients, and finally stir in slowly a tablespoonful of red curaçoa; mix well together for one minute, then pour into the sauce-bowl, and serve.

1166. Caramel Pudding.—Put in a vessel four eggs with three ounces of powdered sugar, mix briskly with the pastry-whip for two minutes, then add one and a half pints of cold milk, and a teaspoonful of lemon essence; then mix well again for one minute, strain this through a sieve into another vessel. Butter and sugar well six small molds as for maraschino pudding (No. 1134), fill them one inch high with caramel (No. 1252), let cool off for five minutes, then pour in the preparation, dividing it equally; place them in a tin pan filled to half the height of the molds with warm but not boiling water, put in a moderate oven, and let steam for forty minutes. Take them out, turn them on a hot dessert-dish, and serve in their own sauce. This pudding may be prepared in cups instead of molds.

1167. Apple Charlotte.—Select four large or six medium-sized Newtown pippins. Peel, core, and cut them into quarters. Put them into a saucepan with two ounces of fresh butter and four ounces of powdered sugar, and place on a moderate fire. Toss them for two minutes, then moisten with a gill of white wine, and grate in the peel of half a lemon. Cover the saucepan, and let cook for ten minutes so that the liquid be almost entirely absorbed by the apples. Remove from the fire, and put aside to cool. Take a three-pint charlotte-mold ; line it, beginning from the bottom, with cut slices of American bread the thickness of a silver dollar. Glaze them well with melted butter, using a hair brush for the purpose, and sprinkle powdered sugar lightly over. Let each slice overlap slightly until the bottom is covered. Then line the sides to the edge in the same way. Fill the mold with the prepared apples, and cover with slices of bread. Lay it on a baking-pan, and place it in a brisk oven for forty-five minutes, or until the bread be a good golden color. Then take it out, lay a hot dessert-dish on top, turn it over, and remove the mold. Heat in a saucepan two ounces of apricot marmalade with two tablespoonfuls of maraschino and one of water. Mix well, pour it over the charlotte, and serve very hot.

1168. Small Apple Charlottes.—Prepare and cook the apples the same as for No. 1167, and when removed from the fire, put it aside to cool. Trim the crust off of a quarter of a loaf of stale American bread. Cut it into slices the thickness of a silver dollar. Butter and sugar well six small, round pudding-molds. Shape the slices of bread carefully, to line the insides. Butter them lightly; place them in a clean baking-pan, and leave in the oven for five minutes to get a brown color. Remove them; let them cool a little, and then line the molds with them. Fill in with the apples, and lay the full molds on a baking-pan in the oven for twenty minutes. Turn the charlottes out on a dessert-dish. Heat half a pint of raspberry juice in a saucepan, pour it over them, and serve hot.

1169. Apples with Rice.—Core and peel neatly six sound, fine Newtown apples. Put into a saucepan with a gill of water and two ounces of sugar. Place it on a hot stove, put the lid on, and let cook for ten minutes. Meanwhile boil four ounces of rice in a pint and a half of milk, with half a saltspoonful of salt. Flavor it with six drops of orange-flower water, and let cook for twelve minutes. Place the cooked apples in a square tin pan, pour the boiled rice over them, and put into a moderate oven for ten minutes. Then have a hot dessert-dish ready, and with a tinned cake-turner dress them carefully on the dish, decorating the sides with the rice. Should a pyramidal shape be desired, place three apples in the centre, two on top of these, and the last one above them all, then fill up the empty space around them with the rice, and serve with half a pint of vanilla syrup in a separate sauce-bowl.

The sauce is made thus: put two pounds of granulated sugar into a saucepan with one quart of cold water, and set it on the hot stove. Stir well for two minutes; add two vanilla-beans split in halves, and boil for ten minutes longer. Remove from the fire; strain through a sieve into another vessel, and use when required. This syrup, when cold, may be poured into bottles, and if corked tightly and put away in a cool place, will keep in good condition for a month at least.

1170. Riz au Lait d'Amandes.—Into one pint of boiling water in a saucepan drop four ounces of well-cleaned rice, with half a saltspoonful of salt, the peel of a quarter of a medium-sized, sound lemon, and two leaves of the almond branch. Let all cook together for twelve minutes. Meanwhile peel four ounces of almonds. Pound them in a mortar with two tablespoonfuls of sweet cream, or the same quantity of cold milk will answer. Tie a clean napkin over a vessel; pour on the pounded almonds, and with a spatula rub the liquid gently through. Remove the rice from the stove; take out the almond-leaves and lemon-peel; then sweeten with three ounces of powdered sugar, and add the almond milk. Return it to the stove, and with a spatula stir gently while cooking for twelve minutes. Pour into a hot china or glass bowl, and send to the table.

1171. Riz au Lait d'Amandes à l'Airolo.—Proceed and prepare the rice exactly as for the above (No. 1170), but after removing it from the stove add immediately half a gill of pure Swiss kirschwasser, mixing it in well with a spatula for five minutes. Pour into a china or glass bowl; cool for one hour at least; then place it in the ice-box until ready to serve.

1172. Riz aux Pommes à la Bonne Femme.—Put a pint of milk in a saucepan on the stove. When boiling, add three ounces of well-cleaned rice and half a saltspoonful of salt. Let cook for twenty minutes, adding one ounce of butter. Mix for one minute; then remove from the fire, and let it cool off for thirty minutes. Add the yolks of two eggs. Beat the whites to a froth in a basin with a wire whip, and add them to the rice. Sweeten with three ounces of powdered sugar and flavor with a teaspoonful of orange-flower water. Mix well together for five minutes. Peel and core four sound Newtown pippin apples, and cut in slices about the thickness of a silver dollar. Butter the sides of a saucepan lightly; then cover the bottom with a layer of the prepared rice half an inch thick; put a layer of sliced apples over this, and so dispose of all the apples and rice in alternate layers. Put on the lid, and put the saucepan into a moderate oven for fifteen minutes. Remove, dress on a hot dish, and serve.

1173. Riz au Pommes à la Czar.—Prepare rice and apples as above (No. 1172), but before putting into the oven, run a larding needle down through it in a dozen places at equal distances, and pour over half a gill of Russian kummel. Put on the lid; place in a moderate oven and let cook for twenty minutes. Remove, and dress it neatly on a dish, sending it to the table with a bowl of sauce à la crême (No. 1133), but using two tablespoonfuls of the kummel instead of the brandy for flavoring, as described in cocoanut pudding (No. 1147).

1174. Turban of Apples au Riz.—Prepare half a pound of boiled rice as for No. 1172. Butter a mold holding three pints. Garnish the bottom and sides with the rice, using a wooden spoon for the purpose. Peel, core, and cut into quarters six fine, sound, Newtown pippin apples. Put them into a saucepan with three ounces of powdered sugar, a gill of cold water, and half a saltspoonful of salt. Place the pan on a hot stove, put on the lid, and let cook for ten minutes. Remove, and fill the mold with eighteen of the pieces, reserving the other six for later use; then put it in a slow oven for twelve minutes. Use an ordinary towel to remove it from the oven. Lay a dessert-dish on top, turn over, and lift off the mold. Decorate the base with the rest of the apples, inclining them slightly; and the top with two ounces of cleaned currants (No. 1080). Garnish between the apples with four ounces of candied fruits, placing some on top. Pears, angelica, and cherries, all sliced, make a pretty effect. Return to the oven for five minutes, and serve.

1175. Iced Timbale au Riz.—Line a timbale-mold holding three pints with a quarter of a pound of pie-paste (No. 1077). Have ready three-quarters of a pound of boiled rice (No. 1172). Peel, core, and cut into quarters three fine, sound apples; put them into a saucepan with two ounces of powdered sugar, one ounce of butter, half a gill of cold water, and half a saltspoonful of salt. Cover, and let cook for ten minutes. Remove the lid, and add to the apples two tablespoonfuls of apricot marmalade (No. 1335). Stir slightly at the bottom for four minutes with the spatula, being careful to avoid breaking the apples. Cover the bottom and sides of the timbale with half a pound of the boiled rice; pour in the apples, lay the remainder of the rice on top, and cover with an ounce and a half of pie-paste. Put the timbale into a moderate oven, and cook for thirty minutes. When the surface is of a good golden color, remove, and put aside to cool thoroughly, leaving it at least two hours. Turn it over onto a dessert-dish, remove the mold, and lay the timbale in a *short, low, wide* freezer; cover, then put it in a tub of nearly the same size, filling it well with chopped ice; sprinkle the top and sides freely with rock salt, and freeze thoroughly for an hour and a half. Remove the cover carefully to avoid any ice or salt falling into the freezer. Take out the timbale, and wipe well the dish. Have ready one pint of whipped cream (No. 1254) with half a gill of maraschino; beat this well for two minutes. Pour it over the timbale, and send immediately to the table. Should there be no freezer handy, the timbale may be cooled by placing in the ice-box for three hours.

1176. Croustade de Riz Méringuée.—On a floured board roll half a pound of feuilletage paste (No. 1076) into an oval shape, and a quarter of an inch thick. Lay it upside down on an oval dish ten inches long by six wide, and with a knife cut away the superfluous paste. Remove the dish, and place the oval paste in a baking-dish; then roll out the pieces which were cut away, and with a small fancy paste-cutter (No. 1) cut it all up. With a small hair pastry-brush dipped in beaten egg, wet the edges of the oval, and arrange the pieces all around, crown-shaped. Bake this croustade in a moderate oven thirty minutes. Have ready six ounces of boiled rice (No. 1172). Peel and core six medium-sized fine apples. Put them into a saucepan with two ounces of powdered sugar, a gill of cold water, and half a saltspoonful of salt. Put on the lid, and let cook on a slow fire for twenty minutes. Arrange half the rice on the croustade, dress the apples over, and fill up the cavities with the rest of the rice. Add to the juice of the apples in the pan two ounces of apricot marmalade (No. 1335). Mix well for two minutes and pour it over the whole. Then set it in a slow oven for fifteen minutes. Remove, and beat up two eggs as for a méringue (No. 1247), mixing in two ounces of powdered sugar. Put this into a pastry-bag (No. 1079), and decorate the surface of the croustade artistically with it, sprinkling a little sugar over. Return it to the oven for five minutes, to get a good color. Pass a knife gently under the croustade, and dexterously slide it from the baking-pan onto a hot dessert-dish, and serve.

1177. Rice with Milk.—Cleanse well a quarter of a pound of fine Italian rice. Place it in a saucepan with half a pint of water, adding half a pinch of salt, the zest of half a lemon, and one bay-leaf. Cook slowly for twenty-five minutes. Then put in three tablespoonfuls of powdered sugar and a pint of hot milk; finish cooking on a slow fire for ten minutes, and serve in a hot, deep dish.

1178. Rice à la Turque.—Wash well a quarter of a pound of rice, and blanch for ten minutes in boiling water. Put it into a saucepan, with a pint of milk, and let cook firmly; adding three tablespoonfuls of powdered sugar, and a lump of sugar onto which has been rubbed the peel of half a small lemon; also half an ounce of good butter, one ounce of cleaned currants (No. 1080), and a saltspoonful of salt. After twenty minutes, remove from the fire and thoroughly stir in the yolks of four eggs. Place this in a croustade, as for 1176, and put it in a slow oven for fifteen minutes. Remove, sprinkle with a little sugar, pass a hot shovel or salamander over the top; glaze it well, and serve at once.

1179. Rice à l'Indienne.—Prepare the rice as for the above (No. 1178), adding the third of a glassful of rum and a small infusion of diluted powdered saffron, to give it a good color. Serve glazed, as for the preceding (No. 1178).

1180. Rice à la Française.—Wash well, and blanch in boiling water for ten minutes, one-quarter of a pound of Italian rice. Boil in a saucepan with an ounce of butter, adding three tablespoonfuls of powdered sugar, a pint of milk, two bitter almond macaroons (No. 1209), half a teaspoonful of orange-flower water, half an ounce of candied orange-peel cut into shreds, about twelve candied cherries cut into halves, and twelve large, seeded, Muscatel raisins (No. 1081); also a quarter of an ounce of thin slices of candied angelica. Finish as for rice à la Turque (No. 1178), and serve with a sauce thickened with a gill of Alicante or Val-de-peras wine, or sherry, kirsch, or rum.

1181. Rice à la Condé.—Boil one pint of milk with one pint of water. When boiling, add four ounces of well-cleaned rice. Boil twenty-five minutes, stirring at the bottom every three minutes with a spatula. Set the saucepan on a table; add half a saltspoonful of salt, four ounces of powdered sugar, and six drops of orange-flower water. Mix well for one minute, break in three whole eggs, and stir again for two minutes. Arrange the rice nicely in a hot dessert-dish, keeping it high in the centre, and decorate with twelve pieces of stewed peaches (No. 1332), two ounces of dried currants (No. 1080), and one ounce of candied angelica cut in small lozenge-shaped pieces; beginning with the peaches on the top, and arranging the remainder of the fruit around.

1182. Nouilles, or Noodles.—Sift onto a table one pound of flour; make a hollow space in the centre, and place therein six egg yolks, half a gill of lukewarm water, one ounce of fresh butter, and half a saltspoonful of salt. Knead these thoroughly for five minutes; then mix in the flour gradually, and knead again for five minutes. Pile up the paste into a lump, flour the table slightly, and use the left hand to press the paste down in the centre, and with the right bring up the edges all around. Continue to repeat this for five minutes. Roll the paste into a ball, put it on a dish, cover with a napkin, and set it in a cool place to rest for fifteen minutes. Roll it out to the thickness of a fifty-cent piece. With a knife cut it into strips two inches wide, and from these, beginning at the end of each, shred it with the knife into narrow pieces resembling matches. Leave these to dry slightly on a floured board for thirty minutes, and they will be ready for use.

1183. Buckwheat Cakes.—Dilute one drachm of compressed yeast with a gill of lukewarm water, and let it rest for ten minutes. Add it to a half pound of buckwheat flour in a basin, pouring in a pint of cold water, and season with a light pinch of salt. Mix thoroughly with the spatula; cover the basin with a cloth, and let rest for four hours.

Have a griddle large enough to hold six cakes. Grease lightly with a piece of fat pork-rind, and place it on a hot stove. Pour half of the batter into the six sections of the griddle, distributing it evenly. Bake two and a half minutes, turn over and bake two and a half minutes longer. Heap them on a hot dessert-dish. Make the other six exactly the same way. Send to the table with honey or maple sugar separately.

1184. Wheat Cakes.—Put into a vessel four ounces of sifted wheat flour, half an ounce of powdered sugar, one drachm of compressed yeast. Break in four whole eggs, and mix well with the spatula for three minutes. Add half a pint of cold milk, and beat well with the pastry-whip for four minutes. Strain through a sieve into another vessel. Place on the stove a small griddle, greasing the surface lightly. Drop about two ounces of the batter onto the griddle; bake ten seconds; turn it with a cake-turner, and bake ten seconds on the other side. See that the cake is a light brown color on both sides. Put them on a hot dish, keeping it warm on a corner of the range, and proceed to make eleven more with the remainder of the batter. Serve very hot, with honey or maple sugar separately.

1185. Batter for all Kinds of Frying.—Put half a pound of flour into a basin. Make a hollow in the centre, and drop into it one egg yolk, half a teaspoonful of sweet oil, a tablespoonful of brandy, and a light saltspoonful of salt. Mix all the ingredients, except the flour, for three minutes, using the hand. Then gradually knead in the flour, meanwhile dropping in, little by little, one gill of cold water. Mix well, moving in the same direction for five minutes. Then put it into a vessel, cover with a cloth, and set aside to rest for three or four hours. When ready to use, beat the whites of three eggs to a froth with a pastry-whip, add it to the batter, and mix together thoroughly with the spatula for two minutes. It will now be ready for use, but should it not all be required, it will keep in a cool place.

1186. French Pancakes.—Sift half a pound of wheat flour into a bowl. Break in three whole eggs. Add one ounce of powdered sugar, and mix well with the spatula, adding half a pint of cold milk, pouring it in very gradually, and mixing for five minutes. Butter lightly a griddle or frying-pan; place it on the stove, and when it is hot, drop on to it two and a half ounces of the batter, and bake two minutes; turn over, and bake the other side as long. Turn the pancake on a hot dessert-dish, and sprinkle over plenty of powdered sugar. Make eleven more out of the remaining batter. Serve very hot.

1187. French Pancakes à la Gelée.—Make the batter exactly the same as for No. 1186. When cooked, arrange the pancakes neatly upon a napkin, and spread over each one about a teaspoonful of currant jelly. Roll them up nicely, and dress on a hot dessert-dish, sprinkling a little powdered sugar over. Then, with a red-hot iron, glaze the surface of each cake in three different parts; wipe the sides of the dish nicely, and send to the table.

French pancakes with apple, apricot, plum, pineapple, strawberry, raspberry, or peach jelly are to be prepared exactly the same, using different jellies.

1188. German Pancakes.—Prepare a batter as for French pancakes (No. 1186); butter an iron pan, one foot in diameter and one and a half inches deep. Place this on a hot stove, and pour all the batter into it, letting it cook for three minutes. Remove to a brisk oven for seven minutes. Take it out, slide the cake carefully on a hot dessert-dish, and send it to the table with six pieces of lemon.

1189. German Pancakes with Apples.—Prepare the batter exactly as for No. 1186. Butter the pan as for the above. When the batter has been poured in, spread over it evenly, one pint of preserved apples, cut into small pieces, and finish cooking exactly as for the plain pancake (No. 1188). When ready, slide it carefully on a hot dessert-dish, sprinkle plentifully with powdered sugar, and send to the table very hot, with six pieces of lemon separately.

1190. Batter for Fritters.—Mix a quarter of a pound of sifted flour in a small basin, with half a pint of lukewarm water, to which three-quarters of an ounce of fresh butter has been added. Place in a saucepan, which should be tilted on the range so that when the water boils the butter can be skimmed off the top. Add, if necessary, a little more water to make a soft paste, beating well with a spatula, to keep it free from lumps, and of a proper consistence; it must be gray and compact-looking. Add just a little warm water to render the paste soft and diluted, although sufficiently thick to cover the objects for which it is intended; that means, it must drop easily from the spoon. Add to this half a pinch of salt and two egg-whites; beat well together for one minute, and use at once.

1191. Apple Fritters.—Take three medium-sized, fine, sound apples; peel and core them neatly. Cut each into six equal round slices. Place them in a vessel, pour over a gill of good brandy, add a light saltspoonful of ground cinnamon, and let all steep for two hours. Strain them through a fine sieve, being careful to keep them whole, and saving the liquid for further use. Prepare a fritter batter, as for No. 1190, dip each slice separately into it, and with a spoon, drop them singly into very hot but not boiling lard, being careful to remove them with a skimmer as soon as they are of a good golden color. Two minutes will be sufficient to have them properly done. Then lay them on a clean cloth, to dry off the grease. Arrange a folded napkin on a hot dessert-dish; arrange the fritters on it, and leave it at the oven door for two minutes. Dredge about an ounce of powdered sugar over, and serve.

1192. Fritters Soufflés à la Vanille.—Infuse in a saucepan half of a vanilla-bean in half a pint of boiling milk, and reduce it to half. Remove the vanilla-bean, and put in one ounce of good butter. Let it come to a boil, then add two ounces of sifted flour, and with the spatula stir briskly, to form a paste so stiff that it will no longer adhere to the saucepan. Remove it to another vessel. Add one ounce of powdered sugar, two egg yolks, and half a saltspoonful of salt. Beat the white of one egg to a stiff froth, and mix it in with half a spoonful of whipped cream (No. 1254); this will form a consistent paste. Roll it on a floured board, besprinkle lightly with flour, and cut out pieces the size of a walnut. With a skimmer drop them into very hot but not boiling fat. Cook quickly for three minutes, until they are a fine golden color. Arrange upon a folded napkin, and serve with powdered sugar sifted over.

1193. Pound Cake.—Put in a vessel half a pound of butter, with half a pound of powdered sugar. Grate in the rind of half a lemon, and with the hand knead well for twenty minutes. Break into a plate five whole raw eggs; add gradually and carefully, kneading sharply with the hand for ten minutes longer. Now add half a pound of well-sifted flour, mixing the whole slowly and thoroughly for five minutes more. Butter a two-quart, round cake-mold, and line it with brown paper at the bottom and sides. Fill it with the preparation, and put it in a slow oven to bake for fully one hour. Remove, and let cool off for about two hours. Unmold, detach the paper, and lay it on a pastry wire-grate. Glaze the top and sides with a preparation as for vanilla éclairs (No. 1245). Lay the cake on a dessert-dish with a fancy white paper. Prepare three ounces of candied cherries, two ounces of angelica, two ounces of red and the same of white pears, both candied; cut the cherries in two, the angelica lozenge-shaped, and the pears each in six parts (except one white one, which is kept whole), keeping the fruits all separate. Place the whole pear on top of the cake in the centre, stem upward. Then decorate thus: at the base of the pear lay two slices of red pear, carefully, one against the other on one side. Repeat on the other side, and arrange in the same way two slices of the white pear in the middle of the space on one side, and two more slices opposite. Now cover the four empty spaces nearest the pear with half a cherry each, and arrange four angelica lozenges in the empty place at the end of the layers of pear. Then on each of the four angelica points lay half a cherry. Begin decorating the edge of the cake all around in a crown-shape with one angelica lozenge, putting near the point one half cherry, then another lozenge, and continue the same all around until joined. Arrange the remaining slices of pear in the empty space near the border, and it will be ready to send to the table.

1194. Wedding Cake.—Place in a large bowl one pound of powdered ugar and one pound of well-washed butter. Grate in the rind of two

DESSERTS.

lemons; and with the hand knead well for ten minutes. Break in ten whole eggs, two at a time, and knead for ten minutes longer. Mix in a plate a teaspoonful of ground cinnamon, a teaspoonful of ground cloves, two of ground allspice, one of mace, and one of grated nutmeg, and add these, with half a gill of confectioners' molasses. Mix well for one minute with the hand. Add one pound of well-sifted flour, stirring for two minutes more. Add two pounds of currants, as for No. 1080, two pounds of Sultana (No. 1080), two pounds of Malaga raisins (No. 1081), one pound of candied citron, finely sliced, one gill of Jamaica rum, and one gill of brandy. Mix the whole well together for fifteen minutes—using both hands, if necessary. Butter the interior of a plain, five-quart, round cake-mold. Line the bottom and sides with paper, leaving it an inch and a half higher than the edge of the mold. Pour in all the preparation, and place it in a very slow oven to bake for five hours. When done, lay it on a table, to cool off for four hours. Unmold, detach the paper, and turn the cake bottom up on a wire pastry-grate. After ten minutes, glaze it with one egg-white which has been beaten in a bowl with four ounces of extra fine sugar, using the spatula; use a knife to apply the glazing. Now lay the cake in a warm place to dry for two hours. Then beat up the white of an egg with four ounces of extra fine sugar for ten minutes, and glaze the cake as before, evenly all around, and lay aside for two hours more. After it is thoroughly dried, lay it on a round wooden board, with a fancy paper over, two inches wider than the board. Procure a fancy wedding-bell, with a miniature bride and groom standing under, lay it in the centre of the cake, fastening it on with glace royale (No. 1206), pressing it through a paper cornet with a fancy tube. Decorate the surface of the cake with ornaments made of the glace; also a fancy border around the edge and base. Let it dry slightly for two hours, and it is ready for use.

1195. Sponge Cake.—Put into a copper basin half a pound of powdered sugar. Break in seven whole eggs, and grate in the rind of half a lemon. Beat well together with the wire whip for one minute; then place it on a slow fire and heat it slightly, stirring it sharply and continually. Take it from the fire, and beat it well until thoroughly cold. Remove the whip, and with a skimmer mix in carefully and slowly half a pound of well-sifted flour; two minutes and a half will be sufficient. Butter the interior of a one-quart, round cake-mold, and line it with paper, keeping it an inch and a half higher than the mold. Then fill it with the preparation, and bake for one hour and fifteen minutes in a moderate oven. Let it cool thoroughly for two hours; unmold, place it on a pastry wire-grate, and glaze it the same as for vanilla éclairs (No. 1245). Decorate artistically with a glace royale (No. 1206), arranging it in any desired fanciful design. Serve on a dessert-dish covered with a fancy paper.

1196. Waffles, with Sugar.—Put in a vessel three ounces of powdered sugar, one pound of flour, three raw eggs, three ounces of melted butter; mix all well together with a spatula for five minutes. Add a pint and a half of sweet cream, and mix again well for two minutes. Have your waffle-iron hot on both sides, and on a clear fire. Grease with melted butter, using a feather for the purpose, and drop into each of the holes two tablespoonfuls of the paste. Bake two minutes on each side, and if they have not a good golden color bake one minute longer on each side. Heap them as fast as cooked on a hot dessert-dish. When all are done, besprinkle plentifully with powdered sugar, and serve very hot.

1197. Savarin Cakes.—Dissolve two drachms of compressed yeast in a gill of lukewarm cream. Add four ounces of sifted flour, knead well for two minutes, and set in a warm place for five minutes. Sift into another vessel six ounces of flour. Make a hollow in the centre, and pour into it two ounces of powdered sugar, four eggs, a gill of lukewarm milk, and a saltspoonful of salt. Knead these well for two minutes, but do not mix in the flour. Add three ounces of melted butter and half a gill of curaçoa (or any other liquor desired), then knead in the flour with the other ingredients, adding the yeast-dough previously laid aside, and mix with the hands, briskly beating the whole in a contrary direction for twenty minutes without ceasing. Cover with a cloth, and set in a warm closet to raise double, which will take about half an hour. Butter a crown-shaped mold holding about three pints. When ready, take two ounces of peeled almonds (No. 1207), mince fine, and add them to the dough, and beat well together for two minutes longer. Then with a spoon drop the paste carefully into the mold ; this not being quite filled to the top. Set aside again in the warm closet until the paste raises to the edge ; then place in a moderately brisk oven for twenty-five minutes. Should the oven be slow, thirty-five minutes will be necessary. To ascertain whether the cake be perfectly baked, thrust the point of a larding-needle into the centre, and should any dough adhere to it, the cake must be left in five minutes longer.

When done, turn it out on a plain, round wire grate, and glaze it with a firm glace à l'eau made as follows : put into a sugar-pan one ounce of granulated sugar, with one tablespoonful of cold water, and let it come to a boil ; remove, and add immediately a tablespoonful of curaçoa, mixing well together. Glaze the cake with this, then let cool. Place a folded napkin on a dessert-dish, dress the cake nicely on top, and serve.

1198. Savarin Cake, hot.—Prepare a savarin cake exactly as for the above (No. 1197), and when unmolded, place it on a wire grate, but do not glaze it. Pour into a saucepan a pint of cold water with five ounces of granulated sugar, and let boil for five minutes. Take it off, and add immediately half a gill of kirsch, mixing it in well. Place the grate with the savarin in a vessel, take hold of the handle with the right hand, and drop the syrup carefully all over the top; lift up the grate and cake. Remove the syrup remaining in the vessel into the pan, boil it again; return the grate and cake to the vessel, and pour over the remaining syrup. Then, lifting the grate on one side, glide the cake carefully onto a dessert-dish. Put into a saucepan four ounces of candied cherries with half a gill of kirsch. Stir it slightly until it comes to a boil and decorate the top of the cake with it ; then serve.

1199. Savarin Cake à l'Anglaise.—Prepare a savarin cake as for No. 1197; when unmolded, place it on a wire grate; do not glaze it. Cut it evenly through the centre, so as to make two equal discs. Garnish the top of the under one with four ounces of apricot marmalade (No. 1335); arrange the other half on top as carefully as possible, so that the cake has its original form. Have a dessert-dish with a folded napkin; dress the cake on top, and serve with a sauce-bowl of crême à l'Anglaise (No. 1200) separately.

1200. Crême à l'Anglaise.—Put into a saucepan two ounces of butter and one ounce of flour. Place on a slow fire, and with a spatula stir slightly for two minutes, adding two ounces of sugar, half a gill of Madeira wine, and one gill of Middletown milk; stir well again for two minutes, to avoid its coming to a boil. Then take it from the fire, and immediately add half a gill of rum, stirring it slightly again. Pour the crême into a sauce-bowl and serve with the savarin.

1201. Brioches.—Take half a pound of sifted flour, put two ounces of it into a vessel. Make a hollow in the centre, and put into this two drachms of compressed yeast and half a gill of lukewarm milk. Dissolve well the yeast with the milk for about one minute, then quickly beat in the flour for one minute. Cover the vessel with a cloth, and let it rest in a warm closet for fifteen minutes. Put in another vessel the remaining six ounces of flour, make a hollow in the centre, and put into it half a saltspoonful of salt, three whole eggs, two tablespoonfuls of sweet cream, two ounces of fresh butter, and one ounce of powdered sugar. Mix thoroughly with the hand, all except the flour, for three minutes, then incorporate the flour gradually, and beat it sharply with the hands for three minutes. Add one egg, beat one minute; add another, and beat one minute longer. Take four ounces of fresh butter, spread it in pieces over the paste, then mix in well for two minutes. The yeast being properly raised double by this time, add it to the other ingredients, and mix the whole carefully by cutting it several times with the hand, being sure to repeat this for at least five minutes. Cover the vessel with a cloth, and lay it in a closet or elsewhere, at a moderate temperature of about eighty degrees, for three hours, when it will be raised to twice the size. Then with the right hand cut it again into pieces in every direction, for about four minutes. Then recover the vessel with the cloth, and leave it in a cool place for thirty minutes. Dredge a board with flour, pour the paste over it; then cut off a three-ounce piece, and lay it aside. With the hands roll up the remaining part of the paste into a ball. Butter well a round, two-quart mold, line it with paper, and put in the paste. Take the piece laid aside, and roll it pear-shaped with the hands. Make a small cavity in the centre of the paste in the mold, using a spoon. Arrange the pear-shaped piece in this, having the larger part on top. Then lay the mold on a baking-sheet; glaze the top lightly with beaten egg, and put it in a moderate oven. After it has been in fifteen minutes, cover it with a buttered paper, close the oven door, and bake for one hour more; test it by thrusting in a larding-needle, and if no dough adheres to this the brioche is thoroughly cooked; if not, leave it in ten minutes longer. Remove from the oven, unmold, and let it cool. Dress on a dessert-dish with a folded napkin, and serve.

1202. Small Brioches.—Prepare the dough as for the above (No. 1201), and when raised to twice the size, lay it upon a board which has been lightly dredged with flour. Cut out a piece of three ounces, and lay it aside until needed, then cut the rest of the paste into twelve equal pieces, and with the right hand roll them into separate balls. Lay these in a pastry baking-pan. Divide the paste laid aside into twelve parts, roll them out, and give each a pear-shape. With a spoon make a cavity in the centre of each ball, and put into each one of the pear pieces, having the larger part on the top. Leave them to rise in a closet for fifteen minutes; glaze them lightly with beaten egg, and put them in a brisk oven for twelve or fifteen minutes, but no longer. Remove, and with a light hair-brush glaze them all over with fresh butter. Keep in a warm place until ready to serve. If the brioches should be required cold, do not glaze them with butter, but dress them on a dessert-dish with a folded napkin. It is better to prepare the paste the evening previous, covering it with a cloth, and leaving it in a cool place over night.

1203. Brioche à la Condé.—Have a brioche cooked as for No. 1201, and when done, cut it in two, crosswise. Then with a spoon spread over the top of the lower half four ounces of apricot marmalade (No. 1335), mixed with one ounce of melted butter. Then replace the other half on top. Put in a saucepan two ounces of candied cherries, four ounces of candied apricots, cut in slices, and four ounces of candied pineapple. Add half a pint of cold water, and boil well together on a hot fire for three minutes. Dress the brioche on a dessert-dish, pour the preparation over, and serve hot.

1204. Brioches Fluttes.—Prepare a brioche paste, as for No. 1203; lay it on a floured board, and cut it into twelve equal pieces. Roll out each one separately with the hands until it is ten inches, or three finger-lengths, long, rounding them into shape. Put them in a pastry baking-pan, and leave them in a closet to rise for ten minutes; take out and glaze them lightly with beaten eggs, sprinkle them over with powdered sugar, and put them in the oven for ten minutes; remove, and dress them on a dessert-dish with a folded napkin, and serve when cool. These brioches will keep well for three or four days, and they are delicious when served with tea, coffee, or chocolate.

1205. Allumettes.—Take three quarters of a pound of feuilletage (No. 1076); spread it out twelve inches long to four inches wide. Cover with a thin layer of glace royale (No. 1206). Divide it into six even pieces; put them in a pan, and let rest for five minutes. Then place in a moderate oven, and bake for forty minutes, until of a good golden color. Serve either hot or cold.

1206. Glace Royale for Allumettes.—Put into a small bowl half the white of a raw egg and two ounces of extra fine sugar, and beat well with a spatula. Drop in carefully just one drop, and no more, of lemon juice; beat again for five minutes, until thickened; it will then be ready for use.

1207. How to Peel and Pound Almonds.—Put the almonds into boiling water; let them soak three minutes; strain, and lay them in cold water to thoroughly cool. Drain well again, and peel by pressing each almond between the thumb and fingers. Then put them into a sieve, and place them at the door of a slow oven to dry for ten minutes. Now pound them gently in a mortar, stirring well to prevent them from getting oily, and taking care to pound them very fine for at least ten minutes. Lay them on a cold dish, and use when needed.

1208. Almond Cake Glacé.—Put a quarter of a pound of powdered sugar and a quarter of a pound of butter into a bowl; beat well together with a wooden spatula for ten minutes. Break in two eggs; beat well, and break in two more; continue beating, and break in two more (six in all), until well mixed together. Then grate in the peel of the third of a small lemon. Add two ounces of peeled and pounded almonds (No. 1207), and a quarter of a pound of flour. Mix gradually together for no longer than two minutes. Butter and sugar a round form holding one quart, and pour the preparation into it. Place it in a slow oven for one hour. See that it gets a good golden color. Take it out; let it get thoroughly cool, and remove from the mold. Lay it on a dish with a folded napkin. Glaze the top lightly with a small hair-bush, as for No. 1206, until it looks well, and send to the table.

1209. Bitter Almond Macaroons.—Take a quarter of a pound of sweet almonds, and two ounces of bitter almonds; peel and pound them as for No. 1307. Put them into a bowl with twelve ounces of powdered sugar and the whites of two eggs. Mix thoroughly with a wooden spatula for at least five minutes. Then take a pastry-bag (No. 1079), slide down to the bottom of it a No. 3 tube (which should not be larger than a five-cent piece), and pour the preparation into the bag. Prepare a pastry baking-pan; lay on it a piece of brown paper the full size of the pan (do not put it on the stove at present); then with the two hands press the preparation down gently into the papered pan, dropping it carefully into bits the size and shape of a silver quarter-dollar, trying to have them as near alike as possible, and taking care that each is entirely separated from the others. Take a damp towel and drop it gently on to the macaroons, so as to shape them perfectly. Then place the pan in a slow oven for twenty minutes. Before lifting them out, be careful that they are a good golden color. Let them get thoroughly cool. To remove the macaroons easily from the paper, wet part of a table; lay the paper over this for two minutes, and the macaroons will detach very easily. The above quantity will make about fifty macaroons. Put aside in a jar those not needed, as they will keep perfectly fresh for several days.

1210. Sweet Macaroons.—Proceed as for bitter macaroons (No. 1209), only omitting the two ounces of bitter almonds, and substituting for them two extra ounces of sweet almonds, or six ounces in all.

1211. Apple Cake.—Peel and core four fine, sound pippin apples.

Put them into a saucepan with two ounces of boiled and peeled chestnuts, and a piece of cinnamon an inch long. Toss well on the fire for ten minutes, then transfer them to a copper basin, stirring in a teaspoonful of corn-starch, and adding a quarter of a pound of powdered sugar. Place on a slow stove for ten minutes, then put aside. When thoroughly cooled, add three egg yolks and one whole one; mix well with a wooden spatula, and the preparation will be ready for use. Take a three-pint, square mold, butter it lightly, and with a small hair-brush sprinkle in a little powdered sugar, and pour in the prepared apple. Place the mold in a tin pastry-pan, filling the latter to half the height of the mold with cold water, and place the whole in a moderate oven for thirty minutes. Take the mold from the pan, and lay on top of it a hot, deep dessert-dish, slightly larger than the cake; turn the mold bottom up, and lift it off, leaving the cake on the dish. While the cake is in the oven, prepare the following sauce: mix in a saucepan two egg yolks, one ounce of powdered sugar, half a pint of water, and half a teaspoonful of ground cinnamon. Place on a brisk fire, and stir constantly for five minutes, not allowing it to boil. When the cream is ready, add half a glassful or a gill of rum, or any other kind of liquor. Mix well for half a minute, pour the sauce over the cake, and serve very hot.

1212. St. Honoré à la Rose Delmonico.—Peel neatly two medium-sized, sound, red oranges. Separate the sections carefully to avoid tearing the skin, as, should they lose any of their juice, they would become useless. Lay a sheet of paper over a tin pan, arrange the pieces of orange on top, and leave them in a warm place to dry for four hours. Wipe neatly twenty-four Malaga grapes, leaving on each about a quarter of an inch of stem, so that they shall remain firm while using them. Beat up a pint and a half of sweet cream à la vanille as for No. 1254, and lay it aside in a cool place until needed. Roll three ounces of pie-paste (No. 1077) into a round piece eight inches in diameter. Lay it on a baking-sheet ten inches wide, and proceed to prepare a pâte-à-chou as follows:

Put into a saucepan a gill of cold milk with one ounce of good butter, place it on a hot fire, and when boiling, add at once three ounces of well-sifted flour. Stir briskly with the spatula all round; take it from the fire, set on a table, and add immediately a saltspoonful of powdered sugar, mixing well for one minute more. Break in an egg, stir briskly for one minute, break in another, mix again, and then another, mixing all together for two minutes. Slide down the pastry-bag (No. 1079) a tube (No. 3), pour in the above preparation, and press down the top with the hands onto the edge of the paste in the baking-sheet, so as to make an even border half an inch high, and with the remainder of the paste press down onto another baking-sheet into twenty-four small, round choux, half an inch in diameter, leaving them one inch apart. Glaze the surfaces with beaten egg, and place them in a brisk oven to bake for twelve minutes. Remove, and let them get thoroughly cold. Spread over the paste, inside the border, two tablespoonfuls of apple sauce (No. 1328); then put it in a moderate oven to bake for twenty-five minutes. Remove, and put to cool for thirty minutes. Make a paper cornet, cut off a quarter of an inch from the point, and put into it three ounces of currant jelly (No. 1326). Press this out gently, dividing it evenly into the twenty-four small choux. Cook one pound of granulated sugar as for No. 1264. Oil two square feet of the surface of a marble table, and place at hand the pan containing the sugar. Plunge one of the grapes into this; remove it immediately with a fork and lay it on the oiled table. Proceed the same with the other twenty-three, being careful to lay them one inch apart from each other. Now dip twelve of the sections of prepared oranges into the sugar, one by one, and lay them on the oiled table exactly the same as the grapes. Dip carefully the surfaces of the small choux into the sugar, and lay them on the same oiled table. Then take the St. Honoré bottom in the baking-sheet, and proceed to arrange it as follows: with the cooked sugar standing on the right, lift the choux up, one by one, dipping one side of each lightly in the cooked sugar, arranging them on top of the pâte-à-chou border close together to form a crown. Should the sugar be too thick, return it to the stove, and let it boil up once; then take it off, and dip the thin part of the oranges lightly in it, and lay them over the small choux, the thick part upward, each one adhering to the other, until they form the crown. Dip the tops of the grapes lightly into the same sugar, and place one on each join of the oranges, with another in the centre, the stems being upward; attach to the small choux the six remaining grapes, dividing them evenly. Arrange a fancy paper on a dessert-dish, and lay the St. Honoré over carefully, then take the froth part only of the whipped cream; transfer it to another vessel, and, with the whip, beat briskly for five minutes, adding half a gill of good cognac, a quarter of a gill of Swiss kirsch, and three ounces of well-pounded and sifted macaroons (No. 1210). Mix well together for two minutes longer, and fill the empty space of the St. Honoré with three-quarters of this preparation, keeping it as high as possible. With the use of the pastry-bag and fancy tube press down the rest of the cream, and decorate artistically the top and sides, taking care not to put any on the oranges, and send to the table.

1213. Gingerbread à la Française.—Make a hollow space in a pound of flour laid on the table. Peel and chop up very fine five ounces of almonds; put them into the hollow with a saltspoonful of grated nutmeg, the same quantity of ground cloves, four ounces of powdered sugar, and seven ounces of fresh honey. Knead the ingredients well for five minutes, then mix in the flour, and knead the preparation with the hands in all directions for fully thirty minutes without ceasing. Finish by forming it into a ball. Lay this on a dish, cover it with a napkin, and place it in a temperature of about 60° for six hours. Lay the paste on a floured table, and roll it out eighteen inches long by twelve wide. Butter well a baking-sheet, lay the paste on top, and put it in a very slow oven to bake for forty-five minutes. Remove, lay the baking-sheet on the table, cut the cake immediately into small pieces, lozenge shaped, one and a half inches long by one inch wide, or any other shape desired; let cool off thoroughly for about twenty minutes, then dress on a glass bowl, and serve. The above cakes can be glazed with a glace à l'eau, as for No. 1197, and served the same.

1214. Strawberry Shortcake.—Put into a vessel half a pound of powdered sugar with half a pound of well-washed butter, grate in the rind of half a sound lemon, and, with the hand, mix well for ten minutes. Break in five whole eggs, one at a time, meanwhile mixing for ten minutes longer, always with the hand. Then add gradually half a pound of well-sifted flour, and mix for three minutes. Cover a baking-sheet with brown paper, place on top three tin cake-rings, nine inches in diameter and one inch high. Divide the preparation equally into the three rings; then place in a moderate oven to bake for thirty minutes. Remove, and allow the cakes thirty minutes more to cool. Lift up the paper, with the cakes, turn it upside down on the table, remove the paper, and detach the cakes from the rings by passing a knife all around. Pick and clean thoroughly three pints of fine, sound, ripe strawberries; have a dessert-dish with a fancy paper over, lay one of the cakes on top of this, spread over evenly two tablespoonfuls of whipped cream (No. 1254), then cover with half the strawberries, nicely and evenly divided. Sprinkle liberally with powdered sugar, then cover with another cake, spread over the same quantity of cream as before, then arrange the other half of the strawberries on top; dredge again with powdered sugar, and lay the last cake over all, sprinkling with more sugar. Slide down a tube (No. 2) into a pastry-bag (No. 1079), put into it six tablespoonfuls of whipped cream à la vanille (No. 1254), and with it decorate the top of the cake in an artistic manner, and send to the table.

1215. Blackberry Shortcake.—Prepare and proceed exactly the same as for strawberry shortcake (No. 1214), only substituting three pints of well-picked, and thoroughly cleaned, fine, sound, ripe blackberries for the strawberries, and serving the same.

1216. Baba.—Have ready half a pound of the best flour, one drachm of compressed yeast, and half a gill of warm water. Put three ounces of the flour into a vessel, make a hollow in the centre, and in it lay the yeast and water; with the hands mix the yeast gently with the water for three minutes, then mix all together gradually for three minutes more. Cover the vessel with a towel, and leave it in the warmest place in the kitchen (not on the stove), and after thirty minutes it will rise to twice the size. Lay the remainder of the flour on the table, make a hollow in the centre, putting in it an ounce of powdered sugar and four raw eggs. Mix the sugar and eggs with the hands; then add a gill of cream and half a gill of good Madeira wine. Season with a drachm of very fine salt, and mix all with the flour for five minutes. Make a hollow in the centre again, and into this put five ounces of good, fresh, soft butter; mix well again for two minutes. If the prepared yeast-dough be now raised to its proper height, mix the two pastes together for at least five minutes; return it to the vessel, leave it in the same warm place, covering it as before. When rested one hour, have ready two ounces of cleaned

Sultana currants (No. 1080), two ounces of cleaned raisins (No. 1081), and one ounce of finely chopped citron. Grease with cold butter the inside of a cylindrical copper or tin form large enough to hold three pints. If the paste be now raised to twice the size, mix in the raisins, currants, and citron, stirring for five minutes; put it in the mold, and lay it in a warm place (not on the stove) for another twenty minutes. Then place it in a moderate oven for one hour. When a good golden color, remove, and let it cool slightly. Place a round dish over the mold, turn upside down, lift off the form, and glaze the cake with a glace à l'eau (No. 1197). Decorate the top and dish with candied fruits, and send to the table.

1217. Baba au Madère.—Prepare a baba cake exactly the same as for the above (No. 1216); but do not glaze it. Slit the cake in two, and remove the top piece. Pour a pint of cold water in a very clean pan, add half a pound of sugar and half a medium-sized sound lemon. Place it on the stove, and boil well for three minutes; then remove, and at once add a gill of good sherry wine and half a gill of curaçoa. Lay the top part of the cake in a round, flat-bottomed vessel. To avoid breaking it, a wire basket is recommended, with which it can be lowered carefully onto the pan. Pour gradually over it the prepared sauce; let it rest for two minutes, then replace it carefully on top of the other half of the cake. Arrange it nicely on a dessert serving-dish, garnish tastefully with candied cherries, and decorate the border with small, thin slices of candied pineapple.

For Baba au Rhum, substitute Jamaica rum for the sherry.

1218. Baba, Crême à la Vanille.—Prepare a baba cake as for No. 1216. When removed from the mold and laid on a dish, cut it into six equal parts. Take six ounces of apricot marmalade (No. 1335), and proceed as follows: take one piece of cake in the left hand, and with a knife in the right, cover both sides, where they were cut, with the marmalade. When finished, arrange the six pieces together on the dish, and give them the same form as before they were cut; to be eaten with the following sauce (No. 1219).

1219. Crême à la Vanille Sauce.—Boil one pint of cold milk in a saucepan; put three egg yolks into a small vessel with two ounces of powdered sugar, one ounce of flour, and a piece of vanilla-bean one inch long. Beat well together with a wire whip for two minutes. Pour this into the boiling milk. Stir again briskly with the whip until it boils once more; remove from the fire, and add half a' gill of maraschino. Beat again for one minute, and pour the cream nicely over the cake before sending to the table.

1220. Home-made Cake.—Put into a bowl half a pound of sugar and half a pound of good butter. Mix thoroughly with the hand for fifteen minutes. Break four eggs, leaving the whites in a basin, and drop the yolks in with the butter and sugar. Mix again. Now beat the whites to a froth and add them to the other ingredients. Grate in half a saltspoonful of nutmeg; add half a pound of flour; mix well again; stir in two ounces of well-cleansed currants (No. 1080), and two ounces of peeled sweet almonds (No. 1207) cut into small pieces. Mingle all well together with the hand for five minutes, and with the other hand drop in one gill of brandy. Have a round cake-mold holding two quarts; butter it lightly with a hair brush, and sprinkle in a little sugar. Drop a third of the preparation into the mold; spread over it two ounces of candied orange, shred into thin slices; then add half of the remaining preparation; spread on top of it two ounces of shred, candied citron, and fill the mold with the rest. Lay a piece of brown paper over, and put the mold into a very moderate oven for two hours. Let it get a good golden color. Remove, and cool off in the mold, which will take about three hours. Remove the cake by turning it bottom up. Arrange a lace paper on a dessert-dish. Glaze the cake with a glacé à l'eau (No. 1197), dress it on the dish, and decorate the top and border tastefully with assorted candied fruits.

1221. Plain Galette.—Knead well and finely together in a vessel one pound of good flour with six ounces of fresh butter, one gill of cold water, and a saltspoonful of salt. After ten minutes, when it becomes soft, roll it into a flat, circular cake—using a rolling-pin, well floured, to prevent its adhering. Place it in a baking-pan. Bake in a very slow oven for thirty-five minutes. When a nice light color, remove and let it cool. Serve it on a dessert-dish, over a folded napkin.

1222. Rice Cake.—Boil two ounces of rice for twenty-five minutes. When well done, drain, and add to it a short paste, made of half a pound of flour, six ounces of butter, two egg-whites, and half a saltspoonful of salt. Pound the paste and rice well together in a mortar, and have a baking-pan covered with a sheet of buttered paper; lay the paste on top, spreading it out about six inches square. Put it in the oven for twenty minutes. Remove it, detach it from the paper, lay it on a dessert-dish, with a folded napkin, and serve hot.

Vermicelli cake is prepared the same way, only the vermicelli should not cook longer than twelve minutes.

1223. Mille-feuilles Cake.—Take a pound of short paste or feuilletage (No. 1076), and divide it into five equal parts. Roll out each piece twelve inches long by four wide, then lay them in a baking-pan, sprinkle a little powdered sugar over, and place them in the oven for ten minutes. Remove, and form the cake by laying these one on top of the other, with layers of preserves between, each layer being of different colored preserves. Put the fifth piece on top of the last layer for a cover. Then cut the cake into six equal pieces ; decorate either with different colored preserves, or with whipped cream (No. 1254), and serve on a dessert-dish with a folded napkin.

1224. Almond Cake.—Make a plain paste in a vessel with four ounces of butter, three egg yolks, half a pound of well-sifted flour, four ounces of powdered sugar, a quarter of a pound of finely pounded almonds (No. 1207), a saltspoonful of salt, and about six drops of orange-flower water. Mix and stir well for five minutes. It will then be of a proper consistency, spread it round about eight inches in diameter on a buttered paper in a pan, and with a light hair-brush moisten the surface slightly with beaten egg. Bake twenty minutes. Remove, detach from the paper, set away to cool, and serve.

1225. Cake de Pithiviers.—Put in a vessel four ounces of pounded almonds (No. 1207), half a pound of powdered sugar, two ounces of chopped, candied lemon-peel, and a quarter of a pound of good, fresh butter. Mix in gradually four eggs, well beaten, and finish as for the almond cake (No. 1224), serving it the same.

1226. Madeleine.—Rub the rind of two small lemons on a lump of sugar; crush it very fine with a roller, mixing three ounces of powdered sugar with it. Put two ounces of this into a saucepan with two ounces of sifted flour, one egg yolk, and two whole eggs, two teaspoonfuls of good brandy, and half a saltspoonful of salt. Stir all together with a wooden spatula, and after two minutes, when the paste is well mixed, stir it again for one minute only. Put two ounces of good butter into a separate saucepan; as soon as the scum rises, stir it carefully for one minute, and let it cool slightly. Then spread it well over the sides of a three-pint madeleine-mold. Put the saucepan containing the preparation on a very slow fire; stir slightly to prevent it adhering to the bottom of the saucepan, and as soon as it becomes liquid take it off, and fill the mold. Lay it in a moderately heated oven for forty-five minutes; remove, and let cool. Unmold it on a dessert-dish over a folded napkin, and serve.

1227. Madeleine Printanière.—Prepare the cake as for the above (No. 1226) until the mold is ready to be filled. Butter the interiors of twelve small madeleine-molds, fill them with the preparation, lay them on a pastry baking-pan, and place them in a moderate oven for twenty minutes. Remove, let them cool, unmold, and turn them up-side down; cut a piece from the thinnest part of the top of each madeleine to serve as a cover. With a dessert-spoon scoop out of each madeleine a cavity one inch deep, fill this with a plombière à la vanille (No. 1294). Replace the covers, lay them on a wire grate, and, with a brush, glaze gently with glace à l'eau (No. 1197), flavored with two tablespoonfuls of strawberry juice, and sprinkle over with three ounces of well-chopped pistache. Place in the oven for one minute more; then dress on a dessert-dish with a folded napkin, and serve.

1228. Milan Cake.—One pound of flour, half a pound of butter, half a pound of powdered sugar, and four whole eggs. Sift the flour on the table. Make a hollow in the centre, and fill it with the sugar and butter, and the grated rind of a lemon. Knead well the butter and sugar for three minutes; add the eggs, one at a time, and incorporate the flour slowly, so as not to burn the paste. Let it rest for about half an hour in a cool place. Then roll out about a quarter of an inch thick. Cut out six pieces with a round cake-cutter; glaze the surfaces with beaten egg and milk, and bake in a moderate oven for twenty minutes. When cold, dress on a dessert-dish with a folded napkin, and serve. Keep the rest of the paste for further use, as it will remain sweet and fresh for two or three days.

1229. Rum Cake.—Half a pound of flour, two ounces of sugar, three whole eggs, one ounce of butter, and two drachms of compressed yeast. Sift the flour on a board. Take one third of it; make a hollow in its centre, and put into it the yeast and half a gill of warm milk. When the yeast is dissolved, mix well for one minute. Then put it into a bowl, cover with a cloth, and let it rise in a warm place until twice the size. Take the rest òf the flour, make a hollow in the centre, and put into it the sugar, eggs, and six drops of orange-flower water. Knead well together, slowly incorporating the flour; then gradually add the butter and the prepared yeast-dough. Mix all together for five minutes; return to the bowl, and again lay it aside to rise to twice its size. Butter well six round rum-cake molds, fill them about three quarters high with the dough, and let it rise until they are full; then lay them on a baking-pan in a moderate oven for twenty minutes. When well browned, remove, unmold, place them on a pastry-wire, and pour over them a sauce made thus: put a quarter of a pound of sugar in a saucepan with half a pint of water, adding half a sliced lemon. When boiling, take from the fire, and pour in half a gill of rum, then throw it over the cakes. Dress on a dish, and serve.

1230. Rice Cake à la Mazzini.—Put a pint of cold milk into a saucepan on a hot stove, and when it boils add half a pound of well-cleaned rice and let it cook slowly for twenty minutes, stirring frequently to the bottom with a spatula. Then set the saucepan in a cool place for thirty minutes. Add six ounces of powdered sugar; mix well for one minute, and break in three whole eggs; flavor with eight drops of orange-flower water, mixing well together for three minutes longer. Take a quarter of a pound of pie-paste (No. 1077), roll it out very thin, and with it line a three-pint, round, channeled mold; fill it with the preparation, and place it in a moderate oven to bake for forty minutes. Remove, and let it become thoroughly cold, which will take an hour. Then unmold, and lay the cake over a round pastry-grate. Have a quarter of a pound of vanilla éclair glazing (No. 1245), put it in a saucepan, adding a teaspoonful of cold water. Place it on the hot range, and with a spatula mix it gently and thoroughly until it becomes lukewarm; then pour it over the cake. Arrange the cake on a dessert-dish, and serve.

1231. Biscuits à la Cuillère, or Lady-fingers.—Put four ounces of powdered sugar and the yolks of five eggs into a small bowl. Beat thoroughly with a spatula for five minutes. Put the whites of the eggs into a copper basin, and with a wire whip beat them to a stiff froth. Add to the sugar and yolks four ounces of flour; mix together gently for half a minute, and immediately add the whites. Beat gently for one minute more, and the preparation will be ready. Take a well-cleaned pastry-bag (No. 1079), slide into it a No. 2 tube, and with a wooden spoon or small skimmer pour the preparation into the bag. When it is all in, close the upper part of the bag very firmly, and lay it aside for one moment. Take two separate sheets of solid, brown paper, each measuring seventeen inches long by five inches wide; lay them on the table, one beside the other. Take hold of the lower part of the bag near the tube with the left hand, and the upper part with the right, press with the latter, and drop the batter on the paper in straight strips four inches long by one inch wide. Make ten of equal size on each paper, being careful to leave an empty space of three quarters of an inch between each. Then with a sugar-dredger sprinkle them lightly with powdered sugar three times, at one minute's interval between each sprinkling. When finished, lift up one paper at a time, keeping it perfectly straight, and shake off the loose sugar, being particular that the biscuits do not detach from the paper. Now lay them in a pastry baking-pan, and let rest for two minutes; put them into a slow oven, and bake for twenty minutes, until of a light golden color. Remove, lift them from the pan, and lay on a table to cool off. Have ready a dessert-dish with a folded napkin, then detaching the biscuits gently from the paper with the hands, dress them neatly on the dish, and send to the table.

1232. Biscuit à la Richelieu.—Put half a pound of sugar, half a pound of peeled and pounded almonds as for No. 1207, and four egg yolks into a bowl, and with a spatula mix well together for two minutes. Place the whites of eight eggs in a copper basin, with half a saltspoonful of salt, and with a wire whip beat them to a stiff froth; add this to the above preparation, with three ounces of melted butter, three ounces of flour, and a teaspoonful of vanilla flavoring. Mix slowly together for three minutes. Butter a plain mold holding three quarts; line the interior thoroughly, and pour in the preparation; place it in a moderate oven for an hour and a half, then remove, and let it cool, and unmold. Dress on a dessert-dish with a folded napkin, and serve.

1233. Biscuit à la Livornaise.—Prepare the paste exactly as for the above (No. 1232), and when ready have a square tin pan, lined all through with paper. Spread the paste over an inch thick with a knife, and put it in a moderate oven for eighteen minutes. Take it out, and when cool lay the cake on a table; detach the paper, sprinkle the surface freely with powdered sugar, and cut it into any shaped pieces desired. Dress on a dessert-dish with a folded napkin, and serve.

1234. Petits Biscuits Ambrosiennes.—Proceed the same as for biscuits à la cuillère (No. 1231). After the paste has been placed in the bag, have a well-cleaned pastry baking-pan, well buttered and lightly sprinkled with flour. Drop the paste carefully into the pan, forming biscuits, each about two inches long, by one inch wide. There should be in all about forty biscuits. Place them in a moderate oven for twenty minutes. Remove, and lay them on a table. With a hair-brush spread over them six ounces of apricot marmalade (No. 1335), and glaze them with a glace à l'eau (No. 1197), flavored with half a gill of white curaçoa. Sprinkle over them four ounces of finely chopped pistaches; shake the pan lightly, and they will adhere to the glace. Set for two minutes in the oven to get dry; remove, and when cool, dress neatly in a glass bowl, and serve.

1235. Almond Biscuits.—Take two ounces of sweet almonds and half an ounce of bitter, peel, and pound them as for No. 1207. Then put them in a vessel with eight ounces of powdered sugar. Add the yolks of five eggs, and beat the preparation thoroughly for five minutes; then separately beat the whites to a froth with a pastry wire whip, and mix in with the yolks and sugar, adding also one ounce of flour. Stir thoroughly with a wooden spatula until perfectly firm, which will require about five minutes. It is now ready. Have six paper boxes, any shape desired, and fill them with the preparation, using a tablespoon for the purpose. Sprinkle the tops with a little finely powdered sugar, arrange them in a pastry baking-pan, and put in a slow oven for fifteen minutes ; they must get a good golden color. Remove, and when cooled off, dress nicely on a dish, and serve.

1236. Chausson Cakes.—Roll half a pound of feuilletage paste (No. 1076) into a piece eighteen inches long by three wide, and pare off the edges lightly. Cut out six square pieces, all the same size, and with a pastry-brush moisten the surfaces with beaten egg. Fold up each piece by laying one corner over the other, so they will have a triangular shape. Put them on a baking-sheet in the oven for twenty minutes; remove them to the oven door ; dredge plenty of powdered sugar over, put them back, and close the door for one minute and a half, to allow the sugar to melt thoroughly. Remove from the oven, and cool for twenty minutes. The cakes will have risen about two inches in front. Then, with the thickest part of a larding-needle, make a hollow in front of each cake. Put three ounces of currant jelly (No. 1326) into a paper cornet, and with it fill the insides of the cakes. Dress them on a dessert-dish with a folded napkin, and serve.

1237. Petites Bouchées des Dames.—Put into a pastry-bag (No. 1079) half the quantity of biscuits-à-la-cuillère preparation (No. 1231). Butter and flour a baking-sheet, and form about fifty small, round biscuits the exact shape of macaroons. Sprinkle slightly with powdered sugar, and place in a brisk oven to bake for twelve minutes. Remove, and set to cool for fifteen minutes. Then lift them from the pan, and lay them upside down on a table. With a knife make a small cavity in the centre of each, half an inch in diameter, and fill these with a pastry cream (No. 1242). Fasten them, two by two, to enclose the cream; they will then be ball-shaped. Dip carefully one after the other into a glace preparation as for chocolate éclairs (No. 1243). Lay them on a pastry-grate to dry for fifteen minutes; then dress on a dessert-dish with a folded napkin, and send to the table.

1238. Petites Bouchées à la Mrs. Astor.—Butter and flour a baking-sheet. Put into a pastry-bag (No. 1079) half the quantity of the biscuits-à-la-cuillère preparation (No. 1231), and drop it on the baking-sheet into Lima-bean-shaped pieces, one and a half inches long by half an inch wide. Sprinkle them lightly with powdered sugar, and place them in a brisk oven to bake for twelve minutes. Take them out and let them cool for fifteen minutes, then put them on a table upside down, and in the middle of each one cut a hole one inch long by a quarter of an inch wide. Fill the holes with apricot marmalade (No. 1335), then unite them, two by two, so as to enclose the marmalade and be the perfect shape of Lima beans. Glaze them neatly by dipping them separately into a glace preparation as for éclairs à la vanille (No. 1245), and lay them at once on a pastry-grate to dry for fifteen minutes. Dress them on a dessert-dish with a folded napkin, and serve. The remainder of the paste may be used the following day.

1239. Fancy Almond Cakes.—Peel and pound half a pound of almonds as for No. 1207; then add two egg whites; when thoroughly pounded, put them into a vessel with ten ounces of powdered sugar, and the grated rind of a good lemon; then, with the hand, knead well together for twenty minutes. Slide a fancy tube (No. 3) into a pastry-bag (No. 1079), and pour in the above preparation. Cover a baking-sheet with brown paper, and holding the top of the bag with the right hand, guide the bottom with the left, and press the paste through onto the paper in small round bits one inch wide and half an inch high. Make ten of these, being careful to keep them one inch apart. Make ten more, shaped like the letter S, using the same quantity as for the others; then ten more, crescent-shaped, or like the letter C; and with the remainder of the paste make ten more, heart-shaped, being careful to keep them from touching one another. Take five candied cherries, cut them in halves, and arrange them on top of the round cakes; have twenty dried currants (No. 1080), and place one on each end of the S. Cut a candied apricot in two, and each half into five slices, and lay them on top of the crescents, and lastly have one ounce of candied angelica cut into very thin strips, and arrange them nicely on the heart-shaped pieces.

It would be advisable to prepare these cakes the evening before they are needed, and lay them aside in a warm place over night. The next morning, glaze them lightly with beaten egg, using a pastry-brush, and place them in a brisk oven to bake for ten minutes. When of a nice brown color, remove, and let them become thoroughly cold. Lift them up carefully with the paper, laying them gently upside down on a table, and with a wet towel moisten the paper, so that the cakes will detach easily. Turn the paper over immediately as it stood before, let rest for two minutes; then remove the cakes. Lay them on a pastry-grate upside down, to allow them to dry for thirty minutes. Dress them on a glass stand with a folded napkin, and send to the table.

1240. Pâte-à-Chou.—Put into a saucepan two gills of cold milk and two ounces of butter. Place it on the range, stir slightly with the spatula, and when boiling, immediately add a quarter of a pound of well-sifted flour; stir briskly for two minutes. Then stand the pan on a table. Break in one egg, mix sharply for two minutes, break in a second egg, mix sharply again; and repeat with a third and a fourth egg; then the pâte-à-chou is ready.

1241. Eclairs.—Arrange in a pastry-bag (No. 1079), a tube (No. 3); put into it the above quantity of pâte-à-chou (No. 1240), and press out upon a baking-sheet fifteen éclairs, each one three inches long. Bake them in a hot oven for twenty minutes. Remove, and let them cool; then with a pair of scissors open each éclair on one side, and with a spoon fill the interiors with a crême patissière (No. 1242).

1242. Crême Patissière.—Put a pint of cold milk into a saucepan, and place it on the stove. Mix in another vessel two ounces of powdered sugar, with one ounce of flour, and half an ounce of corn-starch. Break in two whole eggs, and beat well together with the whip for two minutes. When the milk is boiling, add it to the preparation, and after stirring for one minute longer, put it into another saucepan, and place it on the stove. Beat well until it comes to a boil; then remove from the fire, and add immediately a teaspoonful of vanilla essence. Mix thoroughly again for one minute longer; then pour it into a bowl, and let it get cold.

1243. How to Glaze Eclairs with Chocolate.—Put in a saucepan one pound and three quarters of granulated sugar and a gill of cold water. Place on the stove, and with a spatula mix well until the sugar is thoroughly melted, and when boiling remove from the stove, and pour it gradually on a marble slab, on which it will spread about three feet square. Let it cool off for ten minutes. Then cut two ounces of cocoa into small pieces; put them on a plate, and leave them at the oven door to melt. With a spatula begin working the sugar that is on the marble as rapidly as possible in every direction until it begins to whiten; then add the melted cocoa, mixing it thoroughly again until it becomes hard; remove the spatula, and detach the preparation quickly from the marble with a knife. Put it into a vessel, and covering it with a damp cloth, let it rest for thirty minutes. Then place half of it in a saucepan on the hot stove, and with the spatula mix thoroughly and slowly until it is lukewarm, meanwhile adding a teaspoonful of cold water. Take the éclairs, one by one, and with the hand dip them into this preparation. Lay them on a pastry-grate; let them cool off for five minutes; dress on a dessert-dish with a folded napkin, and serve.

Keep the rest of the preparation for further use. When laid aside in a cool place, and properly taken care of, it will be as good in two weeks' time as when freshly made.

1244. Eclairs au Café.—Have a pâte-à-chou ready, as for No. 1240; then proceed to make the éclairs. Bake, and fill them with a crême patissière (No. 1242) exactly as for the chocolate éclairs; glazing them the same as for No. 1243, only instead of cocoa use half a gill of coffee essence (No. 1263). Serve precisely the same.

1245. Eclairs à la Vanille.—Prepare a pâte-à-chou as for No. 1240. Make the éclairs, bake, and fill them with a crême patissière, as No. 1242. Glaze them as for No. 1243, only substituting two teaspoonfuls of vanilla essence for the cocoa, and serving them the same.

1246. Choux à la Crême.—Prepare a pâte-à-chou as for No. 1240, and put it into the bag. Press it down onto a baking-sheet into six round, equal cakes, about two inches high. Glaze the surface of each with beaten egg. Bake in a moderate oven for thirty minutes. Watch them carefully, and when they are of a good golden color, remove from the oven and let cool for half an hour. Make an incision on one side, about half-way in the cakes, using a pair of scissors. Fill the insides with crême patissière (No. 1242), and close them again. Dredge well with powdered sugar, and dress on a dessert-dish, with a folded napkin, before sending to the table.

1247. Méringues.—Put six egg whites into a copper basin, with a light half saltspoonful of salt, and with a wire whip begin beating slowly, but gradually increase until a stiff froth is obtained. Should it become grainy, beat briskly again, adding half an ounce of powdered sugar. (Eight minutes should suffice to have a proper froth.) Remove the whip. Have on a plate one pound of powdered sugar, and with a spatula drop the sugar slowly and carefully over the froth, mixing, it in meanwhile with the spatula. This should take about two minutes. Flavor it with any desired flavoring, and it will be ready for use.

1248. Apples, Méringuées.—Have six fine apples cooked as for No. 1169; dress them on a dessert-dish, filling the cavities with currant jelly (No. 1326); then decorate all round and the tops with méringue, prepared as for No. 1247, half the quantity being sufficient. Sprinkle them moderately with powdered sugar; lay the dish on a baking-pan, and put it in the oven for five minutes. When a light brown color, remove, and serve either hot or cold.

1249. Small Fancy Méringues à la Ch. C. Delmonico.—Put into a sugar-pan one pound of granulated sugar with half a pint of cold water, and place on the hot stove. Have two quarts of ice-water in a vessel, and when the sugar comes to a boil, dip the fingers of the right hand into the ice-water and pass them quickly around the inside of the pan, and let boil for five minutes. Dip a wooden stick, similar to a pen-holder, in the ice-water, then quickly into the boiling sugar, and again in the ice-water, lifting up the stick to feel the sugar that adheres. Should it not be sufficiently consistent to form into a ball, let boil a little longer; then try once more; and should it be a proper thickness, remove from the fire and set it on the corner of the stove, so that it no longer boils. While the sugar is cooking, beat the whites of five eggs in a copper basin until they are a firm froth; and while beating, have an assistant pour very gradually the prepared sugar into the egg-froth; and when all is added, lay the basin containing the preparation into a vessel half filled with ice-water. Remove the whip, and using a wooden spatula, mix gently for five minutes, adding a teaspoonful of vanilla flavoring. Cover the basin with a napkin, letting it rest for ten minutes. Butter and flour a baking-sheet; slide down a fancy tube (No. 3) into a pastry-bag (No. 1079), fill it with the preparation, press down onto the baking-sheet, giving a C-shape, two inches long by one wide, to forty of them; and then forming twenty more, shaped like the letter D. Sprinkle them lightly with powdered sugar; place in a very slow oven, and let bake for fifteen minutes. When baked, these cakes should be perfectly white. Remove them from the oven, let get thoroughly cold; dress on a glass stand, and send to the table.

1250. Méringue-shells.—Prepare a méringue as for No. 1247. Slide a tube (No. 4) down a pastry-bag (No. 1079); lay a piece of paper over a baking-sheet, and after putting the méringue into the bag, press it out onto the paper, giving it an egg-shape, two and a half inches long by one inch high. There will be enough to make eighteen equal-sized shells. Be careful to keep them one inch apart. Sprinkle over liberally with powdered sugar, and place in a very slow oven to bake thirty minutes. Remove, and set to cool for twenty-five minutes. Then turn the paper containing the shells upside down on the table; and with a wet cloth or brush moisten well the paper; turn them over again, and let rest for two minutes, when the shells will detach easily. With the finger press them gently, one by one, in the bottom, into a perfect shell-shape. Return them to the baking-sheet, laying them upside down, and put them in the oven to dry thoroughly for ten minutes; then leave them to cool for thirty minutes more. Keep them in a dry place, either in a tin or paper box, and use when required. Méringue-shells prepared this way will keep nicely for at least twenty-five days.

1251. Swiss Méringues à l'Helvétienne.—Have a méringue preparation as for No. 1247; slide down in a pastry-bag (No. 1079) a tube (No. 4). Butter and flour a baking-sheet; make on it one design eight inches in diameter; another exactly the same shape, only six inches, and another of the same, only four inches. Put the méringue into the bag, and press it down gently over and around the first design, making the paste three-quarters of an inch thick; repeat the same for the second and third forms. Press down in the pan some more méringue, making a little cone four inches high, two inches in diameter at the base, and tapering gradually to a point at the top. Sprinkle the whole lightly with powdered sugar, and place the pan in a very moderate oven to bake for twenty-five minutes. Take it out, and let it thoroughly cool for half an hour. Have a quart of whipped crême à la vanille (No. 1254), add to it half a gill of Swiss kirsch and half a gill of maraschino, and with a pastry-whip beat the whole together for three minutes. Have ready a round dessert-dish with a fancy paper over, detach carefully the largest form from the pan, lay it on the dish, detach the second, lay it over the first, and fill the hollow space with half of the cream; now detach the third and smallest piece and lay it over the others, filling it entirely with part of the cream, and finally detach the cover, and arrange it nicely on the top. Pour the remaining cream into the pastry-bag containing the fancy tube, and with it decorate the places where the rings are joined. Then send to the table.

1252. Crême Renversée.—Put in a copper sugar-pan three ounces of granulated sugar with half a gill of cold water. Toss the pan briskly to melt the sugar well; then place it on the stove, and let it boil slowly until it becomes a light brown color. If a moderate fire, it will require four minutes, but if a brisk one only two will suffice; this will now be a caramel. Take a pudding-mold holding one quart; line the interior with all the caramel, holding the mold in the left hand, and spreading it evenly all round. Put the mold in a cool place, and let it become thoroughly cold. Have one pint of milk in a bowl; break in four eggs, add a quarter of a pound of powdered sugar and a teaspoonful of lemon essence. Beat well for five minutes; strain through a sieve into another bowl, and fill the mold with this cream. Place it in a tin pan filled with water to half the height of the mold, and place in a very moderate oven for forty-five minutes. When of a good golden color remove, and cool for at least two hours. Turn it on a dessert-dish, and serve with its own juice.

1253. Crême en Mousse au Café.—Take a pint of whipped cream as for No. 1254, add three tablespoonfuls of coffee essence (No. 1263), and beat well together for five minutes. Transfer it to a china bowl, and put it in a cold ice-box. When ready to serve, use a spoon to drop the cream carefully upon the centre of a cold, round dessert-dish, keeping it as high as possible, shaping it into a pretty, artistic dome. Send immediately to the table.

1254. Whipped Cream à la Vanille.—Put a pint of sweet cream into a basin. Have a tub or large dish-pan containing chopped ice and a little water, and lay the basin on top. With a soft wire egg-whip beat the cream slowly at first, and increase in swiftness until it is a firm froth. Sweeten with two ounces of powdered sugar, and add a teaspoonful of vanilla flavoring, beating constantly. Let it rest, and use when needed. Remove all the superfluous milk which may be found with the cream, before using it.

1255. Crême en Mousse au Rhum.—With a pint of fresh, sweet cream proceed as for No. 1254, adding a gill of rum, and beating well together for five minutes. Transfer it into a china bowl, and place in the ice-box until ready to use. When serving, have a cold dessert-dish, and with a wooden spoon drop the cream carefully into the centre of the dish, keeping it piled high as possible so to give it a pretty dome form, and send to the table immediately.

1256. Crême en Mousse au Kirsch.—Proceed as for No. 1255, only substituting a gill of kirsch for the gill of rum; serve in the same manner.

1257. Crême en Mousse au Maraschino.—Prepared the same as crême en mousse au rhum (No. 1255), substituting a gill of maraschino for the rum.

1258. Crême en Mousse au Cognac.—The same as for No. 1255, adding a gill of cognac instead of the rum, but serving the same way.

1259. Créme en Mousse au Curaçoa.—Substituting a gill of curaçoa for a gill of rum, and proceeding precisely the same as for No. 1255.

1260. Crême en Mousse.—To be prepared exactly the same, only using a gill of any other liquor desired, and serving the same as No. 1255.

1261. Charlotte Russe à la Crême.—Take six small, round charlotte russe molds two and a half inches high, three inches in diameter at the top by two at the bottom. When thoroughly cleaned, line them with biscuits à la cuillère (No. 1231), cut them in two, and should they be higher than the mold, trim them off to the edge. Pour the whipped cream (No. 1254) into a pastry-bag (No. 1079), and fill up the molds. Turn them over onto six dessert-plates, spread a little more cream on the top of each, and cover them each with one macaroon (No. 1210). Dress the rest of the cream nicely around the plates, and serve.

1262. Charlotte Russe au Café.—Line and prepare six small charlotte-molds as for the above (No. 1261), adding to the whipped cream two tablespoonfuls of coffee essence (No. 1263). Beat thoroughly together for two minutes, then fill the molds, and serve as for the above.

1263. Coffee Essence.—Take one ounce of good, ground coffee; place it in a small saucepan with half a pint of cold water, and let boil until reduced to about two tablespoonfuls. Then strain through a cloth, pressing it well, and let cool thoroughly. Add it to the cream as described in No. 1262.

1264. How to Cook Sugar.—Put into a sugar-pan one pound of granulated sugar, with half a pint of cold water; place it on a brisk stove. Have a vessel containing two quarts of ice-water, and when the sugar comes to a boil dip the fingers of the right hand into the water, and quickly pass them all around the inside of the pan, being careful to avoid touching the sugar; repeat this two or three times. However difficult this operation may appear, it is essential that it should be done, in order to have the sugar in a perfect condition. Take care to dip the fingers into the ice-water each time. Let the sugar boil; then squeeze in three drops of lemon juice. To know when it is sufficiently boiled, have a thin piece of wood the shape of a larding-needle. Dip the point into the ice-water, and then plunge it into the boiling sugar; remove it quickly, and dip it immediately into the water again. Lift it out, and see whether the sugar adhering to the wood be thoroughly hard. If not, let boil again, and continue to test with the stick as before. To be certain that the sugar is perfectly done, place the point of the stick between the teeth, and bite it. Should the sugar stick to the teeth, it needs more boiling, but if it cracks easily without sticking, it is thoroughly done. Remove it immediately from the fire, and place the bottom of the pan in the ice-water to prevent the sugar from turning brown.

The above cooked sugar can be used for glazing dried fruits and candied fruits of all kinds; also to fasten on pieces of of nougat, and to make any kind of caramels, etc., etc.

1265. Burned Sugar.—Put into a small iron omelet-pan half a pound of granulated sugar, and place on a slow stove, to burn thoroughly for thirty minutes. Remove the pan to the table to cool slightly for five minutes, and then add half a pint of boiling water, mixing well with an iron spoon. Replace the pan on the stove, and boil for five minutes, stirring continually ; then strain the sugar through a sieve into a vessel, and put in a cold place to cool thoroughly. Pour it into a bottle, and use when required. Burned sugar prepared this way will keep in perfect condition for several weeks.

1266. Nougat.—Have ready four ounces of peeled and dried almond (No. 1207). Cut each into four slices, and lay them in a tin pan with a sheet of paper under them. Put the pan in a warm place, but not on the stove. Take a copper sugar-pan, or dropper, put into it six ounces of powdered sugar, and place it on a hot stove ; then with a dry, wooden spatula stir continually, until the sugar is dissolved, being careful to avoid browning it. Remove from the fire, add one drop of lemon juice, and let it cool off slightly for three minutes, stirring constantly; then add the almonds, mixing all gently with the spatula for two minutes. The nougat is now ready for use, and can be molded into cornets-d'abondance, columns, bases, or any shape the fancy may dictate.

1267. Small Pyramid of Nougat.—Oil slightly the interior of a small, round base. Take half the nougat, prepared as for No. 1266, lay it on a marble table (the nougat should always be hot), roll it out very thin with an oiled roller, and with this line the oiled base. Then with a whole lemon sharply press the nougat onto the mold to give it a perfect form, cutting it evenly away all around the edge. Put the pieces with the rest in the pan, and place near the fire to keep hot. Have a small cornet-d'abondance (cornucopia), oil it slightly, and line the inside with half the remaining nougat, rolled out as before, and pressing it the same. Cut away all the superfluous part, and let it cool slightly. Then unmold both the base and cornet. Oil a tartlet-mold, and line it with the rest of the nougat. Lay the base carefully upon a glass stand of suitable size, the covered part uppermost, and fasten to the stand with cooked sugar (No. 1264). With cooked sugar fasten the cornet in the middle, small end uppermost, using cooked sugar for the purpose. Put the remaining piece from the tartlet-mold on top of all, and fasten it in the same way. All this should be done carefully and patiently. Have ready two well-peeled, sound oranges, pull them gently to pieces, looking closely at each separate section to see that the skin is not broken or loosened. Have a quarter of a pound of fresh Malaga grapes, detach them, leaving on each grape about a quarter of an inch of stem. Take also two ounces of candied cherries, plunge the grapes into the cooked sugar (No. 1264), and with a fork lift them up, and immediately lay them on a well-cleaned, oiled, marble table. Treat the pieces of orange and the cherries each the same way. During this time, should the sugar become cool, heat it up once more; fill the cornet with these fruits, dipping one side of each piece into the cooked sugar to make them adhere together. With a part of them fill the tart-shaped piece on top, proceeding in the same manner, and decorate with glace royale (No. 1269).

1269. Glace Royale.—Put the white of one egg into a small bowl. Beat it well with a small spatula, adding six ounces of extra fine sugar, and squeezing in three drops of lemon juice. Then continue beating for twenty minutes. When finished, it should be snow-white and pulpy. Make a small brown paper cornet, cut off the lower end, slide down a small fancy tube, and pour in some of the glace royale, covering the remainder of it with a damp cloth. Then with the cornet decorate the edge of the nougat base as in the preceding (No. 1268), also the upper edge, and all around the edge of the cornet, and finish by decorating artistically the tart-shaped piece on top; then send it to the table.

All nougat pieces, when finished, should be kept in a moderate temperature.

1270. Blanc-manger à la Josephine Delmonico.—Peel neatly six ounces of sweet almonds and two ounces of bitter almonds (No. 1207).

Put in a vessel, cover with cold water, and let them soak for fully one hour. Drain thoroughly through a sieve, and pound them well in a mortar, adding, little by little, a gill of cold water, and continue pounding for ten minutes. Now remove to a vessel and add two gills of lukewarm water, and mix together with the spatula for two minutes. Spread a large napkin over another vessel, pour on the above preparation, lift up the four corners, and holding it with the left hand, squeeze the liquid through with the right. Lay this almond milk aside for further use. Put into a saucepan two gills of cold water, half an ounce of gelatine, a piece of vanilla-bean two inches long and split in two, and four ounces of powdered sugar. Mix well with the spatula for two minutes; remove the spatula, put on the lid, and let infuse for thirty minutes. Then place the saucepan on the hot stove, and stir gently from the bottom, allowing it to boil slowly for four minutes. Remove it from the fire, and let the pan rest on the table for three minutes. Pour in the almond milk, mix again for two minutes, using the spatula, and strain the whole through a fine sieve into another vessel. Have a three-pint, channeled blanc-manger mold; put some broken ice at the bottom of a pail, place the mold on it, arranging more broken ice around the sides, so that the mold be entirely sunk in the ice as far up as the edge. Stir the preparation for one minute, then pour it into the mold, cover the pail with a napkin, and leave it to congeal for one hour. Take up the mold carefully from the pail, wipe off the ice with a towel, and have ready a cold dessert-dish with a folded napkin over. Turn out the blanc-manger onto this; decorate the surface with two ounces of candied cherries and one ounce of angelica, and it is ready for the table.

1271. Vanilla Ice-cream.—Boil in a saucepan one pint of milk with half a vanilla-bean; put in a vessel half a pound of powdered sugar, and six egg yolks, and with a spatula mix thoroughly for ten minutes; then add it to the boiling milk, stirring for two minutes longer, and pour the whole into a copper basin, placing it on a moderate stove to heat for five minutes, stirring at the bottom continually with the spatula, and being careful not to let it boil. Remove from off the fire, place it on a table, and add immediately one pint of sweet cream, still mixing it for two minutes more; let cool off for thirty minutes, then strain through a sieve into an ice-cream freezer; put on the lid, and lay it in an ice-cream tub, filling the freezer all round with broken ice, mixed slightly with rock-salt; then turn the handle on the cover as briskly as possible for three minutes. Lift up the lid, and with a wooden spoon detach the cream from all around the freezer, and the bottom as well. Re-cover it, and turn the handle sharply for three minutes more; uncover, and detach the cream the'same as before, being careful that no ice or salt drops in. Put the lid on, and repeat the same three times more. The ice-cream should by this time be quite firm, so have a cold dessert-dish with a folded napkin, dress the ice-cream over, and send to the table.

This same ice-cream can be formed into a single brick by having a brick-shaped form, filling it with the cream, and pressing it down quickly with a spoon; cover closely, being careful that the form is completely filled, so that no salted water can penetrate into it. Put broken ice at the bottom of a pail, mixing in a little rock-salt, lay the form on top, covering it entirely with broken ice and salt; let freeze for one hour, remove, and bathe it in a vessel containing lukewarm water; wash off the ice and salt that adhere, and lift it out as quickly as possible; remove the cover, and turn it on a dessert-dish with a folded napkin, lift up the mold, and send the ice-cream to the table.

1272. Chocolate Ice-cream.—Prepare and cook exactly the same as for vanilla ice-cream (No. 1271); put in a saucepan two ounces of well-chopped cocoa and an ounce of powdered sugar, add to it half the cream preparation; place the pan on the stove, and with a pastry-whip stir briskly, and let boil for three minutes; take it from the fire, add it to the remaining half of cream, then mix the whole well together for two minutes. Strain through a fine sieve into an ice-cream freezer, let cool for thirty minutes, then proceed to freeze it exactly the same as for the vanilla ice-cream, and serve it also the same.

1273. Coffee Ice-cream.—Put in a vessel half a pound of powdered sugar and six egg yolks; mix well with the spatula for ten minutes, then add one pint of boiling milk, stir for two minutes longer, and pour the whole into a copper basin; place it on the hot stove, and with the spatula stir gently at the bottom until well heated, but it must not boil. Take from off the fire, set it on a table, then immediately add a pint of sweet cream, mixing again for two minutes, and throw in two ounces of freshly ground Mocha coffee, stirring for two minutes longer; return the basin to the stove, beat it up again with the pastry-whip, and lay it on the table once more. Cover with a napkin, so that the coffee can infuse thoroughly for half an hour, then strain through a fine sieve into the freezer, and proceed freezing, and serving exactly the same as for vanilla ice-cream (No. 1271).

1274. Strawberry Ice-cream.—Prepare and proceed exactly the same as for the coffee ice-cream (No. 1273), suppressing the coffee, and when the cream is cooked and cool, add half a pint of well picked and cleaned strawberries. Mix well with the spatula for two minutes, then strain through a fine sieve into the freezer, pressing the strawberries through with a wooden spoon; remove the sieve, cover the freezer, and proceed to freeze, and serve precisely the same as for vanilla ice-cream (No. 1271).

1275. Pistache Ice-cream.—Have two ounces of fine, dried pistaches, using only the best quality; put them into a pie-plate, place it in the oven to let the nuts get a light brown color, which will take about six minutes; remove from the oven, lay the pistaches in a mortar with one ounce of granulated sugar, and pound slightly. Have a cream preparation exactly the same as for coffee ice-cream (No. 1273), suppressing the coffee. When cooked, add the pint of sweet cream and the pistache, then place it on the stove and heat well, stirring continually. Remove from the fire, cover the basin with a napkin, and let get thoroughly cool for thirty minutes. Add three drops of orange-flower water and five drops of spinach-green, mix the whole well for two minutes, then strain through a fine sieve into the freezer, and proceed to freeze and serve exactly the same as for vanilla ice-cream (No. 1271).

1276. Peach Ice-cream.—Put in a vessel half a pound of powdered sugar with six egg yolks, then mix well with the spatula for ten minutes; add a pint of boiling milk, stir for two minutes longer, and pour the whole into a copper basin. Place it on a hot stove, and heat it thoroughly, stirring continually, but not letting it boil; remove, lay it on the table, and mix in immediately one pint of sweet cream; then leave it to cool for thirty minutes. Have six ripe, fine, sound peaches, wipe them nicely, cut them in two, remove the stones, then mash them into the cream, mixing thoroughly for three minutes; strain through a fine sieve into a freezer, pressing the peaches through with a wooden spoon, then proceed to freeze, and serve precisely the same as for the vanilla ice-cream (No. 1271).

1277. Banana Ice-cream.—Prepare and proceed exactly the same as for the peach ice-cream (No. 1276), using four peeled, sound, and ripe bananas instead of the peaches, and finishing exactly the same as for the other.

1278. Lemon Ice-cream.—Put half a pound of powdered sugar into a basin; grate in the rind of two fine lemons, add four egg whites, and mix well with a wire whip for two minutes, then add a pint of cold milk, stirring again for one minute. Place the basin on the hot stove, stir briskly with the whip, and take it off when coming to a boil, lay it on the table, and pour in a pint of sweet cream, mixing well for two minutes. Let it get cool during half an hour, then strain through a fine sieve into a freezer, and finish precisely the same as for vanilla ice-cream (No. 1271).

1279. Lemon Water-ice.—Put in a vessel half a pound of powdered sugar, with one quart of cold water; grate in the rind of a large lemon, or of two small ones, squeezing in the juice of three good-sized ones, or of four if small, and with the spatula beat well together for five minutes. Have a syrup-weigher, place it in the centre of the preparation, and if it be twenty-one degrees it is correct, if not, add a little more powdered sugar; remove the weigher, mix a little more, and then strain through a sieve into the freezer, putting on the cover, and proceed to freeze it precisely the same as for vanilla ice-cream (No. 1271), serving it the same.

1280. Orange Water-ice.—Put into a vessel one quart of cold water, half a pound of powdered sugar, and grate in the rind of two fine, ripe, medium-sized, red oranges, adding their juice besides, the juice of three medium-sized, sound lemons, then finish the same as for lemon water-ice (No. 1279).

1281. Raspberry Water-ice.—Place in a vessel half a pound of powdered sugar, squeeze in the juice of three sound lemons, add a pint of nicely picked and cleaned raspberries, then with the spatula beat briskly for five minutes; add a quart of cold water, mixing again for one minute, and proceed to finish and serve the same as for lemon water-ice (No. 1279).

1282. Cherry Water-Ice.—Procure one pound of sound, solid, sour cherries; put them in a vessel, after picking off the stems nicely, with half a pound of powdered sugar, and squeeze in the juice of three fine lemons. Mix well with the spatula for five minutes, then add a quart of cold water, stirring the mixture for two minutes longer, and strain through a fine sieve into the ice-cream freezer, pressing the cherries down with a wooden spoon. Proceed to freeze, and serve exactly the same as for the vanilla ice-cream (No. 1271).

1283. Pineapple Water-ice.—Cut a small-sized, ripe pineapple in two; put one half away for further use, paring and peeling the other half neatly, then cut it into small pieces; place them in a mortar, and pound them thoroughly to a pulp; ten minutes will suffice for this. Add half a pound of powdered sugar, and pound again for five minutes; transfer the whole into a vessel, squeeze in the juice of three sound lemons, then pour in a quart of cold water, and mix well with the spatula for two minutes. Strain through a fine sieve into the freezer, adding two egg whites, beaten to a stiff froth, then beat well for one minute more. Cover with the lid, and finish it the same as the vanilla ice-cream (No. 1271).

1284. Peach Water-ice.—Procure eight medium-sized, fine, ripe peaches; wipe them neatly, cut in two, remove the stones, then mash them in a vessel with half a pound of powdered sugar; squeeze in the juice of three fine lemons, mix well with the spatula for two minutes, and pour in a quart of cold water, mixing for two minutes more. Strain through a fine sieve into the freezer, cover, and proceed to freeze the cream as for vanilla ice-cream (No. 1271), serving it the same.

1285. Apricot Water-ice.—Have twelve good-sized, fine, sound apricots; wipe them neatly, cut them in two, remove the stones, and put them in a vessel with half a pound of powdered sugar, mashing them thoroughly. Have two ounces of bitter almonds, peel, and pound without drying them; add one gill of cold water and one ounce of powdered sugar, pounding the whole together. Arrange a napkin over the vessel containing the apricot preparation; pour over it the contents of the mortar, pressing the juice through the napkin into the vessel, and mix well together for two minutes with the spatula. Squeeze in the juice of three sound lemons; add a pint and a half of cold water, mix again for two minutes, then strain through a fine sieve into the freezer. Put on the cover, and proceed to finish exactly the same as for the vanilla ice-cream (No. 1271).

1286. Biscuits Glacés.—Put six egg yolks in a copper basin, with two ounces of powdered sugar, half a gill of maraschino, and a quarter of a gill of Swiss kirsch. Then with a pastry-whip beat well together for two minutes. Place the basin on a hot stove, and stir briskly with the whip for five minutes. Remove it from the fire, and immediately put the basin into a vessel containing ice-water, and stir continually for two minutes more. Add a pint and a half of whipped cream à la vanille (No. 1254), and mix well with the rest for three minutes. Then cover the basin with a napkin, and let repose for ten minutes. Have six paper cases, four inches long, two inches wide, and one and a half inches high, and fill equally with the above preparation. Have ready a square biscuit-glacé box, ten inches high by six inches square, and having inside a loose, two-tier frame. Place this box in an ice-cream tub, filling it with broken ice mixed with rock-salt. Wipe the cover neatly, and after lifting it up, remove the frame and place three biscuits on each tier; return the frame to the box, put the cover on, and let freeze for one and a half hours. Have a cold dessert-dish covered with a folded napkin; uncover the box, lift up the frame, and dress the biscuits nicely on the dish, sending them to the table at once.

1287. Biscuits Tortoni.—Prepare and proceed exactly the same as for biscuits glacés (No. 1286), only placing the preparation into six round, fancy paper cases, instead of square ones. When filled, sift evenly over the surfaces two ounces of finely powdered macaroons (No. 1210); lay them on the tiers of the frame, and freeze them, serving them precisely as the biscuits glacés.

1288. Iced Pudding à la Diplomate.—Have a biscuit-glacé preparation exactly the same as for No. 1286; cut ten biscuits à la cuillère (No. 1231) into dice-shaped pieces, and add them to the preparation. Then, with a wooden spoon, mix lightly for two minutes. With this fill a three-pint, melon-shaped form, and place the cover on. Have a pail, with broken ice in the bottom; lay the form on it, and fill the pail with more broken ice and rock-salt, and let it freeze thoroughly for two hours. Have ready a vessel with warm water; take out the mold from the pail, plunge it into the warm water, to wash away the ice and salt; then remove it immediately. unmold it onto a dessert-dish with a fancy paper, and serve.

1289. Plum Pudding Glacé à la Gladstone.—Have ready three ounces of Malaga raisins, prepared as for No. 1081; place them in a stone jar with half a pint of good old sherry, adding three ounces of candied cherries cut into quarters, one ounce of finely chopped candied citron, and two ounces of candied apricots, also cut into small pieces; then with the spatula mix gently together for one and a half minutes. Cover the jar, and let infuse for fully twelve hours. Prepare a chocolate ice-cream, as for No. 1272, and just before removing it from the freezer add the above fruit preparation, mixing well with the spatula for fully two minutes. Put on the cover, and let freeze again for five minutes longer. Take a three-pint melon-form, and with a spoon fill it with the pudding preparation; cover it well, and put it in a pail containing broken ice and rock-salt at the bottom; then fill up the pail with more ice and salt, allowing it to freeze for fully two hours. In the meanwhile prepare the following sauce: put in a saucepan two egg yolks with one ounce of powdered sugar; place it on a slow stove, and with a pastry-whip stir briskly, adding gradually one gill of old English brandy. Heat it well, but it must not boil. Then take from the fire, set the pan on a table, and continue stirring for twelve minutes. Add a pint of well-whipped crème à la vanille (No. 1254), mixing the whole well together with the whip for two minutes, and pour the sauce into a china bowl, placing it in the ice-box. Have a vessel ready containing warm water; lift the mold from the pail, plunge it into the water to remove the ice and salt adhering; then lift it up, unmold the pudding immediately, and place it on a dessert-dish, with a fancy paper cover. Beat well the sauce; transfer it to a silver sauce-bowl, and send it to the table with the plum pudding, serving it separately.

1290. Macaroon Ice-cream.—Take six ounces of macaroons (No. 1210); put them into a tin pan, and place it in a moderate oven to dry for ten minutes. Remove, and lay them on a table to cool off for twenty minutes, then put them in a mortar, pound thoroughly, and sift them over a sheet of paper. Have ready a vanilla ice-cream as for No. 1271, and just before serving add to it the sifted macaroons, and with the spatula mix thoroughly for five minutes, and with this fill a three-pint brick-mold, covering it tightly. Have ready a pail with broken ice and rock-salt at the bottom, lay the mold over, and fill up the pail with more ice and salt. Let it freeze for two hours, and when ready to serve, have ready a vessel with warm water, take up the mold, bathe it in the water, and wash off all the salt and ice that adhere, then unmold the ice-cream onto a dessert-dish with a fancy paper over, and send to the table immediately.

1291. Pudding Glacé à la Frankie Cleveland.—Prepare half the quantity of vanilla ice-cream as for No. 1271; when frozen, let it rest, and prepare also half the quantity of biscuit-glacé preparation (No. 1286), and when ready cover the basin, and let rest also. Have half a pound of marrons glacés (candied chestnuts); break them into pieces onto a plate; take a three-pint melon-form, arrange the vanilla ice-cream all around it, dividing it evenly, and filling up with alternate layers of the biscuit preparation and the marrons glacés; cover the mold tightly, and place it in a pail with broken ice mixed with rock-salt at the bottom, also filling the pail with more ice and salt, then let freeze for fully two hours. Two minutes before serving, bathe the mold in warm water to remove the ice and salt that adhere, unmold, and send to the table immediately with a sauce-bowl full of the following sauce : add to half a pint of whipped cream à la vanille (No. 1254) one gill of strawberry juice, and half a gill, or two ounces, of yellow chartreuse; beat well together with the whip for two minutes, then pour it into the sauce-bowl.

1292. Napolitaine Ice-cream.—Prepare a pint of vanilla ice-cream as for No. 1271; a pint of pistache ice-cream (No. 1275), and a pint of raspberry water-ice (No. 1281). Take a long brick-form holding three pints, put at the bottom of this the raspberry water-ice, arrange the vanilla ice-cream on top, and fill up with the pistache, then cover tightly. Take a pail with broken ice mixed with rock-salt at the bottom, lay the form over, and fill up the pail with more ice and salt, and let freeze for two hours. Plunge the form in warm water to wash off the ice and salt, and unmold the ice-cream onto a piece of paper laid on the table. Dip a long knife in warm water, cut the brick lengthwise through the centre, then each piece into three, so that the Napolitaine will be divided into six equal-sized square pieces, each one having the three kinds of cream. Dress on a cold dessert-dish with a fancy paper over, and serve.

1293. Tutti-frutti.—Prepare a pint of vanilla ice-cream as for No. 1271, half a pint of strawberry ice-cream (No. 1274), and half a pint of lemon water-ice (No. 1279); let them remain in the freezers. Put four ounces of candied cherries onto a plate, cut them in halves, and add two candied apricots cut into small pieces. Take six tutti-frutti molds, open one of them, and lay on the cover a spoonful of strawberry ice-cream, with a spoonful of the lemon water-ice, one beside the other, press the sixth part of the candied fruits onto the ice-cream in the cover of the mold, filling the bottom with vanilla ice-cream, and close together firmly. Lay it immediately into a pail with broken ice and rock-salt at the bottom, cover the mold slightly with more ice and salt, then proceed to prepare the other five molds exactly the same. When they are all in the pail and covered as the first one, fill it up entirely with broken ice and salt, and let it freeze for one hour. Have a vessel containing warm water ready at hand, and prepare six small dessert-plates with a small fancy paper on each, lift up the molds, one after the other, wash them off quickly with the warm water, and unmold the tutti-fruttis onto the cold plates, and serve.

1294. Plombière à la Kingman.—Put together into a saucepan eight egg yolks, half a pound of powdered sugar, a piece of vanilla-bean one inch long and split in two, also a pint of sweet cream, and six ounces of finely grated cocoa. Mix well with the spatula for two minutes, then place the pan on the hot stove, and stir constantly while heating, but under no circumstances must it boil. Remove it from the fire, and lay the pan in a cool place on the table for thirty minutes. Put an ice-cream freezer into a tub, fill it all round with broken ice mixed with rock-salt, remove the cover, and after wiping the freezer well, strain the preparation through a sieve into it, cover it again, and with the hands turn the handle of the cover for five minutes in opposite directions. Lift up the cover, and with the spatula detach the preparation that adheres to the sides, readjust the cover, and turn again the handle, beginning in an opposite direction from the first time; after five minutes, detach from the sides as before, and repeat for the third time the turning process. Finally lift off the cover, and detach the cream from all around, and it will now be thoroughly firm, so cover it again, and let it rest. Beat up to a froth one gill of sweet cream as for No. 1254; take a glass or silver stand, and with an ice-cream spoon remove the cream from the freezer, spoonful by spoonful, and dress it in the centre of the bowl, keeping it as high as possible, and giving it a pretty, pyramid shape. Fill a paper cornet with the whipped cream, cut off the point, and decorate artistically the top and sides of the plombière. Chop up very fine two ounces of pistache, and sprinkle them evenly over the surface, then send to the table.

1295. Parfait au Café à la Parisienne.—Place six ounces of powdered sugar in a saucepan with six egg yolks and a pint of sweet cream, and mix well together for two minutes; set the saucepan on the hot stove, then stir gently and continually from the bottom, using a spatula, until nearly coming to a boil; as this is difficult to determine on account of the briskness of the fire, the best way to tell when it is sufficiently done is to lift up the spatula and see whether the cream adheres thickly to it, if so, remove the saucepan from the fire and lay it on the table, add immediately to it four ounces of freshly roasted Mocha coffee in beans, then stir again well for one minute more. Remove the spatula, cover the saucepan with a napkin, put the lid on, and let infuse for one hour. Beat up one pint of fresh sweet cream as for No. 1254, and let rest until needed. Place an ice-cream freezer in a tub, fill it up all round with broken ice mixed with rock-salt, wipe the cover nicely, and then remove it; strain the infused preparation through a fine sieve into the freezer, put on the cover, then take hold of the handle, and turn the freezer briskly in opposite directions for five minutes; remove the cover, and with the spatula detach all the cream that adheres to the sides and bottom, recover, and turn sharply as before; remove the cover, detach the cream from the sides and bottom, replace the cover, and begin turning again in opposite directions for five minutes longer. The cream should now be thoroughly frozen. Drop the whipped cream into the freezer, very little at a time, meanwhile mixing it gently with the spatula, which should take four minutes to accomplish it; then have ready a three-pint, channeled, ice-cream mold, and with an ice-cream spoon fill the mold with the preparation, and put on the lid. Place some broken ice with rock-salt at the bottom of a pail, lay the mold over, and fill up the pail with more ice and salt, then let freeze for fully one hour. Afterward remove the mold, dip it into lukewarm water, wipe away the ice and salt, and lift it up immediately, take off the cover, and turn the cream onto a cold dessert-dish with a folded napkin, and serve.

1296. Rice and Cream à la Croce.—Put one pint of cold milk into a saucepan, adding one pint of cold water and half a saltspoonful of salt, place the pan on the hot stove, and when boiling, throw in four ounces of well-cleaned, raw rice; then with a spatula stir slowly and continually at the bottom while it is cooking for twenty-five minutes, then take the pan from off the fire, lay it on a table, and add immediately four ounces of powdered sugar and one ounce of fresh butter; mix well together with a spatula for two minutes, then transfer it into another vessel, and set it in a cold place for one hour to have it thoroughly cooled off. Whip to a froth one pint of sweet cream as for No. 1254, cover the basin with a napkin, and let rest for twenty minutes; should there be any milk settled at the bottom, pour it off, and add to the cream two ounces of powdered sugar and one teaspoonful of vanilla flavoring, then with a wire whip beat well together for two minutes longer, and remove the whip. Take the rice from the vessel, drop it gradually into the whipped cream, then mix the whole together slowly and carefully for three minutes. Line a two-quart, tin melon-form with three ounces of peach marmalade (No. 1331), fill the mold with the preparation, put on the cover, and after placing a little broken ice at the bottom of a pail, lay in the mold, and cover it entirely with broken ice (no salt is necessary for this), and let freeze for one hour. Have a vessel with two quarts of lukewarm water; lift up the mold from the pail, dip it into the water, wash off the ice, and raise it up immediately; remove the cover, turn the preparation onto a cold dessert-dish, and send to the table.

1297. Oranges Glacées à la George Renauldt.—Have six fine, solid oranges, and with a pastry-tube, one and a quarter of an inch in diameter, cut off the tops of the oranges, then with a small knife remove the covers gently, laying them aside until later. With either a Parisian-potato cutter or a spoon, empty the insides of the oranges, being careful to avoid breaking any of the skin, for should that occur, they will be useless; the interiors can be used for some other purpose. Arrange the oranges, with their covers on, in a square biscuit-glacé box as for No. 1286; place the box in a tub, filling it with broken ice mixed with rock-salt, and let freeze for one hour. Prepare a champagne punch as for No. 1307, and with it fill the interior of the oranges, put on the covers, and with different colored ribbons tie each one, beginning at the top; when at the bottom, turn the ribbon and bring it back to the top in an opposite direction, then make a graceful bow on top of the covers. Lay them again in the box, and let them freeze for one hour longer, then dress them on a dessert-dish with a folded napkin, and serve.

1298. Macédoine Glacée à la Cavour.—Prepare a pint of lemon ice-cream as for No. 1278, also a pint of coffee ice-cream (No. 1273), leaving them in their freezers. Take two ounces of candied cherries, cut in halves, two ounces of candied apricots, cut in slices, one ounce of candied angelica, cut into very small, lozenge-shaped pieces, two ounces of candied pineapple, cut into very thin slices, and twelve French walnuts, shelled and divided. Have a three-pint, square ice-cream mold, place half the lemon ice-cream at the bottom, arrange a third part of the fruits nicely over, dividing them equally, then cover with half of the coffee ice-cream, and with a spoon press it down well. Lay half the remaining fruits on top of this, and spread over the rest of the lemon ice-cream, then the last of the fruits, and fill up the mold with the balance of the coffee ice-cream. Close very firmly, and lay it into a pail with broken ice mixed with rock-salt at the bottom, and filling it with the same, then let freeze for two hours. Two minutes before serving prepare a vessel with warm water, lift up the mold, and wash off the ice and salt, then unmold the macédoine immediately on a cold dessert-dish with a fancy paper over, and send it to the table.

1299. Charlottes Glacées.—Take six small charlotte-molds, and line them nicely with twelve biscuits à la cuillère (No. 1231) cut crosswise into halves. Have ready one pint and a half of vanilla ice-cream (No. 1271), and fill the interiors of the molds with it, and turn them onto a dessert-dish with a folded napkin over. Divide the remaining ice-cream evenly over the six charlottes, with one macaroon (No. 1210) on top of each, then send immediately to the table.

1300. Charlottes Panachées.—Have six charlotte-molds lined as for charlottes glacées (No. 1299); fill them with a pint of vanilla ice-cream (No. 1271), then turn them onto six cold dessert-plates. Take a pastry-bag (No. 1079), slide down in it a fancy tube (No. 3), and pour into it a pint of whipped crême à la vanille (No. 1254); press a little of this onto the top of the charlottes, arrange over them six macaroons (No. 1210), press a little more cream about the size of a nut on the top of each macaroon, then with the balance of the cream decorate the bottom of the charlottes all around, and serve.

1301. Méringues Glacées.—Prepare a pint and a half of vanilla ice-cream (No. 1271), and with a round ice-cream spoon divide it evenly onto six cold dessert-plates, and arrange over each two méringue-shells (No. 1250), so as to nearly enclose the ice-cream, and then send to the table.

1302. Méringues Panachées.—Have six méringue-shells (No. 1250); divide evenly into them a pint of vanilla ice-cream (No. 1271). Slide into a pastry-bag (No. 1079) a fancy tube (No. 3), and pour into it a pint of whipped crême à la vanille (No. 1254); press half of it into six other méringue-shells, then join them to the other six containing the ice-cream. Lay them on six cold dessert-plates, and decorate the joints nicely with the balance of the cream, then send to the table at once.

1303. Punch à la Lorenzo Delmonico.—Put in a china bowl half a pound of powdered sugar, squeeze in the juice of three fine, sound, large lemons and the juice of a fine, large, red orange, then with a very clean wooden spoon mix together for three minutes. Add half a pint of cold water, a gill of Swiss kirsch, and stir for four minutes more, then strain through a fine sieve into the ice-cream freezer, remove the sieve, and pour into the freezer half a gill of St. Croix rum, a quarter of a gill of Delmonico's fine champagne cognac, and half a pint of Delmonico's champagne. Cover immediately with the lid, and place the freezer in a narrow ice-cream tub, filling the latter all round with broken ice mixed with rock-salt ; then with the handle on the cover turn as sharply as possible for three minutes ; wipe the cover neatly, uncover, and with a wooden spoon detach the punch from the sides of the freezer, as also from the bottom ; cover again, turn the handle for three minutes more, uncover, detach the punch as before, cover, and repeat this three times as explained for the vanilla ice-cream (No. 1271). Have six cold dessert-plates covered with fancy papers, each one having an L. D. designed on it ; fill six punch-glasses with the punch, arrange them on the plates, and send to the table.

1304. Romaine Punch.—Make half the quantity of the preparation the same as lemon water-ice (No. 1279), and before freezing add a gill of Jamaica rum; then finish the same, only serving the romaine punch in six small punch-glasses.

1305. Kirsch Punch.—To be prepared precisely as for the above (No. 1304), only substituting a gill of kirsch for the rum, and serving it the same.

1306. Punch à la Cardinal.—Prepare half the quantity of the preparation as for raspberry water-ice (No. 1281); strain it through a sieve into the freezer, then pour in half a gill of red curaçoa, and half a gill of maraschino; put on the lid, and freeze it the same as for vanilla ice-cream (No. 1271), only serving it in six punch-glasses.

1307. Champagne Punch.—Have half the quantity of preparation described for orange water-ice (No. 1280), strain it through a sieve into the freezer, and add half a pint of good champagne. Place the cover on, and proceed to freeze it exactly as for vanilla ice-cream (No. 1271), serving it in six punch-glasses.

1308. Punch à la Lalla Rookh.—Have ready half the quantity of preparation of vanilla ice-cream (No. 1271); strain it through a fine sieve into the freezer, adding one gill of Jamaica rum; freeze it the same, and serve it in glasses.

1309. Punch en Surprise.—Have six fancy forms; one the shape of a pear, one of an apple, one of a banana, one of a tomato, one of a pineapple, and one of a peach. Fill a tin pan with finely cracked ice well mixed with rock-salt, lay on it the six molds, opened flat, fill them with cold water, also the pan to half its height, and let it all rest for one hour; feel the inside of the molds to find whether a frozen crust adheres to them; if so, continue to finish the punch. Have any kind of desired punch ready; take up each mold separately, empty out the water, and fill them one after another; close tightly, and lay them in a pail previously prepared with broken ice and rock-salt at the bottom; cover them with plenty more ice and salt, and let freeze one hour. Have ready a cold dessert-dish with a folded napkin over; put some warm water in a vessel, take up each mold, one by one, dip them into the water, and hastily wash off any ice or salt which may adhere, unmold them carefully, and lay them nicely on the dessert-dish, and send to the table at once.

1310. Punch à la Française, Hot.—Put in a saucepan on the hot range one pint of Jamaica rum, with twelve ounces of granulated sugar; stir continually with the spatula until reduced to half the quantity. Add the juice of three lemons, the juice of four sweet oranges, then set the pan on the corner of the stove to keep hot. Put into a tea-pot one ounce of green tea, pouring over it a pint of boiling water, and let infuse for ten minutes, then strain into the preparation; return it on the hot place, and when about boiling, skim thoroughly with a skimmer. Take it from the fire, pour it into a punch-bowl, and serve.

1311. Punch à la Française, Iced.—Have a punch à la Française ready as for the above (No. 1310), and let cool off. Pour it into a small freezer, cover it, and lay it in a wooden tub filled with chopped ice all around. Sprinkle the ice well with rock-salt, and with the hands turn the freezer sharply around in opposite directions. While doing this, stop every two minutes to detach the punch from around the freezer (using a spatula), so that it will be perfectly firm. If sharply handled, fifteen minutes will suffice to freeze it thoroughly, then serve in six punch-glasses, dividing it equally.

1312. Punch à la Czarina, Hot.—Place in a copper or tin vessel one pound of granulated sugar, half a pint of Swiss kirsch, four ounces of St. Croix rum, and two ounces of good cognac. Light this mixture with a match, and let it burn until the sugar is dissolved, then pour in a quart of Roederer's champagne, not colder than fifty degrees Fahrenheit. Squeeze in the juice of a good-sized mellow orange, and add twelve thin slices of pineapple; mix the whole well with a ladle, heat it slightly, being careful it does not boil, then pour the punch into a fancy bowl, and serve hot with six punch-glasses.

1313. Champagne Cup.—Squeeze the juice of half a good-sized, sound lemon into a fancy glass pitcher large enough to contain five pints; sweeten with one tablespoonful of powdered sugar, then add two ponies of red curaçoa, one bottle of plain soda, and two slices of cucumber-rind. Pour in three pints of any brand of champagne, adding about a quarter of a pound of ice, then mix thoroughly with a spoon, and ornament the punch nicely with strawberries, very thin slices of pineapple, a finely sliced, medium-sized orange, and half a bunch of fine, fresh mint; send the cup to the table with six champagne-glasses.

1314. Claret Cup.—Have a glass pitcher holding two and a half quarts, or five pints; squeeze in the juice of three medium-sized, sound lemons, add four tablespoonfuls of powdered sugar, two ponies of red curaçoa, and two slices of cucumber-rind, then pour in three pints of claret, and one bottle of plain soda ; or a pint of either Clysmic, Apollinaris, or carbonic water will answer. Mix thoroughly with a spoon, adding a lump of ice weighing about three quarters of a pound; mix again, then decorate with a finely sliced orange, cut into small pieces, berries of any kind, and finally with half a bunch of fresh mint. Serve in six punch-glasses, and the effect will be exceedingly pretty.

1315. Water-melon à la Romero.—Have a fine, sound, large, ripe water-melon, and with a very thin knife cut out a piece in the centre two inches square by three and a half inches deep; remove the piece carefully, and pour gradually into the inside one quart bottleful of champagne; replace the piece of melon in its former position, then lay the melon in the ice-box for six hours to infuse; set it on a silver dessert-dish, and send to the table, cutting it according to taste.

1316. Water-melon à la José Paez.—Proceed and prepare exactly the same as for the above (No. 1315), only substituting one pint of Jamaica rum for the champagne, and serving the same.

1317. Water-melon à la Seward.—Prepare a water-melon as for No. 1315, pouring into it one pint of Delmonico's cognac, instead of the champagne, and serving it the same.

1318. Sherry-wine Jelly.—Put one quart of cold water into a saucepan with half a pound of granulated sugar; break in two ounces of gelatine in small pieces, and grate in the rind of a medium-sized lemon, squeezing in the juice as well. Mix well, and place the saucepan on the hot stove. Beat up in a basin two egg whites, and add them to the other ingredients, then grate in a saltspoonful of nutmeg, adding six cloves, and one bay-leaf, mixing well with the whip for one minute. Have ready a seamless jelly-bag (which can be purchased ready made), tie it on a jelly-stand, or if none handy, two kitchen chairs will answer the purpose. Stir the preparation, and when coming to a boil, set it back to a cooler part of the stove to prevent it overflowing; stir, while boiling, for six minutes. Place a vessel under the jelly-bag, remove the pan from the fire, and pour the whole into the bag, immediately adding to it half a pint of good sherry wine, and a teaspoonful of burned sugar (No. 1265). Let it drain into the vessel, then return it to the bag, placing another vessel underneath, then let it drain through for fully two hours. Have a quart jelly-mold, pour the jelly from the vessel into it, and set it aside in a cool place for two hours, then put it into the ice-box to harden for two hours more. Prepare a cold dessert-dish, and after dipping the mold lightly and carefully to near its edge in lukewarm water, take it up immediately, and turn it onto the dish, wiping neatly the latter all around, then send to the table.

1319. Kirsch Jelly.—This jelly is to be prepared the same as the sherry-wine jelly (No. 1318), omitting the burned sugar, and replacing the sherry wine by a gill of Swiss Kirschwasser, then serving it the same.

1320.—Jamaica-rum Jelly.—Proceed exactly the same as for sherry-wine jelly (No. 1318), only substituting a gill of Jamaica rum for the sherry, then finish and serve the same.

1321. Brandy Jelly.—To be prepared precisely the same as the sherry-wine jelly (No. 1318), substituting a gill of good brandy for the sherry, and served the same as the other jellies.

1322. Champagne Jelly.—To be made the same as the sherry-wine jelly (No. 1318), suppressing the burned sugar, and using half a pint of Delmonico's champagne, instead of the sherry. To be served the same.

1323. Kümmel Jelly.—Prepare and proceed exactly as for sherry-wine jelly (No. 1318), suppressing the burned sugar, and replacing the sherry by a gill of Russian kümmel, sending it to the table the same as for the others.

1324. Rhein-wine Jelly.—The same as for sherry-wine jelly (No. 1318), omitting the burned sugar, and using half a pint of Lieberfraumilch wine, instead of the sherry, and serving the same.

1325. Marcella-wine Jelly à la Castellar.—To be made exactly the same as sherry-wine jelly (No. 1318,) using half a pint of Marcella wine in place of the sherry, and finished the same.

1326. Currant Jelly.—Select sixteen pounds of small, old Dutch currants, not too ripe; those are preferable which are picked at the end of the month of June. Place them in a copper basin on the hot stove, and begin stirring them immediately from the bottom, using a wooden spatula; when they begin to scald, pour them into a clean tub, and with a pounder mash them thoroughly. Strain them through a flannel jelly-bag back into the copper basin, adding to the juice seven pounds of granulated sugar. Return the pan to the fire, and let boil until reduced to about half the quantity, then dip in a skimmer, lift it up, and feel the jelly with the two forefingers; close them, and open them slowly, if the jelly is mucilaginous, then it is done; if not, cook for a few minutes longer. Take it from the fire, and pour a little into every glass jar ready to use, as this will prevent them cracking. Afterwards fill them up. When thoroughly cold, which will be in about two hours, during which time they must not be disturbed; cork them tightly, and put them in a closet. Currant jelly prepared in this way will keep in good condition for two years.

1327. Apple Jelly.—Put six good-sized apples into a saucepan after cutting them into quarters; add a pint of cold water and a quarter of a lemon, then place it on a hot stove, and let boil for fifteen minutes. Place a sieve over a vessel, pour the contents of the pan onto it, and let drain thoroughly for fifteen minutes, then remove the sieve, and pour the apple juice into a saucepan with a pound of granulated sugar. Replace it on the hot stove, and let boil for thirty minutes, so that it be reduced to half, then take it from the fire, and pour it into a stone jar to cool off thoroughly, and use it when required for pies, cakes, or any other desired purpose.

1328. Apple Sauce.—Press the apples cooked in the above (No. 1327) through the sieve into a bowl, add half a pound of powdered sugar, a teaspoonful of ground cinnamon, and mix well together for two minutes, place it in a stone jar, and use when required.

1329. Cranberry Sauce.—Put in a saucepan one quart of fine, red, cleaned cranberries with a gill of water; place it on a hot stove and boil for fifteen minutes, then add five ounces of powdered sugar, and stir lightly with a spatula for five minutes. Remove it from the fire, pour it into a sieve over a vessel, and press well through with a wooden spoon. Transfer it into a stone jar, and use when required.

1330. Stewed Prunes à la Général Dufour.—Procure ten ounces of the best imported prunes (which should invariably be purchased at a responsible dealer's), and put them in a vessel with a quart of cold water, letting them soak for four hours; then thoroughly drain them. Put them in a saucepan with half a pint of cold water, the zest of a sound lemon, a two-inch-length piece of cinnamon, two ounces of fresh butter, and four ounces of powdered sugar. Place the pan on a slow fire, and with the spatula stir carefully and gently once in a while, to avoid breaking them. After letting them cook slowly for two hours, remove the pan from the stove, and add immediately a pint of Bordeaux wine, replace it on the stove to heat thoroughly, but not allowing it to boil again; take from off the fire, pour the prunes into a stone jar, let get cold, then serve.

1331. Peach Marmalade.—Peel and cut into slices twelve good-sized, sound peaches; put into a saucepan half a pound of granulated sugar and a pint of cold water; place it on a hot stove, and let come to a boil, then add the peaches, and cook for twelve minutes, stirring continually with the spatula. Remove from the fire, and strain through a pastry-sieve into a bowl, adding twelve peeled almonds (No. 1207), then let cool off thoroughly. Put it into a china bowl, lay it aside in a cool place, and use when needed. This marmalade will keep for several days if properly prepared.

1332. Stewed Apples.—Take six fine, sound Middletown pippin apples, peel them neatly, and with an apple-corer core them thoroughly, then cut each apple into four quarters, and lay them in a saucepan with a pint of cold water, adding half a pound of granulated sugar. When the contents of the pan come to a boil, skim well, and then flavor with the juice of half an orange, or the same quantity of lemon, and a saltspoonful of ground cinnamon can also be added. When flavored, let cook for five minutes longer, and with a spatula stir slowly from the bottom to avoid mashing the apples. Remove from the fire, pour into a china bowl, and cool off thoroughly before serving.

1333. Stewed Pears.—Are to be prepared and cooked exactly the same as for the above (No. 1332).

1334. Stewed Peaches.—Peel and cut into quarters ten medium-sized, sound, ripe peaches, removing the stones, put them into a saucepan with a pint of cold water, adding half a pound of granulated sugar. Place the pan on the stove, and when boiling skim well; let cook for five minutes, meanwhile stirring them slowly from the bottom, to avoid mashing the fruit; then remove, and immediately add a gill of kirsch, mixing well together for about half a minute. Pour into a china bowl, let get cool, then dress on a dessert-dish, and serve.

1335. Stewed Apricots.—Peel, cut, and stone twelve good-sized apricots, or fifteen if they be small; then proceed to prepare them exactly as for stewed peaches (No. 1334), only substituting a gill of brandy for the kirsch.

1336. Stewed Green-gages.—Have eighteen or twenty solid, ripe, green-gages, peel them neatly, cut them in halves, and stone them. Proceed exactly the same as for stewed peaches (No. 1334), only replacing the kirsch by a gill of red curaçoa, and serving the same.

1337. Stewed Plums.—Proceed exactly the same as for the above (No. 1336), substituting the same quantity of plums for the green-gages.

1338. Stewed Quinces.—Take twelve fine, firm, ripe quinces, peel and core them thoroughly, then cut them into quarters, and put them in a saucepan with a pint of cold water and half a pound of granulated sugar. Place them on the stove; when boiling, skim well, and let cook for fifteen minutes, stirring them gently at the bottom with a spatula to avoid mashing the fruit. Remove from the fire, and immediately add a gill of maraschino; stir lightly again, then pour into a china bowl to let cool. Dress on a dessert-dish and serve.

1339. Syrup for Preserving Fruits.—Put seven pounds of granulated sugar into a sugar-pan, adding five pints of cold water, and when on the hot stove, stir with the spatula until thoroughly heated, but it must not boil. Remove it from the fire, lay it aside, and use when needed for different fruits. The above quantity will produce five quarts at thirty degrees Fahrenheit.

1340. Preserved Peaches.—The best variety for preserving are either the "Crawford Late," or "Smoke." Select one hundred thoroughly ripe, sound, medium-sized peaches; peel them neatly, cut them in halves, and remove the stones with care. Have ready ten patent lightning-glass jars, each holding one quart, or twenty holding only a pint each; then divide the peaches equally into them, and pour into each one pint of syrup prepared as for No. 1339, or half a pint, if using the pint jars, taking care that the peaches floating on the top should be entirely covered, even if it be necessary to press them down lightly. Put on the cover very tight, then bring the larger wire up in the very centre between the two small knobs, and press the smaller one downwards. Place the jars in a large saucepan standing, seeing that they do not touch each other, otherwise they might break, and arrange a little hay or straw between every one. Fill the pan with cold water so as to cover them entirely, and placing it on the hot stove, let boil for ten minutes. Take from off the fire, stand the pan on a table, and with a towel lift up the jars one by one, laying them most carefully on a dry kitchen table, and avoid putting them in a cold place. When all are so arranged, taking the towel into the hand, lift up the smaller wire, so that the gas slightly escapes for one minute, then immediately pull it down again until hermetically sealed. Let them stand till thoroughly cold, then put them away for general use. The right temperature for keeping them is from 65 to 75 degrees. Should the saucepan not be sufficiently large to contain all the jars, boil five at a time.

The best time to select the peaches is from August 20 to September 20.

1341. Preserved Bartlett Pears.—Procure one hundred medium-sized, sound, and fully ripe pears, fit to eat in their natural state; peel them carefully keeping them in their original form, then split in halves, and cut out the cores and seeds. Fill ten lightning-glass jars with the pears, and pour over five quarts of syrup (No. 1339), covering them tightly the same as for the peaches (No. 1340), placing them likewise in the saucepan, but boiling for fifteen minutes instead of ten. When lifted from the pan, proceed precisely as for the peaches. The best time to purchase the fruit is from August 25 to September 20.

1342. Preserved Apples.—Select sixty medium-sized, fine, sound, ripe Newtown pippins, the best time for this being from October 1 to December 1. Peel and core them with a corer, then cut them into quarters, and divide them equally into ten glass jars as for peaches (No. 1340). Fill them up with the syrup at thirty degrees, then cover tightly, put them in the saucepan exactly the same as for the peaches, and boil for fifteen minutes instead of ten. Take from off the fire, and finish the same as for the peaches, putting them away in the same temperature.

1343. Preserved Egg-plums.—Have two hundred medium sized egg-plums, ripe enough to break easily from the stones; wash them carefully, drain, then divide them equally into the ten quart lightning-jars. Fill them up with the thirty-degree syrup (No. 1339), cover tightly, and arrange them in the pan precisely as for peaches (No. 1340). Boil them for eight minutes instead of ten, then take from the stove, and finish preparing them exactly as for the peaches. The best time to procure these is from August 5 to September 1.

1344. Preserved Green-gages.—Procure two hundred and fifty fine, ripe green-gages, selecting those which break easily from the stones;

wash them well in cold water, drain thoroughly, then divide them equally into the ten patent glass jars, exactly as described for peaches (No. 1340). Fill up with five quarts of thirty-degree syrup (No. 1339), and finish preparing them the same as for peaches, but boiling them only for eight minutes instead of ten ; put them away the same as the other fruits. The best time to procure green-gages is from August 1 to September 1.

1345. Preserved Strawberries.—Always purchase the berries from June 7 to July 20, when residing in New York. Have fully the equivalent of ten quarts of well-picked and thoroughly washed, ripe, sound, and perfect strawberries, drain them well. To have these well selected it will doubtless require twenty-two to twenty-five quart baskets of unpicked fruit. When well drained, fill the ten quart lightning-glass jars with the berries, and pour in the thirty-degree syrup (No. 1339), but using it hot instead of cold. Cover them tightly, and proceed precisely the same as for peaches (No. 1340), only boiling them five minutes instead of ten, and putting them away the same.

1346. Preserved Raspberries.—Have ready the equivalent of ten quarts of fine, ripe, solid, well-washed, and thoroughly drained raspberries ; sixteen quart baskets will be about the necessary quantity to purchase. When ready, fill up the ten lightning-glass jars, and proceed to prepare them as explained for peaches (No. 1340), the only exception being that they must be boiled five minutes instead of ten. The proper time to obtain the berries is from July 10 to July 20.

1347. Preserved Cherries.—Purchase twenty-five pounds of fine, sound, ripe, white wax cherries ; pick off the stems neatly, and should there be any unripe or spoilt ones among them, throw them away, as they would likely ruin the rest. When finished, there should be about twenty pounds of sound cherries suitable for preserving. Have ready ten quart lightning-glass jars, same as for the peaches (No. 1340); divide the picked cherries evenly into them, and fill up with the thirty-degree syrup (No. 1339). Cover them tightly and carefully, then arrange them in a large saucepan precisely the same as the peaches, and finish them exactly as described in that number, boiling them for the same length of time. June 15 to July 1 is the best time to obtain the fruit.

1348. How to Roast Coffee.—If practicable, procure a small family coffee-roaster. Have three quarters of a pound of Java, mixed with a quarter of a pound of Mocha, place it in the roaster, and taking one of the lids from off the stove, put the roaster on a moderate fire, and turn the small handle constantly and slowly until the coffee becomes a good brown color; for this it should take about twenty-five minutes; open the cover to see when it is done, then transfer it to an earthen jar, cover it tightly, and use when needed; or, a more simple way, and even more effectual, is to take a tin baking-dish, butter well the bottom, and placing the same quantity of coffee therein, put it in a moderate oven to let get a good golden color; twenty minutes will suffice for this, being careful to toss it frequently with a wooden spoon, then remove to an earthen jar, and cover it well.

Roasting one's own coffee is a sure way of having it always fresh; besides, it retains its full flavor; but care must also be taken to purchase coffee from a responsible, first-class dealer.

1349. How to Make Black Coffee.—Take six light tablespoonfuls of coffee-beans from the jar (No. 1348); grind them in a mill, neither too coarse nor too fine. Have a well-cleaned French coffee-pot, put the coffee on the filter, with the small strainer over, then pour on a pint and a half of boiling water, little by little, recollecting, at the same time, that too much care cannot be taken to impress on those making the coffee, the necessity of having the water boiling thoroughly, otherwise it were as useless to attempt the feat as to try and raise musk-melons at the North Pole, notwithstanding that the coffee be of the very first quality. When all the water is consumed put on the cover, and let infuse slightly, but on no account must it boil again; then serve in six after-dinner cups. Coffee should never be prepared more than five minutes before the time to serve.

1350. Café Noir à l'Alexander the Great.—Put in an earthen pot on the hot range three pints of cold water; when boiling, immediately add four and a half ounces of freshly ground coffee, and as soon as the coffee has been added, put the pot on the corner of the stove to rest for three minutes. Have a piece of hot, red (very red) charcoal the size of a small banana, plunge it into the coffee. (If no charcoal at hand, a piece of red stove-coal will answer). Let rest again for three minutes; then you will see a heavy foam appearing at the surface of the coffee, thoroughly skim it off with a skimmer. Then carefully and gently pour it into a hot coffee-pot, and send to the table with six small, hot demi-tasses; accompanied with six ponies of old Renauldt cognac.

I would recommend that, after the scum has been removed, the coffee should be handled as gently as possible, so that all undesirable elements will remain at the bottom.

1351. Café au Lait (Coffee with Milk).—Have a clean French coffee-filter ready on the hot range; place in it four and a half ounces of freshly ground coffee, as for No. 1349; then gradually pour over it, all around, half a pint of boiling water; let rest for three minutes, then gradually pour over two pints and a half more of boiling water (taking special care that, under no circumstances, should it be allowed to boil again after the water has been poured over). When all dripped down, pour it into a hot coffee-pot. Take three pints of good, freshly and thoroughly heated milk (but do not boil it), pour it into a hot pitcher, send to the table with six hot cups à café au lait, pouring into each cup half coffee and half milk.

1352. Café au Lait à la St. Gottardo.—Place in an earthen pot on the hot range two quarts of very fresh milk, and let it heat until near the boiling-point, then immediately add two and a half ounces of fresh, finely ground coffee (No. 1349). Shuffle the pot in contrary directions until it comes to a boil; then let it rest for three minutes.

Strain it through a clean napkin into a hot serving-pitcher, and serve with six café-au-lait cups.

1353. Café Glacé (Iced Coffee).—Prepare one quart of coffee as for

No. 1349, and also one quart of thoroughly heated milk (not boiled). Pour both coffee and milk into a small ice-cream freezer. Sweeten with three tablespoonfuls of powdered sugar; tightly cover the freezer, place it in a tub containing broken ice and rock-salt a little higher than the height of the coffee, then sharply turn it by the handle of the cover, in different directions, for five or six minutes; neatly wipe the cover of the freezer all around to avoid that any ice should fall in; and with the aid of a ladle pour it into a pitcher, and serve with six coffee-glasses, and powdered sugar separately.

1354. Thé (Tea).—Place in a tea-pot three heaped tablespoonfuls, or one and a half ounces, of the best English-breakfast tea, *purchased from a responsible dealer*. Pour over five pints of boiling water. See to it that the water is boiling, else, even with the best quality of tea, you will never succeed to have it made to perfection. Let infuse for five minutes (but do not boil again), then send to the table with a pint of cold milk, or a pint of sweet cream.

Thé Glacé (Iced Tea).—Prepare the same quantity of tea the same as above, pour into an ice-cream freezer, sweeten, and proceed the same as for iced coffee (No. 1353), (omitting the milk); pour it into a cold pitcher, and send to the table with six coffee-glasses, six slices of sound lemon, and powdered sugar separately.

1355. Thé à la Russe (Russian Tea).—Place in a tea-pot three heaped tablespoonfuls of English-breakfast tea; pour over a little boiling water, just sufficient to cover the tea, about two tablespoonfuls; let infuse for one minute, then draw the water out, but do not use it. Pour in half a pony of good old Jamaica rum and three pints of boiling water; let infuse for four minutes, and then serve in cup with a decanter of old Jamaica rum separately, thin slices of lemon, and powdered sugar.

This is the old Russian style. Later fashion is to flavor it with a little vanilla flavor and a few drops of lemon juice.

1356. How to Make Chocolate.—Select three quarters of a pound of good chocolate (Maillard's is preferable), break it into pieces, and put them in a saucepan on the stove with half a pint of boiling water ; stir well with a wooden spoon, and when the chocolate is thoroughly dissolved pour one quart of boiling water over, using a quart of milk instead of the water when chocolate and milk is desired. Let it cook well for ten minutes, then serve.

1357. Chocolat au Lait à la George Washington.—Have a stone pot on the hot range with half a pint of cold water. Break in six tablets of one ounce each of Maillard's chocolate, sharply mix with a very clean wooden spoon or spatula until it is thoroughly dissolved ; then add two quarts of good cold milk, thoroughly heat until it comes to a boil, mixing lightly with the wooden spoon meanwhile. Pour it into a hot pitcher, and send to the table with cups and powdered sugar separately.

A pinch of salt represents 205 grains, or a tablespoonful.

Half a pinch of pepper represents 38 grains, or a teaspoonful.

A third of a pinch of nutmeg represents 13 grains, or half a teaspoonful.

SUPPLEMENT.

1858. Lobster à la Rushmore.—Select three fine, fresh lobsters, each weighing two pounds; boil them in salted water for ten minutes, then take them out and put to cool for eighteen minutes. Pick out all the meat, leaving the main body-shells intact for further use. Mince up the tail-parts, coral, and claws into pieces a quarter of an inch thick by three quarters of an inch wide. Put a sautoire containing half an ounce of fresh butter on the hot stove; chop up very fine one good-sized, sound shallot, add it to the butter in the pan, also the minced lobster, and season with a light pinch of salt, a light saltspoonful of cayenne pepper, and half a glassful of good white wine; let the whole reduce for ten minutes, stirring it meanwhile with a wooden spoon. Add one tablespoonful of tomato sauce (No. 205), four tablespoonfuls of Espagnole sauce (No. 151), and six mushroom-stalks chopped up very fine. Let cook well for ten minutes longer, then set the sautoire on the corner of the stove to keep warm. Take the three main shells of the lobsters, split them evenly in two, lengthwise, pare the ends off neatly, wash them thoroughly, and wipe them dry. These shells should not be longer than four and a half inches. Fill the six shells with the prepared lobster, lay two mushroom heads on top of each, put them on a tin plate and pour over the remainder of the sauce in the sautoire. Set them in the hot oven to bake for five minutes, then remove and dress them on a hot dish with a folded napkin, and send to the table.

1859. Raw Hamburg Steak.—Chop up two pounds of beef the same as for cooked Hamburg steak (No. 526), only selecting more tender pieces, and return it to the machine two or three times so as to have it finer. Season with one large pinch of salt, half a pinch of pepper, and the third of a pinch of nutmeg. Place the meat on a dish, divide it into six small, flattened steaks, and throw a raw egg yolk over each one; garnish with two shallots, one tablespoonful of parsley, the same quantity of capers, and three anchovies, all finely minced, and arranged in clusters around the dish.

1860. Mignons of Lamb, Sauce Béarnaise.—Procure a fine, tender leg of lamb, bone it with a sharp knife so as to detach the meat from the knuckle, beginning from the hip-side downwards. Cut out from this six even pieces or steaks, one inch thick by two and a half in diameter, pare them nicely, and with a small, keen knife remove any sinews that are liable to adhere to the meat. Lay them on a cold dish, and season with a good pinch of salt and a light pinch of pepper, and roll them well, so that the seasoning be equally distributed. Put half an ounce of good butter in a frying-pan, set it on a brisk fire, and add the pieces, or mignons, immediately, being careful that they do not lay one on top of the other, and cook them very briskly for two and a half minutes on each side. Prepare half a pint of Béarnaise sauce (No. 166), pour it on a hot serving-dish, dress the six mignons nicely over, one overlapping the other, and send to the table immediately.

Any lamb that may be left over after cutting off the mignons can be utilized for minced lamb, soup, or any other purpose desired.

1361. Hind-quarter of Spring Lamb.—Procure a medium-sized, fine, white hind-quarter of lamb; pare it neatly, trim the small handle-bone, and fold the flank over the ribs, to prevent them being overdone; that means that the leg and ribs will be equally cooked the same length of time. Tie it well together, then season with one and a half pinches of salt divided evenly, and envelop it well in its caul or leaf-fat; lay it in a roasting-pan, pouring in one tablespoonful of broth or water, then place it in a moderate oven, and let roast for one hour, basting it occasionally with its own dripping. Take it from the oven, remove the caul, untie, and dress it on a hot dish, adjusting a neat paper ruffle to the handle-bone. Skim the fat from off the gravy, strain the latter over the lamb, and serve.

1362. Chicken, Sauté à la Ch. C. Delmonico.—Select from a good poultry-dealer two fine, tender Philadelphia spring-chickens weighing two pounds each. Singe them over a little alcohol poured onto a plate, draw the entrails, wash well the interiors, then wipe them dry with a clean cloth. Cut each chicken into six pieces, place them in a sautoire with two tablespoonfuls of sweet oil, season with a good pinch of salt and one pinch of pepper, then set the sautoire on a very brisk fire, and let cook until the pieces assume a good, light brown color (ten minutes will suffice), stirring them lightly in the meanwhile. Chop up very fine one sound shallot; cut one green pepper into small, dice-shaped pieces, also the end part only of a medium-sized, peeled carrot; place all these with the chickens, and let cook together for one minute and a half, then add one glassful of good white wine, and let the liquid reduce to one-half, which will take ten minutes on a brisk fire, stirring it occasionally. Now add one gill of Espagnole sauce (No. 151), a tablespoonful of tomato sauce (No. 205), the juice of a good-sized, very sound lemon, and a quarter of an ounce of fresh butter; let all cook for ten minutes longer, stirring it lightly with a spoon. Plunge three canned artichoke-bottoms into very hot water, lift them up immediately with a skimmer, wipe them thoroughly dry with a napkin, then cut each one into four quarters; slice three medium-sized truffles very fine, and add all these to the chickens two minutes before serving. Dress the chickens and sauce on a very hot serving-dish, adjust paper ruffles to the ends of the four legs; garnish the dish artistically with the artichokes star-shaped. Place a slice of truffle on the centre of each artichoke, and a very small, round slice of Spanish sweet pepper on top of each truffle, and send to the table very hot.

1363. Chicken, Sauté à la Ranhofer.—Select two fine, tender chickens weighing two pounds each; singe them well, draw the entrails, wash thoroughly, and wipe very dry; then cut each chicken into six pieces, and season them with a good pinch of salt and a light pinch of pepper. Place the pieces of chicken in a sautoire with three quarters of an ounce of good butter and half a tablespoonful of sweet oil, and set it on a very hot stove. Chop up one shallot very fine, and one sound, green pepper cut in small, dice-shaped pieces; when the chickens are of a light brown color, add the shallot and pepper, and stir well for one minute; then add a wine-glassful of good white wine, and let reduce to one quarter, which will take six minutes. Pour in one gill of tomato sauce (No. 205) and one and a half gills of Espagnole sauce (No. 151), and let cook rather slowly for ten minutes longer, stirring it occasionally. Dress the chickens and sauce on a very hot serving-dish, adjust paper ruffles on the ends of the four legs, and decorate the dish with the following garnishing: take six canned artichoke-bottoms, spread a tablespoonful of Duxelle (No. 215) in the centre of each one; empty the interiors of six fine, sound, medium-sized green peppers, cooked in the oven for five minutes, stuff them with Duxelle garnishing (No. 189), and arrange them on top of the artichokes, their thin part uppermost, so as to give them a pyramidal shape; then lay them on a buttered tin plate or dish, and set them in a slow oven to bake for five minutes; remove them, but while they are baking cut out six round pieces of fresh bread, half an inch thick by two and a half inches in diameter; place them on a hot stove in a frying-pan with half a tablespoonful of butter, and let get a light brown color for two minutes. Arrange the six artichokes and peppers on top of the pieces of bread, garnish the dish nicely, and send to the table at once.

1364. Filets Mignons à la Lorillard.—After preparing six timbales as described below, and when removed from the oven, have ready six fine filets mignons as for No. 509, and serve with the following garnishing and sauce: take six small timbale-molds, measuring one and three quarter inches in diameter and two inches deep; butter well the insides, and set them in the ice-box to get thoroughly cold. Have one medium-sized, cooked carrot, also one cooked turnip; cut them both with a tube a quarter of an inch in diameter by one inch long; have also half a medium-sized, fine, white cabbage, and trim the outer leaves neatly. Put into a stewpan one ounce of salt pork cut into small dice-shaped pieces; add the cabbage, and season with half a pinch of pepper; set the pan on a rather slow fire, cover it tightly, and let cook slowly for thirty minutes, without removing the lid; during this time decorate the six cold timbales by laying a slice of truffle, half an inch in diameter, at the bottom of each, and just in the centre, and with the aid of a larding-needle arrange a row of cooked green peas around this, then decorate half the interior of each timbale with half the prepared carrots and turnips, using the utmost care, and keeping them inclining slightly toward the right, and the other half inclining toward the left. Fill up the timbales with the cooked cabbage, using a spoon to press it in gently, so that they are filled entirely as far as the top. Put them on a roasting-pan, filling it with hot water to half the height of the timbales, then place them in a hot oven, and heat from three and a half to four minutes. Take them from the oven, and leave the pan on the corner of the stove to keep warm. Cut an oval-shaped slice from an American loaf of bread, one inch in thickness, pare the edges neatly, then butter it lightly, and place it in the oven on a tin plate to get a light brown color; two minutes will be sufficient for this; lay it on a very hot dish, and dress the six filets mignons on top of the bread croustade, each one lengthwise and slightly overlapping one another, and so on until all are used. Pour over the mignons half a pint of hot Colbert sauce (No. 190), to which add whatever parings or pieces of truffle remain, one minute before using; then with a towel remove the timbales from the pan, one after the other, turn them upside down, unmold, and with these decorate the dish, placing one at each end and two on each side, then send to the table immediately.

It would be advisable to prepare and cook the fillets after the timbales are removed from the oven.

1365. Flageolets Sautés au Beurre.—Take three quarters of a quart can of fine, French flageolet beans, parboil them in boiling and lightly salted water for one and a half minutes, then drain them on a colander, and place them immediately in a saucepan on the hot stove with an ounce of good butter; season with a teaspoonful of salt, and shuffle lightly with a wooden spoon while cooking for three minutes, and when serving, add half a teaspoonful of finely chopped parsley. Dress them on a hot dish, and serve.

1366. Eggs à la Post.—Wash and scrape neatly one good-sized, sound carrot, then, with a vegetable-scoop, scoop out twelve round pieces; place them in a sautoire with one gill of white broth (No. 99), and a teaspoonful of good butter. Cook them on the hot range for twenty minutes.

Place twelve fine, sound, roasted, and shelled Italian chestnuts into the sautoire with the carrots, let come to a boil. Remove all the skin from two uncooked sausages. Make twelve equal balls out of it, place on a tin plate, and bake in the hot oven four minutes. Remove, and add them to the carrots and chestnuts. Season with a light pinch of salt and the third of a saltspoonful of red pepper; add one gill of Madeira sauce (No. 185). Cook for two minutes longer. Have a silver dish sufficiently large to contain twelve eggs so that they do not touch one another. Place in the centre of the dish half a pint of hot purée of chestnuts (No. 131), then arrange twelve fried eggs over the purée prepared the same as in No. 412. Carefully and equally divide in clusters around the dish, the carrots, chestnuts, and sausage balls, then pour the sauce around the eggs with a spoon, but none over the eggs. Place on top of each egg one thin slice of truffle cut with a tube. Place in the hot oven to heat for one minute. Take from out the oven, and serve.

1367. Oysters Fried à la Arthur Sullivan.—Carefully open thirty large, fine, fresh box-oysters; place them in a saucepan with their own juice, season with the third of a saltspoonful of red pepper, adding half a medium-sized fine, sound lemon, cut into thin slices, one sprig of thyme, a small bay-leaf, and a branch of well-washed parsley. Place on the hot range, and heat up very fast without boiling, for which, on a very brisk fire, it should be done in one minute and a quarter; then place the whole in an earthen bowl to cool.

Beat up one raw egg in a bowl with one gill of cold milk, seasoned with a light pinch of pepper and a light pinch of salt; steep the oysters in this, one by one, then lightly roll them in cracker-dust; give them a nice even shape in the palm of the hand, and lay them on a dish. Heat up thoroughly in a frying-pan on the hot range one gill of clarified butter and half a gill of olive oil (it must be very hot before placing in the oysters), and fry them for one minute on each side. Remove them with a skimmer, dress on a hot dish with a folded napkin, and serve with the following sauce separately:

Strain the juice of the oysters into a saucepan, and reduce it to one half on the hot range, with half a saltspoonful of red pepper, adding also the juice of half a sound lemon and a gill of sauce Espagnole (No. 151). Cook for three minutes, add a teaspoonful of chopped chives, pour it into a sauce-bowl, and send to the table.

1368. Lobster Salad à la Boardman.—Split lengthwise two very fine medium-sized, freshly boiled, and cooled lobsters; pick all the meat out from the shells, as well as from the cracked claws, suppress both intestines and pouch. Cut the meat into very small, equal, square pieces, and place them in a salad-bowl. Finely chop up, as fine as hashed potatoes, three hard-boiled eggs; add them to the lobster. Peel and chop, also very fine, two small, sound shallots, and add to the lobster, with one and a half teaspoonfuls of very fine freshly chopped chives and one and a half teaspoonfuls of finely chopped parsley. Chop also, very fine, one root of thoroughly pared and well-cleaned sound celery (using nothing but the perfect white), add it to the lobster. Season with a light tablespoonful and a half of salt, a teaspoonful and a half of fresh, finely crushed white pepper, half a teaspoonful of Worcestershire sauce, a tablespoonful and a half of olive oil, two tablespoonfuls of very good white vinegar. Mix well, then add three tablespoonfuls of freshly made mayonnaise sauce (No. 206). Gently but thoroughly mix the whole well together; wipe neatly the edges of the salad-bowl with a napkin. Plant right in the centre a branch of parsley-greens, and send to the table.

1369. Game Pie à la Levi P. Morton.—Take one fine partridge, one grouse, and one medium-sized rabbit; pick, draw, and singe well. Thoroughly bone them. Place the fillets in a saucepan with one tablespoonful of clarified butter. Season with one pinch of salt, half a pinch of pepper, and a quarter of a pinch of thyme. Cook on a brisk fire for one minute on each side; then add half a glassful of good Madeira wine, and reduce to one half, which will take five minutes. Place in a bowl and let thoroughly cool. Chop up the bones into fine pieces; place them in a saucepan with one medium-sized, sound onion cut into slices, a small carrot cut the same, one bay-leaf, three cloves, twelve whole peppers, and a blade of thyme. Cook all together with one ounce of butter until it has obtained a light brown color; then add one glassful of Madeira wine, half a medium-sized, sound lemon cut in slices, one quart of white broth (No. 99), and two ounces of gelatine. Let cook one hour. Then strain through a napkin or a fine sieve into a china bowl, and lay aside to thoroughly cool. Chop up very fine a quarter of a pound of lean, raw veal, a quarter of a pound of fresh pork, and six ounces of larding-pork. Season with one good pinch of salt and half a pinch of pepper. Cut into dice-shaped pieces eight truffles, three ounces of cooked smoked beef-tongue; mix well together, and it will be ready for use. Knead well together, on a marble table, wooden board, or in a vessel, half a pound of flour with four ounces of butter, then gradually add a gill of cold water, mixing well until it is a perfect dough, for five minutes at least without ceasing. Then place it in a cool place, and let rest ten minutes before using. Lightly butter the interior of an oval-shaped mold ten inches in length, six inches wide, and four and a half high. Place the mold in an iron roasting-pan. Roll out three quarters of the dough to one quarter of an inch thick, and with it evenly line the inside of the mold, taking special care not to make any holes in the dough. Cut some very thin slices of larding-pork, and line the dough all around with it. Then place one layer of the forcemeat and one layer of the game, and so on, until all is used. Make a hole with a teaspoon right in the centre down to half the depth of the patty (pâté). Roll out the other quarter of dough to the same thickness, quarter of an inch; cut a cover out oval-shaped, and with it cover the pâté, making a small hole in the centre to connect with the other. Decorate the surface with leaves made out of the dough, glaze it with the yolk of one fresh egg and half a gill of cold water. Place in a moderate oven to cook for two hours. Remove from the oven. Put away in the ice-box for six hours.

1370. Plombière à la Hamilton.—Beat up one and a half pints of sweet cream as in No. 1254. Let it rest for half an hour. Neatly pick one and a half pints of sound, ripe strawberries; carefully wash them in cold water, then drain them on a colander. Transfer the whipped cream into another vessel with a skimmer. Briskly beat the cream again for two minutes. Mix in three ounces of powdered sugar, one teaspoonful of vanilla flavor, and half a gill of cognac. Mix the whole well together for one minute longer. Remove the wire whip, add the prepared strawberries, and with the aid of a wooden spoon gently mix for one minute. Pour the preparation into a well-cleaned, two-quart freezer, cover, and lay it into a pail; fill the pail all around with broken ice (but no rock-salt), ánd let freeze for one hour. Have a fruit-stand ready, then with an ice-cream spoon dress the plombière on the stand, giving a dome shape, and immediately send to the table.

The above makes a delicious dessert, also, when served without being frozen.

1371. Tutti-frutti à la Gen. Harrison.—Line the interior of a three-pint melon-form with a pint of vanilla ice-cream (No. 1271). Cut four ounces of candied apricots into small pieces, also four ounces of candied cherries into halves. Mix these together. Evenly spread half the quantity of the fruits all around the ice-cream in the form. Carefully arrange a pint of raspberry water-ice (No. 1281) evenly around the fruits. Spread the balance of the fruits all around the water-ice; then fill the form with a pint of pistache ice-cream (No. 1275). Tightly cover the form. Lay it in a pail with a layer of broken ice and rock-salt at the bottom, and then fill up to the surface with the same. Let freeze for one and a half hours. Unmold the tutti-frutti; dress on a glass stand, and serve with the following sauce: put in a vessel a pint of whipped cream (No. 1254) with two ounces of powdered sugar and a gill of maraschino. Beat the whole well together for two minutes. Pour it over the tutti-frutti, and immediately send to the table.

1372. Frogs' Legs à la Merrill.—Neatly pare off the claws of half a pound of very fine, fat, fresh frogs' legs. Cut them into pieces at each joint. Place them in a saucepan on the hot range, with half an ounce of very good butter. Season with one pinch of salt and half a saltspoonful of red pepper. Cook on a brisk fire for five minutes, then add a wineglassful of Madeira wine, with two finely minced truffles; reduce for three minutes. Crack into a bowl three egg yolks, add 'to it half a pint of sweet cream, beat well together one minute, pour it into the pan with the frogs, then gently shuffle the pan in opposite directions until the sauce thickens, which will take two minutes and a half. Pour into a hot souptureen, and serve.

1373. Strawberries.—After selecting and thoroughly washing the berries, fill the cans and cover with a twenty-five-degree syrup, seal up, and cook five minutes. Open the vent, to let hot air out, about one minute, then close the vent and put away. The best berries are in market between June 7 and 14.

1374. Pineapple.—The best pineapples (the sugar-loaf) come to market between June 15 and July 15. After selecting the ripest fruit, pare and cut all the eyes out, take the core out, cut in slices, and fill cans; cover with a twenty-five-degree syrup; seal up and cook twenty minutes. Open vent to let hot air out, close, and put away.

1375. Asparagus.—The best asparagus for canning is the Colossal, from Monmouth County, New Jersey, and the best time from May 12 to June 12. After selecting the large, perfect spears, wash thoroughly, then scald about ten minutes, and after filling the cans full, cover with a light salt water, and seal the cans up, leaving the vent open; then cook ten minutes; then close the vent and cook two and one half hours. Open vent to let the gas out, and close it again.

1376. Rhubarb, or Pie-plant.—After peeling and cutting the rhubarb in pieces about one inch long, fill cans and cover with a light syrup, seal up, and boil five minutes; open vent to let the air out, close, and put away. The best time is from May 20 to June 1.

1377. Cherries.—The best cherry, the white Ox-heart, ripens between June 20 and July 1. Select the fruit, fill cans, and cover with a twenty-five-degree syrup, seal up, cook fifteen minutes, open vent, close, and put away.

1378. Gooseberries.—Select the berries when green, between June 17 and July 1. After filling the cans, cover with a light syrup, seal up, and bathe five minutes, open vent, close, and put away.

1379. Currant Jelly.—The best jelly can only be made before the currants are fully ripe—between June 25 and July 3. After scalding the currants well, press them through a flannel bag, and while the juice is hot, boil six or seven pounds of the best crushed sugar with one gallon of juice, watching closely until it attains the proper consistency; then pour in molds to cool.

Another way to make a very delicate jelly is to boil one gallon of juice about ten minutes, and while boiling hot stir in eight pounds of granulated sugar, and keep stirring until all dissolved, then pour into molds.

1380. Raspberries.—The best time is between July 5 and 15, and proceed same as strawberries.

1381. Blackberries and Whortleberries between July 15 and August 15. After carefully washing the berries, put on any degree of syrup you wish, as this fruit will make pies or do for the table. Seal up, and cook eight minutes; open vent, close, and put away.

1382. Peas, Corn, and Lima Beans are so hard to keep that it is impossible for a family to put them up. They require a greater heat than boiling water, and have to be cooked in a super-heated steam chest.

1383. Egg-plums and Green-gages are best when nearly ripe—between August 15 and September 1. After filling cans cover with a twenty-five-degree syrup and cook ten minutes, then open the vents, close and put away.

1384. Tomatoes.—Between August 15 and September 15, select thoroughly ripe tomatoes, scald them about two minutes in hot water, so that the skin will peel off very thin to leave the perfect shape of the fruit; then fill the cans as full as you can press them in; seal them and cook twenty minutes, then put away.

1385. Peaches and Bartlett Pears.—Last of August to last of September, select ripe fruit; pare carefully; fill cans and cover with a twenty-five-degree syrup; seal up, cook twenty minutes, then open vent, close and put away.

1386. String Beans are best in October. Select the small refugee beans; after taking strings off, wash and scald well; then fill cans with whole beans, and cover with a light brine. Seal up; cook one half hour, then open vent, close again, and cook three fourths of an hour more, then put away.

1387. Apples.—Newtown pippins are the best about November 15. Pare and quarter; take cores out; then fill cans and cover with any strength syrup required. Seal up, and cook five minutes, open vent, close and put away.

Six pounds of the best crushed sugar to a gallon of water will make a syrup of twenty to twenty-five degrees.

1388. Tenderloin Broil à la Stanton.—Prepare three fillets exactly as in No. 503, and one minute before they are cooked, lightly devil them on both sides ; then broil half a minute on each side.

Chop very fine one small, well-peeled, sound shallot, place it in a small saucepan on the hot range with a teaspoonful of butter, fry for one minute; then add half a glassful of good white wine, and reduce to one half. Add one medium-sized, sound pickle, and one sweet pepper cut into small dice-shaped pieces. Season with half a pinch of salt and half a saltspoonful of red pepper; add half a gill of Spanish sauce (No. 151). Cook for one minute rather briskly, then pour the sauce on a hot serving-dish, dress the fillets over it; arrange six heart-shaped croûtons (No. 133) around the dish, place a slice of truffle on top of each croûton, then a round slice of Spanish sweet pepper, cut with a tube, over each slice of truffle, and send to the table.

1389. Filets Mignons à la Brown.—Chop very fine one medium-sized, sound, peeled shallot, place it in a small saucepan on the hot range, with a teaspoonful of very good butter; heat well for one minute without browning; add half a wine-glassful of good Madeira wine, boil for two minutes, then add half a teaspoonful of freshly chopped tarragon, one good-sized sweet pepper cut in small dice-shaped pieces, twelve stoned and stuffed olives, six whole mushrooms, and one artichoke-bottom, cut in dice-shape, also a gill of sauce Espagnole (No. 151). Season with half a pinch of salt and half a saltspoonful of red pepper. Cook for three minutes and a half, then pour this garnishing on a hot serving-dish. Nicely dress over it six freshly cooked mignons filets as in No. 509, one overlapping another; decorate the dish with six heart-shaped croûtons (No. 133), and serve.

1390. Broiled Grouse à la Pomeroy.—Prepare and broil three fine, tender grouse, precisely the same as for No. 854, but one minute before they are cooked, lightly devil them, and then gently broil again for half a minute on each side.

Place in a small saucepan on the hot range one medium-sized, sound, peeled, and finely chopped shallot, with a tablespoonful of good butter; cook for one minute, then add two chopped mushrooms, one chopped pickle; moisten with a tablespoonful of English sauce; add a light teaspoonful of English mustard; mix all well together. Season with half a pinch of salt and half a saltspoonful of red pepper. Cook for one minute and a quarter. Pour the sauce on a hot serving-dish, place the grouse over it, decorate the dish with six slices of broiled bacon (No. 754), six thin half slices of lemon; arrange six slices of truffles in the centre of the slices of lemon, and serve very hot.

1391. Mazagran à la General Bugeau.—This will be found a superior and pleasantly stimulating summer beverage for ladies, as well as for the sterner sex.

Prepare the same quantity of coffee as in No. 1349. Have six goblets half filled with clean ice, pour in the coffee, evenly divided; add a pony of good cognac to each glass, mix thoroughly with a teaspoon, and serve.

The above is a delicious and healthful after-dinner summer drink, and is enjoyed in nearly all the large cities of Europe, especially by military men, who prefer it to the usual after-dinner demi-tasse, or "gloria," as they call it in Paris.

The name is derived from the village of Mazagran, Province d'Oran, Algeria, famous for a long and heroic siege in 1840, wherein one hundred and twenty-three French soldiers were victorious against twelve thousand Arabs.

1392. Mazagran à la Général Dufour.—The same as above, only substituting a pony of Swiss kirsch instead of cognac.

1393. Smelts à la Van Volkenburgh.—Wash well, and thoroughly dry, eighteen fine, fresh Long Island smelts. Split them right along the backbone in the centre; remove the backbone of each. Season with a pinch of salt and half a pinch of pepper; sprinkle them with half an ounce of flour, then place them in a pan with one ounce of good butter on the hot range, and fry for two minutes on each side, or until they obtain a good light brown color. Dress them on a hot dish; place in a pan one ounce of good butter, fry it until it becomes of a good nut-brown color; add to it a tablespoonful of vinegar, then pour over the smelts; decorate the dish all around with parsley-greens, and serve.

1394. Tomatoes with Rice à la Watson.—Wash in cold water six fine, red, sound, equal-sized tomatoes, wipe them dry, then cut off the top of each tomato (keeping them on a plate until needed); remove the seeds of the tomatoes with a vegetable-scoop. Season the inside of each with half a pinch of pepper and half a pinch of salt.

Place them in a well-buttered pan. Place two ounces of well-picked rice in a cup or in a dish, add to it one teaspoonful of melted butter, half a medium-sized, sound, peeled, and finely chopped shallot; season with half a pinch of salt only, mix all well together, then put into each tomato one teaspoonful of rice; place the tops on as a cover, sprinkle a little clarified butter over, and then cover them with a well-buttered paper. Bake them in a moderate oven for thirty minutes.

Thoroughly wash six large, fresh mushrooms. Cut off the stalks, chop up very fine half a sound, peeled shallot, as well as the mushroom stalks, place in a pan with a tablespoonful of good butter and two drops of lemon juice. Season with half a pinch of salt and half a saltspoonful of pepper. Cook five minutes, without browning, then add the mushroom-tops, with half a glassful of Madeira wine; reduce for two minutes; add now half a gill of demi-glace (No. 185); let cook for five minutes longer.

Dress the tomatoes on a hot serving-dish, place one head of mushroom on top of each tomato, upside down, pour a little of the sauce over the six mushrooms, and the rest on the dish around the tomatoes; arrange a thin slice of truffle on top of each head of mushroom, and send to the table.

HOW TO CARVE.

The art of cookery and carving is an old one. During the Roman Empire it was taught by professors in the schools, and had at that time attained a high standard. France leads all nations in the art of cooking and carving, although the United States is not far behind in this respect.

Good cooking and carving go hand in hand. It is no trifle to prepare and cook a good dinner; but it is an easy matter to spoil the effect, if not the entire dinner, by negligent carving.

The first and most important factor is a strong and very sharp knife.

Chickens.—Lay the roasted chicken (of three to four pounds) on its side. Stick your fork into the leg and lift it up, meanwhile holding down firmly the rest of the chicken. Then cut through the joint on the back; pressing the joint between the leg and second joint, cut through. Stick your fork into the wing so as not to interfere with the knife; cut through the joint and loosen the meat surrounding it; pull down with the fork and press firmly on the carcass with the knife. If done carefully, you can pull all the meat from the breast with the wing. Then cut each breast, crosswise, in half. Turn around, and proceed as in the first operation.

Turkey.—Cut away the leg the same as with a chicken. The leg of a turkey being larger than that of a chicken, it would be advisable to cut into slices the leg and second joint. After the leg is cut off, stick your fork into the breast-bone; hold the fork firmly with the left hand; then, with the sharp knife in your right hand, starting from the outside of the breast, proceed to cut, carefully, thin slices, until you reach the bone. Then turn, and proceed the same as before.

Serve each person with a piece of the dark and a slice of the white meat.

Should the turkey be stuffed, place a little of the stuffing on each plate. A capon, large chicken, or English pheasant should be carved the same way.

Partridges.—In America only the breasts of the birds are generally eaten, the legs being strong and bitter. Stick your fork straight into the breast-bone; cut one slice from the outside breast; then cut close alongside of the breast-bone and around the wing, carefully pushing all the meat from off both breasts, one after the other.

Grouse.—The grouse is generally carved the same way as the partridge.

Canvas-back Duck.—The "King of Birds."—The breast only is carved, served, and eaten. Stick the fork straight and firmly into the middle of the breast-bone. Commence from the neck down to the back, straight to the back-bone, and around the back; then from the point of starting, around the collar-bone. Cut the joint from off the wing. Commence cutting again from the point of starting; carefully and gently carving off the whole breast, so that no meat remains. Proceed precisely the same with the other side. When finished, there will remain only the carcass.

Red-head, black-head, mallard, teal, &c., are carved the same as the canvas-back.

Tame duck, duckling, goose, &c., are carved as a chicken, unless they are over four or five pounds, then they should be carved the same as a turkey or a capon.

For small birds, such as squab, snipe, plover, woodcock, &c., no carving is necessary, as they are generally served whole.

Saddle of Mutton, Lamb, or Venison should always be carved—especially for private families—lengthwise first, on both sides of the spinal bone, then crosswise downward. Special care should be taken to stick the fork right in the centre of the saddle, and holding it firmly while carving with a very sharp knife, and keeping as near the bone as possible, till down to the end on both sides. When all detached, cut it crosswise into small pieces of about half or three-quarters of an inch thick, and serve.

Steak.—Sirloin steak can be carved in various ways—crosswise, lengthwise, in small or large pieces, as desired.

When serving, the cut part should always be laid uppermost. I would suggest, though, carving it diagonally into six fine, even slices, till you reach the fat part. When carved this way it makes it look inviting, and has a beautiful effect. Always place a small piece of the fat on each plate when serving.

Tenderloin, or Fillet.—Fillet is carved straight, in as many pieces as desired, but when serving, the cut part should always be served the same as the sirloin, uppermost.

Roast Beef.—As soon as the rib-beef is roasted to perfection, as mentioned in No. 527, remove it from the hot oven, place it always on a hot dish, with the rib-bones downward; should it be crusty on top, cut off just a little from the surface, which is generally so hard that often it is an impediment in cutting the slices to the desired perfection. Stick in the fork-tines lengthwise, on top of the roast, near the edge, in a slanting manner, so as to avoid pricking the lean part of the roast and the resulting loss of juice or blood; hold firmly the fork with the left hand, and with a large, sharp knife in the right hand, carefully cut, in even, small slices a quarter of an inch thick, right down to the rib-bones; gently make a cut underneath, so as to have each slice separate from one another; then serve.

Roasted Leg of Mutton.—If practicable, when carving a leg of mutton a patent handle should be adjusted to the end bone, which would be a substitute for the fork, and an avoidance of soiling the hands at the same time. Begin carving small, thin, even slices, about quarter of an inch in thickness, straight or diagonally down to the bone, till you come to the end bone, then lengthwise underneath to the end. On account of the much thinner meat on the other side of the leg, carve it diagonally, and serve one piece from each side.

Roasted Leg of Lamb.—Is to be carved exactly the same as the leg of mutton.

CELEBRATED MENUS,

MANY OF WHICH WERE PREPARED

BY

MR. ALESSANDRO FILIPPINI.

SERVICE A LA FRANÇAISE.

IER SERVICE.

Consommé à la Colbert.
Potage à la purée d'asperges vertes.

Saumon à la Chambord.
Longe de veau à la Régence.

Côtelettes de présolé à la chicorée.
Pâte chaud à la Toulouse.
Filets de lièvre à la Romaine.
Cailles à la Dumanoir.

2ME SERVICE.

Galantines de dindes aux truffes.
Faisans piqués, rotis, bread sauce.

Punch à la Romaine.
Artichauts à l'Hollandaise.
Champignons à la Bordelaise.
Timbale de poires à la Duchesse.
Bavarois d'abricots.
Glaces et Dessert.

SERVICE A L'ANGLAISE.

POTAGES.

Potage d'orge à la Princesse.
Potage chasseur aux Grives.

RELEVÉS.

Soles bouillies, sauce persil.
Longe de veau aux légumes.

ENTRÉES.

Faisans à la Périgueux.
Pieds d'agneau, sauce tartare.
Poulets aux Nouilles.
Petites chartreuses à la Royale.

DEUXIEME SERVICE.

ROTIS.

Pintades rôties, cresson.
Selle de chevreuil piquée.

BOUTS.

Tartes aux framboises.
Pommes méringuées.

ENTREMETS.

Artichauts, sauce Hollandaise.
Cailles en chaudfroid à la Gelée.
Bavarois au Café.
Eclairs aux fraises.

SIDE TABLE.

Langue Salée—Bœuf rôti.

SERVICE A LA FRANÇAISE.

IER SERVICE.

Potage à la Palestine.
Consommé aux quenelles de volaille.

Barbue, sauce Hollandaise.
Punch Impérial.
Gigot de mouton, braisé.
Côtelettes d'agneau à la purée de céleri.
Ris de veau à la Toulouse, en croustade.
Bécassines à la maréchale.
Timbale d'homards à la Béchamel.

2ME SERVICE.

Quartier de chevreuil, sauce poivrade.
Dindonneaux rotis.

Soufflé aux pommes.
Cardons à l'Espagnole.
Fonds d'artichauts à la Barigoule.
Gelée d'oranges à la mandarine.
Croquante de Génoise à la crème framboisée.
Glaces et Dessert.

SERVICE A L'ANGLAISE.

POTAGES.

Potage aux moules.
Consommé à la Royale.

RELEVÉS.

Truites grillées, maître d'hôtel.
Bœuf salé aux légumes.

ENTRÉES.

Pâté de poulets à l'Anglaise.
Côtelettes d'agneau à la Villeroi.
Filets de chevreuil au macaroni.
Panpiettes de soles à l'Italienne.

DEUXIEME SERVICE.

ROTIS.

Grouses bardées.
Chapon au cresson.

BOUTS.

Dampfrouilles à la Vanille.
Pommes à la Richelieu.

ENTREMETS.

Chicorée aux œufs pochés.
Salade de queues d'Ecrevisses.
Bavarois aux noix fraiches.
Jambonneaux en biscuit.

SIDE TABLE.

Noix de veau—Langue—Pâté de Gibier.

SERVICE A LA RUSSE.

POTAGES.
Crème d'orge aux ailerons.
Consommé à la Dubarry.

HORS D'ŒUVRES.
Croustades de riz au Salpicon.
Bouchées à la purée de Gibier.

POISSONS.
Turbot, sauce Diplomate.
Pièce de Sandres frits.

RELEVÉS.
Filets de bœuf à la Flamande.
Noix de veau à la Godard.

ENTRÉES.
Escalopes de chevreuil, olives.
Poulardes à la Périgueux.
Galantines de mauviettes.
Buisson de petits homards.
Punch glacé.

ROTIS.
Perdreaux rôtis, sauce pain.
Dindonneaux piqués.

LÉGUMES.
Truffes au champagne.
Fonds d'artichauts, Italienne.

ENTREMETS.
Pouding de cabinet, marasquin.
Charlotte de pommes, vanille.
Gâteau d'amandes à la chantilly.
Gelée moscovite, garni.
Dessert.

SERVICE A LA RUSSE.

POTAGES.
Consommé printanier Royale.
Potage, fausse tortue.

HORS D'ŒUVRES.
Croquettes à la Parisienne.
Bouchées à la Reine.

POISSONS.
Turbot à l'Hollandaise.
Truites, sauce Génevoise.

RELEVÉS.
Longe de veau aux Légumes.
Filet de bœuf au macaroni.

ENTRÉES.
Pâté-chaud de levraut, truffes.
Canetons aux olives.
Mayonnaises des homards.
Timbale de faisans, à la gelée.
Punch à la Romaine.

ROTIS.
Poulardes du Mans au cresson.
Selle de chevreuil, rôtie.

LÉGUMES.
Petits pois garnis de fleurons.
Artichauts à la Barigoul.

ENTREMETS.
Pouding Saxon à la Vanille.
Baba chaud à l'ananas.
Riz à l'Impératrice.
Macédoine de fruits, marasquin.
Dessert.

FAMILLE IMPÉRIALE DE FRANCE.

POTAGES.
Pot-au-feu. Pâtes d'Italie.

HORS D'ŒUVRE.
Petits pâtés au naturel.

GROSSES PIECES.
Saumon à la sauce Génevoise.
Pièce de bœuf à la Jardinière.
Rosbif garni de croquettes.

ENTRÉES.
Tête de veau en tortue.
Petites timbales à la Vallière.
Grenadins à la chicorée.
Suprême de volaille aux pointes d'asperges.
Chaudfroid de foie-gras.
Salade de filets de soles à la ravigote.

ROTIS.
Faisans et chapons au cresson.

ENTREMETS.
Artichauts frits.
Choux-fleurs, sauce au beurre.
Haricots verts sautés.
Epinards, au velouté.
Charlotte Russe au chocolat.
Timbale de poires à l'Italienne.
Gelée macédoine de fruits.
Pains à la Mecque.
Dessert.

FAMILLE ROYALE D'ANGLETERRE.

POTAGES.
A la tortue. Consommé aux quenelles.

POISSONS.
Turbot bouilli, éperlans frits.
Soles à la matelote Normande.

RELEVÉS.
Filets de bœuf aux nouilles.
Poulardes à la Royale.

ENTRÉES.
Rissoles de volailles à la D'Artois.
Mauviettes farcies au gratin.
Côtelettes de mouton à la Soubise.
Epigrammes de volaille aux haricots verts.
Fricandeau à la chicorée.
Boudins de brochet, sauce homard.

ROTIS.
Faisans, ptarmigans, ortolans.

RELEVÉS.
Beignets de griesz, pouding Nesselrode.

ENTREMETS.
Salsifis frits. Croque-en-bouche.
Crème de riz au jus.
Galantine de poulets.
Petits babas chauds.
Bavarois au chocolat.

FAMILLE ROYALE DE PRUSSE.

POTAGES.
Consommé de volaille à la Royale.
Potage tortue à la Française.

HORS D'ŒUVRES.
Tartelettes de nouilles au foie-gras.
Cannelons à la purée de Gibier.

POISSONS.
Turbot garni, sauce aux huîtres.
Dame de saumon, sauce crevettes.

RELEVÉS.
Bœuf fumé de Hambourg, légumes variés.
Longe de veau de Pontoise.
Tomates et cèpes Provençale.

ENTRÉES.
Côtes de daim aux champignons, sauce Venaison.
Filets de poulets aux pointes d'asperges.
Homards à la gelée, sauce Mayonnaise.
Galantines de cailles aux truffes, sauce Cumberland.

ROTIS.
Dindonneaux piqués. Faisans Bohème.

LÉGUMES.
Fonds d'artichauts à la Moëlle.
Petits pois à la Française.

ENTREMETS.
Pouding soufflé à la Vanille.
Croûtes aux cerises à la Montmorency.
Charlotte printanière aux fraises.
Gelée moscovite, garnie d'ananas.
Glaces. Compotes. Dessert.

FAMILLE ROYALE D'ITALIE.

POTAGES.
Potage d'orge à l'Ecossaise.

RELEVÉS.
Turbot à la Bordelaise.
Noix de veau à la Gastronome.

ENTRÉES.
Poulardes aux pointes d'asperges.
Cailles à la Richelieu.
Aspic à la Dominicaine.

LÉGUMES.
Artichauts à la Barigoul

HORS D'ŒUVRE.
Jambon d'York à la gelée.
Punch au Kirsch.

ROTIS.
Faisans piqués.
Venaison à l'Anglaise.
Salades.

ENTREMETS.
Bavarois à la Florentine.
Suédoise d'abricots à l'orientale.
Cussy à la Portugaise.
Glaces aux Fruits.

MAISON IMPÉRIALE D'AUTRICHE.

MAIGRE.
Potage de bisque à la Cardinale.
Sardines à l'huile.
Aprische au Parmesan.
Saumon du Rhin, Génoise.
Omelette aux truffes.
Chicorée garnie de filets de schill.
Sarcelles rôties, au jus d'orange.
Salade mêlée.
Pouding à l'Anglaise.
Crême au marasquin.
Compote mêlée.

GRAS.
Potage Duchesse, quenelles.
Chaudfroid de perdreaux.
Côtelettes d'agneau, papillotes.
Pièce de bœuf à la Napolitaine.
Polpetti et foie-gras, champignons.
Emincée de chevreuil à la Russe.
Chicorée au jus.
Poulets grillés.
Oisons rôtis au cresson.
Salade mêlée.
Gelée au champagne.

FAMILLE ROYALE D'ESPAGNE.

POTAGES.
Crême de perdreaux à la Princesse.
Consommé à l'Impératrice.
Nouilles à la Napolitaine.
Xerès Sec.

HORS D'ŒUVRE.
Petits pâtés à la Béchamel.
Châteaubriand.

RELEVÉS.
Saumon garni, à la Royale.
Jambon, sauce en Malaga.
Madère de Carpenter.

ENTRÉES.
Timbale de foie-gras à la Montesquieu.
Marsala de Sicile.
Suprême de poulets aux truffes.
Triorata.
Salade d'homards en Bellevue.
Vin du Rhin.

LÉGUMES.
Petits pois à la Française.
Côte-Rôtie.

ROTIS.
Chapons garnis de cailles.
Dinde en galantine.
Champagne.

FAMILLE ROYALE DE BELGIQUE.

POTAGES.

Bisque aux écrevisses.
Consommé Printanier.

HORS D'ŒUVRES.

Petites bouchées aux crevettes.
Croquettes de volaille.

RELEVÉS.

Turbot à l'Hollandaise.
Filet de bœuf à la Financière.

ENTRÉES.

Ris de veau aux petits pois.
Cailles à la Bohémienne.
Filets de soles à la Vénitienne.
Mayonnaise d'homards.

Punch au Kirsch.

LÉGUMES.

Asperges, sauce au beurre.
Haricots verts à la maître d'hôtel.

ROTIS.

Selle de sanglier, sauce venaison.
Éperlans frits.

PATISSERIE.

Timbale de fruits.
Pain d'ananas.

FAMILLE ROYALE DE SUEDE.

Potage à l'Impériale.
Madère.
Crème d'asperges.
Xérès.
Corbeilles de truffes à la Lucullus.
Allouettes en caisses.
Turbot à la marinière.
Château d' Yquin.
Saumon à la Régence.
Train de chevreuil, sauce Venaison.
Chapons, truffes.
Château-Margot.
Epigrammes d'agneau, purée d'artichauts.
Château-Rouzan.
Croustades de cailles, à la Talleyrand.
Poulets nouveaux à la Reine.
Purée gelinottes à la Czartoriski.
Tokay.
Punch à l'Impériale.
Bécasses et faisans, rôtis, salade.
Terrine de foie-gras de Strasbourg.
Champagne.
Asperges nouvelles, sauce au beurre.
Fonds d'artichauts à la Lyonnaise.
Vin d' Oporto.
Timbales d'ananas à la Florentines.
Château Laffite.
Gelée de fraises à la Sultane.
Clos-Vougeot.
Plombières, crème de noyau.
Cremant.
Croque-en-bouche, Napolitaine.
Corbeilles Viennoises, Compotes assorties.
Constance.
Dessert.

FAMILLE ROYALE DE GRECE.

POTAGES.

Okra de Sterlets. Tortue de mer.

HORS D'ŒUVRE.

Cromesquis aux truffes. Huîtres grillées.

RELEVÉS.

Truites à la Chambord. Dinde à la chipolata.

ENTRÉES.

Suprême de perdreaux, aux truffes.
Timbale de truffes au champagne.

ROTIS.

Gelinottes et Faisans.

ENTREMETS.

Crème d'ananas (sur socle) garni de pâtisserie.
Glaces.

FAMILLE ROYALE DE PORTUGAL.

POTAGES.

Potage tortue et consommé.

Rissoles à la purée de Gibier.

Rougets grillés, à la maître d'hôtel.
Jambon, sauce Madère.
Petits pois.

Poulets à la chevalière.
Cailles à la Portugaise.
Aspic de crevettes.
Chaudfroid de bécassines.

Poulardes rôties et ortolans.
Salade.

Asperges, sauce au beurre.
Quartiers d'artichauts à la Lyonnaise.
Abricots à la Condé.
Gelée à l'orange et Fruits.
Glaces Variées.

FAMILLE ROYALE A'HOLLANDE.

Potage lié à l'Américaine.
Consommé à la Colbert.

Turbot, sauce Hollandaise et crevettes.
Filet de bœuf à la Flamande.
Endives aux œufs pochés.

Dinde à l'ambassadrice.
Côtelettes de mouton à la Périgueux.
Pain de gibier aux suprêmes.
Homards à la Remoulade.

Petits pois à l'Anglaise.
Perdreaux et chapons rôtis.
Salade de tomates et polonaise.

Croustade de riz à la Duchesse.
Gelée à la clermont.
Glaces. Dessert.

HONNEUR AUX ENFANTS DE LA FRANCE.

Banquet d'Adieu
Offert à Mons. l'Amiral Reajneaud,
Le 16 Novembre, 1863.
Huîtres.
Potage purée de Gibier.

VARIÉS. HORS D'ŒUVRES. VARIÉS.
Bouchées de Tortue.

RELEVÉS.
Saumon Portugaise.
Fillet of beef à la Portugaise.

ENTRÉES.
Dinde, truffes à la Toulouse.
Cailles, purée de céleri.
Côtelettes de Faisans aux champignons.
Pâtés de Gibier. Galantine aux truffes.

SORBET.
A la Régence.

ROTIS.
Bécasses. Canvas-back duck.

ENTREMETS.
Petits pois. Tomates farcies. Flageolets.
Chou-fleur.

SUCRES.
Savarin Chantilly. Gâteaux mille-feuilles.
Charlotte Croque-en-Bouche.
Fruits. Dessert assortie.

Delmonico.

◁ BALL ▷

IN HONOR OF

HIS ROYAL HIGHNESS THE PRINCE OF WALES,

NEW YORK, OCTOBER 12, 1860.

Menu.

Consommé de Volaille.
Huîtres à la Poulette.

Saumon.   Truites.

Au Beurre de Montpelier.

Filets de Bœuf à la Bellevue.   Galantines de Dindes à la Royale.
Pâtés de Gibiers à la Moderne.   Cochons de Lait à la Parisienne.
Pains de Lièvres Anglais Historiés.   Terrines de Nérac aux Truffes.

Jambons de Westphalie à la Gendarme.
Longes de Boeuf à l'Ecarlate.

Mayonnaises de Volailles.   Salades d'Homards à la Russe.

Grouse.

Bécassines.   Bécasses.

Faisans.

Gélées au Madère.   Macédoines de Fruits.
Crêmes Françaises.   Glaces à la Vanille et Citron.
Petits Fours.   Charlotte Russes.

Pêches, Poires, Raisins de Serre, etc.

PIÉCES MONTÉES.

La Reine Victoria et le Prince Albert.

Le Great Eastern.   Le Vase de Flora.

Silver Fountain, etc., etc.

Delmonico.

DINNER BY THE CITIZENS OF NEW YORK,

TO HIS EXCELLENCY

◁ PRESIDENT JOHNSON, ▷

IN HONOR OF

His Visit to the City, Wednesday, August 29, 1866.

Menu.

POTAGES.

Consommé à la Chatelaine. Bisque aux Quenelles.

HORS D'ŒUVRES.

Variés. Timbales de Gibier à la Vénitienne. Variés.

POISSONS.

Saumon à la Livonienne. Panpiettes de Kingfish à la Villeroi.

RELEVÉS.

Selle d' Agneau aux Concombres. Filet de Bœuf à la Pocahontas.

ENTRÉES.

Suprêmes de volaille à la Dauphine. Côtelettes à la Maréchale.
Ballotins de Pigeons à la Lucullus. Ris de Veau à la Montgomery.
Filets de Canetons à la Tyrolienne. Boudins à la Richelieu.

SORBET.

A la Dunderberg.

ROTIS.

Bécasses Bardées. Ortolans Farcis.

ENTREMETS.

Petit Pois. Tomates Farcies.
Aubergines. Artichauts à la Barigoul.

SUCRES.

Pêches à la New York. Abricots Siciliens.
Macédoine de Fruits au Curaçoa. Moscovites aux Oranges.
Bavarois aux Fraises. Gelée Californienne.
Crême aux Amandes. Méringue Chantilly.
Reauséjour au Malaga. Mille-feuilles Pompadour.
Gâteau Soleil. Biscuits Glacés aux Pistaches.

Fruits et Dessert.

PIECES MONTÉES.

Monument de Washington. Fontaine des Aigles.
Temple de la Liberté. Trophée Nationale.
Casque Romain. Colonne de l'Union.
Char de la Paix. Rotonde Egyptienne.
Cassolette Sultane. Cornes d'Abondances.

VINS.

POTAGES.
Amontillado 1824.

POISSONS.
Hochheimerberg.

RELEVÉS.
Champagne.

ENTRÉES.
Château Margaux '48.

ROTIS.
Clos de Vougeot.

ENTREMETS SUCRES.
Tokai Impériale.

DESSERT.
Madère Faguart.

CITY OF MELBOURNE
INAUGURATION DINNER
TO THE
Right Worshipful the Mayor, SAMUEL AMESS, Esq.,
9th November, 1869.

WINES.
Roederer's, Moet's, and Cliquot's Champagne.
D. & J. Squat Hock.
Claret.
Sherry.
Port.

Bill of Fare.

POTAGES.
Mock Turtle.
White Oyster.
Jardinière.

POISSONS.
Murray Cod.
Snapper.
Fillet of Whiting.

RELEVÉS.

Boiled Turkeys, Financier Sauce.	Boiled Chickens, Celery Sauce.
Roast Turkeys à l'Alderman.	Roast Quarters of Lamb.
Hams Braised à la Gelée.	Roast Goslings, Gooseberry Sauce.
Roast Ducklings.	Pigeon Pies.
Roast Fowls.	Saddles of Mutton.
Tongues Garnis des Légumes.	Roast Guinea Fowls.

ENTRÉES.

Les Petites Pâtes aux Huitres.	Côtelettes d'Agneau aux Petits Pois.
Les Karry de Volaille.	Vol-au-Vent au Ris de Veau aux Truffes.
Les Chartreuses des Légumes.	Croquettes de Volaille en Surprise.
Filets de Poulets à l'Ecarlate.	Côtelettes de Mouton à la Reform.

ENTREMETS.

Cabinet Pudding.	Crême au Chocolat.
Gelée au Rhum.	Crême aux Fraises.
Gelée au Citron.	Crême à l'Italienne.
Gelée à l'Orange.	Jamonge.
Gelée à la Victoria.	Grosses Méringues au Crême.
Blanc Mange.	Vol-au-Vent de Pommes.
Les Nougats Françaises.	Gâteaux Napoléon.
Croque-en-bouche.	Puits d'Amour.
Gâteaux Génoise.	Quadrilles à la Princes.
Corbules à la Chantilly.	Macaroni au Gratin.
Canapés en Pyramid.	Pouding à la Nesselrode.
Plum Pudding.	Glaces.
Crême à la Vanille.	

Dinner Given by Sir Morton Peto,
—AT—
DELMONICO'S, OCTOBER 30, 1865.

Menu.

HUITRES.
Barsac.

POTAGES.
Consommé Britannia.
Purée à la Derby.
Xérès J. S., 1815.

VARIÉS. HORS D'ŒUVRES. VARIÉS.
Cassolettes de Foie-gras.
Timbales à l'Ecarlate.

POISSONS.
Saumon à la Rothschild.
Grenadins de Bass, New York.
Steinberger Cabinet.

RELEVÉS.
Chapons, truffes.
Filet de Bœuf à la Durham.
Champagne Napoléon.

ENTRÉES.
Faisans à la Londonderry.
Côtelettes d'Agneau, Primatice.
Cromesquis de Volaille, Purée de Marrons.
Escalops de Canards, en Bigarade.
Rissolettes à la Pompadour.
Turban de Pigeons à la Musulmane.
Château Latour.

ENTRÉES FROIDES.
Volière de Gibier.
Ballotins d'Anguilles en Bellevue.
Chaudfroid de Robins à la Bohémienne.
Buisson de Ris d'Agneau, Pascaline.
Côtes Rôties.

SORBETS.
A la Sir Morton Peto.

ROTIS.
Selle de chevreuil, Sauce Porto-Groseille.
Bécasses Bardées.
Clos de Vougeot.

ENTREMETS.
Choux de Bruxelles ; Haricots Verts.
Artichauts Farcis ; Petits Pois.

SUCRES.
Pudding de Poires à la Madison.
Tokai impériale.
Louisiannais à l'Ananas.
Gelée de Fruits.
Pain d'Abricots à la Vanille.
Moscovite Fouetté, Gelée à l'Indienne.
Vacherin au Marasquin.
Couglakoff aux Amandes.
Mazarin aux Pêches.   Mousse à l'Orange.
Caisses Jardinières.   Glaces Assorties.
Fruits et Dessert.
Madère Faquart.

PIECES MONTÉES.
Cascade Pyramidale.
Corbeille Arabesque.
Ruines de Pœstum : Le Palmier.
Trophé Militaire ; Corne d'Abondance.
Nougat à la Parisienne.

COMPLIMENTARY BANQUET
—TO—
◁GENERAL LATHAM,▷
Late Consul for the United States of America,

CRITERION HOTEL, 12TH OCTOBER, 1869.

WINES.

Roederer's, Moet's, and Cliquot's
Champagne.
D. & J. Squat Hock.
Claret.
Sherry.
Port.

Bill of Fare.

SOUPS.

Mock Turtle.   White Oyster.
Spring.

FISH.

Snapper.   Murray Cod.
Fillet of Whiting.

RELEVÉS.

Boiled Turkeys, Oyster sauce.	Roast Turkeys and Sausages.
Boiled Fowls and Celery sauce.	Roast Fowls en Cresson.
Roast Geese.	Roast Ducks.
Roast Saddles of Mutton.	Roast Quarters of Lamb.
Pigeon Pies.	Raised Chicken Pies.
Hams, Garnished.	Tongues, Garnished.

ENTRÉES.

Ris de Veau à la Sultan.	Côtelettes d'Agneau au Petit Pons Vert.
Côtelettes de Mouton au Tomate.	Vol-au-Vent à la Chevalière.
Filets de Poulet à la Royale.	Turban de Quenelles de Volaille.
Rissoles de Volaille à la Reform.	Croquettes de Veau et Jambon.
Petites Pâtés aux Huîtres.	Timbales de Macaroni à la Princesse.
Fricandeau de Veau, Sauce de Tomate.	Filets de Poulet à l'Ecarlate.

SECOND SERVICE.

ENTREMETS.

Cabinet Pudding.	Macaroni au Gratin.
Newmarket Pudding.	Plum Pudding.
Gelée aux Fraises.	Gelée à la Victoria.
Gelée au Vin de Marasquin.	Gelée à l'Orange.
Puits d'Amour.	Gelée Dantzic.
Pommes Méringuées.	Gâteaux Génoise.
Gâteaux Napoléon.	Tartlets à la Crême.
Crême à la Rose.	Crême à la Vanille.
Crême au Chocolat.	Crême à la Fleur d'Orange.
Corbules à la Chantilly.	Crême aux Framboises.
Canapés en Pyramid.	Tourtes en Caramel.
Gâteaux à la Rutland.	Gâteaux, Neapolitan.

Custards.
Dessert, etc., etc.

◁ BALL, ▷
NOVEMBER 5, 1863, AT THE ACADEMY OF MUSIC.
RUSSIAN FLEET.

Rear-Admiral Lessoffsky, Russian flag-ship *Alexander Wcosky*, 51 guns.
Capt. Kopytor, Russian screw frigate *Peresvat*, 48 guns.
Capt. Bontakoff, Russian screw frigate *Osliaba*, 33 guns.
Capt. Lund (or Lurd), Russian screw sloop *Vitioz*, 77 guns.
Capt. Kremer, Russian screw sloop *Variag*, 17 guns.

Menu.

HORS D'ŒUVRES.
Huîtres à la poulette.   Huîtres en marinade.   Bouchées de gibier.
　　Canapés de filets d'ortolans.　Snit-mitch à la Russe.

GROSSES PIÈCES.
Saumons au beurre de Montpelier.　Truites à la Régence.
Filets de bœuf à la Mazarin.　Pâtés de canvas-back ducks.
Galantine de cochon de lait, garni de hatelets.　Pâtés de gibier sur socles.
Jambons de Westphalie à la moderne.　Galantines de dindes aux truffes.

ENTRÉES.
Salades de volaille à la Russe.　Canetons à la Rouennaise.
Côtelettes de pigeons en Macédoine.　Bordures d'escalopes d'homards.
Chaudfroid de filets de faisans.　Aspics de filets de soles à la Victoria.
Pain de gibier à la royale.　Timbales à la renaissance.
Terrines de nérac de pluviers.　Bécassines à la Geoffroy.

ROTIS.
Cailles aux feuilles de vigne.　　　　　　Bécasses bardées.
　　Faisans piqués.　　　Grouse.

ENTREMETS, SUCRES, ET DESSERT.
Savarins au Marasquin.　Biscuits Moscovites.
Gâteaux de mille-feuilles.　Babas glacés au rhum.
Charlottes Sibériennes.　Charlotte, New York.
　　Méringues panachées et Vanillées.

Gelée macédoine au vin de champagne.　Pains d'abricots à la Béresina.
Gelées Dantzic Orientales.　Blanc manger rubané au chocolat.
Gelées de poires à la maréchale.　Bavarois aux fraises.
Gelées au madère.　Biscuits glacés à la rose.
　Gâteaux assortis.　Petit-fours.　Compotes.　　Fruits.

PIÈCES MONTÉES ET GLACÉS.
Pierre le Grand.　Washington.
Alexandre II.　Lincoln.
Le berceau des palmiers.　La rotunde d'Athènes.
La fontaine moderne.　L'ermitage Russe.
L'arc de triomphe.　Cornes jumelles d'abondance.
Sultane à la Parisienne.　Le pavillon des Aigles.

L'aigle Américain.　Le casque sur socle.　Pouding Nesselrode.
　　　　　　La lionne.
　　Columbus.　Corbeille jardinière.　Les Dauphins.
　　　　Diane.　Madeleines.　Mousses aux amandes.
　Bombes spongade.　Ceylaus au café.　Vanille.　Chocolat.
　　　　　Citrons et Fraises.
　　　etc.　　etc.　　etc.　　etc.

Delmonico.

DÉJEÛNER
DONNÉ PAR
MME. JAMES GORDON BENNETT,
LE 3 DECEMBRE, 1861.

MAISON DORÉE.
Huîtres crues sur Coquilles.

POTAGES.
Aux huîtres,
Consommé à la royale.

POISSONS.
Saumon à l'Impériale.   Truite à la Régence.
Croquettes de Pommes de terre.

HORS D'ŒUVRES.
Petits pâtés à la Parisienne.   Salade d'anchois, olives, sardines.

GROSSES PIÈCES FROIDES.
Hure de sanglier, sur socle à la St. Hubert.
Chaudfroid de foies de Canards de Strasbourg aux truffes.
Perdreaux à la Gelée.
Roast Beef à l'Anglaise.
Jambons de Westphalie, ornementés.
Pâtés de faisans d'Ecosse en Bellevue.
Longe de Bœuf à la Gelée.
Selle de chevreuil et Gelée de Groseille.

ENTRÉES.
Coquilles de Volaille à la Montglas.
Côtelettes d'agneau garnies de pommes.
Asperges.
Boudins à la Richelieu aux truffes.
Brochettes de foies de volaille à l'Anglaise.
Petits pois.
Punch à la Romaine.

ROTIS.
Canvas-back Ducks.
Chapons, Truffes.
Croûte aux champignons nouveaux.
Mayonnaise de Volaille à la Noçoise.
Dindes farcies au cresson.
Cailles bardées au cresson.
Choux de Bruxelles.
Mayonnaise d'Homards à la Nelson.
Buissons d'Ecrevisses.

PIÈCES MONTÉES ET ENTREMETS.
Le Temple de la Paix.
Gâteau Napolitain sur socle.
Nougats à la Parisienne.
Corbeilles de Méringues à la Chantilly
Gelées d'orange à l Orientale.
Macédoine de fruits.
Crème renversée à la vanille.
Gâteau Chateaubriand sur socle.
Croque-en-bouche Génoise.
Charlottes Russes, à la moderne.
Blanc Manger, Rubané.
Mousses aux framboises.
Ladies' Kisses.
Petits fours et Confiserie assortie.

GLACES.
"L'aigle Américain," sur socle.
"Pudding," à la Nesselrode.
"Corbeille" de fruits à la Napolitaine.
"Biscuits," glacés à la vanille.

FRUITS.
Raisins.   Oranges.   Pommes.
Compote de Pommes à la Portugaise.
Poires.

CELEBRATED MENUS. 409

ORANGE BOVEN.

ANNIVERSARY DINNER
OF THE
ST. NICHOLAS SOCIETY,
AT THE
ASTOR HOUSE, DECEMBER 6, 1852.

SOUP.

Green Turtle.   Macaroni with Cheese.

FISH.

Baked Cod, Italian style.   Boiled Striped Bass, Hollandaise sauce.

RELEVÉS.

ROAST.	BOILED.
Turkeys, Giblet sauce.	Partridges, with Sour Krout.
Capons, Truffle sauce.	Leg of Mutton, Dutch Style.
Ham, Cherry-wine sauce.	Leg of Pork, with Cabbage.
Beef, with Croquettes of Potatoes.	Turkey, with Oysters.
Venison, with Currant Jelly.	Leg of Veal with Mushrooms.

Chicken Pot-pie, Farmer's style.

RELISHES.

Olives.   Pickles.   Anchovies.   Sardines.

SIDE DISHES.

Broiled Quails with Green Peas.   Legs of Chickens, in form of birds, Soubise sauce.
Lamb Chops with Mashed Potatoes.   Curry of Veal, Indian mode.
Fillet of Veal, larded, Gardiner's sauce.   Small Cakes of Fish with Oysters.
Breast of Chicken à la Condé.   Fricassee of Chicken, Chevalier style.
Vol-au-Vent, garnished with Veal and Celery.   Côtelettes of Halibut, German style.
Oysters Baked in the Shell.   Mayonnaise of Lobster.
Chartreuse of Game, Madeira sauce.   Turkish Pillau.

COLD ORNAMENTAL DISHES.

American Pâté-de-Foie-Gras with Truffles.   Cheese, made of Veal in Jelly on a Socle.
Bastion made of Fish, with Holland colors.   Stuffed Chickens in form of a Fountain.

Boned Turkey with Jelly.

VEGETABLES.

Plain Boiled Potatoes.   Onions.   Baked Mashed Potatoes.
Cauliflower.   Turnips.   Baked Sweet Potatoes.
Potatoes Fried, German style.   Parsnips.

SMALL PLATES.

Croquettes of Rice.   Fried Oysters.

GAME.

Roast Canvas-back Ducks.   Wild Goose.
Red-head Ducks.   Wild Turkey.
Brant.   Wild Rabbits.

KNICKERBOCKER DISHES.

Rolletjies.   Smoked Goose.
Smoked Sausages.   Spack and Applejes.
Head Cheese.   Krullers.
Kookies.   Doughnuts and Oly Kooks.

PASTRY.

Mince Pie.   Charlotte Russe.   Swiss Méringues.
Blanc Mange.   Rum Jelly.   Apple Pie.
Poor Man's Pudding.

ORNAMENTAL CONFECTIONERY.

Visit of Santa Claus.   City Hall of New Amsterdam.
Stuyvesant and his Dwelling.   Knickerbocker Comfort.
Washington Monument.   Holland Pavilion.

CONFECTS.

Macaroons.   Lady-fingers.
Almond Cakes.   Kisses.
Vanilla Ice-cream.

PRESERVES.

Brandy Peaches.   Ginger.   Chow-Chow.

FRUIT.

Schnaps and Pipes.   St. Nicholas Punch.
Coffee.   Anchovy Toast.

CURIOUS MENUS

OF

VARIOUS NATIONS.

MENU

FROM

CENTRAL AFRICA.

THROUGH the courtesy of a gentleman who has for many years lived in Central Africa, and who has brought with him a young prince, son of one of the powerful chiefs of the Baaili tribe, to be educated in this country, the author is enabled to illustrate the habits and customs now in vogue in the Royal Kitchen there.

As a rule, there is only one principal meal, which is eaten in the early part of the evening. It mostly consists of parrot-soup, roasted or stewed monkeys, alligator eggs (also well liked by Europeans), and birds of every description. They also have moambo or palm-chops, and fish. A great delicacy, so considered by Europeans and natives alike, is elephant's feet and trunk. They have somewhat the taste of veal, and have a very delicious flavor. To prepare them they dig a hole, about five feet deep, in the sand, and build in it a large fire. After the sand is thoroughly heated, the fire is removed, leaving only the ashes in the hole. They place the trunk and feet in this hole, covering them with leaves, and afterward with hot sand; they remain there about two hours, when they are considered done.

All carcasses of animals which are to be cooked, are placed on a block of wood, and pounded until every bone is broken, care being taken not to tear or bruise the skin. They are then boiled or roasted on an open wood-fire, in hot sand or ashes, without removing the hide or feathers.

The cooking is of a very inferior grade; the only spices used being salt and pepper.

The kitchen utensils consist of common earthen or wooden ware.

Very little time is taken for setting or decorating the table; knives, forks, napkins, &c., &c., are dispensed with.

All victuals are served in large wooden vessels. After the members of the chief's household and his guests have assembled, each person is supplied with a wooden spoon, and selects whatever he wishes out of the different vessels, using his hands in eating it.

In the line of vegetables, they have also several dishes well liked by Europeans. N'gutti-N'sengo is a dish eaten all over Africa. It consists of egg-plant, small fish, somewhat like our sardines (N'sengo), and the roots of the cassava or manioca plant (called N'gutti), which have a knotty appearance, and often weigh as much as twenty pounds.

As the latter contains poison, they soak the manioca in water for three to four days, to extract the poisonous substance. They are cut and sliced, adding small tomatoes. All is placed in a vessel with water, and seasoned with salt and pepper, and boiled. Moambo, or, as the Europeans call it, palm-chops, is also a favorite dish. The palm-nuts are first boiled in water, until the pulpy substance loosens from the pit.

Then the shell, which contains a very delicious oil, is placed in a wooden mortar and crushed to obtain the oil. Then whatever the meal consists of, meat, fish, mussels, &c., all is put in a vessel, adding the oil and the pulpy part of the palm-nut, also red pepper and salt, and is boiled.

Roast or boiled squash (Loenge) is generally eaten with it.

Sweet potatoes (M'balla Benga) are more farinaceous, and sweeter than ours, but do not taste so good. They are boiled or roasted in the same way as we do here.

Bananas (Bitaebe) weigh about a half pound each, and are about fifteen inches long. When half ripe they are cut in slices, adding much salt and pepper, and are boiled in water.

N'sensi is a little red bean, which is boiled in water without adding salt or pepper.

Peanut bread (Chisulu): the peanuts are first roasted, then crushed. This mass is then rolled and put into the skin of a banana, adding a little pressure, forming it into a body. It readily retains this shape from the presence of the oily substance in the peanut.

Hongkong Menu.

China.

Bow Ha Mai.
Boiled Prawns in Oil.

Chow Chop Sucy.
Bits of Pork Chops.

Ham ob Dau.
Preserved Eggs with Ducks' Gizzards.

Ob Gau Bow Vo Toway.
Ducks' Livers and Boiled Ham.

Chow Ju Aw.
Boiled Pork, Kidneyed.

Show Ju N Gow.
Roast Pork-tongues.

Bow N Gwei.
Cuttle Fish.

Yen Wo' Gong.
Boiled Pigeon Eggs and Bird-nest Soup.

Bow Hai.
Boiled Crabs.

Bow Yu Chee.
Boiled Shark Fins.

Yuen Tsyai.
Rice Cakes.

Bow Ob.
Duck-tongues and Mushrooms.

Ju Tow N Gow.
Fried Roofs-of-the-Mouths of Pigs.

Chow Ob Jun.
Ducks' Feet.

Chow Gai Pien.
Fried Chicken Wings.

Lein Chi Gong.
Lily-seed Soup.

Hong Yin Gong.
Almond Soup.

Dein Som.
Sweetmeats and Jellies.

Yueh Biung.
Mincemeat Cakes.

Gwoy Zoo.
Fruits.

Kwoh Zuh.
Seeds.

Cha Sam Soo.
Tea, and Rice Whiskey.

As to the Chinese, at their formal dinners or feasts no menus are used. The bill of fare consists of an interminable list of dishes, and which has been arranged by the author in the form of a menu card. The tables are laden with such dishes as shark-fins, bêche-de-mer fish, fish-soup, chicken-soup, duck-soup, rice, rice, rice, and tea, tea, tea, and tea; not forgetting the edible birds' nests, candies, and cakes. One's appetite is almost taken away on entering a Chinese house at which a banquet is to be given—the effect of burning incense and other vile herbs. The Chinese can be extremely polite. Champagne is a favorite drink among Chinese officials at the Treaty Ports, and is always brought out when they have a foreign guest.

Yokohama Menu.
Japan.

Cha.
Tea.

Luimano.	Shirn.	Ohira.
Fish Soup.	Bean Soup.	Vegetable Soup.
Sashimi.	Nizakana.	Teriyaki.
Raw Sliced Fish.	Boiled Fish.	Roast Fish.

Shiwoyaki.
Roasted Fish.

Muchitori.
Boiled Vegetables

Umani.
Fish and Vegetables.

Trubonomoni.
Vegetables.

Gozen.
Boiled Rice.

Tsukemono.
Pickles.

Shoyu.
Sauce.

Saki.
Rice Whiskey.

Cha.
Tea.

A most delicious sauce, called "Shoyu," which is the basis of Worcestershire sauce, is also used to give spice to the food. Throughout the repast the guests are served from time to time with "Saki," a pale liquor made from rice, and which tastes very much like sherry. It is served hot, and is a most insinuating tipple. In a large party you are expected to exchange cups and drink with every one present. The result is that, in nine cases out of ten, you leave the house just a "wee bit fu'," as they say in Scotland. Like the Chinese, no knives, forks, or napkins are used—"chop sticks" only. To smack your lips or belch during the feast is, strange to say of such a supremely polite people, not considered bad form.

Corea Menu.

Cha.
Tea.

Fou Yoon An.
Finely Chopped Ham, with Eggs.

Whey Sum.
Bamboo Shoots, with Mushrooms and Bêche-de-mer Fish.

Chow Kai Goot.
Dice-shaped Spring Chicken-bones, Served in Sweetmeat Pickles.

Chow Lok Zeow.
Finely Sliced Green Peppers, Fried with Cut Beef and Celery.

Gow Jee.
Finely Chopped, Spiced Pork, Wrapped in Thin Dough, then Steamed.

Chow Mien.
A Kind of Boiled Macaroni, Fried with Thin Strips of Chicken, Pork, Mushrooms, and Celery.

Bing Lon.
Betel-nuts Preserved in Rock Candy.

Cha.
Tea.

Sam Soo.
Rice Liquor.

In Corea Chinese fashions are very closely followed. Greasy messes and appetite-destroying smells are their most characteristic features. The food is always conveyed to the mouth by the aid of "chop sticks," and during the progress of a meal the mind becomes catered to by an animated conversation.

Kanaka Menu.
Hawaiian Islands.

FISH.

| Raw Mullet. | Raw Gold-fish. Broiled Taro. | Shell Fish. |

POI.

Chili Peppers.
Small Onions.

ENTRÉES.

| Raw Liver, | | Roast Pig. |
| | Roast Fish. | Stewed Taro. |

VEGETABLES.

Papaias.	Cabbage.	Taro.
	Sweet Potatoes.	

FRUIT.

Bananas.	Oranges.	Guavas.
Mangoes.	Apples.	Hawaiian Tea.
	Kono Coffee.	

LIQUOR.

Ookulian (pronounced O-ku-le-on).
Hawaiian Pipe of Friendship.

Among the Kanakas, the food eaten for breakfast, luncheon, and dinner is about the same, and consists chiefly of the native dish called "POI," which is eaten whenever they (the Kanakas) are hungry.

"POI" is made from a root called "*Taro*," and in shape and size resembles a raw beet, it has a dark skin, and the vegetable itself has a variety of colors—pink, gray, purple, and white.

The "Taro" is cooked in the ground, after the manner of a "New England clam-bake;" after obtaining the softness of a cooked potato it is peeled, and *beaten* with a large stone or iron, made for that purpose, into a pulp. It is then mixed with water until it forms the thickness of paste (and which makes very good paste, as it is often used for sticking bills, etc., when a theatrical company arrives), and after standing for a few days, to allow it to ferment, it is ready to be eaten.

The "Poi" is always eaten out of a "Calabash" (a large gourd about the size of a pumpkin), the natives *always* eating with their fingers, this being done by sticking the two fore-fingers into the "Calabash," giving it one or two twists, and dexterously turning it around in front of their faces, until it looks like a ball of "taffy on a stick" (no pun intended).

"Taro" is sometimes cooked and eaten like potatoes and is considered very wholesome food.

The next important dish is "*Raw Fish*," which are caught along the coast and eagerly eaten by the natives. Fish is also cooked in the ground, and is served on large leaves about the size of palm-leaves, called "Ti" leaves. Raw meat, raw liver, and a fragrant sea-weed form delicate side-dishes.

Coffee, within the last few years, has to a great extent been drunk as a beverage, but not so much as the Hawaiian tea, which tastes and smells like medicine.

Vegetables are also eaten, but sparingly, comprising sweet potatoes, Irish potatoes, cabbages, etc.

Fruit, the product of the Islands, is very much eaten and relished, such as guavas, mangoes, bananas, mountain-apples, oranges, etc.

The Hawaiians when eating always sit on mats. All eat out of the same calabash. After eating, it is the custom to pass the pipe of friendship, which is a small pipe made from shark's teeth.

INDEX.

BEEF.

484, Braised à la Bignon.
483,   en daube.
482,   à la flamande.
479,   à la mode.
478,   à la morlaisienne.
481,   à l'Orsini.
480,   à la Providence.
485,   Russian sauce.
490, Corned, with kale-sprouts.
489,   and spinach.
531,   hash en bordure.
529,   au gratin.
528,   à la polonaise.
530,   à la zingara.
1359, Hamburg steak, raw.
526,   Russian sauce.
502, Minced beef à la Catalan.
501,   à la portugaise.
500,   à la provençale.
512, Mignons filets à la Bernardi.
513,   à la bohémienne.
1389,   à la Brown.
1364,   à la Lorillard.
511,   marinated, Russian sauce.
510,   à la moëlle.
514,   à la parisienne.
515,   aux pommes parisienne.
509,   à la Pompadour.
527, Roast.
539, Roulade à l'écarlate.
498, Sirloin piqué, à la bordelaise.
499,   marrow sauce.
486, Smoked beef à la crême.
524, Steak, porterhouse.
525,   " double.
492,   sirloin, à la béarnaise.
491,   à la bordelaise.
496,   aux cêpes.
494, Steak, duchesse.
497,   green peppers.
493,   à la moëlle.
495,   à la parisienne.
488,   pie à l'américaine.
487,   pie à l'anglaise.
541, Stewed beef, Dufour.
540,   à l'égyptienne.
543,   à la marseillaise.
542,   à la turque.
503, Tenderloin of beef, broiled.
504,   à la chéron.
506,   à la florentine.
508,   aux gourmets.
505,   à la nivernaise.
1388,   à la Stanton.
507,   à la Trianon.
523,   piqué à la Bernardi.
516,   à la duchesse.
521,   à l'égyptienne.
519,   à la Hussard.
517,   à la portugaise.
518,   à la provençale.
522,   à la Richelieu.
520,   à la Sévigne.
532, Tongue of beef à la gendarme.
535,   à la jardinière.
538,   milanaise.
534,   napolitaine.
537,   with risotto.
533,   sauce piquante.
536,   with spinach.
544, Tripe à la bordelaise.
545,   à la créole.
548,   à la lyonnaise.
547,   à la mode de Caen.
546,   à la poulette.

COFFEE, CHOCOLATE, AND TEA.

1263, Coffee, essence.
1348,   how to roast.
1349,   how to make.
1350,   Café noir à l'Alexander the Great.
1351, Café, au lait.
1352,   au lait à la St. Gottardo.
1353,   glacé.
1354, Tea.
1355,   à la Russe.
1356, Chocolate.
1357,   au lait à la George Washington.
1391, Mazagran à la Général Bugeau.
1292,   à la Général Dufour.

DESSERTS:
PASTRY, JELLIES, ICES, PRESERVES, ETC.

1207, Almonds, how to prepare.
1169, Apples, with rice.
1124,   baked.
1190, Batter, for fritters.
1185,   for frying.
1270, Blanc-manger à la Josephine Delmonico.
1205, Cakes, allumettes.
1224,   almond.
1239,   " fancy.
1208,   " glacés.
1211,   apple.
1216,   baba.
1217,   " au madère.
1218,   " crème vanille.
1235,   biscuits, almond.
1234,   "   ambroisienne.
1231,   "   cuillère.
1233,   "   livornaise.
1232,   "   Richelieu.
1201,   brioches.
1203,   " à la Condé.
1204,   " fluttes,
1202,   " small.
1183,   buckwheat.
1236,   chaussons.
1246,   choux à la crème.
1221,   galette.
1213,   gingerbread.
1220,   home-made.
1231,   lady-fingers.
1209,   macaroons, bitter.
1210,   "   sweet.
1226,   madeleine.
1227,   "   printanière.
1228,   Milan.
1223,   mille-feuilles.
1238,   petites bouchées à la Mme. Astor.
1237,   petites bouchées des dames.
1225,   pithiviers.
1193,   pound.
1222,   rice.
1230,   rice à la Mazzini.
1229,   rum.
1197,   savarin.
1199,   " à l'anglaise.
1198,   " hot.
1215,   short, blackberry.
1214,   "   strawberry.
1212,   St. Honoré à la Rose Delmonico.
1195,   sponge.
1196,   waffles.
1194,   wedding.

1184, Cakes, wheat.
1167, Charlotte, apple.
1262,   au café.
1261,   russe.
1168,   small.
1080, Currants, cleaning.
1200, Cream à l'anglaise.
1258,   au cognac.
1259,   au curaçoa.
1256,   au kirsch.
1257,   au maraschino.
1260,   en mousse.
1253,   "   " au café.
1255,   "   " au rhum.
1242,   pâtissière.
1252,   renversée.
1254,   whipped à la vanille.
1176, Croustade of rice.
1313, Cup, champagne.
1314,   claret.
1122, Dumplings, baked apple.
1127,   boiled apple.
1126,   boiled apricot.
1125,   boiled peach.
1241, Eclairs,
1244,   au café.
1243,   au chocolat.
1245,   vanilla.
1191, Fritters, apple.
1192,   vanilla.
1269,   glace, royale.
1206,   "   "   for allumettes.
1277, Ice-cream, banana.
1286,   biscuits glacés.
1287,   biscuits Tortoni.
1299,   charlottes glacées.
1300,   charlottes panachées.
1272,   chocolate.
1273,   coffee.
1278,   lemon.
1290,   macaroon.
1298,   macédoine à la Cavour.
1301,   méringues glacées.
1302,   méringues panachées.
1292,   napolitaine.
1295,   parfait au café.
1276,   peach.
1275,   pistache.
1370,   plombière à la Hamilton.
1294,   "   à la Kingman.
1291,   pudding à la Frances Cleveland.
1288,   pudding à la diplomate.
1289,   plum pudding à la Gladstone.

1274,	Ice-cream, strawberry.	1085,	Pies, rhubarb.
1371,	tutti-frutti à la General Harrison.	1095,	strawberry.
		1342,	Preserves, apples.
1293,	tutti-frutti.	1387,	"
1271,	vanilla.	1381,	blackberries and whortleberries.
1327,	Jelly, apple.		
1321,	brandy.	1347,	cherries.
1322,	champagne.	1377,	"
1326,	currant.	1344,	green-gages.
1379,	"	1378,	gooseberries.
1319,	kirsch.	1340,	peaches.
1323,	kümmel.	1385,	"
1325,	Marcella wine à la Castellar.	1341,	pears.
		1385,	"
1324,	Rhein wine.	1374,	pineapples.
1320,	Jamaica rum.	1343,	egg-plums.
1318,	sherry wine.	1383.	"
1247,	Méringues.	1380,	raspberries.
1248,	apple.	1346,	"
1249,	à la Ch. C. Delmonico.	1376,	rhubarb.
1251,	à l'helvétienne.	1345,	strawberries.
1250,	shells.	1373,	"
1266,	Nougat.	1152,	Puddings, apple à l'helvétienne.
1267,	pyramid.	1151,	apricot à la Richelieu.
1182,	Nouilles or noodles.	1132,	bread.
1297,	Oranges glacées à la Geo. Renauldt.	1164,	cabinet à la Sadi-Carnot.
		1166,	caramel.
1186,	Pancake, French.	1146,	chocolate.
1187	" à la gelée.	1147,	cocoanut.
1188,	German.	1154,	custard.
1189,	" with apples.	1135,	Diaz.
1076,	Paste, feuilletage or puff.	1129,	diplomatic.
1078,	foundation.	1137,	English, baked.
1077,	for pies.	1144,	farina.
1079,	Pastry-bag.	1139,	French à la Delmonico.
1240,	Pâte-à-chou.	1161,	fruit.
1331,	Peach marmalade.	1159,	à la U. S. Grant.
1083,	Pies, apple.	1145,	Indian.
1103,	apple méringue.	1157,	lemon.
1097,	blackberry.	1134,	maraschino.
1098,	cherry.	1155,	Nelson.
1101,	cocoanut.	1158,	orange.
1104,	cranberry.	1150,	peach à la Richelieu.
1090,	fresh currants.	1148,	pineapple à la Richelieu.
1100,	custard.	1163,	plum.
1091,	gooseberry.	1143,	rice.
1093,	green-gage.	1130,	rice and orange.
1089,	huckleberry.	1140,	sago.
1086,	lemon.	1141,	tapioca.
1102,	lemon cream.	1142,	vermicelli.
1105,	Martha Washington.	1306,	Punch à la Cardinal.
1082,	mince.	1307,	champagne.
1092,	peach.	1312,	à la Czarina, hot.
1084,	pear.	1303,	à la Lorenzo Delmonico.
1088,	pear, open.	1310,	à la française, hot.
1087,	pineapple.	1311,	à la française, iced.
1094,	plum.	1305,	kirsch.
1099,	pumpkin.	1308,	à la Lalla Rookh.
1096,	raspberry.	1304,	Roman.

1309, Punch, en surprise.
1170, Rice au lait d'amandes.
1171,   à l'Airolo.
1172,   à la bonne femme.
1181,   à la Condé.
1296,   à la Croce.
1173,   à la Czar.
1180,   à la française.
1179,   à l'indienne.
1177,   with milk.
1175,   timbale, iced.
1178,   à la Turque.
1081, Raisins, cleaning.
1131, Sauce, anglaise à l'orange.
1328,   apple.
1128,   apricot.
1165,   à la Carnot.
1153,   Chaufausen.
1329,   cranberry.
1133,   cream.
1219,   cream à la vanille.
1156,   Daniel Webster.
1136,   Diaz.
1160,   U. S. Grant.
1123,   hard.
1149,   kirsch.
1129,   punch.
1162,   rum.
1138,   sabayon au madère.
1332, Stewed apples.
1335,   apricots.
1336,   green-gages.
1334,   peaches.
1333,   pears.

1337, Stewed plums.
1330,   prunes à la Dufour.
1338,   quinces.
1265, Sugar, burned.
1264,   " cooked.
1339, Syrups for preserving fruits.
1120, Tarts, apple.
1108,   apricot.
1119,   blackberry.
1111,   cherry.
1116,   cranberry.
1121,   Frangipani.
1107,   green-gages.
1114,   gooseberry and currant.
1113,   huckleberry.
1106,   peach.
1109,   pear.
1115,   pineapple.
1110,   plum.
1118,   raspberry.
1112,   rhubarb.
1117,   strawberry.
1174, Turban of apples.
1285, Water-ice, apricot.
1282,   cherry.
1279,   lemon.
1280,   orange.
1284,   peach.
1283,   pineapple.
1281,   raspberry.
1316, Water-melon, à la José Paez.
1315,   à la Romero.
1317,   à la Seward.

EGGS.

443, Eggs à l'alsacienne.
444,   à l'aurore.
416,   à la béchamel.
447,   à la Bennett.
432,   à la bonne femme.
411,   à la bourguignonne.
414,   brown butter.
427,   with celery.
442,   à la chipolata.
449,   duchesse.
423,   en filets.
424,   à la finoise.
418,   au gratin.
448,   à la Hyde.
440,   à l'impératrice.
430,   with livers.
410,   à la Livingstone.
435,   with melted cheese.
437,   à la Meyerbeer.
425,   au miroir.
426,   with mushrooms.

1366, Eggs à la post.
436,   en panade.
431,   au parmesan.
417,   à la pauvre femme.
433,   à la paysanne.
445,   à la polonaise.
422,   à la provençale.
434,   à la régence.
438,   à la reine.
446,   Robert sauce.
429,   with tarragon.
419,   à la tripe.
428,   with truffles.
439,   à la turque.
415,   au soleil.
441,   à la suisse.
420,   à la Vanderbilt.
421,   à la valencienne.
412,   fried.
413,   for garnishing.
458, Omelet, asparagus-tops.

466,	Omelet à la bonne femme.		467,	Omelet, raspail.
477,	célestine.		470,	régence.
460,	with cêpes.		476,	rum.
469,	cheese.		468,	sardine.
464,	chicken liver.		465,	sausage.
455,	crab.		461,	smoked beef.
453,	crawfish.		474,	soufflée.
472,	à l'espagnole.		475,	sweet.
451,	with fine herbs.		456,	tomato.
459,	with green peas.		457,	tomato à la provençale.
462,	ham.		471,	à la Vanderbilt.
463,	kidney.		404,	Poached eggs.
476,	au kirsch.		405,	Scrambled eggs.
454,	lobster.		406,	asparagus-tops.
473,	mexicaine.		409,	à la chicorée.
452,	oyster.		408,	smoked beef.
450,	plain.		407,	truffles.

FISH.

341,	Bass à la bordelaise.		309,	Halibut, boiled.
343,	à la chambord.		310,	steaks, maître d'hôtel.
342,	with white wine.		357,	Lobster à l'américaine.
336,	Bluefish à l'icarienne.		360,	à la bordelaise.
337,	à l'italienne.		361,	en brochette au petit salé,
338,	à la vénitienne.		364,	broiled.
340,	Bouille-à-baisse à la marseillaise.		363,	broiled, ravigote sauce.
			362,	en chevreuse.
301,	Breaded fish; how to prepare.		365,	croquettes.
391,	Canapé Lorenzo.		366,	cutlets, Victoria.
377,	Clams à la marinière.		358,	au curry.
300,	how to serve.		359,	à la Newburg.
376,	stuffed.		1358,	à la Rushmore.
389,	soft shelled à la Merrill,		367,	stuffed.
390,	" " à la Newburg.		329,	Mackerel, broiled, maître
352,	Codfish, boiled, oyster sauce.			d'hôtel.
345,	bonne femme.		331,	aux fines herbes.
346,	picked-up.		330,	en papillotes.
349,	tongues, beurre noir.		378,	Mussels à la marinière.
350,	" fried.		379,	à la poulette.
348,	" how to blanch.		388,	Oysters à la Baltimore.
351,	" à la poulette.		385,	en brochette au petit salé.
373,	Crabs à l'anglaise.		382,	broiled.
370,	deviled.		299,	à l'Alexandre Dumas.
371,	à la St. Jean.		380,	fried.
372,	à la St. Laurent.		386,	à la nali.
369,	soft-shelled, broiled.		384,	à la Pompadour.
368,	" " fried.		383,	à la poulette.
332,	Eels, en matelote.		298,	how to serve.
334,	" normande.		381,	à la Villeroi.
333,	" à la parisienne.		1367,	à la Arthur Sullivan.
335,	how to blanch.		375,	Oyster-crabs fried.
347,	Fish balls.		374,	à la poulette.
347,	à la Mrs. Harrison.		387,	Oyster patties.
398,	Frogs, broiled.		304,	Salmon, Colbert.
401,	à l'espagnole.		364,	croquettes.
400,	fried.		306,	à la génoise.
399,	à la poulette.		303,	oyster sauce.

302,	Salmon, en papillotes.	394,	Snails à l'italienne.
305,	à la régence.	395,	à la provençale.
307,	rolled à l'irlandaise.	324,	Sole, diéppoise.
308,	tails, broiled.	322,	fillets, Jcinville.
344,	Salt Cod à la biscaënne.	323,	fine herbs.
403,	Sardines on toast.	320,	fried, sauce Colbert.
392,	Scallops, brestoise.	319,	au gratin.
326,	Shad, maître d'hôtel.	317,	à l'hollandaise.
327,	with sorrel.	321,	à la Horly.
328,	vert-pré.	318,	normande.
402,	roe, with bacon.	396,	Terrapin à la Baltimore.
339,	Sheep's-head à la créole.	397,	à la Maryland.
325,	Skate au naturel.	397,	à la Newburg.
353,	Smelts à la béarnaise.	312,	Trout à la Cambacères.
356,	au gratin.	313,	à la Chambord.
355,	stuffed.	315,	with fine herbs.
354,	à la toulouse.	314,	maître d'hôtel.
1393,	à la Van Volkenburgh.	316,	en papillotes.
393,	Snails à la bourguignonne.	311,	shrimp sauce.

FORCEMEATS.

229,	Forcemeat, American.	222,	Forcemeat, lobster.
226,	chicken,	228,	partridge.
225,	chicken à la crème.	227,	quenelles of fish.
224,	clam.	220,	sausage.
223,	crab.	218,	Fumet of game.
221,	godiveau.	1372,	Frogs' legs à la Merrill.

GAME.

891,	Antelope chops, port-wine sauce.	847,	Partridge, braised with celery sauce.
890,	steak, Russian sauce.	844,	broiled à l'américaine.
832,	Canapés for roast game.	843,	roasted, bread sauce.
875,	Canvas-back ducks broiled.	849,	chartreuse of.
874,	roasted.	848,	sauté à la chasseur.
833,	Croquettes à la Périgueux.	846,	à la financière.
839,	Doe-birds, broiled.	851,	suprême à la Godard.
841,	roasted à l'africaine.	850,	Périgueux.
840,	à l'américaine.	866,	Plovers, broiled.
838,	plain.	865,	roasted plain.
842,	salmi à la gastronome.	867,	salmi, maison d'or.
1369,	Game pie à la Levi P. Morton.	863,	Ptarmigan, broiled.
894,	Gibelotte of hare.	862,	roasted plain.
854,	Grouse, broiled with bacon.	864,	salmi à la chasseur.
1390,	à la Pomeroy.	836,	Quails, braised, celery sauce.
852,	roasted, plain.	835,	broiled with bacon.
853,	à la Sam Ward.	837,	à la financière.
855,	salmi à la parisienne.	834,	roasted plain.
856,	à la Walter Scott.	876,	Red-head ducks, broiled.
857,	à la florentin.	876,	roasted plain.
858,	suprême à la Richelieu.	877,	Reed-birds.
895,	Hare fillets, poivrade sauce.	869,	Snipe, broiled.
893,	civet à la française.	868,	roasted plain.
892,	roasted plain.	870,	salmi à la moderne.
845,	Partridge, braised with cabbage.	860,	Teal duck broiled.
		861,	salmi à la régence.

859, Teal duck, roasted plain.
878, Venison, saddle, currant jelly.
885, chops, purée of chestnuts.
887, civet à la française.
886, civet, poivrade sauce.
888, civet à la parisienne.
889, pie à l'américaine.
879, steak broiled.
881, Venison steak, Colbert sauce.
884, currant jelly.
880, Londonderry sauce.
883, mashed potatoes;
882, purée of chestnuts.
872, Woodcock broiled.
871, roasted plain.
873, salmi à la chasseur.

GARNISHINGS.

254, Bouquet, how to prepare.
143, Fine herbs cooked.
144, raw.
231, Garnishing Bayard.
243, bordelaise.
242, cêpes.
232, chipolata.
247, à l'écarlate.
246, financière.
238, Godard.
241, gourmets.
237, grecque.
244, marrow.
251, milanaise.
249, Garnishing Montebello.
230, mushrooms.
175½, normande.
240, parisienne.
245, à la Patti.
235, régence.
253, Robinson.
252, rouennaise.
236, St. Nazaire.
248, Stanley.
250, soubise.
239, tortue.
234, valencienne.
233, Vanderbilt.

HORS D'OEUVRES.

285, Anchovies, Norwegian.
284, in oil.
280, on toast.
270, Bouchées à la reine.
269, Canapé Madison.
281, Caviare on toast.
291, Celery, frizzled.
290, in glass.
271, Coquilles of chicken à l'anglaise.
272, of oysters au gratin.
268, Cromesquis aux truffes.
276, Croquettes, chicken, with truffles.
278, foie-gras.
277, of game.
279, of macaroni.
264, Croustades à la régence.
265, de riz à la Victoria.
289, Cucumbers.
274, Lamb sweetbreads en caisses.
287, Mortadella.
275, Oysters en petites caisses.
273, Oysters in shells à l'anglaise.
266, Patties à l'anglaise.
267, ortolans.
292, Radishes, how to prepare.
293, remarks on.
257, Salpicon au chasseur.
256, à la financière.
258, of lobsters, shrimps, &c.
259, montglas.
255, royale.
260, sauce madère.
283, Sardines in oil.
286, Sausage de Lyons.
261, Timbales à l'écossaise.
262, de nouilles à la génoise.
263, à la Schultze.
282, Tunny-fish, pickled.
288, Tomatoes, side dish.
294, Welsh rarebit.
297, au gratin.
296, gherkin-buck.
295, golden buck.

LAMB.

675, Ballotin of lamb, with peas.
702, Breast, jardinière.
674, Brochette à la Dumas.
681, Chops à la Signora.
682, à la Robinson.
683, maison d'or.
684, clichy.
685, maintenon.
686, Villeroi.
687, Masséna.
679, Croquettes à la Patti.
680, Croustades of kidneys with mushrooms.
676, Curry of lamb, asparagus-tops.
678, à la créole.
677, à l'indienne.
690, Epigrammes of lamb à la chicorée.
691, à la louisiannaise.
689, à la macédoine.
692, à la soubise.
672, Fries à la diable.
673, " tomato sauce.
701, Haricot of lamb à la Providence.
700, Hashed lamb à la polonaise.
713, Kidneys, with bacon.

714, Kidneys, with cêpes.
712, Colbert sauce.
715, deviled.
585, Loin of lamb, roasted.
688, Minced lamb à l'anglaise.
1360, Mignons of lamb, sauce béarnaise.
693, Shoulder of lamb à l'africaine.
699, à la flamande.
696, à la jardinière.
697, à la macédoine.
694, à la purée normande.
698, à la rouennaise.
695, stuffed tomatoes.
1361, Spring lamb, roasted.
716, Lamb steak, purée of peas.
717, sauce piquante.
718, à l'américaine.
705, Stewed lamb, Lima beans.
709, string beans.
711, à la créole.
707, aux flageolets.
704, à la française.
710, à la louisiannaise.
703, oyster-plant.
708, à la parisienne.
706, with peas.

MUTTON.

645, Chops à l'africaine.
643, breaded.
644, bretonne.
646, napolitaine.
642, à la provençale.
647, soyer with potatoes.
652, hashed à la zingara.
653, " au gratin.
661, Kidneys aux petit salé.
663, sautés à l'italienne.
662, sauce madère.
648, Leg, roasted plain.
648, à la portugaise.
649, à la Condé.
650, bretonne.
651, caper sauce.

585, Loin, roasted.
665, Saddle of mutton, Colbert.
666, currant jelly.
670, duchesse.
668, Londonderry sauce.
667, sauce poivrade.
671, with potatoes.
664, roasted plain.
669, à la Sévigné.
654, Sheep's feet à la poulette.
655, Stewed Mutton, fermière.
660, Stew, Irish.
657, marseillaise.
658, portugaise.
659, with potatoes.
656, Solferino.

PORK.

754, Bacon, broiled.
719, Black sausages, mashed potatoes.
721, Ham, boiled plain.
753, broiled and fried.
722, for family use.
723, roasted, champagne sauce.
724, " corn à la crême.
725, " with spinach.
726, Pig's cheek, with spinach.
734, Pigs' feet, boned.
730, à la Boston.
729, sauce piquante.
731, à la poulette.
728, sauce Robert.
727, St. Hubert.
733, stuffed, madeira sauce.
732, " Périgueux.
742, Pork Andouillettes.

748, Pork chops, apple sauce.
744, broiled.
747, à la diable.
743, plain.
745, sauce piquante.
749, purée of peas.
750, purée of potatoes.
746, sauce Robert.
752, Pork and beans.
751, roasted.
741, tenderloin.
736, Sausages à l'anglaise.
738, à la bourguignonne.
739, with cabbage.
740, à la gastronome.
737, à l'italienne.
735, with white wine.
720, Suckling pig, apple sauce.

POULTRY.

785, Chicken à la Maryland.
784, with rice.
781, fricassé à l'américaine.
780, à la reine.
779, boiled à la Providence.
756, broiled with bacon.
764, cromesquis à la Richelieu.
765, à la reine.
760, croquettes à l'écarlate.
761, à la Périgourdin.
759, à la Périgueux.
758, à la reine.
762, croustade à la Dreux.
763, of livers au madère.
794, curry à la créole.
793, à l'espagnole.
792, à l'indienne.
766, legs à la diable.
769, livers, with bacon.
770, à l'italienne.
767, au madère.
768, with mushrooms.
783, pillau à la créole.
782, à la turque.
757, pot-pie.
755, roasted plain.
778, sauté à la bohêmienne.
776, à la bordelaise.
775, à la chasseur.
1362, à la Ch. C. Delmonico.
772, à l'hongroise.

771, Chicken sauté, à la marengo.
773, à la parmentier.
777, à la régence.
774, with tarragon.
1363, à la Ranhofer.
787, suprême à la Bayard.
789, à la Patti.
788, à la reine.
790, à la Rothschild.
786, à la toulouse.
823, Duck à l'Américaine.
824, roasted, apple sauce.
825, à la rouennaise.
826, salmi à l'américaine.
829, à la bourgeoise.
828, à la chasseur.
831, à la maréchale.
830, à la montglas.
827, with olives.
808, Goose, stuffed with chestnuts.
815, Pigeon cutlets à la Victoria.
820, Squabs à l'américaine.
818, ballotin à l'italienne.
817, broiled with bacon.
821, à la chipolata.
822, en compote.
819, en crapaudine.
816, roasted, plain.
809, Timbale of foies-gras, lagadère.
791, Turban of chicken à la Cleveland.
795, Turkey à l'anglaise.

799, Turkey, boiled à la Baltimore.
796,   celery sauce.
798,   egg sauce.
797,   oyster sauce.
766, Turkey legs à la diable.
800, Turkey roasted and stuffed.
800,   roasted plain.
813,   boned, à la prosperity of America.
814,   jelly, for boned turkey.

806, Turkey breast a la chipolata.
807,   breast à la Robinson.
802,   hashed à la béchamel.
805,   hashed en bordure.
804,   hashed à la crême.
803,   hashed à la polonaise.
801,   hashed à la royale.
810, vol-au-vent à la financière.
812,   à la reine.
811,   à la toulouse.

SALADS.

1037, Anchovy.
1038, Barbe de Capucine.
1039, Beef.
1040, Cauliflower.
1041, Celery.
1042,   mayonnaise.
1043, Chapon for salad.
1044, Chicken.
1046, Chicory au chapon.
1045,   plain.
1047, Crab.
1050, Dandelion and beet-root.
1051,   à la Contoise.
1049,   with eggs.
1048,   plain.
1053, Doucette with beet-roots.
1054,   with eggs.
1052,   plain.
1055, Escarole.
1074, Herring.
1036, Italienne.

1075, Japanese.
1056, Lamb-tongue.
1059, Lettuce and cream.
1058,   and eggs.
1057,   plain.
1060,   and tomatoes.
1061, Lobster.
1062,   à la Plummer.
1368,   à la Boardman.
1063, Macédoine.
1073, Potato.
1064, Romaine.
1065, Russian.
1066, Salmon.
1067, Shrimp.
1068, String-bean.
1069, Suédoise.
1070, Tomato, French dressing
1071,   mayonnaise.
1072, Watercress.

SAUCES.

146, Butter, anchovy.
150,   crawfish.
148,   horseradish.
149,   lobster.
145,   maître d'hôtel.
147,   ravigote.
210, Sauce allemande.
163,   anchovy.
168,   apple.
182,   a l'aurore.
166,   béarnaise.
154,   béchamel.
186,   bordelaise.
162,   bread.
159,   black butter.
157,   drawn butter.
155,   melted butter.
156,   nut-brown butter.
651,   caper.

200, Sauce celery.
212,   Chambord.
204,   champagne.
197,   chasseur.
190,   Colbert.
199,   crapaudine.
181,   cream.
185,   demi-glace.
198,   diable.
183,   duchesse.
189,   duxelle.
161,   egg.
151,   espagnole.
187,   génoise.
170,   green.
196,   hachée.
160,   hollandaise.
164,   horseradish.
174,   Indian.

INDEX.

188,	Sauce Italian.		184,	Sauce princesse.
15R,	lobster.		209,	remoulade.
185,	madeira.		192,	Robert.
177,	maître d'hôtel, liée.		211,	Russian.
180,	matelote.		193,	salmi.
206,	mayonnaise.		178,	shrimp.
169,	mint.		171,	suprême.
213,	montglas.		172,	tarragon.
202,	mustard.		207,	tartare.
195,	napolitaine.		205,	tomato.
175,	normande.		176,	toulouse.
173,	oyster.		167,	trianon.
165,	percillade.		152,	velouté.
191,	Périgueux.		179,	vénitienne.
203,	piquante.		208,	Victoria.
194,	poivrade.		153,	Villeroi.
598,	poulette.		201,	vinaigrette.

SOUPS.

5,	Beef à l'anglaise.		126,	Consommé Patti.
6,	à l'écossaise.		113,	princesse.
8,	Bisque of clams.		109,	printanier.
9,	of crabs.		121,	printanier Colbert.
10,	of lobster.		124,	printanier royale.
1,	Bouille-à-baisse.		100,	pure.
2,	Brunoise.		129,	aux quenelles.
3,	with rice.		123,	Rachel.
4,	with sorrel.		115,	renaissance.
7,	Busecca.		107,	royale.
65,	Chicken à la créole.		104,	semoule, or tapioca.
64,	à l'hollandaise.		105,	semoule à la crême.
68,	with leeks,		106,	Sévigné.
67,	l'okra.		122,	suédoise.
63,	à la piémontaise.		84,	Cream à l'allemande.
66,	à la portugaise.		72,	of artichokes.
62,	à la Richmond.		70,	of asparagus.
69,	à la turque.		77,	of barley.
14,	Chiffonade.		73,	of cauliflower.
132,	for soups.		71,	of celery.
13,	Chowder, clam.		86,	of celery à l'espagnole.
12,	fish.		82,	of chicken.
116,	Consommé à l'africaine.		83,	of game.
117,	à l'andalouse.		88,	of lentils à la majordomo.
119,	à l'anglaise.		87,	of lettuce.
118,	célestine.		75,	of Lima beans.
128,	chatelaine.		74,	Palestine.
120,	Colbert.		76,	of dried peas.
108,	Deslignac.		78,	of rice.
110,	d'Orleans.		79,	of sorrel.
114,	Douglas.		81,	of sorrel, fermière.
101,	Dubourg.		80,	of sorrel with rice.
125,	duchesse.		85,	of turnips.
112,	Garbaldi.		11,	Croûte-au-pot.
111,	impérial.		134,	Croûtons soufflées.
102,	Masséna.		133,	for soup.
127,	napolitaine.		25,	Frogs à l'espagnole.
103,	aux pâtes.		22,	Giblets à l'anglaise.

21, Giblets with barley
20,   à l'écossaise.
19,   with rice.
16, Green turtle.
18,   clear.
15,   how to prepare.
24, Gumbo of crabs.
23,   with frogs.
28, Jardinière.
27, Julienne.
36, Menestra.
32, Mikado.
17, Mock turtle.
30, Mutton with barley.
31,   à l'écossaise.
34, Mulligatawney.
45,   à la Delmonico.
37, Napolitaine.
130, Onion.
40, Ox-tail à l'anglaise.
38,   with barley.
39,   à l'écossaise.
26, Oyster.
53. Paysanne.
54, Pot-au-feu
52, Printanier chasseur.
51,   grenat.
93, Potage à la diplomate.
96,   à la Dorsay.

95, Potage à la McDonald.
98,   of rice à la maintenon.
97,   à la Montmorency.
94,   à la windsor.
45, Purée bretonne.
91,   of chestnuts à la jardinière.
48,   Condé.
47,   Crécy.
46,   faubonne.
49,   of green peas.
43,   Jackson.
50,   Mongole.
44,   parmentier.
89,   of partridge à la Destaing.
90,   à la gentilhomme.
92,   soubise with white beans.
131,   of chestnuts.
55, Russe.
29, Shin of beef, liée.
41, Sorrel, asparagus-tops.
42,   with rice.
56, Spaghetti with tomatoes.
61, Terrapin.
60,   how to prepare.
58, Tomatoes à l'andalouse.
57,   with rice.
59,   with sago.
33, Westmoreland.
99, White broth.

STOCKS.

217, Chicken essence.
216, Clear gravy.
142, Court'bouillon.
215, Duxelle.
214, Fish broth.
219, Game.
139, Marinade, cooked.

140, Marinade, raw.
137,   white.
141, Meat-glaze
138, Mirepoix.
136, Roux, brown.
135,   white.

VEAL.

549, Blanquette of veal.
553,   à l'ancienne.
552,   with nouilles.
550,   à la reine.
551,   with peas.
591, Braised noix of veal en daube.
590,   à la Providence.
596, Breast of veal à la milanaise.
554, Brisotin of veal.
555,   à l'écarlate.
556,   nantaise.
557, Calf's brain, black butter.
559,   fried, tartare sauce.
558,   à la vinaigrette.
638, Calf's head à la Cavour.

637, Calf's head plain.
639,   à la poulette.
641,   en tortue.
640,   à la vinaigrette.
583, Calf's liver, braised, bourgeoise.
584,   broiled with bacon.
582,   sauté à l'alsacienne.
580,   à l'italienne.
581,   à la provençale.
597, Calf's feet, naturel.
599,   sauce piquante.
598,   à la poulette.
600,   sauce remoulade.
567, Curry of veal à l'indienne.

562, Cutlets à la maréchale.
563,   à la milanaise.
560,   à la Pagasqui.
566,   en papillotes.
565,   à la Philadelphia.
561,   à la St. Cloud.
563,   breaded, tomato sauce.
564,   broiled.
569, Escalops of veal à la duxelle
571,   à la chicorée.
572,   à l'italienne.
568,   plain.
573,   à la provençale.
574,   à la Richelieu.
570,   with stuffed peppers.
579, Fricandeau à la morlaisienne.
577,   with sorrel.
578,   with spinach.
589, Grenadins of veal à l'africaine.
587,   à la chipolata.
586,   purée of peas.
588,   à la Sévigné.
585, Loin of veal, roasted.
576, Minced veal à la biscaënne.
575,   à la Catalan.
595, Panpiette of veal à la duxelle.
594,   purée of chestnuts.
593,   à l'écarlate.
592,   à la faubonne.
601, Sweetbreads, how to blanch.
610,   à la béarnaise.
602,   braised.
616,   à la Catalan.

611, Sweetbreads, aux cêpes.
617,   à la Colbert.
608,   à la duxelle.
603,   à la financière.
614,   à la Godard.
612,   aux gourmets.
615,   à la montglas.
609,   with mushrooms.
613,   à la parisienne.
618,   à la Pompadour.
605,   au salpicon.
604,   with sorrel.
606,   soubise.
607,   with spinach.
622,   coquilles à la cardinal.
621,   à la Dreux.
623,   à la reine..
620,   croquettes with peas.
619,   à la Périgueux.
629, Stewed veal, bourgeoise.
632,   à la chasseur.
626,   à la grecque.
624,   à la Marengo.
630,   with oyster-plant.
631,   with peas.
627,   à la portugaise.
625,   à la provençale.
628,   à la Solferino.
636, Tendron of veal à la chipolata.
635,   à la morlaisienne.
633,   à la nantaise.
634,   with sorrel.

VEGETABLES.

896, Artichokes à la Barigoul.
898,   à la duxelle.
903,   à la florentine.
899,   fried.
900,   with sauce.
897,   stewed.
901,   stuffed.
902,   à la vinaigrette.
904, Asparagus, sauce hollandaise.
906,   à la tessinoise.
905,   à la vinaigrette.
1375, canned.
966, Barley fritters.
950, Beans panachées.
910, Beet-roots, boiled plain.
911,   sautées au beurre.
912,   à la crème.
922, Brussels sprouts au beurre.
923,   à la crème.
917, Cabbage, blanched.
918,   with cream.
920,   for garnishing.

921, Cabbage and pork.
919,   stuffed.
931, Cardons à la moëlle.
927, Carrots and cream.
925, Cauliflower with butter.
926,   au gratin.
928, Celery à la bonne femme.
929,   with cream.
930,   à la moëlle de bœuf.
932, Chicory, cream sauce.
934,   for garnishing.
933,   with gravy.
962, Corn, boiled.
964,   sauté au beurre.
963,   à la crème.
965,   fritters.
1375, canned.
936, Cucumbers à la béchamel.
938,   for garnishing.
936,   à la poulette.
937,   stuffed.
908, Egg-plant, broiled.

907, Egg-plant, fried.
909,   stuffed.
1365, Flageolets sautés au beurre.
976, Green peas à l'ancienne mode.
978,   à l'anglaise.
981,   with bacon.
979,   à la bourgeoise.
980,   with cream.
977,   à la française.
1034, Hominy, boiled.
1035,   fried.
1033, Jardinière.
952, Lima beans.
1375,   canned.
954, Macaroni à la crême.
955,   au gratin.
956,   à l'italienne.
958,   à la milanaise.
957,   à la napolitaine.
1032, Macédoine of vegetables.
913, Mushrooms à la bordelaise.
916,   broiled on toast.
915,   sautés à la crême.
914,   on toast.
1030, Okras, boiled.
1031,   sautés à la créole.
968, Onions, with cream.
969,   fried.
972,   for garnishing.
971,   minced.
970,   stuffed.
1021, Oyster-plant, fried.
1019,   à la poulette.
1018,   sautés au beurre.
1020,   à la crême.
1382, Peas, canned.
988, Potatoes à l'anglaise.
987,   à l'anglaise à crû.
989,   with bacon.
996,   balls.
1001,   bignon.
982,   boiled plain.
983,   broiled.
1009,   château.
997,   croquettes.
1006,   duchesse.
993,   fried.
1000,   gastronome.
984,   génevroise.
1012,   à la Hanna.
1002,   hashed.
1003,   with cream.
1004,   au gratin.

999, Potatoes, hollandaise.
990,   Italian.
1013,   julienne.
991,   lyonnaise.
985,   maître d'hôtel.
998,   mashed.
1014,   en paille.
986,   parisienne.
997,   quenelles.
1007,   à la rice.
1011,   saratoga.
995,   sautées.
995,   au beurre.
1010,   soufflées.
992,   stuffed.
1005,   en surprise.
1008,   Windsor.
951, Red beans à la bourguignonne.
1015, Rice boiled, plain.
1016,   à la Ristori.
1017, Risotto à la milanaise.
1022, Succotash.
974, Sorrel au gras.
973,   au maigre.
924, Sourkrout.
961, Spaghetti, au gratin.
960,   à l'italienne.
959,   à la napolitaine.
940, Spinach à l'anglaise.
939,   blanched.
943,   with gravy.
942,   maître d'hôtel.
941,   vieille mode.
944,   with sugar.
948, String beans à l'anglaise.
947,   au blanc.
945,   blanched.
949,   bretonne.
946,   with cream.
1386,   canned.
953, Stuffed lettuce.
975,   peppers.
1026, Tomatoes à la Bock.
1025,   broiled.
1029,   à la marseillaise.
1024,   à la reine.
1028,   roasted.
1027,   stewed.
1023,   stuffed.
1394,   with rice à la Watson.
1384,   canned.
967, Turnips, with gravy.

www.ingramcontent.com/pod-product-compliance
Lightning Source LLC
Chambersburg PA
CBHW051726300426
44115CB00007B/479